Temporary
MILITARY
LODGING

by

William "Roy" Crawford, Sr., Ph.D.
and
Lela Ann Crawford

Editor: Bryce Thompson
Cover Design: Cover to Cover
Layout Artist: June O. Douglas
Editorial Assistant: Karen Donovan

Marketing Manager: William R. Crawford, Jr.
Office Staff: Jeremy Bingham, Barbara Brown,
Eula Mae Brownlee, Anna Belle Causey, Evelyn DeWald,
Dan Hill, Tom Hogan, Rose McLain

Military Living Publications
P. O. Box 2347
Falls Church, Virginia 22042-0347
(703) 237-0203
FAX (703) 237-2233

NOTICE

The information in this book has been compiled and edited either from the activity/installation listed, its superior headquarters, or from other sources that may or may not be noted by the authors. Information about the facilities listed, including contact phone numbers and rate structures, could change. This book should be used as a guide to the listed facilities with this understanding. Please forward any corrections or additions to: **Military Living Publications, P. O. Box 2347, Falls Church, Virginia 22042-0347.**

This directory is published by Military Marketing Services, Inc., a private business in no way connected with the U.S. Federal or any other government. This book is copyrighted by William Roy and Lela Ann Crawford. Opinions expressed by the publisher and authors of this book are their own and are not to be considered an official expression by any government agency or official. The information and statements contained in this directory have been compiled from sources believed to be reliable and to represent the best current opinion on the subject. No warranty, guarantee, or representation is made by Military Marketing Services, Inc., as to the absolute correctness or sufficiency of any representation contained in this or other publications and we can assume no responsibility.

Cover Photographs: Top Left: Hale Koa Hotel, Honolulu. Top Right: An Air Force TLQ, location unknown. Reader help requested. Lower Left: Navy Lodge, Norfolk Navy Base, VA. Lower Right: U.S. Coast Guard contract hotel (Super 8), Governor's Island, New York City. Picture your military lodging facility on our cover! Please send photos or info to Military Living.

Copyright © 1990 William Roy and Lela Ann Crawford
Second Printing—July 1990
Third Printing—August 1991
MILITARY MARKETING SERVICES, INC.
(T/A MILITARY LIVING PUBLICATIONS)

All rights reserved under International and Pan-American copyright conventions. No part of this book may be reproduced in any form without permission in writing from the publisher, except by a reviewer who wishes to quote briefly from listings in connection with a review written for inclusion in a magazine or newspaper, with source credit to **MILITARY LIVING'S** *TEMPORARY MILITARY LODGING AROUND THE WORLD.* A copy of the review, when published, should be sent to Military Living Publications, P. O. Box 2347, Falls Church, Virginia 22042-0347.

Library of Congress Cataloging-in-Publication Data

```
Crawford, William Roy, 1932-
    Military living's temporary military lodging around the world / by
William "Roy" Crawford and Lela Ann Crawford ; editor, Bryce D.
Thompson.
    p. cm.
    ISBN 0-914862-22-7 : $9.95
    1. United States--Armed Forces--Barracks, and quarters-
-Directories.  2. Military bases, American--Directories.
I. Crawford, Ann Caddell.  II. Thompson, Bryce D.  III. Temporary
military lodging around the world.  IV. Title.
UC403.7'1'02573--dc20                                     90-5504
                                                             CIP
```

INTRODUCTION

This is a book that can pay for itself many times over. All you have to do is use it! There are places to stay on military installations for as little as $4.00 or $5.00 per night. The most common charges we found quoted were in the $10.00-$20.00 price range for a family of five sharing one unit in a transient lodging facility, or $20.00-$30.00 for a Navy Lodge unit, each of which has sleeping space for five, wall-to-wall carpeting, color TV, kitchenette with all utensils, and more. Since our last edition, inflation has caused some military lodging prices to increase; however, they have not increased to the same degree or at the same rate as prices in the civilian sector. In some large cities, the cost of lodging has risen to $150.00 per night, or more. Clearly, *Temporary Military Lodging Around the World* can greatly reduce the high cost of travel experienced by military families.

Before the first edition of this book was published in 1971, there was a big "catch" involved in getting to use temporary lodging facilities. The problem was finding out which installation had what. Military Living Publications has solved that problem by doing the leg work for you. Just glance through the hundreds of listings that follow and you will find out why this book is indispensable if you want to "travel on less per day...the military way."

Ann & Roy Crawford

AREA CODES FOR THE ATVN TELEPHONE SYSTEM

CONUS - 312 (voice) 712 (data)   ALASKA - 317 (voice) 717 (data)
EUROPE - 314 (voice) 714 (data)   PACIFIC - 315 (voice) 715 (data)
CARIBBEAN - 313 (voice) 713 (data)

STANDARD EMERGENCY & SERVICE NUMBERS FROM ALL ARMY DIAL TELEPHONES IN WEST GERMANY/BERLIN

	DDD	ETS
EMERGENCY		
Engineer	91	115
Fire	95	117
Ambulance/Hospital/Clinic	97	116
Military Police	98	114
SERVICE		
Operator	0	0 or 1110
European AUTOVON		314 or thru 112
CONUS AUTOVON		112
Booking	90	112
Information	92	113
Telephone Repair	96	119
Civilian Access	99	99

Note: The Direct Distance Dial (DDD) system (also known as the Military system) is being replaced with the new European Telephone System (ETS). This replacement has been completed in most military communities.

HOW TO USE THIS DIRECTORY

Name of Installation (AL01R2)
Street/PO Box (if required)
City/APO/FPO, State, ZIP Code

TELEPHONE NUMBER INFORMATION: Comm: This is the commercial telephone service for the installation's main or information/operator assistance number. Within the U.S. Area Code System, the first three digits are the area code. For foreign country locations, the first two digits are the Country Code (consult your local directory or operator for specific dialing instructions). The next three digits are the area telephone exchange/switch number. For foreign countries, the exchange number can be either fewer or more digits than in the U.S. system. The last four digits are usually the information or operator assistance number. Again, in foreign countries, this number may be fewer or more than four digits. In the United Kingdom (UK), dialing instructions are given from the telephone exchange serving the installation. These numbers are different for each location in the UK from which you are dialing. Consult the local directory or operator for specific dialing instructions.

ATVN: This is the Department of Defense, worldwide, Automatic Voice Network (ATVN). In most cases, the number given is for information/operator assistance.

ETS: This is the European Telephone System. ETS prefixes for military communities are the same as ATVN prefixes. The ETS system has now largely supplanted the old Direct Distance Dial (DDD) or military system once used throughout West Germany and Berlin (see Mil below).

FTS: This is the Federal Telephone System. The number given is for information/operator assistance. On smaller installations the information/operator assistance number may be the contact number for Temporary Military Lodging.

Location Identifier: Example (AL01R2). The first two characters (letters) are Country/State abbreviations used in Military Living's books (Appendix A). The next two characters are random numbers (00-99) assigned to a specific location. The fifth character is an R indicating region and the sixth character is the region number. The location identifiers for each of the more than 450 listings in this book are keyed to regional maps in Appendix C. The regional maps are designed to provide you with the relative geographic location of each installation worldwide. Detailed driving instructions are contained under **Location** in each listing.

Location: Specific driving instructions to the installation from local major cities, interstate highways and routes are given. More than one routing may be provided. **RM:** is the Rand McNally Road Atlas reference to the location. **HE:** is the Hallwag Europe Road Atlas reference to the location. **NMC:** is the nearest major city. The distance in miles and direction from the installation to the NMC are given.

Billeting Office: The attention line (ATTN:), building number, etc., are for your information and can be added to the address when writing to the

How to Use This Directory, continued

billeting office. The Comm, ATVN/ETS, Mil and/or FTS telephone numbers of the billeting office are given. Hours of operation of the billeting office, main desk, or contact office are listed. Check in/check out points and times are given. Use of Temporary Military Lodging (TML) by government civilian employees on duty is specified. Other helpful general billeting information is detailed. NOTE: Pets are not allowed in temporary lodging facilities unless otherwise noted. Also, all facilities are open to men and women unless otherwise noted.

TML: Each category of TML, i.e., Guest House, Hotel, Army/Navy/Air Force/Marine Corps Lodge, and so on, is listed separately in most cases. The category of occupancy, i.e. all ranks, specific grades, Officer, Enlisted, male, female, is given. Occupancy by leave or duty status is given. Reservation requirements and specific contact telephone numbers are listed. The accommodations, appointments, services and supporting facilities such as kitchens, utensils, television, air conditioning, maid service, cribs, cots, washer/dryer, ice, vending machines, handicapped facilities, etc., are given. Whether the structure is older or modern, its condition and any renovations or improvements are specified. The per day rates are listed for each category of occupant. Please note that rates can change often. Priorities and restrictions on occupancy are listed. Acceptance of household pets is indicated.

DV/VIP: The contact office or person, building, room and telephone number for DV/VIP lodging and other support is given. The grade/status for DV/VIPs at the installation is specified. The use of DV/VIP facilities/services by retirees and lower grades is indicated.

Facilities/Services Support: A list of telephone numbers for key support services at each installation is provided, when available, for military travelers.

Other: Items of interest on the installation or at nearby areas are given along with specific instructions or restrictions.

TML Availability: The best and most difficult times for TML are listed as reported. If possible, call or write regarding availability before you travel or take your chances on space-available use.

Please review Appendix A, Country and State Abbreviations, and Appendix B, General Abbreviations. Also read the other appendices and the questions and answers about TML that supplement the basic TML listings.

A Few Words About Telephone Systems in Germany

Each of the commercial/civilian telephone numbers at the top of all listings in Germany follow the same pattern. The first set of digits is the country code (49 in Germany). The second set of digits is the local area civilian prefix. The next set of digits is the civilian-to-military conversion code. The last set of digits is the line number/extension (or a set of Xs indicating line number/extension). Telephone calls originating on civilian instruments and terminating on military instruments require the conversion code. Telephone

How to Use This Directory, continued

calls originating and terminating on civilian instruments do not require the conversion code. Commercial-to-commercial or commercial-to-military telephone calls originating and terminating in the same local area do not generally require the use of the civilian prefix either. Also, local area civilian prefixes all begin with a "0". The "0" is only used in-country. Drop the "0" if dialing from outside the country.

Commercial/civilian telephone numbers in Germany are frequently identified by a three-letter city identifier followed by the letter "C" indicating civilian. For example, HNUC-55169 in the listing for Hanau Community indicates that 55169 is a civilian extension in Hanau. All ETS numbers consist of a three or four digit prefix and a four or three digit line number.

YOU CAN $AVE THOUSANDS OF DOLLARS WITH THIS BOOK

The one everyone is talking about! Look for this book at military Clothing Sales Stores, Exchanges and air terminal snack bars. If not available, place your credit card order by calling (703) 237-0203.

UNITED STATES

LOCATION IDENTIFIER   **INSTALLATION**   **PAGE**

ALABAMA

AL07R2	Dauphin Island Recreational Complex	1
AL01R2	Fort McClellan (X)	1
AL02R2	Fort Rucker	2
AL04R2	Gunter Air Force Base	3
AL03R2	Maxwell Air Force Base	3
AL06R2	Redstone Arsenal	4

ALASKA

AK04R5	Adak Naval Air Station	5
AK15R5	Eielson Air Force Base	5
AK09R5	Elmendorf Air Force Base	6
AK10R5	Fort Greely	7
AK03R5	Fort Richardson	7
AK07R5	Fort Wainwright	8
AK08R5	Kodiak Coast Guard Support Center	9

ARIZONA

AZ01R4	Davis-Monthan Air Force Base (O)	9
AZ02R4	Fort Huachuca (O)	10
AZ16R4	Gila Bend Air Force Auxiliary Field	11
AZ03R4	Luke Air Force Base	12
AZ09R4	Williams Air Force Base	12
AZ05R4	Yuma Army Proving Ground (O)	13
AZ04R4	Yuma Marine Corps Air Station	14

ARKANSAS

AR01R2	Eaker Air Force Base (X)	15
AR04R2	Fort Chaffee	15
AR02R2	Little Rock Air Force Base	16
AR03R2	Pine Bluff Arsenal	16

CALIFORNIA

CA28R4	Alameda Coast Guard Support Center	17
CA33R4	Alameda Naval Air Station (X)	17
CA13R4	Barstow Marine Corps Logistics Base	18
CA47R4	Beale Air Force Base (O)	18
CA30R4	Camp Pendleton Marine Corps Base	19
CA83R4	Camp San Luis Obispo	20
CA10R4	Castle Air Force Base	21
CA71R4	Centerville Beach Naval Facility	21
CA34R4	China Lake Naval Weapons Center	22

vii

CALIFORNIA (continued)

CA38R4	Coronado Naval Amphibious Base	23
CA03R4	Del Mar Recreation Beach	23
CA48R4	Edwards Air Force Base	24
CA09R4	El Centro Naval Air Facility (X)	25
CA22R4	El Toro Marine Corps Air Station	25
CA37R4	Fort Hunter Liggett	26
CA01R4	Fort Irwin National Training Center	27
CA46R4	Fort MacArthur	27
CA45R4	Fort Mason Officers' Club	28
CA36R4	Fort Ord (X)	29
CA49R4	George Air Force Base (O)	29
CA06R4	Lemoore Naval Air Station	30
CA55R4	Long Beach Naval Station (O)	31
CA39R4	Los Alamitos Armed Forces Reserve Center	31
CA08R4	March Air Force Base (O)	32
CA20R4	Marines' Memorial Club	32
CA12R4	Mather Air Force Base (O)	33
CA35R4	McClellan Air Force Base (O)	33
CA14R4	Miramar Naval Air Station	34
CA15R4	Moffett Field Naval Air Station (X)	34
CA16R4	Monterey Naval Postgraduate School	35
CA43R4	North Island Naval Air Station	36
CA17R4	Norton Air Force Base (O)	36
CA18R4	Oakland Army Base	37
CA41R4	Oakland Naval Hospital (X)	37
CA42R4	Oakland Naval Supply Center (X)	38
CA23R4	Petaluma Coast Guard Training Center	38
CA40R4	Point Mugu Pacific Missile Test Center	39
CA32R4	Port Hueneme Naval Construction Battalion Center	39
CA19R4	Presidio of San Francisco (O)	40
CA26R4	San Diego Naval Station (O)	41
CA79R4	San Diego Naval Submarine Base	41
CA25R4	San Pedro Coast Guard Personnel Support Center	42
CA44R4	Sierra Army Depot	42
CA51R4	Stockton Naval Communications Station	43
CA50R4	Travis Air Force Base	43
CA21R4	Treasure Island Naval Base (X)	44
CA27R4	Twentynine Palms Marine Corps Air/Ground Combat Center	44
CA29R4	Vandenberg Air Force Base	45

COLORADO

CO10R3	Fitzsimons Army Medical Center	46
CO02R3	Fort Carson (O)	47
CO05R3	Lowry Air Force Base (O)	47
CO06R3	Peterson Air Force Base	48
CO07R3	United States Air Force Academy	49

CONNECTICUT

CT01R1	New London Naval Submarine Base	50

DELAWARE

DE01R1	Dover Air Force Base	51
DE02R1	Fort Miles Recreation Area (CLOSED)	52

DISTRICT OF COLUMBIA

DC01R1	Bolling Air Force Base	52
DC03R1	Walter Reed Army Medical Center	53
DC04R1	Washington Navy Yard	54

FLORIDA

FL16R1	Avon Park Air Force Range	54
FL06R1	Cecil Field Naval Air Station	55
FL27R1	Eglin Air Force Base	55
FL17R1	Homestead Air Force Base	56
FL18R1	Hurlburt Field	57
FL08R1	Jacksonville Naval Air Station	57
FL15R1	Key West Naval Air Station	58
FL02R1	MacDill Air Force Base	59
FL13R1	Mayport Naval Station	59
FL09R1	Oak Grove Park Naval Air Station	60
FL11R1	Orlando Naval Training Center	60
FL03R1	Patrick Air Force Base	61
FL14R1	Pensacola Naval Air Station	62
FL04R1	Tyndall Air Force Base	63
FL05R1	Whiting Field Naval Air Station	63

GEORGIA

GA17R1	Albany Marine Corps Logistics Base	64
GA12R1	Athens Naval Supply Corps School	65
GA13R1	Dobbins Air Force Base	65
GA11R1	Fort Benning	66
GA21R1	Fort Gillem	66
GA09R1	Fort Gordon	67
GA08R1	Fort McPherson	68
GA15R1	Fort Stewart	68
GA10R1	Hunter Army Airfield	69
GA03R1	Kings Bay Naval Submarine Base	70
GA02R1	Moody Air Force Base	70
GA14R1	Robins Air Force Base	71

HAWAII

HI10R6	Barbers Point Naval Air Station	72
HI01R6	Barbers Point Recreation Area	72
HI02R6	Bellows Recreation Area	73
HI09R6	Fort Shafter	73
HI08R6	Hale Koa Hotel AFRC	74
HI11R6	Hickam Air Force Base	75
HI06R6	Kaneohe Bay Beach Cottages	76
HI12R6	Kaneohe Marine Corps Air Station	76
HI17R6	Kilauea Military Camp	77

HAWAII (continued)

HI20R6	Pearl Harbor Naval Station (O)	78
HI13R6	Schofield Barracks	78
HI03R6	Tripler Army Medical Center	79
HI05R6	Waianae Army Recreation Center	79

IDAHO

ID01R4	Mountain Home Air Force Base (O)	80

ILLINOIS

IL06R2	Chanute Air Force Base (O)	80
IL04R2	Charles Melvin Price Support Center	81
IL01R2	Fort Sheridan (O)	82
IL03R2	Glenview Naval Air Station	82
IL07R2	Great Lakes Naval Training Center	83
IL02R2	Scott Air Force Base	84

INDIANA

IN03R2	Crane Naval Weapons Support Center	84
IN02R2	Fort Benjamin Harrison (O)	85
IN01R2	Grissom Air Force Base	85

IOWA

NONE

KANSAS

KS04R3	Fort Leavenworth	86
KS02R3	Fort Riley	87
KS03R3	McConnell Air Force Base	87

KENTUCKY

KY02R2	Fort Campbell	88
KY01R2	Fort Knox (O)	89

LOUISIANA

LA01R2	Barksdale Air Force Base	90
LA05R2	England Air Force Base	91
LA07R2	Fort Polk	91
LA11R2	New Orleans Naval Air Station	92
LA06R2	New Orleans Naval Support Activity	93

MAINE

ME10R1	Bangor Air National Guard Base	93
ME07R1	Brunswick Naval Air Station	94
ME06R1	Loring Air Force Base	94
ME09R1	Winter Harbor Naval Security Group Activity	95

MARYLAND

MD11R1	Aberdeen Proving Ground	96
MD02R1	Andrews Air Force Base	96
MD06R1	Bethesda National Naval Medical Center	97
MD01R1	Curtis Bay Coast Guard Yard	98
MD07R1	Fort Detrick (O)	99
MD08R1	Fort George G. Meade (O)	99
MD13R1	Fort Ritchie	100
MD04R1	Indian Head Naval Ordnance Station	101
MD09R1	Patuxent River Naval Air Station	101
MD05R1	Solomons Navy Recreation Center	102
MD10R1	United States Naval Academy/Annapolis Naval Station	103

MASSACHUSETTS

MA10R1	Cape Cod Coast Guard Air Station	103
MA09R1	Fort Devens (O)	104
MA02R1	Fourth Cliff Recreation Area	105
MA06R1	Hanscom Air Force Base	105
MA05R1	South Weymouth Naval Air Station (X)	106
MA03R1	Westover Air Force Base	106

MICHIGAN

MI10R2	Camp Grayling	107
MI02R2	K.I. Sawyer Air Force Base	107
MI01R2	Selfridge Air National Guard Base	108
MI03R2	Wurtsmith Air Force Base	109

MINNESOTA

MN01R2	Minneapolis-St. Paul IAP	109

MISSISSIPPI

MS01R2	Columbus Air Force Base	110
MS03R2	Gulfport Naval Construction Battalion Center	111
MS02R2	Keesler Air Force Base (O)	111
MS04R2	Meridian Naval Air Station	112

MISSOURI

MO03R2	Fort Leonard Wood (O)	113
MO01R2	Lake of the Ozarks Recreation Area	114
MO02R2	Richards-Gebaur Air Force Base	114
MO04R2	Whiteman Air Force Base	115

MONTANA

MT03R3	Malmstrom Air Force Base	116

NEBRASKA

NE02R3	Offutt Air Force Base	117

NEVADA

NV02R4 Fallon Naval Air Station 118
NV01R4 Nellis Air Force Base 118

NEW HAMPSHIRE

NH01R1 Pease Air Force Base (O) (CLOSED).................. 119
NH02R1 Portsmouth Naval Shipyard 120

NEW JERSEY

NJ01R1 Armament Research, Development and Engineering Center (O) . 120
NJ10R1 Bayonne Military Ocean Terminal 121
NJ03R1 Fort Dix Army Training Center (O) 121
NJ05R1 Fort Monmouth (O) 122
NJ08R1 Lakehurst Naval Air Engineering Center 123
NJ09R1 McGuire Air Force Base 123

NEW MEXICO

NM02R3 Cannon Air Force Base (O) 124
NM05R3 Holloman Air Force Base 125
NM03R3 Kirtland Air Force Base (O) 126
NM04R3 White Sands Missile Range 126

NEW YORK

NY06R1 Fort Drum 127
NY02R1 Fort Hamilton 128
NY11R1 Griffiss Air Force Base 128
NY01R1 New York Coast Guard Support Center 129
NY07R1 New York Naval Station (O) 130
NY12R1 Niagara Falls Air Reserve Base 130
NY08R1 Plattsburgh Air Force Base (O) 131
NY17R1 Soldiers', Sailors' and Airmen's Club 132
NY09R1 Stewart Army Sub Post 132
NY16R1 United States Military Academy, West Point 133

NORTH CAROLINA

NC10R1 Camp Lejeune Marine Corps Base 133
NC09R1 Cape Hatteras Coast Guard Recreational Quarters ... 134
NC02R1 Cherry Point Marine Corps Air Station 134
NC03R1 Elizabeth City Coast Guard Support Center 135
NC05R1 Fort Bragg 136
NC06R1 New River Marine Corps Air Station 136
NC01R1 Pope Air Force Base 137
NC11R1 Seymour Johnson Air Force Base 137

NORTH DAKOTA

ND04R3 Grand Forks Air Force Base 138
ND02R3 Minot Air Force Base 139

OHIO

OH02R2	Rickenbacker Air National Guard Base	140
OH01R2	Wright-Patterson Air Force Base	140

OKLAHOMA

OK02R3	Altus Air Force Base	141
OK01R3	Fort Sill	142
OK04R3	Tinker Air Force Base	143
OK05R3	Vance Air Force Base	143

OREGON

OR03R4	Kinglsey Field	144

PENNSYLVANIA

PA08R1	Carlisle Barracks	144
PA04R1	Fort Indiantown Gap	145
PA03R1	Letterkenny Army Depot (O)	145
PA07R1	Mechanicsburg Navy Ships Parts Control Center	146
PA06R1	New Cumberland Army Depot	146
PA09R1	Philadelphia Naval Base	147
PA11R1	Philadelphia Naval Station (X)	147
PA05R1	Tobyhanna Army Depot (O)	148
PA01R1	Willow Grove Naval Air Station	148

RHODE ISLAND

RI01R1	Newport Naval Education & Training Center	149

SOUTH CAROLINA

SC01R1	Beaufort Marine Corps Air Station	150
SC06R1	Charleston Air Force Base	150
SC04R1	Charleston Naval Base	151
SC09R1	Fort Jackson (O)	152
SC07R1	Myrtle Beach Air Force Base (X)	152
SC08R1	Parris Island Marine Corps Recruit Depot	153
SC10R1	Shaw Air Force Base	154

SOUTH DAKOTA

SD01R3	Ellsworth Air Force Base	155

TENNESSEE

TN02R2	Arnold Air Force Base	156
TN01R2	Memphis Naval Air Station	156

TEXAS

TX28R3	Air Force Village	157
TX43R3	Air Force Village II	157

TEXAS (continued)

TX07R3	Belton Lake Recreation Area	158
TX27R3	Bergstrom Air Force Base (X,O)	158
TX26R3	Brooks Air Force Base	159
TX21R3	Carswell Air Force Base	159
TX23R3	Chase Field Naval Air Station (X)	160
TX10R3	Corpus Christi Naval Air Station	161
TX12R3	Dallas Naval Air Station	161
TX14R3	Dyess Air Force Base	162
TX06R3	Fort Bliss (O)	163
TX02R3	Fort Hood	164
TX18R3	Fort Sam Houston	164
TX24R3	Goodfellow Air Force Base (O)	165
TX03R3	Kelly Air Force Base	166
TX22R3	Kingsville Naval Air Station	167
TX25R3	Lackland Air Force Base	167
TX42R3	Laguna Shores Recreation Area	168
TX05R3	Laughlin Air Force Base	168
TX19R3	Randolph Air Force Base	169
TX09R3	Red River Army Depot	169
TX20R3	Reese Air Force Base	170
TX37R3	Sheppard Air Force Base (O)	171

UTAH

UT04R4	Dugway Proving Ground	172
UT02R4	Hill Air Force Base	172
UT05R4	Tooele Army Depot	173

VERMONT

NONE

VIRGINIA

VA02R1	Cheatham Annex Naval Supply Center	174
VA06R1	Dahlgren Naval Surface Weapons Center	174
VA25R1	Dam Neck Fleet Combat Training Center Atlantic	175
VA17R1	Fort A. P. Hill	176
VA12R1	Fort Belvoir (O)	177
VA10R1	Fort Eustis	177
VA15R1	Fort Lee (O)	178
VA13R1	Fort Monroe	179
VA24R1	Fort Myer	180
VA16R1	Fort Pickett	181
VA08R1	Fort Story	181
VA01R1	Judge Advocate General's School	182
VA07R1	Langley Air Force Base	183
VA19R1	Little Creek Naval Amphibious Base	184
VA18R1	Norfolk Naval Base	185
VA09R1	Oceana Naval Air Station	186
VA11R1	Quantico Marine Corps Combat Development Command	186
VA03R1	Vint Hill Farms Station	187
VA14R1	Yorktown Naval Weapons Station	188

WASHINGTON

WA08R4	Bangor Naval Submarine Base	189
WA02R4	Fairchild Air Force Base (O)	189
WA09R4	Fort Lewis (O)	190
WA15R4	Madigan Army Medical Center	191
WA05R4	McChord Air Force Base (O)	192
WA16R4	Pacific Beach Ocean Getaway	193
WA11R4	Puget Sound Naval Shipyard	193
WA10R4	Puget Sound Naval Station (O)	194
WA06R4	Whidbey Island Naval Air Station	195

WEST VIRGINIA

NONE

WISCONSIN

WI02R2	Fort McCoy	195

WYOMING

WY01R4	Francis E. Warren Air Force Base	196

UNITED STATES POSSESSIONS

GUAM

GU03R8	Agana Naval Air Station	198
GU01R8	Andersen Air Force Base	198
GU02R8	Guam Naval Station	199

MIDWAY ISLAND

MW01R8	Midway Island Naval Air Facility	200

PUERTO RICO

PR03R1	Borinquen Coast Guard Air Station	200
PR01R1	Fort Buchanan	201
PR02R1	Roosevelt Roads Naval Station	201

FOREIGN COUNTRIES

ANTIGUA

AN01R1	Antigua Naval Facility	203

AUSTRALIA

AU01R8	Harold E. Holt Naval Communications Station	203

BELGIUM

BE01R7 NATO/SHAPE Support Group (US) 204

BERMUDA

BM01R1 Bermuda Naval Air Station 205

CANADA

CN02R1 Argentia Naval Facility 205
CN03R1 Goose Bay Air Base 206

CUBA

CU01R1 Guantanamo Bay Naval Station 206

GERMANY

GE59R7 Amberg Sub-Community 207
GE60R7 Ansbach/Katterbach Community 207
GE39R7 Augsburg Community 208
GE49R7 Bad Kissingen Community 209
GE01R7 Bad Kreuznach Community 209
GE02R7 Bad Tölz Community 210
GE34R7 Bamberg Community 211
GE03R7 Baumholder Community 211
GE07R7 Berchtesgaden AFRC 212
GE26R7 Berlin Community 213
GE50R7 Bindlach/Bayreuth Sub-Community 214
GE04R7 Bitburg Air Base 214
GE32R7 Bremerhaven Community 215
GE51R7 Butzbach Sub-Community 216
GE08R7 Chiemsee AFRC 216
GE37R7 Darmstadt Community 217
GE05R7 Frankfurt Community 218
GE35R7 Fulda Community 219
GE10R7 Garmisch AFRC 219
GE89R7 Gelnhausen Sub-Community 221
GE23R7 Giessen Community 221
GE06R7 Göppingen Community 222
GE11R7 Grafenwöhr Training Area 222
GE12R7 Hahn Air Base 223
GE13R7 Hanau Community 224
GE33R7 Heidelberg Community 224
GE38R7 Heilbronn Community 225
GE45R7 Hessich-Oldendorf Air Station 226
GE53R7 Idar-Oberstein Sub-Community 226
GE30R7 Kaiserslautern Community 227
GE14R7 Karlsruhe Community 227
GE40R7 Landstuhl Army Medical Center 228
GE41R7 Mainz Community 228
GE43R7 Mannheim Community 229
GE15R7 Munich Community 229
GE54R7 Neubreucke Sub-Community 230

GERMANY (continued)

GE28R7	Neu-Ulm Community	231
GE44R7	Nürnberg Community	231
GE42R7	Pirmasens Community	232
GE24R7	Ramstein Air Base	233
GE16R7	Rhein Main Air Base	234
GE17R7	Schwäbisch Hall Community	234
GE48R7	Schweinfurt Community	235
GE18R7	Sembach Air Base (RUNWAY CLOSED)	235
GE19R7	Spangdahlem Air Base	236
GE20R7	Stuttgart Community	237
GE25R7	Tempelhof Central Airport	237
GE52R7	Wertheim Sub-Community	238
GE27R7	Wiesbaden Community	238
GE86R7	Wildflecken Community	239
GE31R7	Worms/Northpoint/Weierhof Community	239
GE21R7	Würzburg Community	240
GE22R7	Zweibrücken Air Base (X) (CLOSED)	240
GE29R7	Zweibrücken Community	241

GREECE

GR01R9	Hellenikon Air Base (X) (CLOSED)	242
GR02R9	Iraklion Air Station	242

HONG KONG

HK01R8	China Fleet Club	243

ICELAND

IC01R7	Keflavik Naval Station	244

ITALY

IT03R7	Admiral Carney Park	244
IT04R7	Aviano Air Base	245
IT10R7	Camp Darby	245
IT11R7	Comiso Air Station (X)	246
IT13R7	La Maddalena Navy Support Office	247
IT05R7	Naples Naval Support Activity	247
IT07R7	San Vito dei Normanni Air Station	248
IT01R7	Sigonella Naval Air Station	248
IT06R7	Vicenza Palladio	249

JAPAN

JA14R8	Atsugi Naval Air Facility	249
JA07R8	Camp S. D. Butler Marine Corps Base	250
JA06R8	Camp Zama	251
JA12R8	Iwakuni Marine Corps Air Station	251
JA08R8	Kadena Air Base	252
JA03R8	Misawa Air Base	253

JAPAN (continued)

JA01R8	New Sanno US Forces Center	253
JA09R8	Okuma Recreation Center	255
JA10R8	Tama Hills Recreation Center	255
JA02R8	Tokyo Administration Facility	256
JA05R8	Yokosuka Fleet Activities	256
JA04R8	Yokota Air Base	257

KOREA

RK06R8	Chinhae Naval Facility	258
RK09R8	Dragon Hill Lodge	258
RK05R8	Kunsan Air Base	259
RK08R8	Kwang Ju Air Base (X)	259
RK01R8	Naija Hotel Armed Forces Recreation Center	260
RK04R8	Osan Air Base	261
RK03R8	Suwon Air Base (X)	262
RK07R8	Yongsan Army Garrison	262

NETHERLANDS

NT02R7	Schinnen Community	263
NT01R7	Sösterberg Air Base	263

PANAMA

PN02R3	Fort Clayton	264
PN01R3	Howard Air Force Base	265
PN03R3	Quarry Heights Post	265

PHILIPPINES

RP02R8	Camp John Hay USAF Rec Center (CLOSED)	266
RP03R8	Clark Air Base (CLOSED)	267
RP01R8	Grande Island Recreation Center	268
RP04R8	Subic Bay Naval Station	269

PORTUGAL

PO01R7	Lajes Field, Azores	270

SPAIN

SP01R7	Moron Air Base	270
SP02R7	Rota Naval Air Station	271
SP03R7	Torrejon Air Base	272
SP04R7	Zaragoza Air Base	272

TURKEY

TU01R9	Ankara Air Station	273
TU03R9	Incirlik Air Base	273
TU04R9	Izmir Air Station	274
TU02R9	Sinop Army Field Station	275

UNITED KINGDOM

UK01R7	RAF Alconbury	275
UK12R7	RAF Bentwaters/Woodbridge	276
UK02R7	Brawdy Wales Naval Facility	277
UK03R7	Burtonwood Army Depot	277
UK04R7	RAF Chicksands	278
UK06R7	Edzell Naval Security Group Activity	278
UK11R7	RAF Fairford (X) (CLOSED)	279
UK05R7	RAF Greenham Common/Welford (X)	279
UK07R7	RAF Lakenheath	280
UK13R7	London Service Clubs	281
UK08R7	RAF Mildenhall	282
UK09R7	RAF Upper Heyford/Croughton	283
UK10R7	RAF Wethersfield (CLOSED)	284

APPENDICES

APPENDIX A - Country & State Abbreviations 285
APPENDIX B - General Abbreviations 286
APPENDIX C - Regional Maps 288
APPENDIX D - Temporary Military Lodging Questions & Answers 308
APPENDIX E - Billeting Regulations and Navy Lodge Information 311
APPENDIX F - Installations That Did Not Respond 317
Hotel/Motel Directory 319
Coupons 357

NEW TML 363
    California - Tustin Marine Corps Air Station
    Florida - Panama City Naval Coastal Systems Center
    Hawaii - Barking Sands Pacific Missile Range Facility
    Ohio - Defense Construction Supply Center
    Germany - Kitzingen Sub-Community

NOTE: (X) indicates base closures listed in the President's FY 1991 budget. Some bases scheduled for closure or realignment do not have TML and consequently are not listed in this book. (O) indicates bases approved by the Commission on Base Realignment and Closures in 1988. These bases would close or lose or gain 100 or more employees. The schedule for closures and realignments will cover an approximate five year period beginning in 1990.

INFO ON MILITARY LIVING

MILITARY LIVING PUBLICATIONS
(MILITARY MARKETING SERVICES, INC.)

Military Living was founded in 1969. The company publishes **Military Living**, a 30,000-copy circulation monthly magazine distributed on more than twenty military installations in the Washington, D.C. area.

Our travel newsletter, Military Living's **R&R Space-A Report**, has been published since 1971 and is available worldwide by subscription.

Military Living currently publishes seven travel guides and is researching additional titles to improve the quality of life for military personnel and their families. See Central Order Coupons at the back of this book.

HOW TO RECOGNIZE MILITARY LIVING'S BOOKS

All of Military Living's books carry the famous Military Living logo. Military Living is known as "The Morale Booster Publisher." The slogan, "Travel on Less Per Day...The Military Way," is copyrighted by Military Living. Ann Crawford, the founder of Military Living, is a well-known travel writer whose articles reach military families around the world. The president of the parent company, Military Marketing Services, Inc., is William "Roy" Crawford, Sr., Ph.D.

Corporate offices are located at 137 North Washington Street, Suite 201, Falls Church, Virginia 22046-4515. The corporate mailing address is P. O. Box 2347, Falls Church, Virginia 22042-0347. The telephone number is (703) 237-0203. Our FAX number is (703) 237-2233.

Temporary Military Lodging Around the World — 1

UNITED STATES

ALABAMA

Dauphin Island Recreational Complex (AL07R2)
Mobile Coast Guard Base
Mobile, AL 36615-1390

TELEPHONE NUMBER INFORMATION: Main installation numbers: Comm: 205-639-6110, FTS: 537-6110.

Location: Off base. On the Gulf of Mexico approximately 40 miles south of Mobile. I-10 to AL-163 (Dauphin Island Parkway exit). South approximately 35 miles to Dauphin Island. Left at dead end to east end of island. Follow signs to complex. RM: p-5, V/3. NMI: USCG Aviation Training Center, Mobile, 40 miles north. NMC: Mobile, 40 miles north.

Billeting Office: None. Reservations required, by application only, with advance payment. Summer (1 May-30 September): up to 60 days in advance for active CG; up to 30 days, all others. Fall/winter (1 October-30 April): 15-30 days in advance. Address: Dauphin Island Recreational Complex, P.O. Box 436, Dauphin Island, AL 36528-0436. Comm: 205-861-7113.

TML: TLF. 13/3-bedroom cottages, private bath. Bedding and linens not provided. Seven day maximum stay for cottages during summer. Rates: $40.00-$65.00 per day weekends, $50.00-$85.00 per day during week. Reservations as outlined above.

Fort McClellan (AL01R2)
Fort McClellan, AL 36205-5000

TELEPHONE NUMBER INFORMATION: Main installation numbers: Comm: 205-848-4611, ATVN: 865-1110.

Location: Nine miles north of I-20. Take AL-21 north to Fort. Also located 25 miles southeast of I-59. Take US-431 to Fort. RM: p-4, G/11. NMC: Anniston, 3 miles southeast.

Billeting Office: Building 3295, 14th Street & Summerall Road. 24 hours daily. Comm: 848-4338/3546. ATVN: 865-4338/3546. Check in billeting. Check out 1000 hours.

TML: Fort McClellan Lodge. Building 3127. All ranks. Leave or official duty. Check in at lodge. Accessible to handicapped. EX-4916. 50 rooms, two double beds/queen size sofa sleeper, private bath. A/C, free cribs, essentials, ice vending, kitchenette, complete utensils, maid service, special facilities for handicapped American veterans, color TV room & lounge, (.25) washer/dryer. New structure, completed 1989. Rates: $20.00 per night, per room. Maximum 6 persons. Disabled American veterans (if hospital patient) and dependents, and PCS in/out can make reservations. Others Space-A.

TML: VEQ. Buildings 269, 937, 938, 940, 941, 943-946. Enlisted all grades Official duty only. EX-4338. 640 rooms, private and semi-private baths. 1/3-bedroom cottage, semi-private bath. A/C, essentials, ice vending, maid service, refrigerator, color TV, free washer/dryer. Modern structures. Rates: $10.00 per person. Maximum 1 per room.

2 — *Temporary Military Lodging Around the World*

ALABAMA
Fort McClellan, continued

TML: VOQ. Buildings 2275-2277, 3133, 3134, 3136, 3137. Officer all grades. Official duty only. EX-4338. 187/1-bedroom, private bath. 40/1-bedroom, semi-private bath. A/C, community kitchen, essentials, refrigerator, kitchenette (some units), color TV room & lounge, free washer/dryer, ice vending. Older structures. Some rooms remodeled 1989. Renovations anticipated 1990. Rates: $10.00 per person. Maximum 1 per room.

TML: DV/VIP. Buildings 57, 300, 900, 1026. Leave or official duty. Officer 06+. 4/1-bedroom, private bath. 5/2-bedroom, private bath. 3/3-bedroom cottages, private bath. A/C, essentials, ice vending, kitchenette, complete utensils, maid service, refrigerator, color TV, free washer/dryer. Older structures. Remodeled 1989. Leave rates: Sponsor $12.00, adult $12.00, child/infant $3.00. Duty rates: Sponsor $10.00, adult $8.00, child $3.00. Duty can make reservations. Retirees and lower grades Space-A.

DV/VIP: Protocol, USACML+MPCEN+FM, EX-5616. 06+ or GS-13+. Retirees and lower grades Space-A.

Other: Military Police, Natural History, Chemical and WAC Museums.

TML Availability: Best November-December. Difficult, other times.

Cafeteria-820-2000   Enlisted Club-848-5294   Locator-848-3795
Medical-848-2345   NCO Club-848-5294   O'Club-848-5406
Police-848-5555   Snack Bar-820-2000
SDO/NCO-848-3821

Fort Rucker (AL02R2)
Fort Rucker, AL 36362-5000

TELEPHONE NUMBER INFORMATION: Main installation numbers: Comm: 205-255-6181, ATVN: 558-1110.

Location: Ninety miles southeast of Montgomery, midway between the capital city and Florida Gulf Coast, and 7 miles south of Ozark, off US-231 on AL-249. Clearly marked. RM: p-5, Q/12. NMC: Dothan, 22 miles southeast.

Billeting Office: Building 308, 6th Ave. EX-3780. 24 hours daily. For reservations call 598-5216 between 0730-1200 and 1300-1615 M-F. All travelers report to billeting. Check out 1100 hours daily. Government civilian employee billeting in VOQ.

TML: Guest House. Building 124. All ranks. Leave or official duty. 0600-2200 daily. Comm: 598-6352, ATVN: 558-2479. 38 units, 2 double beds, sofa bed, private bath. Kitchen, maid service. Rates: $22.00 per unit. Duty, PCS in/out and family members attending graduation can make reservations. Others Space-A.

TML: VOQ/VEQ/DVQ. Building 308. Officer all grades, enlisted E7-E9. 355/1-bedroom, private bath; 2/2-bedroom cottages, semi-private bath; 5/3-bedroom cottages (3 are DVQ), semi-private bath; 3/4-bedroom cottages (1 is DVQ), semi-private bath; 2 separate bedroom DVQ suites, private bath. Kitchen (50%), refrigerator, A/C, color TV, maid service, free washer/dryer, ice vending. Modern structure, renovated '87. Rates: Sponsor $15.00, others $4.00 ($6.00 per person in cottages). $19.00 maximum per family ($24.00 for cottages). Duty can make reservations. Others Space-A.

DV/VIP: ATTN: Protocol, Building 114 (Post Hq). Comm: 255-3100. ATVN: 558-3400. 06/GS-15+. Retirees and lower grades one night only.

Temporary Military Lodging Around the World — 3

ALABAMA

Fort Rucker, continued

Other: U.S. Army Aviation Museum.

TML Availability: Best, October-April. Limited, May-September.

Enlisted Club-255-5191   Medical-255-7900   NCO Club-255-5191
O'Club-598-2566   Police-255-4175   SDO/NCO-255-3100

Gunter Air Force Base (AL04R2)
Gunter AFB, AL 36114-5000

TELEPHONE NUMBER INFORMATION: Main installation numbers: Comm: 205-279-1110, ATVN: 446-1110.

Location: Take I-65 to Northern bypass, 6 miles to exit on AL-231, continue west 1 mile to AFS. Coming from the opposite direction, from I-85, follow signs and take eastern bypass north 1 mile to AL-231. Then west 1 mile to AFS. RM: p-5, X/7. NMC: Montgomery, 2 miles southwest.

Billeting Office: ATTN: Gunter billeting, Building 1503. 24 hours daily. EX-3360/4611.

TML: VAQ. Buildings 1014-1016. Enlisted all grades. Leave or official duty. Check in at billeting. 247 separate bedroom, semi-private bath; 4 suites, private bath. Refrigerator, A/C, color TV, maid service, free washer/dryer, facilities for disabled American veterans. Modern structure. Check out 1200 hours daily. Rates: $5.00 per person. Duty can make reservations. Others Space-A.

TML: VOQ. Buildings 301, 314, 315 & 1503. Officer all grades. Leave or official duty. Accessible to handicapped. Buildings 301-315 have 33 suites with private bath. Building 1503 has 69 rooms with semi-private bath (Airmen can also use this facility). Refrigerator, A/C, color TV, maid service, free cribs & cots, free washer/dryer, facilities for disabled American veterans. Older buildings. Check out 1200 hours daily. Rates: $5.00 per person (rooms); $10.00 per person (suites). Duty can make reservations. Others Space-A.

TML: TLF. Building 200. All ranks. Leave or official duty. 3/2-bedroom, private bath; 1/3-bedroom apartment, private bath. Kitchen, utensils, A/C, color TV, maid service, free cribs & cots, free washer/dryer. Modern structure. Check out 1200 hours daily. Rates: $17.00 per person. Maximum $17.00 per family. Duty can make reservations. Others Space-A.

DV/VIP: See Maxwell AFB listing.

TML Availability: Good.

Medical-279-4211   NCO Club-279-4804   O'Club-264-1731
Police-446-4250   SDO/NCO-293-2862

Maxwell Air Force Base (AL03R2)
Maxwell AFB, AL 36112-5000

TELEPHONE NUMBER INFORMATION: Main installation numbers: Comm: 205-953-1110, ATVN: 875-1110.

Location: Take I-85 South to I-65, exit on Day St which leads to main gate of base. RM: p-5, Y/4. NMC: Montgomery, 1.5 miles southeast.

Billeting Office: 3800 ABW/SVH, Building 157, West Drive. EX-2401. 24 hours

4 — *Temporary Military Lodging Around the World*

ALABAMA
Maxwell Air Force Base, continued

daily. Check in billeting, check out 1200 hours. Government civilian employee billeting.

TML: TLF. Buildings 46-49. All ranks. Leave or official duty. 30/1-bedroom apartments, private bath. Kitchen, limited utensils, A/C, color TV, maid service, free cribs/cots, free washer/dryer, ice vending. Modern structure. Rates: $20.00 per apartment. Maximum 5 persons. Duty can make reservations. Others Space-A.

TML: VAQ. Building 965. Enlisted all grades. Leave or official duty. 6 SNCO suites, private bath; 38 single rooms, shared bath; 24 double rooms, shared bath. Rates: $5.00-$10.00 per person. Maximum $20.00.

TML: VOQ. Buildings 1412-1419, 1430-1434, 1468, 1470. All ranks. Leave or official duty. 816/1-bedroom, semi-private bath; 342 separate bedroom, private bath. Kitchen, A/C, color TV, maid service, free cribs/cots, free washer/dryer, ice vending. Modern and older structures. Complete renovations in process 1412-1419, 1430-1434. Rates: Sponsor $5.00, adult $5.00. Maximum charge $10.00. Maximum 3 persons per unit. Duty can make reservations. Others Space-A.

TML: Chief Suites. Building 697. Enlisted E-9. Leave or official duty. 5 separate bedrooms, private bath. A/C, essentials, ice vending, maid service, refrigerator, color TV, free washer/dryer, wet bar, microwave. Renovated '87. Rates: Sponsor $10.00, adult $10.00. Maximum charge $20.00. Maximum 3 persons per unit. Duty can make reservations. Others Space-A.

DV/VIP: AU Protocol Office, Building 800. EX-2095. O7+. Retirees Space-A.

TML Availability: Extremely limited year-round.

Enlisted Club-262-8364   Medical-293-2333   NCO Club-262-8364
O'Club-262-8364   Police-293-2766   SDO/NCO-293-2862
Locator-293-5027

Redstone Arsenal (AL06R2)
Redstone Arsenal, AL 35898-5350

TELEPHONE NUMBER INFORMATION: Main installation numbers: Comm: 205-876-2151, ATVN: 746-0011.

Location: Off US-231 South on Martin Rd to main gate with visitor control. For uniformed personnel, Gate 8 is on Drake Ave. Take US-72 East to Jordan Lane, south to Drake. Drake becomes Goss Road at the Arsenal. RM: p-5, E/15. NMC: Huntsville, adjacent north and east sides.

Billeting Office: ATTN: AMSMI-RA-EH-HM-BH. Building 244. Goss Rd. EX-5713/8028. 24 hours daily. Check in facility, check out 1100 hours daily. Government civilian employee billeting.

TML: Guest House. Building 244. All ranks. Leave or official duty. Comm: EX-4130. 1/1-bedroom, private bath; 4 separate bedroom, kitchen, private bath. Refrigerator, community kitchen, limited utensils, A/C, color TV, maid service, free cribs, coin washer/dryer, ice vending. Modern structure, renovated. PCS rates based on BAQ. Unofficial guest, $25.00. Duty can make reservations. Others Space-A.

TML: VOQ/VEQ. Building 131-136. All ranks. Official duty only. 12 separate bedrooms, private bath; 74/2-bedroom, semi-private bath. Kitchen, A/C, color TV, maid service, free washer/dryer. Older structure, renovated. Rates: $15.00 per person. Duty can make reservations. Duty on leave Space-A. Check with billeting for availability.

Temporary Military Lodging Around the World — 5

ALABAMA

Redstone Arsenal, continued

TML: DVQ. Buildings 111, 135. Officer all grades. Leave or official duty. 6 separate bedroom suites, private bath. Refrigerator, A/C, color TV, maid service. Older structure, new furniture/carpets '88. Rates: Sponsor $15.00, $5.00 each additional person. Maximum $25.00 per family. Duty can make reservations. Others Space-A.

DV/VIP: Contact billeting office. 06+. Retirees and lower grades Space-A.

Other: Alabama Space & Rocket Center, Rt 20 west of Huntsville.

TML Availability: Very good, Nov-Feb. More difficult, other times.

Enlisted Club-881-6525   Medical-876-5780   NCO Club-837-0750
Locator-876-3331   O'Club-830-2582   Police-876-2222
SDO/NCO-876-8351/3331

ALASKA

Adak Naval Air Station (AK04R5)
FPO Seattle 98791-5000

TELEPHONE NUMBER INFORMATION: Main installation numbers: Comm: 907-592-8001, ATVN: 317-692-8001.

Location: On Adak Island of the Aleutian Island chain, accessible only by air or ship. RM: p-6, K/7. NMC: Anchorage, 1200 air miles northeast. Note: Closed Station, only assigned personnel and cleared/sponsored guests are allowed on Base Write to Commander for clearance.

Billeting Office: Housing Office, EX-8287, 0800-1700 hours duty days. Check in facility, check out 1000 hours daily. Government civilian employee billeting.
TML: Navy Lodge. All ranks. Leave or official duty. EX-8287/8647. 0800-1700 M-Sa. 14/2-bedroom, living room, private bath. Kitchen, color TV, coin washer/dryer, vending machine. Modern structure. Rates: $18.00 per unit. All categories can make reservations.

TML: Apartments. Officer all grades, enlisted E4-E9. Duty only. 6/2-bedroom apartments, private bath. Kitchen, complete utensils, color TV, free cribs/cots, free washer/dryer. Modern structure. Rates: $18.00 per unit. PCS can make reservations. Others Space-A.

TML Availability: Limited.

Caf (Deli)-592-8491   Enlisted Club-592-8104   Medical-592-8201
NCO Club-592-8393   O'Club-592-8354   Police-592-8051
SDO/NCO-592-4201

Eielson Air Force Base (AK15R5)
Eielson AFB, AK 99702-5000

TELEPHONE NUMBER INFORMATION: Main installation numbers: Comm: 907-377-1110, ATVN: 377-1110.

Location: On the Richardson Highway (AK-2), AFB is clearly marked. RM: p-6, E/7. NMC: Fairbanks, 20 miles northwest.

6 — *Temporary Military Lodging Around the World*

ALASKA
Eielson Air Force Base, continued

Billeting Office: Building 5219 (basement), Coman Street. EX-1844. 24 hours daily. Check in billeting, check out 1200 hours daily. Government civilian employee billeting.

TML: TLQ. Building 3305. All ranks. Leave or official duty. 40 separate bedrooms, private bath (living room has sleeper sofa & chair). Kitchen, complete utensils, color TV, maid service, free cribs, free washer/dryer, facilities for disabled American veterans. Modern structure. Rates: $25.00 per room. Maximum 5 per room. Duty can make reservations. Others Space-A.

TML: VOQ/VAQ. Buildings 5180 & 6 others. All ranks in respective quarters. Leave or official duty. Some buildings accessible to handicapped. 26/1-bedroom, semi-private bath (VOQ). 76 separate bedrooms, private bath (VOQ); 80/1-bedroom, shared bath (VAQ). Community kitchen, limited utensils, refrigerator, cribs, essentials, ice vending, color TV room & lounge, maid service, free washer/dryer. Older structure. Rates: $8.00 per person (VOQ), $6.00 per person (VAQ). Duty can make reservations. Others Space-A.

DV/VIP: Protocol Office, 343TFW/CCE, Building 3112, Room 5, EX-6101. E9/06+. Retirees Space-A.

Other: Mt. McKinley and National Park.

TML Availability: Good, Dec-Mar. Difficult, other times.

Enlisted Club-377-2635
NCO Club-377-2635
B/Bowl A-377-5154
Locator-377-1841
O'Club-377-1121
Snack Bar-377-5154
Medical-377-2296
Police-377-5130

Elmendorf Air Force Base (AK09R5)
Elmendorf AFB, AK 99506-5000

TELEPHONE NUMBER INFORMATION: Main installation numbers: Comm: 907-552-1110, ATVN: 317-552-1110.

Location: Off Glenn Highway. Take Muldoon, Boniface, Post Rd or Government Hill exits. The AFB is next to Ft Richardson. RM: p-6, A/11. NMC: Anchorage, 2 miles southwest.

Billeting Office: Building 31-250, Acacia St. EX-2454. 24 hours daily. Check in facility, check out 1000 hours daily.

TML: TLF. Building 31-250. All ranks. Leave or official duty. 70/1-bedroom, shared bath. Refrigerator, color TV lounge, maid service, coin washer/dryer. Older structure. Rates: $40.00 per unit. Duty can make reservations. Others Space-A.

TML: VOQ. Officer all grades. Leave or official duty. 78/1-bedroom, share bath; 20/1-bedroom, private bath (DV/VIP). Same as TLF except rates: $8.00 per person.

TML: VAQ. Enlisted all grades. Leave or official duty. 269/1-bedroom, share bath. Same as VOQ except rates: $6.00 per person.

DV/VIP: Protocol Office. EX-3210. 06+. Retirees Space-A.

TML Availability: Fairly good. Best, Sep-Jan.

Cafeteria-552-4276
Medical-552-2748
Enlisted Club-753-6131
NCO Club-753-9144
Locator-552-4860
O'Club-753-3131

Temporary Military Lodging Around the World — 7

ALASKA

Elmendorf Air Force Base, continued

Police-552-3421   Snack Bar-552-2994   SDO/NCO-552-3013

Fort Greely (AK10R5)
Fort Greely, AK 98733-5000

TELEPHONE NUMBER INFORMATION: Main installation numbers: Comm: 907-873-1121, ATVN: 317-363-1121.

Location: Off AK-4, 6 miles south of junction of AK-2 & AK-4. Five miles south of Delta Junction. RM: p-6, F/6. NMC: Fairbanks, 105 miles northwest.

Billeting Office: ATTN: Billeting. Building 663, First St. Comm: 873-3285. ATVN: 363-3285. 0730-1600 hours M-F. Others hours, SDO, Building 501, EX-4220. Check in billeting, check out 1100 hours daily. Government civilian employee billeting.

TML: VOQ/VEQ. Building 702. All ranks. Leave or official duty. 32/1-bedroom, share bath (VEQ); 3 separate bedrooms, private bath (VOQ). Refrigerator, color TV, maid service, free cribs/cots, free washer/dryer. Older structure. Rates: $14.00 per person VEQ, $6.00 each additional person; $16.00 per person VOQ, $6.00 each additional person. Duty can make reservations. Others Space-A. Pets boarded at veterinary clinic on post.

TML Availability: Good. Best, Mar-Apr, Dec. More difficult, Jan-Feb.

Cafeteria-869-3110   Enlisted Club-873-3105   Locator-873-4225
Medical-873-4498   NCO Club-873-3105   O'Club-873-3105
Police-873-4323   Snack Bar-869-3110

Fort Richardson (AK03R5)
Fort Richardson, AK 99505-5000

TELEPHONE NUMBER INFORMATION: Main installation numbers: Comm: 907-864-0121, ATVN: 317-864-0121.

Location: Main gate is on Glenn Highway, 5 miles south of Eagle River. RM: p-6, B/12. NMC: Anchorage, 8 miles southwest.

Billeting Office: Building 724, Door 25, Quartermaster Dr. Comm: 862-4279. ATVN: 863-8216. 0600-2230 hours M-F, 1000-1400 Sa. Other times SDO, Building 1, EX-0104. Check in billeting, check out 1200 hours daily. Billeting has 1800 check-in policy. If you plan to arrive after 1800, notify in advance. Government civilian employee billeting in VOQ/DV/VIP.

TML: VOQ. Buildings 57, 58, 345, 1107, 1113. Officer all grades. Leave or official duty. 74 separate bedroom, private bath. Kitchen, refrigerator, color TV, maid service, free cribs/cots, free washer/dryer, ice vending. Older structure. Rates: Sponsor $16.00, others $6.00 each. Reservation 30 days in advance for official TDY or ADT. 15 days in advance for other categories if space available.

TML: VEQ. Building 1114. Enlisted all grades. Leave or official duty. 24/1-bedroom, shared bath; 8 separate bedroom, private bath. Refrigerator, color TV, maid service, free cribs/cots, free washer/dryer, ice vending. Older structure. Rates: Sponsor $14.00, each additional person $6.00. Maximum 5 persons per suite and 3 per room. Reservations policy same as VOQ.

TML: DV/VIP. Building 53 (Igloo). Officer 06+. Leave or official duty. EX-1115. 3/1-bedroom, private bath; 13 separate bedroom suites, private bath; 2/1-bedroom, kitchen, private bath apartments. Refrigerator, limited utensils, color TV, maid

ALASKA
Fort Richardson, continued

service, free cribs/cots, free washer/dryer, ice vending. Older structure, renovated. Rates: Sponsor $23.00, additional person $6.00 each. Reservation policy same as VOQ.

DV/VIP: ATTN: AFVR-GS, Protocol Office, Building 1, Room 111, EX-7204/1115. 06+. Retirees and lower grades Space-A.

Other: Fish & Wildlife Museum, Building 600, EX-8288.

TML Availability: Good, Oct-Apr. Difficult, other times.

Cafeteria-428-1314	Enlisted Club-428-1360	Locator-862-0192
Medical-752-3333	NCO Club-428-1360	O'Club-428-1330
Police-864-0127	Snack Bar-428-1393	SDO/NCO-862-2185

Fort Wainwright (AK07R5)
Fort Wainwright, AK 99703-5320

TELEPHONE NUMBER INFORMATION: Main installation numbers: Comm: 907-353-6113/7500, ATVN: 317-353-6113/7500.

Location: From Fairbanks, take Airport Way East which leads to the main gate of the Post. RM: p-6, E/12. NMC: Fairbanks, 3.5 miles west.

Billeting Office: Building 1045 (Murphy Hall), Gaffney Rd. EX-7726. 0600-2230 hours M-F, Sat 1000-1600 hours. Other hours SDO, Building 1555, EX-7500. Check in billeting, check out 1200 hours daily.

TML: VEQ. Building 4056. Enlisted all grades. Leave or official duty. EX-7291. 27/1-bedroom, private bath (12 suites). Refrigerator, color TV, maid service, free cribs/cots, free washer/dryer, food/ice vending. Older structure. Remodeled '87. Rates: Sponsor $14.00, each additional person $6.00. Duty can make reservations. Others Space-A.

TML: VEQ. Building 4063. Enlisted all grades. Leave or official duty. 10/1-bedroom suites, private bath; 20 single rooms, shared bath. Refrigerator, color TV, maid service, free cribs/cots, free washer/dryer, ice vending. Rates: Sponsor $14.00, each additional person $6.00. Duty can make reservations. Others Space-A.

TML: VOQ. Buildings 4064, 1045. Officer all grades. Leave or official duty. 1045 accessible to handicapped. EX-7291. 3/2-bedroom suites, private bath. Refrigerator, color TV, maid service, essentials, free cribs/cots, free washer/dryer, food/ice vending. Older structures. Remodeled '85. Rates: Sponsor $16.00, each additional person $6.00. Duty can make reservations. Others Space-A.

TML: VIP/VOQ. Building 1045. Officer all grades. Leave or official duty. EX-7291. 27/1-bedroom, living room, private bath; 4 DV/VIP suites (kitchen-one unit). Refrigerator, color TV, maid service, free crib/cots, free washer/dryer, ice vending. Older structure. Rates: Sponsor $23.00, each additional person $6.00. Duty can make reservations. Others Space-A.

DV/VIP: PAO, Building 15550. EX-7118. As designated by Cmdr. Lower grades and retirees Space-A.

Other: Birch Hill Ski Area, Morale Support Activity, No TML. EX-6325.

TML Availability: Fairly good, Oct-Apr. Difficult, other times.

Cafeteria-356-1159	Enlisted Club-353-6716	Locator-353-6586

Temporary Military Lodging Around the World — 9

ALASKA

Fort Wainwright, continued

Medical-353-5110
Police-353-7531
NCO Club-353-6716
Snack Bar-353-7300
Club-356-6109
SDO/NCO-353-7500/6172

Kodiak Coast Guard Support Center (AK08R5)
Kodiak, AK 99619-5000

TELEPHONE NUMBER INFORMATION: Main installation numbers: Comm: 907-487-5267, ATVN: 317-487-5267.

Location: From Kodiak City, take main road southwest for 7 miles. Base is on the left side. RM: p-6, I/5. NMC: Kodiak, 7 miles northeast.

Billeting Office: Administration Building. EX-5310. 0745-1630 duty days. Other hours, Security, Administration Building, EX-5265. Check in facility, check out 1200 hours daily. Government civilian employee billeting.

TML: Guest House. BOQ Building. All ranks. Leave or official duty. EX-5446. 0800-1700 hours daily. 31/1-bedroom, private bath. Some converted to suites. Community kitchen, cable, color TV room & lounge, maid service, free cribs/cots, free washer/dryer, ice vending. Older structure. Rates: $18.00 single, $25.00 double, $30.00 family suite. All categories can make reservations.

TML: BOQ. Officer all grades. Leave or official duty. EX-5446. 19/1-bedroom, private bath. Some converted to suites. Color TV room & lounge, maid service, free cribs/cots, free washer/dryer, ice vending. Older structure. Rates: Suites $50.00, rooms $30.00. Duty can make reservations. Others Space-A. 200 BEQ units. Duty only. No charge.

TML: DV/VIP. BOQ. Officer 05+. Leave or official duty. Reservations accepted. EX-5446. 1 separate bedroom suite, private. Same facilities, rates & occupancy as BOQ above.

DV/VIP: Cmdr. EX-5265. 05+. Retirees Space-A.

TML Availability: Good, Oct-May. Difficult, Jun-Aug.

Cafeteria-487-5783
Locator-487-5252
Police-487-5267
CPO Club-487-5440
Medical-487-5222
Snack Bar-487-5478
Enlisted Club-487-5110
O'Club-487-5440
SDO/NCO-487-5266/7

ARIZONA

Davis-Monthan Air Force Base (AZ01R4)
Davis-Monthan AFB, AZ 85707-5000

TELEPHONE NUMBER INFORMATION: Main installation numbers: Comm: 602-750-3900, ATVN: 361-1110.

Location: Exit I-10 North Palo Verde, circle around to the Golf Links, turn right on Craycroft and proceed to main gate. RM: p-7, P/10. NMC: Tucson, 3 miles northwest.

Billeting Office: Building 2350, 10th St. ATTN: Inn on Davis Monthan, P.O. Box 15013. Comm: 748-1500. ATVN: 361-3230. 24 hours daily. Check in billeting, check out 1200 hours daily. Government civilian employee billeting.

ARIZONA
Davis-Monthan Air Force Base, continued

TML: TLF. Various buildings. All ranks. Leave or official duty. EX-3309. 16/2-bedroom, private bath; 1/4-bedroom, private bath. Kitchen, complete utensils, A/C, color TV, maid service, free cribs/cots, free washer/dryer. Modern structure. Rates: $22.00 per unit. PCS in/out can make reservations. Others Space-A.

TML: VAQ. Buildings 3510, 3511, 4210, 4065. Enlisted all grades (females in 3511 only). Leave or official duty. EX-3309. 207/1-bedroom, 2 beds, latrine bath; 8 separate bedroom Senior Noncommissioned Officer suites, kitchen, private bath; 24/1-bedroom, 2 beds, share kitchen, private bath; 4 separate bedroom Chief Suites, private bath (E9 only). Refrigerator, A/C, color TV room & lounge, maid service, free washer/dryer. Modern structure. Rates: $6.00 per person; Senior Noncommissioned Officer suites, $10.00 per person. Official duty can make reservations. Others Space-A.

TML: VOQ. Buildings 2350, 2550, 4065. Officer all grades. Leave or official duty. EX-3309. 43/1-bedroom, share kitchen, private bath; 16 separate bedroom, kitchen, bar, private bath; 8/2-bedroom, refrigerator, private bath. A/C, color TV room & lounge, maid service, free washer/dryer, ice vending. Modern structure. Rates: $8.00 per person. Maximum $16.00 per family. Official duty can make reservation. Others Space-A.

TML: DV/VIP. Building 4065. Officer 06+. Leave or official duty. EX-3600. 8/2-bedroom suites, 06+, private bath (one special for general/flag officers). Refrigerator, microwave, limited utensils, A/C, color TV, maid service, free washer/dryer, ice vending. Modern structure. Rates: $10.00 per person. Maximum $20.00 per family. All categories can make reservations. Protocol may cancel reservations for non-AD if AD requires space.

DV/VIP: 836 AD/CCP. EX-3600. 06+. Retirees Space-A.

Other: Old Tucson; Reid Park & Zoo; Arizona-Sonora Desert and Pima Air Museum.

TML Availability: Difficult. Best, Aug, Dec.

Cafeteria-790-6150
O'Club-750-3301
Medical-750-3878
Police-750-3200
NCO Club-750-3100
SDO/NCO-750-3121

Fort Huachuca (AZ02R4)
Fort Huachuca, AZ 85613-6000

Telephone Number Information: Main installation numbers: Comm: 602-538-7111, ATVN: 879-0111.

Location: From I-10 take AZ-90 south to Sierra Vista and main gate of Fort. RM: p-8, O/10. NMC: Tucson 75 miles northwest.

Billeting Office: ATTN: ASQH-DEH-H. Building 43083, Service Road. Comm: 533-2222/5361. 24 hours daily. Check in billeting, check out 1100 hrs. Government civilian employee billeting.

TML: Guest House. Buildings 42017, 52054. All ranks. Leave or official duty. 21/1-bedroom, 2 double beds, private bath; 6 separate bedroom, double bed, private bath; 3/2-bedroom, double beds, private bath; 3/3-bedroom, double beds, private bath. Community kitchen, refrigerator, A/C, color TV, maid service, cribs ($1.00 per day), free washer/dryer. Modern structure. Rate: $19.50 per unit. Maximum eight persons in 42017, five persons in 52054. Duty can make reservations. Others Space-A. Pets OK first night only. Must be boarded by second day. On-post kennels available.

Temporary Military Lodging Around the World — 11

ARIZONA

Fort Huachuca, continued

TML: DVQ. Buildings 22102, 22104. Officers 06+. Leave or official duty. 8 suites - 6 separate bedroom, private bath; 2/2-bedroom, private bath. Kitchen, complete A/C, color TV, maid service, cribs $2.00, free washer/dryer. Older structures. Rates: Sponsor $30.00, $2.00 each additional person. Duty can make reservations. Others Space-A.

TML: VOQ/VEQ. Buildings 43083-43086. All ranks. 185/1-bedroom, private bath or semi-private bath. Kitchen & refrigerator in most units, A/C, color TV, maid service, free washer/dryer. Modern structure. Rates: $21.50 per person. Facility restricted to AD.

DV/VIP: Commander, USAISC, ATTN: AS-SGS-P, Room 3209. Comm: 538-6040. 06+. Retirees and lower grades Space-A.

Other: Post Museum. Rock hunting.

TML Availability: Best, Dec. Difficult, other times

Enlisted Club-458-2113   Medical-533-5152   NCO Club-458-2113
O'Club-533-2195   Police-533-2181   SDO/NCO-538-6100

Gila Bend Air Force Auxiliary Field (AZ16R4)
Gila Bend AFAF, AZ 85337-5000

TELEPHONE NUMBER INFORMATION: Main installation numbers: Comm: 602-683-6200, ATVN: 853-5200 (Security Police).

Location: From Phoenix, take I-10 West to AZ-85 south to Gila Bend. The field is four miles out of town. Also off I-8 between Yuma and Casa Grande. RM: P-8, L/5. **NMC:** Phoenix, 65 miles northeast.

Billeting Office: ATTN: Desert Hideaway Inn, P.O. Box 1086, Gila Bend AFAF, AZ 85337. Building 4250. 0700-2000 M-F, by special arrangement on weekends. Check in billeting, check out 1200. Comm: 683-6238. ATVN: 853-5238. Government civilian employee billeting.

TML: Desert Hideaway Inn. All ranks. Leave or official duty. 22/2 beds per unit, semi-private bath. 5 separate bedrooms, semi-private bath. 4/2-bedroom, semi-private bath. 3/3-bedroom, private bath. A/C, community kitchen, free cribs, essentials, maid service, refrigerator, color TV lounge & room, free washer/dryer. Older structure. Remodeled '87. Rates: $5.50 per night. Maximum charge $18.00. Maximum 2 persons. Duty can make reservations. Others Space-A.

TML: TFL. Buildings 114, 118, 122. All ranks. Leave or official duty. Accessible to handicapped. 3/3-bedroom houses, private bath. A/C, cribs, essentials, kitchen, complete utensils, maid service, color TV, free washer/dryer. Older structures. Renovated and remodeled Jan '89. Maximum charge $18.00. Maximum 5 beds per unit. Duty can make reservations. Others Space-A.

TML: VAQ. Building 4250. Enlisted. All grades. Leave or official duty. 22/1-bedroom, semi-private bath, 2 beds per room. 5 separate bedrooms, semi-private bath. A/C, community kitchen, essentials, maid service, color TV lounge & room, free washer/dryer. Older structure. Renovated and remodeled '86. Rates: Sponsor $5.50, adult $5.50. Maximum 2 persons. Duty can make reservations. Others Space-A.

TML: VOQ. Building 2358 A, B, C, D. Officer. All ranks. Accessible to

ARIZONA
Gila Bend Air Force Auxiliary Field, continued

handicapped. 4/2-bedroom, semi-private bath. A/C, community kitchen, essentials, kitchen, maid service, refrigerator, color TV lounge. Older structure. Rates: Sponsor $8.50, adult $8.50. Maximum 2 persons. Duty can make reservations. Others Space-A.

DV/VIP: Protocol Office, 832 CSG/CC, EX-6262, ATVN-5262. Retirees and lower grades Space-A.

TML Availability: Very good. Difficult Oct-Jan.

Cafeteria-853-5240	Medical-853-5270	NCO Club-853-5257
O'Club-853-5257	Enlisted Club-853-5257	Police-853-5220

Luke Air Force Base (AZ03R4)
Luke AFB, AZ 85309-5000

TELEPHONE NUMBER INFORMATION: Main installation numbers: Comm: 602-856-7411, ATVN: 853-0111.

Location: From Phoenix, west on I-10 to Litchfield Rd, north on Litchfield Rd approximately 5 miles. Also, from Phoenix, on I-17 to Glendale Ave, west on Glendale Ave to intersection of Glendale Ave and Litchfield Rd, approximately 16 miles. RM: p-8, K/6. NMC: Phoenix, 20 miles southeast.

Billeting Office: ATTN: Fighter Country Inn, Building 660, 2nd St. Comm: 935-3941, ATVN: 835-3941. 24 hours daily. Check in billeting, check out 1200 hours daily.

TML: VOQ. 6 buildings. Officer all grades. Leave or official duty. 33/1-bedroom; 44 separate bedrooms; 78/2-bedroom. All with private bath. Kitchen, refrigerator, A/C, color TV, maid service. Modern structure. Rates: Moderate.

TML: TLF. 4 buildings. All ranks. Leave or official duty. 40/1-bedroom, private bath. Kitchen, utensils, A/C, color TV, maid service, free washer/dryer. Modern structure. Rates: Moderate.

TML: VAQ. 4 buildings. Enlisted all grades. Leave or official duty. 12/1-bedroom, private bath; 36/2-bedroom, semi-private bath. Kitchen, utensils, A/C, color TV, maid service, free washer/dryer. Older structure. Rates: Moderate. Maximum $11.00 per unit.

TML: DV/VIP. 2 buildings. Officer O7+. Leave or official duty. 2/2-bedroom suites, private bath. Kitchen, utensils, A/C, color TV, maid service. Older facility. Rates: Moderate. Duty can make reservations. Others Space-A.

DV/VIP: Protocol Officer, 832AD. EX-5840. Grades O7+. Retirees and lower grades Space-A on a day-by-day basis.

TML Availability: Best, June-Aug & Dec. Difficult, other times.

Enlisted Club-856-7136	Medical-856-7506	NCO Club-856-7136
O'Club-856-6446	Police-856-6349	SDO/NCO-856-5800

Williams Air Force Base (AZ09R4)
Williams AFB, AZ 85224-5000

TELEPHONE NUMBER INFORMATION: Main installation numbers: Comm: 602-988-2611, ATVN: 474-1110.

Temporary Military Lodging Around the World — 13

Williams Air Force Base, continued ARIZONA

Location: From I-10 exit go east on Chandler Blvd, 17 miles to AFB. RM: p-8, K/7. NMC: Phoenix, 30 miles northwest.

Billeting Office: ATTN: 82 ABG/SVH. Building 321, 7th St at O'Club Circle. EX-5546. 24 hours daily. Check in billeting, check out 1200 hours daily. Government civilian employee billeting.

TML: TLQ. Buildings 775-778. All ranks. Leave or official duty. 40 separate bedrooms, private bath. Kitchen, refrigerator, limited utensils, A/C, color TV, maid service, free cribs, free washer/dryer, ice vending. Modern structure, renovated. Rates: E6 below $14.00 per family; E7+ $18.00 per family. Duty can make reservations. Others Space-A.

TML: BOQ. Buildings 324, 326. All ranks. Leave or official duty. 70/1- bedroom, private bath. Kitchen, refrigerator, limited utensils, A/C, maid service, free cribs, free washer/dryer, ice vending. Modern structure, remodeled. Rates: $17.00 officers, $6.00 enlisted. Duty can make reservations. Others Space-A.

TML: DV/VIP. Building 324. Officer 07+. Leave or official duty. EX-5212. 6/1-bedroom suites, private bath. Kitchen, utensils, A/C, color TV, maid service, free washer/dryer. Modern structure. Rates: $10.00 per pers. Duty can make reservations. Others Space-A.

DV/VIP: 82 FTW/CC, S-1, EX-5212. 07+. Retirees and lower grades Space-A.

TML Availability: Good, Dec-Feb. Difficult, other times.

Cafeteria-988-1970	Enlisted Club-988-6635	Medical-988-5452
NCO Club-988-1501	O'Club-988-5448	Police-988-6993
SDO/NCO-988-6811		

Yuma Army Proving Ground (AZ05R4)
Yuma Army Proving Ground, AZ 85365-9102

Telephone Number Information: Main installation numbers: Comm: 602-328-2151, ATVN: 899-2151.

Location: Northeast of I-8 turn right on US-95. Southwest of I-10 turn left on US-95. US-95 is north/south route which bisects APG. RM: p-8 K/1. NMC: Yuma, 27 miles southwest.

Billeting Office: ATTN: STEYP-EH-H, Building 1003, 5th St & Barranca Rd. EX-2127/2129. 0700-1530 hours. Other hours, SDO, Bldg S-2, EX-2127/2129. Check in billeting, check out 1100 hours daily. Government civilian employee billeting.

TML: Guest House. Building 538. All ranks. Leave or official duty. 10/1-bedroom, private bath. Kitchen, utensils, A/C, color TV room & lounge, maid service, free cribs/cots, free washer/dryer, ice vending. Modern structure. Rates: Sponsor $18.00, each additional person $3.00. Maximum 4 per room. Reservations required. One room accessible to handicapped.

TML: VOQ. Building 1004. All ranks. Official duty only. 24/1-bedroom, semi-private bath; 2/2-bedroom, kitchen, private bath. Community kitchen, A/C, color TV room & lounge, maid service, washer/dryer, ice vending. Modern structure. Rates: Sponsor $21.00, each additional person $4.00. All categories can make reservations.

TML: DV/VIP. Building 1004. Officer 06+. Leave or official duty. 3 suites, private bath. Refrigerator, community kitchen, A/C, color TV room & lounge, maid service, free cribs/cots, free washer/dryer, ice vending, coffee machine, beverages. Older

ARIZONA
Yuma Army Proving Ground, continued

structure. Rates: Sponsor $27.00, each additional person $7.00. 06/GS-13+.

TML Availability: Fairly good, Apr-Sept. More difficult, Oct-Mar.

Cafeteria-328-2591   Enlisted Club-328-3937   Medical-328-2911
NCO Club-328-3937   O'Club-328-3937   Police-328-2790
SDO/NCO-328-2020

Yuma Marine Corps Air Station (AZ04R4)
Yuma MCAS, AZ 85365-5000

TELEPHONE NUMBER INFORMATION: Main installation numbers: Comm: 602-726-2011, ATVN: 951-2011.

Location: From I-8 take Ave 3E south for 1 mile to MCAS on the right. Adjacent to Yuma IAP. RM: p-8, M/1. NMC: Yuma, 3 miles northwest.

Billeting Office: Building 1020, Thomas Ave. Comm: 726-4970. ATVN: 951-3094. 24 hours daily. Check in billeting, check out 1000 hours.

TML: TLQ. Hostess House. Building 1020. All ranks. Leave or official duty. Comm: 726-2262. 13 separate bedroom, private bath. Refrigerator, community kitchen, A/C, color TV, maid service, cribs/cots, ice vending. Older structure. Rates: Station personnel $16.00 per unit, transient personnel $20.00. 7 day limit, then daily. All categories can make reservations.

TML: BEQ. Building 1040. Enlisted E6-E9. Leave or official duty. 52/1-bedroom, semi-private bath; 2 suites, private bath. Refrigerator, A/C, color TV room & lounge, maid service, free washer/dryer, microwave in lounge. Modern structure. Rates: $4.00 per pers. All categories can make reservations.

TML: BOQ. Building 1020. Officer all grades. Leave or official duty. 78/1-bedroom, semi-private bath; 4 separate bedrooms, private bath. Refrigerator, A/C, color TV room & lounge, maid service, free washer/dryer, ice vending. Modern structure. Rates: $6.00 per pers. All categories can make reservations.

TML: DV/VIP. Building 1058. Officer 06+. Leave or official duty. 22/1-bedroom, 3 suites, private bath. Refrigerator, community kitchen, A/C, color TV suites & lounge, maid service, free washer/dryer, ice vending. Modern structure. Rates: $10.00-$30.00 per unit. 06+ may make reservations. All others Space-A. Children not authorized.

DV/VIP: Adjutant. EX-2253. 06/GS-15+. Retirees Space-A.

TML Availability: Good.

Cafeteria-726-2369   Enlisted Club-726-2457   Medical-726-2772
NCO Club-726-2171   O'Club-726-2711   Police-726-2361
SDO/NCO-726-2253

Temporary Military Lodging Around the World — 15

ARKANSAS

Eaker Air Force Base (AR01R2)
Eaker Air Force Base, AR 72315-5000

TELEPHONE NUMBER INFORMATION: Main installation numbers: Comm: 501-762-7000, ATVN: 721-7000.

Location: From I-55 exit to US-61 north through Blytheville to Gosnell to main gate of base. RM: p-9, D/12. NMC: Memphis, 70 miles south.

Billeting Office: Building 702, Memorial Dr. ATTN: Sgt in charge. EX-7461/6163. 24 hours daily. Check in billeting, check out 1200 hours daily. No government civilian employee billeting.

TML: Guest Houses. Various buildings. All ranks. Leave or official duty. Check out 1000 hours. Accessible to handicapped. 5/4-bedroom cottages, private bath. Kitchen, complete utensils, refrigerator, A/C, color TV, maid service, free cribs/cots, free washer/dryer, food/ice vending. Modern structure. Flat rate: $20.00-$21.00 per night. PCS in/out have priority. Others Space-A.

TML: TAQ. Building 702. Enlisted all grades. Leave or official duty. 21 rooms with 2 beds, 2 rooms with 1 bed, private bath. A/C, cots/cots, ice vending, maid service, refrigerator, color TV room and lounge, washer/dryer. Rates: $9.00 per person. Maximum charge $18.00. Duty have first priority. Others Space-A.

TML: DV/VIP/VOQ. Various buildings. All ranks. Leave or official duty. Check out 1200 hours. DV/VIP: 5 houses, private bath. A/C, cots/cribs, ice vending, kitchenette, maid service, color TV room and lounge, utensils, washer/dryer. Rates: $13.00 per person. Maximum charge $26.00. VOQ: 17/1-bedroom, private bath. Refrigerator, A/C, color TV room & lounge, maid service, free cribs/cots, essentials, free washer/dryer, ice vending. Older structure. New carpets '89. Rates: $9.00 per person. Maximum charge $18.00. Duty can make reservations. Others Space-A.

DV/VIP: No separate office. Call billeting. 06+.

TML Availability: Fairly good. Best Oct-Mar. Difficult other times.

Enlisted Club-762-7469	**Medical**-762-7219	**NCO Club**-762-7110
O'Club-762-7111	**Police**-762-7331	**Snack Bar**-762-7109
Locator-762-7260/7461		

Fort Chaffee (AR04R2)
Fort Chaffee, AR 72905-5000

TELEPHONE NUMBER INFORMATION: Main installation numbers: Comm: 501-484-2141, ATVN: 962-2111.

Location: From I-40, take the I-540 exit west in Fort Smith. From I-540, exit onto AR-22 east (Rogers Ave) and continue through the town of Barling to Fort Chaffee, one mile east of Barling. RM: p-9, F/2. NMC: Fort Smith, 6 miles southwest.

Billeting Office: Building 1377, Fort Smith Blvd, 0730-2400 M-F, 0930-1800 weekends, Comm: 501-484-2252, ATVN: 962-2252.

TML: TLF. Rooms for approximately 50 persons. Call for details.

TML Availability: More difficult, summer.

16 — Temporary Military Lodging Around the World

ARKANSAS

Little Rock Air Force Base (AR02R2)
Little Rock AFB, AR 72099-5000

TELEPHONE NUMBER INFORMATION: Main installation numbers: Comm: 501-988-3131, ATVN: 731-1110.

Location: Use US-67/167 to Jacksonville, take AFB exit to main gate. RM: p-9, G/7. NMC: Little Rock, 18 miles southwest.

Billeting Office: P.O. Box 1192, Building 1024, Cannon Circle. EX-6753. 24 hours daily. Check in billeting, check out 1200 hours daily. No government civilian employee billeting.

TML: VOQ/VAQ. Building 1024. All ranks. Leave or official duty. EX-6652. 220/1-bedroom, semi-private bath; 4/2-bedroom, private bath; 68/1-bedroom, semi-private bath. Refrigerator, A/C, color TV, maid service, free washer/dryer, ice vending. Modern structure, remodeled. Rates: VAQ/VOQ $6.00, DV $8.00. Children not authorized. Duty can make reservations. Others Space-A.

DV/VIP: 314 TAW/CCE. EX-6828/3588. 06+. Retirees Space-A, limited.

TML Availability: Extremely limited. Best, Dec.

Cafeteria-988-1139	Enlisted Club-988-1039	NCO Club-988-4121
O'Club-988-1111	Police-988-3221	SDO/NCO-988-3200

Pine Bluff Arsenal (AR03R2)
Pine Bluff, AR 71602-9500

TELEPHONE NUMBER INFORMATION: Main installation numbers: Comm: 501-543-3000, ATVN: 966-3000.

Location: Off US-65 northwest of Pine Bluff. Take AR-256, cross AR-365 into main gate of Arsenal. Or south on US-65 from Little Rock, 35 miles, follow signs. RM: p-9, H/7. NMC: Pine Bluff, 8 miles southeast.

Billeting Office: ATTN: SMCPB-EHH. Building 34-970, Hoadley Rd. EX-3008. 0730-1600 hours daily. Other hours SDO, EX-3505. Check in billeting, check out 1200 hours daily. Government civilian employee billeting.

TML: TQ & BOQ. Buildings 15-330, 15-350. All ranks. Leave or official duty. 6/1-bedroom, private bath; 14 separate bedroom, private bath; 1/2-bedroom, private bath. Refrigerator, community kitchen, utensils, A/C, color TV, maid service, free cribs/cots, free washer/dryer. Older structure, new siding/windows '86, carpets '87. Rates: Sponsor $15.00, adults $1.00, children (13+) $1.00, under 12 free. Duty can make reservations. Others Space-A.

TML Availability: Extremely limited.

Medical-543-3409	Police-543-3505/3506	SDO/NCO-543-3176

Temporary Military Lodging Around the World — 17

CALIFORNIA

Alameda Coast Guard Support Center (CA28R4)
Alameda, CA 94501-5000

TELEPHONE NUMBER INFORMATION: Main installation numbers: Comm: 415-437-3151, ATVN: 536-3151.

Location: Take I-880 south to 23rd St exit, right and straight to causeway and Island. Signs posted. RM: p-11, ND/22. NMC: Oakland, 1 mile east.

Billeting Office: No central billeting office. Housing office in Building 21, McCullough Dr. EX-3437. 0700-1530 hours. No government civilian employees billeting.

TML: Transient Quarters. Buildings 18, 24, 26. All ranks. Official duty only. Reservations not taken. Call for details: BEQ EX-3106, VOQ EX-3303.

TML Availability: Very limited.

Cafeteria-437-3624 Enlisted Club-437-3304 Police-437-3151
SDO/NCO-437-3153

Alameda Naval Air Station (CA33R4)
Alameda NAS, CA 94501-5000

TELEPHONE NUMBER INFORMATION: Main installation numbers: Comm: 415-263-0111, ATVN: 993-0111.

Location: From Nimitz Highway, I-880 south, take the Broadway/Alameda exit. From I-880 north take Broadway exit. Directions to NAS clearly marked. RM: p-11, ND/2. NMC: Oakland, 2 miles northwest.

Billeting Office: Building 17, B St. 24 hours daily. EX-3207. Check in facility, check out 1200 hours daily. Government civilian employee billeting.

TML: Navy Lodge. Building 531. All ranks. Leave or official duty. For reservations call 1-800-NAVY-INN. Check in 0600-2230 hours daily. 70/1-bedroom, 2 beds, living room, private bath. Kitchen, complete utensils, A/C, color TV room & lounge, maid service, free cribs, coin washer/dryer, ice vending. Modern structure. Rates: $30.00 per unit. Maximum 5 persons. All categories can make reservations. Expansion of this facility is planned by summer 1991.

TML: BOQ. Building 17. Officer all grades. Leave or official duty. 163/1-bedroom, semi-private bath; 9 separate bedrooms, private bath; 10 VIP suites for 06+, private bath; 4 VIP suites for 07+, private bath. Refrigerator, color TV room & lounge, free washer/dryer, ice vending. Older structure, renovated. Rates: Sponsor, $6.00, adult $10.00, child no charge. Maximum $16.00 per unit. Duty can make reservations. BEQ facilities also available.

DV/VIP: CO, Building 1. 07+. Retirees Space-A.

TML Availability: Good all year.

Enlisted Club-263-3218 Medical-263-4420 NCO Club-263-3211
O'Club-263-3224 Police-263-3766 SDO/NCO-263-3011

18 — *Temporary Military Lodging Around the World*

CALIFORNIA

Barstow Marine Corps Logistics Base (CA13R4)
Barstow, CA 92311-5000

TELEPHONE NUMBER INFORMATION: Main installation numbers: Comm: 619-577-6211, ATVN: 282-0111

Location: On I-40, 1.5 miles east of Barstow. Take I-15 northeast from San Bernardino, or west from Las Vegas, NV. Signs mark direction to MCLB. RM: p-13, SI/17. NMC: San Bernardino, 75 miles southwest.

Billeting Office: Building 44. EX-6896. 0700-1530 hours daily. Other hours OD, Building 30, Room 8, EX-6611. Check in/out at billeting.

TML: TLF. Buildings 114, 187. All ranks. Leave or official duty. AD 45 days in advance. Special services, Building 44, EX-6896. 9 apartments: 7/1-bedroom, private bath; 2/2-bedroom, private bath. Kitchen, utensils, A/C, BW TV. Older structure. Reservations accepted. Rates: Based on rank & 1/30th of BAQ. Check out 1000 hours daily.

TML: VIP. Building 11-A, 1/2-bedroom, private bath. 06+. Leave or official duty. Kitchen, utensils, A/C, color TV, maid service, free washer/dryer. Older structure. Rates: $25.00 per unit. All categories can make reservations. Check out 1100 hours daily.

DV/VIP: Commanding General, Building 15, EX-6555. 06+. Retired & lower grades Space-A.

Other: Calico Ghost Town, 8 miles east, Solar One, 7 miles east. Lake Delores, 13 miles east.

TML Availability: Good, Oct-Apr. Difficult, other times.

Cafeteria-577-6264	Enlisted Club-577-6495	Locator-577-6663
Medical-577-6588	NCO Club-577-6495	O'Club-577-6432
Police-577-6666	SDO/NCO-577-6653	

Beale Air Force Base (CA47R4)
Beale Air Force Base, CA 95903-5000

TELEPHONE NUMBER INFORMATION: Main installation numbers: Comm: 916-634-3000, ATVN: 368-3000

Location: From CA-70 North exit south of Marysville, to North Beale Rd, continue for 10 miles to main gate of AFB. RM: p-11, NK/10. NMC: Sacramento, 35 miles southwest.

Billeting Office: Building 2156, Warren Shingle Blvd. EX-2084. 24 hours daily. Check in billeting, check out 1200 hours daily. Government civilian employee billeting.

TML: TLF. Buildings 5109-5112, 3120. All ranks. Leave or official duty. 10/2-bedroom, private bath; 6/3-bedroom, private bath; 8/4-bedroom, private bath. Kitchen, complete utensils, A/C, color TV room & lounge, maid service, free cribs/cots, free washer/dryer, microwave, dishwasher. Older structure, new TVs/carpet '87. Rates: $18.00 2 bedroom, $21.00 3 bedroom, $24.00 4 bedroom. Duty can make reservations. Others Space-A.

TML: VAQ. Building 2156. Enlisted E5+. Official duty only. Reservations not taken. Rooms and suites, semi-private and private baths. Community kitchen, A/C, color TV room & lounge, maid service, free washer/dryer, ice vending, microwave.

Temporary Military Lodging Around the World — 19

CALIFORNIA

Beale Air Force Base, continued

Older structure, remodeled. Rates: $50.00-$60.00 per month. Maximum 1 per room.

TML: VOQ. Buildings 2350, 2352. Officer all grades. Official duty only. Reservations not taken. 4/2-bedroom suites, private bath. Kitchen, A/C, utensils, color TV room & lounge, maid service, washer/dryer, microwave. Older structure. Rates: $65.00 per month. Maximum 2 per room.

TML: VOQ. Building 2300 area. Officer all grades. Leave or official duty. 35/4-bedroom, private bath. Kitchen, limited utensils, A/C, color TV room & lounge, maid service, free cribs/cots, free washer/dryer, microwave. Older structure, renovated '88. Rates: $8.00 per person. Maximum $16.00 per room. Maximum 12 per room. Duty can make reservations. Others Space-A.

TML: VAQ. Building 2156. Enlisted all grades. Leave or official duty. 33/1-bedroom, 2 beds, semi-private bath; 3/1-bedroom suites, private bath. Refrigerator, A/C. color TV room & lounge, maid service, free cribs/cots, free washer/dryer, ice vending, microwave. Older structure, remodeled. Rates: $8.00 per person. Maximum $16.00 per room. Maximum 3 per room. Duty, TDY, PCS in can make reservations. Others Space-A.

DV/VIP: Protocol Office, EX-2050. 06+. Retirees and lower grades Space-A.

TML Availability: Good, Sep-May. Difficult, other times.

Cafeteria-788-1070 Locator-634-2657 Medical-634-2992
O'Club-634-4146   Police-634-2131   NCO Club-634-2559
Snack Bar-788-1070 SDO/NCO-634-2883

Camp Pendleton Marine Corps Base (CA30R4)
Camp Pendleton, CA 92055-5001

TELEPHONE NUMBER INFORMATION: Main installation numbers: Comm: 619-725-4111, ATVN: 365-4111.

Location: On I-5 which is adjacent to main gate. Take Camp Pendleton off ramp from I-5 at Oceanside. RM: p-13, SN/16. NMC: Oceanside, adjacent to base on southeast.

Billeting Office: Building 1341, Mainside. From main gate, Vandergrift Blvd 10 miles to right on Rattlesnake Canyon Rd, right at fire station to Vandergrift Blvd again, 3 blocks right at theater, 4 blocks to billeting sign, left to Building 1341. EX-3718/3451/3732. 24 hours daily. Check in as indicated, check out 1100 hours daily. Government civilian employee billeting.

TML: Buildings 1341, 1342, Mainside. Officer all grades, WO1-CW4. EX-3732/3451. Check in at billeting. 20/1-bedroom, single occupancy, semi-private bath; 20 separate bedrooms, private bath. Refrigerator, TV, maid service, cribs ($1.00), washer/dryer. Older structure, renovated. Rates: $12.00 TAD/TDY, $14.00-$14.50 others, $5.00 each additional person. TAD/TDY and PCS in/out can make reservations. Others Space-A.

TML: Guest House. Building 1310. All ranks. Leave or official duty. Reservations accepted. EX-5194. Check in at facility. 64 separate bedrooms, private bath. Kitchen (36 units), limited utensils, A/C, color TV room & lounge, maid service, cribs ($0.50), cots ($1.00), coin washer/dryer, ice vending, facilities for disabled American veterans, swimming pool. Modern structure. Rates: $20.00 with kitchen, $15.00 without kitchen. All categories can make reservations.

TML: TEQ. Building 16146. Enlisted all grades. Leave or official duty. Check out

CALIFORNIA
Camp Pendleton Marine Corps Base, continued

1200. 42/1-bedroom, private bath. Refrigerator, color TV lounge, maid service, free washer/dryer. Older structure. Rates: Sponsor $10.00 TAD/TDY, $11.50 others, $5.00 each additional person over 12 years. Duty can make reservations. Others Space-A. Also TOQ, Buildings 1341, 1342, 210440, 5016. Call for additional information.

TML: DV/VIP. Building 1751. Officer 06+. Leave or official duty. EX-5810. 3/2-bedroom suites, private bath. Kitchen, utensils, A/C, color TV, maid service, washer/dryer, dishwasher. Older structure, remodeled '84. Rates: $25.00 TAD/TDY, $30.00 others, $5.00 each additional person over 12 years. Maximum 6 per suite. TAD/TDY can make reservations. Others Space-A. General/Flag rank have priority.

DV/VIP: ATTN: CG's Sec, Building 1161, EX-5810. 05+. Retirees and lower grades Space-A.

TML Availability: Fairly good, Oct-Mar. More difficult, other times.

McDonald's-725-6233　　Locator-725-4111　　Medical-725-6308
NCO Club-725-2294　　Enlisted Club-725-3066　　O'Club-725-6571
Police-911　　Snack Bar-725-6233　　SDO/NCO-725-5617

Camp San Luis Obispo (CA83R4)
San Luis Obispo, CA 93403-8104

TELEPHONE NUMBER INFORMATION: Main installation numbers: Comm: 805-549-3800, FTS: 629-3800.

Location: Take Highway 1 five miles northwest of the City of San Luis Obispo. RM: p. 12, SH/8. NMC: San Luis Obispo, five miles southeast.

Billeting Office: Building 738, San Joaquin Avenue. ATTN: Billeting Manager, P.O. Box 8104. 805-549-3800. 0800 thru 1630 hours daily. After duty hours 549-3806, Operation. Check in during hours, check out 1200 hours. Government civilian employee billeting.

TML: BOQ. Transient housing. Rooms, apartments, cottages. Officer all grades. Enlisted, E-7 thru E-9. Leave or official duty. 101/1-bedroom, community bath; 39/1-bedroom, hall bath; 3/2-bedroom, private bath; 3/3-bedroom, private bath; 4/various bedroom/bath combinations. Refrigerator, kitchen (some units), limited utensils, color TV, free washer/dryer, maid service. Older structure. Carpets/TV '89. Rates: on leave, Sponsor, $12.00, adult, $12.00, child, $12.00. Rates: on duty, Sponsor, $8.00, adult $12.00, child $12.00. Maximum varies with unit. Duty can make reservations. Others Space-A. NO PETS ALLOWED.

DV/VIP: No separate office. Call billeting. 06+. Retirees, lower grades Space-A.

Other: Small aircraft museum on post, state beaches, wineries, Hearst Castle, San Luis Obispo Mission Plaza and Farmers Market.

TML Availability: Fairly good. Best Sept thru Mar. Difficult other times.

Locator-549-3800　　NCO Club-543-4034　　O'Club-541-6168
Police-911　　SDO/NCO-549-3806

Temporary Military Lodging Around the World — 21

CALIFORNIA

Castle Air Force Base (CA10R4)
Castle AFB, CA 95342-5000

TELEPHONE NUMBER INFORMATION: Main installation numbers: Comm: 209-726-2011, ATVN: 347-1110

Location: From Sacramento, take CA-99 south to Atwater, take Buhach exit to AFB. RM: p-11, NQ/12. NMC: Fresno, 60 miles south.

Billeting Office: Building 1108, 4th & C St. EX-2531. 24 hours daily. Check in billeting, check out 1200 hours daily. No government civilian employees billeting.

TML: Guest House. Building 1109, 1116, 1117. All ranks. Leave or official duty. 12/2-bedroom apartments, private bath. Kitchen, utensils, A/C, color TV, maid service, free washer/dryer. Older structure. Rates: $20.00 per apartment. PCS in/out can make reservations. Others Space-A.

TML: VOQ. Building 427. Officer all grades. Leave or official duty. 20/1- bedroom, private bath. Kitchen, utensils, A/C, color TV, maid service, free washer/dryer. Modern structure. Rates: $5.00 per person. Duty can make reservations. Others Space-A.

TML: VAQ. Buildings 1112-1119, 1131. Enlisted all grades. Leave or official duty. 88/2-bedroom. Kitchen, A/C, color TV, maid service. Modern structure. Rates: $5.00 per person. Duty can make reservations. Others Space-A.

TML: DV/VIP. Building 427. Officer 05+. Leave or official duty. 8/1-bedroom apartments. Kitchen, utensils, A/C, color TV, maid service, free washer/dryer. Modern structure. Rates: $8.00 per person. Duty can make reservations. Others Space-A.

DV/VIP: Contact billeting. 06+. Retirees Space-A.

TML Availability: Limited, all year.

Cafeteria-722-4919
Medical-726-2686
Police-726-2111

Enlisted C-723-4317
NCO Club-726-2259
Snack Bar-722-4919

Locator-726-2011
O'Club-726-2769

Centerville Beach Naval Facility (CA71R4)
Ferndale, CA 95536

TELEPHONE NUMBER INFORMATION: Main installation numbers: Comm: 707-786-9531, ATVN: 896-3381.

Location: Take CA Highway 101 250 miles north of San Francisco to the Ferndale Exit, then 5 miles thru Ferndale on Main Street, then right turn on Ocean Avenue, 5 miles to gate. RM: p-10, NF/3. NMC: Eureka, 23 miles north.

Billeting Office: Building 68, Comm: 786-9531, ATVN: 896-3381. Hours 0730 thru 1630. After duty hours contact: CDO, Quarterdeck, 786-9531. No government civilian employee billeting.

TML: BOQ (with accommodations for families). Building 20. Officer. All ranks. Leave or official duty. EX-216. Accessible to the handicapped. Suites: 4/1-bedroom, private bath; 1/2-bedroom, private bath. Refrigerator, community kitchen, free washer/dryer, color TV, maid service, essentials, cribs. Coffee maker, hair dryer, beverage & Sunday resale in each room, free coffee. Older structure. Renovated 1987, carpeting '89. Porch and BBQ area. Rates: Sponsor, $12.00, adult, $12.00, child, $6.00. All categories can make reservations.

CALIFORNIA
Centerville Beach Naval Facility, continued

TML: Enlisted Transient Quarters (with accommodations for families). Building 23. Enlisted. All ranks. Accessible to the handicapped. 2/1-bedroom, private bath. Room divider, queen hide-a-bed couch, 2 bunks with wardrobe. Refrigerator, food vending, color TV, maid service, free washer/dryer, essentials, cribs, coffee maker, free coffee, hair dryer. Older structure. Remodeled '89. Rates: Sponsor, $4.00, adult, $4.00, child, $2.00. All categories can make reservations.

DV/VIP: No protocol office.

Other: Direct coastal access. Only coastal military installation between Pacific Beach, Washington, and San Francisco. Redwood forests, Victorian village of Ferndale, good local outdoor recreation, hunting and fishing.

TML Availability: Very good. Best in the winter. Difficult in summer.

China Lake Naval Weapons Center (CA34R4)
China Lake NWC, CA 93555-6001

TELEPHONE NUMBER INFORMATION: Main installation numbers: Comm: 619-939-2303, ATVN: 437-2303

Location: From US-395 or CA-14, take CA-178 east to Ridgecrest and the main gate. RM: p-13, SF/15. NMC: Los Angeles, 150 miles southwest.

Billeting Office: Officers, BOQ A, next to O'Club, EX-2383/2789. Enlisted, BEQ 2, EX-3146/3039. 0700-2400 hours daily. Check in facility, most check outs 1200 hours daily. Government civilian employee billeting.

TML: Transient House/Transient Rooms. Many buildings. All ranks. Leave or official duty. 12/3-bedroom, private bath (Transient House/VIP suites); 23/1-bedroom, private bath (Transient Rooms). Transient House: kitchen, limited utensils, A/C, color TV, maid service, free cribs, ice vending. Transient Rooms: refrigerator, color TV, maid service. Rates: $8.00 per person. Max $24.00 per family in house. Duty can make reservations. Others Space-A.

TML: BOQ. Buildings 00496, 00499. Officer all grades. Leave or official duty. 6/1-bedroom, private bath; 17 separate bedrooms, private bath. Refrigerator, A/C, color TV room & lounge, free washer/dryer, ice vending (Building 00496). Older structure. Rates: $8.00 per person. 1 per room. Unaccompanied persons only. Duty can make reservations. Others Space-A.

TML: BEQ. 1915 Mitscher. Building 00484. All ranks. Leave or Official duty. 4/3-bedroom, private bath. Kitchen, limited utensils, A/C, color TV, maid service, free cribs, free washer/dryer. Older structure. Rates: $12.00 per unit. Reservations PCS in/out only. Duty can make reservations. Others Space-A if not used by PCS. Pets allowed.

TML: BEQ. 1805 Harpoon. Building 02340. Enlisted all grades. Leave or Official duty. 39/1-bedroom, private/semi-private baths. Kitchen, limited utensils, A/C, color TV lounge, maid service, free washer/dryer, ice vending. Older structure. Rates: $2.00-$4.00 per person. Unaccompanied person only. Duty can make reservations. Others Space-A.

TML: DV/VIP. Buildings 00662, 00663. Officer 06/GS-15+. Leave or Official duty. 4/3-bedroom suites, private bath. Kitchen, limited utensils, A/C, color TV, maid service. Older structure. Rates: $12.00 unaccompanied, $15.00 accompanied. Maximum 3-4 per unit. Duty can make reservations. Others Space-A.

Temporary Military Lodging Around the World — 23

CALIFORNIA

China Lake Naval Weapons Center, continued

DV/VIP: Protocol Office, EX-1365. O6+. Retirees and lower grades Space-A.

TML Availability: Good.

CPO Club-939-3633
Medical-939-2911
Snack Bar-446-4160

Enlisted Club-939-2581
O'Club-939-3105
SDO/NCO-939-2303

Locator-939-2303
Police-939-3323

Coronado Naval Amphibious Base (CA38R4)
San Diego, CA 92155-5000

TELEPHONE NUMBER INFORMATION: Main installation numbers: Comm: 619-437-2011, ATVN: 577-2011.

Location: From San Diego, I-5 south to Palm Ave (CA-75) west 10 miles. Follow signs to Naval Amphibious Base, Coronado. RM: p-15, O/23. NMC: San Diego, 5 miles north.

Billeting Office: Building 500, Tulagi St, Comm: 437-3860/61 (BOQ); Building 303, Comm: 437-3494 (BEQ). 24 hours daily. Check in billeting, check out 1200 hours daily. No government civilian employee billeting.

TML: BOQ. Buildings 500, 504, 505. Officer all grades. Leave or official duty. Accessible to handicapped. 374/1-bedroom units, private bath; 100 separate bedroom private bath. Refrigerator, color TV, maid service, free washer/dryer, ice vending. Modern structure. Rates: Sponsor $8.00, adult $6.00. Maximum $14.00 per family. Maximum 2 per room. Duty can make reservations. Others Space-A.

TML: BEQ. Building 303. Enlisted all grades. Leave or official duty. Accessible to handicapped. 68/1-bedroom, latrine bath; 4/1-bedroom, private bath. Maid service, refrigerator, color TV, washer/dryer. Rates: $3.00 per person. Duty can make reservations. Others Space-A.

TML: DV/VIP. Building 504. Officers 06-10. Leave or official duty. 10 separate bedroom suites, private bath. Refrigerator, color TV, maid service, free washer/dryer, ice vending. Modern structure. Rates: Moderate. Duty can make reservations. Others Space-A.

DV/VIP: Commander. EX-2777. 06/civilian equivalent+. Retirees Space-A.

Other: Coronado Bay, Pacific Ocean, Seaport Village.

TML Availability: Good most of the year.

Cafeteria-435-3503
Medical-437-2900
SDO/NCO-437-3432

Enlisted Club-437-3185
O'Club-437-3040

Locator-437-2011
Police-437-3432

Del Mar Recreation Beach (CA03R4)
Camp Pendleton Marine Corps Base
Camp Pendleton, CA 92055-5018

TELEPHONE NUMBER INFORMATION: Main installation numbers: Comm: 619-725-7935, ATVN: 365-2463.

Location: Exit I-5 on Harbor Drive/Camp Pendleton. Enter either the Del Mar Gate or the Main Gate on Camp Pendleton. Approximately 2.5 miles from either

CALIFORNIA
Del Mar Recreation Beach, continued

gate. RM: p-13, SN/16. NMC: Oceanside, 1 mile south.

Billeting Office: Building 210595. EX-2463. Check in facility 1300-1630 hours daily. After hours check in with Night Host located in site #0. Check out 1200 hours daily. No government civilian employees billeting.

TML: Mobile Homes. Officer, Enlisted E6+. Leave or official duty. 13/2-bedroom. Kitchen, limited utensils, patron must provide own bedding, towels, and pillows, ice vending, washer/dryer. Rates: $22.00 per night/winter; $25.00 per night/summer. Maximum 6 persons. Reservations by all categories except reservists and national guard personnel. Duty Camp Pendleton can make reservations 5 weeks in advance. Duty other stations 4 weeks. Duty USMC have priority. **Pets allowed but they must remain outside. Not allowed on beach.**

Conv Store: 725-6233. See Camp Pendleton listing for other Support Facilities. 26 mi Pacific Ocean shoreline.

TML Availability: Good, Oct-Apr. Difficult, other times.

Edwards Air Force Base (CA48R4)
Edwards AFB, CA 93523-5000

TELEPHONE NUMBER INFORMATION: Main installation numbers: Comm: 805-277-1110, ATVN: 527-1110

Location: Off CA-14, 18 miles east of Rosamond and 30 miles northeast of Lancaster. Also, off CA-58, 10 miles southwest of Boron. RM: p-13, SI/14. NMC: Los Angles, 90 miles southwest.

Billeting Office: Building 5602. EX-4101/3394. 24 hours daily. Check in facility, check out 1200 hours daily. Government civilian employees billeting.

TML: VOQ. Buildings 5601, 5602. Officer all grades. Leave or official duty. 92/1-bedroom, semi-private bath. Fully furnished, A/C, color TV, maid service, free washer/dryer, ice vending. Older structure, newly furnished. Rates: $8.00 per person. Duty can make reservations. Others Space-A.

TML: DV/VIP. Building 5601. Officer 06+. 10/1-bedroom suites, private bath. A/C, color TV, maid service. Older structure. Rates: $14.00 per person. Duty can make reservations. Others Space-A.

TML: VAQ. Buildings 5604, 2410. All ranks. Leave or official duty. Building 5604: 5/1-bedroom Senior Noncommissioned Officer suites. A/C, color TV, maid service. Older structure. Bldg 2410: 4/1-bedroom Senior Noncommissioned Officer rooms; 28/2-bedroom. A/C, color TV, maid service, free washer/dryer. Older structure, remodeled '85. Rates: $8.00 per person. Duty can make reservations. Others Space-A.

TML: Guest House. Building 7022. All ranks. Leave or official duty. 51/1-bedroom, private bath. Fully furnished, kitchen, complete utensils, A/C, color TV, microwave, free washer/dryer, cribs and roll-aways. Older structure, remodeled '87. Reservations accepted. Rates: $16.00 per unit.

DV/VIP: Protocol Office, ATTN: AFFTC/CCP. Building 2650, Room 200. EX-3326. 07+/SES.

TML Availability: Good, all year.

Cafeteria-258-6678   Locator-277-2777   Medical-277-4427

Temporary Military Lodging Around the World — 25

Edwards Air Force Base, continued   **CALIFORNIA**

NCO Club-277-3230   O'Club-277-2830   Police-277-3340
Snack Bar-277-5987   SDO/NCO-277-3040

El Centro Naval Air Facility (CA09R4)
El Centro, CA 92243-5000

TELEPHONE NUMBER INFORMATION: Main installation numbers: Comm: 619-339-2555, ATVN: 958-8555

Location: Take I-8, 2 miles west of El Centro, to Forrester Rd exit, 1.5 miles to Evan Hewes Hwy left west for 4 miles, Right on Bennet Rd to main gate. RM: p-13, SP/21. NMC: El Centro, 7 miles east.

Billeting Office: Building 270, B & 2nd St's. Comm: 339-2535. ATVN: 958-8535. 24 hours daily. Check in billeting, check out 1000 hours daily. Government civilian employees billeting.

TML: Navy Lodge. Building 387. All ranks. Leave or official duty. For resvervations call 1-800-NAVY-INN. Lodge number is 714-339-2478. 4/2-bedroom trailers, private bath. Community kitchen, utensils, A/C, color TV, maid service, coin washer/dryer. Rates: $22.50 per unit. PCS have priority for reservations.

TML: BOQ. Building 270. All ranks. Leave or official duty. 36/1-bedroom, 2 beds, private bath; 2 separate bedrooms, private bath; 3/1-bedroom suite (DV/VIP), private bath. Refrigerator, limited utensils, A/C, color TV room & lounge, maid service, ice vending. Older structure, remodeled. Rates: $4.00 per person. Duty can make reservations. Others Space-A. Also BEQ rooms and houses. Inquire.

DV/VIP: Contact billeting. 06+. Retirees Space-A.

Other: Winter home of the Blue Angles (Jan-Mar).

TML Availability: Good, Sep-Dec. More difficult,

Cafeteria-339-2654   Enlisted Club-339-2570   Medical-339-2675/2666
O'Club-399-2491   Police-339-2525   Snack Bar-339-2472
SDO/NCO-339-2525

El Toro Marine Corps Air Station (CA22R4)
Santa Ana, CA 92709-5000

TELEPHONE NUMBER INFORMATION: Main installation numbers: Comm: 714-726-3011, ATVN: 997-3011.

Location: Off I-5, take the Sand Canyon Rd exit. Follow the signs to the MCAS. RM: p-15, L/15. NMC: Los Angeles, 40 miles northwest.

Billeting Office: Building 58. EX-3724. 0730-1630 hours daily. Other hours SDO, Building 58, EX-3901. Check in facility, check out 1100 hours daily. No government civilian employee billeting.

TML: TLF. Building 823. All ranks. Leave or official duty. EX-2095. 0700-2000 hours daily. 24 family units. Kitchen, complete utensils, A/C, color TV room & lounge, maid service, cribs ($1.00), coin washer/dryer, ice vending, facility for disabled American veterans. Modern structure. Rates: $20.00 per unit. Maximum 6 per unit. Duty can make reservations. Others Space-A.

TML: VOQ/DV/VIP. Buildings 33, 35, 248, 249. Officers all grades. Leave or

CALIFORNIA
El Toro Marine Corps Air Station, continued

Official duty. EX-3001. 40/1-bedroom, latrine bath; 8 separate bedrooms, private bath; 1/2-bedroom, private bath (VIP); 2/3-bedroom, private bath (VIP). Kitchen (2 units), refrigerator, A/C (VIP), color TV room & lounge, maid service, free cots, washer/dryer, ice vending (Building 248). Older structure. Rates: Sponsor $8.00, each additional person $4.00.

DV/VIP: Building 248, EX-3001. 04+. Retirees and lower grades Space-A.

TML Availability: Good, winter months. Difficult, summer months.

Cafeteria-726-3340	Enlisted Club-726-2476	Locator-726-3736
Medical-726-9911	NCO Club-726-2476	O'Club-726-2464
Police-726-2233	Snack Bar-726-3340	SDO/NCO-726-3901

Fort Hunter Liggett (CA37R4)
Jolon, CA 93928-5000

TELEPHONE NUMBER INFORMATION: Main installation numbers: Comm: 408-385-5911, ATVN: 949-2291.

Location: From US-101 south exit at King City to CA-G-14, south to main gate. RM: p-13, SE/5. NMC: San Luis Obispo, 60 miles south.

Billeting Office: Building T-105, EX-2511/2108. 0800-1630 hours duty days. Other hours SDO, Building 205, EX-2503. Check in billeting, check out 1000 hours daily. Government civilian employee billeting.

TML: Guest House. Building T-101. All ranks. Leave or official duty. 6/1-bedroom, private bath; 5/1-bedroom, hall bath. Refrigerator, color TV lounge, maid service. Older structure. Reservations accepted duty only. Rates: $20.00 with bath, $12.00 without bath. Others Space-A.

TML: VOQ. Building T-105. Officers all grades. 50 separate bedrooms, private bath; 10/1-bedroom, hall bath. Refrigerator, A/C, color TV, maid service. Modern structure. Reservations accepted duty only. Rates: $20.00 per room (1 or 2 people). Others Space-A.

TML: VEQ. Building T-128. Enlisted all grades. 38/1-bedroom, semi-private bath. Rates: $15.00 private, $8.00 each share. Reservations accepted duty only.

TML: DV/VIP. Building T-101. Officers 06+. Leave or official duty. 2 bedroom, 2 bed suites, private bath. Refrigerator, color TV, maid service, free cribs. Older structure. Reservations required. Rates: $21.00 duty, $24.00 off duty. Duty can make reservations. Others Space-A.

DV/VIP: Post Headquarters, Building 205. EX-2505/06. 06+. Retirees and lower grades Space-A.

Other: Famous for yearly return of swallows--just like Capistrano. Old California Hacienda formerly belonged to the Hearst family.

TML Availability: Good, most of the year.

Locator-385-2520	Medical-385-2610	NCO Club-385-2248
O'Club-385-2655	Police-385-2513	Snack Bar-385-2121
SDO/NCO-385-2503		

Temporary Military Lodging Around the World — 27

CALIFORNIA

Fort Irwin National Training Center (CA01R4)
Fort Irwin, CA 92310-5000

TELEPHONE NUMBER INFORMATION: Main installation numbers: Comm:619-386-4111, ATVN: 470-4111.

Location: Take I-15 east from Los Angeles for 125 miles or I-15 west from Las Vegas, NV, for 150 miles. Fort is north of I-15 near Barstow. Watch for signs. RM: p-13, SH/18. NMC: San Bernardino, 60 miles southwest.

Billeting Office: Building 212, 2nd St & C Ave. EX-4599. 0800-1630 hours daily. Other hours SDO, Building 237, EX-3530. Check in billeting or SDO. Check out 1200 hours daily.

TML: Guest House. All ranks. Leave or official duty. Mobile homes, private bath. Kitchen, utensils, A/C, color TV, maid service, free washer/dryer. Reservations accepted. Rates: Moderate. Maximum 7 per unit. All categories eligible, early reservation suggested.

TML: DVQ. Building 99. Officer 06+. Official duty (may take Space-A). EX-3318. 2/1-room w/bed, private bath; 2/2-room suites, private bath. Kitchen, refrigerator, limited utensils, A/C, color TV, maid service, free washer/dryer. Modern structure. Rates: Moderate. Maximum 3-5 per unit. Reservations required.

DV/VIP: Protocol, Building 151. EX-3000. 06+. Lower grades Space-A.

Other: Goldstone Deep Space Station.

TML Availability: Good, winter. Difficult, summer.

Cafeteria-386-2331	Enlisted Club-386-3491	Locator-386-3369
Medical-386-3128	NCO Club-386-3204	O'Club-386-3018
Police-386-3474	Snack Bar-386-2331	SDO/NCO-386-3750

Fort MacArthur (CA46R4)
Los Angeles Air Force Base Annex
Los Angeles, CA 90009-2960

TELEPHONE NUMBER INFORMATION: Main installation numbers: Comm: 213-643-1337, ATVN: 833-1337.

Location: At the end of Harbor 110 Freeway south, left on Gaffey Ave to 22nd St, left to Pacific Ave, right two blocks, left to gate. RM: p-15, L/8. NMC: Los Angeles, 18 miles north.

Billeting Office: ATTN: Billeting Manager, Building 37, Patton Quadrangle, San Pedro, CA 90731-5000. EX-0390/0399. 0600-2200 M-F. 0900-1800 Sa-Su. Other hours Security Police, Main Gate. Check in billeting, check out 1200 hours daily.

TML: TLQ. Building 40. All ranks. Leave or official duty. Reservations required for official duty. Others Space-A. 22 separate bedrooms, private bath. Sofa becomes double bed, chair single bed. Kitchen, utensils, color TV, maid service, free cribs/cots, washer/dryer, ice vending. Older structure, renovated '85. Rates: $16.00 per room. Maximum 3-5 per room. Disabled American veterans can make reservations if outpatient in local VA hospital & have letter from doctor confirming appointment.

CALIFORNIA
Fort MacArthur, continued

TML: VOQ/TAQ. Buildings 33, 36. All ranks. Reservations required for official duty. Others Space-A. 32/1-bedroom, private bath. Kitchen, complete utensils, color TV, maid service, free cribs/cots, free washer/dryer, ice vending. Older structure. Rates: Sponsor $6.00, adult $6.00. Maximum $12.00 per family. Disabled American veterans same as TLQ.

TML: DV/VIP. Cottages 14-17. Officer O6+, Enlisted E9. Leave or official duty. EX-0291. 2 separate bedrooms, private bath; 2/2-bedroom, private bath. Kitchen, utensils, color TV, maid service, free cribs/cots, free washer/dryer. Older structure, renovated '87. Rates: Sponsor $10.00, adult $10.00. Maximum $20.00 per family. Maximum 1-4 per cottage. Duty can make reservations. Others Space-A unless O7+. Contact Protocol Office.

DV/VIP: SD/CSP. Building 105. EX-2030. O6+. Retirees and lower grades served.

Note: Fort MacArthur is a sub-post of the Los Angeles Air Force Base. The phone numbers below are for the AFB.

TML Availability: Best, Nov-Apr. Difficult, other times.

| Locator-643-1000 | Medical-643-2121 | NCO Club-643-2743 |
| O'Club-643-0960 | Police-643-2123 | Snack Bar-414-0083 |

Fort Mason Officers' Club (CA45R4)
San Francisco, CA 94123-5000

TELEPHONE NUMBER INFORMATION: Main installation numbers: Comm: 415-441-7700, ATVN:859-0111.

Location: On Franklin Street, four blocks north of US-101 (Lombard Street). NMC: San Francisco, in the city.

Billeting Office: No central billeting office. Go to Building 1, Bay & Franklin Sts. 0900-1700 hours Tu-Sa. Check in facility, check out 1100 hours daily.

TML: VOQ. Building 1. Officer all grades. Leave or official duty. Reservations required up to 30 days in advance. EX-7700. 2 separate bedroom suites, private bath; 3/1-bedroom, 2 beds each, private bath. Roll-away $10.00, cots $10.00, refrigerator, color TV, maid service, ice vending. Older structure. New TVs and carpeting in '87. Remodeled '88. Rates: Rooms single $23.00, double $30.00; suites single $28.00, double $35.00 + $10.00 each additional person. Active duty, reserves, retirees or GS-7 DoD with orders are eligible. Deposit required.

Other: Fort Mason is a National Park. Offers a magnificent view of Alcatraz Island and San Francisco Bay. Good O'Club.

TML Availability: Difficult, all year. Reserve early. See listing for Marines' Memorial Club at 609 Sutter Street.

Temporary Military Lodging Around the World — 29

CALIFORNIA

Fort Ord (CA36R4)
Fort Ord, CA 93941-5000

TELEPHONE NUMBER INFORMATION: Main installation numbers: Comm: 408-242-2211, ATVN: 929-1110.

Location: From San Francisco, south for 100 miles on US-101, right onto CA-156 for 10 miles to main gate of Post. RM: p-13, SC/11. NMC: Monterey, 7 miles south.

Billeting Office: Building 2798, 2nd Ave & 12th St, EX-3181. 24 hours daily. Check in facility, check out 1000 hours. Government civilian employee billeting.

TML: Guest House. Building 2798. All ranks. Leave or official duty. 175/1-bedroom, latrine bath (23 are double rooms). Refrigerator, community kitchen, color TV lounge, maid service, free cribs, coin washer/dryer, microwave, lounge. Older structure. Rates: Sponsor $4.00, adult $1.00, child $.50. Apartmentss: 10/1-bedroom, private bath; 9/2-bedroom, private bath; 37/3-bedroom, private bath; 2/4-bedroom, private bath (3 apartments located at Presidio of Monterey). Kitchen, refrigerator, limited utensils, color TV, maid service, free cribs. Older structure. Rates: $16.00 (PCS), $20.00 (TDY). Duty can make reservations. Others Space-A. Also, Lightfighter Lodge. 30 hotel-type rooms, sleeps 7. Refrigerator, color TV, maid service, free cribs. Rates: $17.00 per room. Duty can make reservations. Others Space-A.

TML: VOQ. Buildings 4360-4363. Officers all grades. Leave or official duty. 236/1-bedroom, private bath (81/1-bedroom, private bath at Presidio of Monterey). Refrigerator, color TV, maid service, free washer/dryer. Modern structure. Rates: $10.00 per person PCS, $20.00 TDY, each additional person with TDY sponsor $10.00. Duty can make reservations. Others Space-A.

TML: DV/VIP. Building 2789. EX-2367/3042. Officer all grades. Leave or official duty. 6/1-bedroom, private bath cottages (1 located at Presidio of Monterey). Kitchen, refrigerator, limited utensils, color TV, maid service, free cribs. Older structure. Rates: Sponsor $20.00 (PCS), sponsor $21.00 (TDY), each additional person with TDY sponsor $10.00. Duty can make reservations. Others Space-A.

DV/VIP: Protocol Office, Building 2879, EX-2367/3042. O6+.

Other: Beautiful coast line south from Monterey to Big Sur.

TML Availability: Good, most of the year.

Enlisted Club-242-2563
NCO Club-899-2373
Snack Bar-899-1766

Locator-242-2271
O'Club-899-3445
SDO-242-3432/4209

Medical-242-2020
Police-242-7851

George Air Force Base (CA49R4)
George AFB, CA 92394-5000

TELEPHONE NUMBER INFORMATION: Main installation numbers: Comm: 619-269-3000, ATVN: 353-3000.

Location: From I-15 take D St exit and follow signs. From US-395 at Adelanto, exit east on Air Base Rd, 2 miles on left. RM: p-13, SJ/16. NMC: Barstow, 30 miles northeast.

Billeting Office: ATTN: 831 SVS/SVH. Building 454, Mustang St. Reservation Desk, EX-4548. 24 hours daily. Billeting Manager, EX-3938; NCOIC, EX-2514. Check in facility, check out 1200 hours. Government civilian employee billeting.

30 — *Temporary Military Lodging Around the World*

CALIFORNIA
George Air Force Base, continued

TML: TLF. Buildings 246, 247, 249, 250. All ranks. Leave or official duty. TLQ 40/1-bedroom apartments, private bath. Kitchen, color TV, maid service (limited), free cribs, free washer/dryer. Modern structure. Rates $16.00 per unit, maximum 5 persons. Duty can make reservations. Others Space-A.

TML: VAQ. Buildings 162, 458. Enlisted all grades. Leave or official duty. 56 units. Refrigerator, A/C, color TV, maid service, free washer/dryer, ice vending. Rates: $7.50 per person per night. Older structure. Duty can make reservations. Others Space-A.

TML: VOQ. Building 470. top level Building 456. Officer 01-06. Leave or official duty. 45/1-bedroom, private bath. Kitchen, limited utensils, A/C, TV, maid service, free washer/dryer. Modern structure. Rates: $8.00 per person per night. Duty can make reservations. Others Space-A.

TML: DV/VIP. Lower level of Building 456. Officer 06+. Leave or official duty. 1/1-bedroom, private bath; 5/2-bedroom, private bath. Refrigerator, A/C, color TV, maid service, free washer/dryer. Older structure. Rates: $16.00 maximum per unit. Duty can make reservations. Others Space-A.

DV/VIP: Protocol Office, Building 321. EX-2829. 06+.

Other: Permanent displays of F-86, F-100, F-104, F-105D aircraft.

TML Availability: Good, Nov-Mar.

Comm Cntr-269-3233   Locator-269-3208   Medical-269-3069
NCO Club-269-2506   O'Club-269-2501   Police-269-2000
SDO-269-2620

Lemoore Naval Air Station (CA06R4)
Lemoore NAS, CA 93246-5001

TELEPHONE NUMBER INFORMATION: Main installation numbers: Comm: 209-998-2211, ATVN: 949-1110.

Location: On CA-198, 24 miles east of I-5, 30 miles west of CA-99 in the south central part of the state. RM: p-13, SD/9. NMC: Fresno, 40 miles north northeast.

Billeting Office: Barracks 7, Building 852, Hancock Circle. EX-3266. 24 hours daily.

TML: Navy Lodge. Building 908/909. All ranks. Leave or official duty. For reservations call 1-800-NAVY-INN. Lodge number is 998-5791. Check out 1200 hours daily. 46 efficiency rooms, private bath, 2 double beds. Kitchen, utensils, A/C, color TV, maid service, coin washer/dryer, ice vending. Modern structure. Rates: Sponsor $27.00. Maximum 5 per room. All categories can make reservations. Military member may sponsor guest.

TML: BEQ. Building 852. Enlisted all grades. Leave or official duty. Check in and out (1200 hours daily) at billeting office. 32 male rooms, 2 female rooms. 3 per room. Refrigerator, A/C, 45" color TV in lounge, maid service-5 days, free washer/dryer. Modern structure. Rates: Sponsor $3.00. Retirees & disabled American veterans Space-A. Duty can make reservations.

TML: BOQ. Building 800. Officer all grades. Leave or official duty. EX-3014. Check in and out (1200 hours daily) front desk of facility. 60 rooms, private bath. Refrigerator, community kitchen, A/C, color TV, maid service, free washer/dryer, ice vending, 50" TV in lounge. Modern structure. Rates: On orders $7.00. Retirees,

Temporary Military Lodging Around the World — 31

CALIFORNIA
Lemoore Naval Air Station, continued

disabled American veterans, reservists Space-A. Others can make reservations.

DV/VIP: Commanding Officer. EX-3121. 06+. Retirees Space-A.

TML Availability: Good all year.

Cafeteria-998-3084	**Enlisted Club-998-3331**	**Locator-998-3059**
Medical-998-4256/4257	**CPO Club-998-3130**	**O'Club-998-3550**
Police-998-3362	**Snack Bar-998-3479**	**SDO/NCO-998-3360**

Long Beach Naval Station (CA55R4)
Long Beach NS, CA 90822-5000

TELEPHONE NUMBER INFORMATION: Main installation numbers: Comm: 213-547-7924, ATVN: 360-0111.

Location: Take Long Beach Freeway, CA-710, to Terminal Island exit to Naval Station. Clearly marked. RM: p-15, L/9. NMC: Long Beach, 2 miles east.

Billeting Office: Building 422, Military Support. Comm: 547-7924. ATVN: 360-7928. 24 hours. 7 days. Check out 1200 hours.

TML: Navy Lodge. All ranks. Leave or official duty. Check in 24 hours daily. Check out 1200 hours. For reservations call 1-800-NAVY-INN. Lodge number is 833-2541. 50/1-bedroom, 2 double beds, private bath, washer/dryer, ice vending. Rates: $28.00 per room. All categories can make reservations.

TML: BOQ. Building 257. Officer. All ranks. Leave or official duty. Check in 24 hours daily. Check out 1200 hours. Accessible to the handicapped. 81/1-bedroom rooms and suites, private and semi-private baths. Refrigerator, food vending, ice vending, maid service, color TV, washer/dryer. Older structure. New phone system and cable TV. Rates: $5.00 (room), $8.00 (suite). Maximum one person. Duty can make reservations. Others Space-A.

TML: Enlisted quarters. Building 422. All ranks. 600/1-bedroom, private and semi-private baths. Refrigerator, food vending, maid service, color TV, washer/dryer. Modern structure '89. Rates: Sponsor, $2.00. Maximum 3 per unit. Duty can make reservations. Others Space-A.

TML Availability: Extremely limited. Best Nov-Jan. Difficult May-July.

Cafeteria-547-7100	**Enlisted Club-547-7007**	**Locator-547-6002**
Medical-547-7979	**NCO Club-547-8206**	**O'Club-547-7208**
Police-547-7731	**Snack Bar-519-5100**	**SDO/NCO-547-6721**

Los Alamitos Armed Forces Reserve Center (CA39R4)
Los Alamitos, CA 90720-5001

TELEPHONE NUMBER INFORMATION: Main installation numbers: Comm: 213-493-8000, California National Guard, ATVN: 972-2000.

Location: Off I-605 east of Long Beach. Clearly marked. RM: p-15, K/12. NMC: Los Angeles, 35 miles northwest.

Billeting Office: Hq Armed Forces Reserve Center. Check in facility, check out 1200 hours daily. Comm: 213-493-8124/8125, ATVN: 972-2124/2125.

TML: TLF. All ranks. Leave or official duty. 1 bedroom, 2 beds, shared bath. Duty

CALIFORNIA
Los Alamitos Armed Forces Reserve Center, continued

can make reservations. Others Space-A.

TML Availability: Limited, call ahead.

March Air Force Base (CA08R4)
March AFB, CA 92518-5000

TELEPHONE NUMBER INFORMATION: Main installation numbers: Comm: 714-655-1110, ATVN: 947-1110.

Location: Off CA-60 and on I-215 which bisects AFB. RM: p-15, I/23. NMC: Riverside, 11 miles southwest.

Billeting Office: Building 100, Myers & DeKay. EX-5241. 24 hours daily. Check in billeting office, check out 1100 hours daily.

TML: VOQ/TLQ/TAQ. Buildings 100, 102, 125, 501, 2418, 2419, 2420, 2421. All ranks. Leave or official duty. Rooms, apartments, & suites. Refrigerator, kitchen, utensils, A/C, color TV room & lounge, maid service, free cots & washer/dryer, ice vending. Modern structure. Rates: VOQ, Sponsor $11.00; VAQ, Sponsor $9.00-$11.00; TLF, Sponsor, $23.00. Duty can make reservations. Others Space-A.

DV/VIP: HQ 15th Air Force, Protocol, March AFB. ATVN: 947-4764. O6+. DVQ Rate: $13.00-$14.00.

TML Availability: Good, Oct to Feb. More difficult, May-Sep.

Locator-655-3192   Medical-655-4266   NCO Club-653-1153
O'Club-653-2121   Police-655-2981   SDO/NCO-655-2944

Marines' Memorial Club (CA20R4)
609 Sutter Street
San Francisco, CA 94102-5000

TELEPHONE NUMBER INFORMATION: Main installation numbers: Comm: 415-673-6672, 1-800-3-MARINE (Reservations, in California), 1-800-5-MARINE (Reservations, outside California), 415-562-7463 or 415-673-6604 (direct). ATVN: None.

Location: Use CA-101 or CA-580. Take CA-580 north to SF, cross the Bay Bridge. Take 5th St exit, go up 5th St until you reach O'Farrell. Turn right and proceed to Powell St. Turn left, proceed to Sutter St, turn left. At the corner of Sutter and Mason. Author's Note: This is NOT "military lodging" in the sense that we list other military installations in this book. The Marines' Memorial Club is a club/hotel exclusively for uniformed services personnel, Active duty & retirees and their guests. The club is not a part of the government but is a private, non-profit organization and is completely self-supporting. This club/hotel is a living memorial to Marines who lost their lives in the Pacific during WWII. It opened on the Marine Corps' Birthday, 10 Nov 1946, and chose as its motto "A tribute to those Marines who have gone before; and a service to those who carry on."

Office: Check in and out at lobby desk. Check out 1200 hours daily. Occupancy limited to two weeks except when vacancies exist. 24 hours daily. For brochure or more info write to the above ATTN: Club Secretary, or call 673-6672.

Temporary Military Lodging Around the World — 33

Marines' Memorial Club, continued CALIFORNIA

TML: Hotel. 143 guest rooms; 12 deluxe suites; family suites. All ranks. Leave or official duty. Reservations required. Deposit $30.00 per room. Courtesy coffee/tea in room, free ice each floor, soft drinks vending each floor, large closets. Rates: Average room $55.00. Average suite $100.00. Rates higher for guests of members. All active duty considered as members. Club facilities include, library/museum, swimming pool, gym, coin-operated launderette, valet, exchange store, package store, rooms for private parties, and a dining room and lounge in the beautiful Skyroom on the 12th floor, overlooking San Francisco. Convenience store/news stand and coffee shop are outside hotel adjacent to entrance. Hotel discount parking on Sutter St. Ask at desk. Beautiful city by the bay. Great seafood is at Tadich Grill, 240 California St. Hours 1130-2030. No reservations, go early for shorter line.

TML Availability: Best, winter months. Make reservations well in advance.

Mather Air Force Base (CA12R4)
Mather AFB, CA 95655-5000

TELEPHONE NUMBER INFORMATION: Main installation numbers: Comm: 916-364-1110, ATVN: 674-1110.

Location: In Rancho Cordova, US-50 to Mather Field Rd direct to main gate. RM: p-11, NM/10. NMC: Sacramento, 12 miles west.

Billeting Office: ATTN: 323 ABG/SVH, Building 2750, "A" Ave at Gilbert St. EX-2457. 24 hours daily. Check in at billeting, check out 1200 hours daily.

TML: TLQ/VOQ/VAQ/UOQ/VIP. Building 2750. All ranks. Leave or official duty. Rooms and suites. Kitchen, refrigerator, complete utensils, A/C, color TV room & lounge, maid service, free cribs, free washer/dryer, ice vending. Rates: Moderate. Duty can make reservations. Others Space-A. Advance reservations for TDY/PCS.

TML Availability: Fairly good, Dec-Feb. Difficult, other times.

Enlisted Club-364-4993   Locator-364-2597   Medical-364-3213
NCO Club-362-8122   O'Club-362-3257   Police-364-2200

McClellan Air Force Base (CA35R4)
McClellan AFB, CA 95652-5000

TELEPHONE NUMBER INFORMATION: Main installation numbers: Comm: 916-643-2111, ATVN: 633-1110.

Location: Off I-80 North. From I-80 take Madison Ave exit. Clearly marked. RM: p-11, NK/25. NMC: Sacramento, 10 miles southwest.

Billeting Office: Building 89, Palm & 30th St, Gate 3. EX-6223. 24 hours daily. Check in billeting, check out 1200 hours daily. Government civilian billeting.

TML: Guest House. Building 1430. All ranks. Leave or official duty. 7/1-bedroom, private bath; 14/2-bedroom, private bath. Kitchen, limited utensils, A/C, color TV, maid service, free cribs/cots, free washer/dryer, ice vending. Modern structure. Rates: $16.00 per unit. Duty can make reservations. Others Space-A. Also, VOQ/VAQ available for single occupancy only, EX-6223.

DV/VIP: Protocol, Building 200, EX-4311. 06+. Retirees/lower grades Space-A.

34 — Temporary Military Lodging Around the World

CALIFORNIA
McClellan Air Force Base, continued

TML Availability: Good, winter months. Difficult, summer months.

Cafeteria-929-9295
Medical-643-4733
Police-643-6160

Enlisted Club-643-2259
NCO Club-922-9657
Snack Bar-920-939

Locator-643-4113
O'Club-927-5013

Miramar Naval Air Station (CA14R4)
San Diego, CA 92145-5000

TELEPHONE NUMBER INFORMATION: Main installation numbers: Comm: 619-537-1011, ATVN: 577-1011.

Location: Fifteen miles north of San Diego, off I-15. Take Miramar Way exit. RM: p-15, K/23. NMC: San Diego, 15 miles southwest.

Billeting Office: No central billeting office. Check in facility, check out 1200 hours daily.

TML: Navy Lodge. Building 516. All ranks. Leave or official duty. For reservations call 1-800-NAVY-INN. Lodge number is 271-7111. 24 hours daily. 90 units, private bath. Kitchen, A/C, color TV, free cribs, coin washer/dryer, maid service. Modern structure. Rates: $32.00 per unit. All categories can make reservations. Kennels near lodge.

TML: BEQ. Building 638. All ranks. Official duty only. EX-1174. 24 hours daily. 206 units, semi-private bath. Color TV in lounge, free washer/dryer. Older structure. No reservations. Rates: $4.00 per person.

TML: BOQ. Building M-312. All ranks. Leave or official duty. EX-4235. 24 hours daily. Rooms & suites, private bath. Color TV, maid service, free washer/dryer. Older structure. Rates: $8.00 per person. Duty on orders can make reservations. Others Space-A.

DV/VIP: Comm: 537-1221. O6+. Retirees Space-A.

TML Availability: Very good all year.

Cafeteria-695-7278
McDonalds-271-0481
Police-537-4059

Enlisted Club-537-6171
Medical-537-4656
SDO/NCO-537-1227

Locator-537-6017
NCO Club-537-4820

Moffett Field Naval Air Station (CA15R4)
Moffett Field, CA 94035-5000

TELEPHONE NUMBER INFORMATION: Main installation numbers: Comm: 415-966-5411, ATVN: 462-5411.

Location: On Bayshore Freeway, US-101, 35 miles south of San Francisco, CA. RM: p-11, NK/25. NMC: San Jose, 7 miles south.

Billeting Office: Building 583. EX-5911. 0800-1600 hours daily. Other hours OD, EX-5326.

TML: Navy Lodge. All ranks. Leave or official duty. For reservations call 1-800-NAVY-INN. Lodge number is 962-1542. 0700-2300 hours daily. 50/1-bedroom, 2 double beds, kitchen, private bath. Maid service, washer/dryer, ice vending. Modern structure. Rates: $34.00 per unit. All categories can make reservations.

Temporary Military Lodging Around the World — 35

CALIFORNIA

Moffett Field Naval Air Station, continued

Other: Historic Hangar One. Former home of USS Macon.

TML Availability: Limited.

Enlisted Club-966-5471
CPO Club-966-5471
Snack Bar-940-6200
Locator-966-5061
O'Club-966-5306
SDO/NCO-966-5326
Medical-966-5112
Police-966-5141

Monterey Naval Postgraduate School (CA16R4)
Monterey, CA 93943-5000

TELEPHONE NUMBER INFORMATION: Main installation numbers: Comm: 408-646-0111, ATVN: 878-0111.

Location: Take CA-1 to central Monterey exit, right at light onto Camino Aguajito. Left at stop sign onto Thomas Drive, left at light onto Sloat Avenue and to Base entrance. Or north on CA-1, Aguajito Rd exit to Mark Thomas Dr, to left on Sloat Ave, right at 3rd St gate. RM: p-13, SB/22. NMC: Monterey, in city limits.

Billeting Office: Building 220, Herrmann Hall, Middle Rd. EX-2060/69. 24 hours daily. Check in billeting 1500 hours, check out 1100 hours daily. Duty billets available during school vacations.

TML: BOQ. Building 220. Officers all grades. Official duty only. 65/1-bedroom, private bath. 52/1-bedroom, semi-private bath. Refrigerator, community kitchen, complete utensils, essentials, color TV in lounge/room, maid service, free washer/dryer, food/ice vending, microwave. Older structure. Rates: Sponsor on official duty $7.00, Space-A $7.00. Duty can make reservations. No children. Kennel listing available.

TML: BOQ. Buildings 221 & 222. Officers all grades. Leave or official duty. 74/1-bedroom, private bath; 28/1-bedroom, semi-private bath; 2 separate bedrooms, private bath. Refrigerator, community kitchen (in 221), cable color TV, maid service, free washer/dryer, ice vending. Telephone in '88. Rates: $5.00 official duty, $7.00 Space-A. Duty can make reservations. No children. Kennel listing available.

TML: BEQ. Building 259. Enlisted E1-E6. Check out anytime. 34 shared, hall baths. Refrigerator, community kitchen, limited utensils, color TV in lounge, free washer/dryer. Older structure, renovations in near future. Rates: No charge. Duty can make reservations.

DV/VIP: Building 220. Officers O6+. Leave or official duty. 4/1-bedroom, private bath; 2 separate bedrooms, private bath. Kitchen, utensils, cable color TV, maid service, free washer/dryer, ice vending. Older structure. Rates: $5.00 official duty; $20-$25.00 Space-A. Maximum 4 per room. Duty can make reservations. Others Space-A.

DV/VIP: Building 220. EX-2513/2514. O6+. Retirees & lower grades Space-A.

Other: Pebble Beach, 17 mile drive, Steinbeck's Cannery Row, Fisherman's Wharf and Carmel Mission.

TML Availability: Best, Christmas during school vacation and June. Other times, extremely limited.

Enlisted Club-646-2358
Police-646-2555
Locator-646-2441
Medical-911
O'Club-373-1339
SDO/NCO-646-2441

CALIFORNIA

North Island Naval Air Station (CA43R4)
San Diego, CA 92135-5000

TELEPHONE NUMBER INFORMATION: Main installation numbers: Comm: 619-524-1011, ATVN: 735-0444.

Location: From I-5 north or south exit at Coronado Bridge (toll). Also, from CA-75 north to CA-282 to Base. In Coronado. RM: p-15, N/22. NMC: San Diego, 4 miles northeast.

Billeting Office: Building 1 for Officer, EX-7545. Building 773 for Enlisted, EX-9551. 24 hours daily. Check in facility (between 1500-1800 for confirmed reservations at Navy Lodge), check out 1200 hours daily. Government civilian employee billeting.

TML: Navy Lodge. Building 1402. All ranks. Leave or official duty. For reservations call 1-800-NAVY-INN. Lodge number is 545-6940. 90/1-bedroom, 2 double beds, studio couch, private bath. Kitchen, limited utensils, A/C, color TV, maid service, free cribs, coin washer/dryer, ice vending. Modern structure, renovated '87. Rates: $32.00 per unit. Maximum 5 per room. All categories can make reservations.

DV/VIP: PAO. EX-8167. O6+. Retirees and lower grades if approved by Commander.

TML Availability: Good, except Oct-Mar.

Cafeteria-522-7265	Enlisted Club-545-2881	Locator-694-3155
McDonalds-435-0074	Medical-545-4306	O'Club-545-6945
Police-545-7423	Snack Bar-522-7278	Petty O'Club-545-7205
SDO/NCO-545-8123		

Norton Air Force Base (CA17R4)
Norton AFB, CA 92409-5000

TELEPHONE NUMBER INFORMATION: Main installation numbers: Comm: 714-382-1110, ATVN: 876-1110.

Location: From I-10 in Loma Linda take Tippecanoe exit north to Base, approximately 1.5 miles. RM: p-15, E/24. NMC: San Bernardino, 3 miles northwest.

Billeting Office: Building 512, 3rd St. EX-5531. For reservations call EX-4855. 24 hours daily. Check in billeting, check out 1200 hours daily.

TML: TLQ. Buildings 901-904. All ranks. Leave or official duty. 40 separate bedrooms, private bath, sleeps 4 persons. Kitchen, A/C, color TV, maid service, free cribs, free washer/dryer. Older structure, remodeled '85. Rates: $15.00 per unit. Maximum 4 per unit. Duty can make reservations. Others Space-A.

TML: VAQ. Buildings 512, 515. Enlisted all grades. Leave or official duty. 162/1-bedroom, semi-private bath; 5 separate bedroom suites, private bath. Refrigerator, A/C, color TV, maid service, free washer/dryer. Older structure. Rates: $7.00 per person. Maximum 1 per room. Duty can make reservations. Others Space-A.

TML: VOQ. Buildings 503, 517, 561-563. Officer O1-O5. Leave or official duty. 162/1-bedroom, private and semi-private baths; 15 separate bedrooms, private bath. Kitchen (some), refrigerator, A/C, color TV, maid service, free washer/dryer. Older structure. Rates: $8.00 per person. Duty can make reservations. Others Space-A.

Temporary Military Lodging Around the World — 37

Norton Air Force Base, continued   CALIFORNIA

TML: DV/VIP. Building 504. EX-7615. 06+. Leave or official duty. 16 separate bedroom suites, private bath. Kitchen, A/C, color TV, maid service, free washer/dryer. Older structure. Rates: $10.00 per person. Duty can make reservations. Others Space-A.

DV/VIP: Building 673, 63 MAW/CCP. EX-7615. 06+. Retirees & lower grades Space-A.

TML Availability: Good, Oct-Apr. Difficult, other times.

Cafeteria-885-4741   Enlisted Club-382-5769   Locator-382-5381
Medical-382-7818   NCO Club-889-0635   O'Club-889-4451

Oakland Army Base (CA18R4)
Oakland, CA 94626-5000

TELEPHONE NUMBER INFORMATION: Main installation numbers: Comm: 415-466-9111, ATVN: 859-9111.

Location: Near junction of I-80, I-580, and CA-880, south of the San Francisco-Oakland Bay Bridge. RM: p-11, NC/22. NMC: Oakland, 2 miles southeast.

Billeting Office: Building 650. Comm: 444-8107. ATVN: 859-3113. 24 hours daily. Check in front desk, check out 1100 hours daily. Government civilian employee billeting.

TML: Guest House, Building 650. All ranks. Leave or official duty. 23/1-bedroom, double beds, private bath; 25 double rooms, queen-size bed, living room, sofa bed, private bath; 4 suites with bedroom, living room, den with sofa bed, private bath. Community kitchen, refrigerator, cable color TV room & lounge, cribs ($1.00), cots ($5.00), maid service, free washer/dryer, ice vending, video movies, irons and ironing boards, complimentary coffee, some non-smoking rooms. Modern structure, renovated '86. Rates: Single $19.00-$24.00, double $28.00-$33.00, suites $36.00-$44.00. Sofa beds $7.00-$10.00. All categories can make reservations.

TML Availability: Good.

Cafeteria-465-3175   Enlisted Club-466-2791   Medical-466-2918
NCO Club-466-2791   O'Club-441-7701   Police-466-3333

Oakland Naval Hospital (CA41R4)
8750 Mountain Blvd
Oakland, CA 94627-5000

TELEPHONE NUMBER INFORMATION: Main installation numbers: Comm: 415-633-5000 (After duty hours EX-6200), ATVN: 855-6200.

Location: Off I-580 south from San Francisco-Oakland Bridge, take either Keller Ave or Golf Links Rd exit. Clearly marked. RM: p-11, ND/24. NMC: Oakland, 38 miles northwest.

Billeting Office: No central billeting office. Check in facility, check out 1200 hours daily.

TML: Navy Lodge. All ranks. Leave or official duty. Reservations required. For reservations call 1-800-NAVY-INN. Lodge number is 633-6096. 0800-1700 hours daily. 18/1-bedroom, semi-private bath. Refrigerator, A/C, color TV lounge, maid

CALIFORNIA
Oakland Naval Hospital, continued

service, free cribs/cots, coin washer/dryer, facility for DAVs. Older structure. Rates: $14.00 per unit. All categories can make reservations.

TML: Other. 1 DV/VIP suite at Officers' Club. Call Flag Lt for use, EX-2112. Also 18/1-bedroom in Building 690, EX-2181. Enlisted billeting in Building 501, EX-3078.

TML Availability: Limited.

Medical-633-5440

Cafeteria, Snack B, Clubs, EX-5440 for numbers.

Oakland Naval Supply Center (CA42R4)
Oakland, CA 94625-5000

TELEPHONE NUMBER INFORMATION: Main installation numbers: Comm: 415-466-0112, ATVN: 836-4011.

Location: Can be reached from I-880 north or south and CA-24 from east. Clearly marked. RM: p-11, NC/22. NMC: San Francisco, 6 miles north.

Billeting Office: Building 521, Navy Lodge. EX-6187. 0730-1630 hours M-F, 0900-1700 hours Sa, Su, Hol. Others hours, SDO, EX-5713. Check in facility, check out 1100 hours daily. Government civilian employee billeting.

TML: Navy Lodge. Building 521. All ranks. Leave or official duty. For reservations call 1-800-NAVY-INN. 20/1- & 2-bedroom, private bath (4 suites with kitchen, complete utensils). Refrigerator, color TV, maid service, free cribs/cots, coin washer/dryer, ice/snack vending. Rates: $21.00-$22.00. Maximum 2 per single, 4 per suite. All categories can make reservations.

TML Availability: Fairly good, winter. More difficult, summer.

Locator-466-0112   SDO-466-5713

Petaluma Coast Guard Training Center (CA23R4)
Petaluma, CA 94952-5000

TELEPHONE NUMBER INFORMATION: Main installation numbers: Comm: 707-765-7211, FTS: 623-7211.

Location: Exit US-101 north to East Washington Ave West. Follow Washington Ave 9 miles west to Coast Guard Training Center. RM: p-11, NN/6. NMC: San Francisco, 49 miles south.

Billeting Office: Building T-134, Nevada Ave. EX-7247. 0730-1600 hours daily. Other hours Security, EX-7211. Check in at facility, check out time discussed with manager. Government civilian employee billeting, maximum stay 2 weeks.

TML: TLQ. Building 134. All ranks. Leave or official duty. 8/1-bedroom, private bath; 1/4-person unit, semi-private bath. Refrigerator, color TV, free cribs, washer/dryer, ice vending, microwave. Older structure. Rates: $16.00-$19.00 per room. Maximum $16.00 per family. All categories can make reservations. PCS have priority.

DV/VIP: One room in Harrison Hall for special Coast Guard personnel. EX-7173.

Temporary Military Lodging Around the World — 39

CALIFORNIA

Petaluma Coast Guard Training Center, continued

TML Availability: Generally good. Difficult, summer months.

Medical-765-7200
SDO/NCO-765-7215
Police-765-7215
Snack Bar-765-7254

Point Mugu Pacific Missile Test Center (CA40R4)
Point Mugu, CA 93042-5000

TELEPHONE NUMBER INFORMATION: Main installation numbers: Comm: 805-989-1110, ATVN: 351-1110.

Location: Eight miles south of Oxnard and 40 miles north of Santa Monica, on Coast Highway, CA-1. RM: p-13, SL/11. NMC: Los Angeles, 50 miles southeast.

Billeting Office: Building 27. D Street, between Sixth and Seventh Streets. EX-7510/7470. 24 hours daily. Check in facility, check out 1000 hours daily. Government civilian employee billeting. Note: Point Mugu Rec Area has 5 cabins and 11 motel-type rooms with kitchenette. Call 805-989-8349 for details.

TML: BOQ. Building 27. Officer all grades. Leave or official duty. 22/1-bedroom, 2 single beds, latrine bath. 4/1-bedroom, 1 single bed, male only, latrine bath. Roll-a-way cots available, $6.00. Refrigerator, color TV, maid service, free washer/dryer, essentials, food vending. Older structure. Rates: $6.00 per person. Maximum charge $24.00. Duty can make reservations. All others Space-A.

TML: BEQ. Building 27. Enlisted all grades. Leave or official duty. 52 units with one to three beds per room, baths vary. Refrigerator, color TV, maid service, essentials, food vending, free washer/dryer. Older structure. Rates: $4.00 per person. Duty only can make reservations. Unaccompanied retirees Space-A. No dependents.

TML: DV/VIP. Building 170. Officer 06+. Leave or official duty. 8/1-bedroom suites, private bath. Community kitchen, fully furnished. Older structure. Rates: $8.00 per person. Duty can make reservations. Others Space-A.

DV/VIP: Command Protocol, Building 36. EX-8672. 06+.

TML Availability: Fair. Difficult, Mar-Sep.

Cafeteria-989-7189
Locator-989-7938
O'Club-989-8407
CPO Club-989-7517
Medical-911
Police-911
Enlisted Club-989-7391
NCO Club-989-8570
Snack Bar-989-8898

Port Hueneme Naval Construction Battalion Center (CA32R4)
Port Hueneme, CA 93043-5000

TELEPHONE NUMBER INFORMATION: Main installation numbers: Comm: 805-982-4711, ATVN: 360-4711.

Location: Seven miles west of US-101. Take Victoria Ave exit in Ventura to Channel Islands Blvd (turn left), to Ventura Road (turn right), to Pleasant Valley Road (turn right). Enter at Pleasant Valley Gate. RM: p-13, SL/11. NMC: Los Angeles, 40 miles southeast.

Billeting Office: ATTN: Code 61, Building 1435, Pacific Road. EX-4497. 24 hours daily. Check in at facility. Government civilian employee no billeting.

40 — *Temporary Military Lodging Around the World*

CALIFORNIA
Port Hueneme Naval Construction Battalion Center, continued

TML: Navy Lodge. Building 1172. All ranks. Leave or official duty. Reservations required. For reservations call 1-800-NAVY-INN. Lodge number is 985-2624. 22/1-bedroom studio efficiency, private bath. Kitchen, utensils, color TV, maid service, free cribs, coin washer/dryer, ice vending, special facilities DAVs. Modern structure, remodeled. Rates: $27.00 per unit. Maximum 4 persons. Duty and retirees can make reservations. Others Space-A.

TML: BEQ: Duty only, EX-4497. BOQ: Duty only, EX-5705. Female enlisted quarters: Duty only, EX-4497. May have TML Space-A.

TML: DV/VIP. Guest House. Buildings 39, 1201, 1435. Officers O6+. Leave or official duty. Reservations required. EX-5785. Check in Building 1164. Building 39, 1 cottage (Doll House), private bath. Kitchen, utensils, color TV, maid service. Older struc (1925), patio back yard. Duty can make reservations. Others Space-A.

DV/VIP: Plan & Mob Office. Building 14, Room 204, EX-4401. 07/GS-16+.

Other: SEABEE Museum at center.

TML Availability: Good, winter months. Difficult, summer months.

Cafeteria-982-4435	Enlisted Club-982-5293	Locator-982-4711
Medical-982-3332	NCO Club-982-5207	O'Club-982-4468
Police-982-4591	Snack B-982-4687	

Presidio of San Francisco (CA19R4)
San Francisco, CA 94129-5000

TELEPHONE NUMBER INFORMATION: Main installation numbers: Comm: 415-561-2211, ATVN: 586-1110.

Location: At the South end of the Golden Gate Bridge. From US-101 North exit onto Lombard St. From US-101 South exit onto Merchant Rd, follow signs to Lombard St and Presidio. RM: p-11, ND/19. NMC: San Francisco, south & east in city limits.

Billeting Office: Building 42, Lincoln Blvd. ATTN: AFZM-DEH-HB. EX-3411. 0730-1615 hours daily. Check in at desk of facility, 24 hours daily. Check out 1100 hours daily.

TML: Guest House. Building 42, Pershing Hall; Building 951, Scott Hall. All ranks. Leave or official duty. Pershing, 2/2-bedroom apartments, private bath; 12/1-bedroom apartments, private bath; Scott, 16/2-bedroom, semi-private bath; 2/1-bedroom, semi-private bath. Kitchen in some, limited utensils, color TV, room & lounge, maid service, cribs $1.50, free & coin washer/dryer, ice vending. Older structure. Rates: Pershing: 2 bedroom unit $24.00, each additional person $3.50; 1 bedroom $12.00, each additional person $3.50. Maximum $38.00 per family. Maximum $15.00 per family. Scott: single $9.00, double $19.00. Maximum $23.00 per family. PCS & medical outpatient can make reservations 30 days in advance. Retirees, military widows, and dependents Space-A.

DV/VIP: Protocol Office, Building 38. EX-3950/2540. O6+. Retirees & lower grades Space-A at discretion of Protocol.

Other: Golden Gate Bridge, City of San Francisco.

TML Availability: Good, Sep-Nov, Mar. Difficult, other times.

| Cafeteria-922-3546 | Enlisted Club-561-2250 | Locator-561-4431 |

Temporary Military Lodging Around the World — 41

CALIFORNIA

Presidio of San Francisco, continued

Medical-561-5656
Police-561-2251/2252
NCO Club-921-6896
Snack Bar-922-3546
O'Club-921-1612
SDO-561-2045/3601

San Diego Naval Station (CA26R4)
San Diego NS, CA 92136-5000

TELEPHONE NUMBER INFORMATION: Main installation numbers: Comm: 619-556-1011, ATVN: 526-1011.

Location: Off I-5, 7 miles south of San Diego. Take 28th St exit. NAVSTA is at 28th & Main St's. **RM:** p-15, O/23. NMC: San Diego, 7 miles south. Billeting Office: Building 3362 (BEQ), Building 254 (BOQ). Comm: 556-2745 (BEQ). Comm: 556-6134 (BOQ). 0730-1630 hours daily. Other hours, Watch Section/Central Assignments, Building 3362. Check in facility, check out 1200 hours daily. Government civilian employees billeting.

TML: Navy Lodge. Building 3191. All ranks. Leave or official duty. For reservations call 1-800-NAVY-INN. Lodge number is 234-6142. 24 hours daily. Check in 1500-1800 hours. Check out 1200 hours. 45/1-bedroom units, private bath. Each room has 2 double beds, couch, sleeps 5. Kitchen, utensils, A/C, color TV, telephone, coin washer/dryer, ice vending, vending machine, playground, maid service, free cribs. Facilities for disabled American veterans. Rates: $26.00 per room. Government civilian employees billeting only if 02+ equivalent with ID and orders. All categories can make reservations. Note: facility will expand to 100 units by Summer 1991. Two rooms converted to give access to the handicapped.

TML: BEQ. Building 8. Enlisted all grades. Official duty only. 3500 beds, semi-private bath (E7+ private bath). TV lounge, maid service, free washer/dryer, ice vending. Rates: $2.00 per person. Dependents not authorized. Reservations required.

TML: BOQ. Building 254. Officers all grades. Official duty only. 75/1-bedroom, private bath; 57 separate bedrooms, private bath. Refrigerator, color TV, maid service, free washer/dryer, ice vending. Rates: $4.00 per person. Maximum 2 per room. Children not authorized. Duty can make reservations. Others Space-A.

Other: Sea World, San Diego Zoo, Balboa Park, beaches, Sea Port Village.

TML Availability: Good except PCS rotations, summer months.

Cafeteria-544-2287
NCO Club-556-7050
SDO/NCO-556-1246
Enlisted Club-556-1918
O'Club-556-7948
Medical-556-1801
Police-556-1526

San Diego Naval Submarine Base (CA79R4)
San Diego, CA 92106-3521

TELEPHONE NUMBER INFORMATION: Main installation numbers: Comm: 619-553-1011, ATVN: 933-1011.

Location: From I-5 take Rosencrans west onto base. RM: p-13, SQ/17. NMC: San Diego, 2 miles west.

Billeting Office: BOQ. Building 601. EX-9381. Check in facility. Check out 1200 hours.

TML: BOQ. Building 601. Officer. All ranks. Leave or official duty. Enlisted E7-E9. Official duty only. 75/1-bedroom, private bath; 55 separate bedrooms, private bath;

CALIFORNIA
San Diego Naval Submarine Base, continued

6 VIP suites, private bath. Cots, essentials, food/ice vending, kitchenette (suites), limited utensils, maid service, refrigerator, color TV, free washer/dryer. Modern structure. Rates: Sponsor $6.00, VIP suites $15.00. Maximum 2 persons. Duty can make reservations. Others Space-A.

TML: BEQ. Building 300. Enlisted. E1-E6. Official duty only. EX-7535. Rooms with various bath combinations. Food/ice vending, maid service, refrigerator, color TV lounge, free washer/dryer. Modern structure. Rates: Sponsor $3.00.

TML Availability: Fairly good. Best Dec. Difficult May-Aug.

CPO Club-553-7597   Enlisted Club-553-7519   O'Club-553-9384
Police-553-7070   SDO/NCO-553-7208

San Pedro Coast Guard Personnel Support Center (CA25R4)
San Pedro, CA 90731-0208

TELEPHONE NUMBER INFORMATION: Main installation numbers: Comm: 213-514-6450, FTS: 795-6450.

Location: On Coast Guard Base, Terminal Island, San Pedro, CA, 6 miles west of Long Beach. RM: p-15, L/9. NMC: Long Beach, 2 miles east.

Billeting Office: Local Housing Authority, Long Beach, P. O. Box 8, Terminal Island Station, San Pedro, CA 90731-0208. EX-6450. 0700-1600 M-F. Check in facility, check out 1400 hours daily. No government civilian employee billeting.

TML: Guest House. All ranks. Leave or official duty. 2/2-bedroom, private bath. Kitchen, complete utensils, color TV, free washer/dryer. Modern structure. Rates: vary by rank. Duty and retired can make reservations.

TML Availability: Good year round.

SDO/NCO-514-6401

Sierra Army Depot (CA44R4)
Herlong, CA 96113-5000

TELEPHONE NUMBER INFORMATION: Main installation numbers: Comm: 916-827-2111, ATVN: 855-4910.

Location: 55 miles north of Reno, NV, off US-395. Right on CA-A26 from Reno. When traveling south on US-395, left on CA-A25. RM: p-11, NH/13. NMC: Reno, 55 miles southeast.

Billeting Office: Building T-26, EX-4544 duty hours. Other hours, Sec Radio Room, Building P-100, EX-4345. Check in facility, check out 1100 hours daily. Government civilian employee billeting.

TML: Guest House. Building T-26 (O'Club). All ranks. Leave or official duty. 2/1-bedroom, semi-private bath; 2/2-bedroom apartments, private bath (DV/VIP); 8/1-bedroom (VOQ/VEQ), semi-private bath. Kitchen in apartments, refrigerator, community kitchen, limited utensils, maid service, cribs/cots $1.00, free washer/dryer. Older structure. Rates: Sponsor $8.00, each additional person $3.00. Duty can make reservations. Others Space-A.

Temporary Military Lodging Around the World — 43

CALIFORNIA

Sierra Army Depot, continued

DV/VIP: PAO, EX-4544. Determined by Commander.

TML Availability: Good, winter. Difficult, summer.

Cafeteria-827-6166
NCO Club-827-2504
Snack Bar-827-3140

Locator-827-4328
O'Club-827-2771/5231
SDO/NCO-827-4345/4555

Medical-827-4141/4575
Police-827-4345

Stockton Naval Communications Station (CA51R4)
Stockton, CA 95203-5000

TELEPHONE NUMBER INFORMATION: Main installation numbers: Comm: 209-944-0284/0343, ATVN: 466-7284/7343.

Location: From I-5 north exit at Rough & Ready Island, right at Fresno St to Washington St to Station. RM: p-11, NO/10. NMC: Stockton, in the city.

Billeting Office: Building 128. Hooper Dr & McCloy Ave. EX-0284/0343. 0730-1600 M-F. Other hours. DMAA Office, Building 128. Check in facility, check out 1200 hours daily. No government civilian employee billeting.

TML: TLQ/BOQ/BEQ. Buildings 24, 128, 129. All ranks. Leave or official duty. 13/1-bedroom, private and semi-private baths; 2 separate bedrooms, private bath; 30/2-bedroom, hall bath; 6 separate rooms, 4 beds, hall bath. Male E6 & below 4 per room; male E7+ one per room; female 2 per room. Refrigerator, A/C, TV, maid service (BOQ only), washer/dryer, game room (Building 128 & BOQ only). Rates: $4.00 per person. Under 12 free. Maximum 4 per room. Duty can make reservations. Others Space-A.

TML Availability: Fairly good, winter months and holidays. Difficult, summer.

Cafeteria-944-0380
Locator-944-0284/0343
O'Club-944-0552

CPO Club-944-0552
Medical-944-0445
Police-944-0451

Enlisted Club-944-0522
NCO Club-944-0552
Snack Bar-944-0522

Travis Air Force Base (CA50R4)
Travis AFB, CA 94535-5000

TELEPHONE NUMBER INFORMATION: Main installation numbers: Comm: 707-424-5000, ATVN: 837-1110.

Location: Off I-80 North, take Travis AFB Parkway exit. RM: p-11, NN8. NMC: San Francisco, 45 miles southwest.

Billeting Office: Building 404, Sevedge Dr. Comm: 424-2987. ATVN: 837-2987. 24 hours daily. Check in facility, check out 1200 hours daily. Government civilian employee billeting.

TML: TLQ. Building 404. All ranks. Leave or official duty. 40 studio apartments, private bath. Kitchen, color TV, A/C, maid service, telephone. Modern structure. Rates: $16.00 per unit. Duty can make reservations. Others Space-A.

TML: VOQ. Building 404. Officer all grades. Leave or official duty. 231/1-bedroom, semi-private bath. Refrigerator, A/C, TV, maid service. Older structure. Rates: $6.00 per person. Duty can make reservations. Others Space-A.

TML: VAQ. Building 239. Enlisted all grades. Leave or official duty. Reservations accepted. 172/1-bedroom, semi-private bath. Same as VOQ above.

44 — *Temporary Military Lodging Around the World*

CALIFORNIA
Travis Air Force Base, continued

TML: DV/VIP. Building 404. Officer 06+. Leave or official duty. ATVN: 837-3185. 23/1-bedroom suites, private bath. A/C, color TV, maid service. Older structure. Rates: $10.00 per person. Duty can make reservations. Others Space-A.

DV/VIP: DV lounge at Air Term. ATVN: 837-3185. 06+. Retirees Space-A.

TML Availability: Very limited, summer. Good, other times.

Cafeteria-424-2092   Enlisted Club-424-5659   Locator-424-2026
Medical-423-3462   NCO Club-424-5071   O'Club-424-3368
Police-438-2011   SDO/NCO-438-5517

Treasure Island Naval Base (CA21R4)
San Francisco, CA 94130-5001

TELEPHONE NUMBER INFORMATION: Main installation number: Comm: 415-765-6411/6232, ATVN: 869-6232.

Location: On Treasure Island in San Francisco Bay off Hwy I-80 (Oakland Bay Bridge), take exit from left lane. RM: p-11, NC/20. NMC: San Francisco, 3 miles southwest.

Billeting Office: BOQ, Building 369, California Ave. EX-5236. BEQ, Building 452. EX-6556/7. 24 hours daily. Check in facility, check out 1100 hours daily. Space-A call after 1800 hours.

TML: BOQ/BEQ. All ranks. Leave or official duty. 300 rooms, private and semi-private baths. Refrigerator, color TV room & lounge, maid service, free washer/dryer. Older structure, renovated buildings. Rates: Sponsor $14.00, each additional person $4.00. Duty can make reservations. Others Space-A.

DV/VIP: Protocol Office, Code 120, Building 1. EX-6941. 07+. Retirees Space-A.

TML Availability: Good, Dec. Other times, limited.

Cafeteria-765-6087   Enlisted Club-765-5121   Locator-765-6433
Medical-765-5223   NCO Club-765-6284   O'Club-765-5445
SDO/NCO-765-6232

Twentynine Palms Marine Corps Air/Ground Combat Center (CA27R4)
Twentynine Palms, CA 92278-5000

TELEPHONE NUMBER INFORMATION: Main installation numbers: Comm: 619-368-6000, ATVN: 952-6000.

Location: From west on I-10 exit on CA-62 NE to Base. From east on I-40 exit south at Amboy. RM p-13, SK/20. NMC: Palm Springs, 60 miles southwest.

Billeting Office: Building 1565, 5th St near O'Club. EX-7375/6642. 24 hours daily. Check in facility, check out 1100 hours daily. Government civilian employee billeting.

TML: BOQ/BEQ. All ranks. Leave or official duty. 4 VIP Quarters (04/GS-10+); 121 CG Guest House rooms; 16 rooms (04+); 69 rooms (03-); 40 Senior Noncommissioned Officer rooms. Community kitchen, A/C, color TV room & lounge, maid service, free washer/dryer, ice vending. Older structure. Rates: Adults $9.00.

Temporary Military Lodging Around the World — 45

CALIFORNIA
Twentynine Palms Marine Corps Air/Ground Combat Center, continued

Maximum $30.00 per family. Duty can make reservations. Others Space-A.

TML: TLF. Building 690. EX-6573/6583. One bedroom family units, trundle beds, private bath. Kitchen, washer/dryer, BBQ, playground. Rates: $16.80-$30.00 per unit. Call for reservations information.

DV/VIP: Protocol Office. EX-6109. 04+. Retirees and lower grades Space-A.

Other: Joshua Tree national monument.

TML Availability: Good, winter months. Difficult, summer months.

Enlisted Club-368-6691	Locator-368-6853	Medical-368-7254
NCO/CPO Club-368-669	O'Club-368-6610	Police-368-6800
Snack Bar-368-7253	SDO/NCO-368-7200	

Vandenberg Air Force Base (CA29R4)
Vandenberg AFB, CA 93437-5000

TELEPHONE NUMBER INFORMATION: Main installation numbers: Comm: 805-866-1110, ATVN: 276-1110.

Location: From south on US-101, west on CA-246, north on CA-S20 to AFB. From north on US-101, west on US-1 from Gaviota, north on CA-S20 to AFB. RM: p-7, SJ/7. NMC: Santa Maria, 22 miles north.

Billeting Office: ATTN: Shuttle Inn, Box 5579. Building 13005, Oregon at L St. EX-1844. 24 hours daily. Check in billeting, check out 1200 hours daily. Government civilian employee billeting.

TML: TLF. Building 13007. All ranks. Leave or official duty. Accessible to the handicapped. 15/1-bedroom, private bath. Kitchen, complete utensils, cable color TV, maid service, free cribs/cots, free washer/dryer, essentials. Older structure, renovated '88. New TVs '89. Rates: $22.00 per room. Maximum 5 per room. Duty can make reservations. Retirees can make reservations for medical appointments only. Others Space-A.

TML: VAQ. Building 13140. Enlisted all grades. Leave or official duty. 76 separate bedrooms, semi-private baths (E1-E8); 4/1-bedroom, private bath (E9 only). Color TV, maid service, free washer/dryer, vending machines, essentials. Older structure. Remodeled recently. New TVs. Rates: $9.00 per person. Maximum 2 persons in E9 rooms. Duty can make reservations. Others Space-A.

TML: VOQ. 11000 area. Officer all ranks. Leave or official duty. Accessible to handicapped. 78/1-bedroom, private bath. 16/1-bedroom, private bath. 224/2-bedroom, semi-private bath. Color TV, maid service, free cribs/cots, free washer/dryer, essentials, ice vending, special facilities disabled American veterans. Modern structure. Rates: $9.00 per person. Maximum 2 persons per unit. Duty can make reservations. Others Space-A.

TML: VOQ. Building 13000 area. Officers all grades. Leave or official duty. 16/1-bedroom suites, private bath; 224/2-bedroom, semi-private bath. Refrigerator, community kitchen, color TV, maid service, free cots, free washer/dryer, special facilities disabled American veterans. Older structure. Rates: $9.00 per person. Duty can make reservations. Others Space-A.

TML: BOQ. Building 13800. Officers all grades. Official duty only. Reservations not taken. 10/2-bedroom apartments, private bath. All other same as VOQ above. Maid service optional.

CALIFORNIA
Vandenberg Air Force Base, continued

TML: DV/VIP. Marshallia Ranch, Building 1338. Officers 06/GS-17+. Leave or official duty. EX-3711. 5/1-bedroom, private bath, suites. Kitchen, utensils, A/C, color TV, maid service, free washer/dryer, ice vending. Older structure. Rates: $14.00 per person. All categories can make reservations.

DV/VIP: 1 STRAD/CSP, Building 10577. EX-3711. 06+.

TML Availability: Best, Nov-Jan. Difficult Apr-Oct.

Cafeteria-734-1488	Enlisted Club-734-4375	Locator-866-1841
Medical-866-1847	NCO Club-734-4375	O'Club-734-4311
Police-866-3911	Snack Bar-734-1228	SDO/NCO-866-9961

COLORADO

Fitzsimons Army Medical Center (CO10R3)
Aurora, CO 80045-5000

TELEPHONE NUMBER INFORMATION: Main installation numbers: Comm: 303-361-8241, ATVN: 943-8241, FTS: 337-8241.

Location: From I-70 take Peoria Ave (281), exit south on Peoria Ave, 1 mile to left on Colfax Ave, Center on left. From I-25 take I-225 north to Colfax Ave, west on Colfax Ave to Center on right. RM: p-17, C/26. NMC: Denver 8 miles east.

Billeting Office: Building 400, West Bruns Ave. EX-8903. 0730-1930 hours M-F. 0930-1630 Sa-Su. Other hours, Guest House, Building 407, EX-8068. Check in/out at facility.

TML: VOQ/VEQ: Building 400. All ranks. Leave or official duty. Check out 1200 hours daily. 44/1-bedroom, private bath; 85 separate bedroom, private bath; 1/2-bedroom, private bath. Refrigerator, color TV room & lounge, maid service, free cribs, free washer/dryer, ice vending. Older structure. Rates: $10.00 single, $15.00 double, $2.50 per roll-away. TDY can make reservations. Others Space-A.

TML: Guest House. Building 407. All ranks. Leave or official duty. Check in at facility 24 hours daily. Check out 1100 hours daily. EX-8068. 12/1-bedroom, private bath; 28 separate bedrooms, private bath. Color TV lounge, maid service, free cribs & cots, free washer/dryer, ice vending. Older structure. Rates: Sponsor $10.00, adult $15.00, $1.00 each additional person. All categories can make reservations.

TML: O'Club. Building 24. Officer all grades. Leave or official duty. Check in facility, 0800-2200 hours daily. Check out 1100 hours daily. One deluxe suite, private bath; 10 separate bedrooms, private bath. Refrigerator, A/C, color TV, maid service, free cribs, cable TV. Older facility. Rates: $16.00 single, $20.00 double, each additional person over 12 $6.00, under 12 $1.50. All categories can make reservations.

DV/VIP: Commander's office. Comm 361-8824. ATVN: 942-8824. 06+. Retirees Space-A.

Other: Near Stapleton Int'l Arpt, Lowry AFB, Rocky Mountain Arsenal & Buckley ANG Base.

TML Availability: Good, Oct-Dec. More difficult other times.

Temporary Military Lodging Around the World — 47

COLORADO

Fitzsimons Army Medical Center, continued

Locator-361-8223
O'Club-361-8061
SDO/NCO-361-8234

Medical-361-8350
Police-361-3791

NCO Club-361-8961
Snack Bar-361-8475

Fort Carson (CO02R3)
Fort Carson, CO 80913-5000

TELEPHONE NUMBER INFORMATION: Main installation numbers: Comm: 719-579-3431, ATVN: 691-3431.

Location: From Colorado Springs, take I-25 or CO-115 south. Clearly marked. RM: p-17, J/24. NMC: Colorado Springs, 6 miles north.

Billeting Office: Building 6227, Prussman St. Red Ivy Inn. EX-4832. 24 hours daily. Check in facility, check out 1100 hours daily. Government civilian employee billeting.

TML: BOQ. Building 7305. Officer. All ranks. Leave or official duty. 6/1-bedroom, private bath. A/C, free cribs/cots, essentials, kitchen, maid service, color TV in room, free washer/dryer. Older structure. New carpets/paint '90. Rates: Sponsor, $17.50, adult $7.00, child $1.00. Maximum charge $45.00. Maximum 4 persons. Duty can make reservations. Others Space-A.

TML: VOQ. Buildings 7303 and 7305. Officer. All ranks. Leave or official duty. 48/1-bedroom, private bath. Description same as BOQ above.

TML: VEQ. Buildings 6227, 6228, 7301, 7302. Enlisted. All grades. Leave or official duty. 135/1-bedroom, private bath. 33 rooms, with single bed, semi-private bath. A/C, community kitchen, free cribs/cots, essentials, kitchen in unit, maid service, refrigerator, color TV in room, free washer/dryer. Older structure. New carpets/paint '90. Rates: Sponsor $15-$17.50, adult $3-$7.00, child $1.00. Maximum charge $45.00. Maximum 4 persons. Duty can make reservations. Others Space-A.

TML: VIP/DV. Buildings 6227, 6215. Officer 04+. Enlisted E8-E9. Leave or official duty. 3/2-bedroom, private bath; 2/3-bedroom, private bath. A/C, free cribs/cots, essentials, maid service, color TV in room, free washer/dryer. Older structures. Repaint '90. Rates: Sponsor $21.50, adult $10.50, child $6.00. Maximum charge $45.00. Maximum 8 persons. All categories can make reservations.

DV/VIP: Protocol Office, Building 1430, EX-4601. 05+. Retirees and lower grades Space-A.

Other: Pikes Peak, Royal Gorge, Cripple Creek mining town.

TML Availability: Difficult. Best Nov-Apr.

Cafeteria-576-6670
Medical-9-911
Police-579-2333

Enlisted Club-576-7119
NCO Club-576-7540
SDO/NCO-579-3400

Locator-579-3341/4275
O'Club-579-6646

Lowry Technical Training Center (CO05R3)
Lowry AFB, CO 80230-5000

TELEPHONE NUMBER INFORMATION: Main installation numbers: Comm: 303-676-1110, ATVN: 926-1110.

Location: From I-70 take I-225 south to 6th Ave, west 3 miles to "E" gate of Base at 6th Ave & Dayton St. RM: p-17, D/25. NMC: Denver, 6 miles west.

48 — Temporary Military Lodging Around the World

COLORADO
Lowry Air Force Base, continued

Billeting Office: 3415 ABG/SVH, ATTN: Reservation Clerk, Building 1400, Lowry Dr. EX-7255. 24 hours daily. Check in billeting, Check out 1200 hours daily.

TML: TLF. Buildings 572, 574, 576, 578. All ranks. Leave or official duty. 40/1-bedroom apartments, private bath. Kitchen, complete utensils, A/C, color TV, maid service, free cribs, free washer/dryer, ice vending. Modern structures. Rates: $16.00 per room E1-E6, $20.00 per room E7+. Maximum 4 per room. Duty can make reservations. Others Space-A.

TML: VOQ. Buildings 1111, 1112, 1113, 1119. Officer 01-03. Leave or official duty. 216/1-bedroom, semi-private bath (8 units private bath). Refrigerator, A/C, color TV, maid service, free washer/dryer, ice vending. Modern structures, new furniture '86. Rates: $6.00 per person. Maximum 2 per room. Duty can make reservations. Others Space-A.

TML: VOQ. Buildings 405, 406. Officer 04-06. Leave or official duty. 100/1-bedroom, private bath. Kitchen, A/C, color TV, maid service, free washer/dryer, ice vending, microwave. Modern structures. Rates: $6.00 per person. Maximum 2 per room. Duty can make reservations. Others Space-A.

TML: VAQ. Building 963. Enlisted E7-E9. Leave or official duty. 87/1-bedroom, semi-private bath. Refrigerator, A/C, color TV, maid service, free washer/dryer, ice vending, microwave in lounge. Modern structures, new TVs/carpets in '87. Rates: $5.00 per person. Maximum 2 per room. Duty can make reservations. Others Space-A.

TML: VAQ. Building 1400. Enlisted E1-E6. Leave or official duty. 873/1-bedroom, semi-private bath. Refrigerator, A/C, color TV, maid service, free washer/dryer, ice vending, microwave in lounges. Modern structure, new carpets '87. Rates: $5.00 per person. Maximum 2 per room. Duty can make reservations. Others Space-A.

DV/VIP: Protocol Office, Building 349. EX2261. 06/GS-15+. Retirees and lower grades Space-A.

Other: Denver mint.

TML Availability: Good, Nov-Jan. More difficult, other times.

Cafeteria-388-4625 Enlisted Club-388-0827 Locator-370-4171
Medical-370-2193   NCO Club-320-4483   O'Club-320-4002
Police-370-2000   SDO/NCO-370-2950

Peterson Air Force Base (CO06R3)
Peterson AFB, CO 80914-5000

TELEPHONE NUMBER INFORMATION: Main installation numbers: Comm: 719-554-7321, ATVN: 692-7321.

Location: Off US-24 (Platte Ave) east of Colorado Springs. Clearly marked. RM: p-17, I/26. NMC: Colorado Springs, 4 miles west.

Billeting Office: Building 1042, Stewart Ave. Comm: 719-554-7851. ATVN: 692-7851. For reservations call EX-6293. 24 hours daily. Check in facility, check out 1200 hours daily. Government civilian employee billeting.

TML: TLQ. Buildings 1091-1094. All ranks. Leave or official duty. Accessible to the handicapped. 40/1-bedroom, private bath. Refrigerator, kitchen, complete utensils, color TV, A/C, maid service, free cribs, free washer/dryer, ice vending. Older structure. New carpets/TVs. Rates: $20.00 per unit, sleeps 5 persons. Duty

Temporary Military Lodging Around the World — 49

Peterson Air Force Base, continued   COLORADO

can make reservations. Others Space-A. Space-A policies same as VOQ below.

TML: VOQ. Buildings 1026, 1030. Officer all grades. Leave or official duty. Accessible to handicapped. 32/1-bedroom, private bath; 33/1-bedroom suites, private bath (DV/VIP). Kitchen, free cots, essentials, ice vending, refrigerator, A/C, color TV, maid service, free washer/dryer. Modern structures. Rates: Sponsor/Adult, Building 1026 $8.00 per person, Building 1030 $10.00 per person. Maximum 2 persons per unit. Maximum charge $16.00 (Building 1026), $20.00 (Building 1030). No children, no infants. Duty can make reservations. Others Space-A. Space-A released at 1700 hours Sat-Thurs, Fridays at 2000 hours. First come, first served. Unaccompanied dependents may only be Space-A if an active duty or retired person signs them in.

TML: VAQ. Building 1143. Enlisted E-1 to E-6. Leave or official duty. 64/1-bedroom, double occupancy, semi-private; 18/1-bedroom, double occupancy, private bath; 7 Senior Noncommissioned Officer suites, private bath. A/C, color TV room & lounge, refrigerator, maid service, free washer/dryer, ice/food vending, essentials. Modern structure. Rates: VAQ, Sponsor/Adult, $5.00 per person. No children, no infants. Maximum 2 persons per unit. Maximum charge $10.00. Rates: Senior Noncommissioned Officer suites, Sponsor/Adult, $10.00 per person. Maximum 2 persons per unit. Maximum charge $20.00. No children, no infants. Duty can make reservations. Others Space-A. Space-A policies same as VOQ above.

TML: DV/VIP. Buildings 999, 1026, 1030. Officer 07+. 10/1-bedroom, private bath. A/C, free cots, essentials, ice vending, kitchen w/complete utensils, maid service, refrigerator, color TV, free washer/dryer. Building 999 has been renovated '89 with new A/C. Building 1030 has new carpets '89. Rates: Sponsor/Adult, $10.00 per person. Maximum 2 persons per unit. Maximum charge $20.00 on leave, $10.00 active duty. No children, no infants. Rooms only for protocol reservations.

DV/VIP: Protocol, Building 1, 554-5007, 07+. Retirees Space-A. See VOQ above for Space-A policies.

Other: Great skiing and camping. NORAD, Space Command HQ, Pikes Peak, USAF Academy.

TML Availability: Difficult. Best Dec-Feb.

Snack Bar-554-7769	Locator-554-4020	Medical-554-4333
NCO Club-554-7876	O'Club-554-4100	Police-554-4000

United States Air Force Academy (CO07R3)
Colorado Springs, CO 80840-5231

TELEPHONE NUMBER INFORMATION: Main installation numbers: Comm: 719-472-1818, ATVN: 259-3110.

Location: West of I-25 north from Colorado Springs. Two gates, about 5 miles apart, provide access from I-25 and are clearly marked. RM: p-17, F/24. NMC: Colorado Springs, 5 miles south.

Billeting Office: ATTN: Reservations. Building 3130, Academy Dr. EX-3060. 24 hours daily. Check in facility, check out 1100 hours daily. Government civilian employee billeting.

TML: DVQ. Building 3130. Officer 07+. Leave or official duty. EX-3060. 8/1-bedroom, private bath. Kitchen, study, living room, refrigerator, utensils, color TV, maid service, free washer/dryer, free cribs/cots, ice vending, facilities for disabled American veterans. Modern structure, renovated, new carpets '89. Rates: Sponsor $10.00, adult $10.00. Maximum 2 per family. Most reservations handled

50 — *Temporary Military Lodging Around the World*

COLORADO
United States Air Force Academy, continued

through protocol office for 07+ and equivalent.

TML: VOQ. Building 3130/3134. Officer all grades. Leave or official duty. EX-3060. 10/1-bedroom, private bath; 14 separate bedrooms, semi-private bath; 16/2-bedroom, semi-private bath. Refrigerator, color TV in lounge, maid service, free cribs/cots, free washer/dryer, ice vending, facilities for disabled American veterans. Modern structures. New carpets '87. Rates: Sponsor $6.00, adult $6.00, child $6.00, infant up to 2 years free. Maximum capacity depends on type of room. Duty can make reservations. Others Space-A.

TML: TLF. Building 4700/02. All ranks. Official duty only. EX-3060. 26/3-bedroom houses. Kitchen, complete utensils, color TV, maid service, free cribs/cots, free washer/dryer. Modern structures. Rates: E1-E5 $15.00 per night, E6+ $22.00 per night. TDY persons not eligible. Family quarters intended primarily for use by PCS in/out. Others Space-A on day-to-day basis.

DV/VIP: Protocol Office, Harmon Hall, Building 2304, Room 328. EX-3540. 07+.

Other: New Visitors Center: movie, gift shop, and exhibits, EX-2555. 2 million annual visitors, guided tours. Two 18 hole golf courses and picnic area. Cadet Wing holds noon formation for marching to lunch in Cadet Area at 1130 hrs. Visitors can watch from the chapel wall.

TML Availability: Best, Jan-Apr. Difficult, other times.

Cafeteria-472-2825	Enlisted Club-472-4377	Locator-472-4262
Medical-472-5000	NCO Club-472-4377	O'Club-472-4677
Police-472-2000	Snack Bar-472-4709	SDO/NCO-472-1818

CONNECTICUT

New London Naval Submarine Base (CT01R1)
Groton, CT 06349-5000

TELEPHONE NUMBER INFORMATION: Main installation numbers: Comm: 203-449-3011, ATVN: 241-3011, FTS: 648-3011.

Location: From I-95 north take exit 86 to CT-12. Go left on Pleasant Valley Rd, then right on Lestertown Rd. Base clearly marked. RM: p-19, I/17. NMC: Hartford, 50 miles northwest.

Billeting Office: None.

TML: Navy Lodge. 77 Dewey Ave, Groton, CT 06340. All ranks. Leave or official duty. Check in 1500-1800 daily, check out 1100 hours daily. For reservations call 1-800-NAVY-INN. Lodge number is 446-1160. 68/1-bedroom, 2 double beds, private bath. Kitchen, refrigerator, limited utensils, A/C, color TV room & lounge, maid service, free cribs, coin washer/dryer. Modern structure, renovated. Rates: $32.00 per unit. Maximum 5 persons. All categories can make reservations.

TML: BOQ. Buildings D, 379, M, L. All ranks. Leave or official duty. Comm: 449-3416. Check in 24 hours daily, check out 1100 hours daily. 67/1-bedroom, private bath; 21/1-bedroom suites, private bath; 106/1-bedroom, semi-private bath; 54/1-bedroom, hall bath. Refrigerator, community kitchen, A/C (suites only), color TV (suites only), color TV lounge, maid service. Older structure. Rates: $7.00 per person. Duty can make reservations. Others Space-A.

CONNECTICUT

New London Naval Submarine Base, continued

DV/VIP: No office. EX-3416. 07+.

Other: Mystic seaport, USCG Academy, U.S.S. Nautilus Memorial/Submarine Force Library and Museum.

TML Availability: Fairly good, Navy Lodge, all year.

Cafeteria-449-3679 Enlisted Club-449-3142 Locator-449-4761
Medical-449-3666   NCO Club-449-3237   O'Club-449-3352
Police-449-3222   SDO/NCO-449-3444

DELAWARE

Dover Air Force Base (DE01R1)
Dover AFB, DE 19902-5000

TELEPHONE NUMBER INFORMATION: Main installation numbers: Comm: 302-677-2113, ATVN: 445-3000.

Location: Off US-113. Clearly marked. RM: p-41, F/24. NMC: Dover, 5 miles northwest.

Billeting Office: Building 805, 14th St (across from O'Club). EX-6329. 24 hours daily. Check out 1200 hours daily. Space-A billeting roll call at 1700 hours daily.

TML: Guest House. Building 803. All ranks. Leave or official duty. 14/2-room family suites, private bath. Kitchen, refrigerator, A/C, color TV, maid service, free cribs/cots, free washer/dryer, ice vending. Older structure. Rates: Maximum $20.00 per family. PCS/TDY can make reservations. Others Space-A.

TML: VOQ. Building 803-806. Officer all grades. Leave or official duty. 151/1-bedroom, semi-private bath. Refrigerator, A/C, color TV, maid service, free washer/dryer. Modern structure. Rates: $6.00 per person. Maximum 4 per room. No children.

TML: VAQ. Buildings 472, 474, 481, 482, 801. Enlisted all grades. Building 802 air crew quarters. Building 474, upstairs, female enlisted quarters. 608 beds total. 400 series buildings have latrine bath, color TV, refrigerator, clock radio, coffee makers. 800 series buildings have room/bath room configuration. Rates: $6.00 per person. No children.

DV/VIP: Suites. 06+. Leave or official duty. 16/1-bedroom, private bath. A/C, color TV, maid service, free washer/dryer. Modern structure. Rates: $10.00 per person.

DV/VIP: Building 201, Room 101. EX-6649/6610. 06+. Retirees and lower grades Space-A.

TML Availability: Very good, Oct-Apr. Limited, other times.

Cafeteria-677-3923 Enlisted Club-677-6342 Locator-677-2841
Medical-735-2600   NCO Club-677-6342   O'Club-677-6023
Police-677-6664   Snack Bar-674-3380

DELAWARE

Fort Miles Recreation Area (DE02R1)
Fort Meade, MD 20755-5071
CLOSED

DISTRICT OF COLUMBIA

Bolling Air Force Base (DC01R1)
1100 Air Base Wing
Bolling AFB, DC 20332-5000

TELEPHONE NUMBER INFORMATION: Main installation numbers: Comm: 703-545-6700, ATVN: 297-0101.

Location: Take I-95 (east portion of Capital Beltway, I-495) north or south, exit to I-295 north, exit to Portland St and main entrance to AFB. Also, I-395 (Southeast Freeway) north, exit South Capitol St, cross Anacostia River on South Capitol St, main entrance to AFB on right. Clearly marked. RM: p-42, I/8. NMC: Washington, in southeast section of the city.

Billeting Office: Building 602, Theisen St. EX-5316/5741. 24 hours daily. Check in billeting, check out 1100 hours daily.

TML: TLQ. Apartments. All ranks. Leave or official duty. 50 separate bedrooms, private bath. Kitchen, A/C, color TV room & lounge, maid service, free washer/dryer, ice vending. Older structure. Reservations TDY. Rates: $25.00 per room. Maximum 4 persons. Unaccompanied dependents not authorized. Others Space-A.

TML: VOQ. Officer 01-06. Leave or official duty. 8 suites, private bath; 52/1-bedroom, semi-private bath. Refrigerator, A/C, color TV room & lounge, maid service, free washer/dryer, ice vending. Older structure. Rates: $10.50 per person. Reservations TDY only. Others Space-A.

TML: TAQ. Blanchard Barracks #1302. Enlisted E1-E6. EX-4600. 25/1-bedroom, latrine bath. Refrigerator, color TV room & lounge, maid service, free washer/dryer, cable TV. Older structure. Reservations TDY. Rates: $6.00 per person. Others Space-A.

Temporary Military Lodging Around the World — 53

Bolling Air Force Base, continued **DISTRICT OF COLUMBIA**

TML: VIP. 07+. 23 suites, private bath. Refrigerator, A/C, color TV, maid service, free washer/dryer. Older structure. Rates: $10.50 per person. Duty can make reservations. Also 6 Senior Noncommissioned Officers' quarters, $6.00 per person, reservations via Protocol. Others Space-A.

DV/VIP: Protocol Office, Building P-20. EX-4264/65. 07+. Retirees Space-A.

Other: Capital City, national monuments & parks.

TML Availability: Difficult. Better during winter months.

Cafeteria-562-4419   Locator-767-4522   Medical-767-5233
NCO Club-563-1400   O'Club-563-8700   SDO/NCO-767-1111

Walter Reed Army Medical Center (DC03R1)
Washington, DC 20307-5000

TELEPHONE NUMBER INFORMATION: Main installation numbers: Comm: 202-576-3501/02, ATVN: 291-3501/02.

Location: 6900 Georgia Ave, NW. From I-495 (Capital Beltway) take Georgia Ave/Silver Spring exit south to Center, enter first or second gate. To reach the Forest Glen support facilities from Georgia Ave, south, right turn on to Linden Lane, cross over B&O railroad bridge, support facility on left (.75 miles from Georgia Ave). RM: p-42, F/8. NMC: Washington, DC, in the city.

Billeting Office: ATTN: Housing Referral, Main Dr, Building 1, Room G-01. EX-3117/18/19. 0800-1530 daily. Check in facility, check out 1100 hours daily. No government civilian employee billeting.

TML: Guest House. Building 17. All ranks. Leave or official duty. EX-3044 or 882-1000. 65 rooms, latrine baths, semi-private bath, private bath. A/C, color TV room & lounge, maid service, free cribs/cots, coin washer/dryer, ice vending, facilities for disabled American veterans. Older structure. Rates: $13.00-$17.00 per unit. Maximum 3 per unit. Priority to members of immediate family of seriously ill patients and to MEDEVAC/AIRVAC personnel, out-patients, and PCS. Others Space-A.

TML: VOQ. Building 18. All ranks. Leave or official duty. EX-2076/2096. Check out 1100 hours daily. 68/1-bedroom, semi-private bath; 5 separate bedrooms, semi-private bath. Kitchen, complete utensils, A/C, color TV room & lounge, maid service, free cots, coin washer/dryer, ice vending. Modern structure, remodeled '85. Rates: $25.00 per unit. Maximum 3 per room. Duty can make reservations. Others Space-A.

DV/VIP: Chief, Housing Management Division, Building 1, Room G-01. EX-3117/18. 06+. Retirees and lower grades Space-A.

TML Availability: Best, Mar-Apr & Sep-Oct. Difficult, others times.

Cafeteria-829-0240   Enlisted Club-829-8932   Locator-576-3501/02
Medical-576-1199   NCO Club-829-8932   O'Club-576-2216
Police-576-2511   Snack Bar-829-0240   SDO/NCO-576-2309

54 — *Temporary Military Lodging Around the World*

DISTRICT OF COLUMBIA

Washington Navy Yard (DC04R1)
Washington, DC 20374-5000

TELEPHONE NUMBER INFORMATION: Main installation numbers: Comm: 202-545-6700, ATVN: 222-6700.

Location: The Hq is in the Washington Navy Yard, 9th & M Sts SE. The TML is in the NDW Anacostia complex adjacent to Bolling AFB. From I-95 (beltway) take I-295 north exit at South Capitol St. NDW Anacostia is clearly marked. NMC: Washington, DC, in the city.

Billeting Office: ATTN: Anacostia CMAA: NAVSTA, Comm: 433-3232. 0730-1600 hours daily. Other hours, 433-2193. Check in 1500-1800, check out 1200 hours daily. No government civilian employees billeting.

TML: Navy Lodge. Located Bellevue Navy Housing Community. All ranks Leave or official duty. For reservations call 1-800-NAVY-INN. Lodge number is 563-6950. 50/1-bedroom, private bath. Utensils, A/C, color TV, free cribs, high chairs, ironing boards, dining/living room areas, sleeps up to 5 persons (2 double beds, 1 converted sofa). Modern structure. Rates: $34.00 per unit. PCS can make reservations 5-90 days in advance. Others 5 days in advance.

Other: Navy Memorial Museum, Display Ship Barry (DD-933), Marine Corps Museum (with famous flags raised over Mt. Suribachi, Iwo Jima), Combat Art Gallery.

TML Availability: Good, Dec-Apr. Difficult, other times.

Enlisted Club-433-2048   Locator-694-3155   Medical-433-2204
CPO Club-433-2523   O'Club-433-3401   Police-433-2411
SDO/NCO-433-2607

FLORIDA

Avon Park Air Force Range (FL16R1)
Avon Park, FL 33825-5000

TELEPHONE NUMBER INFORMATION: Main installation numbers: Comm: 813-452-4191, ATVN: 968-1110-EX-191.

Location: Off FL-64, 10.5 miles east of Avon Park, 15.5 miles northeast of Sebring. RM: p-21, N/13. NMC: Orlando, 60 miles north.

Billeting Office: Building 475. EX-4114. 0800-1600 hours duty days. Other hours contact SP Desk Sgt, Building 424. Check in facility, check out 1100 hours daily. Government civilian employee billeting.

TML: Mobile Homes. All ranks. Leave or official duty. 30 days in advance. EX-4251. 5/2-bedroom, private bath mobile homes, fully furnished. Kitchen, complete utensils, A/C. Rates: $20.00 per unit. TML for single enlisted, Building 240. Duty can make reservations. Others Space-A.

TML: VOQ. Building 447. Officer all ranks. Leave or official duty. Accessible to the handicapped. 4/1-bedroom apartments, private bath. A/C, kitchen, limited utensils, maid service, color TV. Modern structure. Rates: Sponsor, $8.00. Maximum 2 persons. Maximum charge $16.00. Duty can make reservations. Others Space-A.

Temporary Military Lodging Around the World — 55

FLORIDA

Avon Park Air Force Range, continued

TML: VAQ. Building 240. Enlisted all grades. Leave or official duty. 13/1-bedroom, private and semi-private bath. A/C, ice/food vending, maid service, refrigerator, color TV lounge/room, free washer/dryer. Older structure. Rates: Sponsor, $8.00. Duty can make reservations. Others Space-A.

DV/VIP: Protocol, Building 236, 56CSS/CCE, EXT-191, 06+. No DV or VIP suites.

TML Availability: Fairly good. Best May-Nov. Difficult other times.

Cafeteria-452-4113	Locator-452-4120	Medical-452-4140
NCO Club-452-4116	O'Club-452-4116	Enlisted Club-452-4116
Police-454-4194	Snack Bar-454-4265	SDO/NCO-968-1110
		EX-194

Cecil Field Naval Air Station (FL06R1)
Cecil Field NAS, FL 32215-5000

TELEPHONE NUMBER INFORMATION: Main installation numbers: Comm: 904-778-5626, ATVN: 860-5626.

Location: Take Normandy exit west off I-295 and follow Normandy (FL-228) to main gate. RM: p-21, E/11. NMC: Jacksonville, 20 miles east.

Billeting Office: Building 331, D Ave & 4th St. Comm: 771-0641. ATVN: 860-5255/5258. 24 hours daily M-F. Check in facility, check out 1400 hours daily.

TML: BOQ. Building 331. Officer all grades. Leave or official duty. 45/1-bedroom, private bath; 86 separate bedroom, private bath. Refrigerator, A/C, essentials, color TV, maid service, free cribs/cots, free washer/dryer, food/ice vending. Modern structure. New AC/carpets/TVs '89. Rates: Sponsor on leave $8.00, sponsor on duty $4.00, adult $4.00, child $4.00, under 3 years no charge. Maximum charge $16.00 on leave, $12.00 on duty. Duty can make reservations. Others Space-A.

TML: BEQ. Building 92. Enlisted. All grades. Leave or official duty. Check out 1200 hours. EX-6191/92. 10/1-bedroom, private bath. 28 rooms with 2 or more beds. A/C, essentials, food vending, maid service, color TV lounge, free washer/dryer. Older structure. Renovated and remodeled Nov '89. Rates: Sponsor $4.00. Duty can make reservations. Others Space-A.

DV/VIP: BOQ, Building 331. EX-5255. 06+. Retirees and lower grades Space-A.

Other: St Augustine 45 miles south. Beaches, Jacksonville seaport.

TML Availability: Good, Dec-Feb, Sep-Oct. More difficult, other times.

Cafeteria-778-5225	Enlisted Club-778-6154	Locator-778-5240
Medical-778-5508/5378	NCO Club-778-5193	O'Club-778-5110
Police-778-5381	SDO/NCO-778-5626/27	

Eglin Air Force Base (FL27R1)
Eglin AFB, FL 32542-5000

TELEPHONE NUMBER INFORMATION: Main installation numbers: Comm: 904-882-6668, ATVN: 872-1110.

Location: Exit I-10 at Crestview, & follow posted signs to Niceville and Valparaiso, (Eglin AFB). RM: p-21, W/5. NMC: Fort Walton Beach, 14 miles west.

FLORIDA
Eglin Air Force Base, continued

Billeting Office: Building 11001, Boatner Rd, Comm: 882-8761. ATVN: 872-8761. 24 hours daily. Check in billeting, check out 1000 hours daily. Government civilian employee billeting.

TML: All ranks. Leave or official duty. VAQ under renovation until late 1991-call for availability of rooms. VSNCOQ has 6 private bath units and 16 shared bath units at $8.00 per person. TLF has 40/1-bedroom units, 32/2-bedroom units and 1/3-bedroom unit at $14.00-$18.00 per unit. VOQ has 114 rooms and several suites at $8.00 per person for rooms, $10.00-$14.00 per person for suites. A/C, color TV, refrigerator, microwave, maid service, ice vending. Duty can make reservations. Others Space-A.

DV/VIP: HQ MSD/CSP, Building 1 (Command Section). EX-3011.

Other: Armament Museum, beaches, sport fishing, dog races.

TML Availability: Very good, Nov-Jan. Difficult, other times.

Cafeteria-651-4821	Locator-882-4478	Medical-882-7227
NCO Club-678-5127	O'Club-651-1010	Police-882-2502
Snack Bar-651-4821		

Homestead Air Force Base (FL17R1)
Homestead AFB, FL 33039-5000

TELEPHONE NUMBER INFORMATION: Main installation numbers: Comm: 305-257-8011, ATVN: 791-0111.

Location: Off Florida Turnpike, US-1, take Homestead exit. Clearly marked. RM: p-21, V/15. NMC: Miami, 25 miles north.

Billeting Office: Building 945. Saint Nazair St. Comm: 257-5831. ATVN: 791-8224. 24 hours daily. Check in facility, check out 1200 hours daily. Government civilian employee billeting.

TML: TLF. Mango Way Apartments (located off-base). All ranks. Leave or official duty. EX-8224. 19/1-bedroom, private bath. Kitchen, complete utensils, A/C, color TV, limited maid service, free cribs. Older structures. Rates: $21.00 per unit, with $40.00 deposit (refundable upon checkout if there is no damage and appliances are clean). Reservations for PCS in/out. Others Space-A.

TML: VOQ. Buildings 945, 947, 951. Officer all grades. Leave or official duty. EX-8224. 90/1-bedroom, semi-private bath. Refrigerator, community kitchen, limited utensils, A/C, color TV, maid service, free washer/dryer, ice vending. Older structures. Rates: $8.00 per person. Maximum 1 per unit. Duty, retired, disabled American veterans, Reservists on orders can make reservations. No dependents.

TML: VAQ. Buildings 434, 435. Enlisted all grades. Leave or official duty. EX-8224. 128/1-bedroom, 2 beds, semi-private bath; 6/1-bedroom Senior Noncommissioned Officer suites, 1 bed, living room, private bath (E7-E9); 6/1-bedroom Chief suites, 1 bed, living room, private bath (E9). Refrigerator, A/C, color TV, maid service, free washer/dryer. Older structures. Rates: $5.50 per person. Maximum 2 per unit. Reservations for PCS in/out and official TDY only. Others Space-A. No dependents.

TML: DV/VIP. Buildings 963, 938. Officer 06+. Leave or official duty. EX-7212. 36/1-bedroom suites, private bath; 10/2-bedroom suites, private bath; 2 separate

Temporary Military Lodging Around the World — 57

Homestead Air Force Base, continued FLORIDA

bedrooms, private bath. Kitchen, complete utensils, A/C, color TV, maid service, free cribs, free washer/dryer. Older structures. Rates: $8.00 per person. Reservations for PCS in/out or official TDY only. Others Space-A.

DV/VIP: Protocol Office, Building 931, Conference Center. EX-7212. 06+. Retirees Space-A.

TML Availability: Limited. Best, May-Nov. Difficult, Dec-Apr.

Cafeteria-257-5117	Enlisted Club-257-7197	Locator-257-7621
Medical-257-7233/7668	NCO Club-257-7197	O'Club-257-8791
Police-257-7867	Snack Bar-257-5117	SDO/NCO-257-8425

Hurlburt Field (FL18R1)
Hurlburt Field, FL 32544-5000

TELEPHONE NUMBER INFORMATION: Main installation numbers: Comm: 904-882-1110, (Eglin Base Info) ATVN: 579-1110.

Location: Off US-98, 5 miles west of Fort Walton Beach. Clearly Marked. RM: p-21, X/4. NMC: Pensacola, 40 miles west.

Billeting Office: Building 90509, Simpson St. Comm: 884-6245 & 581-1627. ATVN: 579-6245. 24 hours daily. Check in billeting, check out 1200 hours daily. Government civilian employee billeting.

TML: VAQ/VOQ. Buildings 90344-90346, 90507, 90508. All ranks. Leave or official duty. Accessible to the handicapped. 179/1-bedroom, private and semi-private bath; 29 separate bedrooms, private bath. Kitchen, limited utensils, A/C, color TV, maid service, free cribs/cots, essentials, free washer/dryer, ice vending, VOQ stocked wet bar. Older structure. Rates: Sponsor, $6.00; DVs, $10.00. Maximum 2 persons per unit. Duty can make reservations. Others Space-A. See Eglin AFB listing for other TML.

DV/VIP: Protocol Office, Building 1, EX-2308. 06+. Retirees and lower grades Space-A.

TML Availability: Difficult. Best, Dec-Mar.

Locator-884-6333	Medical-884-7882	NCO Club-884-6468
O'Club-581-3110	Police-884-6423	Enlisted Club-884-6468
SDO/NCO-884-7774		

Jacksonville Naval Air Station (FL08R1)
Jacksonville NAS, FL 32212-5000

TELEPHONE NUMBER INFORMATION: Main installation numbers: Comm: 904-772-2345, ATVN: 942-2345.

Location: Access from US-17 south (Roosevelt Blvd). On the St Johns River. RM: p-21, E/15. NMC: Jacksonville, 9 miles northeast.

Billeting Office: ATTN: Box 27, Building 11. EX-4050/51/52. 24 hours daily. Check in facility, check out 1200 hours daily. Government civilian employee billeting.

TML: Navy Lodge. All ranks. Leave or official duty. For reservations call 1-800-NAVY-INN. Lodge number is 772-6000. 0700-2300 daily. 50/1-bedroom, 2

FLORIDA
Jacksonville Naval Air Station, continued

double beds, studio couch, private bath. Kitchen, A/C, color TV, maid service, coin washer/dryer, food/ice vending. Modern structure. Rates: $25.00 per unit. Duty can make reservations. Others Space-A.

TML: BOQ. Buildings 11, 845. Officer all grades. Leave or official duty. EX-3147/3427. 119/1-bedroom, private bath; 95 separate bedrooms, private bath. Refrigerator, community kitchen, A/C, essentials, color TV room & lounge, maid service, free cribs/cots, free washer/dryer, food/ice vending, gym, sauna, fishing dock, barbecue pit. Building 11, older structure. New carpets in halls and lobby '89. Rooms painted. Building 845, modern structure. A/C and plumbing to be renovated '90. Rates: $7.00 per person including children 13 years or older. Duty can make reservations. Note: BEQ facilities also available. Call billeting for information.

DV/VIP: PAO, EX-3147/3427. 06/GS-15+. Retirees and lower grades Space-A.

TML Availability: Fairly good. Difficult, summer months.

Cafeteria-771-7035
O'Club-772-3041
SDO/NCO-772-2338

Enlisted Club-772-2209
Police-772-2662

Locator-772-2340
Snack Bar-772-0411

Key West Naval Air Station (FL15R1)
Key West NAS, FL 33040-5000

TELEPHONE NUMBER INFORMATION: Main installation numbers: Comm: 305-296-3561, ATVN: 483-3561.

Location: Take Florida Turnpike, US-1 south to exit signs for Key West NAS on Boca Chica Key 7 miles north of Key West. RM: p-21, Z/11. NMC: Miami, 150 miles north.

Billeting Office: No central billeting office. BOQ at Trumbo Point Annex, Bldg 2076. Comm: 294-5571. 24 hours daily. Check in facility, check out 1200 hours daily. Government civilian employee billeting.

TML: Guest House. Building 220. Enlisted E1-E6. Leave or official duty. 0800-1600 daily. Check out 1000. 6/1-bedroom, semi-private bath. Refrigerator, community kitchen, maid service, cribs/cots, free washer/dryer. Older structure. Rates: $12.00-$15.00 per person. Duty can make reservations. Others Space-A.

TML: BOQ/BEQ. Officer and enlisted. All ranks. Leave or official duty. Accessible to handicapped. Reservations required. BOQ: 196/1-bedroom, private bath. Community kitchen, free cots/cribs, essentials, ice/food vending, maid service, refrigerator, color TV lounge/rooms, free washer/dryer. Older structure. New carpets '89. Rates: Sponsor/Adult/Child, $6.00. Maximum 4 persons per unit. BEQ: 350/2 or 3 beds per room, hall bath. Rates: Sponsor, $4.00. Maximum 3 persons per unit.

TML: DV/VIP. C.O. Secretary, NAS Key West, FL 33040. 06+. Retirees Space-A.

TML Availability: Extremely limited. Best in summer.

NOTE: 26 unit new Navy Lodge now available. 305-292-7556.

Locator-292-2256
NCO Club-292-2807
SDO/NCO-292-2268

Medical-292-2601
Police-292-2114

O'Club-294-5571
Snack Bar-292-2976

FLORIDA

MacDill Air Force Base (FL02R1)
MacDill AFB, FL 33608-5000

TELEPHONE NUMBER INFORMATION: Main installation numbers: Comm: 813-830-1110, ATVN: 968-1110.

Location: Take I-75 south to I-275 south. Exit at Dale Mabry west, 5 miles south to MacDill AFB main gate. RM: p-21, 9/4. NMC: Tampa, 5 miles north.

Billeting Office: 56 CSG/SVH/Billeting, P. O. Box 6826, Building 411, Corner Garden Dr & Tampa Blvd. EX-4259. 24 hours daily. Check in billeting, check out 1200 (TLQ 1100) hours daily. No government civilian employee billeting.

TML: TLQ. Buildings 890-893, 905-906. All ranks. Leave or official duty. Accessible to the handicapped. 60/1-bedroom, private bath. Kitchen, refrigerator, utensils, A/C, color TV, cots/cribs, maid service, essentials, free washer/dryer, food/ice vending, special facilities for disabled American veterans. Older structure (pre-fab). Rates: $18.00 per family. Maximum 5 persons. Duty can make reservations. Others Space-A.

TML: VAQ. Buildings 372, 375. Enlisted E1-E6. Leave or official duty. 60/1-bedroom, latrine bath. Refrigerator, A/C, color TV room & lounge, maid service, free washer/dryer. Older structure. Rates: $8.00 per person. Maximum 2 persons. Duty can make reservations. Others Space-A.

TML: VOQ. Buildings 312, 366, 390, 411. Officer all grades. Leave or official duty. 56/1-bedroom, private bath; 44/1-bedroom, semi-private bath; 28 separate bedroom, private bath; 85 room w/kitchen; 44 rooms, refrigerator. A/C, color TV, maid service, free washer/dryer, ice vending. Modern structure. Rates: Sponsor $8.00 per person. Maximum 2 persons. No children. Duty can make reservations. Others Space-A.

DV/VIP: 56th TTW/CCP, Building P-9, EX-2056. 06+.

Other: Busch Gardens, Epcot, Disney World, Sea World, Circus World.

TML Availability: Extremely limited. Best Oct-Jan.

Cafeteria-840-0511
Medical-830-3334
Police-830-3322
Enlisted Club-830-3357
NCO Club-830-3357
Snack Bar-840-2211
Locator-830-2444
O'Club-837-1031

Mayport Naval Station (FL13R1)
Mayport NS, FL 32228-5000

TELEPHONE NUMBER INFORMATION: Main installation numbers: Comm: 904-246-5011, ATVN: 960-5011.

Location: From Jacksonville, FL on Atlantic Blvd (FL-10) east to Mayport Rd (FL-A1A) left (north) to Naval Station. RM: p-21, E/15. NMC: Jacksonville, 10 miles west.

Billeting Office: No central billeting office. Check in facility, check out 1200 hours daily. Government civilian employee billeting.

TML: BOQ. Building 425. Officer all grades. Leave or official duty. EX-5581. Kitchen (DV/VIP), refrigerator, A/C, color TV lounge, maid service, free washer/dryer, ice vending. Modern structure. Rates: $5.00 per person. Duty can make reservations. Others Space-A.

FLORIDA
Mayport Naval Station, continued

TML: BEQ. Building 1586. Enlisted all grades. Leave or official duty. EX-5581. 244/1-bedroom, hall and private baths; 1 separate bedroom. DV/VIP with kitchen. Rates: $2.00 per person. Duty can make reservations. Others Space-A.

TML: Navy Lodge. All ranks. Leave or official duty. For reservations call 1-800-NAVY-INN. Lodge number is 246-5554. Check in duty hours. Check out 1200 hours daily. 19/2- & 3-bedroom mobile homes, private bath, kitchen, complete utensils, A/C, color TV, free cribs/cots, maid service, coin washer/dryer. Rates: $23.00 per unit. All categories can make reservations.

DV/VIP: Cmdr/DO. Comm: 246-5401. E9, O6+.

TML Availability: Very good, Nov-Mar. Difficult, other times.

CPO Club-246-5432	Enlisted Club-246-5300	Locator-246-5401
Medical-246-5631	O'Club-246-5313	Police-246-5583
Snack Bar-246-5670	SDO-246-5401	

Oak Grove Trailer Park (FL09R1)
Pensacola Naval Air Station
Pensacola, FL 32508-5000

TELEPHONE NUMBER INFORMATION: Main installation numbers: Comm: 904-452-0111, ATVN: 922-0111.

Location: From I-10, south on I-110, Garden Street Exit to Navy Blvd. to front gate. RM: X/3, p. 21. NMC: Pensacola, 2 miles northeast.

Billeting Office: None.

TML: Recreational Cabins. Officer and enlisted. All ranks. Leave or official duty. Accessible to handicapped. EX-2535. Check in 1200-1530 hours. Check out 0730-1000 hours. 12/1-bedroom cabins, private bath. A/C, cots/cribs ($2.00 daily), kitchen, complete utensils, refrigerator, special facilities for disabled American veterans. Modern structures built Apr '89. All categories can make reservations. Rates: $25.00. Maximum 5 persons per unit.

DV/VIP: No Protocol Office.

Other: Naval Aviation Museum.

TML Availability: Best, Oct-Apr. Difficult other times.

Cafeteria-453-5111	Medical-452-4256	O'Club-455-2276
Enlisted Club-452-3251	Police-452-2353	SDO/NCO-452-2353

Orlando Naval Training Center (FL11R1)
Orlando, FL 32813-5005

TELEPHONE NUMBER INFORMATION: Main installation numbers: Comm: 407-646-4111, ATVN: 791-4111.

Location: On Bennet Rd, .5 miles north of FL-50 (Colonial Dr). Bennet Rd is about 3 miles from I-4 on FL-50. RM: p-21, J/4. NMC: Orlando, in the city.

Billeting Office: Building 2010, Hibiscus St. EX-5163/5722. 0730-1600 hours duty days. Other hours, SDO, Building 2702, EX-4501. Check in facility. Government civilian employee billeting (GS-7+).

FLORIDA

Orlando Naval Training Center, continued

TML: Navy Lodge. Building 2543. All ranks. Check out 1200 hours daily. Leave or official duty. For reservations call 1-800-NAVY-INN. Lodge number is 646-5722. 5/1-bedroom, latrine bath; 22 separate bedroom, private bath; 4/2-bedroom, private bath; 1/3-bedroom, private bath; 3/1-bedroom, living room, private bath. 27 units, NTC; 8 units, McCoy Annex, 5 miles south of Orlando. Kitchen & utensils (17 units), refrigerator (18 units), A/C, color TV, maid service, free cribs/cots, coin washer/dryer, food/ice vending (NTC). Older structure. Rates: $19.00-32.00 per unit. All categories can make reservations. Expansion/replacement of existing rooms planned but still not scheduled as of early 1990.

TML: BEQ. Building 375. Enlisted all grades. Official duty only. EX-5614. Check out 1000 daily. 130/1-bedroom, 3 beds, private bath. A/C, color TV lounge, free washer/dryer. Modern structure, new TVs '87. Rates: $4.00 per person. Duty on official orders Space-A.

TML: BOQ. Building 2404A. Officer all grades. Leave or official duty. EX-5150/5153. 0630-2300 hours daily. Check out 1000 hours daily. 28/1-bedroom, semi-private bath; 22 separate bedrooms, private bath; 1/2-bedroom cottage, private bath (senior VIPs/Flag Officers). Refrigerator (12 units), A/C, color TV, maid service, free cots, free washer/dryer. Older structure, renovated late '87. Rates: $6.00-$8.00 per person. Duty can make reservations. Others Space-A.

DV/VIP: CO, Code NTC-00A, Building 2002. EX-5063. Recruit reviewing officials 06+. Otherwise, 07+. Lower grades and retirees Space-A.

Other: Disney World. Cypress Gardens.

TML Availability: Best, Aug-Nov, Jan-Apr.

Cafeteria-646-5826	CPO Club-646-5050	Enlisted Club-646-4127
Locator-646-4501	Medical-646-4911	O'Club-646-4867
Police-646-5380	Snack Bar-646-4330	SDO/NCO-646-4501

Patrick Air Force Base (FL03R1)
Patrick AFB, FL 32935-5152

TELEPHONE NUMBER INFORMATION: Main installation numbers: Comm: 407-494-1110, ATVN: 854-1110.

Location: Take I-95 south to exit 73 (Wickham Rd), 3 miles to FL 404 (Pineda Causeway, toll-20), left on South Patrick Dr to Patrick AFB. RM: p-21, L/15. NMC: Cocoa Beach, 2 miles north.

Billeting Office: ATTN: 6550 ABG/SVH, Building 400, C St between 1st & 2nd Sts. EX-2593. 24 hours. Check in billeting, check out 1100 hours daily. Government civilian employee billeting.

TML: TLQ. Buildings 1046, 1048, 1050, 1056. All ranks. Leave or official duty. EX-2075. 24/2-bedroom, private bath; 7/3-bedroom, private bath. Kitchen, utensils, A/C, color TV, maid service, free cribs/cots, free washer/dryer. Older structure, renovated. Rates: $18.00 per unit. Duty can make reservations. Others Space-A. Used primarily for PCS families.

TML: VAQ. Buildings 255, 504, 557, 734, 738. Enlisted E1-E4. Leave or official duty. 280/1-bedroom, hall bath. Refrigerator, A/C, color TV room & lounge, maid service, free cribs/cots, free washer/dryer, ice vending, microwave. Older structure, renovated. Rates: $7.00 per person. Maximum 2 persons. Duty can make reservations. Others Space-A.

62 — Temporary Military Lodging Around the World

FLORIDA
Patrick Air Force Base, continued

TML: VOQ. Buildings 250, 251, 253, 264, 265, 400, 404. Officer all grades. Leave or official duty. EX-5428. 71/1-bedroom, semi-private bath; 183/2-bedroom, mixed private and semi-private baths. Kitchen, utensils, A/C, color TV, maid service, free cribs/cots, free washer/dryer, ice vending. Older structure, renovated. Rates: $8.00 per person. Duty can make reservations. Others Space-A.

DV/VIP: ESMC/CEP, Building 423. EX-4506. 07+. Retirees Space-A.

Other: Kennedy Center, Disney World, Sea World, Epcot Center.

TML Availability: Good, Nov-Jan. Limited, other times.

Cafeteria-494-4458	Locator-494-4542	Medical-494-8133
NCO Club-494-7491	O'Club-494-4011	Police-494-7777
Snack Bar-494-283	SDO/NCO-494-7001	

Pensacola Naval Air Station (FL14R1)
Pensacola, FL 32508-5000

TELEPHONE NUMBER INFORMATION: Main installation numbers: Comm: 904-452-0111, ATVN: 922-0111.

Location: Off US-98, 4 miles south of I-10. Take Navy Blvd from US-98 or US-29 directly to NAS. RM: p-21, X/3. NMC: Pensacola, 8 miles north.

Billeting Office: Family Housing Office. Building 735. EX-4540/4549. 0830-1600 hours daily. Check in facility, check out 1200 hours daily. Government civilian employee billeting if on orders. No civilian dependents.

TML: Navy Lodge. Buildings 221 & 3448. All ranks. Leave or official duty. For reservations call 1-800-NAVY-INN. Lodge number is 456-8676. 0800-2000 daily. After duty hours, OD, EX-2353. 38 efficiency apartments, private bath. Kitchen, complete utensils, A/C, color TV room & lounge, maid service, free cribs/cots, coin washer/dryer, ice vending, facilities for disabled American veterans. Modern structure. Lodge 221 renovated '87. Rates: $24.00 per unit. No maximum per unit. All categories can make reservations.

TML: BOQ. Building 600. Officer all grades. Leave or official duty. EX-2755. 24 hours daily. No stated check-out time. Approximately 780/1-bedroom, private bath; some have 2 bedrooms. Refrigerator, A/C, color TV in lounge, cots, free washer/dryer. Building renovated '86-87. Older structure. Rates: $6.00 per room, VIP $10.00. Active duty, retired, Reservists can make reservations. Others Space-A.

TML: BEQ. Buildings 3468-3475 (3474/5 female). Enlisted E1-E6. EX-4609. 24 hours daily. 513 male beds, 189 female beds, 969 transient beds. 2 or 3 beds per room, 4 rooms per suite. Refrigerator, A/C, color TV in lounge, free washer/dryer, ice vending, microwave. Modern structure. Rates: $2.00 for temporary attached duty, leave, retired. Student and staff personnel free. Maximum 11 per suite. Active duty, retired, Reservists can make reservations. Other Space-A.

DV/VIP: Protocol, Building 45-M, Room M-7. EX-2311. 08+. Retirees Space-A.

Other: Blue Angels. Aviation Museum. USS Lexington.

TML Availability: Good, all year. Best, during winter.

Cafeteria-456-9956	CPO Club-452-3251	Enlisted Club-452-3251
Locator-452-4693	Medical-452-2492	O'Club-455-2276
Police-452-2653	Snack Bar-456-9956	SDO/NCO-452-2353

Temporary Military Lodging Around the World — 63

FLORIDA

Tyndall Air Force Base (FL04R1)
Tyndall AFB, FL 32403-5000

TELEPHONE NUMBER INFORMATION: Main installation numbers: Comm: 904-283-1110, ATVN: 523-1110.

Location: Take I-10, exit US-231 south to US-98 east, signs mark the AFB. RM: p-21, Y/8. NMC: Panama City, 10 miles northwest.

Billeting Office: P.O. Box 40040, Bldg. 1332, Suwannee & Oak Dr. Comm: 286-6200. ATVN: 523-4211, 24 hours daily. Check in billeting, check out 1200 hours daily. Government civilian employee billeting.

TML: VAQ/VOQ/DV/TLF. All ranks. Leave or official duty. EX-2394. 240 separate bedrooms, kitchen, private bath (VOQ); 460/1-bedroom, semi-private bath (VAQ); 40 efficiency apartments, private bath, sleeps 5 cribs/roll-away available (TLF). A/C, color TV room and lounge, maid service, free washer/dryer, ice vending. Modern structure. Rates: $20.00 per unit TLF, $6.00 per person VOQ & VAQ. $10.00 per person VIP. Official duty should make reservations. Others Space-A.

Note: Tyndall Fam-Camp has 3/2-bedroom cottages. Rates: $32.00 Sponsor, $2.00 each additional person. Call 904-283-2798 for more information and reservations.

DV/VIP: Hq, Building 647. EX-2232. 06+. Retirees and lower grades Space-A.

Other: Beautiful white-sand beaches.

TML Availability: Very good, Jan & Dec. Fair, other times.

Locator-283-2138/4210   Medical-283-7523   NCO Club-283-4444
O'Club-283-2986   Police-283-4124   SNCO-283-2965
SDO/NCO-283-4145

Whiting Field Naval Air Station (FL05R1)
Milton, FL 32570-5000

TELEPHONE NUMBER INFORMATION: Main installation numbers: Comm: 904-623-7011, ATVN: 868-7011.

Location: From US-90 east exit, FL-87 north 7 miles to NAS. RM: p-21, W/4. NMC: Pensacola, 40 miles southwest.

Billeting Office: Building 2942, Lexington Circle. EX-7605/06. 24 hours daily. Check in facility, check out 1200 hours daily. Government civilian employee billeting.

TML: BOQ/BEQ. Building 2942. All ranks. Leave or official duty. 52 rooms & suites, private bath. Refrigerator, A/C, color TV lounge, maid service, free cribs, washer/dryer, ice vending. Modern structure, renovated. Rates: $8.00 per room single, $12.00 per room double, $16.00 suite. Husband & wife only. Duty can make reservations. Others Space-A.

DV/VIP: Admiral's Office, Building 1401. EX-7201. 06+. Retirees Space-A.

TML Availability: Good, Dec-Feb. Limited, other times.

Cafeteria-623-0118   Enlisted Club-623-7591   Locator-623-7011
Medical-623-7584   NCO Club-623-2339   O'Club-623-7311
Police-623-7387   Snack Bar-623-5897   SDO/NCO-623-7437

GEORGIA

Albany Marine Corps Logistics Base (GA17R1)
Albany, GA 31704-5000

TELEPHONE NUMBER INFORMATION: Main installation numbers: Comm: 912-439-5000, ATVN: 567-5000.

Location: Off US-82, take Mock Rd south from 5-Points to Fleming Rd. Go east to main gate. RM: p-23, P/6. NMC: Albany, 3 miles west.

Billeting Office: Housing Office, Building 3600. EX-5614. 0800-1630 hours daily. Check in billeting, check out 1130 hours daily. Government civilian employee billeting.

TML: TLQ. Buildings 9257 A & B, 9259 A & B. All ranks. Leave or official duty. Accessible to handicapped. 4/3-bedroom apartments, private bath. Kitchen, complete utensils, A/C, color TV, cots/cribs (free), essentials, free washer/dryer. Older structures. TVs '89. Rates: 1/30th BAQ with dependent rate (active duty); $30.00 per unit (retirees). Maximum 6 per unit. Primarily for PCS in/out. Duty can make reservations. Others Space-A.

TML: TEQ. Buildings 7964 and 7966. Enlisted, E6 to E9. Leave or official duty. 4/1-bedroom, private bath. A/C, cots/cribs (free), essentials, maid service, refrigerator, color TV, free washer/dryer. Rates: Sponsor $7.00 on official duty, $12.00 in non-duty status including leave/retirees, Space-A. Maximum 4 persons per unit.

TML: TOQ. Buildings 10201 and 10202. Officer all ranks. Leave or official duty. Accessible to handicapped. 7/1-bedroom, 1/3-bedroom and 1/4-bedroom, private bath. A/C, cribs/cots (free), essentials, kitchen, complete utensils, maid service, special facilities for disabled American veterans, color TV, free washer/dryer. Modern structures. Renovated Jan '89. Rates: Sponsor $10.00-$20.00 on official duty, $15.00-$30.00 in non-duty status including leave/retirees, Space-A.

TML: DV/VIP. Building 10300. Officer 06+. Leave or official duty. Accessible to handicapped. 1/2-bedroom, completely furnished detached house, private bath. A/C, cots/cribs (free), essentials, kitchen, complete utensils, maid service, color TV, free washer/dryer. Modern structure. Renovated '89. Rates: $Sponsor $25.00 on official duty, $35.00 in non-duty status including leave/retirees, Space-A.

DV/VIP: Protocol Office, Building 3600. EX-5204. 05+. Retirees and lower grades Space-A.

TML Availability: Fairly good. Best Oct-May.

Enlisted Club-439-5223
NCO Club-439-5231
Snack Bar-435-1471
Locator-439-5270
O'Club-439-5239
SDO/NCO-439-5206
Medical-439-5911
Police-439-5181

Temporary Military Lodging Around the World — 65

GEORGIA

Athens Navy Supply Corps School (GA12R1)
Athens, GA 30606-5000

TELEPHONE NUMBER INFORMATION: Main installation numbers: Comm: 404-354-1500, ATVN: 588-7305.

Location: From Athens take bypass, exit to Prince Ave, continue 1 mile to Base at intersection of Prince & Oglethorpe Avenues. RM: p-23, G/8. NMC: Atlanta, 70 miles west.

Billeting Office: Brown Hall. Comm: 354-7360. 0800-1600 hours duty days. Check in facility, check out 1200 hours daily. Government civilian employee billeting.

TML: VOQ. Officer all grades. Leave or official duty. 2/1-bedroom, private bath; 4/2-bedroom suites, private bath. Refrigerator, A/C, color TV room & lounge, maid service, free washer/dryer, ice vending, microwave. Older structure. Rates: $15.00 family suites, $8.00 rooms. Duty can make reservations. Others Space-A.

TML Availability: Good, Nov-Feb. Difficult, other times.

Medical-354-7321   SDO/NCO-354-1500

Dobbins Air Force Base (GA13R1)
Dobbins AFB, GA 30069-5000

TELEPHONE NUMBER INFORMATION: Main installation numbers: Comm: 404-421-5000, ATVN: 925-1110.

Location: From I-75 north exit to GA-280 west to AFB. Clearly marked. RM: p-24, B/1. NMC: Atlanta, 17 miles northwest.

Billeting Office: ATTN: SVH, Building 800, Atlantic St. 24 hours daily. EX-4745. Check in facility, check out 1200 hours daily. Government civilian employee billeting.

TML: VAQ. Building 801. Enlisted. E1-E6. Leave or official duty. 75/1-bedroom, semi-private bath. Refrigerator, A/C, cribs, essentials, color TV, free washer/dryer, ice vending. Older structure. New TVs '89. Renovation scheduled '90. Rates: $6.00 per person. Maximum 2 persons. Duty, retirees, and disabled American veterans can make reservations. Others Space-A.

TML: DV/VIP. Building 401. Officer 06+, available to lower grades Space-A. Leave or official duty. 4/1-bedroom suites, private bath. 2 separate bedrooms, private bath, and sitting room. Refrigerator, A/C, free cribs, essentials, ice vending, maid service, color TV, free washer/dryer. Older structure. Renovated and remodeled '88. Rates: $10.00 per person. Maximum charge $20.00. Maximum 4 persons. Duty can make reservations. Others Space-A.

TML: Senior NCO Quarters. Building 800. 4 suites (2 rooms). Rate: $10.00 per person per night. 25 other SNCO rooms, single occupancy, share bath. Rate: $6.00 per person per night.

DV/VIP: PAO, EX-5055/1110. 06+. Retirees and lower grades Space-A.

TML Availability: Good, Nov-Mar. More difficult, Apr-Oct.

Locator-421-5000   Medical-421-5302   Police-421-4907
SDO/NCO-421-5000

66 — *Temporary Military Lodging Around the World*

GEORGIA

Fort Benning (GA11R1)
Fort Benning, GA 31905-5065

TELEPHONE NUMBER INFORMATION: Main installation numbers: Comm: 404-544-2011, ATVN: 784-2011.

Location: Off I-185 and US-27/280. RM: p-23, Y/5. NMC: Columbus, 5 miles northwest.

Billeting Office: Building 399. Comm: 689-0067. ATVN: 835-3145/46. 24 hours daily. Check in facility, check out 1200 hours daily. Government civilian employee billeting.

TML: Guest House. Buildings 36-38. EX-2820. All ranks. Leave or official duty. Reservations accepted. 50/1-bedroom suites, private bath. Refrigerator, A/C, color TV, maid service, free cribs/cots, free washer/dryer. Living room 2 sofa beds. Older structure. Rates: $16.00 per unit.

TML: VOQ/VEQ. Buildings 17, 73, 75, 83, 399. All ranks, primarily for TDY/PCS, may have Space-A for transients. Check by calling EX-2505. Children not authorized.

TML: DV/VIP. McIver St. Officer 06+. Leave or official duty. 10/1-bedroom, 2 beds, private bath suite. Refrigerator, A/C, color TV, maid service, free cots, free washer/dryer. Older structure. Rates: $20.00 per unit. Duty can make reservations. Others Space-A.

DV/VIP: Protocol. Comm: 545-1214. 06+. Ret and lower grades Space-A.

TML Availability: Good, all year.

Enlisted Club-689-0887   Locator-545-5216   Medical-544-2041
NCO Club-687-0600   O'Club-682-0640   Police-545-5222
Snack Bar-687-6013   SDO/NCO-545-2218

Fort Gillem (GA21R1)
Fort Gillem, GA 30050-5000

TELEPHONE NUMBER INFORMATION: Main installation numbers: Comm: 404-363-5000, ATVN: 797-1001.

Location: From I-75, east on I-285 to US-23 (Moreland Ave/Macon Hwy), S for 3 miles to the main gate. Fort is 5 miles from Hartsfield IAP. RM: p-24, J/5. NMC: Atlanta, 10 miles northwest.

Billeting Office: Building 817, Hood Ave. EX-5431. 0730-1600 hours duty days. Check in facility, check out 1000 hours daily. Government civilian employee no billeting. This is a sub-post of Fort McPherson.

TML: VOQ/VEQ. Buildings 131, 134. All ranks. Leave or official duty. 7 separate bedrooms, private bath; 1/2-bedroom, private bath. Kitchen, complete utensils, A/C, color TV, maid service, free washer/dryer, ice vending. Older structure. Rates: $20.00 per apartment. Duty can make reservations. Others Space-A.

DV/VIP: Billeting Office, EX-5431. 06/GS-15+. Retirees and lower grades Space-A.

TML Availability: Extremely limited.

Enlisted Club-363-3530   NCO Club-363-3530   O'Club-363-3830
Police-363-5582

Temporary Military Lodging Around the World — 67

GEORGIA

Fort Gordon (GA09R1)
Fort Gordon, GA 30905-5000

TELEPHONE NUMBER INFORMATION: Main installation numbers: Comm: 404-791-0110, ATVN: 780-0110.

Location: Between US-78/278 and US-1. Gates are on both US-78 & US-1. RM: p-23, H/13. NMC: Augusta, 12 miles northeast.

Billeting Office: Griffith Hall, Building 250, Chamberlain Ave. 0730-2400 hours daily. Toll free reservations 1-800-962-8589. Check in facility, check out 1100 hours daily. Government civilian employee billeting.

TML: Guest House (Stinson). Newly constructed Guest House Annex. 24 hours daily. EX-7160/9029. All ranks. Leave or official duty. 19/1-bedroom suites, private bath; 1 handicapped room, private bath; 12 rooms with kitchenettes. 75/1-bedroom, 2-double beds, private bath. Refrigerator, A/C, color TV, maid service, cribs/cots ($2.00), coin washer/dryer, ice vending, facilities for disabled American veterans. Modern structure, new carpets '87. Rates: $19.50 per room. Rates Guest House Annex: $24.00 per room. PCS and hospital visitors can make reservations 60 days in advance. Others Space-A reservations 2 days in advance.

TML: Guest House. Building 34602. Enlisted E1-E4. Check in billeting. 4/1-bedroom, latrine bath; 15 separate bedroom, private bath. Refrigerator, A/C, color TV room & lounge, maid service, washer/dryer. Older structure. Rates: $5.00 single, $8.00 double, children free. Maximum 2-3 per room. PCS and hospital visitors can make reservations. Others Space-A.

TML: Guest House. Building 18404. Enlisted E7-E9. Check in billeting. 2/2-bedroom apartments, private bath. Kitchen, utensils, A/C, color TV, maid service. Modern structure. Rates: $20.00 per room. PCS and hospital visitors can make reservations. Others Space-A.

TML: VOQ. Buildings 250, 36700. Officer all grades. Check in billeting. Leave or official duty. 435/1-bedroom, private bath; 23 separate bedrooms, private bath. Kitchen, A/C, color TV room & lounge, maid service, free washer/dryer, ice vending. Modern structure, new carpets '87. Rates: $18.00 single, $2.00 each additional person. Maximum 2 per room. Duty can make reservations. Others Space-A.

TML: VEQ. Buildings 28410, 28411. Enlisted. All grades. Leave or official duty. 68/1-bedroom, private bath. Refrigerator, A/C, color TV, maid service, free washer/dryer. Duty can make reservations. Others Space-A.

TML: DVQ. Buildings 34503/04/06, 3460, 34605. Officer 06+. 5 separate bedrooms, private bath. Kitchen, complete utensils, A/C, color TV, maid service, free cots. Older structure. Rates: $20.00 single, $2.00 each additional person. Duty can make reservations. Others, including lesser ranks, Space-A.

DV/VIP: Protocol Office, 10th floor, Signal Towers, EX-5376/5138. 06+. Retirees and lower grades (03+) Space-A.

TML Availability: Good.

Cafeteria-793-8161   Enlisted Club-791-2207   Locator-791-4675
Medical-911   NCO Club-791-6780   O'Club-791-2205
Police-791-4380   SDO/NCO-791-4517

68 — *Temporary Military Lodging Around the World*

GEORGIA

Fort McPherson (GA08R1)
Fort McPherson, GA 30330-5000

TELEPHONE NUMBER INFORMATION: Main installation numbers: Comm: 404-752-3113, ATVN: 572-1110.

Location: Off I-75 take Lakewood Freeway (GA-166), exit to US-29 (Main St exit). Main gate is at Main St exit. RM: p-24, H/3. NMC: Atlanta, in city limits.

Billeting Office: Building T-22. EX-2253. 0630-2330 hours duty days. Other hours, SDO, Building 65, EX-2980. Check in facility, check out 1000 hours daily. Government civilian employee billeting.

TML: Transient Quarters. Building T-109 (Chalet). All ranks. Leave or official duty. 8/1-bedroom, semi-private bath. Community kitchen, complete utensils, A/C, color TV lounge, maid service, cribs, free washer/dryer. Older structure. Rates: $14.00 officer, $12.00 enlisted, $15.00 TDY. Duty can make reservations. Others Space-A.

TML: VOQ/VEQ. Building T-22 (Chateau). All ranks. Leave or official duty. 22/1-bedroom, private bath. Community kitchen, A/C, color TV room & lounge, maid service, cribs/cots $1.00, free washer/dryer, ice vending. Older structure. Same rates and occupancy as above. Building 168. 10/3-bedrooms, private bath; 2/2-bedrooms, private bath. A/C, free cots/cribs, food/ice vending, kitchen, maid service, special facilities for disabled American veterans, color TV in room, telephone in room, free washer/dryer. Modern structure. Renovated '88, remodeled '89, new carpets/TVs. Same rates as above. Duty can make reservations.

TML: DV/VIP. Lee Hall. Officer 06+. Leave or official duty. EX-4145. 8 various size suites, private bath. Refrigerator, community kitchen, A/C, color TV room & lounge, maid service, cribs/cots $1.00, ice vending. Older structure. Call for rates. Duty can make reservations. Others Space-A.

DV/VIP: Protocol Office, Building 200, EX-5388/5398. 06+. Retirees and lower grades Space-A.

TML Availability: Good. Best Dec-Feb.

Enlisted C-753-4575
NCO Club-753-4540
SDO/NCO-752-2980/3602

Locator-752-2743/4174
O'Club-753-4520

Medical-752-3139
Police-752-3050

Fort Stewart (GA15R1)
Fort Stewart, GA 31314-5000

TELEPHONE NUMBER INFORMATION: Main installation numbers: Comm: 912-767-1110, ATVN: 870-1110.

Location: Accessible from US-17 or I-95. Also GA-119 or GA-144 crosses the Post. RM: p-23, N/14. NMC: Savannah, 35 miles northeast.

Billeting Office: ATTN: AFZP-DEH-B. Building 4951. Comm: 368-4184. ATVN: 870-8384. 0730-2345 hours daily. Other hours, SDO, Building 01, EX-8666. Check in billeting, check out 1100 hours daily. Government civilian employees billeting.

TML: Guest House. Building 4951. All ranks. Leave or official duty. EX-8384. 70/1-bedroom, dining room, private bath (sleeps 6). Kitchen, A/C, color TV, maid service, free cribs/cots, essentials, special facilities for disabled American veterans, coin washer/dryer, ice vending. Modern structure. New carpets/TVs '89. Duty and disabled American veterans can make reservations. Rates: $20.00 per room per

GEORGIA

Fort Stewart, continued

night. Others Space-A.

TML: BOQ/VOQ. Building 4950. EX-8384. Officer all grades. Official duty only. Reservations accepted (VOQ), not taken (BOQ). 35/1-bedroom, private bath (VOQ). Kitchen, A/C, color TV, maid service (VOQ), washer/dryer, ice vending. Modern structure. Rates: $19.00 per room per night (VOQ), N/A (BOQ). Maximum 1 per room.

TML: DVQ. Officer O6+. Leave or official duty. EX-8610. 2/2-bedroom cottages, private bath. A/C, free cots/cribs, essentials, ice vending, kitchen, complete utensils, maid service, special facilities for disabled American veterans, color TV, free washer/dryer. Active and retirees can make reservations. Rate: $20.00. Others Space-A.

TML: TLQ. Building 4950. All ranks. Leave or official duty. Accessible to handicapped. EX-8384. 35/1-bedroom, private bath. A/C, essentials, ice vending, kitchen, maid service, special facilities for disabled American veterans, color TV, free washer/dryer. Being remodeled. New carpets/TVs '89. Duty can make reservations. Rate: $19.00. Maximum 2 per unit. Others Space-A.

DV/VIP: Protocol, Building 01, EX-8610. O6+. Retirees and lower grades Space-A.

TML Availability: Fairly good. Best Nov-Apr. More difficult, other times.

Enlisted Club-767-8715	Locator-767-2862	Medical-767-6666
NCO Club-368-2212	O'Club-368-2212	Police-767-2822
SDO/NCO-767-8666		

Hunter Army Airfield (GA10R1)
Hunter Army Airfield, GA 31409-5023

TELEPHONE NUMBER INFORMATION: Main installation numbers: Comm: 912-352-6521, ATVN: 971-1110.

Location: From I-95 to GA-204 east for 13 miles to Savannah. Turn left onto Stephenson Ave, proceed straight into Wilson Ave Gate to Installation. RM: p-23, Z/14. NMC: Savannah, in southwest part of city.

Billeting Office: ATTN: AFZP-DEH-B(H). Building 6010, Duncan and Leonard Sts. 0700-2400 hours M-F, 0800-1700 hours Sa, Su. Comm: 352-5910/5834 or 355-1060 (reservations). After hours, SDO, Building 1201, Comm: 352-5140. Check in facility, check out 1100 hours daily. Government civilian employee billeting.

TML: Guest House/VOQ/VEQ. Buildings 6005, 6010. All ranks. Leave or official duty. EX-5910/5834. 32/2-bedroom suites, private bath; 9/1-bedroom, semi-private bath. Kitchen, complete utensils, essentials, A/C, color TV room & lounge, maid service, free cribs/cots, free washer/dryer, food/ice vending, facilities for disabled American veterans. Older structures. Renovated and remodeled. New carpets/TVs/telephones '89. Rates: $20.00 per family. All categories can make reservations. PCS have priority.

DV/VIP: Cmdr, 24th Inf Div, ATTN: AFZP-CS-P, Building 1. Comm: 767-8610. ATVN: 870-8610. 05+. Retirees Space-A.

TML Availability: Very good, all times.

Cafeteria-352-6209	Enlisted Club-352-5262	Locator-767-2862
Medical-352-5551	NCO Club-352-5262	O'Club-352-5270
Police-352-6133	Snack Bar-352-5484	SDO/NCO-352-5000

GEORGIA

Kings Bay Naval Submarine Base (GA03R1)
Kings Bay, GA 31547-5015

TELEPHONE NUMBER INFORMATION: Main installation numbers: Comm: 912-673-2000, ATVN: 860-2000.

Location: Off I-95 north of GA/FL border. Take exit 1 which leads right into base, or exits 2A or 2B, east to Kings Bay and follow road north to base. RM: p-23, R/14. NMC: Jacksonville, 40 miles south.

Billeting Office: ATTN: Housing Office N53. Building 1051-N, James Madison Rd. EX-2056. 0800-1630 hours M-F. Check in billeting, check out 1200 hours daily.

TML: Navy Lodge. Building 0158. All ranks. Leave or official duty. For reservations call 1-800-NAVY-INN. Lodge number is 882-6868. Check in facility, 0700-2000 hours daily. 26/1-bedroom, 2 beds, private bath. Kitchen, complete utensils, A/C, color TV, maid service, free cribs, coin washer/dryer, ice vending, facilities for handicapped, cable HBO. Modern structure. Rates: $32.00 per room. Maximum 5 per room. Duty and retirees can make reservations.

TML: BEQ. Building 1041. Enlisted all grades. Leave or official duty. EX-2163/2164. 142/1-bedroom, private bath. A/C, free cots, essentials, food/ice vending, maid service, refrigerator, color TV lounge & room (CPO &VIP), free washer/dryer. Microwave & coffee pot (CPO &VIP). Modern structure. Rates: VIP $10.00 for one person, $15.00 for two or more; all others $4.00 for one person, $10.00 for two or more. Maximum charge VIP & family suite $15.00. Maximum charge for rooms $10.00. Maximum 4 persons. Duty can make reservations. Others Space-A.

TML: BOQ. Building 1056. Officer. All ranks. Leave or official duty. EX-2165/2169. Accessible to handicapped. 38/1-bedroom, private bath; 98 separate bedroom, private bath. A/C, free cots, essentials, food/ice vending, maid service, color TV in room, free washer/dryer. Modern structure. Rates: $8.00-$15.00 per person. Maximum charge $16.00-$20.00. Maximum 4 persons. Duty can make reservations. Others Space-A.

TML Availability: Good. Best Oct-Dec. Difficult June-Sept.

Cafeteria-882-6229 Enlisted C-882-4567 Medical-882-5109
NCO Club-882-4566 O'Club-882-4563 Police-882-2265
Snack Bar-882-2049 SDO-673-4703

Moody Air Force Base (GA02R1)
Moody AFB, GA 31699-5000

TELEPHONE NUMBER INFORMATION: Main installation numbers: Comm: 912-333-4211, ATVN: 460-1110.

Location: On GA 125, 10 miles north of Valdosta. Also can be reached from I-75 via GA-122. RM: p-23, R/9. NMC: Valdosta, 10 miles south.

Billeting Office: Building 320, Cooney St. EX-3893. 24 hours daily. Check in billeting, check out 1200 hours. Government employee off base contract quarters.

TML: TLF. Building 325. All ranks. Leave or official duty. 12/2-bedroom, private bath. Kitchen, A/C, color TV, maid service, free cribs/cots, free washer/dryer. Community motel design. Rates: $16.00 for 2 bedroom. PCS in/out, TDY can make reservations. Others Space-A.

TML: VAQ. Building 325. Enlisted all grades. Leave or official duty. 29 units, private bath. Refrigerator, A/C, color TV, maid service, free washer/dryer.

Temporary Military Lodging Around the World — 71

GEORGIA

Moody Air Force Base, continued

Community motel design, '62. Rates: $6.00 per person. PCS in/out, TDY can make reservations. Others Space-A.

TML: VOQ. Building 213. Officer all grades. Leave or official duty. 23/1-bedroom, private bath. Kitchen, refrigerator, A/C, color TV, maid service, free washer/dryer. Community motel design. Rates: $6.00 per person. PCS in/out, TDY can make reservations. Others Space-A.

TML: DV. Buildings 213/325. Officer O6+, E8-E9. Leave or official duty. 5/1-bedroom suites, private bath (Officer); 1/2-bedroom suite, private bath (Officer); 2/1-bedroom suites, private bath (E8-E9). Kitchen, A/C, color TV, maid service, free washer/dryer. Community motel design, '62. Rates: $10.00 per person. PCS in/out, TDY can make reservations. Others Space-A.

DV/VIP: Protocol Office, 347 CSG/CCE, Building 101. EX-3480. O6+, E9. Retirees and lower grades Space-A.

TML Availability: Good, May, Sep, Dec. Difficult, Jun-Aug.

Cafeteria-333-4814	Enlisted Club-333-3792	Locator-333-3585
Medical-333-3232	NCO Club-333-3794	O'Club-333-3351
Police-333-3280	Snack Bar-333-3101	SDO/NCO-333-3503

Robins Air Force Base (GA14R1)
Robins AFB, GA 31098-5000

TELEPHONE NUMBER INFORMATION: Main installation numbers: Comm: 912-926-1110, ATVN: 468-1001.

Location: Off US-129 on GA-247 at Warner Robins. Access from I-75 south. RM: p-23, K/7. NMC: Macon, 18 miles northwest.

Billeting Office: Building 557, Club Dr. EX-2100. 24 hours daily. Check in facility. Government civilian employee billeting.

TML: TLF. Building 1180-1183. All ranks. Leave or official duty. Check out 1000 hours. 40 separate bedroom, private bath. Kitchen, complete utensils, A/C, color TVs, maid service, free cots/cribs, ice vending, washer/dryer. Older structure. Rates: E4- $14.00, E5+ $18.00. Maximum family rate $14.00-$18.00. Maximum 5 per unit. Duty and retired can make reservations. Others Space-A.

TML: VOQ. Buildings 551/2/3/7. Officer all grades. Leave or official duty. Accessible to handicapped. Check out 1200 hours. 51 separate bedroom, private bath; 47/2-bedroom, semi-private bath. Kitchen, complete utensils, A/C, refrigerator, color TV, maid service, free cribs/cots, washer/dryer. Older structure, renovation on-going. Rates: $7.00-$8.00 per person. Maximum family rate $16.00. Maximum 4 per unit. If more than one unit needed, 2nd unit is free. Duty and retired can make reservations. Others Space-A.

TML: VAQ. Building 755. Enlisted all grades. Leave or official duty. Check out 1200 hours. 28/1-bedroom, shared bath; 39/2-bedroom, shared bath; seven separate bedroom, private bath. Refrigerator, A/C, color TV, maid service, washer/dryer, ice vending. Older structure. Rates: $6.00 per person. Duty and retired can make reservations. Others Space-A.

DV/VIP: Building 215, EX-2761. O6+.

TML Availability: Good, Oct-May. Difficult, other times.

GEORGIA
Robins Air Force Base, continued

Cafeteria-922-8635
Medical-926-3845
Police-926-2187
Enlisted Club-923-5581
NCO Club-923-5581
Snack Bar-922-4715
Locator-926-6027
O'Club-922-3011

HAWAII

Barbers Point Naval Air Station (HI10R6)
Barbers Point NAS, HI 96862-5050

TELEPHONE NUMBER INFORMATION: Main installation numbers: Comm: 808-684-6266, ATVN: 484-6266.

Location: Take HI-I West (toward Waianee) to Barbers Point NAS/Makakilo exit, south for 2.5 miles to main gate. RM: p-7, I/3. NMC: Honolulu, 12 miles east.

Billeting Office: Building 1788, Bealleau Woods, off Enterprise. EX-2248/2290. 24 hours daily. Check in facility, check out 0900 hours daily. Government civilian employee billeting.

TML: BOQ. Building 77. Officer all grades. Leave or official duty. EX-3191. 80/1-bedroom, shared bathroom; 28 separate bedroom, private bath. Refrigerator, A/C, color TV room & lounge, maid service, free washer/dryer, ice vending. Modern structure. Rates: Sponsor $4.00, adult $4.00. No children. Maximum 2 persons per room. Duty can make reservations. Others Space-A.

TML: BEQ. Building 1784. Enlisted all grades. Leave or official duty. EX-2290. 60/1-bedroom, private bath. Refrigerator, A/C (some), color TV room & lounge, maid service, free washer/dryer, vending machine. Modern structure. Rates: $2.00 per person. No children. Duty can make reservations. Others Space-A.

DV/VIP: Commander Naval Base, P.O. Box 110, Pearl Harbor, HI 96860. EX-1181. 05+.

Other: Great beaches on the NAS.

TML Availability: Good, winter months. Difficult, summer months.

CPO Club-682-3083
O'Club-682-4925
Enlisted Club-682-5243
Police-684-6222
Medical-684-8245
SDO/NCO-684-6266

Barbers Point Recreation Area (HI01R6)
Barbers Point Naval Air Station, HI 96862-5050

TELEPHONE NUMBER INFORMATION: Main installation numbers: Comm: 808-684-6266, ATVN: 484-6266.

Location: Take HI-1 West to Barbers Point/Makakilo exit. Left at sign then go through main gate. Turn right on Shangrila, then turn into the parking lot on the left. Reservations office is in Building 19 (Fitness Center). RM: p-7, I/2. NMC: Pearl Harbor, 10 miles northeast.

Billeting Office: Recreation Service Dept, Building 55, ATTN: Beach Cottages, Barbers Point NAS, HI 96862-5050. Comm: 808-682-2019. ATVN: 430-0111. 0800-1700 hours M-F for reservations. Reservations 4 weeks in advance. After confirmation, payment in full is required. Reservations for 3 days F-M, 4 days

Temporary Military Lodging Around the World — 73

HAWAII

Barbers Point Recreation Area, continued

M-F, 7 days M-M or F-F. Check in at area 1400 hours daily, check out 0900 hours daily. Cottages cannot be used as party facility. Operates year round.

TML: Rec Cottages. All ranks. Leave only. Accessible to handicapped. 14 enlisted cottages, 6 officer cottages, 2 VIP cottages (06+). Kitchen, complete utensils, color TV (VIP only), cribs/cots, BBQ grills. Rates: Enlisted $25.00 per unit, Officer $30.00 per unit, VIP $34.00 per unit. Maximum 8 persons. All categories can make reservations by written application.

DV/VIP: Administration Office, Building 1, EX-4103. 07/GS-16+. Retirees and lower grades Space-A.

Other: Complete beach rec area. Check with Special Services, Ticket Office for tourist/island activities. Complete support facility at NAS. For full details see Military RV, Camping & Rec Areas Around The World.

TML Availability: Good, Jan-Apr & Oct-Nov. Difficult, other times.

Bellows Recreation Area (HI02R6)
Bellows AFS, HI 96795-1010

TELEPHONE NUMBER INFORMATION: Main installation numbers: Comm: 808-259-8841, ATVN: 259-8841.

Location: From Honolulu take I-HI Easy to HI-61 North to HI-72 South to the AFS. Clearly marked. RM: p-7, H/7. NMC: Kailua, 9 miles northwest.

Billeting Office: P. O. Box 1010, Waimanalo, HI 96795. AD AF on HI, 90 days in advance. Other AD AF, 75 days in advance. Other services, 60 days in advance. Retirees 45 days in advance. Maximum 14 day occupancy. Sponsor or spouse must register. Reservations 0930-1730 daily. Check in 1400 hours, check out 0900-1200 hours. Comm: 259-8841.

TML: Cottages. All ranks. Leave only. See above. 101 cottages, private bath, single & duplex units. Kitchen, complete utensils, color TV, cots/cribs $1.00, dishes, linens, towels, bedding all furniture. Rates: Studio $20.00, backrow $25.00, oceanview $30.00.

Other: Large beach front rec center. For complete details see Military RV, Camping & Rec Areas Around The World.

TML Availability: Good, Oct-Apr. Difficult, other times.

Enlisted Club-259-5915   Locator (Mgr)-259-5428   O'Club-259-5915
Police-259-5955

Fort Shafter (HI09R6)
Fort Shafter, HI 96858-5000

TELEPHONE NUMBER INFORMATION: Main installation numbers: Comm: 808-471-7110, ATVN: 430-0111.

Location: Take HI-1 West exit at Fort Shafter. Clearly marked. RM: p-7, J/8. NMC: Honolulu, 7 miles east.

Billeting: 453B, Burr Rd. EX-1102. 0730-1600 hours duty days. Other hours, DSO, Building T-100, EX-9912 or PMO, Building T-118, EX-9877. Write to: USASCH Billeting Fund, 692 McCornack Rd, Wahiawa, HI 96786. Check in billeting or

HAWAII
Fort Shafter, continued

facility, check out 1200 hours daily. No government civilian employee billeting.

TML: Guest House. Building 453B, Burr Rd. All ranks. Leave or official duty. EX-1507. 8/2-bedroom (4 units no kitchen), shared bath; 4/3-bedroom, shared bath. Kitchen, complete utensils, color TV, maid service, free cribs/cots, free washer/dryer. Older structure. Rates: Sponsor $23.00 with kitchen, $19.00 without kitchen, adult $4.00, children free. Maximum 7 per unit. PCS can make reservations and have priority; PCS out 5 days maximum, PCS in 10 days maximum. Others Space-A.

TML Availability: Fair, most of the year.

Cafeteria-845-9636	Locator-438-1904	NCO Club-848-0431
O'Club-847-6468	Police-438-2885	Snack Bar-848-0477
SDO/NCO-438-2255		

Hale Koa Hotel AFRC (HI08R6)
2055 Kalia Road
Honolulu, HI 96815-1998

TELEPHONE NUMBER INFORMATION: Main installation numbers: Comm: 808-955-0555 (24 hours), 800-367-6027 (0800-1600 hours daily HI time, except holidays).

Location: At 2055 Kalia Road, Waikiki Beach, Honolulu, HI. The installation, Fort De Russy, is on Waikiki Beach, between the Ala Moana Blvd, Kalakaua Ave and Saratoga Road, approximately 9 miles east of Honolulu International Airport. RM: p-7, NMC: Honolulu, in the city.

Description of Area: This morale-boosting, all ranks hotel, was opened in October 1975. The hotel has 14 stories with 420 air-conditioned guest rooms with views of the Pacific Ocean and Koolau Mountains. All rooms are identical in size and each has its own private lanai, color TVs, room-controlled air-conditioning, and most have two double beds. Some rooms are specially fitted for handicapped veterans. Coin-operated washers & dryers are available. The hotel has a swimming pool, fitness center, landscaped gardens, and offers indoor and outdoor sports activities on the most beautiful golden sand beach in Waikiki. Also available: cocktail lounges, snack bar, Post Exchange, Show Room, Hale Koa fine dining room, meeting rooms and conference facilities, sauna & locker rooms, coffee house, barber & beauty shops, and rental cars. With nine magnificent dining, cocktail, and entertainment rooms, the Hale Koa is one of the island's most complete resorts. In addition, ocean and pool swimming, snorkeling, tennis, volleyball, sail boats, racquet ball, and paddle tennis are available at your door, plus one of the world's largest shopping centers. Dress is aloha-wear at all times. Facilities are accessible to the handicapped. The 1988-89 double rates are quoted below.

Season of Operation: Year round.

Reservations: Required. Write for free reservation and information packet: 2055 Kalia Road, Honolulu, HI 96815-1998.

Eligibility: Active duty, retired, DoD civilian on official business.

HAWAII

Hale Koa Hotel AFRC, continued

1989-90 double rates are quoted below:

Categories* for both Active and Retired	I Active/Retired E-1 to E-5	II Active/Retired E-6 to E-9 WO-1 to CW-3 0-1 to 0-3 all TDY, TLA DAV**, Widow(s)	III Active/Retired CW-4 0-4 to 0-10 Foreign Others
Standard	$35.00	$44.00	$57.00
Superior	$41.00	$50.00	$67.00
Partial Oceanview	$46.00	$60.00	$78.00
Oceanview	$52.00	$65.00	$83.00
Ocean Front	$63.00	$77.00	$90.00

A limited number of ocean front rooms (with king bed only) are available upon request at additional cost. Daily rates are based on room location (generally the higher floors reflect increased rate) and the number of occupants (maximum of 4 persons permitted per room). Add $10.00 for each additional person over age 2. Cribs are available at $4.00 per night. Most rooms are furnished with two double beds. Reservations may be made for a maximum stay of 30 days. Extensions permitted on a space available basis.

* Active and Retired (DD form 2 Retired-Gray or Blue) and dependents (DD1173), all services, all ranks, family & guests meeting eligibility requirements.

** Must have DD1173. Note: Widows(ers) can take guest. Write or call Hotel for more information. The Luau at the Hale Koa is every Thursday evening right on the beach (Monday and Thursday June-August). Adult $22.95, children under 12 $12.95. ID cardholders can sponsor guests.

NOTE: A new "tower" is under construction at the Hale Koa as we go to press. Watch Military Living's R&R Space-A Report for details.

Hickam Air Force Base (HI11R6)
Hickam AFB, HI 96853-5000

TELEPHONE NUMBER INFORMATION: Main installation numbers: Comm: 808-471-7110, ATVN: 471-7110.

Location: Adjacent to the Honolulu IAP. Accessible from HI-1 or HI-92. Clearly marked. RM: p-7, L/7. NMC: Honolulu, 6 miles east.

Billeting Office: ATTN: 15 ABW/SVH. Building 1153. Commercial and ATVN: 449-2603. 24 hours daily. Check in facility, check out 1200 hours daily. Government civilian employee billeting.

TML: VOQ. 8 buildings adjacent to O'Club. Officer all grades. Leave or official duty. 24/1-bedroom, private bath; 88/2-bedroom apartments, living room, private bath. Kitchen, microwave TV, maid service. Older structure. Rates: $10.00 per person. Maximum $40.00 per family. Duty can make reservations. Others Space-A.

TML: VAQ. Buildings 470, 471, 920. Senior Enlisted E7+. Leave or official duty. 16/2-bedroom apartments, private bath (kitchen, microwave, TV); 24 single rooms,

HAWAII
Hickam Air Force Base, continued

private bath. Maid service. Older structure. Rates: $6.00 per person. Maximum $24.00 per family. Duty can make reservations. Others Space-A.

TML: VAQ. Building 1153 (female); Buildings 1166, 1168 (male). Enlisted E1-E6. Leave or official duty. 147/2-bedroom, 2 persons per room, communal bath. Maid service. Older structure. Rates: $6.00 per person. Duty can make reservations. Others Space-A.

TML: DV/VIP. Building 728. Officer 07+. Leave or official duty. 33/2-bedroom apartments, living room, private bath. Kitchen, microwave, TV, maid service. Older structure. Rates: $10.00 per person. Maximum $30.00 per family. Duty can make reservations. Others Space-A.

DV/VIP: PACAF Protocol Office, 07+. Comm: 449-1781. Building 1153, Comm: 449-2603.

TML Availability: Difficult, most of the year.

Cafeteria-422-8000	Locator-449-9480	Medical-449-6333
NCO Club-449-1092	O'Club-449-1998	Police-449-6373

Kaneohe Bay Beach Cottages (HI06R6)
Kaneohe Bay MCAS, HI 96863-5001

TELEPHONE NUMBER INFORMATION: Main installation numbers: Comm: 808-471-1110, ATVN: 430-0111.

Location: Take H-3 to MCAS. Cottages are across from the airstrip along the coast line, near Pyramid Rock overlooking Kaneohe Bay. RM: p-7, G/6. NMC: Honolulu, 14 miles southwest.

Billeting Office: Temporary Lodging Facility, Building 3038, MCAS Kaneohe Bay, HI 96863-5018. For reservations for cottages call Comm: 808-254-2716/2806.

TML: Beach Cottages. All ranks. 12/2-bedroom, living room, dining areas, private bath; 1 CB cottage, private bath. Kitchen, complete utensils, color TV, lanai. Completely furnished. Rates: $25.00 per day (2 bedroom cottages); $27.00-$31.00 (CB cottage). All categories can make reservations.

Other: MCAS full support facilities. For details see Military Living's Military RV, Camping & Rec Areas Around The World.

TML Availability: Fairly good.

Kaneohe Marine Corps Air Station (HI12R6)
Kaneohe MCAS, HI 96863-5001

TELEPHONE NUMBER INFORMATION: Main installation numbers: Comm: 808-471-7110, ATVN: 471-7110.

Location: At end of H-3 on the windward side of Oahu. Off Mokapu Blvd and Kaneohe Bay Drive. Clearly marked. RM: p-7, G/6. NMC: Honolulu, 14 miles southwest.

Billeting Office: Hostess House. Building 3038. 0630-1800 hours M-F, 0900-1800 hours Sa, Su, holidays. Comm: 254-2716. ATVN: 457-2808. Other hours, OD, Building 215, EX-1829. After hours Station Officer of the Day 257-1823. Check in facility, check out 1000 hours daily. Government civilian employee billeting.

Kaneohe Marine Corps Air Station, continued

TML: Hostess House. Building 3038. All ranks. Leave or official duty. 24/2-, 3- & 4-bedroom, private bath. Also, 45/1-bedroom SNCO suites, private bath. Older structure. Rates: $24.00 per unit. Duty can make reservations. Others Space-A.

TML: BOQ. Building 503. Officer all grades. Leave or official duty. EX-2409. 37 suites, private bath. Refrigerator, community kitchen, utensils, color TV room & lounge, maid service, free cots, free washer/dryer, ice vending, spa/jacuzzi. Older structure. Rates: Sponsor $12.50, each additional person over 10 years $4.00. Maximum $16.50 per family. Maximum 5 per room. Duty can make reservations. Others Space-A.

TML: Studios. All ranks. Leave or official duty. 24 studios, living/dining areas, kitchen, private bath. Rates: $25.00 per day.

DV/VIP: FMF PAC Protocol, Camp Smith, HI 96861. Building 1, Room 200. Comm: 477-6891. 06+. Retirees Space-A.

Other: See Kaneohe Bay Beach Cottages listing.

TML Availability: Good. Best, Mar-Apr. More difficult, May-Jun.

Cafeteria-254-2663	Enlisted Club-254-5703	Locator-257-2008
Medical-257-2505	NCO Club-254-5481	O'Club-254-4785
Police-257-2123	Snack Bar-254-5602	SDO/NCO-257-1829

Kilauea Military Camp AFRC (HI17R6)
Hawaii National Park, HI 96718-5000

TELEPHONE NUMBER INFORMATION: Main installation numbers: Comm: 808-967-7315, ATVN: None.

Location: On island of Hawaii, 216 air miles southeast of Honolulu, 32 miles from Hilo IAP. Scheduled bus transport to Camp, reservations required Hilo to KMC. RM: p-7, H/11. NMC: Hilo, 32 miles northwest.

Billeting Office: ATTN: Reservations Office, Hawaii Volcanoes National Park, HI 96718. Comm: 967-8333. Reservations required. FCFS basis regardless of rank. Include name, grade, service, status & list children & guest(s) when applying for reservation. Priority I, AD, 90 days in advance; priority II, retirees, 60 days in advance; priority III, DOD civilian and other authorized personnel, 45 days. Reservations Office, 0800-1600 daily. Located at 4000 feet, temperature 50-65 degrees F. Check in 1400, check out 1100 hours daily. From Oahu, call toll free Comm: 438-6707 (0800-1600 daily).

TML: Apartments & Cabins (some woodburning fireplaces). All ranks. Leave or official duty. Reservations required. 32/1-bedroom, private bath; 18 separate bedroom, private bath; 13/2-bedroom, private bath; 1/3-bedroom, private bath; 1/4-bedroom cabin, private bath; dormitory has open-bay sleeping and latrine bath/showers. Kitchen (some cabins), refrigerator, complete utensils (kitchen only), color TV, maid service, cribs ($1.00 per night), rollaways ($3.00 per night), coin laundry. Rates: $19.00 E1-E5; $25.00 E6-E9, WO1-CW3, O1-O3; $31.00 CW4, O4+ and civilians up to two persons. $4.00 for each additional person. No charge for children under age 3. Kitchens $7.00 more per night. Dorms $5.00 per person.

Other: Great rec area. For details see Military RV, Camping & Rec Areas Around The World.

TML Availability: Good, fall, winter, spring. More difficult, summer.

78 — *Temporary Military Lodging Around the World*

HAWAII
Kilauea Military Camp AFRC, continued

Cafeteria-967-8355   Medical-967-8367   Snack Bar-967-8350
SDO/NCO-976-7315

Pearl Harbor Naval Station (HI20R6)
Pearl Harbor, HI 96860-5020

TELEPHONE NUMBER INFORMATION: Main installation numbers: Comm: 808-471-7411, ATVN: 430-0111.

Location: Off H-1 adjacent to Honolulu International Airport. Clearly marked. RM: p-7, H/4. NMC: Honolulu, 10 miles east.

Billeting Office: Building 1315, B Ave. EX-5210. 24 hours daily. Check in at facility, check out 1300 hours daily. Government civilian employee billeting BOQ.

TML: BOQ. Buildings 3721, 1315. Officer all grades. Leave or official duty. Accessible to handicapped. 138/1-bedroom, private bath. A/C, refrigerator, color TV, maid service, free washer/dryer, food/ice vending, room telephones. Modern structure. New TVs/carpets '89. Rates: Sponsor $6.00, adult $3.00. Maximum 2 persons. Duty can make reservations. Others Space-A. No children.

TML: BEQ. Buildings 1623, 1507. Enlisted all grades. Leave or official duty. Accessible to handicapped. Singles only. 84/1-bedroom, private bath. Refrigerator, color TV, maid service, free washer/dryer, food/ice vending, telephones in room. Modern structure. New TVs/carpets '89. Rates: $3.00 per person. Duty can make reservations. Others Space-A. No dependents.

DV/VIP: CINCPAC FIT Protocol. EX-7256. 07+. Only 06 Space-A.

Other: Arizona Memorial. USS Bowfin. Aloha Stadium.

TML Availability: Difficult. Best Dec-Jan.

Cafeteria-423-3243   CPO Club-474-8183   Enlisted Club-471-0841
Locator-474-6249   Medical-471-9541   O'Club-471-3041
Police-474-1237   SDO/NCO-471-1222

Schofield Barracks (HI13R6)
Schofield Barracks, HI 96786-5000

TELEPHONE NUMBER INFORMATION: Main installation numbers: Comm: 808-655-4930, ATVN: 455-4930.

Location: Off H-2 or HI-99 in the center of the Island of Oahu. Clearly marked. RM: p-7, F/3. NMC: Honolulu, 20 miles southeast.

Billeting Office: Building 692, McCornack Rd. Comm: 624-9877. 0730-1600 hours daily. Check in facility, check out 1200 hours daily. Government civilian employee billeting.

TML: Guest House. Grant Hall. All ranks. Leave or official duty. 57 separate bedrooms, shared bath; 1/2-bedroom suite, private bath. Refrigerator, community kitchen, color TV room & lounge, maid service, free cribs/cots, free washer/dryer, ice vending, playground, game room, snack vending. Older structure. Rates: Sponsor $17.00-$32.00, adult $4.00, child $4.00, infant free. Maximum 3 per room. Reservations from PCS only. Others Space-A.

Temporary Military Lodging Around the World — 79

Schofield Barracks, continued　　　　　　　　　　HAWAII

DV/VIP: Protocol Office, Fort Shafter, Building T-100. Comm: 808-438-1577. 06+. Retirees and lower grades Space-A. Primarily for TDY.

TML Availability: Good, most of the year.

Burger King-624-2785　　Enlisted Club-655-9672　　Locator-471-7411
Medical-655-4747/48/49　　NCO Club-624-5360　　　O'Club-655-9795
Police-655-5116　　　　　　Snack Bar-624-2692

Tripler Army Medical Center (HI03R6)
Tripler AMC, HI 96859-5000

TELEPHONE NUMBER INFORMATION: Main installation numbers: Comm: 808-433-6661, ATVN: 433-6661.

Location: Take H-1 West from Honolulu to Tripler exit. Turn right on Jarrett White Rd to Tripler AMC. RM: p-7, J/8. NMC: Honolulu, 3 miles southeast.

Billeting Office: Building 228B, Jarrett White Rd. Comm: 433-6963, ATVN: 433-6905. 0600-2200 M-F, 0800-1600 Sa, Su. Other hours, info desk in hospital lobby, EX-6661. Check in billeting, check out 1100 hours daily. Government civilian employee billeting.

TML: Guest House. Building 228B, 226E, 222C, 220D. All ranks. Leave or official duty. 53/1-bedroom, 2 beds, shared bath; 42 separate bedroom, 2 beds, living room, private bath. Refrigerator, community kitchen, microwave, color TV, maid service, free cribs/cots, free washer/dryer, food/ice vending, playground. Older structure, renovated. Rates: $20.00 with private bath, $15.00 without private bath, $4.00 each additional person. Maximum 5 persons with private bath, 3 without. Child under 1 no charge. All categories Space-A.

Other: Arizona Memorial. Pearl Harbor.

TML Availability: Difficult. Best, winter.

Cafeteria-833-1259　　Locator-433-6661　　　Medical-433-6620
NCO Club-433-6661　　O'Club-833-1268　　　Police-438-7116
Snack Bar-833-1259　　SDO/NCO-433-6661

Waianae Army Recreation Center (HI05R6)
Waianae, HI 96792-5000

TELEPHONE NUMBER INFORMATION: Main installation numbers: Comm: 808-696-2494/2883, ATVN: None.

Location: Located on west coast of Oahu. Take I-H1 West to HI-93 (Farrington Hwy) West to Waianae. RM: p-7, G/1. NMC: Honolulu, 35 miles southeast.

Billeting Office: Waianae Army Recreaton Center, Building 4004, 85-010 Army St, Waianae, HI 96792-5000. Comm: 696-2494/2883. 0900-1600 M-F. AD Army 60 days in advance. Other military personnel/retirees 40 days in advance. Reservist/DoD civilian 20 days in advance. 14 day occupancy limit in a 60 day period. Year round operation.

TML: Cabins. 9 delux 2- and 3-bedroom cabins with kitchen ($40.00-$45.00 daily); 25 standard cabins with kitchen ($26.00-$31.00 daily); 10 standard cabins without kitchen ($13.00-$15.00 daily). Utensils, dishes, bedding, tableware all furrnished. Bring bath & dish towels and personal items.

HAWAII
Waianae Army Recreation Center, continued

Other: For details see Military RV, Camping & Rec Areas Around The World.

TML Availability: Good all year.

Beach Club-696-4778   Police-696-2811   SDO/NCO-696-2494/2883

IDAHO

Mountain Home Air Force Base (ID01R4)
Mountain Home AFB, ID 83648-5000

TELEPHONE NUMBER INFORMATION: Main installation numbers: Comm: 208-828-2111, ATVN: 857-1110.

Location: From Boise, take I-84 southeast, 39 miles to Mountain Home exit, follow road through town to Airbase Rd, 10 miles to main gate. RM: p-25, N/4. NMC: Boise, 51 miles northwest.

Billeting Office: Building 2604, F St. Comm: 832-4661. ATVN: 857-6451. 24 hours daily. Check in facility, check out 1100 hours daily. No government civilian employees billeting.

TML: Motel. Building 2640. All ranks. Leave or official duty. 105/1-bedroom, semi-private bath; 11/2-bedroom, private bath; 4/3-bedroom, private bath; 1/4-bedroom, private bath. 15 units designated DV/VIP. Refrigerator, community kitchen, limited utensils, A/C, color TV room & lounge, maid service, free cribs/cots, free washer/dryer, ice vending, cable TV. Older structure. Rates: $6.00 per person. Maximum 12.00-18.00 per family. Duty can make reservations. Others Space-A.

DV/VIP: 366 TFW/CCE, Building 1506, EX-2016. 06+. Retirees Space-A.

TML Availability: Very good, winter. Difficult, Jun-Aug.

Enlisted Club-828-2105   Medical-828-2319   NCO Club-832-4311
O'Club-828-2597   Police-828-2256   Snack Bar-832-4424
SDO/NCO-828-2071

ILLINOIS

Chanute Air Force Base (IL06R2)
Chanute AFB, IL 61868-5225

TELEPHONE NUMBER INFORMATION: Main installation numbers: Comm: 217-495-1110, ATVN: 862-1110.

Location: North of Champaign (14 miles) at Rantoul. Access from I-57 and US-45. RM: p-27, J/14. NMC: Chicago, 120 miles north.

Billeting Office: Building 200. 24 hours daily. EX-2277. Check in facility, check out 1200 hours daily. Government civilian employee billeting.

Temporary Military Lodging Around the World — 81

ILLINOIS

Chanute Air Force Base, continued

TML: TLQ. Buildings 593, 594. All ranks. Leave or official duty. 24/2-bedroom, private bath apartments; 8 separate bedrooms, private bath apartments. Kitchen, A/C, limited utensils, color TV, maid service, facilities for disabled American veterans. Older structures, renovated '87. Rates: $16.00 E1-E6, $20.00 E7+. Maximum 4 per family. Duty can make reservations. Others Space-A.

TML: VOQ. Buildings 581, 583, 596-599. Officer all grades. Leave or official duty. 240/1-bedroom, private bath. Kitchen, A/C, color TV, maid service, free washer/dryer, ice vending. Modern structures. Rates: $6.00 per person. Duty, disabled American veterans, dependents of disabled American veterans can make reservations. Others Space-A.

TML: VAQ. Building 200. Enlisted all grades. Leave or official duty. 846/1-bedroom, semi-private bath. Refrigerator, A/C, color TV, maid service, free washer/dryer, ice vending. Modern structure. Rates: $5.00 per person. Duty can make reservations. Others Space-A.

TML: DV/VIP. Cottages. Officer O6+. Leave or official duty. EX-2277. 2/1-bedroom, private bath. A/C, color TV, maid service, free washer/dryer. Older structure. Rates: $10.00 per person. Duty can make reservations. Others Space-A.

DV/VIP: PAO. EX-2400. O6+. Retirees and lower grades Space-A.

TML Availability: Good, Oct-Jan. Difficult, Jun-Sep.

Enlisted Club-893-3138　Locator-495-3545　Medical-495-3133
NCO Club-495-3064　O'Club-495-3088　Police-495-3100
Snack Bar-893-8450　SDO-495-4566

Charles Melvin Price Support Center (IL04R2)
Granite City, IL 62040-1801

TELEPHONE NUMBER INFORMATION: Main installation numbers: Comm: 618-452-4211, ATVN: 892-4211.

Location: From I-70 take McKinley Bridge exit, cross Mississippi River, follow signs to Center. From I-270, cross river bridges and take first Granite City exit (IL-3) south to Center. RM: p-27, R/7. NMC: St. Louis, 7 miles west.

Billeting Office: Building 102, Niedringhaus St. EX-4287. 0730-1615 hours daily. Other hours: Security Office, Building 221, EX-4224. Check in facility, check out 1000 hours daily. No government civilian employee billeting.

TML: Guest House. Buildings 101, 116. All ranks. Leave or official duty. EX-4287. 5 separate bedrooms, private bath; 2/2-bedroom, private bath. Microwave in 5 rooms, refrigerator, limited utensils, A/C, color TV, maid service, free cribs/cots, free washer/dryer. Older structure. New furniture, drapes, bedspreads. New windows in '88. Rates: Sponsor $17.00. Maximum $19.00 per family. Maximum 3-5 persons. PCS reservations 90 days in advance. Others 15 days in advance.

TML Availability: Good, Nov-Mar. Difficult, May-Aug.

Enlisted Club-452-5595　　NCO Club-452-5595　　O'Club-452-5595

ILLINOIS
Charles Melvin Price Support Center, continued

Police-452-4224   SDO/NCO-452-4247

Fort Sheridan (IL01R2)
Fort Sheridan, IL 60037-5000

TELEPHONE NUMBER INFORMATION: Main installation numbers: Comm: 708-926-4111, ATVN: 459-4111.

Location: Take US-41 to Old Elm Rd (Lake Forest) exit, east 1.5 miles to main gate of Post. Or I-294 to Half-Day Rd exit, east to US-41 and proceed north as above. RM: p-28, D/8. NMC: Chicago, 28 miles south.

Billeting Office: ATTN: AFKE-ZO-DE-H, Building 205. EX-5506/2735. 0730- 1900 hours M-F, 0730-1600 Sa-Su. Other hours SDO, Building 140, EX-3095/6. Check in billeting, check out 1100 hours daily. Government civilian employee billeting at Guest House.

TML: Guest House. Buildings 31, 32. All ranks. Leave or official duty. 12 separate bedrooms, private bath; 3/2-bedroom, private bath; 1/4-bedroom, private bath. Kitchen (4 units), refrigerator, microwave, limited utensils, A/C, color TV, maid service, free cribs/cots, free washer/dryer. Older structures. Rates: $24.00 per night in Building 31, $32.00 per night in Building 32. Maximum of 5 persons. All categories can make reservations.

TML: VOQ/VEQ. Several buildings . Officer & E7-E9. Leave or official duty. Separate bedrooms, semi-private bath. Community kitchen, color TV lounge, maid service, free washer/dryer. Older structures. Rates: Sponsor $8.00. 1 person per unit.

DV/VIP: Army Protocol, Building 140, EX-5426. 07+. Retirees and lower grades Space-A.

Other: Great America 12 miles from post. City of Chicago.

TML Availability: Good, Oct-Mar. Difficult, other times.

Enlisted Club-926-3864   Locator-926-2274   Medical-926-3861
O'Club-926-2565   Police-926-2112   Snack Bar-433-4779
SDO/NCO-926-3095

Glenview Naval Air Station (IL03R2)
Glenview NAS, IL 60026-5000

TELEPHONE NUMBER INFORMATION: Main installation numbers: Comm: 708-657-1000, ATVN: 932-0111.

Location: From I-294 north, exit Willow Rd, east two traffic lights, right on Phingston Rd to West Lake Ave, left to NAS main gate. RM: p-28, F/8. NMC: Chicago, 10 miles southeast.

Billeting Office: Office in Building 45, Fowler Dr, EX-2275. Enlisted in Barracks 55, Ave B, EX-2453. Both 24 hours daily. Check in facility, check out 1300 hours daily. Government civilian employee billeting.

TML: BOQ/BEQ. BOQ, Building 45. BEQ, Building 55. All ranks. Leave or official duty. 15/1-bedroom, private bath; 52 separate bedroom, semi-private bath; 6/2-bedroom, private bath. Kitchen (2 rooms only), refrigerator, utensils (2 rooms only), A/C, color TV room & lounge, maid service, free cribs/cots, free

Temporary Military Lodging Around the World — 83

ILLINOIS

Glenview Naval Air Station, continued

washer/dryer, ice vending. Older structures, some remodeled '88. Rates: $9.00 2-bedroom with kitchen, $7.00 without kitchen; $4.00 per person all others. Double, $6.00, single $8.00. For BOQ, PCS in and reservists on orders can make reservations. Others Space-A.

DV/VIP: CO, Building 41, EX-2136. 06+. Retirees Space-A.

Other: Museum of Science & Industry. Museum of Natural History.

TML Availability: Limited. Best, winter. No TML for enlisted dependents.

Cafeteria-657-2280	CPO Club-657-2396	Enlisted Club-657-2396
Locator-657-1000	Medical-657-2222	O'Club-657-2339
Police-657-2476	Snack Bar-657-2471	

Great Lakes Naval Training Center (IL07R2)
Great Lakes, IL 60088-5000

TELEPHONE NUMBER INFORMATION: Main installation numbers: Comm: 708-688-3500, ATVN: 792-2002.

Location: From I-94 north or US-41 north of Chicago, exit to IL-137 east to NTC. Clearly marked. RM: p-28, B/7. NMC: Chicago, 30 miles south.

Billeting Office: Building 62. Comm: EX-3777. 24 hours. 7 days. Check in facility, check out 1300 hours. Government civilian employee billeting.

TML: Navy Lodge. Building 2500. All ranks. Leave or official duty. 50/1-bedroom, 2 double beds, private bath. Kitchen, complete utensils, A/C, color TV, maid service, free cribs/cots, coin washer/dryer, food/ice vending. Modern structure. Rates: $34.00 per room. Maximum 5 per room. All categories can make reservations.

TML: BEQ. Building 178. Enlisted all grades. Leave or official duty. EX-2374. 144/1-bedroom, hall bath/latrine bath. 22/1-bedroom, private bath. A/C, essentials, community kitchen, refrigerator, color TV lounge, maid service, free washer/dryer, food vending. Older structure. New TVs '89. Rates: Sponsor, $4.00. Duty can make reservations. All others Space-A.

TML: BOQ/VOQ. Building 62. Officer all grades. Leave or official duty. Comm: 689-2565/688-3777. ATVN: 792-3777. 57/1-bedroom, semi-private bath; 111 separate bedroom, private bath; 1/2-bedroom, private bath. Refrigerator, community kitchen, essentials, A/C (some), color TV room & lounge, maid service, free cribs/cots, free washer/dryer, food/ice vending, game and exercise room. Older structure. New A/C and TVs '89. Rates: Sponsor $8.00, adult/child over 6, $3.00. Maximum 5 per unit. Duty can make reservations. Others Space-A.

DV/VIP: Cmdr, Building 1. EX-3400. 06+. Retirees and lower grades Space-A.

TML Availability: Fairly good. Best, winter months.

Cafeteria-578-6103	CPO Club-688-6928	Enlisted Club-688-4641
Locator-688-2014	Medical-688-5618	O'Club-688-6946
Police-688-3333	Snack Bar-688-5612	SDO/NCO-688-3939

ILLINOIS

Scott Air Force Base (IL02R2)
Scott AFB, IL 62225-5000

TELEPHONE NUMBER INFORMATION: Main installation numbers: Comm: 618-256-1110, ATVN: 576-1110.

Location: Off I-64 east or west, exit 19E or 19A west to Il-158 south, 2 miles and watch for signs to AFB entry. RM: p-27, S/8. NMC: St Louis, 25 miles west.

Billeting Office: Building 1510, Scott Dr. Comm: 744-1200 or EX-3224/3225 (front desdk); EX-2045 (reservations). 24 hours daily. Check in billeting, check out 1200 hours daily. Government civilian employee billeting in VOQ.

TML: TLF/VOQ/VAQ. Buildings 1508-1551. All ranks. Leave or official duty. 64/1-bedroom, semi-private bath; 176/1-bedroom, private bath; 70/2-bedroom, private bath; 3 double rooms, private bath. 2 handicapped rooms, private bath; 36 family units, private bath. Refrigerator, A/C, color TV, maid service, free washer/dryer, ice vending. Rates: TLF $20.00, VOQ $8.00, VAQ $6.00. TDY can make reservations. Others Space-A.

DV/VIP: MAC protocol. EX-5555. 06+. Retirees Space-A.

TML Availability: Fairly Good, Nov-Jan. Difficult, other times.

Cafeteria-746-4199	Enlisted Club-744-4328	Locator-256-4108
Medical-256-7595	NCO Club-744-0300	O'Club-744-1333
Police-256-2223	SDO/NCO-256-5891	

INDIANA

Crane Naval Weapons Support Center (IN03R2)
Crane NWSC, IN 47522-5000

TELEPHONE NUMBER INFORMATION: Main installation numbers: Comm: 812-854-2511, ATVN: 482-1110.

Location: From US-231 north or south exit to IN-45 or IN-645 to enter the Center from the west. RM: p-31, S/7. NMC: Bloomington, 22 miles northeast.

Billeting Office: Building 2682. EX-1176. 0730-1530. After duty hours, EX-1225/1222, Building 1. Check in billeting.

TML: BOQ/VIP. Building 2681. Officer. All ranks. Leave or official duty. Accessible to handicapped. 11/1-bedroom, private bath; VIP suites, 2 separate bedrooms, private bath, kitchen, living room. A/C, essentials, food vending, refrigerator, maid service, cable color TV lounge/room, free washer/dryer. Modern structure. Renovated and remodeled '87. New TVs '89. Rates: $8.00 per night, VIP suites $15.00 per night. Maximum 2 persons. All categories can make reservations.

TML: BEQ. Building 2682. Enlisted. All grades. Leave or official duty. Accessible to handicapped except for wheelchair. Rooms, semi-private bath. A/C, essentials, food vending, maid service, refrigerator, cable color TV room/lounge, free washer/dryer. Modern structure. Renovated '89. New TVs/carpets. All categories can make reservations. Rates: $4.00.

DV/VIP: Building 1. EX-1210. 06+. Retirees Space-A.

Temporary Military Lodging Around the World — 85

INDIANA

Crane Naval Weapons Support Center, continued

TML Availability: Very good, all year.

Cafeteria-854-1381 Locator-854-2511 Medical-854-1220
Police-854-3300 O'Club-854-1501 Enlisted Club-854-1501
SDO/NCO-854-1222

Fort Benjamin Harrison (IN02R2)
Fort Benjamin Harrison, IN 46216-5450

TELEPHONE NUMBER INFORMATION: Main installation numbers: Comm: 317-546-9211, ATVN: 699-1110.

Location: Take I-465 east to Fort Harrison exit 40, east on 56th St, or take Pendleton Pike (IN-67/US-36) exit 42 to Post Rd and North Fort Harrison. RM: p-29, K/26. NMC: Indianapolis, 8 miles southwest.

Billeting Office: Building T-609, Green Ave (Post Rd). Comm: 549-5455. 24 hours daily. Check in facility, check out 1200 hours daily. Government civilian employee billeting. Contract motels available through billeting.

TML: Guest House. Building T-51. All ranks. Leave or official duty. 14/1-bedroom, 2 full-size beds, private bath; 2/1-bedroom, 1 bed, facilities for handicapped, private bath. All have sleeper sofas. Kitchen, complete utensils, A/C, color TV, maid service, free cribs/cots, free washer/dryer, ice vending. Modern structure. Rates: $25.00-$30.00 per room per night. PCS in/out have priority. Others Space-A.

DV/VIP: Protocol Office. Building 600. ATVN: 542-4186. O6/GS-15+. Retirees Space-A with approval of Protocol Office.

TML Availability: Extremely limited. Best, end of Dec.

Enlisted Club-542-4485 Locator-542-4537 Medical-549-5194/5
NCO Club-542-4425 O'Club-542-2582 Snack Bar-549-5699
SDO/NCO-542-4541

Grissom Air Force Base (IN01R2)
Grissom AFB, IN 46971-5000

TELEPHONE NUMBER INFORMATION: Main installation numbers: Comm: 317-689-5211, ATVN: 928-1110.

Location: On US-31, 15 miles north of Kokomo and 7 miles south of Peru. RM: p-31, G/10. NMC: Indianapolis, 72 miles south.

Billeting Office: Building 550, Lancer St. EX-2596. 24 hours daily. Check in facility, check out 1200 hours daily.

TML: TLF. Building 313. All ranks. Leave or official duty. 13 separate bedrooms, private bath; 6/2-bedroom, private bath. Kitchen, utensils, A/C, color TV, maid service, free cribs, free washer/dryer, ice vending. Modern structure. Rates: $23.00 per unit. Duty can make reservations. Others Space-A.

TML: VAQ. Building 550. Enlisted all grades. Leave or official duty. 10/1-bedroom, semi-private bath (E7+); 21/2-bedroom, semi-private bath (E6-). Refrigerator, A/C, color TV room & lounge, maid service, free washer/dryer, ice vending. Older structure. Rates: Sponsor $5.50, adult $5.50. Duty can make reservations. Others Space-A.

86 — *Temporary Military Lodging Around the World*

INDIANA
Grissom Air Force Base, continued

TML: VOQ. Officer all grades. 29/1-bedroom, semi-private bath (10 are VIP rooms; 2 suites separate bedrooms for VIP). Rates: $6.50 per person. Space-A in BOQ Building 551 & UNCOQ Bldg 311.

DV/VIP: CSG/ESO, Building S-1, EX-3144. O6+. Retirees Space-A.

Other: Miniature White House. Aircraft Museum on base.

TML Availability: Good, Oct-May. Difficult, summer months.

Enlisted Club-689-9804 Locator-689-3032 Medical-689-3302
NCO Club-689-9151 O'Club-689-9135 Snack Bar-689-2504

IOWA

NONE

KANSAS

Fort Leavenworth (KS04R3)
Fort Leavenworth, KS 66027-5000

TELEPHONE NUMBER INFORMATION: Main installation numbers: Comm: 913-684-4021, ATVN: 552-4021.

Location: From I-70 take US-73 north to Leavenworth. Fort is adjacent to city of Leavenworth. RM: p-35, D/23. NMC: Kansas City, 30 miles southeast.

Billeting Office: Building 695, Grant Ave. EX-4091. 24 hours daily. Check in billeting after 1400 hours, check out 1000 hours daily. Government civilian employee billeting.

TML: Guest House. Building 427. All ranks. Leave or official duty. Comm: 651-9522. ATVN: 552-4091. 12/2 & 3 bedroom, private bath. Kitchen, complete utensils, A/C, color TV, maid service, free cribs/cots, room telephones, ice vending, free washer/dryer. Older structure, renovated. Rates: Sponsor $18.00, flat rate. Duty can make reservations. Others Space-A.

TML: VOQ. Hoge Barracks, Truesdell Hall, Root & Schofield Hall. Officer all grades. Leave or official duty. 750 units, private and semi-private bath. Kitchen (some), A/C, color TV, maid service, room telephones, ice vending, free washer/dryer. Rates: Sponsor $18.00-$20.00, each additional person $5.00. TDY can make reservations. Others Space-A.

TML: DV/VIP. Building 22 (Cooke Hall), Building 3 (Thomas Custer House), Building 213 (Otis Hall). Officer O6+. Leave or official duty. EX-4064. 8/1-bedroom, private bath; 14 separate bedrooms, private bath. Kitchen (some), refrigerator (some), utensils, A/C, TV, maid service, room telephones, ice vending, free washer/dryer. Older structure. Rates: Sponsor $20.00, each additional person $5.00. Duty can make reservations. Others Space-A.

DV/VIP: Executive Services. EX-4064. O6+. Retirees and lower grades Space-A.

TML Availability: Difficult. Best Jul & Dec. Limited, other times.

Temporary Military Lodging Around the World — 87

KANSAS

Fort Leavenworth, continued

Cafeteria-684-5147
NCO Club-651-6852
Snack Bar-651-6586

Locator-684-3651/4021
O'Club-651-7013
SDO-684-4154

Medical-684-6100
Police-684-3456

Fort Riley (KS02R3)
Fort Riley, KS 66442-5000

TELEPHONE NUMBER INFORMATION: Main installation numbers: Comm: 913-239-3911, ATVN: 856-1110.

Location: On KS-18 and off I-70 in the central part of the state. Junction City, 5 miles southwest and Manhattan, 10 miles northeast. RM: p-35, E/18. NMC: Topeka, 50 miles east.

Billeting Office: Building 45, Barry Ave. EX-2830. 24 hours daily. Check in facility, check out 1100 hours daily. Government civilian employee billeting.

TML: Guest House. Building 5309. EX-5229. All ranks. Leave or official duty. 27/2-room suites, 3 single rooms, private bath. Community kitchen, free cribs, free washer/dryer. Older structure. Rates: $18.00 suites, $15.00 rooms. Duty on PCS orders can make reservations. Others Space-A.

TML: VOQ/VEQ. Carr Hall, Buildings 621, 541. All ranks. Leave or official duty. 23/2-room suites, living room, private bath; 37 single rooms, kitchenette. Color TV, free cribs, free washer/dryer. Older structure. Rates: $22.00-$25.00 per unit. Duty on PCS/TDY can make reservations. Others Space-A.

TML: Guest House. Building 170. All ranks. Leave or official duty. 6/1-bedroom, living room, kitchen, private bath. 2/2-bedroom, living room, kitchen, private bath. Older structure. Rates: $22.00-$25.00 per unit. Duty on PCS orders can make reservations. Others Space-A.

TML: DV/VIP. Building 510 (Grimes Hall), Building 28 (Bacon Hall). Officer O6+. Leave or official duty. EX-3926/3037. Bacon Hall has 3 bedroom house for $35.00 per night; Grimes Hall has Custer Suite for $35.00 per night; 6/1-bedroom suites for $30.00 per night; 2 single rooms in basement for $10.00 per night. Kitchen, washer/dryer. Older structure. All categories can make reservations.

TML Availability: Very good.

Enlisted Club-784-4075
NCO Club-239-2222
SDO/NCO-239-2222

Locator-239-9867
O'Club-784-5999

Medical-239-7777
Police-239-3053/MPMP

McConnell Air Force Base (KS03R3)
McConnell AFB, KS 68221-5000

TELEPHONE NUMBER INFORMATION: Main installation numbers: Comm: 316-652-6100, ATVN: 743-1110.

Location: Take I-35 south to Wichita, exit at Kellogg St (US-54) east to Rock Rd south and McConnell AFB. RM: p-35, Q/4. NMC: Wichita, 6 miles northwest.

Billeting Office: Building 193, Manhatten St. Comm: 683-7711. ATVN: 743- 6500. 24 hours daily. Check in billeting, check out 1200 hours daily. Government civilian employee billeting in contract quarters.

TML: TLF. Building 193. All ranks. Leave or official duty. 3/1-bedroom, private

88 — *Temporary Military Lodging Around the World*

KANSAS
McConnell Air Force Base, continued

bath; 21 separate bedroom, private bath. Community kitchen, A/C, color TV room & lounge, maid service, free washer/dryer, ice vending. Older structure. Rates: 1 bedroom $18.00. All categories Space-A.

TML: VOQ/VAQ. Buildings 202, 320. All ranks. Leave or official duty. 18 rooms (VOQ); 30 rooms (VAQ). A/C, color TV, maid service, free washer/dryer. Rates: VOQ, $8.00 per person; VAQ, $7.00. Duty can make reservations. Others Space-A.

TML: DV/VIP. Building 202. Officer 06+. Leave or official duty. 4/1-bedroom suites, private bath. Kitchen, limited utensils, A/C, color TV, maid service, free washer/dryer, ice vending. Rates: $10.00 per person. Maximum $20.00 per family. Duty can make reservations. Others Space-A.

DV/VIP: Hq. EX-3107. 06+. Retirees & lower grades Space-A.

TML Availability: Good, Nov-Feb. Difficult, other times.

Enlisted Club-681-5004   Locator-681-6322   Medical-681-5743
NCO Club-681-5004   O'Club-681-5070   Police-681-5851
SDO-681-5218

KENTUCKY

Fort Campbell (KY02R2)
Fort Campbell, KY 42223-1291

TELEPHONE NUMBER INFORMATION: Main installation numbers: Comm: 502-798-2151, ATVN: 635-1110.

Location: In the southwest part of KY, 4 miles south of intersection of US-41A and I-24. 10 miles northwest of Clarksville, TN. RM:p-37, P/4. NMC: Hopkinsville, 15 miles north.

Billeting Office: Building 2601, 26th St & Indiana Ave. Reservations for all TML call Comm: 615-431-5107, ATVN: 635-2865. 24 hours. Check in facility, check out 1000 hours daily. Government civilian employee billeting.

TML: Guest House. Clifford C. Sims. Building 2601. All ranks. Leave or official duty. Accessible to handicapped. 74/1-bedroom, 2 double beds, private bath. Community kitchen, refrigerator, A/C, color TV room & lounge, maid service, free cribs/cots, washer/dryer, food/ice vending. Modern structure. Rates: Sponsor $16.00, each additional person $2.00. Maximum 6 per unit. All categories can make reservations.

TML: Guest House Annex. Buildings 109 & 111. Enlisted all grades. Families only. Reservations accepted. 68 separate bedrooms, private bath. Community kitchen, refrigerator, A/C, color TV, maid service, free cribs/cots, washer/dryer, ice vending. Older structure, renovated '86. Rates: Sponsor $8.00, each additional person $2.00. Maximum $14.00 per family.

DV/VIP: Protocol Office, Building T-39. EX-8924. 06+.

TML Availability: Fairly good, Oct-May. Difficult, other times.

Cafeteria-439-3779   Enlisted C-615-431-3610   Locator-798-7196
Medical-798-8388   NCO Club-615-431-3610   O'Club-615-431-5604
Police-798-2677   SDO/NCO-798-8722/8688

Temporary Military Lodging Around the World — 89

KENTUCKY

Fort Knox (KY01R2)
Fort Knox, KY 40121-5000

TELEPHONE NUMBER INFORMATION: Main installation numbers: Comm: 502-624-1181, ATVN: 464-0111.

Location: From I-65 north in Louisville, exit Jefferson Freeway, 841 west to 31 west go south to Fort Knox. From I-64, exit I-264 west (Waterson) to I-65 south, to Jefferson Fort Knox to US-31W north to Fort Knox. From I-71, exit I-65 south to exit Jefferson Freeway 841, west to 31 west then south to Fort Knox. RM: p-37, J/10. NMC: Louisville, 25 miles north.

Billeting Office: ATTN: ATZK-EH-H, Building 4770 (Newgarden Tower), Dixie Highway 31 west. Reservations: Comm: 502-624-3138, ATVN: 464-3138. 24 hours daily. Check in/out as indicated. Government civilian employee billeting.

TML: Guest House. Building 6597, Wickam Guest House. All ranks. Leave or official duty. Comm: 942-0490. Check out 1200 hours daily. 42/1-bedroom, 1 single, 2 double beds, private bath; 34/1-bedroom, 2 double beds, private bath. Refrigerator, community kitchen, limited utensils, color TV room & lounge, maid service, cribs $1.50, free washer/dryer, ice vending. Modern structure. Rates: $16.50 2 persons, $18.50 3 persons, $20.00 4 persons, $21.50 5-6 persons, $23.00 maximum 6 persons. All categories can make reservations.

TML: Guest House. Loriann Annex. Building 6525. 1/1-bedroom, private bath; 4/2-bedroom, private bath; 12/1-bedroom, 2 double beds, private bath. Refrigerator, community kitchen, color TV lounge, maid service, coin washer/dryer. Older structure. Rates: $5.50 1-2 person, $6.50 for 3 or more. Maximum 6 persons. All categories can make reservations.

TML: VOQ. Apartments. Officer O1-O6. Leave or official duty. Check out 1200 hours daily. Kitchen, A/C, color TV, maid service, free washer/dryer, ice vending, alarm clock/radio. Modern structure. Rates: Sponsor $18.50, each additional person $5.00. Maximum based on beds available. Duty can make reservations. Others Space-A.

TML: VEQ. Apartments. Building 4770. Enlisted E7-E9. Leave or official duty. Check out 1200 hours daily. Kitchen, color TV room & lounge, maid service, free washer/dryer, ice vending, elevator, alarm clock/radio. Modern structure. Rates: Sponsor $18.50, each additional person $5.00. Duty can make reservations. Others Space-A.

TML: DV/VIP. Building 1102, Henry House. Officer O7+. Leave or official duty. Comm: 624-2744. ATVN: 464-2744. Check out 1100 hours daily. 1/3-bedroom house, private bath. Kitchen, color TV, maid service, free washer/dryer. Older structure. Rates: Sponsor $20.00, adult $5.00 each. Duty can make reservations. Others Space-A.

TML: DV/VIP. Building 1117, Yeomans Hall. Enlisted E9. Leave or official duty. Comm: 624-5240/6540/6951. ATVN: 464-2744. Check out 1000 hours daily. 2/1-bedroom, queen beds, private bath; 8/1-bedroom, twin beds, private bath. Sitting room. Refrigerator, A/C, color TV room & lounge, maid service, free cots, free washer/dryer. Older structure. Sponsor $20.00, $5.00 each additional person. Two military persons $5.00 each. Duty can make reservations. Others Space-A.

DV/VIP: Protocol Office, Building 1102, Henry House, Room 104. EX-2744. O6+. Retirees and lower grades Space-A at discretion of Protocol.

Other: Patton Museum of Cavalry & Armor, U.S. Bullion Depository (viewed from outside only).

KENTUCKY
Fort Knox, continued

TML Availability: Good. Best, Nov-Mar. More difficult, other times.

Cafeteria-942-0805/0230
Medical-624-9999/6450
O'Club-942-8383
SDO/NCO-624-6450

Enlisted Club-942-0581
NCO Club-942-8067
Police-624-2111

Locator-624-1141/1336
SNCO Club-942-3410
Snack Bar-942-8038

LOUISIANA

Barksdale Air Force Base (LA01R2)
Barksdale AFB, LA 71110-5000

TELEPHONE NUMBER INFORMATION: Main installation numbers: Comm: 318-456-2252, ATVN: 781-1000.

Location: Exit I-20 at Airline Dr, go south to Old Minden Rd (.25 mile), left on Old Minden Rd (1 block), then right on North Gate Dr (1 mile) to North Gate of AFB. RM: p-38, A/13. NMC: Shreveport, 1 mile west. Co-located with Bossier City and Shreveport.

Billeting Office: Building 5155, second building on left after entering North Gate on Davis Ave. Comm: 747-4708, ATVN: 781-3091. 24 hours daily. Check in facility, check out 1200 hours daily. Government civilian employee billeting.

TML: VAQ. Barksdale Inn. Building 5155. All ranks. Leave or official duty. Accessible to Handicapped. 10/1-bedroom, private bath; 17 separate bedroom, shared bath; 10/2-room Senior NCO suites, private bath (E7-E9). Refrigerator, A/C, black/white TV, color TV lounge, maid service, free cribs, free washer/dryer, ice vending. Older structure, renovated. Rates: $8.00 per adult, $4.00 per dependent. Maximum $12.00 per unit. Duty can make reservations. Others Space-A.

TML: VOQ. SAC Inn. Buildings 5167, 5224, 5243. Officer all grades. Leave or official duty. 84/1-bedroom, private bath. Kitchen, complete utensils, A/C, color TV, maid service, free cribs/cots, free washer/dryer, ice vending. Older structure. Rates: $8.00 per adult, $4.00 per dependent. Duty can make reservations. Others Space-A. Note: Large and small TLF units for families available for $19.00-$21.00 per night.

TML: VAQ. Enlisted all grades. Leave or official duty. 9/1-bedroom, 1 bed, private bath; 61/1-bedroom, 2 beds, private bath. A/C, color TV, maid service, free washer/dryer, ice vending. Older structure. Rates: $5.50 per person. Maximum $11.00 per room. Duty can make reservations. Others Space-A.

TML: DV/VIP. Officer 06+. Leave or official duty. 1/3-bedroom house, fully furnished, duty 07+ only, no retirees. 16/1-bedroom suites, private bath. Kitchen, complete utensils, A/C, color TV, maid service, free cribs/cots, free washer/dryer, ice vending. Older structure. Rates: $10.00 per adult, $5.00 per dependent. Duty can make reservations. Others Space-A.

DV/VIP: PAO, 2nd BMW. Comm: 456-4447. 06+. Retirees Space-A.

TML Availability: Good, all year.

Enlisted Club-456-3190
NCO Club-746-3366
Snack Bar-746-5441

Locator-456-2252
O'Club-746-2203
SDO/NCO-456-2151

Medical-456-4051
Police-456-2551

Temporary Military Lodging Around the World — 91

LOUISIANA

England Air Force Base (LA05R2)
England AFB, LA 71303-5000

TELEPHONE NUMBER INFORMATION: Main installation numbers: Comm: 318-448-2100, ATVN: 683-1110.

Location: From Alexandria take LA-1 to Airbase Rd, enter main gate. Or LA-28 to Vandenburg Dr (LA-3054) and enter back gate. RM: p-38, F/5. NMC: Alexandria, 5 miles northwest.

Billeting Office: Building 1421B, Oliver Drive. EX-5313. 24 hours daily. Check in billeting, check out 1200 hours daily. Government civilian employee billeting VOQ.

TML: VOQ/VIP. Building 1423. VOQ: Officer all grades. Leave or official duty. Accessible to handicapped. 23/1-bedroom, private bath. Shared kitchen, limited utensils, essentials, refrigerator, A/C, color TV, maid service, free cribs/cots, free washer/dryer, ice vending. Modern structure. Renovated Oct '88. Rates: $18.00 per unit. Duty can make reservations. Others Space-A. VIP: Officer O4+. Leave or official duty. 4 rooms with bed, private bath. Rates: Sponsor, $8.00; all others, $8.00. Maximum charge $16.00. Maximum 2 persons per unit. Description same as VOQ above. Also 2- and 4-bedroom units in TLF facilities, $18.00 per unit.

TML: VAQ. Building 1102. Enlisted all grades. Leave or official duty. Accessible to handicapped. 16 rooms with two beds, semi-private bath. Cots/cribs, essentials, refrigerator, A/C, color TV, maid service, free washer/dryer, food/ice vending, coffee in room. Older structure, renovated. New furniture. Rates: Sponsor, $8.00; all others, $8.00. Maximum charge $18.00. Duty can make reservations. Others Space-A.

TML: DV. Building 1422. Officer O6+. Leave or official duty. EX-5181. 2/1-bedroom suites, private bath. 2/2-bedroom suites, private bath. Kitchen, complete utensils, A/C, cots/cribs, essentials, food/ice vending, color TV, maid service, free washer/dryer. Older structure. Rates: Sponsor $10.00; all others $10.00. Maximum charge $20.00. Maximum 3 persons per unit. All categories can make reservations.

DV/VIP: 23rd TFW/CC, Building 1830. EX-5181. O6+. Retirees Space-A.

TML Availability: Difficult. Best, winter. Limited, summer.

Enlisted Club-448-2525   Locator-448-5313   Medical-448-5809
NCO Club-448-2525   O'Club-448-2422   SDO/NCO-448-5222

Fort Polk (LA07R2)
Fort Polk, LA 71459-5000

TELEPHONE NUMBER INFORMATION: Main installation numbers: Comm: 318-531-2911, ATVN: 863-1110.

Location: Off US-171, at LA-10, 9 miles south Leesville. RM: p-38, G/4. NMC: Alexandria, 45 miles northeast.

Billeting Office: Magnolia House. Building 522, Utah Ave. Comm: 531-2941 or 537-9591. 24 hours daily. Check in Magnolia House, check out 1000 hours daily. Government civilian employee billeting.

TML: Guest House. Building 522, Magnolia House. All ranks. Leave or official duty. 70/1-bedroom, sleep sofa, private bath. Kitchen, color TV, maid service, washer/dryer, vending machine. Rates: $22.00 for military personnel, $25.00 non-military per unit. Active duty on PCS, visiting relatives and guests of patients in the hospital, and active and retired military receiving outpatient care can make

LOUISIANA
Fort Polk, continued

reservations. Others Space-A.

TML: VOQ/VEQ. 22 rooms in Woodfill Hall, Building 350, and 8 cottages (VOQ); Building 2830, Red Devil Inn (VEQ). Enlisted E4 and below with families in a PCS status. Off duty only. 7/1- and 2-bedroom cottages and 22 rooms, private bath (VOQ); 10/1-bedroom, private bath (VEQ). A/C, color TV, maid service, free cribs, free washer/dryer. Older structure, renovated. Rates: $12.00 first person, $2.00 each additional person (VOQ); $4.00 for first room, $2.00 each additional room if needed (VEQ). Inquire about reservations.

TML: DV/VIP. Buildings 8-10, 15, 17, 18, 5674. Officer 06+, DOD civilian GS-15+, and Sergeant Major of the Army. Official duty only. 3/4-bedroom, private bath; 4/2-bedroom, private bath. Kitchen, complete utensils, A/C, color TV, maid service. Older structure, renovated. Rates: $17.00 first person, $5.00 each additional person. Upon request, personnel in grades 05+, on PCS in/out, may be given tentative, unconfirmed reservations.

TML Availability: Good, Oct-Mar. More difficult, other times.

Cafeteria-531-2385	Enlisted Club-531-6695	Locator-531-6622
Medical-531-3368/9	NCO Club-531-7943	O'Club-531-4440
Police-531-2677	Snack Bar-537-3540	SDO/NCO-531-2228

New Orleans Naval Air Station (LA11R2)
New Orleans NAS, LA 70143-5000

TELEPHONE NUMBER INFORMATION: Main installation numbers: Comm: 504-393-3011, ATVN: 363-3011.

Location: Off LA-23 in Belle Chase. Clearly marked. RM: p-38, J/11. NMC: New Orleans, 13 miles north.

Billeting Office: BEQ/BOQ. Building 22, 2nd St; Building 40, 4th St. EX-3841. 24 hours daily. Check in facility, check out 1300 hours daily. Government civilian employee billeting.

TML: BEQ/BOQ. Buildings 22, 40. All ranks. Leave or official duty. Accessible to handicapped. 5/1-bedroom, private bath (DV/VIP w/queen size beds); 75/1-bedroom, 2 beds, semi-private bath; 194/1-bedroom, 3 beds, hall bath. Refrigerator, A/C, color TV (BOQ), color TV lounge, maid service, cribs/cots ($2.00), free washer/dryer, ice vending. Older structures, renovated. Rates: $6.00 per person BOQ (infant $2.00), $3.00 per person BEQ. Military widows and unaccompanied dependents of active duty on leave Space-A. Others can make reservations.

DV/VIP: CO, Building 46, EX-3201. 06+. $8.00 per night for VIP rooms. Retirees Space-A.

Other: Downtown New Orleans, Bourbon Street.

TML Availability: Good, except on drill weekends.

Enlisted Club-393-3508	Locator-393-3253	Medical-393-3663
O'Club-393-3844	Police-393-3265	SDO/NCO-361-8822

LOUISIANA

New Orleans Naval Support Activity (LA06R2)
New Orleans, LA 70142-5000-5010

TELEPHONE NUMBER INFORMATION: Main installation numbers: Comm: 504-948-5011, ATVN: 485-5011.

Location: On the west bank of Mississippi River. From I-10 east take Canal Street Mississippi River Bridge exit, right on Clairborne Ave, right at Gretna exit. Take Gen DeGaulle east exit after passing over bridge and turn left at Shirley Dr which leads to NSA. RM: p-38, F-17. NMC: New Orleans, 5 miles east.

Billeting Office: Navy Lodge. Building 702, Hebert Dr. 0700-2000 hours daily. Check in Lodge, check out 1200 hours. All ranks. Leave or official duty. For reservations call 1-800-NAVY-INN. 22/1-bedroom, private bath. Kitchen, utensils, A/C, color TV, maid service, free cribs, coin washer/dryer, ice vending, ramps for disabled American veterans, irons/ironing boards, free clocks. Modern structure, remodeled. Rates: $32.00 per unit. Maximum 5 persons. All categories can make reservations.

TML Availability: Good, Nov-Jan. Difficult, Apr-Sep.

Cafeteria-361-2160
O'Club-361-2279
SDO/NCO-361-2655

Enlisted Club-361-2219
Police-361-2570

Medical-361-2692
Snack Bar-361-2739

MAINE

Bangor Air National Guard Base (ME10R1)
Bangor, ME 04401-3099

TELEPHONE NUMBER INFORMATION: Main installation numbers: Comm: 207-947-0571, ATVN: 698-7700.

Location: Located in Bangor city limits. Northbound from I-95 take exit 43 Ohio Street, drive west 2 blocks and turn left 1 block to right turn on Union Street (ME-222), pass Bangor IAP, turn left on Griffin Road, entrance is 300 yards on right. RM: p-39, L/7. NMC: Bangor, in city limits.

TML: The Army National Guard operates "Pine Tree Inn" for military members, retirees, and their families. Comm: 207-942-2081. Check out 1200 hours. 3/1-bedroom, semi-private bath. Community kitchen, essentials, food/ice vending, maid service, refrigerator, color TV lounge, free washer/dryer. Older structure. Anticipate renovations in '91. Rates: On leave sponsor $8.00, adult $8.00, child $8.00. On duty sponsor $4.00, adult $8.00, child $8.00. Duty can make reservations. Others Space-A.

DV/VIP: No Protocol Office.

TML Availability: Fairly good any time.

SDO/NCO-941-2211

MAINE

Brunswick Naval Air Station (ME07R1)
Brunswick NAS, ME 04011-5000

TELEPHONE NUMBER INFORMATION: Main installation numbers: Comm: 207-921-1110, ATVN: 476-1110.

Location: From I-95 north exit US-1 north to Brunswick, Old Bath Rd (Rt24) to main gate of BNAS. RM: p-39, I/4. NMC: Portland, 30 miles southwest.

Billeting Office: Building 220, ATTN: MSCS(SW), Orion St. EX-2245. 24 hours daily. Check in facility, check out 1100 hours (Navy Lodge 1000 hours). No government civilian employee billeting.

TML: Navy Lodge. Topsham Annex. All ranks. Leave or official duty. For reservations call 1-800-NAVY-INN. Lodge number is 921-2206. 0730-2200 hours. Other hours check with OD, EX-2214. 17/1-bedroom, private bath. Community kitchen, complete utensils, color TV lounge, maid service, coin washer/dryer. Older structure. Rates: $27.00 per unit. All categories can make reservations.

TML: BOQ/BEQ. All ranks. Leave or official duty. 10/1-bedroom, private bath; 24 separate bedroom, private bath. Refrigerator, community kitchen, limited utensils, color TV room & lounge, maid service, free cots, free washer/dryer, ice vending, picnic tables, tennis courts, sauna, gym. Older structure. Rates: Sponsor $5.00, adult $5.00, child $2.00, under 10 years no charge. Maximum 3 per room. Duty can make reservations. Others Space-A. Kennels in town.

TML: Transient BOQ/BEQ. Buildings 220, 512. Official duty only. Officer 06+. Enlisted E-8 to E-9. 5 rooms, private bath. 3/2-bedroom, private bath. 28/3-bedroom, private bath. Essentials, food vending, maid service, refrigerator, color TV, free washer/dryer. VIP suites have VCR, water beds, bar, hair dryers, clock radios. Older and modern structures. Older renovated and remodeled '88 and '89. Rates: $20.00 per night, $5.00 (VIP), families not authorized. Maximum 3 persons. Duty can make reservations.

DV/VIP: Brunswick NAS, Building 512. EX-2214. 05+. Retirees Space-A.

TML Availability: Good, Sep-Jan. Difficult, Apr-Aug.

Cafeteria-921-2455   CPO Club-921-2291   SDO/NCO-921-2214
Enlisted Club-921-2121   Locator-921-1110   Medical-921-2610
O'Club-921-2591   Police-921-2585

Loring AFB (ME06R1)
Loring AFB, ME 04751-5000

TELEPHONE NUMBER INFORMATION: Main installation numbers: Comm: 207-999-1110, ATVN: 920-1110.

Location: Take I-95 to Houlton, exit to US-1 north to Caribou (50 miles). The AFB is 1 miles north of ME-89 & ME-223 intersection. Clearly marked. RM: p-39, B/17. NMC: Caribou, 3 miles southwest.

Billeting Office: Building 2501, Virginia Place. EX-2227/8. 24 hours daily. Check in billeting, check out 1200 hours daily. Government civilian employee billeting.

TML: TLF. Buildings 2101, 2103, 2105, 2107, 4100, 4116. All ranks. Leave or official duty. 8 separate bedrooms, private bath; 16/2-bedroom, private bath. Kitchen, limited utensils, color TV, maid service, free cribs/cots, free washer/dryer, microwave. Older structures. Remodeled. New TVs/carpets '89. Rates: $20.00-$24.00 per family. Duty can make reservations. Others Space-A.

MAINE

Loring Air Force Base, continued

TML: VAQ. Building 6550. Enlisted all ranks. Leave or official duty. 19/1-bedroom, 2 beds, semi-private bath; 2 separate bedroom suites, private bath (E9). Refrigerator, color TV room & lounge, maid service, free cribs/cots, free washer/dryer, food/ice vending. Older structure. Remodeling began summer '90. Rates: $9.00 per person. Maximum $13.50 per room. Maximum 2 persons. Duty can make reservations. Others Space-A.

TML: VOQ. Building 2501. Officer all grades. Leave or official duty. 40/1-bedroom, semi-private bath; 3 separate bedroom, private bath (O5+). Kitchen, essentials, refrigerator, color TV room & lounge, maid service, free washer/dryer, food/ice vending. Modern structure, remodeled lounge, new TVs/carpets '89. Rates for private rooms: Sponsor $13.00. Maximum $19.50 per room. Maximum 2 persons. Rates for semi-private rooms: Sponsor $10.00. Maximum $15.00 per room. Maximum 2 person. Duty can make reservations. Others Space-A.

TML: DV/VIP. Building 2112. Officer O6+. Leave or official duty. 4 separate bedrooms, private bath. Kitchen, complete utensils, color TV, maid service, free cribs/cots, free washer/dryer, ice vending, microwave. Older structure. Rates: $14.00 per room. Maximum $21.00 per family. Occupancy subject to CO's approval. Duty can make reservations.

DV/VIP: Wing XO, 42 BMW/CCE. Building 5100. EX-2275. O6+.

TML Availability: Difficult. Best, winter. Limited, other times.

Locator-999-2100 Medical-999-5316 NCO Club-328-7334
O'Club-999-7136 Police-999-7155 Snack Bar-328-6602
SDO-207-999-2170 Enlisted Club-328-7334 Cafeteria-328-4110

Winter Harbor Naval Security Group Activity (ME09R1)
Winter Harbor, ME 04693-0900

TELEPHONE NUMBER INFORMATION: Main installation numbers: Comm: 207-963-5534/35, ATVN: 476-9011.

Location: From Ellsworth, take US-1 north to ME-186 east to Acadia National Park. Naval Security Station is on Schoodic Point in the park. RM: p-39, G/9. NMC: Bangor, 45 miles northwest.

Billing Office: No central billeting office. Building 84. Comm: 963-5534/35-EX-223. ATVN: 476-9223. 0730-2230 daily. Check in billeting, check out 1200 hours daily. Government civilian employee billeting.

TML: BEQ. Building 84. Enlisted all grades. Official duty only. 16/3-bedroom, hall bath (E1-E4); 6/2-bedroom, hall bath (E5-E6); 1/1-bedroom, semi-private bath (E7-E9). Refrigerator, community kitchen, color cable TV room & lounge, free washer/dryer. Older structure, new TVs/carpets '87. Rates: no charge.

TML: BOQ. Building 192. Officer all grades. Leave or official duty. 4/1-bedroom, private bath. Kitchen, limited utensils, color TV, maid service, free washer/dryer, cable TV. Modern structure. Rates: Sponsor $4.00 per person. Maximum 2 per room. Duty can make reservations. Others Space-A.

TML Availability: Good, Nov-Mar. Difficult, May-Sep.

Cafeteria-EX-255 Locator-963-5534/5535 Medical-EX-297
Police-EX-202 Snack Bar-963-2223

MARYLAND

Aberdeen Proving Ground (MD11R1)
Aberdeen, MD 21005-5001

TELEPHONE NUMBER INFORMATION: Main installation numbers: (Aberdeen Area) Comm: 301-278-5201, (Aberdeen Area) ATVN: 298-1110, (Edgewood Area) Comm: 301-671-5201, (Edgewood Area) ATVN: 584-1110.

Location: Aberdeen Area: take exit 5 east from I-95 north on MD-22 east for 2 miles to main gate. Also, from US-40 north to right on Maryland Blvd, entrance to main gate. NMC: Baltimore, 23 miles southwest. Edgewood Area: take exit 4 from I-95 north on MD-24 east for 2 miles to main gate. Also, from US-40 right on MD-24 to main gate. RM: p-41, D/20. NMC: Baltimore, 13 miles southwest.

Billeting Office: Building 2207, ATTN: STEAP-SV-H, Bel Air St. 24 hours daily. EX-4373. Check in billeting, check out 1100 hours. Government civilian employee billeting.

TML: Guest House. Building 3322. All ranks. Leave or official duty. EX-3856. 37/1-bedroom, 2 double beds, private bath; 8/2-bedroom apartment, private bath. Refrigerator, A/C, color TV, maid service, free cribs, cots ($2.00), free washer/dryer, ice vending. Modern structure. Rates: Sponsor $25.00, each additional person $3.00, infant no charge. TDY and visiting $25.00, $3.00 each additional person. Maximum $37.00 and 5 persons in room. Maximum $40.00 and 6 persons in apartment. Duty can make reservations. Others Space-A. 35 additional units in contracted off-post motel.

TML: VOQ. Building 2207. Officer all grades. Official duty only. Reservations accepted. 204/1-bedroom, private bath; 68 separate bedroom, semi-private bath. Kitchen, A/C, color TV, maid service, free washer/dryer. Older structure, remodeled. Rates: $25.00 per room. Maximum 1 per room.

TML: VEQ. Building 2207. Enlisted all grades. Official duty only. Reservations accepted. 64/1-bedroom, private bath. Community kitchen, A/C, color TV, maid service, washer/dryer. Older structure, renovated. Rates: $25.00 per room. Maximum 1 per room.

TML: DV/VIP. Building 2207. Officer O6+. Leave or official duty. 2 separate bedrooms, private bath; 4/2-bedroom, private bath; 2/3-bedroom, private bath. Kitchen, complete utensils, A/C, color TV, maid service, free cribs/cots. Check out 1300 hours daily. Older structure. Rates: Sponsor $20.00, each additional person $5.00, infant no charge. Duty can make reservations. Others Space-A.

DV/VIP: TECOM Protocol, Ryan Building, EX-5156. Or USAOC&S Protocol, Building 3071, EX-5595. O6+. Retirees Space-A.

TML Availability: Good, Nov-Jan. Difficult, other times.

Cafeteria-278-6339 Enlisted Club-272-8873 Locator-278-5138
Medical-278-3332   NCO Club-272-8873   O'Club-278-3062
Police-278-5291   Snack Bar-676-1313   SDO/NCO-278-4500

Andrews Air Force Base (MD02R1)
Andrews AFB, MD 20331-5000

TELEPHONE NUMBER INFORMATION: Main installation numbers: Comm: 301-981-1110, ATVN: 858-1110.

Temporary Military Lodging Around the World — 97

MARYLAND

Andrews Air Force Base, continued

Location: From I-95 (east portion of Capital Beltway, I-495) north or south, exit 9, first traffic light after leaving exit ramp turn right into main gate of AFB. Also, from I-395 north, exit South Capitol St, cross Anacostia River on So Capitol St, bear left to Suitland Parkway east, exit Parkway at Morningside on Suitland Rd east to main gate of AFB. Clearly marked. RM: p-42, J/11. NMC: Washington, DC 6 miles northwest.

Billeting Office: ATTN: 1776 SVS/SVH, Building 1375, Arkansas Rd. EX-4614/24. 24 hours daily. Check in billeting, check out 1200 hours daily. Government civilian employee billeting. No walk-in reservations taken.

TLM: TLF. Buildings 1801-1804, 1328, 1330. All ranks. Leave or official duty. 60 separate bedrooms, private bath; 8/2-bedroom, private bath. Kitchen, limited utensils, A/C, color TV, maid service, free cribs, free washer/dryer, ice vending. Modern structure. Rates: $18.00 1-bedroom, $24.00 2-bedroom. Maximum 5 per room. Duty can make reservation. Others Space-A.

TML: DV/VIP. Building 1349. Officer 06+. Leave or official duty. 41/1-bedroom & 15/2-bedroom suites, private bath. Kitchen, A/C, color TV, maid service, free washer/dryer. Older structure. Rates: $8.00 per person. Duty can make reservations. Others Space-A.

TML: Other. 128 VOQ units; 56 VAQ units; 5 chief units (EX-2606/7). Reservations required for duty personnel. Rates: $8.00 per person.

DV/VIP: Protocol, 76 ALB/CCP. EX-4525. 07+. Retirees Space-A.

Other: Aerial gateway to Washington, DC. Home of "Air Force One", the President's aircraft.

TML Availability: Best, Dec. Difficult, Jun-Aug.

Cafeteria-568-2381
NCO Club-568-3100
Snack Bar-568-0180

Locator-981-6161
O'Club-420-4744
SDO/NCO-981-5058

Medical-981-2333
Police-981-2000/01

Bethesda National Naval Medical Center (MD06R1)
8901 Wisconsin Avenue
Bethesda, MD 20889-5000

TELEPHONE NUMBER INFORMATION: Main installation numbers: Comm: 301-295-5385/2075, ATVN: 295-5960/2075.

Location: From I-495 (Capital Beltway) take exit 25, Wisconsin Ave (Md-335, Rockville Pike) south for 1 mile to Naval Medical Center on left. Enter first gate, Wilson Dr, for support facility. Also, can enter the center from Jones Bridge Rd off Wisconsin Ave. RM: p-42, F/7. NMC: Washington, DC 1 mile southeast.

Billeting Office: ATTN: Manager, Housing Referral Office, Building 8. Comm: 295-1138. 0800-1630 hours daily. Check in facility, check out 1200 hours daily. No government civilian employee billeting.

TML: Navy Lodge, Building 52. All ranks. Leave or official duty. For reservations call 1-800-NAVY-INN. Lodge number is 654-1795. 0800-2200 hours daily. Only for family members of in-patients. 22/1-bedroom, private bath. Kitchen, A/C, color TV room & lounge, maid service, free cribs, coin washer/dryer, ice vending. Modern structure. Rates: $30.00 per unit. Maximum 5 per unit. Guest must live in excess of 50 miles from hospital. Family members of in-patients can make reservations.

MARYLAND
Bethesda National Naval Medical Center, continued

TML: BOQ. Building 11. Officer all grades. Official duty. Reservations required. EX-1111. 89/1-bedroom, latrine bath; 4 separate bedrooms, kitchen, private bath (DV/VIP). Refrigerator, community kitchen, utensils, A/C, color TV lounge, maid service, free cots, free washer/dryer, ice vending. Older structure. Rates: $4.00 per person, $8.00 DV/VIP. Maximum 2 per room. Quarters are inadequate & substandard.

DV/VIP: Cmdr, NAVMEDCOM NATCAPREG, Building 1, Room 5156A. EX-5800. 06+ Retirees Space-A.

TML Availability: Very limited.

Cafeteria-295-5349	Enlisted Club-652-0256	Locator-295-5385
Medical-666	NCO Club-652-0256	O'Club-652-6318
Police-295-1246	Snack Bar-530-8068	SDO/NCO-295-4611
SNCO-295-5960		

Curtis Bay Coast Guard Yard (MD01R1)
Curtis Bay, MD 21226-1797

TELEPHONE NUMBER INFORMATION: Main installation numbers: Comm: 301-789-1600, ATVN: None, FTS: 922-6000.

Location: Take I-695 to exit 1, bear to your right, right on Hawkins Point Rd, left into Coast Guard Yard. RM: p-41, P/5. NMC: Baltimore, 5 miles northwest.

Billeting Office: No central billeting office. ATTN: BOQ Manager. Building 28A (BOQ), Comm: 636-7356. Building 33 (Transient Family Lodging), Comm: 636-4194. 0700-2300 M-F. After duty hours, OOD, Building 33, Ex-7356 (if reservations already made). Check in facility, check out 1000 hours daily. No government civilian employee billeting.

TML: TFL. Building 84. All ranks. Leave or official duty. Accessible to handicapped. 5/3-bedroom suites, private bath. Kitchen, complete utensils, A/C, color TV, free cribs, free washer/dryer, playground. Older structure. Rates: 1 bedroom $12.00, 2 bedroom $16.00. 2 bedroom units can be combined into 3 bedroom units for $20.00. Maximum 8 per family. All categories except widows and unaccompanied dependents can make reservations. PCS in/out have priority.

TML: BOQ. Building 28A. Officer all grades. Official duty only. Reservations required. EX-439. 0830-1500. After duty hours, OOD, Building 33, EX-488. 5/1-bedroom, 2 beds, private bath. A/C, color TV lounge, microwave, refrigerator, pool table and VCR in lounge, free washer/dryer. Modern structure. Rates: Sponsor $5.00. Maximum 2 persons per unit.

TML Availability: Good, Oct-Apr. More difficult, other times.

CPO Club-EX-7383	Enlisted Club-EX-7383	Locator-EX-4147
Medical-EX-3144	Police-EX-7476	SDO/NCO-EX-7356
NCO Club-EX-7382	O'Club-EX-7382	

Temporary Military Lodging Around the World — 99

MARYLAND

Fort Detrick (MD07R1)
Frederick, MD 21701-5000

TELEPHONE NUMBER INFORMATION: Main installation numbers: Comm: 301-663-8000, ATVN: 343-1110.

Location: From Washington, DC, take I-270 north to US-15 north. From Baltimore, take I-70 west to US-15 north. From US-15 north, in Frederick, exit Seventh St. Clearly marked to Post. RM: p-41, D/13. NMC: Baltimore, 50 miles east and Washington, DC, 50 miles southeast.

Billeting Office: Building 901, Sultan St & Doughten Dr. EX-2154. 0745-1630 hours M-F. Check out 1000 hours daily. No government civilian employee billeting.

TML: Guest House. Buildings 800-802. All ranks. Leave or official duty. 1/2-bedroom, private bath; 5/3-bedroom, private bath. Kitchen, limited utensils, A/C, color TV, free cribs/cots, free washer/dryer. Older structure. New carpet '87. Rates: $24.00 per room. PCS can make reservations. Others Space-A.

TML: VOQ. Building 660. Officer all grades. Leave or official duty. 1-bedroom suites, private bath. Kitchen, limited utensils, A/C, color TV, maid service, free washer/dryer, soda machine, pay telephone. Older structure, remodeled. Rates: $13.00 per room. TDY can make reservations. Others Space-A.

TML: DVQ. Building 715. Officer all grades. Leave or official duty. 1 suite, private bath. Kitchen, limited utensils, A/C, color TV, maid service. Older structure, remodeled '86. Rates: $18.00 per night. TDY can make reservations. Others Space-A.

DV/VIP: Hq Ft Detrick EX-7114. 06+. Retirees and lower grades Space-A.

Other: Historic sites, near ski resorts and Fort Ritchie.

TML Availability: Good, Oct-Mar. Difficult, Jun-Aug.

Cafeteria-662-9653	Enlisted Club-662-9653	Locator-663-2061
Medical-663-2200	NCO Club-662-9653	Police-663-7114
SDO/NCO-663-7114		

Fort George G. Meade (MD08R1)
Fort George G. Meade, MD 20755-5115

TELEPHONE NUMBER INFORMATION: Main installation numbers: Comm: 301-677-6261, ATVN: 923-6261.

Location: Off Baltimore-Washington Parkway, I-295, exit MD-198 east which is Fort Meade Rd. Clearly marked. RM: p-42, C/12. NMC: Baltimore and Washington, DC, 30 miles from each city.

Billeting Office: ATTN: AFKA-ZI-EH-HB, Building 4707, Brett Hall, Ruffner Rd. EX-6529/5884. 24 hours daily. Check in billeting, check out 1200 hours daily. Government civilian employee billeting.

TML: Guest House. Building 2793, Abrams Hall. All ranks. Leave or official duty. Accessible to handicapped. Reservations accepted from PCS only. EX-2045. Check in 24 hours daily. 54 rooms with 2 beds, private bath. 11/2-bedroom, private bath. Refrigerator, community kitchen, A/C, essentials, color TV room & lounge, maid service, free cribs/cots, washer/dryer, food/ice vending, cable TV, in-room telephone, microwaves. Older structure. Completely renovated '89. Rates: PCS in/out $17.00 per room, others $22.50. Maximum charge PCS $20.00, others $26.50. Maximum 5

MARYLAND
Fort George G. Meade, continued

persons per unit. Duty can make reservations. Others Space-A. **Pets are allowed if customer is blind.**

TML: VOQ. Buildings 4703, 4704, 4707, 4709. Officer all grades. Leave or official duty. 142/1-bedroom, semi-private bath; 4/1-bedroom, private bath; 16 separate bedroom suites, private bath. Kitchen (8 units), refrigerator, A/C, color cable TV, maid service, free washer/dryer, ice vending. Older structures. Bathrooms renovated '88-'89. Rates: $22.50 per room. Maximum 1 per room. TDY can make reservations. Others Space-A.

TML: SEBQ. Building 4705. Enlisted E7-E9. Official duty only. 30 separate bedroom, private bath. Modern structure. Rates: No charge. For Senior Noncommissioned Officers PCS to Ft. Meade only.

TML: BOQ. Buildings 4717, 4720, 4721. Officer all grades. Official duty only. 62 separate bedrooms, private bath. Modern structure. Rates: No charge. PCS to Ft. Meade only.

TML: DVQ. Building 4415. Officer 05+. Leave or official duty. Check in 0800-1600. After hours SDO, Building 4420. 5 separate bedrooms, private bath; 2/2-bedroom, private bath. Kitchen, limited utensils, A/C, color TV, maid service, free cots, washer/dryer. Older structure. Rates: $15.00-$26.50 per room. No maximum capacity. Duty can make reservations. Others Space-A.

DV/VIP: 1st U.S. Army/SGS, Pershing Hall, Building 4550, EX-3420. 05+ and GS-14+. Retirees Space-A.

TML Availability: Good. Best months, Oct-Mar.

Enlisted Club-677-3983	Loc:677-AR-4547;NA-6354;MC-3233;AF-3295	
Medical-677-2570	NCO Club-677-3983	O'Club-677-5358
Police-677-6622	SDO/NCO-677-4805	

Fort Ritchie (MD13R1)
Fort Ritchie, MD 21719-5010

TELEPHONE NUMBER INFORMATION: Main installation numbers: Comm: 301-878-1300, ATVN: 988-1300.

Location: From US-15 north exit at Thurmont, to MD-550 north for 7 miles to Cascade and main gate. Also, from Hagerstown, take MD-64 east to MD-491 north to MD-550 north to Cascade and main gate. RM: p-41, B/12. NMC: Hagerstown, 16 miles southwest, Baltimore, 50 miles southeast, Washington, DC, 55 miles southeast.

Billeting Office: Building 520, West Banfill & Cushman. Comm: 241-4445 or 878-5171. ATVN: 277-5171. 0800-1845 M-F, 0800-1645 Sa-Su, holidays. Other hours, SDO in basement of Building 200. Check in facility, check out before 1130 hours daily. Government civilian employee billeting.

TML: Guest House. Building 520. All ranks. Leave or official duty. 21/ 1-bedroom, private bath. Kitchen (9 units), refrigerator (12 units), complete utensils, color TV, maid service, free cribs/cots, coin washer/dryer, ice vending. Modern structure. Rates: PCS without kitchen $12.00, with kitchen $14.00; TDY $20.00; visitors without kitchen $17.00, with kitchen $20.00. Maximum 5 per room. PCS can make reservations. Others Space-A.

Temporary Military Lodging Around the World — 101

Fort Ritchie, continued MARYLAND

TML: VOQ/VEQ. Building 800. Officer all grades. Enlisted E7-E9. Leave or official duty. 10/1-bedroom, private bath (VOQ); 1/1-bedroom, private bath (VEQ); 1/1-bedroom suite, private bath (DVQ). Refrigerator, community kitchen, color TV room & lounge, maid service, free washer/dryer. Rates: VOQ/VEQ $12.00, $2.00 each additional person; DVQ $20.00, $3.00 each additional person. TDY can make reservations. Others Space-A.

DV/VIP: HQ 7th SIG, Building 307. EX-5754. 06+. Retirees Space-A.

Other: Beautiful small post. Great location for ski resorts in the area. NSF Thurmont nearby.

TML Availability: Good, most of the year. Best, Mar-Jun.

Locator-878-5685   Medical-878-4132   O'Club-878-4361
Police-878-4228   Snack Bar-878-4192   SDO/NCO-878-5626

Indian Head Naval Ordnance Station (MD04R1)
Indian Head, MD 20640-5000

TELEPHONE NUMBER INFORMATION: Main installation numbers: Comm: 301-743-4000, ATVN: 364-4000.

Location: Take I-495 (Capital Beltway) east, exit to MD-210 south for 25 miles to station. RM; p-41, J/14. NMC: Washington, DC 25 miles north.

Billeting Office: None.

TML: BOQ. Building 969. All ranks. Leave or official duty. EX-5543. Open 24 hours. 52 officer/enlisted rooms, semi-private baths. Most are 2 bedroom. Kitchen, limited utensils, A/C, color TV lounge, maid service, free washer/dryer, food vending. Older structure, renovated '86. Rates: $4.00 permanent/students, $6.00 transient. Duty can make reservations. Others Space-A.

TML: BEQ. Building 902. All ranks. Leave or official duty. EX-4845. Open 24 hours. 108 rooms with 2 beds, semi-private bath. A/C, color TV lounge, maid service, free washer/dryer, food vending. Rates: $4.00 per day. Duty can make reservations. Others Space-A.

DV/VIP: PAO. Building 20, EX-4627. Inquire about qualifying grade. Retirees Space-A.

TML Availability: Fair, Jan-May, Sept-Dec. Difficult, other times.

Enlisted Club-743-4648   Locator-743-4303   Medical-743-4601
O'Club-743-4557   Police-743-4381   SDO/NCO-743-4438
CPO Club-743-4648

Patuxent River Naval Air Station (MD09R1)
Patuxent River, MD 20670-5000

TELEPHONE NUMBER INFORMATION: Main installation numbers: Comm: 301-863-3000, ATVN: 326-0111 or 326-1000.

Location: From I-95 (east portion of Capital Beltway, I-495) exit 7A to Branch Ave (MD-5) south. Follow MD-5 until it turns into MD-235 near Oraville, on to Lexington Park, and the NAS. Main gate is on MD-235 and MD-246 (Cedar Point Rd). RM: p-41, L/18. NMC: Washington, DC, 65 miles west.

MARYLAND
Patuxent River Naval Air Station, continued

Billeting Office: No central billeting office. Check in facility, check out 1200 hours daily. No government civilian employee billeting.

TML: Navy Lodge. Building 2119. For reservations call 1-800-NAVY-INN. Lodge number is Comm: 737-2400. 50 units, private bath. A/C, cots/cribs, ice vending, kitchen, maid service, color TV, utensils, washer/dryer. Rates: $35.00 per unit. Maximum 2 adults. All categories can make reservations.

TML: BOQ. Building 406. Officer all grades. Leave or official duty. Reservations only from persons on TAD orders. EX-3601. 45 rooms/suites, private, semi-private baths. Refrigerator, A/C, color TV, maid service, cots, free washer/dryer, ice vending, telephone. Rates: $6.00 per person, child up to 12 free.

TML: DV/VIP. EX-7503. 3/1-bedroom, king-size bed suites, dining room, living room, private bath, kitchen.

TML: DV/VIP. Crowe's Nest (located at Officers' Club). 1 suite, private bath. For reservations contact Cmdr, ATTN: Code CT001. EX-3601. O6+.

DV/VIP: PAO. EX-7503. 07+. Retirees Space-A.

Other: Excellent outdoor recreational facility.

TML Availability: Fairly good, winter. More difficult, Jun-Aug.

Enlisted Club-863-3643   Locator-863-1036   Medical-863-3353
O'Club-863-3656   Police-863-3911   SDO/NCO-863-1097
CPO Club-863-3685

Solomons Navy Recreation Center (MD05R1)
Solomons, MD 20688-0147

TELEPHONE NUMBER INFORMATION: Main installation numbers: Comm: 301-356-3566, DC area 261-2816.

Location: Off base, on Patuxent River. From US-301, take MD-4 southeast to Solomons; or take MD-5 southeast to MD-235, then MD-4 northeast to Solomons. RM: p-41, L/18. NMC: Washington, DC, 65 miles northwest.

Billeting Office: Building 411. 0800-2200 Sat-Thurs, May 1 to Oct 15. 0800-2400, 0800-2200 Fri. and 0800-2000 Sat-Thurs, Oct 16 to April 30. Late check-in if arranged in advance. All ranks. Leave or official duty. Check in billeting, check out 1200 hours daily.

TML: Units are bungalows, apartments & cottages. 4/1-bedroom, private bath; 6/2-bedroom, private bath; 14/3-bedroom, private bath; 13/4- &2/5-bedroom, private bath. Kitchen, limited utensils, A/C, color TV lounge (Building 6), pay cribs/cots, coin washer/dryer, food/ice vending. Older structure. Rates: 1 bedroom, E1-E5 $10.00, E6-E9 $15.00, Officer $21.00; 2 bedroom, E1-E5 $12.00, E6-E9 $17.00, Officer $23.00; 3 bedroom, E1-E5 $14.00, E6-E9 $19.00, Officer $25.00; 4 bedroom, E1-E5 $16.00, E6-E9 $21.00, Officer $27.00; 5 bedroom, E1-E5 $18.00, E6-E9 $23.00, Officer $29.00. Maximum 3 persons per bedroom. All categories except unaccompanied dependents can make reservations. Call for information about when reservations will be accepted for summer months.

Other: Complete river recreational area. Full support facility available at nearby Paxtuxent River NAS. For complete details see Military RV, Camping & Rec Areas Around The World. St. Maries City, Calvert Cliffs, Calvert Marine Museum, Farmers' Market, charter fishing, Point Lookout State Park.

Temporary Military Lodging Around the World — 103

MARYLAND

Solomons Navy Recreation Center, continued

TML Availability: Good, Oct-Apr. Difficult, other times.

SDO/NCO-356-3566   Police-326-2436

United States Naval Academy/ Annapolis Naval Station (MD10R1)
Annapolis, MD 21402-5054

TELEPHONE NUMBER INFORMATION: Main installation numbers: Comm: 301-267-6100, ATVN: 281-0111, FTS: 930-0111.

Location: Two miles off US-50/301. Two exits to Academy clearly marked. Main gate on King George St in Annapolis. Naval Station is across Severn River off US-50/301 east, first exit. Clearly marked. RM: p-41, I/6. NMC: Annapolis, in city.

Billeting Office: No billeting office. Contact Officers' Club, EX-3906. 0730-1600 hours daily. Check in/out at Officers' Club. Government civilian employee billeting.

TML: Officers' Club. Third deck of O'Club. Officer all grades. Leave or official duty. Most rooms are for permanent residents; Space-A only between occupancies. 1 VIP suite, private bath, with kitchen (07+); 1 transient suite, private bath. Refrigerator, coffee bar (06-); 16 separate bedroom, private bath (permanent resident or Space-A). A/C, color TV, maid service, free washer/dryer. Older historic structure, remodeled. Rates: VIP suite, sponsor $10.00, accompanied $16.00; transient suite, sponsor $6.00, accompanied $12.00; permanent resident room, sponsor $4.00, accompanied $10.00. Duty can make reservations. Other Space-A.

TML: BOQ/BEQ. Building 2. All ranks. Leave or official duty. Comm: 267-3972. 2/1-bedroom, private bath; 5 separate bedroom, private bath. Refrigerator, community kitchen, complete utensils, A/C, TV, maid service, free cots, free washer/dryer. Older structure, renovated. Rates: $6.00 single, $10.00 double. All categories can make reservations.

DV/VIP: Superintendents Building. EX-2403. 07+. Retirees Space-A.

TML Availability: Best, Sep-Apr. Difficult, summer months.

Cafeteria-757-0005   CPO Club-267-3660   Enlisted Club-267-3660
Locator-267-2385   Medical-267-2535/2061 O'Club-263-8280
Police-267-2886/2887 SDO/NCO-267-3972

MASSACHUSETTS

Cape Cod Coast Guard Air Station (MA10R1)
Otis ANGB, MA 02542-5000

TELEPHONE NUMBER INFORMATION: Main installation numbers: Comm: 508-968-1000, ATVN: 557-1000, FTS: 829-1000.

Location: Take MA Military Reservation exit off MA-28, south on Connley Ave approximately 2 miles to Bourne Gate. RM: p-45, M/22. NMC: Boston, 50 miles northwest.

Billeting Office: ATTN: Temporary Quarters, Building 5204. EX-5461. 0800-1600 hours M-F. 1200-1600 hours Sat & Sun. Check in billeting. Check out 1100 hours.

MASSACHUSETTS
Cape Cod Coast Guard Air Station, continued

TML: TLF/BOQ. All ranks. Leave or official duty. Accessible to handicapped. Advance payment required. 4 units with kitchen, private bath; 4/2-bedroom townhouses, private bath; 3/1-bedroom, private bath (BOQ); 16/1-bedroom efficiency apartments, private bath. Free cots/cribs, essentials, food vending, maid service, refrigerator, color TV lounge & room, utensils, coin washer/dryer, small child's playroom. Older structure. Some units have new carpets '89. Remodeled '89. Rates: Moderate, determined by rank. Reservations: PCS 90 days in advance, TDY 60 days in advance, others 30 days. In summer vacationers 2 weeks in advance.

Other: Otis has 9-hole golf course and driving range. Newport mansions, beaches, Martha's Vineyard, Nantucket Islands nearby.

TML Availability: Good. Best Oct-Apr.

Medical-968-5570   Police-968-5208   Enlisted Club-968-5929
Snack Bar-968-5454

Fort Devens (MA09R1)
Fort Devens, MA 01433-5000

TELEPHONE NUMBER INFORMATION: Main installation numbers: Comm: 508-796-3911, ATVN: 256-3911.

Location: From Boston follow MA-2 west and exit at Fort Devens, about 5 miles west of I-495. In Ayer. RM: p-45, D/14. NMC: Boston, 35 miles southeast.

Billeting Office: ATTN: AFZD-DEH-B, Bldg P-22, Sherman Ave. EX-3353. 0500-2400 hours daily. Other hours, Duty Officer, Building P-1, EX-3711. Check in billeting, check out 1100 hours daily. Government civilian employee billeting.

TML: Guest House. Buildings T-3595-3597, T-150. All ranks. Leave or official duty. 24 separate bedrooms, private bath; 12 separate bedrooms, semi-private bath. Refrigerator, color TV, maid service, free cribs/cots, free washer/dryer. Older structure. Rates: E1-E5 $13.00; E6-E8, W1, 01-02 $17.00; E9, W2-W4, 03-04 $20.00; 05-010 $22.00. Duty can make reservations. Others Space-A.

TML: VEQ. Building P-22, Washington Hall. All ranks. Leave or official duty. 55 single rooms, semi-private bath; 4 suites. Adequate facilities. Rates: $12.00 single rooms, $15.00 suites. All categories can make reservations.

TML: VOQ. Building P-19, Rogers Hall. WO1+. Leave or official duty. 14 rooms; 6 suites. 12 rooms have kitchen. Adequate facilities. Rates: $18.00 rooms with kitchen, $16.00 rooms without kitchen; $18.00 suites 2 & 8; $20.00 suites 1, 10, 11, 12, $5.00 each additional person. Maximum $30.00 per family. All categories can make reservations.

TML: DVQ. Building 314, Prescott House. 06+. Leave or official duty. 6 suites, private bath. Adequate facilities. Rates: Sponsor $22.00, each additional person $5.00. Maximum $32.00 per family. Per diem occupants $22.00. Reservations accepted through Protocol.

DV/VIP: Protocol Office, Building P-1, EX-3711. 05+. Retirees Space-A

Other: Historic towns, Groton, Concord & Lexington.

TML Availability: Good, Dec-Mar. Difficult, summer.

Temporary Military Lodging Around the World — 105

MASSACHUSETTS

Fort Devens, continued

Cafeteria-772-4828
Medical-796-6816
Police-796-3333

Enlisted Club-796-2119
NCO Club-796-2535
Snack Bar-772-5955

Locator-796-7954/2748
O'Club-796-2149

Fourth Cliff Recreation Area (MA02R1)
Hanscom Air Force Base, MA 01731-5000

TELEPHONE NUMBER INFORMATION: Main installation numbers: Comm: 617-377-4441, ATVN: 478-4441.

LOCATION: Off base. I-95 or I-93 to MA-3, approximately 30 miles south of Boston; south to exit 12; MA-139 east to Marshfield. 1.5 miles to Furnace St; turn left. Continue to "T" intersection; turn left on Ferry St. Stay on Ferry St to Sea St; right over South River Bridge; left on Central Ave and proceed to gate. Check in at Building 7. RM: p-45, H/20. NMI: South Weymouth NAS, 15 miles northwest. NMC: Boston, 30 miles north.

Billeting Office: None. Reservations are required with payment in full (ask for map). Address: Fourth Cliff Recreation Area, PO Box O, Humarock, MA 02047. Comm: 617-837-9269 (0800-1630 M-F) or 1-800-468-9547. Rec area operates Memorial Day through Columbus Day. 13 cabins operate year round.

TML: 18 1-3 bedroom cabins. All ranks. Leave or official duty. Rates: $30.00-$65.00 daily. All categories can make reservations. **Pets not allowed in cabins but may be leashed in other areas.**

TML Availability: Limited. Book early.

Hanscom Air Force Base (MA06R1)
Hanscom AFB, MA 01731-5000

TELEPHONE NUMBER INFORMATION: Main installation numbers: Comm: 617-377-4441, ATVN: 478-4441.

Location: From I-95 north take exit 31A, MA-2A west for 2 miles to right on Hartwell Rd which bisects the AFB. RM: p-43, E/2. NMC: Boston, 17 miles southeast.

Billeting Office: Building 1427, EX-2112. 24 hours daily. Check in facility, check out 1200 hours daily. Government civilian employee billeting.

TML: TLF. Building 1423. Officer all grades. Leave or official duty. EX-2044. Accessible to handicapped. 30/1-bedroom, sofa bed, pullout lounge chair, private bath. Kitchen, complete utensils, A/C, maid service, free cribs, free washer/dryer. Modern structure. Rates: $16.00 per unit. TLF is used for PCS in/out only. 30 days PCS in, 7 days PSC out. Also VOQ for TDY personnel only. Call for details.

DV/VIP: Protocol Office, Building 1606, EX-5151. O6/GS-15+. Retirees Space-A.

TML Availability: Difficult. Best in Oct, Nov, Feb, Mar.

Cafeteria-377-2189
NCO Club-377-2123
Snack Bar-377-5258

Locator-377-5111
O'Club-377-3799
SDO/NCO-377-5144

Medical-377-2333
Police-377-2315

106 — *Temporary Military Lodging Around the World*

MASSACHUSETTS

South Weymouth Naval Air Station (MA05R1)
South Weymouth NAS, MA 02190-5000

TELEPHONE NUMBER INFORMATION: Main installation numbers: Comm: 617-786-2500, ATVN: 478-5980.

Location: From MA-3 (Pilgrims Highway) exit 16 to MA-18 (Main St). Base is approximately two miles ahead. Main gate is on left side of MA-18. RM: p-45, H/19. NMC: Boston, 15 miles northwest.

Billeting Office: Building 31, Shea Memorial Dr. EX-2928. 24 hours daily. Check in facility, check out 1000 hours daily. Government civilian employee billeting (limited).

TML: TLQ. Building 31. All ranks. Leave or official duty for Officer. Official duty only for Enlisted. 3 separate bedroom suites, latrine bath (Officer); 2/2-bedroom apartments, latrine bath (Enlisted). Kitchen (Enlisted), refrigerator (suites), complete utensils, color TV, maid service (Officer), free cribs, free washer/dryer, ice vending. Older structure. Rates: $4.00 per person. Maximum 4 per room. Enlisted must be on PCS orders to S. Weymouth. Duty can make reservations. Others Space-A.

DV/VIP: Executive Officer Secretary, Administration Building. EX-2601. 06+. Retirees Space-A.

Other: Historic Quincy near by.

TML Availability: Extremely limited.

Enlisted Club-786-2898   Medical-786-2674   SDO/NCO-786-2933
O'Club-786-2938/2932   Police-786-2610   Snack Bar-786-2980

Westover Air Force Base (MA03R1)
Westover AFB, MA 01022-5000

TELEPHONE NUMBER INFORMATION: Main installation numbers: Comm: 413-557-1110, ATVN: 589-1110.

Location: Take exit 5 off I-90 (MA Turnpike) in Chicopee. Westover is on MA-33, north of I-90. Signs mark way to Base. RM: p-45, H/7. NMC: Springfield, 8 miles south.

Billeting Office: Building 2200, Outer Drive. VOQ/TAQ: Comm: 413-593-5421, EX-3006, ATVN: 589-2695/3032, EX-3006 weekends only. Check in billeting, check out 1200 hours daily. Government civilian employee billeting.

TML: VOQ. Buildings 2200, 2201. Officer. All ranks. Leave or official duty. 10/1-bedroom, semi-private bath; 29/2-bedroom suites, semi-private bath. A/C, essentials, color TV lounge & room, maid service, free washer/dryer, ice vending. Older structure. New A/C '89. Rates: $6.00 per person, under 12 free. Maximum 4 persons. Maximum depends on number per family. Duty can make reservations. Others Space-A.

TML: TAQ. Buildings 5101-5105. Enlisted. E-1 thru E-7. Leave or official duty. 400 rooms. Food/ice vending, maid service, refrigerator, color TV, free washer/dryer. Older structure. Rates: $6.00 per person. Maximum 2 persons. Duty and retirees can make reservations.

DV/VIP: Building 2200. Comm: 593-5421. 05+ or unit commander. Retirees and lower grades Space-A.

Westover Air Force Base, continued

MASSACHUSETTS

TML Availability: Good, except Jun-Sep.

Medical-557-3565
Snack Bar-557-3990
NCO Club-593-5531
SDO/NCO-557-3571
Police-557-3557

MICHIGAN

Camp Grayling (MI10R2)
Grayling, MI 49738-0001

TELEPHONE NUMBER INFORMATION: Main installation numbers: Comm: 517-348-8200, ATVN: 722-8200.

Location: On I-75 take Grayling exit. Camp Grayling is 4 miles west of Grayling. RM: p-46, M/10. NMC: Traverse City, 60 miles west.

Billeting Office: Officers' Club, Comm: 517-348-9033, ATVN: 722-8621 EX-3225. Building 311. 0900-1600 hours. Check out 1000 hours.

TML: Lakefront Cottages and Mobile Homes. Buildings 177-182. Officer. All ranks. Leave or official duty. Accessible to handicapped. 4 cottages and 2 mobile homes. 6/2-bedroom, private bath. Kitchen, complete utensils, maid service. Modern structure. Renovated '88. New carpets '89. Rates: Cottages $25.00, Mobile Homes $20.00. Maximum 6 persons. Duty can make reservations. Others Space-A.

TML: VOQ. Building 311. Officer. All ranks. Leave or official duty. 10 rooms with 2 beds, hall bath. Maid service, color TV lounge. Older structure. New carpets '89. Rates: $6.00 per person. Maximum 4 persons. Duty, retirees, disabled American veterans, and accompanied dependents of duty persons can make reservations. Others Space-A.

TML Availability: Good. Closed Nov-Mar.

K.I. Sawyer Air Force Base (MI02R2)
K.I. Sawyer AFB, MI 49843-5000

TELEPHONE NUMBER INFORMATION: Main installation numbers: Comm: 906-346-1110, ATVN: 472-1110.

Location: In the MI upper peninsula. From US-41 south of Marquette, take MI-460 west to gate 2. RM: p-47 F/2. NMC: Marquette, 23 miles northwest.

Billeting Office: Building 801, A St. EX-2145. 24 hours daily. Check in facility, check out 1200 hours daily. Government civilian employee billeting.

TML: VAQ. Building 801. Enlisted all grades. Leave or official duty. 36 rooms with 2 beds, semi-private bath. 2 separate bedrooms, semi-private bath. 2/1-bedroom, private bath. Refrigerator, essentials, color TV room & lounge, maid service, free washer/dryer, ice vending, microwave. Older structure, renovated '86. Rates $5.00 per person. Maximum 2 per room. Duty, widows, retirees, unaccompanied dependents can make reservations. Others Space-A.

TML VOQ. Building 802, 806. Officer 02-05. Leave or official duty. 4/1-bedroom suites, private bath; 20 separate bedrooms, semi-private bath; 2/4-bedroom, semi-private bath. Kitchen, color TV, maid service, washer/dryer, ice vending. Older

MICHIGAN
K.I. Sawyer Air Force Base, continued

structure, renovated. Rates: $7.00 per unit. Duty can make reservations. Others Space-A.

TML: TLF. Buildings 1200-1203, 1244-1245. All ranks. Leave or official duty. 20/1-bedroom, private bath. 3/2-bedroom, private bath. 12/3-bedroom, private bath. Free cribs/cots, essentials, ice vending, kitchen, complete utensils, maid service, special facilities for disabled American veterans, color TV, free washer/dryer. Older structures. Renovation '90. Rates: $15-$20.00 per family. All categories except duty Reservists and National Guard personnel can make reservations.

TML: DV/VIP House. Building 807. Officer O6+. Leave or official duty. 2 bedroom, private bath. Kitchen, color TV, maid service, free washer/dryer. Older structure. Rates: $10.00 per person. Duty can make reservations. Others Space-A.

DV/VIP: PAO, Building 807/8. EX-2763. O6+. Retirees and lower grades Space-A.

TML Availability: Fairly good, fall, winter. Difficult, summer.

Cafeteria-346-2513
Medical-346-2233
Police-346-2131
Enlisted Club-346-9273
NCO Club-346-9273
Snack Bar-346-3518
Locator-346-2605
O'Club-346-2480

Selfridge Air National Guard Base (MI01R2)
Selfridge ANG Base, MI 48045-5004

TELEPHONE NUMBER INFORMATION: Main installation numbers: Comm: 313-466-4011, ATVN: 273-4011.

Location: Take I-94 north from Detroit, to Selfridge exit, then east on MI-59 to main gate of Base. RM: p-48, D/12. NMC: Detroit, 25 miles southwest.

Billeting Office: Building 410, ATTN: AMSTA-CYACH, George Ave. Operated by U.S. Army MWR. 0630-2300 hours daily. EX-4062. Check in billeting, check out 1200 hours daily. Government civilian employee billeting.

TML: Guest House. Building 916. All ranks. Leave or official duty. 7/2-bedroom, living room, dining room, private bath; 8/1-bedroom, living room, dining room, private bath. Kitchen, complete utensils, color TV, cribs, washer/dryer. Older structure. Rates: $14.00 1 bedroom, $17.00 2 bedroom. Maximum 3 in 1 bedroom, 5 in 2 bedroom. Duty can make reservations. Others Space-A. **Pets OK, $3.00 per day.**

TML: VOQ/VEQ. Building 410. All ranks. Leave or official duty. 23 separate bedrooms, private bath. Community kitchen, color TV, maid service, food/ice vending, free washer/dryer. Older structure. Renovations and remodeling completed Oct '89. Rates for leave status: Sponsor $19.00, adult $7.00, under 18 free. Rates for duty status: Sponsor $21.50, adult $7.00, under 18 free. Rates for 2 bedroom VIP suites: $32.00-$37.00 up to four persons. Duty can make reservations. Others Space-A.

TML: DV/VIP. Suites. Controlled by base IO, Building 304, Room 101. EX-5576/4735. O6+. Retirees and lower grades Space-A.

TML Availability: Fairly good.

Cafeteria-469-3660
O'Club-468-0879
Medical-466-4650
Police-466-4673
NCO Club-465-5321
SDO/NCO-466-4011

Temporary Military Lodging Around the World — 109

MICHIGAN

Wurtsmith Air Force Base (MI03R2)
Wurtsmith AFB, MI 48753-5360

TELEPHONE NUMBER INFORMATION: Main installation numbers: Comm: 517-739-2011, ATVN: 623-1110.

Location: Off US-23, 2 miles northwest of Oscoda. On F-41. Clearly marked. RM: p-47, N/14. NMC: Bay City, 65 miles southwest.

Billeting Office: Building 1600, Skeel Ave. EX-6033/6692. 24 hours daily. Check in billeting, check out 1200 hours daily. Government civilian employee billeting.

TML: TLF. Building 1750. All ranks. Leave or official duty. 3/2-bedroom, private bath; 4/3-bedroom, private bath; 6/4-bedroom, private bath. Kitchen, complete utensils, color TV, maid service, free cribs, washer/dryer. Older structure, remodeled. Rates: $20.00 per unit. Duty can make reservations. Others Space-A.

TML: VAQ. Building 1600. All ranks. Leave or official duty. 16/1-bedroom, 2 beds, semi-private bath. Refrigerator, color TV room & lounge, maid service, free washer/dryer, ice vending, facilities for disabled American veterans, microwave in lounge. Older structure, renovated. Rates: $4.50 per person. Maximum $9.00 per family. Children not authorized. Duty can make reservations. Others Space-A.

TML: VOQ. Building 1602. All ranks. Leave or official duty. 16/1-bedroom, semi-private bath; 2 separate bedrooms, private bath. Kitchen, color TV, maid service, free washer/dryer, facilities for disabled American veterans. Older structure, renovated. Rates: $7.00 per person. Maximum $14.00. Maximum 2 per room. Children not authorized. Duty can make reservations. Others Space-A.

TML: DV/VIP. Buildings 1600, 1602. Officer 06+, Enlisted E8-E9. Leave or official duty. 4 separate bedroom suites, private bath. Kitchen, complete utensils, color TV, maid service, ice vending, facilities for disabled American veterans. Older structure, renovated. Rates: $10.00 per person. Maximum 2 per room. Children not authorized. Duty can make reservations. Others Space-A.

DV/VIP: Protocol Office, Building 5006. EX-6416. 06/GS-15+. Retirees Space-A.

Other: Vacationer's paradise. Lake Huron, Van Etten Lake, and historic Au Sable River for swimming, boating and excellent fishing. Ice fishing and snowmobile trails.

TML Availability: Fair. Limited from Memorial Day through Labor Day and from 1 Nov-10 Dec because of hunting season.

Cafeteria-747-6382	Locator-739-2011	Medical-747-6333
NCO Club-747-6493	O'Club-747-6300	Police-747-6023
Snack Bar-747-6100		

MINNESOTA

Minneapolis-St. Paul IAP (MN01R2)
Minneapolis, MN 55450-5000

TELEPHONE NUMBER INFORMATION: Main installation numbers: Comm: 612-725-5011, ATVN: 825-5100.

MINNESOTA
Minneapolis-St. Paul IAP, continued

Location: From I-35 west to crosstown MN-62 to 34th Ave and entrance. Follow signs to AFB. RM: p-49, J/6. NMC: Minneapolis-St Paul, in the city.

Billeting Office: ATTN: 934 TAG/SVH. Building 711, EX-5320. 0700-2200 hours M-F, 0630-1700 Sa, closed Su & holidays. Check in billeting, check out 1200 hours. Government civilian employee billeting.

TML: VOQ/TAQ. Building 711. All ranks. Leave or official duty. 188/1-bedroom, private, semi-private, hall, and latrine baths. Refrigerator, A/C, color TV room & lounge, maid service, washer/dryer, ice vending. Older structure, renovated '85. Rates: $6.00 per person. Maximum 2 per room. Duty can make reservations. Others Space-A. Dependent must be spouse. No children.

Other: Minnehaha Falls, 2 miles from base. Ft. Snelling, .5 miles from base.

TML Availability: Good, Oct-Jan. Difficult, May-Sep.

SDO-725-5402	Locator-725-5011	Medical-725-5402
NCO Club-725-5390	O'Club-725-5403	Police-725-5402

MISSISSIPPI

Columbus Air Force Base (MS01R2)
Columbus AFB, MS 39701-5000

TELEPHONE NUMBER INFORMATION: Main installation numbers: Comm: 601-434-7322, ATVN: 742-7322.

Location: Off US-45 north, 60 miles west of Tuscaloosa, AL via US-82. RM: p-52, E/11. NMC: Columbus, 10 miles south.

Billeting Office: ATTN: 14th ABG/SVH, Building 956, B St. EX-2548/2844. 24 hours daily. Check in billeting, check out 1200 hours daily. Government civilian employee billeting.

TML: TLF. Building 955. All ranks. Leave or official duty. 20 separate bedrooms, private bath. Kitchen, utensils, A/C, color TV, maid service, free cribs/cots, free washer/dryer, ice vending, facilities for disabled American veterans. Modern structure. Rate: $14.00 per unit E1-E6, $18.00 E7+. Duty can make reservations. Others Space-A.

TML: VOQ. Building 954. Officer all grades. Leave or official duty. 18/1-bedroom (2 DV/VIP rooms), private bath. Color TV, maid service, free washer/dryer, ice vending. Older structure. Rates: $7.00 per person, $10.00 per person DV/VIP. Maximum $30.00 per room. Duty can make reservations. Others Space-A.

TML: VAQ. Building 956. Enlisted all ranks. Leave or official duty. 30/1-bedroom, semi-private bath; 3 SNCO suites, private bath. Color TV, maid service, free washer/dryer, ice vending. Older structure. Rates: $6.00 per person, $10.00 SNCO. Maximum $30.00 per room. Duty can make reservations. Others Space-A.

DV/VIP: PAO. Building 722. EX-7974. 06+. Retirees and lower grades Space-A.

TML Availability: Very good. Best, Nov-Jan. More difficult, other times.

Enlisted Club-434-7927	Locator-434-2841	Medical-434-2244
NCO Club-434-7927	O'Club-434-2489	Police-434-7129

Temporary Military Lodging Around the World — 111

MISSISSIPPI

Columbus Air Force Base, continued
Snack Bar-434-6498   SDO/NCO-434-7020

Gulfport Naval Construction Battalion Center (MS03R2)
Gulfport, MS 39501-5000

TELEPHONE NUMBER INFORMATION: Main installation numbers: Comm: 601-865-2121, ATVN: 363-2121.

Location: Take US-49 south to Gulfport. Follow signs to Center. From US-90 exit to US-49 (Broad Ave). From I-10 exit to US-49. RM: p-52, P/1. NMC: New Orleans, LA, 70 miles west.

Billeting Office: ATTN: Code 450. Building 85, 2nd St. EX-2586. 0700-1700 hours daily. Other hours, SDO, Building 1, EX-2555. Check in facility, check out 1200 hours daily. Government civilian employee billeting.

TML: Navy Lodge. All ranks. Leave or official duty. For reservations call 1-800-NAVY-INN. Lodge number is 864-3101. 0800-1830 hours daily. Others hours SDO, Building 1. 17/1-bedroom, private bath. Kitchen, utensils, A/C, color TV, maid service, coin washer/dryer. Modern structure. Rates: $26.00 per unit. Maximum 5 per room. All categories can make reservations.

TML: BOQ. Building 301. Officer all grades. Leave or official duty. EX-2226. 36/1-bedroom, private bath. (2 VIP rooms). Kitchen, A/C, color TV room & lounge, maid service, free cribs/cots, free washer/dryer, ice vending. Modern structure. Rates: $4.00 per person. Maximum 3 persons. Duty can make reservations.

TML: BEQ. Building 317. Enlisted all grades. Leave or official duty. EX-2506. 90/1-bedroom (4 beds), latrine bath; 1/3-bedroom (female only), latrine bath. A/C, color TV lounge, free washer/dryer. Modern structure. Rates: $4.00 per person. Duty can make reservations. Others Space-A.

DV/VIP: BOQ. Building 301, EX-2226. 06+. Retirees and lower grades Space-A.

TML Availability: Good, Sep-Mar. Difficult, other times.

Cafeteria-864-5530   Enlisted Club-865-2396   Locator-865-2286
Medical-865-2809   NCO Club-865-2245   O'Club-865-2616
Police-865-2361   Snack Bar-864-5530   SDO/NCO-865-2555

Keesler Air Force Base (MS02R2)
Keesler AFB, MS 39534-5000

TELEPHONE NUMBER INFORMATION: Main installation numbers: Comm: 601-377-1110, ATVN: 597-1110.

Location: From I-10 exit 46, follow signs to Base. From US-90, north on White Ave to main gate. RM: p-52, P/4. NMC: Biloxi, in the city.

Billeting Office: Building 2101, Muse Manor. EX-3309/4200. 24 hours. Check in facility, check out 1200 hours. Government civilian employee billeting.

TML: Guest House. Building 0470. All ranks. Leave or official duty. EX-3663/3774. 21/2-bedroom, living room, dining room, semi-private bath. Refrigerator, maid service, free cribs, free washer/dryer, ice vending. Rates: $18.00 per 2-bedroom unit or $9.00 per bedroom. Primarily for hospital patients and families of patients.

MISSISSIPPI
Keesler Air Force Base, continued

TML: VAQ. Buildings 2101, 2002, 5025. Enlisted all grades. Leave or official duty. EX-2631/3244. 638/1-bedroom, 2 beds, semi-private bath; 8 separate bedrooms, semi-private bath for E7+; 112/1-bedroom, 1 bed, semi-private bath for E7+. Refrigerator, A/C, color TV, maid service, free washer/dryer, food/ice vending. Modern structure, renovated. Rates: $5.00 per person. Maximum 3 per room. Duty can make reservations. Others Space-A.

TML: TLF. 0300 block. All ranks. Leave or official duty. EX-3663(VEQ)/3774(VOQ). 55 separate bedrooms, private bath. Kitchen, utensils, A/C, color TV room & lounge, maid service, essentials, free washer/dryer, food/ice vending, playground rear of facility. Modern structure, renovated. Rates: $15.00 E1-E6, $19.00 E7+. Maximum 5 persons. Duty can make reservations. Others Space-A.

TML: VOQ. Building 3821. Officer all grades. Leave or official duty. EX-3663/3774. 224/1-bedroom, private bath; 328/1-bedroom, semi-private bath; 12/2-bedroom, semi-private bath; 6 DV suites, private bath. Kitchen (98 rooms), A/C, color TV, maid service, washer/dryer, ice vending. Modern structure. Rates: $6.00 per person rooms. Maximum $18.00 per room. $10.00 per person suites. Maximum $20.00 per suite. Duty can make reservations. Others Space-A.

DV/VIP: KTTC/CCP, EX-3359. E9+ & 06+. Retirees and lower grades Space-A.

TML Availability: Fairly good, all year. Best, Dec-Jan.

Enlisted Club-377-2424 Locator-377-2798 Medical-377-6555
NCO Club-377-4146 O'Club-377-2219 Police-377-3720
Snack Bar-435-5284 SDO/NCO-377-1110

Meridian Naval Air Station (MS04R2)
Meridian NAS, MS 39309-5000

TELEPHONE NUMBER INFORMATION: Main installation numbers: Comm: 601-679-2211, ATVN: 446-2211.

Location: Take MS-39 north from Meridian for 12 miles to 4-lane access rd. Clearly marked. Right for 3 miles to NAS main gate. RM: p-52, I/11. NMC: Meridian, 15 miles southwest.

Billeting Office: Building 218 (CBQ), Fuller Rd. EX-2186. 24 hours daily. Check in facility, check out 1300 hours daily. Government civilian employee billeting.

TML: Family Quarters. Building 208. Enlisted all grades. Leave or official duty. 25 separate bedrooms, private bath. Refrigerator, community kitchen, A/C, color TV, maid service, free cribs/rollaways, free washer/dryer. Older structure, renovated in '88. Rates: $13.00 per room per night first 3 persons, $1.00 each additional person. Maximum 5 per room. Duty can make reservations. Others Space-A.

TML: BEQ. Buildings 218. Enlisted all grades. Leave or official duty. Accessible to handicapped. 12/1-bedroom, semi-private bath; 18/1-bedroom, private bath. Refrigerator, community kitchen, A/C, color TV, maid service, free washer/dryer, food/ice vending. Older structure. Remodeled '89. New lounge. Rates: E1-E6 $3.00; E7-E9 $4.00. Maximum 2 per room. Duty can make reservations. Others Space-A.

TML: VOQ. Building 218. Officer all grades. Leave or official duty. Accessible to handicapped. 40 separate bedrooms, private bath. Community kitchen, A/C, color TV, maid service, free cribs, free washer/dryer, ice vending. Older structure. Remodeled '89. Rates: $8.00 per night single, $15.00 per night up to three persons, $1.00 each additional occupant.

MISSISSIPPI

Meridian Naval Air Station, continued

TML: DV/VIP. Building 218. Officer 06+. Leave or official duty. Accessible to handicapped. 4/2-bedroom, private bath. 2 units have kitchen, 1 has refrigerator only. Community kitchen, limited utensils, A/C, color TV lounge & room, maid service, free cribs, free washer/dryer, ice vending. Older structure. Remodeled '89. Rates: $18.00 per room. Maximum charge $18.00. Maximum 3 per room. Duty can make reservations. Others Space-A.

TML Availability: Good, Oct-Dec. Difficult, other times.

CPO Club-679-2650 Enlisted Club-679-2636 Locator-679-2301
Medical-679-2683   O'Club-679-2667   Police-679-2528
McDonalds-679-7632 SDO/NCO-679-2528

MISSOURI

Fort Leonard Wood (MO03R2)
Fort Leonard Wood, MO 65473-5000

TELEPHONE NUMBER INFORMATION: Main installation numbers: Comm: 314-596-0131, ATVN: 581-0110.

Location: Two miles south of I-44, adjacent to St Robert & Waynesville, at Ft Leonard Wood exit. RM: p-55, L/16. NMC: Springfield, 85 miles southwest.

Billeting Office: Building 315, Room 126, MO Ave. EX-6169/1635. 24 hours daily. Check in billeting, check out 1000 hours daily. Government civilian employee billeting.

TML: Guest House. 12 buildings. Officer Building 315. All ranks. Leave or official duty. Accessible to handicapped. 10/1-bedroom, private bath; 8 separate bedrooms, private bath; 43/2-bedroom, 19 (private bath), 24 (semi-private bath). Kitchen (9 units), refrigerator, utensils (9 units), A/C (51 units), color TV, maid service, essentials, free cribs/cots, special facilities for disabled American veterans. Older structure. Rates: Sponsor $12.00, each additional person $1.00. Reservations accepted from PCS in/out, persons with hospital appointments, and families of graduating soldiers. Others Space-A. Pets allowed in 26 units at $3.00 per day. **Note: 70 new units will be added in the Spring of 1991.**

TML: TDY. 14 buildings. All ranks. Official duty only. 500/1-bedroom, private bath. A/C, essentials, food/ice vending, kitchen, limited utensils, maid service, refrigerator, color TV, free washer/dryer. Modern structure. Rates: Sponsor $20.00, each additional person $3.50. Maximum 2 persons. Duty can make reservations. Others Space-A.

TML: VOQ. Buildings 4102, 4104. Officer all grades. TDY only. 74/1-bedroom, private bath; 8 separate bedroom suites, private bath. Kitchen (8 units), refrigerator (74 units), A/C, color TV, maid service, free washer/dryer, ice vending, coffee makers, irons/ironing boards. Modern structure, remodeled. Rates: Sponsor $20.00, each additional person $3.50. Maximum 2 per room. Duty can make reservations. Others Space-A.

TML: DV/VIP. Building 315. Officer 06+. Leave or official duty. 8 separate bedroom suites, private bath; 1/3-bedroom suite, private bath. Kitchen, utensils, A/C, color TV, maid service. Modern structure. Rates: Sponsor $20.00, each additional person $3.50. Maximum 2 per room. Duty can make reservations. Others Space-A.

MISSOURI
Fort Leonard Wood, continued

DV/VIP: Protocol Office. EX-5161. 06/GS-15+. Retirees and lower grades Space-A.

TML Availability: Good. Best Dec. Difficult May-Oct.

Cafeteria-329-3611	Enlisted Club-329-3477	Locator-596-2151
Medical-596-9741	NCO Club-329-6533	O'Club-329-6565
Police-596-6141	Snack Bar-329-3266	

Lake of the Ozarks Recreation Area (MO01R2)
Fort Leonard Wood, MO 65473-5000

TELEPHONE NUMBER INFORMATION: Main installation numbers: Comm: 314-596-0131, ATVN: 581-0110.

Location: Offpost. From I-70 at Columbia, take US-54 southwest to Linn Creek area, left at County Rd A for 6 miles to Freedom, left on Lake Rd A-5 for 4.7 miles to travel camp. From I-44 northeast of Springfield, MO-7 northwest to Richland, right on County Rd A and travel 19.8 miles to Freedom, right on Lake Road A-5 4.7 miles to travel camp. RM: p-55, J/14. NMC: Jefferson City, 40 miles northeast.

Billeting Office: Fort Leonard Wood LORA, Rt 1, Box 380, Linn Creek, MO 65052. All ranks. Leave only. Reservations required. Comm: 314-346-5640. 30-45 days in advance, Apr-Sep. Reservations accepted starting 2nd week in March. Full service members weekend-Labor Day weekend. Check in facility, check out 1200 hours day of departure.

TML: Mobile Homes. 42/2-&3-bedroom, fully equipped, A/C. Rates: $26.00-$34.00 per unit.

Other: Large fully equipped recreational area. For complete details see Military RV, Camping & Rec Areas Around The World.

TML Availability: Fairly good, in season. Very good, off season.

Richards-Gebaur Air Force Base (MO02R2)
Richards-Gebaur AFB, MO 64030-5000

TELEPHONE NUMBER INFORMATION: Main installation numbers: Comm: 816-348-2000, ATVN: 463-1110.

Location: From US-71 south take Belton-Air Base exit, west on County Line Rd (or 155th St) to Base. Between Granview & Belton. RM: p-55, H/9. NMC: Kansas City, 17 miles north.

Billeting Office: ATTN: 442 CSG/SVH. Building 250, Kensington St. EX-2125. 0630-2330 daily. After hours Security Police, Building 602, EX-2118. Check in billeting, check out 1200 hours daily. No government civilian employee billeting.

TML: VOQ/VAQ/VIP. Buildings 250/252/243. All ranks. Leave or official duty. EX-2125/7. 24/1-bedroom, semi-private bath; 120/2-bedroom, semi-private bath; 8/1-bedroom suites, private bath; 4/1-bedroom DV suites, private bath (06+). Refrigerator, A/C, color TV, maid service, free cribs, free washer/dryer, ice vending, coffee pots, ironing boards and irons. Older structure. Rates: $6.00 per person and DV $8.00 per person. DV require advance approval. Duty can make reservations. Others Space-A.

Temporary Military Lodging Around the World — 115

MISSOURI

Richards-Gebaur Air Force Base, continued

Other: Harry S. Truman Library and Home, Crown Center, the Plaza.

TML Availability: Best Mon-Thur. Units train on weekends. A USAFR training base.

Enlisted Club-331-1601 O'Club-331-1601/2053 Police-348-2118
Medical-348-2114   Locator-348-2000/1110

Whiteman Air Force Base (MO04R2)
Whiteman AFB, MO 65305-5000

TELEPHONE NUMBER INFORMATION: Main installation numbers Comm: 816-687-1110, ATVN: 975-1110.

Location: From I-70 east exit to US-13 south to US-50 east for 10 miles, then left on Route J which leads to AFB. RM: p-55, H/12. NMC: Kansas City, MO 60 miles west.

Billeting Office: Building 3006, Mitchell Ave. EX-1844. 24 hours daily. Check in billeting, check out 1200 hours daily. Government civilian employee billeting.

TML: TLF. Buildings 3003, 3005. All ranks. Leave or official duty. Accessible to handicapped. 4/3-bedroom apartments, private bath. Kitchen, complete utensils, A/C, essentials, refrigerator, color TV, maid service, free cribs/cots, free washer/dryer, ice vending. Older structure. Renovated '87. New carpets/TVs '89. Rates: $21.00 per family. PCS in/out can make reservations (60 days in advance recommended). Others Space-A.

TML: Military Hospital. All ranks. Leave or official duty. Check in facility. 25/1-bedroom, semi-private bath. A/C, black/white TV, special facilities for disabled American veterans. Modern structure. Rates: $6.50 per person. Duty can make reservations. Others Space-A.

TML: VOQ. Building 3006. Officer all grades. Leave or official duty. 18/1-bedroom, living room, private bath. Refrigerator, A/C, essentials, color TV, maid service, free cribs/cots, special facilities for disabled American veterans. Older structure. Renovated '85. New TVs '89. Rates: $8.00 1 person, $12.00 2 persons, $16.00 3 or more persons. Duty can make reservations. Others Space-A.

TML: TAQ/VAQ. Building 1551. Enlisted all grades. Leave or official duty. Accessible to handicapped. 11/1-bedroom, semi-private bath. 12 separate bedrooms, semi-private bath. 5 suites, private bath. Refrigerator, A/C, essentials, color TV room & lounge, maid service, free cots/cribs, ice vending, free washer/dryer. Modern structure '86. Rates: Sponsor $7.50-$8.00 for suites, adult $4.00. Maximum charge $16.00. Maximum 5 persons in suites. Duty can make reservations. Other Space-A.

TML: DV/VIP. Building 3006. Officer 06+. Leave or official duty. 1/3-bedroom house (Truman House), 2 baths, beautifully furnished. All amenities. 1/1-bedroom suite (Chadwell Suite), private bath. Kitchen, all amenities. Rates: $10.00 1 person, $15.00 2 persons, $20.00 3 or more persons (Truman House), $8.00 1 person, $12.00 2 persons, $16.00 3 or more persons (Chadwell Suite). Duty can make reservations. Others Space-A.

DV/VIP: 351 SMW/CCP, EX-6543. 06+. Retirees and lower grades if other quarters are full.

TML Availability: Good all year except late July/early Aug because of State Fair. Best, winter.

116 — *Temporary Military Lodging Around the World*

MISSOURI
Whiteman Air Force Base, continued

Cafeteria-687-3170   Enlisted Club-563-2241   Locator-687-5098
Medical-687-2186   NCO Club-563-2242   O'Club-563-2273
Police-687-3700

MONTANA

Malmstrom Air Force Base (MT03R3)
Malmstrom AFB, MT 59402-5000

TELEPHONE NUMBER INFORMATION: Main installation numbers: Comm: 406-731-1110, ATVN: 632-1110.

Location: From I-15 north or south take 10th Ave south exit to AFB. From east take Malmstrom exit off US-87/89 to AFB. Clearly marked. RM: p-57, P/22. NMC: Great Falls, 1 mile west.

Billeting Office: ATTN: 341 CSG/SVH. Building 1680, 5th St. EX-3394. 24 hours daily. Check in billeting, check out 1200 hours daily. Government civilian employee billeting.

TML: TLF. Buildings 1210, 1212, 1214, 1216. Across from billeting office. All ranks. Leave or official duty. 40 separate bedrooms, private bath. Kitchen, utensils, A/C, color TV, maid service, free cribs/cots, free washer/dryer, ice vending. Older structure, renovated. Rates: $20.00 per unit. Maximum 5 per unit. Duty can make reservations. Others Space-A.

TML: VOQ. Building 1680. Officer all grades. Leave or official duty. 36/1-bedroom, semi-private bath; 8 separate bedroom suites, private bath (DV/VIP). Refrigerator, color TV, maid service, washer/dryer, ice vending. Older structure, renovated. Rates for leave status: $24.00 per person. Rates for duty status: E-1 to E-4 $16.00, E-5 to 02, $20.00, 03+ $24.00. Maximum charge $24.00. Maximum 5 per room. Children not authorized. Duty can make reservations. Others Space-A.

TML: VAQ. Building 737. Enlisted all grades. Leave or official duty. 23/1-bedroom, private bath. 2 separate bedroom suites. A/C, free cribs/cots, essentials, ice vending, kitchen, complete utensils, refrigerator, color TV, free washer/dryer. Rates: $7.00 single, $10.00 suite. Maximum charge $24.00. Maximum 2 persons. No children. Duty can make reservations. Others Space-A.

DV/VIP: Protocol Office. 40 AD/CCE, Building 500, EX-2026. 06+. Retirees Space-A.

Other: Facility won SAC Innkeeper Award for 1987. Malmstrom Museum on Base.

TML Availability: Good, winter. Difficult, Jul-Sep.

Cafeteria-727-0671   Enlisted Club-761-4155   Locator-731-4121
Medical-731-3483   NCO Club-761-4155   O'Club-761-6431
Police-731-3829   Snack Bar-727-0671

NEBRASKA

Offutt Air Force Base (NE02R3)
Offutt AFB, NE 68113-5000

TELEPHONE NUMBER INFORMATION: Main installation numbers: Comm: 402-294-1110, ATVN: 271-1110.

Location: From I-80 exit to US-73/75 south to AFB exit, 6.5 miles south of I-80/US-73/75 interchange. RM: p-59, L/24. NMC: Omaha, 8 miles north.

Billeting Office: Building 44, Grants Pass St. EX-3671. 24 hours daily. Check in 1200 hours, check out 1400 hours daily. No government civilian employee billeting.

TML: TLF. Buildings 5089-5093. Platte River Lodge. All ranks. Leave or official duty. 60/2- or 3-room cottages. Kitchen, utensils, A/C, color TV, maid service, free cribs, free washer/dryer, ice vending. Older structure, renovated. Rates: $21.50 per family. Maximum 5 per unit. PCS in/out can make reservations. Others Space-A.

TML: VOQ. Building 479. Offutt Inn. Officer all grades. Leave or official duty. 40/1-bedroom, private bath; 5 separate bedroom suites, private bath (VIP). Refrigerator, A/C, color TV, maid service, free washer/dryer, ice vending. Rates: $10.00 per person. Maximum 2 per unit. Duty can make reservations. Others Space-A.

TML: VOQ. Building 432. Officer all grades. Leave or official duty. 36 separate bedroom suites, private bath. Refrigerator, A/C, color TV, maid service, free washer/dryer, ice vending. Older structure, renovated mid-'88. Rates: $12.00 per person. Maximum 2 per unit. Duty can make reservations. Others Space-A.

TML: VOQ. Building 436. O'Malley Inn. Officer all grades. Leave or official duty. 79/1-bedroom, private bath. Refrigerator, A/C, color TV, maid service, free washer/dryer, ice vending, special facilities for disabled American veterans. Modern structure. Rates: $10.00 per person. Maximum 2 per unit. Duty can make reservations. Others Space-A.

TML: VAQ. Building 402. McCoy Inn. Enlisted all grades. Leave or official duty. 35/1-bedroom, semi-private bath; 1/1-bedroom, private bath; 5 separate bedrooms, private bath (E9 suites); 41/1-bedroom, 2 beds, semi-private bath. Refrigerator, A/C, color TV room & lounge, maid service, free washer/dryer, ice vending, microwave each floor. Older structure. Rates: $7-$8.00 per person. Maximum 2 per unit. Duty can make reservations. Others Space-A.

TML: DVQ. Fort Crook House. Officer 06+. Leave or official duty. 2/2-bedroom, private bath. Kitchen, A/C, color TV, maid service. Historic building - 1900. Rates: $12.00 per person. Maximum 2 persons per unit. Duty can make reservations. Others Space-A.

TML: DVQ. Quarters 13 A & B. Officer 06+. Leave or official duty. 8 separate bedroom suites, private bath. Refrigerator, utensils, A/C, color TV, maid service, free washer/dryer, microwave. Historic building - 1900. Rate: $12.00 per person. Maximum 2 per unit. Duty can make reservations. Others Space-A. Protocol VIP quarters.

DV/VIP: HQ SAC, CINCSAC/CSP, Building 500. EX-4212. 07+. Retirees Space-A.

TML Availability: Good. Best, Dec-Jan. More difficult, other times.

Cafeteria-291-9596
Medical-294-3000
Police-294-3000
Enlisted Club-291-6785
NCO Club-292-1600
Locator-294-5125
O'Club-292-1560

NEVADA

Fallon Naval Air Station (NV02R4)
Fallon NAS, NV 89406-5000

TELEPHONE NUMBER INFORMATION: Main installation numbers: Comm: 702-426-5161, ATVN: 830-2110.

Location: From US-50 exit to US-95 south at Fallon, for 5 miles to left on Union St to NAS. RM: p-60, G/4. NMC: Reno, 72 miles west.

Billeting Office: Central billeting office EX-2809. BEQ-EX-2515. BOQ-EX-2491. Navy Lodge-EX-2583. BEQ/BOQ open 24 hours daily. Lodge open 0800-1630 M-F. Other hours, BOQ. Check in facility, check out 1100 hours (Lodge), 1000 hours BEQ/BOQ. Government civilian employee billeting.

TML: Navy Lodge. All ranks. Leave or official duty. Reservations: 1-800-NAVY-INN. Or write to Navy Exchange 120-151, Building 308, Fallon NAS, NV 89406-5000. 1/2-bedroom, living room, private bath; 5/3-bedroom, living room, private bath. Kitchen, A/C, color TV, maid service. Renovated structure. Rates: $23.00-$24.00 per unit. Maximum 6 per unit. Duty can make reservations.

TML: BEQ. Barracks 5, 6, 7. Enlisted all grades. Leave or official duty. 68/1-bedroom, private bath; 336/1-bedroom, 2 beds, hall bath. Refrigerator, A/C, color TV lounge, maid service, free washer/dryer, ice vending. Modern structure. Rates: $2.00 per person. Duty can make reservations. Retired and leave Space-A.

TML: BOQ. Building 468. Officer all grades. Leave or official duty. 96/1-bedroom, semi-private bath; 226 separate bedrooms, private bath; 8 DV/VIP suites, private bath. Kitchen (136 units), refrigerator, A/C, color TV, maid service, free washer/dryer, ice vending. Modern structure. Rates: Sponsor $6.50, each additional person $3.50. Duty can make reservations. Others Space-A.

DV/VIP: Administration Office, Building 350. EX-2615. 06+. Retirees Space-A.

TML Availability: Good, winter. Difficult, other times.

Cafeteria-426-2501	CPO Club-426-2449	Enlisted Club-426-2449
Locator-426-5161	Medical-426-3100	NCO Club-426-2483
O'Club-426-2454	Police-426-2803	SDO/NCO-426-2483

Nellis Air Force Base (NV01R4)
Nellis AFB, NV 89191-5000

TELEPHONE NUMBER INFORMATION: Main installation numbers: Comm: 702-652-1110, ATVN: 682-1110.

Location: Off I-15 north of Las Vegas. Also accessible from US-91/93. Clearly marked. RM: p-60, N/10. NMC: Las Vegas, 8 miles southwest.

Billeting Office: Building 780, Fitzgerald St. Comm: 702-643-2710. ATVN: 682-9174. 24 hours daily. Check in billeting, check out 1200 hours daily. Government civilian employee billeting.

TML: TLF. 2900's (9 buildings). All ranks. Leave or official duty. Accessible to handicapped. 60/1-bedroom, private bath. Sofa couch in living room makes into queen size bed. A/C, refrigerator, kitchen, complete utensils, color TV, maid service, free cribs/cots, playground for children, free washer/dryer, food/ice vending. Modern structure. New TVs/sofa beds/dining room furniture '89. Rates: $18.00. Maximum

NEVADA

Nellis Air Force Base, continued

charge $18.00. Maximum 5 persons per unit. Duty can make reservations. Others Space-A.

TML: VAQ. Buildings 536 and 552. Enlisted. All grades. 258/1-bedroom, semi-private bath. 5 SNCO rooms, private bath. 1 Chief's suite, private bath. 8 single rooms (1 double bed), private bath. Refrigerator, A/C, color TV, maid service, free washer/dryer, essentials, food/ice vending, microwave, room telephone, clock radio. Modern structure. New carpets '89. Rates: $6.00 per person. Maximum charge $12.00. Maximum 2 persons per unit. Children not authorized during deployments. Duty can make reservations. Others Space-A.

TML: VOQ. Buildings 523, 538, 540, 545. Officer all grades. Leave or official duty. 153/1-bedroom, private bath; 5 VIP suites, private bath. Kitchen, utensils only in suites, essentials, refrigerator, A/C, color TV, maid service, free washer/dryer, microwave, room telephone, clock radio, iron/ironing boards. Modern structure. Building 545 renovated '87. New A/C/carpets '88-'89. Rate: $9.00 per person, $10.00 per person VIP suites. Maximum charge $18.00. Maximum 2 persons per unit. No children. Duty can make reservations. Others Space-A.

DV/VIP: Protocol Office, Building 620, Room 112. EX-2987. 06+.

Other: Home of the Thunderbirds. Gambling resort of Las Vegas nearby.

TML Availability: Extremely limited. Best, spring & Nov-Dec. Difficult other times.

Cafeteria-644-2391
Medical-652-2343
Police-652-2311

Enlisted Club-652-9732
NCO Club-652-9732
Snack Bar-643-2391

Locator-652-1841
O'Club-644-2582
SDO/NCO-652-2755

NEW HAMPSHIRE

Pease Air Force Base (NH01R1)
Pease AFB, NH 03801-5000
CLOSED
NOTES

120 — *Temporary Military Lodging Around the World*

NEW HAMPSHIRE
Pease Air Force Base, continued

CLOSED

Portsmouth Naval Shipyard (NH02R1)
Portsmouth Naval Shipyard, NH 03804-5000

TELEPHONE NUMBER INFORMATION: Main installation numbers: Comm: 207-438-1000, ATVN: 684-0111.

Location: From I-95 north exit 2 to US-1 to NH-103 (Walker St) to gate 1. Located on an island on Piscataqua River between Portsmouth and Kittery, ME. RM: p-61, O/12. NMC: Boston, 60 miles south.

Billeting Office: Building H-23. EX-1513/2015. 24 hours. Check in billeting, check out 1100 hours daily. Government civilian employee billeting.

TML: BOQ/BEQ/CPOQ. Several buildings. All ranks. Leave or official duty. Accessible to handicapped. Refrigerator, community kitchen, free cribs/cots, ice vending, maid service, color TV room & lounge, free washer/dryer, special facilities disabled American veterans. Older structures. Rates: Officer $8.00, Enlisted $3.00. Maximum 4 persons. Duty can make reservations. Others Space-A.

DV/VIP: Protocol Office, Building 86. EX-3800. Commanders+. Retirees and lower grades Space-A.

Other: Near White Mountain. Shopping outlets.

TML Availability: Fairly good. Depends on number of boats at shipyard.

CPO Club-438-2455	Enlisted Club-438-2565	Medical-438-2444
O'Club-438-2269	Police-438-2351	Snack Bar-438-1727
SDO/NCO-438-1900		

NEW JERSEY

Armament Research, Development and Engineering Center (NJ01R1)
Picatinny Arsenal, NJ 07806-5000

TELEPHONE NUMBER INFORMATION: Main installation numbers: Comm: 201-724-4021, ATVN: 880-4021.

Location: Take I-80 west, exit 34B, follow signs to Center, 1 mile N. From I-80 east, exit 33 follow signs to Center. RM: p-63, E/10. NMC: Newark, 30 miles east.

NEW JERSEY

Armament Research, Development and Engineering Center, continued

Billeting Office: ATTN: SMCAR-ISE-H, Building 3359, Belt Rd. EX-2633/3506. 0800-1630 M-F. Check in billeting, check out 1100 hours daily. After hours, persons with reservations may check in with Desk Sgt, Building 173, EX-6666. Government civilian employee billeting.

TML: Guest House/DVQ. Building 110. All ranks. Leave or official duty. 1/4-room, 3 bed DVQ suite, kitchen, living room, dining area, private bath; 2/2-room apartments, private bath; 1/1-room apartment, private bath. Community kitchen, refrigerator, A/C, color TV room & lounge, maid service, free cribs/cots, free washer/dryer. Older structure, renovated '88. Rates: Sponsor Guest House single $10.00, double $15.00; DV single $22.00, double $25.00, children $1.00 per child, under 2 no charge, over 12 $5.00 per child. Duty can make reservations. Others Space-A.

DV/VIP: Protocol Office, SMCAR-GSP, Building 1, 4th fl, EX-7026/27. O6+. Retirees and lower grades Space-A.

TML Availability: Fairly good, Oct-Apr. More difficult, other times.

Cafeteria-989-2420	Locator-724-2852	Medical-724-2113
NCO/EM Club-724-2639	O'Club-989-2460	Police-724-6666

Bayonne Military Ocean Terminal (NJ10R1)
Bayonne, NJ 07002-5302

TELEPHONE NUMBER INFORMATION: Main installation numbers: Comm: 201-823-5111, ATVN: 247-0111.

Location: From New Jersey Turnpike, exit 14A to NJ-169 east to main gate. Follow green and white signs. RM: p-65, Q/7. NMC: New York City, 10 miles northeast.

Billeting Office: None.

Guest House: Liberty Lodge, opened June 1990. 40 double rooms, with two double beds, television, phone individually controlled heating and air conditioning and private bath. Rates are $40.00 per night. All ranks, retirees on a Space-A basis. Call 201-823-5666 or 823-8700 for reservations and information.

TML: VOQ/VEQ. Several buildings. All ranks. Leave or official duty. Call for rates and additional information. EX-7202.

TML Availability: Fair.

Locator-823-5111/0111	Medical-823-7371	Police-823-6666/6000
SDO/NCO-823-7207		

Fort Dix Army Training Center (NJ03R1)
Fort Dix, NJ 08640-5000

TELEPHONE NUMBER INFORMATION: Main installation numbers: Comm: 609-562-1011, ATVN: 944-1110.

Location: From NJ Turnpike (I-95), exit 7, right onto NJ-206, short distance left on NJ-68 and continue to General Circle and main gate. RM: p-63, O/10. NMC: Trenton, 17 miles northwest.

NEW JERSEY
Fort Dix Army Training Center, continued

Billeting Office: ATTN: ATZD-EH-H. Building 5255, Maryland Ave & First St. EX-3188. 24 hours daily. Check in facility, check out 1100 hours daily. No government civilian employee billeting.

TML: Guest House (Doughboy Inn). Building 5997. All ranks. Leave or official duty. EX-6663. 10 cottages, kitchen, living room, private bath; 78/1-bedroom, 2 double beds, private bath. Community kitchen, A/C, color TV, telephone, maid service, free cribs/cots, free washer/dryer, ice vending. Modern structure. Rates: $30.00 double, $35.00 3 persons, $40.00 4 or more. All categories can make reservations.

TML: VOQ/VEQ. Building 5255. All ranks. Leave or official duty. 65/1-bedroom, semi-private bath (VEQ); 10 separate bedrooms, private bath (VOQ). Refrigerator, A/C, color TV room & lounge, maid service, free cribs/cots, free washer/dryer, ice vending. Older structure, renovated. Rates: TDY $30.00 per night, $5.00 each additional person; leave $20.00. All categories can make reservations.

TML: DVQ. Building 5256. Officer 06+. Leave or official duty. 4/1-bedroom suites, private bath; 4/2-bedroom apartments, private bath. Kitchen (apartments), refrigerator (suites), utensils, A/C, color TV room & lounge, maid service, free cribs/cots, free washer/dryer, ice vending. Modern structure. Rates: TDY $34.00, leave $25.00, $5.00 each additional person. All categories can make reservations.

DV/VIP: HQ USATC & Ft Dix, ATTN: Office of The Secretary General Staff. EX-5059/6293. 06/civilian equivalent +. Retirees Space-A.

TML Availability: Good, Oct-Mar. Difficult, other times.

Cafeteria-723-2671	Enlisted Club-562-3315	Locator-562-1011
Medical-562-2695	NCO Club-723-3272	O'Club-723-7700
Police-562-6001	SDO/NCO-562-2643/2645	

Fort Monmouth (NJ05R1)
Fort Monmouth, NJ 07703-5000

TELEPHONE NUMBER INFORMATION: Main installation numbers: Comm: 201-532-9000, ATVN: 992-9000.

Location: Take NJ Turnpike to I-95; east to Garden State Parkway; north to exit 105 for Eatontown and Fort Monmouth. RM: p-63, L/14. NMC: New Brunswick, 23 miles northwest.

Billeting Office: ATTN: SELHI-EH-H, Building 270, Allen & Barton Ave. EX-1092. 0745-2400 hours daily. Other hours, SDO, Building 1209, EX-1100. Check in billeting office, check out 1000 hours daily. Government civilian employee billeting.

TML: Guest House. Buildings 360, 364, 1077. All ranks. Leave, official or unofficial duty. 34/1-bedroom, private bath; 34 suites, private bath; 4/2-bedroom suites, private bath; 33 double occupancy rooms, private baths. All have color TV, TV lounge, maid service, free cots, washer/dryer and ice vending. All have a kitchen or access to a community kitchen. Rates: $8.50 - $10.50 single, $14.50 - $16.50 double. PCS can make reservations. Others Space-A. **Sixty new units will be added Spring '91.**

TML: VOQ. Building 363, 270, 1202. Officers, TDY civilians, Senior NCO's on official duty. 60/1 bedroom, private bath; 60 rooms, kitchenette, private bath; 9 suites, kitchenettes, private bath. Inquire about rooms and services. Modern structure, renovated. $25.00 single, $37.00 double. No children. Duty can make reservations. Others Space-A.

TML: DVQ. Building 259, Blair Hall. Officer 06+. Leave or official duty. Inquire

Temporary Military Lodging Around the World — 123

NEW JERSEY

Fort Monmouth, continued

about rooms and services available. Modern structure, renovated. Rates: $25.00 single, $37.50 double. Duty can make reservations. Others Space-A.

DV/VIP: CECOM Protocol Office, EX-4015. 06/GS-15+. Retirees and lower grades Space-A.

Other: Seashore resort area; Monmouth Park race course.

TML Availability: Difficult, all year.

Cafeteria-542-7399	Enlisted Club-542-7267	Locator-532-1492
Medical-532-2952	NCO Club-532-4520	O'Club-532-4561
Police-532-1112	Snack Bar-532-3805	SDO/NCO-532-1100

Lakehurst Naval Air Engineering Center (NJ08R1)
Lakehurst, NJ 08733-5085

TELEPHONE NUMBER INFORMATION: Main installation numbers: Comm: 201-323-2011, ATVN: 624-1110.

Location: Take Garden State Parkway south to NJ-70 west to junction of NJ-547 right and proceed 1 mile to Base. RM: p-63, O/11. NMC: Trenton, 30 miles northwest.

Billeting Office: Navy Lodge. 1000-2200 M-F. EX-1103. Other hours Mini-Mart, EX-2909. Check in facility, check out 1100 hours daily. Government civilian employee billeting.

TML: Navy Lodge. All ranks. Leave or official duty. For reservations call 1-800-NAVY-INN. Lodge number is 323-1103. 9/2-bedroom, living room, private bath. Kitchen, A/C, color TV, maid service, coin washer/dryer. Older structure, renovated. Rates: $29.00 per unit. All categories can make reservations.

TML Availability: Difficult, summer months.

Cafeteria-323-2291/2554	Enlisted Club-323-2475	Locator-323-2170
Medical-323-2231	O'Club-323-2340	Police-323-2457/2332
Snack Bar-323-2717		

McGuire Air Force Base (NJ09R1)
McGuire AFB, NJ 08641-5000

TELEPHONE NUMBER INFORMATION: Main installation numbers: Comm: 609-724-1110, ATVN: 440-0111.

Location: From New Jersey Turnpike, exit 7 to NJ-68 southeast to AFB. Adjacent to Fort Dix. Clearly marked. RM: p-63, O/9. NMC: Trenton, 18 miles northwest.

Billeting Office: All-American Inn/SVH, Building 1902. EX-2954. 24 hours daily. Check in facility, check out 1200 hours daily. Government civilian employee billeting.

TML: TLQ. Buildings 2418/19. All ranks. Leave or official duty. EX-3336/37 0745-1600 hours M-F. Other hours, EX-2954. 30/2-bedroom, private bath. Kitchen, A/C, maid service, free washer/dryer. Older structure. Rates: $20.00 per unit. PCS have priority. Others Space-A.

NEW JERSEY
McGuire Air Force Base, continued

TML: Base Motel TLF. All ranks. Leave or official duty. EX-3167. 160/1-bedroom, private bath. A/C, color TV, maid service. Modern structure. Rates: $8.00 per unit. All categories can make reservations.

TML: VOQ/VAQ. Buildings 1903 (VAQ), 2704/07 (VOQ). All ranks. Leave or official duty. EX-3167. 186/1-bedroom, semi-private bath (VOQ); 244/1-bedroom, semi-private bath (VAQ). A/C, color TV, maid service. Older structure. Rates: $8.00 officers, $5.00 enlisted. All categories can make reservations.

TML: DV/VIP. Building 19-02. Officer 06+. Leave or official duty. EX-2340. 13/1-bedroom suites, private bath. 1 unit kitchen, A/C, color TV, maid service. Older structure. Rates: $8.00 per person. All categories can make reservations.

DV/VIP: Protocol Office, EX-1110/0111. 06+.

TML Availability: Good, Oct-Apr. Difficult, other times.

Cafeteria-723-2450	Enlisted Club-723-0203	Locator-724-2345
Medical-724-3615	NCO Club-724-2396	O'Club-724-3296
Police-724-2001	SDO/NCO-724-3935	

NEW MEXICO

Cannon Air Force Base (NM02R3)
Cannon AFB, NM 88103-5000

TELEPHONE NUMBER INFORMATION: Main installation numbers: Comm: 505-784-3311, ATVN: 681-1110.

Location: From Clovis west on US-60/84 to AFB. From NM-467 enter the Portales Gate. RM: p-70, H/11. NMC: Clovis, 7 miles east.

Billeting Office: ATTN: 27SVS/SVH, Building 1801B, Olympic St. EX-2918. 24 hours daily. Check in billeting, check out 1200 hours daily. Government civilian employee billeting.

TML: TLF. Buildings 1812, 1818. All ranks. Leave or official duty. 8 separate bedrooms, private bath; 23/2-bedroom, private bath. Kitchen, utensils, A/C, color TV, housekeeping service, washer/dryer, ice vending. Older structure. Rates: $18.00 per room. PCS in/out can make reservations. Others Space-A.

TML: VOQ. Building 1800B. Officer all grades. Leave or official duty. 4/1-bedroom, private bath. 4 rooms share community living area & kitchen. A/C, color TV room and lounge, housekeeping service, washer/dryer, ice vending. Older structure. Rates: $8.00 per person. Maximum $16.00 per family. Duty can make reservations. Others Space-A.

TML: VOQ. Building 1816. Officer all grades. Leave or official duty. 16/1-bedroom, shared kitchen, private bath; 4 separate bedroom suites, private kitchen, private bath. A/C, color TV, housekeeping service, washer/dryer, ice vending. Older structure. Rates: $8.00 per person. Maximum $16.00 per family. Duty can make reservations. Others Space-A.

TML: VAQ. Building 1812. Enlisted all grades. Leave or official duty. 16/1-bedroom, shared kitchen, private bath; 4 separate bedrooms, private kitchen, private bath. A/C, color TV room and lounge, housekeeping service, washer/dryer, ice vending. Older

NEW MEXICO

Cannon Air Force Base, continued

structure. Rates: $8.00 per person. Maximum charge $16.00 per family. Duty can make reservations. Others Space-A.

TML: DV/VIP. Buildings 1800A and 1812. EX-2727. Officer O6+. Leave or official duty. 6 separate bedroom suites, private bath. Kitchen, complete utensils, color TV, housekeeping service, washer/dryer, ice vending. Older structure. Rates: $10.00 per person. Maximum charge $20.00. Duty can make reservations. Others Space-A.

DV/VIP: 27TFW/CCEP, Building 1, EX-2727, O6+. Retirees Space-A.

TML Availability: Good, Nov-Feb. Difficult, other times.

Cafeteria-784-3621	Locator-784-2424	Medical-784-4033
O'Club-784-2477	Police-784-4111	SDO/NCO-784-2253
Snack Bar-784-2280		

Holloman Air Force Base (NM05R3)
Holloman AFB, NM 88330-5000

TELEPHONE NUMBER INFORMATION: Main installation numbers: Comm: 505-479-6511, ATVN: 867-1110.

Location: Exit US-70/82, 8 miles southwest of Alamogordo NM. Clearly marked RM: p-70, K/6. NMC: La Cruces, 50 miles southwest.

Billeting Office: Building 583, west New Mexico Ave. Comm: 479-6123. ATVN: 867-3311/3468. 24 hours daily. Check in facility, check out 1200 hours daily. Government civilian employee billeting.

TML: TLF. Buildings 17, 583. All ranks. Leave or official duty. 14/2-bedroom, private bath; 10 separate bedrooms, private bath. Kitchen, complete utensils, A/C, color TV room, maid service, free cribs/cots, free washer/dryer, ice vending. Older structure. Rates: $14.00 per unit. PCS in/out can make reservations. Others Space-A.

TML: VAQ. Buildings 342, 518. Enlisted all grades. Leave or official duty. 100/1-bedroom, semi-private bath; 4 separate bedrooms, private bath. Refrigerator, A/C, color TV, maid service, cribs/cots, free washer/dryer, ice vending. Modern structure. Rates: $8.00 per person. Maximum 2 per room. TDY, PCS in/out can make reservations. Others Space-A.

TML: VOQ. Buildings 582, 584-587. Officer all grades. Leave or official duty. 40/1-bedroom, private bath; 120 separate bedrooms, private bath; 20/2-bedroom, semi-private bath. Kitchen, A/C, color TV, maid service, free cribs/cots, free washer/dryer, ice vending. Modern structure. Rates: $8.00 per person. TDY, PCS in/out can make reservations. Others Space-A.

DV/VIP: CSG/CC, Building 29. ATVN: 867-5573/74. E9/O6+/GS-15+.

TML Availability: Good, Dec-Jan. Difficult, other times.

Cafeteria-479-2698	Enlisted Club-479-3226	Locator-479-7510
Medical-479-3268	NCO Club-479-3226	O'Club-479-3611
Police-479-7397	Snack Bar-479-2779	SDO/NCO-479-3226

NEW MEXICO

Kirtland Air Force Base (NM03R3)
Kirtland AFB, NM 87117-5000

TELEPHONE NUMBER INFORMATION: Main installation numbers: Comm: 505-844-0011, ATVN: 244-0011.

Location: From I-40 east, exit on Wyoming Blvd, south for 2 miles to Wyoming gate to AFB. RM: p-70, P/10. NMC: Albuquerque, NM, 1 mile southeast.

Billeting Office: KAFB Billeting Fund, Box 5418, Kirtland AFB, NM 87185. Building 22010, Club Dr. EX-2936. 24 hours daily. Check in billeting, check out 1200 hours daily. Government civilian employee billeting.

TML: TLF. All ranks. Leave or official duty. 24 separate bedroom suites, private bath. Kitchen, limited utensils, A/C, color TV, maid service, cots, ice vending, special facilities for disabled American veterans. Older structure, renovated. Rates: $15.00 per suite. PCS in/out can make reservations. Others Space-A.

TML: Guest Cottages/Suites. All ranks. Leave or official duty. 15/3-bedroom, private bath; 1/4-bedroom, private bath; 24 suites, private bath. Kitchen, limited utensils, A/C, color TV, maid service, cots, special facilities for disabled American veterans. Older structure, renovated. Rates: $18.00 per cottage, $15.00 per suites. PCS in/out can make reservations. Others Space-A.

TML: VOQ. Buildings 1901, 1902, 19011, 22001, 22003, 22010-22012, 23225. Officer all grades. Official duty only. 229 separate bedrooms, private bath. Refrigerator, A/C, color TV, maid service, free washer/dryer, ice vending. Older structure. Rates: $6.00 per person. Duty can make reservations.

TML: VAQ. Buildings 920, 20101, 22002, 23226. Enlisted all grades. Leave or official duty. 24 suites, private bath (E7-E9); 225 beds, semi-private bath (E1-E6). Refrigerator, A/C, color TV, maid service, free washer/dryer, ice vending. Older structure, renovated. Rates: $4.00 per person. Duty can make reservations. Others Space-A.

TML: DV/VIP. Buildings 1900, 22000. Officer 07-10. Leave or official duty. 9 suites, private bath. Older structure, renovated. Rates: $10.00 per person. All categories can make reservations.

DV/VIP: 1606 ABW/CC. Building 22000, EX-0408. 07+ & GS-16/SES+ and AD Wing Cmdrs and equivalent if 06+. Retirees and lower grades (with certain considerations) Space-A.

Other: National Atomic Museum, Old Town Albuquerque, ghost towns.

TML Availability: Best, late fall and winter. Friday and Saturday nights always better than during the week.

Cafeteria-265-4304
Medical-265-1711
Snack Bar-265-4304
Enlisted Club-844-9089
O'Club-265-7512/3488
SDO/NCO-844-4676
Locator-844-0011
Police-844-4618

White Sands Missile Range (NM04R3)
White Sands Missile Range, NM 88002-5076

TELEPHONE NUMBER INFORMATION: Main installation numbers: Comm: 505-678-2121, ATVN: 258-2211.

Location: From Las Cruces, east on US-70, 30 miles to WSMR. From Alamogordo west on US-70, 45 miles to WSMR. RM: p-70, L/10. NMC: El Paso, 45 miles south.

Temporary Military Lodging Around the World — 127

NEW MEXICO

White Sands Missile Range, continued

Billeting Office: ATTN: STEWS-EL-H. Building 501, Aberdeen Ave. EX-4559. 0745-1515 hours daily. Other hours SDO, Building 100, EX-2031. Check out 1100 hours daily. Charge for late checkouts.

TML: VOQ/DVQ. Buildings 501, 502. All military and DOD civilians on official duty. 3/1-bedroom, private bath; 43 suites, private bath; 8/3-bedroom houses, private bath. Refrigerator, community kitchen, complete utensils, A/C, color TV, maid service, free cribs, free washer/dryer. Rates: TDY $21.50, spouse $6.00 additional. Reservations confirmed only for TDY or PCS military families in/out. No pets.

TML: Guest House. Building 506. All ranks. PCS, official duty, leave and retired military. 15/1-bedroom, 2 beds, sofa bed, private bath. Kitchen, complete utensils, A/C, color TV, free cribs, free washer/dryer, ice vending (in 501, 502), special facilities for disabled American veterans (2 units). Modern structure. PCS rates (per unit)-$21.50 per night first four nights for all ranks, after four nights $21.50 per unit for 04+ and W3, W4, $18.00 per unit 01-03, W1, W2 and E7-E9, $15.00 per unit E5-E6, and $13.00 E1-E4; all others, Space-A and TDY personnel $21.50 per unit. Maximum 6 per room. PCS in/out may confirm reservations.

DV/VIP: CG, WSMR, ATTN: STEW-PC, Building 100, Room 227. EX-1028. 06/GS-15+ Retirees and lower grades Space-A.

Other: White Sands National Monument, Aerospace Museum, Alamogordo, NM.

TML Availability: Very good.

Cafeteria-678-2081
Medical-678-2882
Police-678-1234

Enlisted Club-678-2061
NCO Club-678-2061
SDO/NCO-678-2031

Locator-678-2121
O'Club-678-2057

NEW YORK

Fort Drum (NY06R1)
Fort Drum, NY 13602-5000

TELEPHONE NUMBER INFORMATION: Main installation numbers: Comm: 315-772-6900, ATVN: 341-6011.

Location: From Syracuse, take I-81 north to exit 48, past Watertown, and follow signs to Fort Drum. RM: p-67, EG/6. NMC: Watertown, 8 miles southwest.

Billeting Office: ATTN: Building T-2227, Officers' Loop. 24 hours daily. EX-5435. Check in billeting, check out 1100 hours daily. Government civilian employee billeting.

TML: Guest House. Building 2340. All ranks. Leave or official duty. 9 separate bedrooms, private bath; 5/2-bedroom, private bath. Kitchen, complete utensils, color TV, maid service, free cribs/cots, free washer/dryer. Older structure. Rates: Sponsor $12.00, adult $5.00, child $1.00, infants no charge. All categories Space-A.

TML: VOQ/VEQ. All ranks. Leave or official duty. 22/2-bedroom, private bath; 13/3-bedroom, private bath. Kitchen, complete utensils, color TV, maid service, free cribs/cots, free washer/dryer, laundry. Rates: Same as Guest House. Contact billeting for more information.

NEW YORK
Fort Drum, continued

TML: TLF. The Inn. All rank. Leave or official duty. (315)-773-7777. 111 rooms, 64 with kitchenettes and microwaves. Queen size beds, remote control cable color TV, room telephones, individual A/C/heating. Rates: $44.00 single, $47.00 double queen with kitchen; $49.50 double occupancy, $54.00 double queen with kitchen. Lower rates for PCS on an extended stay.

DV/VIP: Protocol Office, Building T-3, EX-5010. 06+. Retirees and lower grades Space-A.

Other: Sackets Harbor Battle Ground, site of war of 1812 battle.

TML Availability: Good, Oct-Apr. Difficult, other times.

Cafeteria-772-2112	Locator-772-5869	Medical-772-5236
O'Club-772-6222/6218	Police-772-5156	SDO/NCO-772-5647

Fort Hamilton (NY02R1)
Brooklyn, NY 11252-5330

TELEPHONE NUMBER INFORMATION: Main installation numbers: Comm: 718-630-4101, ATVN: 232-1110.

Location: From Belt Parkway, exit 2 (Fort Hamilton Parkway) to 100th St, right to Fort Hamilton Parkway, right to main gate. RM: p-65, S/8. NMC: New York, in the city.

Billeting Office: Building 109, Schum Ave. EX-4052. 0800-1630 hours daily. Other hours, SDO, Building 302, EX-4546. Check in facility after 1400 hours daily. Check out 1000 hours daily. No government civilian employee billeting.

TML: Guest House. Adams, Building 109. All ranks. Leave or official duty. EX-4052. 36/1-bedroom, private bath. Kitchen, A/C, color TV room & lounge, coin washer/dryer, ice vending. Older structure. Rates: $36.00 single, $42.00 two or more. Duty can make reservations. Others Space-A.

TML: DV/VIP. Building 209. Officer 06+. Leave or official duty. EX-4324. 5 separate bedrooms, private bath. Refrigerator, color TV, coffee/bar set up, A/C, maid service. Rates: $18.00 single, $24.00 two or more. Duty can make reservations. Others Space-A.

DV/VIP: For Liaison & Protocol Office, Building 302, Room 13, EX-4324. 06+. Retirees Space-A.

TML Availability: Good, winter months. Difficult, summer months.

Cafeteria-748-6232	Locator-630-4958	Medical-630-4615
NCO Club-630-4361	O'Club-630-4361	Police-630-4456
Snack B-748-3440/x18	SDO/NCO-630-4565/96	

Griffiss Air Force Base (NY11R1)
Griffiss AFB, NY 13441-5000

TELEPHONE NUMBER INFORMATION: Main installation numbers: Comm: 315-330-1110, ATVN: 587-1110.

Location: Off NY-49 in Rome. Entrance off NY-49 and from Chestnut St, Floyd St, and East Dominick St. RM: p-67, EK/8. NMC: Utica, 17 miles southeast.

NEW YORK

Griffiss Air Force Base, continued

Billeting Office: Building 704, Wright Dr. EX-4391. 24 hours daily. Check in facility, check out 1200 hours daily. Government civilian employee billeting.

TML: TLF. Buildings 490, 491, 492. All ranks. Leave or official duty. 35 separate bedrooms, sleeps 5 persons, private bath. Kitchen, A/C, free cribs/cots, color TV, maid service, free cribs, free washer/dryer. Modern structures. Renovated '89. Rates: $21.50/22.50 per room, maximum charge. Maximum 5 persons per unit. Duty can make reservations. Others Space-A.

TML: VAQ. Building 438. All ranks. Leave or official duty. 44/1-bedroom, semi-private bath. 3 separate bedrooms (Chief suites), private bath. Kitchen, A/C, free cribs/cots, color TV, maid service, food/ice vending, free washer/dryer. Rates: Sponsor $9.00, Maximum charge $13.50. Chief suites $13.00. Maximum charge $19.50. Maximum 2 persons suites, others 1 person. Duty can make reservations. Others Space-A.

TML: VOQ. Buildings 704, 712. Officers. Grades 01-05. Leave or official duty. Accessible to handicapped. 40/1-bedroom, private bath. A/C, free cribs/cots, essentials, maid service, refrigerator, special facilities for disabled American veterans, color TV room & lounge, free washer/dryer. Older structures. Renovated '88. New air conditioning/carpets/TVs '89. Rates: $9.00 per person. Maximum charge $18.00. Maximum 4 persons per unit. Duty can make reservations. Others Space-A.

TML: DV/VIP. Building 712. Officer 06+. Enlisted 09. Leave or official duty. 4 separate bedrooms suites, private bath. 1/2-bedroom, private bath (DV family quarters, living room, dining room, kitchenette). Kitchen, complete utensils, essentials, A/C, color TV, maid service, free cribs/cots, free washer/dryer, bar. Older structure. New carpets/TVs '89. Rates: $13.00 per person. Maximum charge $26.00. Duty can make reservations. Others Space-A.

DV/VIP: PAO, EX-7415. 06+. Retirees Space-A.

TML Availability: Good. Best Dec-Mar. Difficult, other times.

Cafeteria-330-7945	Enlisted Club-330-7057	Locator-330-2231
Medical-330-4108	NCO Club-330-7055	O'Club-330-7915
Police-330-2200	SDO/NCO-330-1110	Snack Bar-330-2123

New York Coast Guard Support Center (NY01R1)
Governors Island, NY 10004-5000

TELEPHONE NUMBER INFORMATION: Main installation numbers: Comm: 212-668-7000, FTS: 664-7000.

Location: Take free Governors Island Ferry from Battery Park area of Manhattan. RM: p-65, P/8. NMC: New York, 1 mile northwest.

Billeting Office: Building S-293, opposite O'Club. Comm: 212-269-8878. Check in facility, check out 1100 hours daily. No government civilian employee billeting.

TML: Super 8 Motel. Building 293. All ranks. Leave or official duty. 11/1-bedroom, 1 bed, private bath; 38/1-bedroom, 2 beds, private bath; limited number of efficiency apartments, private bath. 2 VIP suites (06+), private bath. Kitchen (8 units), A/C, color TV, maid service, free cribs, cots ($7.00), ice vending, special facilities for disabled American veterans. Modern structure. Rates: single and double rooms $35.00 first person, $5.00 each additional person; efficiency apartments $40.00 first person, $5.00 each additional person; suites $50.00-$60.00 first person, $5.00 each additional person; + 8 1/4% tax, under 12 no charge. All categories can make reservations.

NEW YORK
New York Coast Guard Support Center, continued

TML: BOQ. Officer all grades (and occasionally enlisted personnel may use if special circumstances warrant). Leave or official duty. Comm: 668-3452. Single person only. No families. Be prepared to share room. Rates: $7.00 per person.

DV/VIP: CO, EX-7251. 07+.

TML Availability: Good, Oct-May. Difficult, other times.

Burger King-825-04656
Medical-668-7167
Police-668-7474
Enlisted Club-668-7270
NCO Club-668-7266
SDO/NCO-668-7015
Locator-668-7000
O'Club-668-7400

New York Naval Station (NY07R1)
Brooklyn, NY 11251-5000

TELEPHONE NUMBER INFORMATION: Main installation numbers: Comm: 718-834-2000, ATVN: 456-2000.

Location: In Brooklyn, .25 miles west of I-278, at Flushing & Washington Avenues (207 Flushing Avenue). RM: p-65, T/12. NMC: New York, in the city.

Billeting Office: Building RG, North Rd. Comm: 834-2298. Check in 0600-2300 hours daily, check out 1000 hours daily. No government civilian employee billeting.

TML: BOQ. Building RG. Officer all grades, Enlisted E7-E9. Leave or official duty. 5 separate bedrooms, private bath; 5 separate bedrooms, hall bath; 1/3-bedroom, living room, dining room, kitchen, private bath. A/C, refrigerator, color TV, maid service, free cots, free washer/dryer, ice vending. Rates: Cottage $20.00, suite $10.00, room $6.00, additional person $4.00. No maximum capacity. Duty can make reservations. Others Space-A.

TML Availability: Good, winter months. Difficult, summer months.

Note: 50 new Navy Lodge units available now at Staten Island Navy base, State Island, NY 10305-5097. Call 718-442-0413.

Cafeteria-834-2432
Medical-834-2222
Snack Bar-834-2430
Enlisted Club-834-2430
O'Club-834-2215
Locator-834-2609
Police-834-2323

Niagara Falls Air Reserve Base (NY12R1)
Niagara Falls International Airport
Niagara Falls, NY 14304-5000

TELEPHONE NUMBER INFORMATION: Main installation numbers: Comm: 716-236-2000, ATVN: 489-3011.

Location: Take I-190 to Niagara Falls, exit Packard Rd and turn right to base. Take US-62 to Walmore Rd north to base. RM: p-69, WD/12. NMC: Niagara Falls, 6 miles west.

Billeting Office: Building 312, Flint Ave. 0700-2300 hours daily. EX-2014. Other hours, Base Ops, EX-2000. Check in facility, check out 1200 hours daily. Government civilian employee billeting.

TML: VOQ. Building 312. Officers all grades. Leave or official duty. 43/1 bedroom, private bath, telephone, refrigerator, AC, color TV and other essentials. Maid service, washer/dryers, ice vending, crib and cots. Older structure renovated 1984. Lounge with

Temporary Military Lodging Around the World — 131

NEW YORK

Niagara Falls Air Reserve Base, continued

microwave. Rates: $6.00 per person. Duty can make reservations. Others Space-A.

TML: VAQ/VIP. Building 312, Officer O-5 and above, GS/GM 13 and above. Leave or duty. 6 living rm/ bedroom suites, private bath, A/C, telephone, color TV, refrigerator and other essentials. Maid service. Rate: $8.00 per person. Duty can make reservations, others Space-A.

TML: VAQ: Buildings 502 and 504. Enlisted all grades, leave or official duty. 34/1 bedroom, 2 beds per room each building, TV, A/C refrigerator and other essentials. Older structure renovated. Rates: $6.00 per person. Duty can make reservations, others Space-A.

TML: VAQ: Building 508. Enlisted all grades 31/1 bedroom semi-private bath, 5/1 bedroom private bath, TV, A/C refrigerator and other essentials. Maid service, washer, dryers and ice vending. Older structure renovated 1984. Senior NCO quarters available, 2 living/bedroom suites, private bath. TV, A/C, refrigerator, telephone and other essentials. Rates $8.00 per person.

Other: Niagara Falls, Winter Gardens, Power Vista, Old Fort Niagara, Our Lady of Fatima Shrine, Native American Center for the Living Arts, amusement parks, aquarium and scenic area surrounding the Niagara Frontier.

TML Availability: Good, Oct-Mar. Difficult, Apr - Sep.

Locator-236-2002　　Medical-236-2086/7　　NCO Club-236-2027
Police-236-2278　　　Snack Bar-236-2328

Plattsburgh Air Force Base (NY08R1)
Plattsburgh AFB, NY 12903-5000

TELEPHONE NUMBER INFORMATION: Main installation numbers: Comm: 518-565-5000, ATVN: 689-5000.

Location: From I-87 take exit # 36. Directions to AFB are clearly marked. RM: p-67, EC/15. NMC: Plattsburg, 4 miles northwest.

Billeting Office: Building 381, Club Rd. EX-7614. 24 hours daily. Check in billeting, check out 1200 hours daily. Government civilian employee billeting VOQ.

TML: TLF. Building 164. All ranks. Leave or official duty. 15 apartments, all private bath: 4/1-bedroom, private bath; 8 separate bedrooms, private bath; 2/2-bedroom, private bath; 1/3-bedroom, private bath. Kitchen (11 units), community kitchen, complete utensils, color TV room & lounge, maid service, free cribs/cots, free washer/dryer, food/ice vending. Modern structure, renovated. Rates: $8.00 1 bedroom, $14.00 separate bedrooms, $20.00 2-bedroom, $25.00 3-bedroom. Duty can make reservations. Others Space-A.

TML: VOQ. Building 381. Officer all grades. Leave or official duty. 40/1-bedroom, semi-private bath; 4 DV (06+) suites, private bath. Refrigerator, community kitchen, free cribs/cots, essentials, color TV room & lounge, maid service, free washer/dryer, ice vending. Older structure. Renovated '87-'89. Rates: Sponsor and adult $6.00 per person. Maximum $12.00 per room. Maximum 2 per room. Children not authorized. Duty can make reservations. Others Space-A.

TML: VAQ. Building 1944. Enlisted all grades. Leave or official duty. 16/1-bedroom, semi-private bath. Refrigerator, free cribs/cots, community kitchen, color TV room & lounge, free washer/dryer, food/ice vending. Older structure, renovated '87. Rates: Sponsor and adult $8.00 per person. Maximum 2 per roomn. Maximum charge $17.00. Children not authorized. Duty can make reservations. Others Space-A.

NEW YORK
Plattsburgh Air Force Base, continued

DV/VIP: 380th BW Cmdr's Sec. EX-5171. 06+. Retirees Space-A.

TML Availability: Very good. Best winter months. Difficult, other times.

Locator-565-5579   Medical-565-7223   NCO Club-563-3956
O'Club-563-4780   Police-565-7111   Snack Bar-561-9141
SDO/NCO-565-5000

Soldiers', Sailors' and Airmen's Club (NY17R1)
283 Lexington Avenue
New York, NY 10016

TELEPHONE NUMBER INFORMATION: Main installation numbers: Comm: 212-683-4353, ATVN: None. In U.S. toll free 1-800-678-TGIF.

Location: In mid-town Manhattan on Lexington Avenue between 36th and 37th Sts. RM: p-65, Y/15. NMC: New York, in the city.

Author's Note: The Soldiers', Sailors' and Airmen's Club is a tax exempt, not-for-profit organization founded in 1919 to serve the needs of service personnel while visiting New York and is the only club of its kind in the city.

Office: Check in and out at the lobby desk. 24 hours daily. Check out 1230 hours.

TML: Hotel. Enlisted all grades. Active duty, reservists, spouses, dependents 12 years and older and cadets and midshipmen of service academies and ROTC sponsored by US government are eligible. Enlisted and Officer Retirees, family members 12 and over, Reserve, Guard and family members with ID card may stay on a Space-A basis. Note: unaccompanied spouses with ID may use facilities on a Space-A basis, widows, too! 29 bedrooms (most have 2 beds). Facilities include lounges, library, TV rooms, pool room, and dining room. Older structure, renovations on-going. Rates: $20.00 per person per night. Reservations are suggested for weekends.

Other: Continental breakfast on weekends $1.00. Discount tickets to Broadway shows.

Stewart Army Sub-Post (NY09R1)
Newburgh, NY 12550-9999

TELEPHONE NUMBER INFORMATION: Main installation numbers: Comm: 914-564-6309, ATVN: 247-3524.

Location: From I-87 take Newburgh exit to Union Ave, south to NY-207. Follow signs to Stewart IAP and Sub-Post. RM: p-67, EU/13. NMC: Newburgh, 4 miles northwest.

Billeting Office: Building 626, Westpoint, NY. Comm: 914-563-3311, ATVN: 688-3009. 0800-1630, M-F. Check out 1000 hours daily. Government civilian employee billeting if TDY.

TML: Guest House. Building 2605, Five Star Inn. All ranks. Leave or official duty. Accessible to handicapped. 18/1-bedroom, private bath; 34 bedrooms, semi-private bath. Kitchen in apartments, limited utensils, A/C, food vending, color TV room & lounge, refrigerator, free cribs, cots ($4.00), free washer/dryer, ice vending. Older structure. Renovated 88. Rates: Sponsor $18.00, adult and child $4.00, under 2 years free. Maximum 3 per room. All categories can make reservations. Others Space-A.

TML: VOQ. Building 2609. All ranks. Official duty only. Reservations required. Comm: 938-4500. ATVN: 688-4500. 12/1-bedroom, semi-private bath. Color TV, maid service. Older structure. Rates: $22.00 per person with orders.

Temporary Military Lodging Around the World — 133

NEW YORK

Stewart Army Sub-Post, continued

TML Availability: Fairly good, Oct-Mar. Difficult, other times.

Medical-563-3430 NCO Club-564-7590 O'Club-563-3341
Police-564-0580 Enlisted Club-564-7590

United States Military Academy, West Point (NY16R1)
West Point, NY 10996-5000

TELEPHONE NUMBER INFORMATION: Main installation numbers: Comm: 914-938-4011, ATVN: 688-1110.

Location: Off I-87 or US-9 west. Clearly marked. RM: p-67, EU/14. NMC: New York City, NY 36 miles south.

Billeting Office: Building 674. Comm: 446-4731. 24 hours daily. Check in facility, check out 1200 hours daily. No government civilian employee billeting.

TML: Hotel Thayer. Comm: 914-446-4731, or toll free 1-800-247-5047. ATVN: 688-2632. 200/1-bedroom, private bath. A/C, color TV room & lounge, maid service, cribs/cots $5.00 each, ice vending. Older structure, new furniture '86, renovation anticipated '90-'92. Rates: Single room with shower $49.00-$54.00, double room with shower $64.00-$70.00, suites with kitchenette $85.00-$140.00. Open to public. Reservations accepted 1 year in advance.

DV/VIP: Protocol Office, Building 600. EX-4315/4316. 07/GS-16+. Retirees Space-A.

Other: Part of the U. S. Armed Forces Recreation System. Overlooks the Hudson River. Group facility 10-300.

TML Availability: Good, except during special holiday events at USMA.

Enlisted Club-446-5507 Locator-938-4412 Medical-938-3637
NCO Club-446-5507 O'Club-446-5504 Police-938-3333
SDO/NCO-938-3500

NORTH CAROLINA

Camp Lejeune Marine Corps Base (NC10R1)
Camp Lejeune, NC 28542-5000

TELEPHONE NUMBER INFORMATION: Main installation numbers: Comm: 919-451-1113, ATVN: 484-1113.

Location: Main gate is 6 miles east of junction of US-17 and NC-24. RM: p-73, J/19. NMC: Jacksonville, 3 miles northwest.

Billeting Office: Building 2617, Seth-Williams. EX-2146/1385. 24 hours daily. Check in billeting, check out 1300 hours daily. Government civilian employee billeting.

TML: Hostess House. Building 896, off Holcomb Ave near MCBX. Check in after 1400 hours daily. 24 hour desk. All ranks. Leave or official duty. 90/1-bedroom, 2 double beds, semi-private bath, fold-out couch, sleeps 5 persons. Kitchen, utensils, A/C, color TV, maid service, cots ($1.00), coin washer/dryer, many extras. Modern

134 — *Temporary Military Lodging Around the World*

NORTH CAROLINA
Camp Lejeune Marine Corps Base, continued

structure, motel type. Rates: $18.00 per unit. Duty can make reservations. Others Space-A.

TML: BOQ/BEQ. Building 2617 (BOQ), EX-2146/1385. Officer all grades. Building HP-53 (BEQ), EX-5262. Enlisted E6-E9. Leave or official duty. 38/1-bedroom, semi-private bath; 27 separate bedrooms, living room, private bath; 1/2-bedroom, private bath, 23/1-bedroom, SNCO transient billeting. Refrigerator, community kitchen, limited utensils, A/C, color TV room & lounge, maid service, free cribs/cots, free washer/dryer, ice vending, facilities for disabled American veterans, free coffee & coffee maker. Older structure, renovated '87. Rates: $11.00-$21.00 per unit. Duty can make reservations. Others Space-A.

TML: DV/VIP. Building 2601: 1/2-bedroom suite, private bath, kitchen; 2/1-bedroom suites, private bath, kitchen. Building 2607, EX-2146: 3 separate bedroom suites, private bath, community kitchen. All have A/C, maid service, free washer/dryer, free cribs. Rates: 06+ $11.00-$18.00 per unit; DV $11.00-26.00. All categories can make reservations.

DV/VIP: Protocol Office, EX-2523. 06+. Retirees and lower grades Space-A.

TML Availability: Limited, year round.

Cafeteria-451-5867   Enlisted Club-451-2872   Locator-451-3074
Medical-451-4551   NCO Club-451-1534   O'Club-451-2465
Police-451-2555   Snack Bar-451-2394   SDO/NCO-451-2528

Cape Hatteras Coast Guard Recreational Quarters (NC09R1)
Group Cape Hatteras
Buxton, NC 27920-0604

TELEPHONE NUMBER INFORMATION: Main installation numbers: Comm: 919-995-6435.

Location: On base. From US-158 or US-64, take NC-12 to Buxton (approximately 50 miles south of Nags Head). Check in with USCG Group exchange or JOOD on Old Lighthouse Road. RM: p-73, G/26. NMC: Elizabeth City, 110 miles northwest.

Billeting Office: None. Reservations required with advance payment, 30-90 days in advance by mail. Address: Cape Hatteras Recreational Quarters, Group Cape Hatteras, P.O. Box 604, Buxton, NC 27920-0604. Comm: 919-995-6435.

TML: 6 rooms that sleep 3, rollaway available, community kitchen, private bath; 1 suite that sleeps 6, kitchen, private bath; 1 VIP suite (E7+), sleeps 6, private bath. Rates: $17.00-$24.00 for the first 6 rooms, $21.00-$29.00 for regular suite, $34.00-$40.00 for VIP suite. All categories can make reservations.

TML Availability: Limited. Book early.

Cherry Point Marine Corps Air Station (NC02R1)
Cherry Point, NC 28533-5001

TELEPHONE NUMBER INFORMATION: Main installation numbers: Comm: 919-466-2811, ATVN: 582-1110.

Location: On NC-101 between New Bern and Morehead City, NC. US-70 south connects with NC-101 at Havelock, NC. RM: p-73, I/21. NMC: Morehead City, 18

Temporary Military Lodging Around the World — 135

NORTH CAROLINA

Cherry Point Marine Corps Air Station, continued

miles southeast.

Billeting Office: Building 487 (Officer), Building 214 (Enlisted). EX-3601. 24 hours daily. Check in facility, check out 1100 hours daily. Government civilian employee billeting.

TML: Guest House (DGQ). O6+. Leave or official duty. EX-2848. 4-bedroom, private bath. Kitchen, complete utensils, A/C, color TV, maid service, free cribs/cots, washer/dryer. Rates: $20.00 (TDY), $5.00 each additional person.

TML: BOQ. Building 487, 496, 498 (E6-E9). Officer all grades, Enlisted E6-E9. Leave or official duty. Comm: 466-5169/5245. ATVN: 582-5169. Check out 1200 hours. 47/1-bedroom, private bath; 29 separate bedroom suites, private bath. Refrigerator, A/C, color TV, maid service, free cribs, free washer/dryer, ice vending. Older structure, renovated. Rates: Single $10.00, suite $13.00, each additional person over 2 years $5.00. Duty, leave, retired can make reservations. Others Space-A.

TML: DV/VIP. Building 313. Officer O6+. Leave or official duty. 3 bedroom suites. Kitchen, complete utensils, A/C, color TV, maid service. Older structure. Rates: $15.00 (TDY), $5.00 each additional person. All categories can make reservations.

DV/VIP: BOQ. Buildings 487, 496. Comm: 447-1220. ATVN: 582-5169. O6+. Retirees Space-A.

TML Availability: Very good all year.

Cafeteria-466-4381	Enlisted Club-466-2997	Locator-466-2109
Medical-466-4410	NCO Club-466-3087	O'Club-447-2303
Police-466-3615	Snack Bar-447-4233	SDO/NCO-466-5236

Elizabeth City Coast Guard Support Center (NC03R1)
Elizabeth City, NC 27909-5006

TELEPHONE NUMBER INFORMATION: Main installation numbers: Comm: 919-338-6115, FTS: 931-0115.

Location: Take I-65 east to VA-104S to US-17 south to Elizabeth City, left on Halstead Blvd; 3 miles to main gate of Center. RM: p-73, C/23. NMC: Elizabeth City, in the city.

Billeting Office: Building 5. Comm: 335-6397. FTS: 931-0115. 0800-1630 hours daily. Other hours duty persons, Building 5, Comm: 338-6115. Check in facility, check out 1200 hours daily. No government civilian employee billeting.

TML: Mobile homes. 16A-F. All ranks. Leave or official duty. 3/2-bedroom, private bath; 3/3-bedroom, private bath. Kitchen, limited utensils, A/C, black/white TV, coin washer/dryer. Modern structure. Rates: $20.00 per night, sleeps 6. Duty can make reservations. Other Space-A.

TML Availability: Good, Oct-Apr. Difficult, other times.

Enlisted Club-335-6403	Locator-335-6130	Medical-335-6460
NCO Club-335-6389	O'Club-335-6226	Police-335-6398
SDO/NCO-335-6130		

136 — *Temporary Military Lodging Around the World*

NORTH CAROLINA

Fort Bragg (NC05R1)
Fort Bragg, NC 28307-5000

TELEPHONE NUMBER INFORMATION: Main installation numbers: Comm: 919-396-0011, ATVN: 236-0011.

Location: From I-95 exit to NC-24 west which runs through Post as Bragg Blvd. From US-401 (Fayetteville Bypass) exit to All American Expressway, 5 miles to Fort. RM: p-72, H/13. NMC: Fayetteville, 15 miles southeast.

Billeting Office: Building D-3601 (Moon Hall), Room 101, off Bastogne Dr. EX-5575. 24 hours daily. Check in facility, check out 1100 hours daily. Government civilian employee billeting.

TML: Guest Houses. All ranks. Leave or official duty. Delmont House, Bastogne Dr, Building D-4215, EX-2211 (Comm), EX-4496 (ATVN). Normandy House, Totten & Armistead St, Building 1-4228, EX-2250 (Comm), EX-1970 (ATVN). Leal House, Reilly Rd across from main PX, Building 5-5047, EX-3033 (Comm), EX-8770 (ATVN). 111/1-bedroom, private bath; 7 separate bedroom suites, private bath. Kitchen (some), refrigerator, community kitchen, A/C, color TV room & lounge, maid service, free cribs/cots, free washer/dryer, ice vending, facilities for disabled American veterans (Delmont House). Modern structures. Rates: E1-E4 $12.00, E4+ $16.00, suites $17.00. PCS can make reservations. Others Space-A.

TML: VOQ/VEQ. Buildings D-3601, D-3705. All ranks. Leave or official duty. EX-7700. 520/1-bedroom, private bath; 27 separate bedroom suites, private bath. Kitchen (suites), refrigerator, A/C, color TV, maid service, free washer/dryer, ice vending, facilities for disabled American veterans. Modern structures. Rates: $12.00 (E1-E4), $16.00 (E5+), $17.00 suites. Maximum 2 per unit. Duty can make reservations. Others Space-A.

TML: DV/VIP. Building 1-4425. Officer O7+. Leave or official duty. EX-2804. 1/3-bedroom suite, private bath. Kitchen, complete utensils, A/C, color TV, maid service, free cribs/cots, free washer/dryer. Modern structure. Rates: $17.00 per suite. All categories can make reservations.

DV/VIP: Protocol Office. EX-2804. O7+. Retirees Space-A.

TML Availability: Good, Sep-Apr. Difficult, other times.

Cafeteria-436-0160   Enlisted Club-436-4200   Locator-396-1461
O'Club-436-1700/1945   Police-396-0391   SDO/NCO-396-6100

New River Marine Corps Air Station (NC06R1)
Jacksonville, NC 28545-5000

TELEPHONE NUMBER INFORMATION: Main installation numbers: Comm: 919-451-1113, ATVN: 484-1113.

Location: Off US-17, 2 miles south of Jacksonville. Clearly marked. RM: p-73, J/19. NMC: Jacksonville, 2 miles northeast.

Billeting Office: Duty Office, Building 705, Flounder Road. EX-6621/6903. 24 hours. Check in at facility, check out 1200 hours daily. Government civilian employee billeting.

Temporary Military Lodging Around the World — 137

NORTH CAROLINA

New River Marine Corps Air Station, continued

TML: BOQ. Building 705. Officer. All ranks. Enlisted 6+. Leave or official duty. 44/1-bedroom, private bath; 11 separate bedrooms, private bath. Refrigerator, A/C, color TV room & lounge, maid service, cribs/cots $2.00, essentials, free washer/dryer, food/ice vending, coffee makers, microwave. Modern structure. Carpets '89. Remodeled '88. Rates leave status: $10.00 single room, $15.00 2 room suite, $2.00 each additional person. Rates active duty status: Sponsor $6.00, each additional person $2.00. Maximum 4 persons per unit. Duty can make reservations. Others Space-A.

Other: Beirut Memorial.

TML Availability: Good. Best Sept-Mar. Difficult other times.

Enlisted Club-451-0589 Locator-451-6568 Medical-451-6532
NCO Club-451-6707 O'Club-451-6409 Police-451-6111
SDO/NCO-451-6524

Pope Air Force Base (NC01R1)
Pope AFB, NC 28308-5225

TELEPHONE NUMBER INFORMATION: Main installation numbers: Comm: 919-394-0001, ATVN: 486-1110.

Location: Take I-95, exit to NC-87/24 W. Signs point the direction to AFB and Ft Bragg. RM: p-73, H/14. NMC: Fayetteville, 12 miles southeast.

Billeting Office: Building 235, Ethridge St. EX-4131. 24 hours daily. Check in billeting, check out 1200 hours daily. Government civilian employee billeting with reservations.

TML: VOQ. Buildings 229-247. All ranks. Leave or official duty. 96/1-bedroom, private bath; 12 separate bedroom, private bath; 8/8-bedroom units. Community kitchen, refrigerator, A/C, color TV, maid service, free cribs, washer/dryer, ice vending. Older structure. Rates: Sponsor $6.00, adult $6.00. TDY can make reservations. Others Space-A.

TML: VAQ. Building 287. Enlisted all grades. Leave or official duty. 68/1-bedroom, share bath; 4 separate bedroom, private bath. Refrigerator, A/C, color TV, maid service, free washer/dryer, ice vending. Older structure. Rates: $6.00 per person. TDY can make reservations. Others Space-A.

TML: DV/VIP. Building 219. Officer 06+. Leave or official duty. EX-4739. 4/1-bedroom, private bath. Kitchen, utensils, A/C, color TV, maid service, free washer/dryer, ice vending. Older structure. Rates: $10.00 per person. All categories can make reservations.

DV/VIP: Protocol Office. Building 309, EX-4739. 06+. Retirees Space-A.

TML Availability: Good, winter. Difficult, other times.

Locator-394-1110/4131 Medical-394-2232 NCO Club-497-4051
O'Club-394-2154 Police-394-2800

Seymour Johnson Air Force Base (NC11R1)
Seymour Johnson AFB, NC 27531-5000

TELEPHONE NUMBER INFORMATION: Main installation numbers: Comm: 919-736-5400, ATVN: 488-1110.

138 — *Temporary Military Lodging Around the World*

NORTH CAROLINA
Seymour Johnson Air Force Base, continued

Location: From US-70 in Goldsboro take Seymour Johnson exit onto Berkeley Blvd to main gate. Clearly marked. RM: p-73, G/17. NMC: Raleigh, 50 miles northwest.

Billeting Office: ATTN: 4SVS/SVH. Building 3804, Wright Ave. EX-6705. 24 hours daily. Check in billeting, check out 1200 hours daily. Government civilian employee billeting VOQ.

TML: TLF. Building 3802. All ranks. Leave or official duty. 3/1-bedroom, private bath; 22/separate bedrooms, private bath; 2/2-bedroom, private bath. Kitchen, limited utensils, A/C, color TV, maid service, free washer/dryer, ice vending. Modern structure, renovated. Rates: $16.00 per unit. Maximum based on size of unit. Duty can make reservations. Others Space-A.

TML: VOQ. Building 3803. Officer all grades. Leave or official duty. 38/1-bedroom, private and semi-private baths; 6 separate bedrooms, private bath. Kitchen (1 unit), A/C, color TV room & lounge, maid service, free washer/dryer, ice vending. Modern structure, renovated. Rates: $8.00 per person. Maximum 2 persons. Duty can make reservations. Others Space-A.

TML: VAQ. Building 3804. Enlisted all grades. Leave or official duty. 21/1-bedroom, private and semi-private baths; 3 separate bedrooms, private bath; 5/1-bedroom, private bath. Color TV, maid service, free washer/dryer, ice vending. Modern structure, renovated '85. Rates: $8.00 per person. Maximum 2 persons. Duty can make reservations. Others Space-A.

TML: DV/VIP. Building 2820. Officer 06+. Leave or official duty. 2 separate bedrooms suites, private bath. Kitchen, color TV, maid service, free washer/dryer. Older structure. Rates: $8.00 per person. Duty can make reservations. Others Space-A at discretion of Wing Commander.

TML Availability: Good, Nov-Apr. Difficult, other times.

Enlisted Club-736-3905 Locator-736-5584 Medical-736-5577
NCO Club-734-2753 O'Club-735-8457 Police-736-6413
Snack Bar-736-6406

NORTH DAKOTA

Grand Forks Air Force Base (ND04R3)
Grand Forks AFB, ND 58205-5000

TELEPHONE NUMBER INFORMATION: Main installation numbers: Comm: 701-747-3000, ATVN: 362-3000.

Location: From I-29 take US-2 west exit for 14 miles to Grand Forks, County Rd B-3 (Emerado/Air Base) 1 mile to AFB. RM: p-71, D/15. NMC: Grand Forks, 15 miles east.

Billeting Office: ATTN: 842CSG/SVH, Building 117, Holzapple & 6th Ave. EX-3069/70. 24 hours daily. Check in billeting, check out 1200 hours daily. Government civilian employee billeting.

TML: TLF. Across street from billeting. All ranks. Leave or official duty. 40 efficiency apartments, private bath. Kitchen, limited utensils, A/C, color TV, maid

Temporary Military Lodging Around the World — 139

NORTH DAKOTA

Grand Forks Air Force Base, continued

service, free washer/dryer, ice vending. Modern structure. Rates: $21.00 per unit. PCS in/out reservations required. Duty can make reservations. Others Space-A.

TML: VOQ. Building 117. Officer all grades. Leave or official duty. 9/2-bedroom suites, private bath; 8/1-bedroom, semi-private bath. Refrigerator, A/C, color TV, maid service, free washer/dryer, ice vending. Rates: $9.00 per person. PCS in/out reservations required. Duty can make reservations. Others Space-A.

TML: VAQ. Building 117. Enlisted all ranks. Leave or official duty. 10/1-bedroom, semi-private bath; 10/2-bedroom suites, private bath. Refrigerator, color TV, maid service, free washer/dryer, free ice. Rates: $9.00 per person. PCS in/out reservations required. Duty can make reservations. Others Space-A.

TML: DV/VIP. Building 132. Officer 06+. Leave or official duty. 1/4-bedroom house, private bath. Kitchen, living room, dining room, free washer/dryer. Rates: $14.00 per person. For reservations contact Protocol (see below).

TML: DV/VIP. Building 117. Enlisted E8-E9. Leave or official duty. 2/2-bedroom suites, private bath. Living room, refrigerator, color TV, A/C, maid service, free washer/dryer, ice vending. Rates: $13.00 per person. For reservations contact Protocol (see below).

DV/VIP: 42 AD Protocol Office, Building 305. EX-4155. 06+. Retirees and lower grades Space-A.

TML Availability: Good, winter. Difficult, spring and summer.

Cafeteria-594-6729	Enlisted Club-594-6527	Locator-747-3344
Medical-747-5600	NCO Club-747-3392	O'Club-747-3131
Police-747-5351	Snack Bar-594-5941	

Minot Air Force Base (ND02R3)
Minot AFB, ND 58705-5000

TELEPHONE NUMBER INFORMATION: Main installation numbers: Comm: 701-723-1110, ATVN: 453-1110.

Location: On US-83, north of Minot. RM: p-71, B/7. NMC: Minot, 15 miles south.

Billeting Office: ATTN: 857 SVS/SVH, Billeting. Building 173. Missile Ave and Summit Dr. Comm: 727-6161. ATVN: 453-2184. 24 hours daily. Check in billeting, check out 1200 hours daily.

TML: TLF. Buildings 158-161. All ranks. Leave or official duty. EX-2184. 40 separate bedroom apartments, private bath. Kitchen, complete utensils, A/C, color TV, maid service, free cots, free washer/dryer. Modern structure. Rates: $19.00 per unit. Active duty Reservists can make reservations. Others Space-A.

TML: VOQ. Buildings 169, 170, 175, 182. Officer all grades. Leave or official duty. EX-2184. 44 rooms, semi-private bath. A/C, color TV, maid service, free washer/dryer, ice vending. Modern structure. Rates: $9.00 per person. Duty and active duty reservists can make reservations. Others Space-A.

TML: VAQ. Building 173. Enlisted all grades. Leave or official duty. EX-2184. 19/1-bedroom, semi-private bath; 3 separate bedrooms, private bath. Refrigerator, A/C, color TV, maid service, free washer/dryer, ice vending. Modern structure. Rates: $9.00 per person. Active duty Reservists can make reservations. Others Space-A.

140 — *Temporary Military Lodging Around the World*

NORTH DAKOTA
Minot Air Force Base, continued

TML: DVQ. Building 171. Officer 06+. Official duty only. EX-2184. 8 suites, semi-private bath. Kitchen, complete utensils, A/C, color TV, maid service, free washer/dryer, ice vending. Rates: $14.00 per person. Maximum $28.00 per suite. Duty can make reservations. Others Space-A.

DV/VIP: STAO/CCP Protocol Office, Building 167, EX-3474. 06+.

TML Availability: Generally good. Difficult Jul - Oct.

Cafeteria-727-4652	Enlisted Club-727-6158	Locator-723-1841
Medical-723-5300	NCO Club-727-6158	O'Club-727-6103
Police-723-3096	Snack Bar-727-4652	SDO/NCO-723-3102

OHIO

Rickenbacker Air National Guard Base (OH02R2)
Rickenbacker ANGB, OH 43217-5000

TELEPHONE NUMBER INFORMATION: Main installation numbers: Comm: 614-492-8211, ATVN: 950-1110.

Location: From I-270 take Alum Creek exit south to ANGB. Also, accessible off US-23 onto OH-317. Clearly marked. RM: p-77, SC/12. NMC: Columbus, 13 miles northwest.

Billeting Office: Building 92, EX-4545/46. 24 hours daily. Check in facility, check out 1100 hours daily. Government civilian employee billeting.

TML: VOQ/VAQ. Building 92. All ranks. Leave or official duty. 47/1-bedroom, semi-private bath. Refrigerator, A/C, color TV, maid service. Older structure. Rates: $6.00 per person. Duty can make reservations. Others Space-A.

TML: DV/VIP. Building S-9. Ofc 06+. Leave or official duty. 5 separate bedrooms, private bath. A/C, maid service. Older structure. Rates: $8.00 per person. Duty can make reservations. Others Space-A.

DV/VIP: PAO, EX-8211/1110. 06+.

TML Availability: Good, Oct-May.

Locator-492-8211/1110   Medical-492-3165   Police-492-4727

Wright-Patterson Air Force Base (OH01R2)
Wright-Patterson AFB, OH 45433-5000

TELEPHONE NUMBER INFORMATION: Main installation numbers: Comm: 513-257-1110, ATVN: 787-1110.

Location: South of I-70, off I-675 at Fairborn. Also, access from OH-4, AFB clearly marked. RM: p-77, SN/12. NMC: Dayton, 10 miles northwest.

Billeting Office: ATTN: 2750 SVS/SVH. Building 825, Schlatter Dr & Childlaw Rd. EX-3451. 24 hours daily. Check in billeting, check out 1200 hours daily. Government civilian employee billeting.

OHIO

Wright-Patterson Air Force Base, continued

TML: TLQ. Building 40. All ranks. Leave or official duty. EX-3810. 40/1-bedroom, private bath. Kitchen, complete utensils, A/C, color TV, maid service, free cribs, free washer/dryer, ice vending. Modern structure '74, renovated '84/85. Rates $16.00 per unit. Sleeps 5. Duty can make reservations. Others Space-A.

TML: TAQ. Building 1217. All ranks. Leave or official duty. Check out 1300 hours. 97/1-bedroom, 2 beds, semi-private bath; 11 separate bedrooms, private bath. Refrigerator, A/C, color TV, maid service, free washer/dryer, ice vending. Remodeled '86. Rates: Sponsor $6.00. No families. Duty can make reservations. Others Space-A.

TML: VOQ. Building 825. All ranks. Leave or official duty. 108/1-bedroom, private bath; 492/1-bedroom, semi-private bath. Refrigerator, A/C, color TV, maid service, washer/dryer, ice vending. Rates: $8.00 per person. Maximum $16.00 per family. Maximum 3 per room. Duty can make reservations. Others Space-A.

TML: DV/VIP. Building 826. Call about eligibility, EX-3118. Leave or official duty. 22/2-bedroom suites, private bath. Refrigerator, A/C, color TV, maid service, cribs/cots, free washer/dryer, ice vending, microwaves. Rates: $10.00 per person. Maximum 5 per suite. Duty can make reservations.

DV/VIP: Protocol, 2750 ABW/CCP, Building 10. EX-3118. 07/GS-16+. Retirees and lower grades Space-A.

TML Availability: Good, Nov-Apr. Difficult, other times.

Cafeteria-879-4317	Enlisted Club-257-2001	Locator-257-3231
Medical-257-2968	NCO Club-257-7292	O'Club-257-7407
Police-257-6841	Snack Bar-879-4317	

OKLAHOMA

Altus Air Force Base (OK02R3)
Altus AFB, OK 73523-5000

TELEPHONE NUMBER INFORMATION: Main installation numbers: Comm: 405-481/482-8100, ATVN: 866-1110.

Location: Off US-62 south of I-40 and west of I-44. From US-62 traveling west from Lawton, turn right at 1st traffic light in Altus and follow road to main gate northeast of Falcon Rd. RM: p-79, J/12. NMC: Lawton, 56 miles east.

Billeting Office: Building 82, EX-7356. 24 hours daily. Check in billeting, check out 1400 hours daily except TLF 1200 hours daily. Government civilian employee billeting.

TML: VOQ. Buildings 81-85. Officer all grades. 96/1-bedroom, private bath; 30 separate bedrooms, private bath. Kitchen, A/C, color TV, maid service, free washer/dryer. Modern structure, hotel type. Rates: $6.00 per person. Duty can make reservations. Others Space-A.

OKLAHOMA
Altus Air Force Base, continued

TML: VAQ. Building 82. Enlisted all grades. 198/1-bedroom, latrine bath. A/C, color TV room & lounge, maid service. Modern structure. Rates: $5.00 per person. Duty can make reservations. Others Space-A.

TML: DV/VIP. Building 81. Officer O4+. Leave or official duty. 6 separate bedrooms, private bath. Kitchen, A/C, color TV, maid service, free washer/dryer. Modern structure, hotel type. Rates: $6.00 per person. Duty can make reservations. Others Space-A.

DV/VIP: Wing EXO, Building 1. EX-7554. O6+. Retirees and lower grades Space-A.

TML Availability: Good, Dec. Difficult, other times.

Enlisted Club-481-7034　　Locator-481-6392　　Medical-481-5213
NCO Club-481-7034　　　　O'Club-481-6224　　Police-481-7444
SDO/NCO-481-7444

Fort Sill (OK01R3)
Fort Sill, OK 73508-5100

TELEPHONE NUMBER INFORMATION: Main installation numbers: Comm: 405-351-8111, ATVN: 639-7090.

Location: From I-44 at Lawton take US-62/277, 4 miles northwest to Post. Clearly marked. RM: p-79, J-14. NMC: Lawton, adjacent to city.

Billeting Office: ATTN: ATZR-EHB. Building 5676, Fergusson Rd. 24 hours daily. Comm: 353-5007, 351-5000. ATVN: 639-5000. Check in billeting, check out 1200 hours daily. Government civilian employee billeting DV/VOQ.

TML: Guest House. Office in Building 5690. Geronimo Road. 24 hours daily. Comm: 351-3214, ATVN: 639-3214. Check in Building 5690. All ranks. Leave or official duty. 75 rooms. Refrigerator, microwave, kitchen, A/C, color TV in room & lounge, maid service, cribs/cots, free washer/dryer, ice vending. Rates: E1-E4, $12.00 per room; E5, E6, W1, & O1, $17.00 per room; E7-E9, W2-W4, 02-03, $22.00 per room; 04-05, Guests, $25.00 per room. PCS can make reservations. Others Space-A. New structure opened Dec 1988.

TML: BOQ/BEQ. E7+. Official duty only. Reservations not taken. Waiting list maintained. Must be signed into unit to get on waiting list. 138 spaces in BOQ, 40 spaces in BEQ. Modern structure, renovated '87. Rates: No charge for room; maid fee $2/$3 per day. Maximum 1 per room. Dependents not authorized.

TML: VOQ/VEQ. Both take overflow from Guest House. All ranks. Official duty only. 649 spaces in VOQ, 246 spaces in VEQ and 11 VIP suites. Modern structure, renovated '86. Rates: Sponsor $17.50, adult $7.00, VOQ/VIQ, and $20.50-$25.00 VIP suites. No children. Billeting recommends that children stay in guest house with spouse. Duty can make reservations. Others Space-A.

TML: DVQ. Building 460. Officer O6/GS-15+. Leave or official duty. 351-5511. Kitchen, complete utensils. Modern structure, renovated. Rates: Sponsor $25.00 at Comanche House (Building 460); all other DVQs $20.50, additional adult $7.00. Duty can make reservations. Others Space-A.

DV/VIP: Protocol Office, Building 460. 351-4825. O6/GS-15+. Retirees Space-A.

TML Availability: Fairly good, fall, winter, spring. Difficult, summer.

Temporary Military Lodging Around the World — 143

OKLAHOMA

Fort Sill, continued

Cafeteria-353-6209
Medical-351-4878
Police-351-2102

Enlisted Club-357-8145
NCO Club-248-7602
Snack Bar-248-7025

Locator-351-6172
O'Club-355-9112
SDO/NCO-351-4912

Tinker Air Force Base (OK04R3)
Tinker AFB, OK 73145-5000

TELEPHONE NUMBER INFORMATION: Main installation numbers: Comm: 405-732-7321, ATVN: 884-1110.

Location: Southeast Oklahoma City, off I-40. Use gate 1 off Air Depot Blvd. Clearly marked. RM: p-79, O/6. NMC: Oklahoma City, 12 miles northwest.

Billeting Office: ATTN: 2854 SVS/SVH. Building 5604. Comm: 405-734-2822. 24 hours daily. Check in billeting, check out 1300 hours daily for DV, VOQ, and VAQ. 1100 hours daily for TLQ. Government civilian employee billeting.

TML: TLF. Buildings 5024/26/28/30/32. All ranks. Leave or official duty. 40 rooms. Refrigerator, A/C, color TV, maid service, washer/dryer. Rates: $18.00 per unit. Duty can make reservations. Others Space-A.

TML: VOQ/VAQ. Buildings 5604/05/06. Officer all grades. Enlisted all grades. Leave or official duty. Approximately 130 rooms, private and semi-private baths. Refrigerator, A/C, color TV, maid service, free washer/dryer. Rates: $6.00 per person. Duty can make reservations. Others Space-A.

TML: SNCO Quarters. Building 5915. Enlisted E7-E9. Leave or official duty. 21 rooms. Call about types of facilities available. Rates: $8.00 per room. Duty can make reservations. Others Space-A.

DV/VIP: OC-ALC/CCP, Building 3001. Comm: 734-5511. 07/GS-16+. Retirees and lower grades Space-A.

TML Availability: Good all year.

Cafeteria-734-3161
NCO Club-734-3435
Snack Bar-734-3486

Locator-734-2456
O'Club-734-3418

Medical-734-8249
Police-734-2151

Vance Air Force Base (OK05R3)
Vance AFB, OK 73705-5000

TELEPHONE NUMBER INFORMATION: Main installation numbers: Comm: 405-237-2121, ATVN: 962-7110.

Location: Off US-81 south of Enid. Clearly marked. RM: p-79, D/15. NMC: Oklahoma City, 90 miles southeast.

Billeting Office: Building 714, Goad St. 249-7358. 24 hours daily. Check in billeting, check out 1200 hours daily. Government civilian employee billeting.

TML: TLF. Building 790. All ranks. Leave or official duty. 10 separate bedrooms, private bath. Kitchen, utensils, A/C, color TV, maid service, free cribs, washer/dryer, ice vending. Rates: E6-$14.00 per unit, E7+ $18.00 per unit. Duty can make reservations. Others Space-A.

TML: VOQ/TAQ. Building 714. All ranks. Leave or official duty. 20/1-bedroom, private bath; 1 separate bedroom suite, private bath (DV/VIP); 2/2-bedroom suites,

OKLAHOMA
Vance Air Force Base, continued

private bath (DV/VIP). Kitchen, microwave, A/C, color TV room & lounge, maid service, washer/dryer, ice vending, facilities for disabled American veterans. Modern structure. Rates: $7.00 per person ($10.00 DV/VIP). Maximum $21.00 per family ($30.00 DV/VIP). Duty can make reservations. Others Space-A.

DV/VIP: Wing EXO, Building 500, Ex-7202. 06+. Retirees Space-A.

TML Availability: Difficult. Best, Dec, Jan.

Locator-249-7791   Medical-249-7416   NCO Club-237-7311
O'Club-237-2326   Police-249-7200

OREGON

Kingsley Field (OR03R4)
Klamath Falls, OR 97603-0400

TELEPHONE NUMBER INFORMATION: Main installation numbers: Comm: 503-885-6365, ATVN: 830-6110.

Location: On Highway 140. RM: p-80, P/9. NMC: Klamath Falls, 5 miles west.

Billeting Office: Building 208. Kingsley Street. Hours 0730-1530. EX-6365. After hours extra keys at Security Gate.

TML: VOQ. All ranks. Leave or official duty. 20 suites, private bath. 40 rooms with two beds, semi-private bath. Older structure, renovated. Rates: suites $8.00 per person, single rooms $6.00 per person. Students have priority in reservations. Others Space-A.

Other: Trappers Inn Restaurant nearby.

TML Availability: Difficult, except for holidays.

NOTE: Both VOQ and restaurant operated under contract to Commission for the Blind.

PENNSYLVANIA

Carlisle Barracks (PA08R1)
Carlisle Barracks, PA 17013-5002

TELEPHONE NUMBER INFORMATION: Main installation numbers: Comm: 717-245-3131, ATVN: 242-4141.

Location: From I-81 exit 16 to US-11, 2 miles southwest to Carlisle, signs clearly marked to Barracks and Army War College. RM: p-85, ES/3. NMC: Harrisburg, 18 miles north.

Billeting Office: ATTN: ATZE-DI-GH. Building 7, Ashburn St. EX-4245. 0700-1800 hours weekdays, 0900-1600 hours weekends. Other hours Building 400, pick up key at MP desk. Check in billeting, check out 1100 hours daily.

Temporary Military Lodging Around the World — 145

PENNSYLVANIA

Carlisle Barracks, continued

Government civilian employee billeting. Note: only family members with valid ID card can stay at this facility.

TML: Guest House. Buildings 7, 37. All ranks. Leave or official duty. 14 rooms, private bath; 4 rooms, shared bath; 6 rooms, community bath; 4 VIP suites, private bath (1 night only). Community kitchen, A/C, color TV room & lounge, maid service, $2.00 cribs/cots, ice vending. Rates: $5.00-$25.00 with private bath, $5.00-$20.00 with shared bath, $5.00-$15.00 with community bath, $25.00-$30.00 suites PCS and guests of USAWC have priority. All categories can make reservations.

Other: Gettysburg Battlefields.

TML Availability: Good, Jan-May. Difficult, other times.

Enlisted Club-245-4961
NCO Club-245-4961
SDO/NCO-245-4342
Locator-245-3131
O'Club-245-3215
Medical-245-3915/3400
Police-245-4315

Fort Indiantown Gap (PA04R1)
Annville, PA 17003-5011

TELEPHONE NUMBER INFORMATION: Main installation numbers: Comm: 717-865-5444, EX-2512, ATVN: 277-2512.

Location: From I-81 take exit 29 west, north on PA-934 to facility. RM: p-85, EQ/7. NMC: Harrisburg, 20 miles southwest.

Billeting Office: ATTN: AFKA-ZQ-DE-H, Building T-0-1, Fisher Ave at traffic light, EX-2512. 0800-2330 hours daily. Check in billeting, check out 1100 hours daily. No government civilian employee billeting.

TML: VOQ/BEQ. Building T-0-1. Officer all grades, Enlisted E7-E9. Leave or official duty. 26/1-room, latrine bath; 5 separate bedroom, private bath. A/C, color TV, maid service, washer/dryer, facilities for disabled American veterans. Older structure, renovated. Rates: $7.00 and $9.00 per room. No dependents.

DV/VIP: Admin Office, Building T-0-1, EX-2552. 06 in command position and above.

TML Availability: Difficult, most of the time. Best, Nov-Mar.

Enlisted Club-865-2450
O'Club-865-2460
Locator-865-5444
Police-865-2160
NCO Club-865-2450
SDO/NCO-EX-2444

Letterkenny Army Depot (PA03R1)
Chambersburg, PA 17201-4150

TELEPHONE NUMBER INFORMATION: Main installation numbers: Comm: 717-267-8111, ATVN: 570-1110.

Location: From I-81 exit 8 west on PA-997 to PA-233 on left and enter depot at Gate 6. RM: p-83, WT/17. NMC: Harrisburg, 45 miles northeast.

Billeting Office: ATTN: SDSLE-EH, Building 663. EX-8890. 0730-1600 hours M-F. Other hours call security at 267-8800. Check in billeting, check out 1000 hours daily. Government civilian employee billeting.

PENNSYLVANIA
Letterkenny Army Depot, continued

TML: Guest House. Building 539. All ranks. Leave or official duty. 3 apartments. 1/1-bedroom, private bath; 1 separate bedroom, private bath; 1/2-bedroom, private bath. Kitchen, limited utensils, A/C, color TV, maid service, free cribs/cots, free washer/dryer. Older structure, renovated. Rates: 1 bedroom $12.00, separate bedroom $14.00, 2 bedroom $17.00. Duty, disabled American veterans, military widows can make reservations. Others Space-A.

DV/VIP: ATTN: SDSLE-CA. Building 500, EX-8659. DV/VIP determined by CO. Retirees Space-A.

Other: Gettysburg Battlefield.

TML Availability: Best, Sept-March.

Cafeteria-264-1321
Police-267-8800
Locator-264-1413
SDO/NCO-267-8792
O'Club-264-141

Mechanicsburg Navy Ships Parts Control Center (PA07R1)
Mechanicsburg, PA 17055-0788

TELEPHONE NUMBER INFORMATION: Main installation numbers: Comm: 717-790-2900, ATVN: 430-2900.

Location: From I-83 exit 20 to US-11, 4 miles. Or from PA Turnpike (I-76), exit 16 (Carlisle), 8 miles to Center. RM: p-75, EY/1. NMC: Harrisburg, 10 miles northeast.

Billeting Office: Building 214. Operated by Navy Exchange EX-2608. 0800-1600 hours daily. Other hours, OD, Building 310, EX-4444. Check in billeting, check out 1100 hours daily. No government civilian employee billeting.

TML: Navy Lodge. Building 17. All ranks. Leave or official duty. For reservations call 1-800-NAVY-INN. Lodge number is 766-0507. 2 apartments, sleeps 6, private bath; 2 apartments, sleeps 4, private bath; 4 rooms, sleeps 4, private bath; 1 room, sleeps 2, private bath. Kitchen (apartments), refrigerator, A/C, color cable TV, maid service, free cribs/cots, coin washer/dryer, ice vending. Older structure. Rates: $28.00 apartments, $25.00 rooms. All categories can make reservations.

DV/VIP: PAO, Building 311, EX-3338. 08/GS-16/SES +.

Other: Hershey Park.

TML Availability: Good. Limited, summer months.

Cafeteria-790-3537
NCO Club-790-3104
SDO/NCO-790-4444
Locator-790-2000
O'Club-790-3505
Medical-790-3461
Police-790-3351

New Cumberland Army Depot (PA06R1)
New Cumberland, PA 17070-5001

TELEPHONE NUMBER INFORMATION: Main installation numbers: Comm: 717-770-6011, ATVN: 977-6011, FTS: 589-6011.

Location: From I-83 take exit 18 to PA 114. East for 1 mile to Old York Rd, L .75 mile to Ross Ave, right for 1 mile to main gate. RM: p-85, EZ/4. NMC:

Temporary Military Lodging Around the World — 147

PENNSYLVANIA

New Cumberland Army Depot, continued

Harrisburg, 7 miles northeast.

Billeting Office: ATTN: SDSNC-EH, Building 268, J Ave, EX-7035. 0700-1700 hours daily. Other hours Security Office, Building 102, EX-6279. Check in billeting, check out 1200 hours daily. Government civilian employee billeting in VOQ.

TML: VOQ/DV/VIP. Building 268. All ranks. Leave or official duty. 18/1-bedroom, shared bath; 1 separate bedroom, private bath; 1/2-bedroom, private bath. Refrigerator, community kitchen, A/C, color TV, maid service, free cribs, cots ($2.00), free washer/dryer. Older structure. New carpeting, TVs, A/C. Rates: VOQ $20.00, DVQ $24-$26.00, each additional person $4.00. Duty with TDY orders can make reservations. Others Space-A. Maximum 2 adults and 1 child per unit.

DV/VIP: Protocol Office. Building 81, EX-7192. 06/GS-15+. Retirees and lower grades Space-A.

Other: Hershey Park, Dutch Country, Gettysburg National Military Park, Lee's Headquarters and Museum.

TML Availability: Good, Oct-Dec and Feb-Mar. Difficult, other times.

Cafeteria-770-7165　　Locator-770-6011　　Medical-770-7281
NCO Club-770-7802　　O'Club-770-7802　　Police-770-6222
SDO/NCO-770-6601

Philadelphia Naval Base (PA09R1)
Philadelphia, PA 19112-5098

TELEPHONE NUMBER INFORMATION: Main installation numbers: Comm: 215-897-5000, ATVN: 443-5000.

Location: Exit I-95 North at Broad St. Base gate is 20 yards south of exit. RM: p-67, I/6. NMC: Philadelphia, in the city.

Billeting Office: Building 889, 24 hours daily. EX-5318/17/16. Check in facility, check out 1100 hours daily. No government civilian employee billeting.

TML: Navy Lodge. For reservations call 1-800-NAVY INN. Lodge number is 215-465-9001. All ranks. Leave or official duty. 50/1-bedroom, 2 double beds, private bath. Kitchen, color TV, convenience store, vending machines. Rates: $32.00 per room. All categories can make reservations.

TML: BOQ. Officer WO1-O10. Official duty only. Call for room and rate info. EX-5316/17/18.

TML Availability: Limited.

Philadelphia Naval Station (PA11R1)
Philadelphia, PA 19112-5098

TELEPHONE NUMBER INFORMATION: Main installation numbers: Comm: 215-897-5000, ATVN: 443-5000.

Location: From I-95 North exit at Broad St. Facility gate 200 yards south of exit. RM: p-87, I/6. NMC: Philadelphia, in the city.

Billeting Office: Office, Building 889, Patrol Rd & 2nd St East., EX-5317/8. Enlisted Building 1031, EX-5160/1. 24 hours. Check in facility, check out 1100

PENNSYLVANIA
Philadelphia Naval Station, continued

hours daily. No government civilian employee billeting.

TML: BOQ. Buildings 886, 887. Officer all grades. 136/1-bedroom, shared bath; 4 separate bedroom, private bath. Refrigerator, A/C, color TV room & lounge, maid service, free washer/dryer, ice vending. Modern structure, renovated. Rates: $4.00 per person. Duty can make reservations. Others Space-A.

TML: BEQ. Buildings 974, 1006, 1031. Enlisted all grades. Leave or official duty. 48/1-bedroom, latrine bath (female & E7-E9 male private bath). Refrigerator, A/C, color TV lounge, free washer/dryer. Modern structure. Rates: $2.00 per person. Duty can make reservations. Others Space-A.

DV/VIP: ATTN: Flag Lt. Bldg 6, EX-7622. O6+. Retirees Space-A.

Other: Liberty bell. Many historic exhibits and museums.

TML Availability: Good, winter months. Difficult, other times.

Cafeteria-952-5061	CPO Club-897-5274	Enlisted Club-897-5274
Locator-897-5550	Medical-897-6837	O'Club-467-1810
Police-897-4242	SDO/NCO-897-5120	

Tobyhanna Army Depot (PA05R1)
Tobyhanna, PA 18466-5058

TELEPHONE NUMBER INFORMATION: Main installation numbers: Comm: 717-894-7000, ATVN: 795-7110.

Location: I-80 East or West to I-380 North, exit 7 to Depot. RM: p-85, EK/13. NMC: Scranton, 24 miles northwest.

Billeting Office: ATTN: SDSTO-EH-F, Building 1001, Admin Loop. EX-7647. 0800-1630 hours daily. Other hours Security, Building 20, EX-7550. Check in billeting, check out 1200 hours daily. Government civilian employee billeting.

TML: Guest House. Building 1013; VOQ Building 1005; BOQs Buildings 1004-5. All ranks. Leave or official duty. 1/2-bedroom, private bath; 1/3-bedroom, private bath; 1/4-bedroom, private bath; 9 separate bedrooms, private bath. Kitchen, limited utensils, color TV, maid service, free cribs, free washer/dryer. Older structure. Rates: Sponsor $11.00, each additional person $3.00. Maximum $25.00 per family. Duty can make reservations. Others Space-A.

DV/VIP: ATTN: Protocol Office. Building 11-2, EX-6223. O6+. Retirees and lower grades Space-A.

Other: In the Pocono Mountains Resort Area. Excellent skiing and fishing.

TML Availability: Good, Apr-Nov. More difficult, other times.

Cafeteria-894-7998	Cons Club-894-8283	Locator-894-7000
Medical-894-7121	Police-894-7550	SDO/NCO-894-7550

Willow Grove Naval Air Station (PA01R1)
Willow Grove, PA 19090-5010

TELEPHONE NUMBER INFORMATION: Main installation numbers: Comm: 215-443-1000, ATVN: 991-1000.

Temporary Military Lodging Around the World — 149

PENNSYLVANIA

Willow Grove Naval Air Station, continued

Location: Take PA Turnpike (I-276), exit 27 north on PA 611 5 miles to NAS. RM: p-87, I/6. NMC: Philadelphia, 21 miles south.

Billeting Office: Building 609, EX-6038/6041. 24 hours daily. Check in facility, check out 1200 hours daily. Government civilian employee billeting at BOQ.

TML: BOQ. Building 5. Officer all grades. Official duty only. EX-6038/6041. 20/1-bedroom, latrine bath. Refrigerator, color TV, maid service. Older structure. Rates: $4.00 per person.

TML: BEQ. Building 609, Enlisted all grades. Leave or official duty. 40/1-bedroom, shared bath; 5/2-bedroom suites, private bath. A/C, maid service, refrigerator, color TV, free washer/dryer. Rates: $4.00 per person over 12 years, $2.00 per person under 12. Maximum 5 per unit. Duty can make reservations. Others Space-A.

DV/VIP: PAO. Building 1 top deck, EX-6060/6076. DV/VIP determined by PAO. Retirees and lower grades Space-A.

TML Availability: Fair except weekends when extremely limited due to Reserve Unit and individual training.

Enlisted Club-443-6088   Locator-443-6053   Medical-443-1600
O'Club-443-6081   Police-443-6007   SDO/NCO-443-6454

RHODE ISLAND

Newport Naval Education & Training Center (RI01R1)
Newport, RI 02841-5000

TELEPHONE NUMBER INFORMATION: Main installation numbers: Comm: 401-841-2311, ATVN: 948-1110.

Location: From US-1 exit to RI-138 East over Jamestown/Newport bridge (toll) to Newport. Follow signs to Naval base, gate # 1. RM: p-19, H/24. NMC: Newport, 2 miles south.

Billeting Office: No central billeting office. Officer, Building 684, EX-3157. Enlisted, Building 447, EX-4410. Both 24 hours daily. Check in facility. Officer check out 1200 hours daily. Enlisted check out 1400 hours daily. No government civilian employee billeting in BEQ.

TML: BOQ/BEQ. 575/1-bedroom, private/shared bath; 4 separate bedrooms, private bath. Full facility. Rates: Moderate. No families. Duty can make reservations. Others Space-A.

TML: Navy Lodge. Building 685. All ranks. Leave or official duty. For reservations call 1-800-NAVY-INN. Lodge number is 849-4500. 0700-2300 hours daily. Check out 1200 hours daily. 67 studio apartments, 2 double beds, 1 studio couch, sleeps 5, private bath. Kitchen, complete utensils, A/C, color TV room & lounge, maid service, free cribs, coin washer/dryer, ice vending. Modern structure. Rates: $30.00 per unit. All categories can make reservations.

DV/VIP: Contact CO, EX-3456.

Other: Sailing events. Naval War College Museum.

TML Availability: Good, winter months. Difficult, summer months.

150 — *Temporary Military Lodging Around the World*

RHODE ISLAND
Newport Naval Education & Training Center, continued

Cafeteria-841-3994   CPO Club-841-3877   Enlisted Club-841-3994
Locator-841-4001   Medical-841-3111/2222   O'Club-846-2515
Police-841-3241   Snack Bar-846-7671   SDO/NCO-841-3456

SOUTH CAROLINA

Beaufort Marine Corps Air Station (SC01R1)
Beaufort, SC 29904-5000

TELEPHONE NUMBER INFORMATION: Main installation numbers: Comm: 803-522-7100, ATVN: 832-7100.

Location: From I-95 exit at Pocataligo to SC-21, 4 miles to MCAS. Clearly marked. RM: p-88, K/10. NMC: Savannah, 40 miles south.

Billeting Office: BOQ, Building 431. EX-7676 (reservations), EX-7674 (front desk). 24 hours daily. Check in facility, check out 1200 hours daily. Government civilian employee billeting.

TML: Hostess House. Building 1108. Comm: 522-1663. All ranks. Leave or official duty. Accessible to handicapped. 21/1-bedroom, private bath; 21 separate bedroom, private bath. Kitchen (in separate bedroom), A/C, cots ($5.00), cribs, ice vending. maid service, special facilities for disabled American veterans, color TV, complete utensils, washer/dryer, playground, picnic area with grills. Modern structure. Rates: $21.00 E5- and $26.00 for E6+ with an extra $10.00 for units with kitchen. Maximum 5 per unit. All categories can make reservations. Non-military personnel visiting relatives stationed at Beaufort may stay on a space-available basis.

TML: BOQ. Building 431. Officer all grades, Enlisted E6-E9. Leave or official duty. 39 rooms, 5 suites, shared bath/private bath. Refrigerator, community kitchen, limited utensils, A/C, color TV room & lounge, maid service, free cribs, free washer/dryer, ice vending. Modern structure, renovated. Room and suite rates: Moderate. Duty can make reservations. Others Space-A.

DV/VIP: Contact CO, Building 601. EX-7158. Retirees and lower grades Space-A.

Other: Historic homes in Beaufort.

TML Availability: Very good, most of the year. Best, Sept-April.

Cafeteria-522-7895   Enlisted Club-522-7592   Locator-522-7188
Medical-522-7311   O'Club-522-7541   Police-522-7373
Snack Bar-522-7895   SDO/NCO-522-7121

Charleston Air Force Base (SC06R1)
Charleston AFB, SC 29404-5415

TELEPHONE NUMBER INFORMATION: Main installation numbers: Comm: 803-566-6000, ATVN: 673-2100.

Location: From I-26 East exit to West Aviation Ave to traffic light, continue through light to 2nd light on right, follow Rd around end of runway to Gate 2 (River Gate). RM: p-88, I/12. NMC: Charleston, 5 miles southeast.

SOUTH CAROLINA

Charleston Air Force Base, continued

Billeting Office: Building 322, Davis Dr. Comm: 552-9900. ATVN: 673-2640. 24 hours daily. Check in facility, check out 1200 hours daily. Government civilian employee billeting in contract quarters.

TML: VOQ/DV/VIP. Buildings 343, 346, 362. Officer all grades. Leave or official duty. 102/1-bedroom, shared bath; 7/1-bedroom suites, private bath (06+). Kitchen, refrigerator, A/C, maid service, free cribs/cots, free washer/dryer, ice vending. Modern structure. Rates: $6.00 per person. Maximum $12.00 per room. Maximum 5 per room. Duty can make reservations. Others Space-A.

TML: VAQ. Building 300, 302, 304. Enlisted all grades. Leave or official duty. 370/1-bedroom, hall bath. A/C, color TV, maid service, free washer/dryer, ice vending. Rates: $6.00 per person. Duty can make reservations. Others Space-A. No dependents.

DV/VIP: Office of the Wing CO, Building 103, Room 1. EX-3203. 06+. Retirees Space-A.

TML Availability: Good, Nov-Dec. Difficult, other times because of duty traffic.

Cafeteria-566-4307 Locator-566-3282/3574 Medical-566-2775
NCO Club-566-3837 O'Club-566-3925 Police-566-3642
Snack Bar-566-3343 SDO/NCO-566-0230

Charleston Naval Base (SC04R1)
Charleston, SC 29408-5006

TELEPHONE NUMBER INFORMATION: Main installation numbers: Comm: 803-743-4111, ATVN: 563-4111.

Location: From I-26 take Cosgrove Ave exit to Spruill Ave, right for 3 miles to main gate of NB. RM: p-88, J/16. NMC: Charleston, 5 miles north.

Billeting Office: Building 54, Osprey St. 24 hours daily. EX-5268/5528. Check in billeting, check out 1200 hours daily. Government civilian employee billeting.

TML: Navy Lodge. Building 225. All ranks. Leave or official duty. For reservations call 1-800-NAVY-INN. Lodge number is 747-7676. 24 hours daily. 48/1- & 2-bedroom, private bath. Kitchen, complete utensils, A/C, color TV, maid service, free cribs, free washer/dryer, ice vending. Modern structure. Rates: $26.00 per unit. Maximum 5 per unit. All categories can make reservations. Note: expansion of this facility planned by 1990.

TML: BOQ/BEQ. All ranks. Leave or official duty (BOQ), official duty only (BEQ). 540 units, hall bath/private bath. Refrigerator, A/C, color TV room & lounge, maid service, washer/dryer. Rates: No charge. Duty on orders and on leave can make reservations. Active duty Reservists Space-A. Others not authorized.

TML: VOQ/DV/VIP. Building 28. Officer all grades. Leave or official duty. EX-5394/3939. 24 hours daily. Check out 1200 hours daily. 179/1-bedroom, private bath; 47 separate bedroom, private bath. Refrigerator, A/C, color TV room & lounge, maid service, free cribs/cots, free washer/dryer, ice vending. Modern structure. Rates: Depends on status. Duty can make reservations. Others Space-A.

DV/VIP: CO's Office, EX-4111. E9, 07+.

Other: Patriots Point Maritime Museum, Gardens, Historic Charleston.

TML Availability: Very good all year.

152 — Temporary Military Lodging Around the World

SOUTH CAROLINA
Charleston Naval Base, continued

Cafeteria-743-5328	Enlisted Club-743-5266	Locator-743-4111
Medical-743-5130	NCO Club-743-5526	O'Club-743-6376
Police-743-5555	Snack Bar-743-5416	SDO/NCO-743-5430

Fort Jackson (SC09R1)
Fort Jackson, SC 29207-5000

TELEPHONE NUMBER INFORMATION: Main installation number: Comm: 803-751-7511, ATVN: 734-1110.

Location: Exit from I-20 north of the Fort or from US-76/378 south of the Fort or US-601 east of the Fort. From I-20 take Ft Jackson or Two Notch Rd exit, left on Decker Blvd, right on Percival Rd to Fort entrance. RM: p-88, E/9. NMC: Columbia, SC 12 miles southwest.

Billeting Office: Building 2785, Semmes Rd & Lee Rd. Toll free reservations 1-800-221-3503. 24 hours daily. Check in billeting, check out 1000 hours daily. Government civilian employee billeting.

TML: Guest House. Palmetto Lodge. Building 6000. All ranks. Leave or official duty. EX-4779. 70/1-bedroom, private bath. Sleeps 6 persons. Kitchen, limited utensils, A/C, color TV room & lounge, maid service, washer/dryer, ice vending. Rates: $24.00 per couple, $2.00 child over 6. Duty can make reservations. Others Space-A.

TML: Kennedy Hall. Building 2785. All ranks. Leave or official duty. 96/1-bedroom, 2 beds, private bath (transient units); 62 BOQ units. Refrigerator, A/C, color TV, maid service, free washer/dryer. Modern structure, remodeled. Rates: Sponsor $13.50, adult $5.00. Maximum 2 per unit. No children. Duty can make reservations. Others Space-A.

TML: VEQ. Building 2464. Enlisted all grades. Leave or official duty. 12/1-bedroom, 3 beds, private bath. Refrigerator, color TV, maid service. Modern structure. Rates: Sponsor $13.50, adult $5.00, maximum 3 persons. Duty can make reservations. Others Space-A.

TML: DV/VIP. Cottages. Building 3640-3645, 4410. Legion Landing & Dozier House. Officer 05+. Leave or official duty. Check out 1100 hours. 2/1-bedroom, private bath, suite; 4/2-bedroom, private bath; 1/3-bedroom, private bath (separate house, Dozier). Kitchen, utensils, A/C, color TV, maid service. Modern structure. Rates: Sponsor $18.00, adult $5.00, 3rd occupant $2.00. Maximum 2-6 persons. Duty can make reservations. Others Space-A.

DV/VIP: Protocol Office, Hq Building. Comm: EX-6618. ATVN: EX-5218. 06+. Retirees and lower grades Space-A.

TML Availability: Very good, Oct-May. Difficult, other times.

Enlisted Club-782-1932	Locator-751-7671	Medical-911
NCO Club-782-1932	O'Club-751-4906	Police-751-3113
Snack Bar-751-4759	SDO/NCO-751-7613/4	

Myrtle Beach Air Force Base (SC07R1)
Myrtle Beach AFB, SC 29579-5000

TELEPHONE NUMBER INFORMATION: Main installation numbers: Comm: 803-238-7211, ATVN: 748-7211.

Temporary Military Lodging Around the World — 153

SOUTH CAROLINA

Myrtle Beach Air Force Base, continued

Location: From I-95 exit east on US-501, right on US-17 (business) to AFB. Clearly marked. RM: p-88, F/15. NMC: Myrtle Beach, in city limits.

Billeting Office: ATTN: 354 CSG/SVH. Building 126, A Ave & 4th St. Comm: 238-5101. ATVN: 748-7691. 24 hours daily. Check in billeting, check out 1200 hours daily. Government civilian employee billeting.

TML: TLQ. Buildings 115, 127. All ranks. Leave or official duty. 12/2-bedroom, private bath; 2/1-bedroom, private bath. Kitchen, complete utensils, A/C, color TV, maid service, free cribs/cots, free washer/dryer. Modern structure. Rates: $18.00 per family. PCS in/out can make reservations. Others Space-A.

TML: VOQ. Building 126. All ranks. Leave or official duty. 34/1-bedroom, shared bath; 2/1-bedroom, private bath. Refrigerator, A/C, color TV, maid service, free washer/dryer, ice vending. Modern structure, renovated. Rates: $9.00 per room per night. Maximum 1 per room. TDY can make reservations. Others Space-A.

TML: TAQ. Building 249. All ranks. Leave or official duty. 36/1-bedroom, 2 beds, shared bath. Same facility as VOQ. Modern structure, new carpeting, TVs, drapes in '87. Rates: $7.00 per person. Maximum 2 per room. TDY can make reservations. Others Space-A. 1/1 bedroom Chief suite, private bath.

TML: DV/VIP. Building 126. Officer 06+. Leave or official duty. Comm: EX-7673/5101. ATVN: EX-7673/7691. 2/1-bedroom, private bath; 1/2 bedroom suite, private bath. Kitchen, complete utensils, A/C, color TV, maid service, free cribs/cots, free washer/dryer, ice vending. Modern structure, renovated. Rates: $10.00. Maximum charge $20.00 (1 bedroom), $40.00 (2 bedroom). Duty can make reservations. Others Space-A.

DV/VIP: 354 TFW/CCE. Building 104. EX-7673. 06/GS-15+. Retirees Space-A.

Other: Beautiful beach on Atlantic Ocean.

TML Availability: Good, Nov-Feb. Difficult, other times.

Cafeteria-238-7027   Locator-238-7056   Medical-238-7333
NCO Club-238-7799   O'Club-238-7133   Police-238-7659
Snack Bar-238-5722

Parris Island Marine Corps Recruit Depot (SC08R1)
Parris Island, SC 29905-5000

TELEPHONE NUMBER INFORMATION: Main installation numbers: Comm: 803-525-2111, ATVN: 832-1110.

Location: From I-95 South exit at Beaufort to SC-170 or US-21, both east to SC-280 to SC-281 which leads to main gate of Depot. RM: p-88, K/10. NMC: Savannah, 43 miles southwest.

Billeting Office: No central billeting office. Check in facility, check out 1100 hours. Government civilian employee billeting in Hostess House.

TML: Hostess House. Building 200. All ranks. Leave or official duty. EX-2976/3460. 30/1-bedroom, 2 beds, sleep sofa, private bath. Kitchen, limited

SOUTH CAROLINA
Parris Island Marine Corps Recruit Depot, continued

utensils, A/C, color TV, room & lounge, maid service, free cribs, washer/dryer, ice vending, facilities for disabled American veterans. Modern structure, new TVs '87, new carpets '89. Rates: Officer/enlisted $25.00, $30.00 double, $35.00 3 persons. PCS rates: $22.50, $27.50 (with kitchenette). Non-PCS $10.00 additional. All categories can make reservations.

TML: TLQ. Building 254. Officer all grades. Leave cr official duty. EX-2976. 6/1-bedroom, private bath. Kitchen, complete utensils, A/C, color TV room & lounge, maid service, free cots, washer/dryer, ice vending. Older structure, renovated '87. Rates: $25.00-$35.00 per room. Maximum 4 persons. All categories can make reservations.

TML: BEQ. Building 331. Enlisted E6-E9. EX-2976/2744. 71/1-bedroom, private bath. Refrigerator, A/C, optional maid service, free washer/dryer, ice vending. Modern structure. Rates: $4.00 per person. Maximum 1 per room.

TML: BOQ. Building 289. Officer all grades. Leave or official duty. EX-2976/3460. 21/1-bedroom, hall bath; 15 separate bedrooms, private bath. A/C, color TV, free washer/dryer, ice vending. Older structure. Rates: depends on status. Maximum 1 per room. Duty and retirees can make reservations. Dependents not authorized.

DV/VIP: Building 254. Officer O6+. Leave or official duty. Attn: Protocol Office. EX-2594. 1/2-bedroom suite, completely furnished, kitchen, private bath. Complete utensils, A/C, color TV, maid service, free cribs, free washer/dryer, ice vending. Rates: $40.00 per room. Maximum 4 per room. Duty, retired, disabled American veterans, military widows, accompanied dependents of retirees can make reservations.

TML Availability: Good except graduation days.

Enlisted Club-525-3653　　Locator-525-3358　　Medical-525-3351
NCO Club-525-2452　　　　O'Club-525-2905　　　Police-525-3444
Snack Bar-525-2810　　　　SDO/NCO-525-3712

Shaw Air Force Base (SC10R1)
Shaw AFB, SC 29152-5000

TELEPHONE NUMBER INFORMATION: Main installation numbers: Comm: 803-668-8110, ATVN: 965-1110.

Location: Off US-76/378 8 mi west of Sumter, SC. Clearly marked. RM: p-88, E/10. NMC: Columbia, 35 miles west.

Billeting Office: Building 929, Myers St. EX-3210. 24 hours daily. Check in facility, check out 1200 hours daily. Government civilian employee billeting.

TML: TLF. Buildings 931-934. All ranks. Leave or official duty. Accessible to handicapped. 40 separate bedrooms, sleeper sofa, private bath. Kitchenette, A/C, color TV (HBO & Disney), maid service, free cribs/cots, free washer/dryer. Modern structure. Rates: $20.00 per unit. Maximum 5 per apartment. Duty can make reservations. Others Space-A.

TML: VAQ. Buildings 900, 929. Enlisted all grades. Leave or official duty. 64/1-bedroom, 2 beds, shared bath (3 SNCO rooms have private bath). A/C, color TV (HBO), maid service, free cribs/cots, free washer/dryer, ice vending. Modern structure. Rates: $7.50 per person. Maximum 2 per room. Duty can make reservations. Others Space-A.

Temporary Military Lodging Around the World — 155

SOUTH CAROLINA

Shaw Air Force Base, continued

TML: VOQ. Buildings 911, 924, 927. Officer all grades. Leave or official duty. 68/1-bedroom, private bath; 14 separate bedroom suites, private bath. Kitchen, limited utensils, A/C, color TV (HBO), maid service, free cribs/cots, free washer/dryer, ice vending. Older structure. Rates: $8.00 per person. Maximum 2 per room. Duty can make reservations. Others Space-A.

TML: DV/VIP. Building 924. Officer O6+. Leave or official duty. 6 separate bedroom suites, private bath. Kitchen, complete utensils, A/C, color TV (HBO), maid service, free cribs/cots, free washer/dryer, ice vending. Older structure, remodeled. Rates: $10.00 per person. Maximum $20.00 per room. Duty can make reservations. Others Space-A.

DV/VIP: Protocol Office. Comm: 668-2156/2311. ATVN: 965-2156/2311. O6+. Retirees Space-A.

TML Availability: Good. Best, Dec-Mar.

Enlisted Club-666-3651
NCO Club-666-3651
Snack Bar-668-3553

Locator-668-2166
O'Club-666-3661
SDO/NCO-668-3330

Medical-668-2571
Police-668-3628

SOUTH DAKOTA

Ellsworth Air Force Base (SD01R3)
Ellsworth AFB, SD 57706-5000

TELEPHONE NUMBER INFORMATION: Main installation numbers: Comm: 605-385-1000, ATVN: 675-1000.

Location: Off I-90, 10 miles east of Rapid City. Clearly marked. RM: p-89, F/4. NMC: Rapid City, 10 miles west.

Billeting Office: Building 1103, 6th St, across from gym. 24 hours daily. Comm: 923-5861. ATVN: 675-2844. Check in facility, check out 1200 hours daily (TLF 1000 hours). No government civilian employee billeting.

TML: TLF. Building 4101. All ranks. Leave or official duty. EX-1362. 4/1-bedroom, shared bath; 21 double rooms, shared bath. Refrigerator, community kitchen, color TV, free cribs, cots, maid service, free washer/dryer, ice vending. Older structure. Rates: $15.00 per unit. Duty can make reservations. Others Space-A.

TML: VOQ/VAQ. Building 1103. All ranks. Leave or official duty. 51/2-bedroom, private bath (VOQ); 70/1-bedroom, 1 bed each room, shared bath (VAQ). Refrigerator, A/C, color TV room & lounge, maid service, free washer/dryer, ice vending. Older structure. Rates: $8.00 per person VOQ, $6.00 per person VAQ. Maximum $16.00 per room. Maximum 3 per room. Duty can make reservations. Others Space-A.

TML: DV/VIP. Building 4100. Officer O6+. Leave or official duty. Comm: 923-5861. 6 separate bedroom suites, private bath. Color TV, maid service. Older structure. Rates: $8.00 per person. Duty can make reservations. Others Space-A.

DV/VIP: Protocol Office. Building 1103. Comm: 923-5861. ATVN: 675-2844. O6+. Retirees and lower grades Space-A with approval of Protocol.

TML Availability: Good, Oct-Apr. More difficult, other times.

SOUTH DAKOTA
Ellsworth Air Force Base, continued

Cafeteria-385-1625
NCO Club-923-1442
Snack Bar-923-1455

Locator-385-1379
O'Club-385-1764

Medical-385-3430
Police-399-4001

TENNESSEE

Arnold Air Force Base (TN02R2)
Arnold AFB, TN 37389-5000

TELEPHONE NUMBER INFORMATION: Main installation numbers: Comm: 615-454-3000, ATVN: 340-3000.

Location: From Tullahoma, take AEDC access highway. From I-24 take AEDC exit 117, 4 miles south of Manchester. Clearly marked. RM: p-91, G/17. NMC: Chattanooga, 65 miles southeast; Nashville, 65 miles northwest.

Billeting Office: Building 3027. EX-5498. M-F 0600-2200, Sa 1000-2000, Su 1200-2200. Other hours, SDO EX-7752. Check in billeting, check out 1200 hours. No government civilian employee billeting.

TML: VOQ. Building 3027. All ranks. Leave or official duty. 40/1-bedroom, shared bath; 5 separate bedroom, shared bath (DV/VIP). Refrigerator, community kitchen, limited utensils, A/C, color TV room & lounge, maid service, free cribs, free washer/dryer, ice vending. Older structure. Rates: $8.00 per person, $14.00 DV/VIP. Duty can make reservations. Others Space-A.
DV/VIP: Commander's Office. 06+.

TML Availability: Good, all year.

Locator-454-3000
O'Club-454-7601

Medical-454-5351
Police-454-5222

NCO Club-454-6113
SDO/NCO-454-7752

Memphis Naval Air Station (TN01R2)
Millington, TN 38054-5000

TELEPHONE NUMBER INFORMATION: Main installation numbers: Comm: 901-873-5500, ATVN: 966-5500.

Location: From US-51 North at Millington, exit to Navy Rd, right to first gate on right, main gate. RM: p-90, G/3. NMC: Memphis, 20 miles southwest.

Billeting Office: Building S-61, EX-5459/5384. 24 hours daily. Check in facility, check out 1200 hours daily. Government civilian employee billeting GS-9+.

TML: Navy Lodge. Building N-762. All ranks. Leave or official duty. For reservations call 1-800-NAVY-INN. Lodge number is 872-0121. 8 separate bedroom, private bath; 7/2-bedroom, private bath; 4/3-bedroom, private bath; 22/1-bedroom, private bath. Kitchen, complete utensils, A/C, color TV, maid service, coin washer/dryer. Modern structure. Rates: $23.00 per unit. All categories can make reservations. Pets allowed in area adjacent to lodge.

TML: BOQ/BEQ. Building S-61. All ranks. Leave or official duty. Check in at facility. 873-5346. Officer 100/1-bedroom, private bath; Enlisted 296/1-bedroom, private bath. Some shared bath. Refrigerator, A/C, color TV room & lounge, maid service, free washer/dryer, ice vending, special facilities for disabled

Temporary Military Lodging Around the World — 157

TENNESSEE

Memphis Naval Air Station, continued

American veterans. Modern structure. Rates: BOQ $8.00-$15.00 per person, BEQ $6.00-$9.00 per person. Dependents must use Navy Lodge. Duty can make reservations. Others Space-A.

DV/VIP: Cmdr, EX-5101/2. O6+. Retirees Space-A.

TML Availability: Good, Dec. Difficult, other times.

NOTE: 22 new Navy lodge units to be available August 1990.

Cafeteria-872-1170
Locator-873-5111
Police-873-5533

CPO C-873-5442
Medical-911
SDO/NCO-873-5500

Enlisted Club-873-5131
O'Club-873-5115

TEXAS

Air Force Village (TX28R3)
4917 Ravenswood Drive
San Antonio, TX 78227-4352

TELEPHONE NUMBER INFORMATION: Main installation numbers: Comm: 512-673-2761, ATVN: None.

Location: Off I-410 (Loop), take exit 4 (Lackland/Valley-Hi), near Lackland AFB, TX. RM: p-95, EM/7. NMC: San Antonio, 6 miles northeast.

Billeting Office: Write or call for information to address and telephone number above.

TML: Guest Rooms. Officers all grades. Duty or retired. 8 guest rooms, private bath; 1/2-bedroom apartment, private bath, kitchen, living room, furnished. For guests of residents. Others Space-A.

TML Availability: Limited. Call in advance.

Air Force Village II (TX43R3)
5100 John D. Ryan Boulevard
San Antonio, TX 78245

TELEPHONE NUMBER INFORMATION: Main installation numbers: Comm: 512-677-8666. ATVN: None.

Location: Eight miles west of San Antonio on US-90 West. RM: p-95, EO/5. NMC: San Antonio, eight miles east.

Billeting Office: Check in at front desk of main building. 24 hours daily. Same number as above. Air Force Village II is a retirement community with limited number of guestrooms and cottages. Check out 1300 hours. No government civilian employee billeting.

TML: Cottages and guestrooms. Officers all grades. Leave or official duty. Accessible to handicapped. 9/1-bedroom, private bath; 2/2-bedroom cottages with kitchen, private bath. A/C, cribs/cots ($3.00), maid service, refrigerator, color TV, limited utensils in cottages. Modern structure. Rates: $39.00-$55.00 per night. Call for reservations information.

158 — *Temporary Military Lodging Around the World*

TEXAS
Air Force Village II, continued

TML Availability: Very difficult all year.

Belton Lake Recreation Area (TX07R3)
Fort Hood, TX 76544-5000

TELEPHONE NUMBER INFORMATION: Main installation numbers: Comm: 817-287/288-1110, ATVN: 737/738-1110.

Location: From I-35 take Killeen/Ft Hood exit; west on US-190, right on Hood Rd, right on North Ave, left on Martin Dr, to right on North Nolan Rd. Area marked. RM: p-94, EJ/7. NMC: Austin, 60 miles south.

Billeting Office: ATTN: AFZF-PA-CRD-OR-BLORA, Fort Hood, TX 76544-5056. Comm: 817-287-8303, ATVN: 737-8303. Check in cottages 1400-1600 hours, check out 0730-1100 hours.

TML: Cottages. All ranks. Leave or official duty. 10/1-bedroom, private bath, sleeps 4 persons. Kitchen, no utensils, A/C, color TV, fully equipped. Rates: 15 Apr-15 Oct $20.00-$25.00 daily; 14 Oct-14 Apr $15.00-$20.00 daily. All categories can make reservations. $25 deposit required. **Pets OK.**

TML Availability: Good, winter months. Difficult, May-Sep.

Bergstrom Air Force Base (TX27R3)
Bergstrom AFB, TX 78743-5000

TELEPHONE NUMBER INFORMATION: Main installation numbers: Comm: 512-369-4100, ATVN: 685-1110.

Location: From US-183 or TX-71. Clearly marked. RM: p-93, WZ/10. NMC: Austin, 7 miles northwest.

Billeting Office: Building 3508, Sixth St. Comm: 369-2207. ATVN: 685-2207. For reservations: Comm: 369-2207, ATVN: 685-2207. 24 hours daily. Check in facilities, check out 1200 hours daily. Government civilian employee billeting.

TML: VOQ/VAQ. Bergstrom Inn, Building 2104 (VAQ), Buildings 3708-3709 (VOQ). All ranks. Leave or official duty. VAQ as follows. 48 double bedrooms, shared bath; 6 SNCO rooms, shared bath; 6 suites, private bath. A/C, color TV, washer/dryer, lounge, maid service. VOQ as follows: 60 single bedrooms, private bath; 30 suites, private bath. Kitchen, A/C, color TV, maid service, free washer/dryer, lounge. Older structure, remodeled. Rates: $6.00-$8.00 per person. Duty can make reservations.

TML: TLF. Buildings 3542-3548. All ranks. Leave or official duty. Accessible to handicapped. 40 separate bedroom, private bath. A/C, cribs/cots, ice vending, kitchenette, maid service, special facilities for disabled American veterans, complete utensils, washer/dryer. Modern structure. Rates: $20.00 per unit. Duty can make reservations. Others Space-A.

TML: DV/VIP. Building 109. Officer 06+. Leave or official duty. 6 suites, private bath. Kitchen, living room, A/C, color TV, maid service, free cots/cribs, free washer/dryer. Rates: $8.00 per person. Duty can make reservations.

DV/VIP: PAO. EX-3710. 06+. Retirees and lower grades Space-A.

TML Availability: Good, Jan, Apr, May, Sep.

Temporary Military Lodging Around the World — 159

TEXAS

Bergstrom Air Force Base, continued

Locator-369-2214
O'Club-369-2403
SDO/NCO-369-3375

Medical-369-2333
Police-369-2604

NCO Club-369-3545
Snack Bar-385-2126

Brooks Air Force Base (TX26R3)
Brooks AFB, TX 78235-5000

TELEPHONE NUMBER INFORMATION: Main installation numbers: Comm: 512-536-1110, ATVN: 240-1110.

Location: At intersection of I-37 and Loop 13 (Military Drive). RM: p-95, EY/16. NMC: San Antonio, 5 miles northwest.

Billeting Office: Building 214, 6th St. EX-1844. 24 hours daily. Check in facility, check out 1200 hours daily. Government civilian employee billeting.

TML: TLF. Building 211. All ranks. Leave or official duty. Accessible to handicapped. 8/1-bedroom, private bath. Kitchen, living room, free cribs, A/C, utensils, linen, maid service, washer/dryer. Rates: $16.00 (E1-E6), $20.00 (E7+). Duty can make reservations. PCS in 30 day limit. PCS out 7 day limit. PCS have priority. Others Space-A.

TML: VAQ. Building 718. EX-3031. Enlisted all grades. Leave or official duty. 2 separate bedrooms, private bath; 52/2-bedroom, shared bath. A/C, community kitchen, cribs/cots, ice vending. maid service, refrigerator, color TV, free washer/dryer. Modern structure. Rates: $8.00-$12.00 per person. Duty can make reservations. Others Space-A.

TML: VOQ. Buildings 212, 214, 218, 220. EX-3031. Officer all grades. Leave or official duty. 109 separate bedrooms, private bath; 50/2-bedroom, shared bath. A/C, cribs/cots, ice vending, maid service, refrigerator, color TV, free washer/dryer. Modern structure. Rates: Sponsor $8.00-$14.00. Maximum $20.00 per family. Duty can make reservations. Others Space-A.

TML: DV/VIP. Officer O6+. Leave or official duty. EX-3278. 6 separate bedrooms, living room, private bath. Maid service, free washer/dryer. Rates: $14.00 per unit. Duty can make reservations. Others Space-A.

DV/VIP: PAO Office, EX-3238. O6+. Retirees Space-A.

TML Availability: Limited. Base has contract hotel/motel billeting. Contact Billeting Office, EX-1844.

Enlisted Club-536-2782
NCO Club-532-2782

Locator-536-1841
O'Club-532-3782

Medical-536-3278
SDO/NCO-536-3278

Carswell Air Force Base (TX21R3)
Carswell AFB, TX 76127-5000

TELEPHONE NUMBER INFORMATION: Main installation numbers: Comm: 817-782-5000, ATVN: 739-1110.

Location: On TX-183. From Fort Worth, west on I-30, exit at Carswell AFB/Horne St. Follow signs to main gate. RM: p-96, D/2. NMC: Fort Worth, 7 miles east.

Billeting Office: ATTN: 7th SVS/SVH. Building 3140, corner 6th St & Meandering Rd. Comm: 731-7003. 24 hours daily. Check in facility, check out 1200 hours daily. Government civilian employee billeting.

TEXAS
Carswell Air Force Base, continued

TML: TLF. Buildings 3112/13/14. All ranks. Leave or official duty. 18/1-bedroom apartments, private bath. A/C, color TV, maid service, free cribs, free washer/dryer. Modern structure. Rates: $18.00 per unit. Maximum 5 per apartment. Duty can make reservations. Others Space-A. **Kennel facility 2 miles from main gate.**

TML: VOQ. Buildings 3110/15, 3140. Officer all grades. Leave or official duty. 64/1-bedroom, private bath; 16/2-room suites, living room, private bath; 8 additional suites, shared living room, private bath. Kitchen (microwave), limited utensils, A/C, color TV, maid service, free cribs, free washer/dryer, ice vending. Modern structure, renovated '87. Rates: $7.00 Sponsor, $3.00 each additional person. Maximum 2 per unit. TDY can make reservations. Others Space-A.

TML: VAQ. Building 1565. Enlisted all grades. Leave or official duty. 38/1-bedroom, 2 beds, shared bath; 4 separate bedroom suites, private bath (SNCO). Refrigerator, A/C, color TV room & lounge, maid service, free washer/dryer, ice vending. Modern structure, renovated. Rates: $6.50 per person. Single occupancy only. No families. Duty can make reservations. Others Space-A.

TML: DV/VIP. Building 3140. Officer 06+. Leave or official duty. 6/2-bedroom suites, shared bath. Refrigerator, A/C, color TV, maid service, free cribs, ice vending. Modern structure. Rates: $7.00-$10.00 Sponsor, #3.50-$5.00 each additional person. Duty can make reservations. Others Space-A.

DV/VIP: Protocol, EX-5377. 07+. Retirees and lower grades Space-A.

Other: Ft. Worth Stockyards, Six Flags Over Texas, Botanical Gardens, Opera.

TML Availability: Good. Best, Aug-Mar.

Enlisted Club-782-5293   Locator-782-7082   Medical-782-4051
NCO Club-782-5293   O'Club-782-5631   Police-782-5200
SDO/NCO-782-5555

Chase Field Naval Air Station (TX23R3)
Chase Field NAS, TX 78103-5000

TELEPHONE NUMBER INFORMATION: Main installation numbers: Comm: 512-354-5119, ATVN: 861-1110.

Location: Off US-181, 5 miles southeast of Beeville. Clearly marked. RM: p-95, ER/7. NMC: Corpus Christi, 45 miles south/southeast.

Billeting Office: Building 2168, Constitution Street, Comm: 362-0884, ATVN: 861-5480. 24 hours daily. Other hours Security Office, Building 1011, EX-5412. Check in facility, check out 1300 hours daily. Government civilian employee billeting.

TML: VOQ. Building 2135. All ranks. Leave or official duty. Accessible to handicapped. 48/1-bedroom, private bath. A/C, community kitchen, free cribs, ice vending, maid service, refrigerator, color TV, free washer/dryer. 6 family suites, 2 rooms w/private bath and kitchen. Rates: $6.00 per person Officer, $4.00 per person Enlisted. Duty can make reservations. Others Space-A.

DV/VIP: Commanding Officer, EX-5213. 06+. Retirees Space-A.

Temporary Military Lodging Around the World — 161

TEXAS

Chase Field Naval Air Station, continued

TML Availability: Good all year.

Enlisted Club-354-5374 Locator-354-5011/1110 Medical-354-5292
O'Club-354-5484 Police-354-5412 SDO/NCO-354-5119

Corpus Christi Naval Air Station (TX10R3)
Corpus Christi, TX 78419-5000

TELEPHONE NUMBER INFORMATIN: Main installation numbers: Comm: 512-939-2811, ATVN: 624-1110.

Location: On TX-358, on southeast side of Corpus Christi. The South gate is on NAS Drive. RM: p-95, ET/8. NMC: Corpus Christi, 10 miles northwest.

Billeting Office: Office: Building 1281, Ocean Dr, EX-2388/89. Enlisted: Building 1739, Ave East, EX-2187. Navy Lodge: Building 101, 937-6361. BOQ/BEQ 24 hours. Navy Lodge 0800-1900 hours M-F, 0900-1700 hours Sa-Su, holidays. Other hours contact OD, Building 2, EX-2383. Check in facility, check out 1300 hours daily (1200 Navy Lodge). No government civilian employee billeting.

TML: Navy Lodge. Building 1281. All ranks. Leave or official duty. For reservations call 1-800-NAVY-INN. 21 suites and 1 bedroom units, private bath. Singles have double bed. Suites have double bed, living room with sofa bed. Kitchen, complete utensils, A/C, color TV, maid service, coin washer/dryer, ice vending. Modern structure. Rates: $26.00 (singles), $32.00 (suites). All categories can make reservations.

TML: BOQ/BEQ. Officer Building 1746, Enlisted Building 1732. All ranks. Leave or official duty. 80/1-bedroom, private bath. Refrigerator, A/C, color TV room & lounge, maid service, free washer/dryer. Modern structure, renovated. Rates: $5.50 (TDY), $20.00 (leave), child no charge. Maximum 3 persons. Duty can make reservations. Others Space-A.

DV/VIP: Protocol Office. Building 1281, Room 10. EX-2380/2389/3285. Commander's discretion. Retirees and lower grades Space-A.

Other: Padre Island National Seashore. King Ranch. Confederate AF Flying Museum.

TML Availability: Very Good, Jan-Mar & Jun-Dec. Difficult, Apr-May.

Enlisted Club-939-3867 Locator-939-2383 Medical-939-3735/3839
NCO Club-939-2240 O'Club-939-2541 Police-939-3460
Snack Bar-939-3444 SDO/NCO-939-2383

Dallas Naval Air Station (TX12R3)
Dallas, TX 75211-5000

TELEPHONE NUMBER INFORMATION: Main installation numbers: Comm: 214-266-6111, ATVN: 874-6111.

Location: Exit from I-30 at loop 12 west of Dallas, go south on loop 12 to Jefferson Ave exit. NAS on left, south side, of Ave. Near Grand Prairie. RM: p-96, E/7. NMC: Dallas, 15 miles northeast.

Billeting Office: Building 209, Hutchins Hall, Halsey Ave. EX-6155. 24 hours daily. Check in facility, check out 1400 hours daily. Government civilian employee billeting.

TEXAS
Dallas Naval Air Station, continued

TML: BOQ. Building 8. Officer all grades. Leave or official duty. EX-6134/5. 80/1-bedroom, hall bath. Free washer/dryer. Older structure well maintained. Rates: $6.00 per person (shared room); $8.00 per person (suites); $12.00 (VIP suites). 1 family room on Space-A basis at $15.00. Duty can make reservation. Others Space-A.

TML: BEQ. Buildings 209, 231. Enlisted all grades. Leave or official duty. EX-6155. 564 beds, hall bath. Rates: $4.00 per day. Duty can make reservations. Others Space-A.

DV/VIP: PAO, EX-6140. Commander's discretion.

Other: Six Flags Over Texas. Dallas Cowboys. Cotton Bowl.

TML Availability: Difficult & unpredictable.

Cafeteria-266-6405/6400	CPO Club-266-6413	Enlisted Club-266-6426
Locator-266-6111	Medical-266-6283	O'Club-266-6134
Police-266-6105	Snack Bar-266-6405	SDO/NCO-266-6120

Dyess Air Force Base (TX14R3)
Dyess AFB, TX 79607-5000

TELEPHONE NUMBER INFORMATION: Main installation numbers: Comm: 915-696-3113, ATVN: 461-1110.

Location: Six miles southwest of Abilene. Main gate is 3 miles east of I-20. Accessible from I-20 & US-277. RM: p-94, EG/2. NMC: Abilene, 6 miles northeast.

Billeting Office: Building 7409, Dyess Inn, Fifth St. Comm: 692-8610. ATVN: 461-2681. 24 hours daily. Check in facility, check out 1200 hours daily. Government civilian employee billeting.

TML: TLF. Building 6240. All ranks. Leave or official duty. Accessible to handicapped. 40 separate bedroom, private bath (sleeps 5). Kitchen, complete utensils, A/C, color TV room & lounge, free cribs/cots, free washer/dryer, ice vending, facilities for disabled American veterans. Modern structure. Rates: $19.00 per room. Duty can make reservations. Others Space-A.

TML: VAQ. Building 7218. Enlisted all grades. Leave or official duty. 70 double rooms, shared bath. Refrigerator, A/C, color TV, maid service, free washer/dryer, ice vending. Rates: $9.00. Duty can make reservations. Others Space-A.

TML: VOQ. Buildings 7403/07/09, 7420-22. Officer all grades, Senior Enlisted only. Accessible to handicapped. Leave or official duty. 174/1-bedroom, shared bath, 20 separate bedroom DV/VIP suites, private bath. Kitchen (suites only), refrigerator, A/C, color TV, maid service, free washer/dryer, ice vending. Older structure, remodeled. Rates: $9.00 - $14.00 per person. Maximum 2 per room. Duty can make reservations. Others Space-A.

DV/VIP: 96/BMW. Protocol Office. Comm: 696-5610. O6+. Retirees and lower grades Space-A.

TML Availability: Very good all year.

Cafeteria-698-1720	Enlisted Club-696-4311	Locator-696-3098
Medical-696-2334	O'Club-692-9577	Police-696-2131

Temporary Military Lodging Around the World — 163

TEXAS

Fort Bliss (TX06R3)
Fort Bliss, TX 79916-6200

TELEPHONE NUMBER INFORMATION: Main installation numbers: Comm: 915-568-2121, ATVN: 978-0831.

Location: From I-10 take airport exit to Robert E Lee gate. From US-54 take Pershing Road to Ft Bliss. RM: p-93, WW/4. NMC: El Paso, within city limits.

Billeting Office: Building 504A, Pershing Rd. EX-4888. 24 hours daily. Check in billeting, check out 1100 hours daily.

TML: Guest House. The Inn at Fort Bliss. Comm: 565-7777. All ranks. Leave or official duty. 36 deluxe kitchenette units with microwave and coffeemaker and additional standard units. Cable color TV, A/C, cribs ($2.00), maid service, ice vending. Rates: For standard rooms, $31.75 single, $37.50 double, $5.00 each additional person; for deluxe rooms, $34.25 single, $41.00 double, $5.00 each additional person. Call for reservation information.

TML: Transient Facilities. Officer and Senior Enlisted. Leave or official duty. EX-4888/2703. Bldg 504-A for check-in. Shared bath, private bath, refrigerator, A/C, color TV, maid service. Also, 4 duplex brick cottages, 8 units each, separate units, private bath. Refrigerator, color TV, bedding. Rates: Sponsor $18.00 single occupancy. Cottages $22.50 double occupancy. TDY to Fort Bliss can make reservations, all others Space-A.

TML: Guest House (Wm Beaumont AMC, Ft Bliss control). Building 7008. E-4 and below. Official duty. EX 2381. Check in 1300-1600 hours, check out 1100 hours daily. After 1600 hours, check-in at Billeting Office, Bldg 504-A. 8/1-bedroom, shared bath; 7/2-bedroom, shared bath; 1/3-bedroom, private bath. Refrigerator, A/C, color TV, maid service, free cribs/cots, coin washer/dryer. Older structure. Rates: Sponsor $10.00 shared bath, $3.00 each additional person. Private bath, $13.00, $3.00 each additional person. PCS can make reservations, all others Space-A.

TML: Armed Services YMCA (Wm Beumont AMC, Ft Bliss control). All ranks. Leave or official duty. (915)-562-8461. 52 separate bedrooms with two double beds or a king size bed, private bath. Individual A/C heating, color TV, room telephones, modern kitchenette (most rooms), 24 hour laundromat, food/ice vending, playground, meeting rooms for parties/receptions. Rates: $22.00 without kitchen, $24.00 with kitchen. PCS, dependents, retirees, Reservists/Reservists' families, military widows/widowers, non ID-card holders visiting relatives and friends can make reservations. Reservations held until 1800 hours.

TML: DV/VIP. 3 houses, 4 suites. Officer O7+. Leave or official duty. EX-5319. Completely furnished DV/VIP facility. Rates: variable; call. All categories can make reservations.

DV/VIP: Protocol Office, EX-5319/5225. O7+. Retirees and lower grades Space-A.

Other: Numerous military museums on post. Juarez, Mexico, largest city on Mexican border, walking distance from El Paso.

TML Availability: Good, Nov-Jan. Difficult, other times.

Cafeteria-562-2071	Enlisted Club-568-2715	Locator-568-1113
Medical-569-2331	NCO Club-568-2715	O'Club-568-2738
Police-568-2115	Snack Bar-562-2551	SDO/NCO-568-4233/1501

TEXAS

Fort Hood (TX02R3)
Fort Hood, TX 76544-5000

TELEPHONE NUMBER INFORMATION: Main installation numbers: Comm: 817-288-1110, 287-1110, ATVN: 737/738-1110.

Location: From I-35 North exit to US-190 West, 9 miles to Killeen. Main gate is clearly marked. RM: p-94, EK/7. NMC: Killeen, at main entrance.

Billeting Office: Building 36006, Wratten Dr. EX-2700. 24 hours daily. Check in facility, check out 1100 hours daily. Government civilian employee billeting.

TML: Poxon Guest House. Building 111. All ranks. Leave or official duty. EX-3067. 75/1-bedroom, private bath. Refrigerator, community kitchen, A/C, color TV room & lounge, maid service, free cribs/cots, free washer/dryer, ice vending, special facilities for disabled American veterans. Older structure, renovated '89. Rates: $12.00 single, $18.00 double, $1.00 each additional person. Maximum $24.00 per family. Duty can make reservations. Others Space-A. Kennels available.

TML: VOQ. Building 36006. Officer all grades. Leave or official duty. 225/1-bedroom, private bath. Refrigerator, A/C, color TV, maid service, free cribs/cots, free washer/dryer, ice vending. Older structure renovated. Rates: $19.50 TDY, $13.50 PCS, $5.00 2nd person, $1.00 each additional person. Duty can make reservations. Others Space-A.

TML: VEQ. Buildings 5786/88/90/92. Enlisted all grades. Leave or official duty. 226/1-bedroom, shared bath. Refrigerator, community kitchen, A/C, color TV, maid service, free washer/dryer, ice vending. Older structure, renovated. Rates: $19.50 TDY, $13.50 PCS, $5.00 2nd person, $1.00 each additional person. Duty can make reservations. Others Space-A.

TML: Junior Guest Quarters. Buildings 2305/06/07. Enlisted E1-E4. Leave or official duty. EX-3067. 48/1-bedroom, shared bath. Refrigerator, community kitchen, A/C, color TV room & lounge, maid service, free cribs/cots, free washer/dryer. Older structure. Rates: $4.00 two persons, $5.00 3 persons. Maximum $6.00 per family. Duty can make reservations. Others Space-A.

TML: DV/VIP. Building 36006. Officer 06+. Leave or official duty. EX-5001. 10/2-bedroom, private bath. Kitchen, utensils, A/C, color TV, maid service, free cribs/cots, free washer/dryer, ice vending. Older structure, remodeled '88. Rates: $19.50 1st TDY, $13.50 PCS, $6.00 2nd person, $3.00 each additional person. Duty can make reservations. Others Space-A.

DV/VIP: Executive Service. Building 1, EX-5001. 06/GS-15+. Retirees Space-A.

TML Availability: Good, winter months. Difficult, May-Sep.

Enlisted Club-532-2887 Locator-287-2137 Medical-288-8133
NCO Club-287-5825   O'Club-532-5073   Police-287-2176
SDO/NCO-287-2520

Fort Sam Houston (TX18R3)
Fort Sam Houston, TX 78234-5000

TELEPHONE NUMBER INFORMATION: Main installation numbers: Comm: 512-221-1110/1211, ATVN: 471-1110/1211.

Location: Accessible from I-410 or I-35/US-81. RM: p-95, EW/16. NMC: San Antonio, northeast section of city.

TEXAS

Fort Sam Houston, continued

Billeting Office: Building 367, Stanley Rd. EX-6125/5946. 24 hours daily. Check in facility, check out 1300 hours daily. Government civilian employee billeting.

TML: Guest House. Building 1002, Gorgas Circle. All ranks. Leave or official duty. EX-2744. 144 rooms, private bath. 2-room suites, kitchen, private bath. Refrigerator, A/C, color TV, maid service, free cribs, coin washer/dryer, rollaway $1.00. Rates: $13.00-$17.00 rooms, $20.00 suites. Duty can make reservations. Others Space-A.

TML: VOQ. Building 1384. Officer all grades. Leave or official duty. 300 units, private bath. Community kitchen, refrigerator, A/C, color TV, maid service, free washer/dryer. Older structure. Rates: Sponsor $22.50, each additional person $11.25. Duty can make reservations. Others Space-A.

TML: VOQ. Building 592. Officer all grades. TDY only. 150 rooms, private bath. Community kitchen, refrigerator, A/C, color TV, maid service, free washer/dryer. Rates: Sponsor $22.50, each additional person $11.25.

TML: DV/VIP. Buildings 48 (Staff Post Rd), 107 (Artillery Post). Officer 06+. Leave or official duty. EX-6125/5946. 27/2- & 3-bedroom suites, complete furniture. Breakfast served (M-F) in Building 48. Refrigerator, A/C, color TV, maid service. Older structure. Rates: $20.25 two persons (Building 107); $33.75 two persons (Building 48). All categories can make reservations. All are subject to bump except TDY.

TML: Other. 50 BOQ rooms, 51 SEQ rooms. Call for additional information.

DV/VIP: PAO. EX-1211. 06+. Retirees & lower grades (General's aide, etc.) Space-A.

TML Availability: Good. Best Oct-Mar.

Enlisted Club-224-2721
NCO Club-224-2721
Snack Bar-228-9071

Locator-221-2948
O'Club-224-4211
SDO/NCO-221-3810

Medical-221-4104/6466
Police-221-6363

Goodfellow Air Force Base (TX24R3)
Goodfellow AFB, TX 76908-5000

TELEPHONE NUMBER INFORMATION: Main installation numbers: Comm: 915-654-3231, ATVN: 477-3217.

Location: Off US-87 or US-277. Clearly marked. RM: p-93, WO/16. NMC: San Angelo, 2 miles northwest.

Billeting Office: Building 3305, Kearney Blvd. 24 hours daily. EX-3332. Check in facility, check out 1200 hours daily. Government civilian employee billeting.

TML: TLF. Buildings 910, 920, 922, 924. All ranks. Leave or official duty. Accessible to handicapped. 22 separate bedrooms, private bath. Kitchen, complete utensils, color TV, maid service, free cribs, free washer/dryer, ice vending, special facilities for handicapped American veterans. Modern structure. Rates: $14.00 E6-, $18.00 E7+. PCS can make reservations. Others Space-A.

TML: VAQ. Buildings 3307, 3311. Enlisted all grades. Leave or official duty. Accessible to handicapped. 100/1-room with bed, private bath; 270/1-room with 2 beds, shared bath. Refrigerator, microwave, A/C, color TV, maid service, washer/dryer. Modern structure. Rates: $5.00 per person. Duty can make reservations. Others Space-A.

TEXAS
Goodfellow Air Force Base, continued

TML: VOQ. Buildings 702, 711. Officer all grades. Leave or official duty. 115 separate bedrooms, private bath. Kitchenette, microwave, A/C, color TV, maid service, free washer/dryer, microwave. Modern structure. Rates: $6.00/$10.00 per person. TDY can make reservations. Others Space-A.

TML: DV/EV. Building 910 (DV), Building 3307 (EV). Officer O6+, Enlisted E9. Leave or official duty. 10 separate bedrooms, private bath. Kitchen, complete utensils, A/C, color TV, maid service, washer/dryer, ice vending. Modern structure. Rates: $10.00 per person. Duty can make reservations. Others Space-A.

DV/VIP: Protocol Officer, EX-5400. O6+, E9. Retirees Space-A.

TML Availability: Fairly good all year.

Cafeteria-654-3356	Enlisted Club-654-3256	Medical-654-3145
NCO Club-654-3256	O'Club-654-5327	Police-654-3504
SDO/NCO-657-3044		

Kelly Air Force Base (TX03R3)
Kelly AFB, TX 78241-5000

TELEPHONE NUMBER INFORMATION: Main installation numbers: Comm: 512-925-1110, ATVN: 945-1110.

Location: All of the following, I-10, I-35, I-37, I-410 intersect with US-90. From US-90 take either the Gen Hudnell or Gen McMullen exit and go south to Kelly AFB. RM: p-95, EY/13. NMC: San Antonio, 7 miles northeast.

Billeting Office: Building 1676 (O'Club), Gilmore Rd. Comm: 925-8931, 924-7201. ATVN: 945-8931. 24 hours daily. Check in billeting, check out 1300 hours daily. Government civilian employee billeting.

TML: VOQ. Building 1676. Officer all grades. Leave or official duty. 47/1-bedroom, private bath. Kitchen (shared), A/C, color TV, maid service, free washer/dryer, ice vending. Older structure. Rates: $6.00 per person. Maximum 2 persons. Duty can make reservations. Others Space-A.

TML: VAQ. Building 1650. Enlisted all grades. Leave or official duty. 2/1-bedroom, shared bath (E7-E8); 2 separate bedroom, private bath (E9); 22/1-bedroom, 2 beds, latrine bath (E1-E6). Refrigerator, A/C, color TV, maid service, free washer/dryer, ice vending. Older structure. Rates $6.00 per person. Maximum 2 persons. Duty can make reservations. Others Space-A.

TML: DV/VIP. Building 1676. Officer 07+. Leave or official duty. 6 separate bedrooms, private bath. Kitchen, A/C, color TV, maid service, free cribs/cots, free washer/dryer, ice vending. Older structure. Rates: $10.00 per person. Maximum 4 persons. Duty can make reservations. Others Space-A.

DV/VIP: Protocol Office, Building 1680, EX-7678. 07/GS-16+. Retirees and lower grades Space-A.

TML Availability: Fairly good all year.

Cafeteria-925-3875	Locator-925-1841	Medical-925-4544
NCO Club-924-4511	O'Club-924-7127	Police-925-6811
SDO/NCO-925-6906		

Temporary Military Lodging Around the World — 167

TEXAS

Kingsville Naval Air Station (TX22R3)
Kingsville NAS, TX 78363-5000

TELEPHONE NUMBER INFORMATION: Main installation numbers: Comm: 512-595-6136, ATVN: 861-6136.

Location: Off US-77 South, exit to TX-425 Southeast to main gate. RM: p-95, ET/7. NMC: Corpus Christi, 30 miles northeast.

Billeting Office: Officer, Building 2700, EX-6321. Enlisted, Building 3730, EX-6309. 24 hours daily. Check in facility, check out 1100 hours daily. No government civilian employee billeting.

TML: BOQ/MOQ/BEQ/MEQ. Buildings 2700, 3729, 3755, 3730W. All ranks. Accessible to handicapped. 26 separate bedrooms, private bath; 10/2-bedroom, private bath. Refrigerator, community kitchen, kitchenette, limited utensils, A/C, TV, maid service, free cribs/cots, washer/dryer, food/ice vending, microwave. Older structure. Rates: Officer/enlisted $7.00, second adult $6.00, child (up to 17) $1.00; DoD civilian $24.00. Maximum charge $29.00. Maximum 5 persons. Duty can make reservations. Others Space-A.

DV/VIP: Protocol Office, Building 700, EX-6481. 06+. Retirees Space-A. One VIP room.

TML Availability: Very good overall.

Cafeteria-595-6718	CPO Club-595-6413	Enlisted Club-595-6413
Locator-595-6136	Medical-595-6434	O'Club-595-6121
Police-595-6217	Snack Bar-595-6196	SDO/NCO-595-6136

Lackland Air Force Base (TX25R3)
Lackland AFB, TX 78236-5000

TELEPHONE NUMBER INFORMATION: Main installation numbers: Comm: 512-671-1110, ATVN: 473-1110.

Location: Off US-90 South. Loop 13 (Military Drive) bisects Lackland AFB. RM: p-95, EY/12. NMC: San Antonio, 6 miles northeast.

Billeting Administrative Office: Building 10203, west side of base. 24 hours daily. EX-2523. Check in facility, check out 1200 hours daily. Government civilian employee billeting.

TML: TLQ/VAQ. Building 10203. West side of base, Feymoyer Street. 24 hours daily. EX-4270/4277. Check in facility, check out 1200 hours daily. All ranks. 160 separate bedrooms, private bath; 770/2 person rooms, semi-private baths and 78 SNCO rooms, semi-private baths. A/C, color TV, maid service, free cribs, free washer/dryer, ice vending. Special facilities for handicapped. Modern structure. Rates: TLQ $16.00 - $20.00 per unit, VAQ $5.00 - $10.00 per unit. Duty can request reservations. All others Space-A.

TML: VOQ/DV/VIP: Building 2604. 24 hours daily. EX-3622. Officer all grades. Leave or official duty. 32 separate bedrooms, shared bath; 96 separate bedrooms, private bath. Microwave, refrigerator, A/C, color TV, maid service, free washer/dryer, ice/snack vending. 16/1-bedroom suites, private bath (DV/VIP); 7/2-bedroom suites, private bath (DV/VIP). Refrigerator, 8 units have kitchen, A/C, color TV, maid service, free washer/dryer, ice vending. Older structure, remodeled. Rates: $6.00/$10.00 per person. Duty can make reservations. Others Space-A.

DV/VIP: Protocol Office, EX-2423. 06+. Retirees Space-A.

168 — Temporary Military Lodging Around the World

TEXAS
Lackland Air Force Base, continued

TML Availability: Good. Difficult, Jun-Aug.

Cafeteria-674-0950	Enlisted Club-670-7331	Locator-671-1110
Medical-670-7100	NCO Club-673-5953	O'Club-673-5881
Police-671-2018	SDO/NCO-671-2593	

Laguna Shores Recreation Area (TX42R3)
Kelly Air Force Base, TX 78241-5000

TELEPHONE NUMBER INFORMATION: Main installation numbers: Comm: 512-925-1110, ATVN: 945-1110.

Location: On Corpus Christi Naval Air Station. Take I-37 to exit 4A west of Corpus Christi; east on TX-358 approximately 17 miles to NAS. Enter at South Gate; follow Laguna Shores signs to office. RM: p-95, ET/8. NMC: Corpus Christi, in city limits.

Billeting Office: None. Reservations required with payment in full (first month's payment for stays of 1 month or more). Write to Tickets and Tours, 2851 ABG/SSRT, Building 1662, Kelly AFB, TX 78241-5000. Comm: 512-925-4585. ATVN: 945-4585. Laguna Shores office for information only call Comm: 512-939-7783.

TML: 38/2-bedroom apartments, private bath. A/C, cable TV. Bring your own towels. Rates: $26.00 per day up to 4 persons. $3.00 each additional person.

TML Availability: Best during winter.

Laughlin Air Force Base (TX05R3)
Laughlin AFB, TX 78843-5000

TELEPHONE NUMBER INFORMATION: Main installation numbers: Comm: 512-298-3511, ATVN: 732-1110.

Location: Take US-90 West from San Antonio, 150 miles or US-277 South from San Angelo, 150 miles to Del Rio area. The AFB is clearly marked off US-90. RM: p-93, WU/15. NMC: Del Rio, 8 miles northwest.

Billeting Office: Building 470, 7th St. EX-5731. 24 hours. Check in billeting, check out 1200 hours daily. No government civilian employee billeting.

TML: TLQ. Buildings 460-463. All ranks. Leave or official duty. 20 separate bedroom, private bath. Kitchen, utensils, A/C, color TV, maid service, free cribs, free washer/dryer (Building 463), ice vending, special facilities for disabled American veterans. Modern structure. Rates: E1-E6 $15.00 per unit, E7-010 $19.00 per unit. Duty can make reservations. Others Space-A.

TML: VOQ/VAQ. Building 470. All ranks. Leave or official duty. 13/1-bedroom, shared bath (Officer all grades); 18/1-bedroom, shared bath (Enlisted all grades). Refrigerator, A/C, color TV room & lounge, maid service, free cribs/cots, free washer/dryer, ice vending. Older structure, renovated. Rates: $7.00 per person VOQ, $6.00 per person VAQ. Duty can make reservations. Others Space-A.

TML: DV/VIP. Building 470. Officer 06+, Enlisted E7-E9. Leave or official duty. 2 separate bedroom, private bath; 4/3-bedroom, private bath. Kitchen, utensils, color TV, maid service, free cribs/cots, free washer/dryer, ice vending. Older structure, renovated. Rates: $7.00 per person. Duty can make reservations. Others Space-A.

Temporary Military Lodging Around the World — 169

TEXAS

Laughlin Air Force Base, continued

DV/VIP: 47 TFW/CCP, Building 338, Room 1. EX-5041. O6+ & E7+. Retirees and lower grades Space-A.

TML Availability: Good, Nov-Jan. Difficult, other times.

Cafeteria-298-5295	Enlisted Club-298-5474	Locator-298-5195
Medical-298-5225/3416	NCO Club-298-3573	O'Club-298-3675
Police-298-5102	Snack Bar-298-2711	SDO/NCO-298-5167

Randolph Air Force Base (TX19R3)
Randolph AFB, TX 78150-5000

TELEPHONE NUMBER INFORMATION: Main installation numbers: Comm: 512-652-1110, ATVN: 487-1110.

Location: From I-35 take exit 172, Pat Booker Rd. From I-10 take exit 587, TX FM-1604. RM: p-95, EO/6. NMC: San Antonio, 6 miles south.

Billeting Office: Building 118. EX-1844. 24 hours daily. Check in billeting, check out 1200 hours daily. Government civilian employee billeting.

TML: TLF. Building 112, 152-155. All ranks. Leave or official duty. One handicapped room. 7/1-bedroom, private bath; 33 separate bedrooms, private bath. Kitchen (34 units), microwave, refrigerator only (6 units), A/C, color TV, maid service, free cribs/cots, free washer/dryer, ice vending. Older structure, renovated '86. Rates: $8.00-$20.00 per person depending on unit and rank. Duty can make reservations. Others Space-A.

TML: VOQ. Buildings 110, 111, 120, 161, 162, 381. Officer all grades. Leave or official duty. 200/1-bedroom, private bath; 76 separate bedrooms, private bath; 2/2-bedroom, private bath. A/C, cribs/cots, ice vending, maid service, refrigerator, color TV, limited utensils in some rooms, free washer/dryer. Some modern, some older structures. Rates: $7.00-$10.00 per person. Duty can make reservations. Others Space-A.

TML: VAQ. Buildings 862. Enlisted all grades. Leave or official duty. 22/1-bedroom, two beds, private bath; 48/1-bedroom, queen bed, private bath; 2/1-bedroom, queen bed, shared bath. A/C, cribs/cots, ice vending, maid service, refrigerator, color TV rooms and lounge, free washer/dryer, microwave (some). Modern structure. Rates: $7.00 per person. Maximum $21.00 per room. TDY can make reservations. Others Space-A.

DV/VIP: Protocol. Building 900, Room 306. EX-4126. O7+/SES. Retirees and lower grades Space-A.

TML Availability: Good, Nov-Feb. Difficult, other times.

Cafeteria-658-1338	Locator-652-1841	Medical-911
NCO Club-658-3557	O'Club-658-7445	Police-652-5700
Snack Bar-658-1338	SDO/NCO-652-1859	

Red River Army Depot (TX09R3)
Texarkana, TX 75507-5000

TELEPHONE NUMBER INFORMATION: Main installation numbers: Comm: 903-334-2141, ATVN: 829-4110.

TEXAS
Red River Army Depot, continued

Location: From I-30 East or West, take Red River Army Depot exit. Route clearly marked. RM: p-94, ED/14. NMC: Texarkana, 20 miles east.

Billeting Office: ATTN: SDSRR-GH. Building 228, Texas Ave. 0645-1715 M-Thu. EX-3227. Other hours, contact SDO/NCO, Building S-04, or SP EX-2911. Check in billeting, check out 1100 hours daily. No government civilian employee billeting.

TML: BOQ. Building S-40. All ranks. Leave or official duty. 1/1-bedroom, private bath; 5 separate bedrooms, private bath. Community kitchen, A/C, color cable TV room & lounge, maid service, cribs, free washer/dryer. Older structure, renovated. New building & furnishings anticipated in '90. Rates: Sponsor $5.00, adult $4.00, child $4.00, infant $4.00. Maximum per family $12.00. Maximum five per room. Duty can make reservations. **Small pets if leashed outside OK.** Note: New Building open w/ 5 additional bedrooms and a 2 bedroom DVQ.

TML: DV/VIP. Building S-40. Officer 06+. Leave or official duty. Report to Protocol Office. 2 separate bedrooms, private bath. Rooms adjoin and may be used as a single, 2-bedroom unit. 1 has kitchen, 1 has refrigerator. Limited utensils, A/C, color TV room & lounge, maid service, free cribs, free washer/dryer. Older structure. New building anticipated '90. Rates: Same as BOQ. Duty can make reservations. Others Space-A.

DV/VIP: Protocol Office, ATTN: SDSRR-AP, Building 15, EX-2316. 06+, GS-14+. Must be approved by Commander. Retirees and lower grades Space-A.

TML Availability: Extremely limited. Best, Nov-Mar. Difficult, Apr-Oct.

Cafeteria-334-2341   Medical-911   NCO Club-334-2350
Police-334-2911   SDO/NCO-334-2911   Enlisted Club-334-2350
O'Club-334-2350

Reese Air Force Base (TX20R3)
Reese AFB, TX 79489-5000

TELEPHONE NUMBER INFORMATION: Main installation numbers: Comm: 806-885-4511, ATVN: 838-1110.

Location: From west side of Loop 289 at Lubbock take 4th St West, 6 miles. Road terminates at AFB. Main gate is one block north. RM: p-92, WJ/12. NMC: Lubbock, 12 miles east.

Billeting Office: Building 1142, K St. EX-3155. 24 hours daily. Check in billeting, check out 1200 hours daily. No government civilian employee billeting.

TML: TLF. Building 1150. All ranks. Leave or official duty. 25/1-bedroom, private bath. Units 1 & 2 dedicated for disabled American veterans. Kitchen, microwave, limited utensils, color TV, maid service, free cribs/cots, free washer/dryer, ice vending. Modern structure. Rates: E6- $15.00 per unit, E7+ $19.00 per unit. PCS can make reservations. Others Space-A.

TML: BAQ. Building 1030. Enlisted E1-E7. Leave or official duty. 16 efficiency apartments, private bath. Kitchen, microwave, limited utensils, A/C, color TV, maid service, free washer/dryer, ice vending. Modern structure. Rates: $6.00 per unit. TDY/PCS can make reservations. OtherS Space-A.

TML: BAQ. Building 1030. E8-E9. Leave or official duty. 4/1-bedroom SNCO suites, living room, private bath. Kitchen, microwave, limited utensils, A/C, color TV, maid service, free cribs/cots, free washer/dryer, ice vending. Modern structure.

TEXAS

Reese Air Force Base, continued

Rates: $6.00 per person. TDY/PCS can make reservations. Others Space-A.

TML: DV/VIP. Building 1030. Officer 06+. Leave or official duty. 2/1-bedroom suites. Kitchen, microwave, limited utensils, A/C, color TV, maid service, free cribs/cots, free washer/dryer, ice vending. Modern structure. Rates: $7.00 per person. TDY/PCS can make reservations. Others Space-A.

DV/VIP: Wing XO, Building 800, Room 203. EX-3409. 06+.

TML Availability: Good, winter months. Difficult, summer months.

Cafeteria-885-6027	Enlisted Club-885-3156	Locator-885-3678
Medical-885-3373	NCO Club-885-3156	O'Club-885-3466
Police-885-3332	Snack Bar-885-3556	SDO/NCO-885-3754

Sheppard Air Force Base (TX37R3)
Sheppard Air Force Base, TX 76311-5000

TELEPHONE NUMBER INFORMTION: Main installation numbers: Comm: 817-676-2511, ATVN: 736-1001.

Location: Take US-281 North from Wichita Falls, exit to TX-325 which leads to main gate. Clearly marked. RM: p-92, WA/6. NMC: Wichita Falls, 5 miles southwest.

Billeting Office: ATTN: 3750 SVS/SVH, Building 776, Ave H. Comm: 855-7370. ATVN: 736-6359/4351. 24 hours daily. Check in billeting, check out 1200 hours daily. Government civilian employee billeting.

TML: TLF. Buildings 160-165. All ranks. Leave or official duty. Comm: 676-2707. 50 separate bedrooms, private bath. Kitchen, utensils, A/C, color TV, maid service, free cribs/cots, free washer/dryer, ice vending. Modern structure. Rates: $14.00 E1-E6, $18.00 E7+. Maximum 4 per unit. Duty can make reservations. Others Space-A.

TML: VAQ. Building 776. Enlisted all grades. Leave or official duty. Comm: 676-2707. ATVN: 736-1844. 437/1-bedroom, two beds, private bath; 7 separate bedrooms, private bath, 49 1-bedroom, 1 bed, private bath. A/C, ice vending, maid service, refrigerator, color TV, washer/dryer, microwaves in lounges. Modern structure. Rates: $5.00 per person standard room, $10.00 per person suites. Maximum 2 per room. Duty can make reservations. Others Space-A.

TML: VOQ. Buildings 331, 332, 333, 370. Ave G. Officer all ranks. Leave or official duty. Comm: 676-2707. ATNV: 736-1844. 220/1-bedroom, private bath; 12 separate bedrooms, private bath. Refrigerator, A/C, color TV, free washer/dryer. Rates: $6.00 per person standard room, $10.00 per person suite. Maximum 2 per room. Duty can make reservations. Others Space-A.

TML: DV/VIP. Building 332. Officer 06+. Leave or official duty. Comm: 676-2123. ATVN: 736-2123. 6 separate bedroom suites, private bath. A/C, kitchenette, maid service color TV, utensils, free washer/dryer. Modern structure. Rates: $10.00 per person. Maximum 2 per room. Duty can make reservations. Others Space-A.

DV/VIP: ATTN: STTC/CCEX, Stop 1, Building 400. Comm: 676-2123. ATVN: 736-2123. 06+. Retirees and lower grades Space-A.

TML Availability: Good during winter months, difficult Apr - Sep.

TEXAS
Sheppard Air Force Base, continued

Cafeteria-855-5451	Enlisted Club-676-6427	Locator-676-4403
Medical-676-2333	NCO Club-855-6427	O'Club-855-9241
Police-676-6302	SDO/NCO-676-2083	

UTAH

Dugway Proving Ground (UT04R4)
Dugway Proving Ground, UT 84022-5000

TELEPHONE NUMBER INFORMATION: Main installation numbers: Comm: 801-831-2151, ATVN: 789-2151.

Location: Isolated but can be reached from I-80. Take Skull Valley Rd (exit 77) for 40 miles south. RM: p-97, E/3. NMC: Salt Lake City, 80 miles northeast.

Billeting Office: Building 5228, Valdez Circle. 0630-1900 M-Th, 0800-1600 Friday. EX-2333/2334. Other hours, MP Station, Building 5438, EX-2933. Check in billeting, check out 1300 hours daily. Government civilian employee billeting.

TML: VOQ/DVQ. Buildings 5228, 5226. Officer and Enlisted. All ranks. Leave or official duty. Accessible to handicapped. 54/1-bedroom, semi-private bath; 9 separate bedrooms. Refrigerator, A/C (in Building 5228), color TV room & lounge, maid service, cots no charge, essentials, free cribs, free washer/dryer, ice vending. Older structures. 5228 remodeled '88. 5226 remodeled Aug '89. Rates: Sponsor, $25.00 single room; suite $30.00. $5.00 each additional occupant. Children under 17 free. Maximum $30.00 per single room. Maximum $35.00 per suite people. Maximum 2 persons per unit. Duty can make reservations. Others including contractors and social guests Space-A.

DV/VIP: STEDP-AG. Building 5450. EX-2020. O5/GS-14+. Retirees and lower grades Space-A.

TML Availability: Good. Best, fall and winter.

Enlisted Club-831-2901	Locator-831-2151	Medical-831-2222
O'Club-831-2901	Police-831-2933	SDO/NCO-831-3535

Hill Air Force Base (UT02R4)
Hill AFB, UT 84056-5000

TELEPHONE NUMBER INFORMATION: Main installation numbers: Comm: 801-777-7221, ATVN: 458-1110.

Location: Adjacent to I-15 between Ogden and Salt Lake City. Take exit 336, east on UT-193 to South Gate. RM: p-96, P/7. NMC: Ogden, 8 miles north.

Billeting Office: ATTN: 2849 ABGp/SVH. Bldg 146, D St. EX-2601. 24 hours daily. Check in billeting, check out 1200 hours daily. Government civilian employee billeting.

TML: TLF. Building 472. All ranks. 40 separate bedrooms, private bath. Kitchen, complete utensils, A/C, color TV, limited maid service, free cribs, free washer/dryer, ice vending, facilities for disabled American veterans. Modern structure. Rates: $15.00. Maximum 5 per room. PCS/TDY can make reservations. Others Space-A.

Temporary Military Lodging Around the World — 173

UTAH

Hill Air Force Base, continued

TML: VOQ. Buildings 141, 142, 150, 480. Officer all grades. Leave or official duty. 52/1-bedroom, semi-private bath; 5/1-bedroom, private bath; 36 separate bedrooms, semi-private bath; 6 separte bedrooms, private bath. Kitchen, A/C, color TV, maid service, free cots, free washer/dryer, ice vending. Older structures, renovated. Rates: $6.00 per person. No families. TDY can make reservations. Others Space-A.

TML: VAQ. Building 521. Enlisted all grades. Leave or official duty. Accessible to handicapped. 64 rooms, semi-private bath. 6 suites, semi-private bath. Refrigerator, A/C, color TV room & lounge, maid service, free cots, free washer/dryer, ice vending. Older structure, renovated '88. Rates: $5.50 per person. No families. Duty can make reservations. Retirees Space-A.

TML: DV/VIP. Building 1118. Officer O6+. Leave or official duty. 6 separate bedrooms, private bath. Kitchen, limited utensils, A/C, color TV, maid service, free cots, free washer/dryer, ice vending. Older structure, renovated. Rates: $6.00 per person. No families. Duty can make reservations. Others Space-A.

DV/VIP: Protocol ALC/CCP. Building 1102. EX-5565. O6+. Retirees Space-A.

TML Availability: Difficult.

Cafeteria-777-2043	Locator-777-1841	Medical-911
NCO Club-777-3841	O'Club-773-4924	Police-777-3056
Snack Bar-773-1207		

Tooele Army Depot (UT05R4)
Tooele, UT 84074-5008

TELEPHONE NUMBER INFORMATION: Main installation numbers: Comm: 801-833-1110, ATVN: 790-1110.

Location: From west I-80, exit 99 to UT-36 south for 15 miles to main entrance. RM: p-97, E/5. NMC: Salt Lake City, 40 miles northeast.

Billeting Office: ATTN: SDSTE-ELH. Building 1, Hq Loop, EX-2124. 0630-1700 hours M-Th. Closed on Fridays. Other hours, SDO, Building 1, EX-2304. Check in billeting, check out 1200 hours daily. Government civilian employee billeting.

TML: VOQ/DVQ. Building 35. All ranks. Leave or official duty. 2 separate bedrooms, private bath; 8/2-bedroom apartments, private bath. Kitchen, complete utensils, A/C, cable color TV, maid service, free cribs, free washer/dryer. Also 10/1-bedroom, VOQ; 17/1-bedroom, VEQ. Older structure, renovated. New carpets '89. Rates for leave status: Sponsor $12.00, adult $6.00, child no charge. Maximum $18.00 per family. Rates for active status: Sponsor $20.25, adult $2.25, child no charge. Maximum charge $22.50. Duty can make reservations. Others Space-A.

Other: Salt Lake City, Mormon Temple, Pioneer Memorial Museum, ski resorts.

Military Discount Lodging: Great American Inn, 491 S. Main, Tooele (801) 882-6100. Best Western Inn (801) 882-5010.

TML Availability: Good. Best, Dec-Mar.

Locator-833-2094	Medical-833-2572	Police-833-2314/2559
Snack Bar-833-3311	SDO/NCO-833-2304	

VERMONT

NONE

VIRGINIA

Cheatham Annex Naval Supply Center (VA02R1)
Williamsburg, VA 23187-8792

TELEPHONE NUMBER INFORMATION: Main installation numbers: Comm: 804-887-4000, ATVN: 953-4000.

Location: From I-64 take exit 57-B on US-199 east to main gate of Cheatham Annex. RM: p-99, B/19. NMC: Williamsburg, 6 miles west.

Billeting Office: MWR, Building 284, D Street. EX-7224/7101/02. 0800-1630 hours week days. After duty hours, Building 235, EX-7453. No government civilian employee billeting.

TML: Recreation Cabins. Cabins 161, 163-165, 167-170, 261, 262. Active duty and retirees only. All ranks. Leave only. Accessible to handicapped. Reservations required. 11 cottages, private bath. Kitchen, complete utensils, refrigerator, cribs ($1.00), color TV, A/C, woodburning stove, boat, electric motor, battery charger, paddles, cushions. No woodburning stove in mobile homes. Rates: Winter 1 Nov thru 31 Mar - cabins, $29.00-48.00 daily/$174.00-288.00 week. Summer 1 Apr thru 31 Oct - cabins, $35.00-51.00 daily/$192.00-306.00 week. All categories can make reservations, first call first serve basis. Maximum 6 to 8 people per unit.

DV/VIP: Commander's Office, EX-7108. O6+.

Other: Colonial Williamsburg/Jamestown. Many Museums. Busch Gardens. Great deer hunting, contact Special Services. Complete recreational area, for more details see Military RV, Camping & Rec Areas Around The World.

TML Availability: Good, Nov-Mar. Difficult, other times.

Medical-887-7222   Police-887-7222

Dahlgren Naval Surface Weapons Center (VA06R1)
Dahlgren, VA 22448-5000

TELEPHONE NUMBER INFORMATION: Main installation numbers: Comm: 703-663-8531, ATVN: 249-1110.

Location: From I-95 in Fredericksburg, VA, east on VA-3 to VA-206 (17 miles), left at Arnolds Corner, east to Dahlgren (11 miles). Also, US-301 south to VA-206, east to main gate of Center. RM: p-99, J/21. NMC: Washington, DC, 38 miles north.

Billeting Office: Building 960. EX-7671/72. 24 hours daily. Check in billeting, check out 1200 hours daily. Government civilian employee billeting.

Temporary Military Lodging Around the World — 175

VIRGINIA

Dahlgren Naval Surface Weapons Center, continued

TML: BOQ. Buildings 217, 962. Officer. All ranks. Leave or official duty. 12/1-bedroom, private bath; 20 separate bedrooms, private bath; 1/2-bedroom, private bath. Community kitchen, limited utensils, refrigerator, A/C, free cribs/cots, essentials, ice vending, color TV room & lounge, maid service, free washer/dryer. Older structures, renovated. Rates: Sponsor $5.00, suite $6.00 (+free market rate $5.00); $3.00 12 year+, $1.00 6-11 years. Maximum 4 persons. Duty can make reservations. Others Space-A.

TML: BEQ. Building 962 A wing. Enlisted. All grades. Leave or official duty. 53/1-bedroom, hall bath. A/C, essentials, ice vending, maid service, refrigerator, color TV room & lounge, free washer/dryer. Rates: $2.00 per room, per night. Duty can make reservations. Others Space-A.

TML: TLQ. Building 909, 962 D wing. All ranks. Leave or official duty. 10/1-bedroom, private bath. 4/2-bedroom, private bath. A/C, community kitchen, free cribs/cots, essentials, ice vending (962), kitchen (909), maid service, refrigerator (962), color TV room & lounge (962), complete utensils (909), free washer/dryer (962). Older structures. New TVs (962). Remodeled '89. Rates: Building 909 rates vary with pay grade. Rates: Building 962 D wing, Sponsor $5.00 (+$5.00 free market rate), adult $1.00, children free. Maximum charge $6.00. Maximum 3 persons per unit. Duty can make reservations. Others Space-A.

DV/VIP: Public Affairs Office. EX-8513. 06/SES equivalent +. Retirees Space-A.

Other: Washington's birthplace, Lee's birthplace, historic Fredericksburg.

TML Availability: Difficult. Best Nov-Feb.

Cafeteria-663-3841	CPO Club-663-7566	Enlisted Club-663-8785
Locator-663-8216/8701	Medical-663-8241	O'Club-663-2610
Police-663-8500	Snack Bar-663-7261	SDO/NCO-663-8531

Dam Neck Fleet Combat Training Center Atlantic (VA25R1)
Virginia Beach, VA 23461-5000

TELEPHONE NUMBER INFORMATION: Main installation numbers: Comm: 804-433-2000, ATVN: 433-2000.

Location: On the oceanfront, 2 miles southeast of Oceana NAS, off Oceana Blvd. RM: p-99, P/24. NMC: Virginia Beach, 2 miles northeast.

Billeting Office: Building 566-C. Comm: 433-6041. ATVN: 433-6691. Check in facility, check out 1000 hours daily. Government civilian employee billeting.

TML: BOQ. Buildings 225, 241. Officer all grades. Leave or official duty. EX-6366. 96/1-bedroom, private bath; 53/1-bedroom, living room, private bath; 4 DV/VIP suites, private bath (EX-6542). Kitchen (some), refrigerator, limited utensils, A/C, color TV, maid service, free cots, free washer/dryer, ice vending. Modern structures. Rates: $6.00 per person. Under 8 no charge. Duty on orders can make reservations. Others Space-A.

TML: BEQ. Buildings 550, 532, 566. Total 1,336 rooms including 27 Chief's rooms with refrigerator, A/C, color TV, maid service, free washer/dryer, pool tables.

VIRGINIA
Dam Neck Fleet Combat Training Center Atlantic, continued

Enlisted all grades. Reservations accepted for official orders. Others Space-A. Modern structures. Rates: Duty $2.00, others $4.00. Mess across street. Sundeck, BBQ, phone, cable, free washer/dryer, maid service.

DV/VIP: Protocol Office, Taylor Hall. EX-6542. 07/civilian equivalent+. Retirees Space-A.

TML Availability: Because this is a training command, availability is usually poor and only fair at best.

Cafeteria-433-7753	Enlisted Club-433-6146	Locator-433-2000
Medical-433-6327	NCO Club-433-6146	O'Club-433-6366
Police-433-6302	Snack Bar-433-7753	CDO-433-6234

Fort A.P. Hill (VA17R1)
Bowling Green, VA 22427-5000

TELEPHONE NUMBER INFORMATION: Main installation numbers: Comm: 804-633-5041, ATVN: 934-8710.

Location: From I-95, take Bowling Green/Fort A.P. Hill exit, US-17 (bypass) east to VA-2 south to Bowling Green, take VA-301 northeast to main gate. Also, exit I-95 to VA-207 north to VA-301 north and to main gate. RM: p-99, K/20. NMC: Fredericksburg, 14 miles northwest.

Billeting Office: Building TT-0114, 4th St. EX-8335. 0800-1630 hours M-F. Other hours, SDO, Building TT-0101, EX-8201. Check in billeting, check out 1200 hours. Government civilian employee billeting.

TML: Guest House. All ranks. Leave or official duty. Same facilities as DV/VIP. One handicapped suite. Rates: $20.00 per unit.

TML: VOQ/VEQ. Buildings TT-0117-0119, TT-0125, TT-0146. Officer all grades, Enlisted E7-E9. Leave or official duty. 39/1-bedroom, semi-private bath. Community kitchen, limited utensils, A/C, color TV, maid service, ice vending. Older structures. Rates: $20.00 per person. TDY can make reservations. Others Space-A.

TML: VOQ. Cottages. Officer all grades, Enlisted E7-E9. Leave or official duty. 4/1-bedroom, private bath; 2/2-bedroom, private bath; 1/3-bedroom, private bath; 1/5-bedroom, private bath. Kitchen, complete utensils, A/C, color TV, maid service, roll-aways ($10.00). Older structures. Rates: $20.00 per person. TDY can make reservations. Others Space-A.

TML: DV/VIP. Buildings SS-0252-0254, PO-0290. Officer 06+. EX-8205. 2 separate bedrooms, private bath; 1/2-bedroom, private bath; 1/3-bedroom, private bath. Kitchen, complete utensils, A/C, color TV, maid service, roll-aways ($10.00). Rates: $20.00 per person. TDY can make reservations. Others Space-A.

TML: Recreation Lodge. Building SS-0251. All ranks. Leave or official duty. EX-8219. 1/9-bedroom, semi-private bath. Sleeps 18. Kitchen, complete utensils, freezer, ice maker, color TV, roll-aways ($10.00), 2 woodburning fireplaces, lounge chairs. Rates: $150.00 per day for groups of 6 or less, $25.00 each additional person. All categories can make reservations.

Temporary Military Lodging Around the World — 177

Fort A.P. Hill, continued　　　　　　　　　　　VIRGINIA

TML: Recreation Cabins. Buildings PO-0292/93/94. All ranks. EX-8219. Report to Building TT-0106, Comm Rec Div. Check out 1100 hours. 3/3-bedroom, private bath. Kitchen, complete utensils, A/C, color TV, washer/dryer. Modern structures. Rates: $10.00 per adult and $5.00 per child E1-E6, $20.00 per adult and $10.00 per child E7-E8, $13.00 E9+ and TDY. Maximum 6 persons per family. All categories can make reservations.

DV/VIP: Commander's Office, Building TT-0101, EX-8205. 06+.

TML Availability: Good, Oct-Mar. Difficult, other times.

Cons Club-633-8389　　　Medical-633-8216　　　SDO/NCO-633-8205

Fort Belvoir (VA12R1)
Fort Belvior, VA 22060-5000

TELEPHONE NUMBER INFORMATION: Main installation numbers: Comm: 703-664-6071, ATVN: 354-6071.

Location: From I-95 south or US-1 south take Fort Belvoir exits. Clearly marked. RM: p-99, I-21. NMC: Washington, DC, 10 miles northeast.

Billeting Office: Building 470, Gaillard Road. EX-2456/2565. Billeting Manager, EX-2005. 24 hours daily. Check in billeting, check out 1200 hours daily. Government civilian employee billeting VOQ.

TML: VOQ/VEQ. Various buildings. Officer all grades. Leave or official duty. 231/1-bedroom, private bath (VOQ); 92/1-bedroom, semi-private bath (VOQ); 8 separate bedroom, private bath (VOQ); 9/2-bedroom, private bath (VEQ); 16 double rooms for E1-E6, shared bath (VEQ); 8 single rooms for E7-E9, private bath (VEQ). Some kitchen/refrigerator, color TV, maid service, free washer/dryer, free cribs/rollaways. Modern structure. Rates: Sponsor $27.00-$22.00, spouse $5.00, child $3.00. Maximum $30.00 per family. TDY and PCS can make reservations.

TML: DV/VIP. Building 20 (O'Club), 470. Officer 06+. Leave or official duty. 4 separate bedroom suites, private bath. Kitchen, complete utensils, A/C, color TV, maid service, free cribs/cots. Modern structure. Rates: Sponsor $27.00, spouse $5.00, child $3.00. Maximum $35.00 per family. Duty can make reservations.

TML Availability: Good, Dec. Difficult, May-Sep.

Cafeteria-360-1966　　　Enlisted Club-780-0962　　Locator-664-3096
Medical-664-1938　　　　NCO Club-780-0962　　　O'Club-780-0930
Police-664-1251　　　　　Snack Bar-781-7080/82　　SDO/NCO-664-5001

Fort Eustis (VA10R1)
Fort Eustis, VA 23604-5337

TELEPHONE NUMBER INFORMATION: Main installation numbers: Comm: 804-878-1110, ATVN: 927-1110.

Location: From I-64, exit 60A to VA-105, west to Fort. RM: p-99, N/22. NMC: Newport News, 13 miles southwest.

VIRGINIA
Fort Eustis, continued

Billeting Office: ATTN: Billeting Office, ATZF-EHH. Building 2110, Pershing Ave. EX-2337/5807. 24 hours daily. Check in billeting, check out 1000 hours daily. Government civilian employee billeting.

TML: VOQ/VEQ/DVQ/TLQ. Building 2110. All ranks. Leave or official duty. Accessible to handicapped. 24 suites & 7 cottages for transient persons; 273/1-bedroom, semi-private baths; 51 separate bedrooms, private bath. Refrigerator, community kitchen, kitchen (cottages only), limited utensils, A/C, essentials, color TV in room & lounge, maid service, free cribs/cots, free washer/dryer, food/ice vending, facilities for disabled American veterans. Older structure, remodeled. Rates for leave status: Sponsor $22.00, each additional person $6.00. Maximum charge $22.00. Maximum 4 persons per unit. Rates for active duty: Sponsor $16.00, DVQ $22.00. Maximum charge $16.00 PCS only. Priorities for VOQ are for officers attending Transportation Officer Basic Course. Priorities for VEQ are for enlisted personnel attending Advanced Non-commissioned Officer Course and Basic Non-commissioned Officer Course. Duty can make reservations. Others Space-A. Space-A rented at 1800 hours. **Pets allowed ($3.00 ea per day).**

DV/VIP: Protocol Office. Building 210, Room 207, EX-6010/30. 06+. Retirees and lower grades Space-A.

Other: Army Transportation Museum. Yorktown Battlefield. Colonial Williamsburg.

TML Availability: Good. Best Oct-May.

Enlisted Club-887-0985 Locator-878-5215   Medical-878-4555
NCO Club-887-0985   O'Club-887-0191   Police-878-4555
Snack Bar-887-0494   SDO/NCO-878-5897

Fort Lee (VA15R1)
Fort Lee, VA 23801-5000

TELEPHONE NUMBER INFORMATION: Main installation numbers: Comm: 804-734-1011, ATVN: 687-0111.

Location: From I-95 take Fort Lee/Hopewell exit, and follow VA-36 to main gate. RM: p-99, N/20. NMC: Petersburg, 3 miles west.

Billeting Office: Building P-8025, Mahone Ave. Comm: 733-4100. ATVN: 687-4023/1877. 24 hours daily. Check in billeting, check out 1200 hours daily. Government civilian employee billeting VOQ.

TML: Guest House. Buildings P-9001, P-9002. All ranks. Leave or official duty. 5/1-bedroom, 1 bed, private bath; 25/1-bedroom, 2 beds, sofa bed, living room, private bath. Refrigerator, A/C, color TV, maid service, free cribs/cots, free washer/dryer. Modern structures. Rates: Sponsor $8.00-$10.00, 2nd person $2.00, child no charge. Maximum $14.00-$16.00 per family. Duty can make reservations. Others Space-A. Note: primarily for PCS in/out. **Note: 40 additional units will be added during the early Spring of 1990.**

VIRGINIA

Fort Lee, continued

TML: VOQ. Buildings P-8025/26, P-9051-55, P-4229. Officer all grades, E7-E9. Leave or official duty. 482/1-bedroom, private bath. Kitchen, A/C, color TV, maid service, free washer/dryer, ice vending, special facilities for handicapped (2 units). Modern structures. Rates: Sponsor $20.00, 2nd person $5.00. Maximum 2 per room. Duty can make reservations. Others Space-A. Note: primarily for TDY personnel.

TML: DV/VIP. Building P-9052. Officer 06+, Enlisted E9. Official duty only. 16 apartments, living room, dining room, private bath. Kitchen, complete utensils, A/C, color TV, maid service, free washer/dryer, ice vending. Modern structure. Rates: Sponsor $20.00, 2nd person $5.00. Maximum 2 per room. Duty can make reservations. Others Space-A.

DV/VIP: Protocol Office, Building P-5000, Room 221, EX-3475. 06/GS-15+. Retirees and lower grades Space-A.

Other: Quartermaster Museum. Battlefield Park, rich in Civil War history.

TML Availability: Difficult. Best Dec, also on weekends and holidays.

Cafeteria-861-6480	Enlisted Club-861-8797	Locator-734-2021
Medical-734-3637	NCO Club-734-3521	O'Club-734-2210
Police-734-2072	Snack Bar-861-6172	SDO/NCO-734-2326

Fort Monroe (VA13R1)
Fort Monroe, VA 23651-5000

TELEPHONE NUMBER INFORMATION: Main installation numbers: Comm: 804-727-2111, ATVN: 680-2111.

Location: From I-64 exit Hampton and follow tour signs through Phoebus to Fort Monroe. RM: p-99, B/4. NMC: Hampton, 1 mile southeast.

Billeting Office: ATTN: ATZG-EHH. Building 28, Murray St. EX-2128. 0800-1645 hours M-F. Check in billeting. Check out 1000 hours. No government civilian employee billeting.

TML: VEQ. Buildings 61, 136. Enlisted all grades. Leave or official duty. 2/2-bedroom suites, private bath; 2 separate bedrooms, private bath. Kitchen, complete utensils, A/C, color TV, maid service, cribs/cots, washer/dryer. Older Victorian, renovated. Rates: TDY sponsor $15.00, other sponsor $15.00, spouse $4.00/$5.00, child $1.00/$2.00. Duty can make reservations. Others Space-A.

TML: VOQ. Building 137. Officer all grades. Leave or official duty. 2 separate bedrooms, private bath, with sleeper sofa in living room. Kitchen, complete utensils, A/C, color TV, cribs/cots, washer/dryer. New TVs, carpets, A/C in '87. Rates: TDY sponsor $15.00, other sponsor $15.00, spouse $4.00, child $1.00. Maximum family charge $20.00 except TDY. No number limit if family. Duty can make reservations. Others Space-A.

TML: DV/VIP. Building 80. Officer 06+. Leave or official duty. EX-4401. Check in Building 11, 0700-1645. 4/2-bedroom suites, private bath. Kitchen, complete utensils, A/C, color TV, maid service, free washer/dryer. Older Victorian, remodeled. Rates: TDY $22.00, others $22.00, spouse $10.00, child up to 16 $2.00. Maximum

180 — *Temporary Military Lodging Around the World*

VIRGINIA
Fort Monroe, continued

$38.00 per family. Duty can make reservations. Others Space-A. Check out 1100 hours daily.

DV/VIP: ATTN: Protocol Office, Building 11. EX-4401. 06+.

Other: Historic Fort. Jefferson Davis, President of the Confederate States of America, was imprisoned here after the Civil War.

TML Availability: Fairly good, Oct-Apr. More difficult, May-Sep.

SDO/NCO-727-2174	Locator-727-2598	Medical-727-2840
NCO Club-727-2796	O'Club-727-2406	Police-727-2238
Snack Bar-722-3862		

Fort Myer (VA24R1)
Fort Myer, VA 22211-5050

TELEPHONE NUMBER INFORMATION: Main installation numbers: Comm: 703-545-6700, ATVN: 227-0101.

Location: Adjacent to Arlington National Cemetery. Take Fort Myer exit from Washington Blvd, at 2nd St, or enter From US-50 (Arlington Blvd) first gate. Also, exit from Boundary Drive to 12th St north entrance near the Iwo Jima Memorial. RM: p-42. I/7. NMC: Washington, DC, 1 miles northeast.

Billeting Office: Building T-49, Jackson St. 24 hours daily. Comm: 696-3576. ATVN: 226-3576. Check in billeting, check out 1200 hours daily. Government civilian employee billeting.

TML: VOQ/VEQ. Buildings T-49, T-52. All ranks. Leave or official duty. VOQ: 16/1-bedroom, semi-private bath; 4 separate bedrooms, private bath. VEQ: 20 rooms, 2/3/4 beds in some rooms, semi-private bath. Refrigerator, A/C, color TV room & lounge, maid service, cribs/cots $3.00, free washer/dryer, microwave in lobby. Rates: Sponsor $11.00, adult $11.00, spouse $3.00, child/infant $3.00. Duty can make reservations. Others Space-A.

TML: DV/VIP. Building 50. Officer 07+. Leave or official duty. 18/1-bedroom suites, living room, private bath. Refrigerator, bar, A/C, color TV, telephone, maid service, free cots, free washer/dryer. Older structure. Rates: Sponsor $20.00, adult $20.00, spouse $5.00, child/infant $5.00. Duty can make reservations. Others Space-A.

DV/VIP: Write to: DA Protocol, Pentagon. Building 50. Comm: 697-7091. ATVN: 227-7091. 07+. Retirees & lower grades Space-A.

Other: Arlington National Cemetery. Stables of ceremonial horses used in military funerals. Old Guard Museum. Home of U.S. Army Band.

TML Availability: Good. Best, Nov-Dec.

Enlisted Club-696-3394	Locator-545-6700	Medical-696-3628
NCO Club-696-3394	O'Club-524-7000	Police-696-3525
Snack Bar-528-1039	SDO/NCO-696-3250	

Temporary Military Lodging Around the World — 181

VIRGINIA

Fort Pickett (VA16R1)
Blackstone, VA 23824-5000

TELEPHONE NUMBER INFORMATION: Main installation numbers: Comm: 804-292-8621, ATVN: 438-8621.

Location: On US-460, 1 mile from Blackstone. Clearly marked. RM: p-99, O/18. NMC: Richmond, 60 miles northeast.

Billeting Office: ATTN: AFZA-FP-EH. Bldg T-469, Military Rd. EX-8309/8320. 0730-1600 duty days. Other hours, PMO, Building T-471, EX-8444. Check in billeting, check out 1000 hours daily. Government civilian employee billeting. Note: confirm all reservations by phone at least 24 hours in advance.

TML: VOQ. Cottages. Officer all grades, E6-E9. Leave or official duty. 13/1-bedroom, 2 beds, private bath. Community kitchen, complete utensils, A/C, color TV lounge, maid service, free cribs, cots $5.00 per adult. Older structures. Rates: $17.50-$20.00 per unit. Maximum 4 persons. Maximum 3 guests per sponsor. Duty can make reservations. Others Space-A. **Pets allowed outside.**

TML: VOQ. Officer all grades. Leave or official duty. 28/1-bedroom, latrine bath; 4/1-bedroom suites, 2 beds, private bath. Community kitchen, complete utensils, A/C, color TV lounge, maid service, free cribs, cots $5.00 per adult, free washer/dryer. Older structures. Rates: $7.00-$11.00 per adult. Maximum 3 guests per sponsor. Duty can make reservations. Others Space-A. **Pets allowed outside.**

TML: VEQ. Enlisted all grades. Leave or official duty. 28/1-bedroom, latrine bath; 4/1-bedroom suites, 2 beds, private bath. Community kitchen, complete utensils, A/C, color TV lounge, maid service, free washer/dryer. Older structure. Rates: $7.00-$11.00 per adult. Maximum 3 guests per sponsor. Duty can make reservations. Others Space-A. **Pets allowed outside.**

DV/VIP: PAO, Building 472, EX-8303/2454. O5+. Retirees and lower grades Space-A.

Other: Great hunting area. Reserve/NG training post.

TML Availability: Good, Sept.-Mar. Difficult, other times.

Enlisted Club-292-2336	Locator-292-2266/8525	Medical-292-2528
NCO Club-292-2336	O'Club-292-2336	Police-292-8444
Snack Bar-292-5273	SDO/NCO-292-2560	

Fort Story (VA08R1)
Fort Story, VA 23459-5000

TELEPHONE NUMBER INFORMATION: Main installation numbers: Comm: 804-422-7305, ATVN: 438-7305.

Location: From south exit of Chesapeake Bay Bridge-Tunnel (US-13) east on US-60 (Atlantic Ave), to Fort Story. Clearly marked. From I-64 take US-60 east. From VA-44 (Norfolk-VA Beach Expressway) exit US-58, left turn to north on

VIRGINIA
Fort Story, continued

Atlantic Ave (US-60) to 89th St entrance to Fort Story. RM: p-98, D/6. NMC: Virginia Beach, 7 miles south.

Billeting Office: Building 300, Atlantic & Guadalcanal Rd. EX-7321. 0730-2330 hours daily. Check in billeting, check out 1000 hours daily. Government civilian employee billeting.

TML: TLQ. Buildings 511, 526, 537. All ranks. Leave or official duty. 1/1-bedroom, private bath; 2 separate bedrooms, private bath. Kitchen, refrigerator, community kitchen, limited utensils, A/C, color TV room & lounge, maid service, essentials, free cribs/cots, free washer/dryer, special facilities for disabled American veterans (1 unit). Older structures. Redecorated. Rates: Sponsor $18.00, each additional person $8.00. Duty can make reservations. Others Space-A.

TML: DV/VIP. Cottages. 06+. Memorial day-Labor day. Office of the Commander, Fort Eustis, VA 23604. Comm: 804-878-4802. ATVN: 927-4802. 6/2-bedroom, private bath; 2/4-bedroom, private bath. Fully equipped, linens, towels, all utensils. Rates: $24.00. Leave only. All categories can make reservations. Cottages on Chesapeake Bay/Atlantic Ocean.

DV/VIP: Handled by Fort Eustis as indicated above.

Other: Old Cape Henry Lighthouse. Douglas MacArthur Memorial. World's largest naval base. Virginia Beach.

TML Availability: Good, Oct-Mar. Difficult, other times.

Enlisted Club-428-7405   Locator-422-7682   Medical-422-7802
NCO Club-428-7405   O'Club-425-6631   Police-422-7696
SDO/NCO-422-7454

Judge Advocate General's School (VA01R1)
Charlottesville, VA 22903-1781

TELEPHONE NUMBER INFORMATION: Main installation numbers: Comm: 804-972-6300, ATVN: 274-7110.

Location: On the grounds of the University of Virginia at Charlottesville. Take the 250 bypass off I-64 to the Barracks Road exit, then turn right at light, then right onto Midmont, then right onto Arlington Blvd, then right at the top of the hill to the school. RM: p-99, K/17. NMC: Charlottesville, within city limits.

Billeting Office: ATTN: JAGS-SSL-H. Basement of TJAGS. Room B017. Comm: 972-6450. 0750-1650. Other hours, SDO front desk. Check in facility, check out 1200 hours. Government civilian employee billeting only on orders to TJAGS.

TML: VEQ/VOQ. All ranks. Leave or official duty. Accessible to handicapped. 36/1-bedroom, one bed, private bath; 36/1-bedroom, two beds, private bath. A/C, community kitchen, cots ($2.00), ice vending, maid service, refrigerator, color TV, washer/dryer. Modern structure. Rates: For personnel on leave/vacation: Sponsor $15.00-$20.00, dependents $3.00; for personnel on active duty status: Sponsor $10.00-$15.00, dependents $5.00. Maximum 4 persons. Duty can make reservations. Others Space-A. Most space reserved for TJAGS students.

Temporary Military Lodging Around the World — 183

VIRGINIA

Judge Advocate General's School, continued

DV/VIP: ATTN: JAGS-SSJ-V. EX-6301. 06+. Retirees and lower grades Space-A. For PCS families only.

Other: Monticello. Ash Lawn. Michie Tavern.

TML Availability: Very limited, last two weeks in June. Difficult, other times.

O'Club-972-6448

Langley Air Force Base (VA07R1)
Langley AFB, VA 23665-5000

TELEPHONE NUMBER INFORMATION: Main installation numbers: Comm: 804-764-9990, ATVN: 574-1110.

Location: From I-64 east in Hampton take Armistead Ave exit, go right to stop light; right onto La Salle Ave and enter AFB. RM: p-98, A/2. NMC: Hampton, 1 mile west.

Billeting Office: 1 CSG/SVH. Building 75, Nealy Ave. EX-4051. 24 hours daily. Check in billeting, check out 1200 hours daily. Government civilian employee billeting.

TML: TLQ. Buildings 78, 79, 94, 95. All ranks. Leave or official duty. 39 separate bedrooms, private bath. Kitchen, complete utensils, A/C, color TV, maid service, free cribs/cots, free washer/dryer, ice vending. Modern structures, renovated. Rates: $18.50 per unit, sleeps 5. Duty can make reservations. Others Space-A.

TML: TLQ. Buildings 1092-1098. All ranks. Leave or official duty. 39/1-bedroom, private bath. Kitchen, complete utensils, A/C, color TV, maid service, free cribs/cots, free washer/dryer, ice vending. Modern structures. Rates: $18.50 per unit, sleeps 4. Duty can make reservations. Others Space-A.

TML: VOQ. Buildings 67, 68. Officer 01-05. Leave or official duty. 78/1-bedroom, private bath. Kitchen, A/C, color TV, maid service, free cots, free washer/dryer, ice vending, special facilities for disabled American veterans. Modern structures. Rates: $9.00 per person. Duty can make reservations. Others Space-A.

TML: VAQ. Building 75. Enlisted all ranks. Leave or official duty. 65/1-bedroom, 2 beds, latrine bath; 5 separate bedrooms, private bath for SNCOs. Refrigerator, A/C, color TV, maid service, free washer/dryer, ice vending. Modern structure, renovated. Rates: $6.00 per person. Maximum 2 per room. Duty can make reservations. Others Space-A.

TML: DV/VIP. Buildings 472 (Lawson Hall), 448 (Dodd Hall). Officer 06/GS-15+. Leave or official duty. EX-Lawson-3467, EX-Dodd-5044. Lawson: 11 separate bedroom suites, private bath. Dodd: 10 separate bedroom suites, private bath. Kitchen, limited utensils, A/C, color TV, maid service, free cribs/cots, free washer/dryer, ice vending. Older structures, renovated. Rates: $10.00 per person. Maximum 2 per unit. Duty can make reservations. Others Space-A.

DV/VIP: Protocol Office, Building 703. EX-3467. 06+. Retirees and lower grades Space-A.

Other: Colonial Williamsburg. Busch Gardens. Virginia Beach. Mariners' Museum.

184 — *Temporary Military Lodging Around the World*

VIRGINIA
Langley Air Force Base, continued

TML Availability: Good, winter months. Difficult, summer months.

Cafeteria-851-7837   Enlisted Club-851-4220   Locator-764-5615
Medical-865-6800   NCO Club-851-4220   O'Club-851-3833
Snack Bar-851-7837   SDO/NCO-764-7771

Little Creek Naval Amphibious Base (VA19R1)
Norfolk, VA 23521-5000

TELEPHONE NUMBER INFORMATION: Main installation numbers: Comm: 804-464-7000, ATVN: 680-7000.

Location: From I-64 south through Hampton Roads Bridge Tunnel take Northampton Blvd exit, 5 miles to Base, exit VA-225. From Chesapeake Bay Bridge Tunnel proceed west on US-60 to Base. RM: p-98, D/5. NMC: Norfolk, 11 miles southwest.

Billeting Office: ATTN: Code N73. Officers in Building 3408, A St, EX-7522. Enlisted in Building 3601, 6th & 3rd Sts, EX-7577. Check in facility, check out as indicated. Government civilian employee billeting.

TML: Navy Lodge. Building 3531. All ranks. Leave or official duty. For reservations call 1-800-NAVY-INN. Lodge number is 464-6215. Check in prior to 1800 to avoid cancellation. Check out 1200 hours daily. 90/1-bedroom, 2 beds/studio couch, private bath. Kitchen, complete utensils, A/C, color TV, maid service, coin washer/dryer, ice vending. Modern structure. Rates: $32.00 per unit. All categories can make reservations. **No pets except birds in cages, fish in tanks.**

TML: BOQ. Building 3408. Officer all grades. Leave or official duty. EX-7522. Check out 1330 hours daily. 271/1-bedroom, private bath; 18 separate bedroom suites, private bath. Kitchen, limited utensils, A/C, color TV room & lounge, maid service, free washer/dryer, ice vending. Modern structure, renovated '87. Rates: $5.00 per person. No accompanied members until Navy Lodge is full. Duty can make reservations. Others Space-A.

TML: BEQ. Building 3601. Enlisted all grades. Leave or official duty. EX-7577. Check out 1100 hours daily. 17/1-bedroom, private bath; 20/1-bedroom, 2 beds, private bath; 155/1-bedroom, 3 beds, private bath. Refrigerator, A/C, color TV lounge, maid service, free washer/dryer, ice vending. Modern structure, renovated. Rates: $2.00 per person. Dependents not authorized. Duty can make reservations. Others Space-A.

TML: DV/VIP. Building 3186. Officer 07-010. Leave or official duty. Comm: 444-5901. Check out 1200 hours daily. 4 separate bedroom suites, private bath. Queen beds, refrigerator, community kitchen, limited utensils, A/C, color TV, maid service, free cots, ice vending. Older structure, remodeled. Rates: $8.00 per person active duty. Maximum $32.00 per day.

DV/VIP: Commander, EX-7000. 07+. Retirees Space-A.

Other: Beautiful Virginia beaches nearby. Colonial Williamsburg 1 hour north.

VIRGINIA

Little Creek Naval Amphibious Base, continued

TML Availability: Good, Oct-Dec. Difficult, Jun-Aug.

Cafeteria-464-7546	CPO Club-464-7789	EnlistedClub-464-7949
Locator-464-7226	Medical-464-7879	O'Club-460-1111
Police-464-7621	Snack Bar-464-2663	SDO/NCO-464-7385

Norfolk Naval Base (VA18R1)
Norfolk, VA 23511-5000

TELEPHONE NUMBER INFORMATION: Main installation numbers: Comm: 804-444-0000, ATVN: 564-0111, FTS: 954-0111.

Location: From north take I-64 east, take Naval Base exit, follow signs. From south take I-64 exit to I-564 into Gate 2. RM: p-98, C/3. NMC: Norfolk, in city limits.

Billeting Office: BEQ: Billeting Code 06, Building I-A, Pocahontas & Bacon Sts. EX-4425. 0730-1600 hours daily. Other hours, Central Assignment Building A-48. BOQ: BOQ Billeting Fund, Building A-128, Powhattan St off Maryland Ave. EX-4151/3250. 24 hours daily. Check in facility, check out 1000 hours daily. Government civilian employee billeting.

TML: Navy Lodge. SDA-314. All ranks. Leave or official duty. For reservations call 1-800-NAVY-INN. Comm: 489-2656. 24 hours daily. Check out 1200 hours daily. 90/1-bedroom, 2 double beds, studio couch, private bath. Kitchen, complete utensils, A/C, color TV, HBO, maid service, free cribs, coin washer/dryer, ice vending. Modern structure. Rates: $24.00 per unit. All categories can make reservations. Note: 200 units were added to the Lodge as of July 1989. Navy Lodge is located 1 mi south on Hampton Blvd. directly across from the Armed Forces Staff College.

TML: BOQ. Buildings A-125, A-128. Officer all grades. Leave or official duty. 274/1-bedroom, private bath; 3 separate bedrooms, kitchen, private bath. Refrigerator, A/C, cable color TV room & lounge, maid service, cots ($2.00), free washer/dryer, ice vending, sauna/exercise room, jacuzzi, sun deck. Modern structures. Rates: $7.00 per unit, $13.00 double. Duty can make reservations. Others Space-A.

TML: BEQ. Buildings I-A (NAVSTA), U-16 (NAS). Enlisted all grades (No E7+ at NAS). Leave or official duty. NAVSTA EX-4425, NAS EX-4983.152/1-bedroom, hall bath (NAVSTA); 5 buildings, hall bath (NAS). Check out NAVSTA 1300 hours daily, NAS 1000 hours daily. Both: Refrigerator, A/C, color TV room & lounge, maid service, free washer/dryer, ice vending. Modern structures. Rates: $4.00 per person. Duty can make reservations. Others Space-A.

DV/VIP: COMNAVBASE Building KBB, EX-2788. CINCLANTFLT Camp Elmore, EX-6323. 07+. Retirees Space-A. 4 suites used for O6+ with BOQ manager's permission.

Other: Largest naval base in the world. Tour given daily. Ship launchings. Hampton Roads Naval Museum. MacArthur Memorial. Busch Gardens. Williamsburg. Jamestown and Yorktown Visitor Centers.

TML Availability: Good, fall & winter. More difficult, other times.

186 — *Temporary Military Lodging Around the World*

VIRGINIA
Norfolk Naval Base, coantinued

Cafeteria-440-0199/7026	CPO Club-444-2125	Enlisted Club-444-4014
Locator-444-0000	Medical-444-1531	O'Club-423-8450
Police-444-2361	Snack Bar-444-4118	SDO/NCO-444-7097

Oceana Naval Air Station (VA09R1)
Virginia Beach, VA 23460-5120

TELEPHONE NUMBER INFORMATION: Main installation numbers: Comm: 804-433-2000, ATVN: 433-2000.

Location: From I-64 exit to Norfolk-Virginia Beach Expressway (VA-44 east), east on Virginia Beach Blvd. Bordered by Oceana Blvd (VA-615) and London Bridge Rd. Also, bordered by Potters and Harper Rds. RM: p-98, F/7. NMC: Virginia Beach, in city limits.

Billeting Office: Building 460. G St across from O'Club. EX-3293. 24 hours daily. Check in billeting, check out 1100 hours daily. Government civilian employee billeting.

TML: BOQ. Building 460. Officer all grades. Leave or official duty. 102/1-bedroom, private bath (28 rooms with semi-private bath); 48 separate bedroom suites, living room, private bath. A/C, community kitchen, cots ($4.00), essentials, ice/food vending, small kitchens (suites), maid service, refrigerator, color TV room & lounge, free washer/dryer. Older structure. New carpets '87. Hotel type telephone systems. Rates: Sponsor $6.00, (suite) $7.00, (VIP suite) $8.00, adult double Sponsor rates, child over 2 years $4.00, infant no charge. No maximum charge. Maximum 4 in suites, 2 in rooms. Duty can make reservations. Reservations not taken for non-duty during summer months. Others Space-A.

DV/VIP: Building 460. EX-3293. 06+. Retirees and lower grades Space-A.

Other: Largest jet base on east coast. Great beaches at Virginia Beach. Try the seafood at the Lighthouse Restaurant, south end of beach on Atlantic Ave.
TML Availability: Good, winter months. Difficult, summer months.

Cafeteria-491-4260	Enlisted Club-433-2112	Locator-491-4260
Medical-433-2221/2	NCO Club-433-2637	O'Club-428-0036/7
Police-433-9111	Snack Bar-433-3197	SDO/NCO-433-2366

Quantico Marine Corps Combat Development Command (VA11R1)
Quantico, VA 22134-5001

TELEPHONE NUMBER INFORMATION: Main installation numbers: Comm: 703-640-2121, ATVN: 278-2121.

Location: From I-95 north or south take Quantico/Triangle exit # 50A. US-1 north/south is adjacent to Base. Clearly marked. RM: p-99, I/20. NMC: Washington, DC, 40 miles north.

Billeting Office: Building 2034, Little Hall, Barnett Ave. EX-2681. 24 hours daily. Housing Office, 0800-1630 M-F. EX-2711. Check in billeting, check out 1000 hours (1200 hours Hostess House). Government civilian employee billeting.

Temporary Military Lodging Around the World — 187

VIRGINIA
Quantico Marine Corps Combat Development Command, continued

TML: Hostess House. Building 3072. All ranks. Leave or official duty. Deposit required first day for PCS prior to occupancy. Maximum stay 15 days. EX-2983/7959. 73/1-bedroom, semi-private bath. A/C, color TV lounge, maid service, cribs .50, cots $1.00, free washer/dryer, vending machine. Older structure. Rates: $23.00 per person, $18.00 PCS with orders.

TML: SNCO Quarters. Building 3229, Shuck Hall. Enlisted E6-E9. Leave or official duty. EX-3148-3149. 24/1-bedroom, private bath; 1 separate bedroom suite, private bath (reservations made through Cmd Sgt Maj). Kitchen (suite only), refrigerator, A/C, color TV, maid service, free cribs/cots, free washer/dryer, ice vending. Older structure. Rates: $4.00 per room, $10.00 per suite. Maximum 1 per room, 4 per suite. Duty on orders or leave, retired, and dependents only.

TML: BOQ. Building 15, Liversedge Hall. Officer all grades. Leave or official duty. EX-3148/3149. 72/1-bedroom, semi-private bath; 12 separate bedrooms, private bath (DV/VIP suites). Kitchen (6 units), refrigerator, community kitchen (Building 15), limited utensils, A/C, cable color TV room & lounge, maid service, free cribs/cots, free washer/dryer, ice vending, O'Club with bar at Building 15. Older structure. Rates: Transient $10.00, TAD/TDY $5.00, suites $10.00 with orders, $20.00 without orders. All categories can make reservations.

TML: DV/VIP. Building 17. Officer O6+. Leave or official duty. EX-2786. 1/1-bedroom suite, private bath; 2/2-bedroom suite, private bath. Refrigerator, community kitchen, A/C, color TV, maid service, free cribs/cots, washer/dryer, ice vending, cash bar in suites. Older structure. Rates: $10.00 with orders, $20.00 without orders. Duty on orders or leave, retirees, and dependents only.

DV/VIP: Protocol, Building 3250, EX-2786. O6+. Retirees and lower grades Space-A.

Other: On the Potomac River. Near the capital city of Washington, DC.

TML Availability: Good, Oct-Apr. Difficult, summer months.

Enlisted Club-640-2780
NCO Club-640-3166
Snack Bar-640-7171
Locator-640-2121
O'Club-640-6115
SDO/NCO-640-2707
Medical-640-2525
Police-640-2251

Vint Hill Farms Station (VA03R1)
Warrenton, VA 22186-5013

TELEPHONE NUMBER INFORMATION: Main installation numbers: Comm: 703-349-6000, ATVN: 229-6000.

Location: From Washington, DC area take I-66 west to VA-29/211 south, proceed 4 miles to to VA-215 (Mitchell Rd), left for 2 miles to Station main gate. RM: p-99, I/19. NMC: Washington, DC 35 miles northeast.

Billeting Office: Building 163, Helms St. EX-6670. 0730-2300 hours M-F. 0800-1600 Sat, Sun, Holidays. Other hours, Building 162, EX-6323. Check in facility, check out 1100 hours daily. No government civilian employee billeting.

TML: Guest House. Building 150. All ranks. Leave or official duty. EX-6670. 11/1-bedroom, hall bath; 2/2-bedroom (mobile homes), private bath. Community kitchen, limited utensils, refrigerator, essentials, A/C, color TV room & lounge,

VIRGINIA
Vint Hill Farms Station, continued

cribs, free washer/dryer, ice vending. Older structure. Rates: Sponsor $10.50, adult $2.00. Mobile homes $20.00. Duty can make reservations. Others Space-A.

TML: VOQ/VEQ. Building 163. All ranks. Leave or official duty. 10/1-bedroom, private bath. 2/1-bedroom, semi-private bath. A/C, maid service, refrigerator, color TV room & lounge, free washer/dryer, ice vending. Modern structure. Rates: $20.00 per room, per night. No children. No families. Duty can make reservations. Others Space-A.

TML: DV/VIP. Building 247, 2nd floor. Officer 06+. Leave or official duty. EX-6670. Second floor O'Club. 1 separate bedroom suite, private bath. Refrigerator, A/C, color TV, maid service. Older structure, remodeled. Rate: Sponsor $25.00, each additional person $2.00. Duty can make reservations. Others Space-A.

DV/VIP: Protocol Office same as Billeting Office EX-6670. 06+/GS-15+/E9. Retirees and lower grades Space-A.

Other: Near Bull Run Battlefield Park, Shenandoah Valley, Blue Ridge Mountains.

TML Availability: Fairly good. Best Oct-May. Difficult, June-Sep.

Note: 14 unit Guest House to be opened August 1991.

| Locator-347-6400 | Medical-347-6543 | NCO Club-349-1895 |
| O'Club-347-6322 | Police-347-6543 | SDO/NCO-347-6323 |

Yorktown Naval Weapons Station (VA14R1)
Yorktown, VA 23691-5000

TELEPHONE NUMBER INFORMATION: Main installation numbers: Comm: 804-887-4000, ATVN: 953-4000.

Location: From I-64 exit to US-143 west, .5 miles to US-238 left, .5 miles to gate 3, Skiffes Creek. RM: p-99, D/19. NMC: Newport News, 15 miles southeast.

Billeting Office: ATTN: Housing Officer. Building 1970. Comm: 887-2424. 0800-1530 M-F. Check in facility, check out 1000 hours. Government civilian employee billeting if GS-7+ with advance reservations.

TML: BOQ. Building 704. Officer all grades. Leave or official duty. EX-7621. After duty hours EX-7557. 1/1-bedroom, private bath, suite (DV/VIP); 16 separate bedroom suites, private bath. Community kitchen, A/C, color TV room & lounge, maid service, free cots, free washer/dryer, ice vending, refrigerator. Modern structure. Rates: Sponsor $8.00. Maximum $16.00 per family. Duty can make reservations. Others Space-A.

TML: BEQ. Building 706, 707. Enlisted all grades. 92/1-bedroom, semi-private bath. Lounge, recreational area. Rates: $4.00 per person.

DV/VIP: PAO, Building 31-A, EX-4141. 06/GS-15+.

Other: Historic Williamsburg, Yorktown, Jamestown, Mariners' Museum.

TML Availability: Good, winter months. Limited, summer months.

VIRGINIA

Yorktown Naval Weapons Station, continued

Cafeteria-887-4646
O'Club-887-4272
Enlisted Club-887-4646
Police-887-4677
Medical-887-7404
SDO/NCO-887-4545

WASHINGTON

Bangor Naval Submarine Base (WA08R4)
Bremerton, WA 98315-5000

TELEPHONE NUMBER INFORMATION: Main installation numbers: Comm: 206-396-1110, ATVN: 744-1110.

Location: Approximately 15 miles north of Bremerton, on WA-3, exits to Base clearly marked. RM: p-100, G/10. NMC: Tacoma, 40 miles southeast.

Billeting Office: Building 2300, Scorpion St. EX-6686. 24 hours daily. Check in facility, check out 1200 hours daily. No government civilian employee billeting.

TML: BOQ. Building 2750. Officer all grades. Leave or official duty. EX-6581. 66/1-bedroom, private bath (some suites). Kitchen, complete utensils, color TV room & lounge, essentials, cribs/cots, maid service, free washer/dryer, food/ice vending, computer, jacuzzi. Modern structure. Rates: Sponsor $8.00, adult $4.00, child under 12 $4.00, infant $4.00. Maximum 4 persons per unit. Duty, retirees, reservists can make reservations. Others Space-A.

TML: BEQ. Building 2200. Enlisted all grades. Leave or official duty. EX-4035. 600/1-bedroom, semi-private bath, 1-3 beds depending on grade. 8/1-bedroom, private bath. Refrigerator, color TV in lounge, maid service, free cribs/cots, free washer/dryer, food/ice vending, microwave. Modern structure. Rates: Sponsor $4.00, adult $3.00, child $3.00, infant $3.00. Duty can make reservations. Others Space-A.

TML: VIP Cottage. Building 4189. Officer 06+. Leave or official duty. EX-6581. 1 bedroom cottage, private bath. Kitchen, complete utensils, maid service, free cribs/cots, color TV. Renovated and remodeled '89. Rates: Sponsor $8.00, adult $4.00, child $4.00, infant $4.00. Maximum 4 persons. Duty can make reservations. Others Space-A.

DV/VIP: PAO, Building 1100, Room 213. EX-4843. 06+. Civilians determined by Commander. Retirees Space-A.

TML Availability: Fairly good. Best Oct-Mar.

Cafeteria-779-3365
Medical-396-4222
Police-396-4312
Enlisted Club-779-9907
NCO Club-779-9907
Snack Bar-779-9907
Locator-396-6008
O'Club-779-9907
SDO/NCO-396-4800

Fairchild Air Force Base (WA02R4)
Fairchild AFB, WA 99011-5000

TELEPHONE NUMBER INFORMATION: Main installation numbers: Comm: 509-247-1212, ATVN: 657-1110.

WASHINGTON
Fairchild Air Force Base, continued

Location: Take US-2 exit from I-90 west of Spokane. Follow US-2 through Airway Heights, after 2 miles left to Base main gate and Visitors' Control Center. RM: p-101, G/23. NMC: Spokane, 12 miles east.

Billeting Office: ATTN: 92CSG/SVH. Building 2392, Short St. EX-5737/5519. 24 hours daily. Check in billeting, check out 1100 hours daily. Government civilian employee billeting official duty only.

TML: VOQ. Building 2392/93. All ranks. Leave or official duty. 27/1-bedroom, private bath; 8 separate bedrooms, private bath; 11/2-bedroom, private bath. Kitchen, color TV room & lounge, maid service, free cribs/cots, free washer/dryer, ice vending, irons, ironing boards. Older structures. Building 2393 renovated '87. Rates: $9.00 per person. Maximum $13.50 per family. (DV/VIP $12.00 per person, $24.00 maximum per family). Duty can make reservations. Others Space-A.

TML: VAQ. Building 2272. Enlisted all ranks. Leave or official duty. 29/1-bedroom, semi-private bath. Refrigerator, A/C, color TV, maid service, free washer/dryer. Modern structure. Rates: $9.00 per room. Maximum 2 per room. TDY can make reservations. Others Space-A.

TML: TLF. Building 2393. All ranks. Leave or official duty. 8/1-bedroom suites, private bath. Kitchen, complete utensils, color TV, maid service, cribs/cots, free washer/dryer, ice vending. Older structure, renovated. Rates: $21.50-$22.50 per room. Maximum 2 per room. TDY only can make reservations. Others Space-A.

DV/VIP: Building 2392, EX-2127. 06+. Retirees and lower grades Space-A.

Other: Spokane Riverfront Park.

TML Availability: Good, Sep-Mar. More difficult, other times.

Cafeteria-244-2022
NCO Club-244-3622
Snack Bar-244-3061
Locator-247-5875
O'Club-244-3644
Medical-247-5661
Police-247-5493

Fort Lewis (WA09R4)
Fort Lewis, WA 98433-5000

TELEPHONE NUMBER INFORMATION: Main installation numbers: Comm: 206-967-1110, ATVN: 357-1110.

Location: On I-5 in Puget Sound area, 14 miles north of Olympia. Clearly marked. RM: p-100, J/10. NMC: Tacoma, 12 miles north.

Billeting Office: ATTN: AFZH-DEH, Building 5228, between Teak and Hemlock Sts. EX-7862/2815. 24 hours daily. Check in facility, check out 1000 hours. Government civilian employee billeting.

TML: Guest House. Fort Lewis Lodge. All ranks. Leave or official duty. EX-0211/5051. 75/1-bedroom, private bath. 8/1-bedroom, private bath & 2/2-bedroom, private bath cottages, fully furnished for Enlisted PCS families. Rates: Same as above. Color TV, maid service, recreation room, lounge, cribs/cots, coin washer/dryer, ice vending. Modern structure. Rates: Based on sponsor's BAQ/VHA allowance according to rank. Maximum 5 per room. TDY can make reservations. Others Space-A. Pets allowed in kennel ($1.50 per space).

WASHINGTON

Fort Lewis, continued

TML: VOQ/VEQ. Buildings 2492, 4292 (Clark House). All ranks. Leave or official duty. Clark House (for PCS in/out families): 3/1-bedroom, private bath; 5 suites, private bath. Building 2492 (for Officer/civilian on official TDY): 3/1-bedroom, private bath; 27 suites, private bath. Community kitchen on each floor (2492), limited utensils, color TV room & lounge, maid service, washer/dryer, irons/ironing boards on request. Older structures. Rates: Sponsor $19.25, each additional person $2.00. TDY can make reservations. Others Space-A.

TML: DV/VIP. Building 1020. Bronson Hall. Officer 04+. Leave or official duty. 16/2-room suites, private bath; 3 VIP suites, private bath. Refrigerator, color TV, maid service, washer/dryer. Older structure. Rates: Sponsor $15.00-$22.00, each additional person $2.00. Duty can make reservations. Others Space-A.

TML: VOQ/VEQ. Building 9906. Lincoln Street. Officer. All ranks. 28 single rooms. TV, refrigerator, community kitchen, maid service. Duty can make reservations.

TML: Officer Cabins. PCS in/out families. Klatawa Village, Main Post. 6 family units. Small kitchen, limited utensils, color TV, maid service.

TML: Enlisted Cabins. PCS in/out families. 11 family units. Small kitchen, limited utensils, color TV, maid service.

DV/VIP: Protocol Office, Building 2025. EX-5834. 07+.

Other: Mt. Rainier, Puget Sound, Mt. St. Helens.

TML Availability: Fair, Oct-Apr. Difficult, other times.

Cafeteria-964-4424
Medical-967-6972
Police-967-3107
Enlisted Club-964-0144
NCO Club-964-2555
Locator-967-6221
O'Club-964-0331

Madigan Army Medical Center (WA15R4)
Tacoma, WA 98431-5000

TELEPHONE NUMBER INFORMATION: Main installation numbers: Comm: 206-967-5151, ATVN: 357-5151.

Location: From I-5 north or south take the Madigan exit. Clearly marked. RM: p-100, I/10. NMC: Tacoma, 12 miles north.

Billeting Office: Building 9901, Lincoln St, EX-2664. 0730-2300 hours daily. Other hours SDNCO, Building 9901, information desk, EX-7082. Check in billeting, check out 1000 hours daily. Government civilian employee billeting.

192 — *Temporary Military Lodging Around the World*

WASHINGTON
Madigan Army Medical Center, continued

TML: Guest House. Building 9901. All ranks. Leave or official duty. Reservations not taken. 4/1-bedroom, semi-private bath; 18 separate bedrooms, semi-private bath. Community kitchen, refrigerator, limited utensils, maid service, cribs/cots, coin washer/dryer. Older structure. Rates: Sponsor $6.00-$12.00, each additional person $3.00. Maximum 3 per unit. MEDEVAC have priority.

TML: VOQ/VEQ. Building 9906. All ranks. Leave or official duty. 27/1-bedroom, semi-private bath. Community kitchen, refrigerator, limited utensils, maid service, free washer/dryer. Older structure. Rates: $6.00-$12.00 per person. TDY/medical students can make reservations. Others Space-A.

TML: DV/VIP. Building 9938. Officer 03+. Leave or official duty. 4 separate bedrooms, private bath; 1 suite, private bath (06+ only). Refrigerator, community kitchen, limited utensils, A/C, color TV, maid service, cribs/cots. Older structure. Rates: Sponsor $8.00, each additional person $3.00 (rooms); Sponsor $15.00, each additional person $5.00 (suite). Maximum 3 per unit. TDY/MEDEVAC personnel can make reservations. Others Space-A.

DV/VIP: CO's Office, Building 9900. EX-6921. 03+. Retirees Space-A.

TML Availability: Fairly good. Best, Oct-May.

Cafeteria-964-3456	Enlisted Club-964-2555	Locator-967-6221
Medical-967-6972	NCO Club-964-3671	O'Club-964-4054
Police-967-3107	Snack Bar-964-3456	

McChord Air Force Base (WA05R4)
McChord AFB, WA 98438-5000

TELEPHONE NUMBER INFORMATION: Main installation numbers: Comm: 206-984-1910, ATVN: 976-1110.

Location: From I-5 exit 125. Clearly marked. RM: p-100, I/10. NMC: Tacoma, 8 miles north.

Billeting Office: Building 166, Main St. Comm: 584-1471. 24 hours daily. Check in facility, check out 1200 hours daily. No government civilian employee billeting.

TML: VOQ/VAQ. Many buildings. All ranks. Leave or official duty. 172/1-bedroom, private, semi-private, & latrine baths; 18 separate bedrooms, private bath; 19/2-bedroom, private bath. Kitchen (VOQ), refrigerator (all), limited utensils, color TV, maid service, free cribs/cots, free washer/dryer, ice vending, facilities for disabled American veterans. Older structures. Rates: $6.00 per person. Maximum 2 room suite $16.00, 1 room $8.00. Duty can make reservations. Others Space-A.

TML: DV/VIP. Building 116. Officer 06+. Leave or official duty. EX-2621. 6/1-bedroom suites, private bath; 17/2-bedroom suites, private bath; 48/1-bedroom, private bath. Kitchen, complete utensils, color TV, maid service, free cribs/cots, free washer/dryer, ice vending. Older structure. Rates: $8.00 per person. Maximum $16.00 2 bedroom suite. Duty can make reservations. Others Space-A.

DV/VIP: EXO 62/MAW/CCE, Building 100, EX-2621. 06/GS-12+. Retirees and lower grades Space-A.

TML Availability: Good, Nov-Feb. Difficult, Jun-Aug.

McChord Air Force Base, continued

WASHINGTON

Enlisted Club-984-2918 Locator-984-2474 Medical-984-5601
NCO Club-584-1371 O'Club-582-4222/5581 Police-984-5624
Snack Bar-582-2092

Pacific Beach Ocean Getaway (WA16R4)
Puget Sound NS, WA 98115-5014

TELEPHONE NUMBER INFORMATION: Main installation numbers: Comm: 206-526-3211, ATVN: 941-3211.

Location: Located on the coast in Pacific Beach, WA, 150 miles southwest of Seattle. Accessible from US-101 (Coastal Highway) and US-12 from Yakima. RM: p-101, I/6. NMC: Seattle, 150 miles northeast.

Billeting Office: On board Naval Station Seattle in Building 193N. 1000-1600 hours M-F. 1000-1400 Sat. Check out 1100 hours. Reservations made over the phone are tentative until request forms and full payment are returned within 10 working days of phone request. Send request forms to OCEAN GETAWAY: Recreation Services, PO Box O, Pacific Beach, WA 98571-5000, 800-626-4414 or 206-276-4414. Make checks payable to:Recreation Services. Cancellations must be in writing and received by Recreation Services 10 days prior to reservation date. Notices received less than 10 working days will be assessed one day's rental. Reservations not paid within 10 working days will automatically be cancelled. Reservation Priority: (1 reservation per request) Active duty-90 days, other military personnel 60 days, all other authorized personnel 30 days.

TML: Cabins and suites. All ranks. Leave or official duty. 28 furnished Capehart cabins (2-, 3-, or 4-bedroom) and four suites are available. Basic cabin rate: E1-E5 $22.00, E6-E9 $35.00, Officer $40.00, DOD $45.00. 3 bedroom cabin rate: E1-E5 $27.00, E6-E9 $40.00, Officer $45.00, DOD $50.00. 4 bedroom cabin rate: E1-E5 $32.00, E6-E9 $45.00, Officer $50.00, DOD $55.00. Suite rate: E1-E5 $12.00, E6-E9 $15.00, Officer $18.00, DOD $20.00. Each cabin unit sleeps two people per bedroom. Oceanside cabins add $2.00 per day, cabins with fireplace add $5.00 per day. Cribs are available upon request ($2.00). Crib linens are not provided. Lodging can be reserved from 2 nights up to 2 weeks. Extensions granted when space is available. Minimum of 2 nights required (F-Sun), and 3 nights (Sun-F). Holiday weekends minimum of 3 nights (F-Mon). All other requests on a Space-A basis. Note: Sponsor must accompany guest during stay.

TML Availability: Fairly good. Best in winter months.

Puget Sound Naval Shipyard (WA11R4)
Bremerton, WA 98314-5000

TELEPHONE NUMBER INFORMATION: Main installation numbers: Comm: 206-476-3711, ATVN: 439-3711.

Location: Take WA-16 West to end of freeway, PSNS clearly visible 3 miles north. RM: p-100, E/10. NMC: Seattle, 60 miles southeast.

WASHINGTON
Puget Sound Naval Shipyard, continued

Billeting Office: Building 865, Comm: 476-7660, ATVN: 439-2637. 24 hours daily. Check in facility, check out 1300 hours daily. Government civilian employee billeting.

TML: BEQ. Buildings 865, 885, 942. Enlisted all grades. Leave or official duty. Comm: 476-7619, ATVN: 439-7627. 447/1-bedroom, shared bath; 72 additional rooms, hall bath. Color TV room & lounge, maid service, free washer/dryer, ice vending. Modern structure. Rates: $3.00 per person. BEQ facilities for AD and retirees only. Duty can make reservations. Others Space-A. Six family rooms available at $10.00 per day.

TML: BOQ. Building 847. Officer all grades & GS-7+. Leave or official duty. Comm: 476-2840. 70/1-bedroom, private bath; 5 VIP/family suites, private bath. Kitchen (VIP), refrigerator, color TV room & lounge, maid service, free cribs/cots, free washer/dryer, ice vending. Older structure, renovated '88. Rates: $6.00 per person. Maximum 4 per room. Duty can make reservations. Others Space-A.

DV/VIP: BOQ, Building 847. EX-2840. O6+. Retirees Space-A.

TML Availability: Fairly good, Nov-Mar. More difficult, Jun-Sep.

Cafeteria-476-2527
Locator-476-3582
Police-476-3393
CPO Club-476-3391
Medical-911
Enlisted Club-476-2546
O'Club-373-5014

Puget Sound Naval Station (WA10R4)
Seattle, WA 98115-5000

TELEPHONE NUMBER INFORMATION: Main installation numbers: Comm: 206-526-3211, ATVN: 941-3211.

Location: From I-5 take 45 Street exit, then take Highway 513 north to main gate. Located on Sand Point Way. RM: p-101, G/11. NMC: Seattle, 6 miles southwest.

Billeting Office: Building 224, B Street. EX-3883. 24 hours daily. Check in billeting, check out 1200 hours daily. Government civilian employee billeting.

TML: BOQ/BEQ. Eagles & Crows Nest I- All ranks. Leave or official duty. Accessible to handicapped. 36 ... ooms, private bath. 6/2-bedroom, private bath. Community ... erator, color TV, maid service, free cribs, food vending, free washe ... Older structure, new TVs '89. Rates: Sponsor $8.00; (VIP) $12.00, adult $8.00, child/infant $4.00. Duty can make reservations. Others Space-A.

TML Availability: Fairly good. Best, Nov-Mar.

Cafeteria-527-7818
Medical-526-3274
Snack Bar-527-7818
CPO Club-526-3578
O'Club-Burned
SDO/NCO-526-3212
Enlisted Club-526-3539
Police-526-3212

WASHINGTON

Whidbey Island Naval Air Station (WA06R4)
Oak Harbor, WA 98278-5000

TELEPHONE NUMBER INFORMATION: Main installation numbers: Comm: 206-257-2211, ATVN: 820-0111.

Location: Take WA-20 to Whidbey Island, 3 miles west of WA-20 on Ault Field Road. RM: p-100, E/10. NMC: Seattle, 90 miles southeast.

Billeting Office: Building 973, McCormick Center, EX-2529, Officer/CPO. Building 2701, 8th Street, EX-5513, Enlisted. Check in facility, check out 1200 hours daily. Government civilian employee billeting.

TML: BOQ. Building 973. Officer all grades. Leave or official duty. 140/1-bedroom, private bath. Refrigerator, maid service, essentials, food/ice vending, color TV room & lounge, free washer/dryer. Older structure. New carpets '89. Rates: Sponsor $6.00, adult/child over 12 $6.00, infant free. Maximum 2 persons per unit. Duty can make reservations. Others Space-A.

TML: BEQ. Building 2552. All grades. Leave or official duty. 36 beds, 3 per room, shared bath. Refrigerator, color TV room & lounge, maid service, ice/food vending, kitchen (suite), free washer/dryer. Older structure. Rates: $4.00 per person. Duty can make reservations. Others Space-A.

DV/VIP: C.O. Secretary, Building 108. EX-2345. 06+.

Other: Home of the EA-6B "Prowlers".

TML Availability: Difficult on weekends due to Reserve Training. Best during winter.

Cafeteria-257-2716　　CPO Club-257-2892　　Enlisted Club-257-3309
O'Club-257-2521　　　Police-257-3122　　　　SDO-257-2631
Snack Bar-679-5291

WEST VIRGINIA

NONE

WISCONSIN

Fort McCoy (WI02R2)
Sparta, WI 54656-5000

TELEPHONE NUMBER INFORMATION: Main installation numbers: Comm: 608-388-2222, ATVN: 280-1110.

WISCONSIN
Fort McCoy, continued

Location: From west on I-90 to north on WI-27 to northeast on WI-21 to Fort. From east on I-90, to west on WI-21 to Fort. RM: p-103, O/7. NMC: La Crosse, 35 miles southwest.

Billeting Office: ATTN: AFZR-DLH-B, Building 2168, 8th St, EX-2107. 24 hours daily. Check in billeting, check out 1100 hours daily. Government civilian employee billeting.

TML: TLQ. All ranks. Leave or official duty. 230/1-bedroom, shared bath; 70/1-bedroom, private bath; 3/2-bedroom and 1/4-bedroom, private bath (4 units are trailers). Kitchen, complete utensils, A/C, color TV, free cribs, cots ($3.00), essentials, free washer/dryer. Older structure, new trailers. Rates: vary according to rank, status and quarters occupied. Call for details. All categories can make reservations.

DV/VIP: Protocol Office, Building 100. EX-3607. 06+. Retirees and lower grades Space-A.

Other: Ski Hill on installation has cross country and downhill skiing. Mid-Dec thru Feb. Equipment rental, Building 8061, EX-4498/3360.

TML Availability: Fairly good, Jan-May and Sep-Dec. Difficult, other times.

Cafeteria-269-4335	Locator-388-3116	Medical-116 (emerg)
NCO Club-388-2777	O'Club-388-2065	Police-115 (emerg)
Snack Bar-269-4968	SDO/NCO-269-2216/7	

WYOMING

Francis E. Warren Air Force Base (WY01R4)
Francis E. Warren AFB, WY 82005-5000

TELEPHONE NUMBER INFORMATION: Main installation numbers: Comm: 307-775-1110, ATVN: 481-1110.

Location: Off I-25, 2 miles north of I-80. Clearly marked. RM: p-104, J/2. NMC: Cheyenne, adjacent to the city.

Billeting Office: Building 216, Randall St. 24 hours daily. EX-1844. Check in facility, check out 1100 hours daily. Government civilian employee billeting.

TML: Guest House. Buildings 74, 129, 202, 238. All ranks. Leave or official duty. 18/2-bedroom apartments, private bath. Kitchen, living room, maid service, free cribs, free washer/dryer, color TV (3 apartments), black & white TV, refrigerator in all, cable for TV. Older structures, renovated. Rates: $22.00 per unit. Duty can make reservations. Others Space-A.

TML: VOQ/VAQ/DV/VIP. All ranks. Leave or official duty. 1 DV house; 8/1-bedroom apartments, private bath. Kitchen (some), refrigerator, color TV, maid service, free cribs, free washer/dryer. Older structure, renovated. Total 10 VOQ, 29

WYOMING

Francis E. Warren Air Force Base, continued

VAQ. 1 DV/VIP unit for E8-E9. Rates: VOQ $8-$10.00 per person; VAQ $8.00 per person. Duty can make reservations. Others Space-A.

DV/VIP: PAO. EX-2137/3052. E8+/O6+. Retirees Space-A.

TML Availability: Good, except last week of July for Cheyenne Frontier Day Rodeo.

Enlisted Club-638-8993
NCO Club-638-8993
Snack Bar-634-1593
Locator-775-1841
O'Club-632-9286
SDO/NCO-775-3921
Medical-775-3461
Police-775-3501

The complete military guide to Europe!
Look for this book
at military Exchanges and
military Clothing Sales Stores.
If not available, place your credit card
order by calling (703) 237-0203.

UNITED STATES POSSESSIONS

GUAM

Agana Naval Air Station (GU03R8)
FPO San Francisco 96637-5000

TELEPHONE NUMBER INFORMATION: Main installation numbers: Comm: 671-351-1110. ATVN: 322-1110.

Location: Naval Air Station is in the middle of the island of Guam, on Marine Drive. Clearly marked. NMC: Agana, 3 miles southwest.

Billeting Office: BOQ/BEQ. Comm: 344-5227. Check in at facility, check out 1300 hours daily. No government civilian employee billeting.

TML: BOQ. Building 1300. Officer all grades. Leave or official duty. 81/1-bedroom, shared bath; 3 separate bedrooms, private bath. Refrigerator, A/C, color TV lounge, maid service, free washer/dryer, ice vending. Older structure. Rates: $4.00 per person, plus $10.00 fair market rental fee, family maximum $16.00, plus $8.00 fair market rental fee. Duty can make reservations. Others Space-A.

TML: BEQ. Building 15. Enlisted all grades. Leave or official duty. 850 beds, shared bath. A/C, color TV lounge, maid service, free washer/dryer. Older structure. Rates: $4.00 per person. No dependents. Duty can make reservations. Others Space-A.

DV/VIP: OD. 06/GS-15+. Retirees Space-A.

TML Availability: Good, Apr-Dec. Difficult, other times.

Cafeteria-344-5174	Enlisted Club-342-2274	Locator-344-6161
Medical-344-8201/4140	O'Club-342-2124	Police-344-5160
SDO/NCO-344-6114		

Andersen Air Force Base (GU01R8)
APO San Francisco 96334-5000

TELEPHONE NUMBER INFORMATION: Main installation numbers: Comm: 671-351-1110, ATVN: 322-1110.

Location: On the north end of the island, accessible from Marine Dr which extends entire length of the island of Guam. NMC: Agana, 15 miles south.

Billeting Office: Building 27006, 4th & Marian Sts. Comm: 366-8201. ATVN: 366-8144. 24 hours daily. Check in billeting, check out 1200 hours daily. Government civilian employee billeting.

TML: VOQ. Buildings 27003, 27005, 27006. Officer all grades. Leave or official duty. 120/1-bedroom, shared bath. Refrigerator, A/C, color TV, maid service, free

Andersen Air Force Base, continued   GUAM

washer/dryer, ice vending. Older structure. Rates: $9.00 per person. Duty can make reservations. Others Space-A.

TML: VAQ. Building 25003. Enlisted all grades. Leave or official duty. Reservations accepted. 76 rooms, shared bath. Refrigerator, A/C, color TV, free washer/dryer. Older structure. Rates: $6.50 per person. Duty can make reservations. Others Space-A.

TML: DV/VIP. Building 27006. Officer O6+. Leave or official duty. 6/1-bedroom, private bath; 5 separate bedroom, private bath suites. A/C, color TV, maid service, free washer/dryer. Rates same as VOQ. Duty can make reservations. Others Space-A.

DV/VIP: Protocol Office, 633 ABW, EX-4228. 07+. Retirees Space-A.

Other: An island paradise. World War II history.

TML Availability: Good, year round.

Cafeteria-362-3247   Enlisted Club-366-9236   Medical-363-2978
NCO Club-366-8204   Officer Club-362-4269   Snack Bar-36-3149
SDO/NCO-363-2981

Guam Naval Station (GU02R8)
FPO San Francisco 96630-0051

TELEPHONE NUMBER INFORMATION: Main installation numbers: Comm: 671-351-1110. ATVN: 322-1110.

Location: South on Marine Drive. Clearly marked. NMC: Agana, 10 miles north.

Billeting Office: None. Contact BOQ, Building 2000, Chapel Rd. Comm: 339-5259. 24 hours daily. Check in facility, check out 1200 hours daily. Government civilian employee billeting.

TML: BEQ. Barracks 7. Enlisted all ranks. Leave or official duty. Comm: 339-5259. 12/1-bedroom, private bath; 68/1-bedroom, shared bath. Refrigerator, A/C, maid service, free washer/dryer. Older structure, renovated. Rates: $2.00 per person. Maximum 4 per room. Duty can make reservations. Others Space-A. Note: space for families is very limited.

TML: BOQ. Building 2000. Officer all grades. Leave or official duty. Reservations accepted. 77/1-bedroom, private bath. Refrigerator, A/C, color TV room & lounge, maid service, free washer/dryer, ice vending. Older structure. Rates: $4.00 per person. Duty can make reservations. Others Space-A.

DV/VIP: Flag Lt, EX-5202. 07+.

Other: Scuba diving, war relics, monuments.

TML Availability: Fairly good. Best, December. Most difficult, Jul-Aug.

Cafeteria-332-1217   Enlisted Club-332-8193   Locator-321-1110
Medical-344-9351   NCO Club-342-2274   O'Club-342-2124
Police-349-5216   Snack Bar-332-7182   SDO/NCO-333-2980

MIDWAY ISLAND

Midway Island Naval Air Facility (MW01R8)
FPO San Francisco 96114-1200

TELEPHONE NUMBER INFORMATION: Main installation numbers: Comm: Call small island operator, ask for Midway Island, EX-415/400/814, ATVN: 430-0111.

Location: On Midway Island in the Pacific Ocean, 1,300 air miles northwest of Honolulu, HI. NMC: Honolulu, 1,300 miles southeast.

Billeting Office: This station is in a Naval Defensive Sea Area and requires entry approval to visit, which is obtained thru the Comdt, 14th Naval District, Honolulu, 45 days in advance. Entry is usually restricted to personnel visiting relatives on the island, and TDY personnel. No central billeting office. Contact BOQ, lower deck BOQ Building "B". 0800-1630 hours duty days, EX-436. Other hours, OD, EX-777. Check in facility, check out 1000 hours daily. Government civilian employee billeting.

TML: BOQ. Building "B". EX-648. 24 hour desk at MAC Term. Officer all grades. Leave or official duty. 6/1- & 2-bedroom apartments, private bath. Kitchen, free washer/dryer. Some 1 bedroom, shared bath. Older structure. Rates: $4.00 per person. Enlisted check BEQ, EX-437.

Other: Base has exchange, cafeteria, snack bar, all clubs, package store, theater.

TML Availability: Good, Feb-Aug.

PUERTO RICO

Borinquen Coast Guard Air Station (PR03R1)
Aquadilla, PR 00604-5000

TELEPHONE NUMBER INFORMATION: Main installation numbers: Comm: 809-882-3500, FTS: 498-3500.

Location: At old Ramey AFB, north of Aguadilla. Take PR-2 from San Juan or north from Mayaguez to PR-110 North to CGAS. RM: p-119, B/18. NMC: San Juan, 65 miles east.

Billeting Office: La Plaza, Room 26. 0800-1600 duty hours. EX-3127. Other hours, Duty Officer, EX-2581. Check in billeting, check out 1200 hours daily. Government civilian employee billeting.

TML: Guest House. All ranks. Leave or official duty. 5/1-bedroom, shared bath and private bath; 3/3-bedroom, private bath. Kitchen, complete utensils, A/C (2 units), color TV room & lounge, maid service, free cribs, free washer/dryer. Older structure. Rates: Sponsor $14.00, each additional person $2.00. Duty and retirees can make reservations. Others Space-A. PCS have priority. Personnel on leave/anyone on vacation should apply at least 15 days in advance. **Pets OK.**

TML Availability: Very limited. Best, Jan-Apr.

Cafeteria-890-2581	Medical-882-3500	Police-890-2020.
SDO/NCO-882-3500		EX-1500

Temporary Military Lodging Around the World — 201

PUERTO RICO

Fort Buchanan (PR01R1)
Fort Buchanan, PR 00934-5042

TELEPHONE NUMBER INFORMATION: Main installation numbers: Comm: 809-783-2424, ATVN: 740-2424.

Location: From Munoz Rivera International Airport take highway 26 west toward Bayamon to highway 22 to the Fort Buchanan sign. NMC: San Juan, 6 miles southwest.

Billeting Office: Building 119. Comm: 792-7977. ATVN: 740-7221. For reservations/information dial the Guest House direct at Comm: 809-792-7977. 0700-1700 hours daily. Other hours SDO, Building 390, EX-7123. Check in facility, check out 1100 hours daily. No government civilian employee billeting.

TML: Guest House. Su Casa. Building 119. All ranks. Leave or official duty. Accessible to handicapped. 29/1-bedroom, private bath (each with double bed and sleeper sofa). Refrigerator, community kitchen, A/C, cable color TV, maid service, cribs, cots, facilities for disabled American veterans. Older structure, remodeled. Rates: $27.00 first person, $5.00 each additional person. PCS may make reservations once they have their orders. Other active duty one week in advance. Others Space-A.

DV/VIP: Commander's Office. Building 399, EX-7265. 06+. Active duty TDY only.

Other: Capital of Puerto Rico, El Morro Castle, Plaza las Americas Shopping Center, El Condado, Bacardi Rum Distillers, beaches.

TML Availability: Good, Aug-Nov, Feb-May. Difficult, summer months, Christmas holidays.

Cafeteria-792-7049
Medical-EX-8888
Snack Bar-792-8116

Enlisted Club-792-8431
NCO Club-792-8431
SDO/NCO-792-7777

Locator-EX-8296
O'Club-792-6234

Roosevelt Roads Naval Station (PR02R1)
Box 3010, FPO Miami 34051-5000

TELEPHONE NUMBER INFORMATION: Main installation numbers: Comm: 809-865-2000, ATVN: 831-2000.

Location: From San Juan International Airport, turn left onto PR-26 for 20 minutes, turn left onto PR-3 (Carolina exit) for 30 minutes, then turn left after Puerto Del Rey Marina into NS. RM: p-119, C/26. NMC: San Juan, 50 miles northwest.

Billeting Office: Building 729 (Officers), Building 1708 (Enlisted). Comm: 865-2000-EX-4334/3364 (Officers), Ex-4145/4147 (Enlisted). 24 hours daily. Check in billeting, check out 1200 hours daily. Government civilian employee billeting.

TML: BOQ/BEQ. All ranks. Leave or official duty. Accessible to handicapped. 8/2-bedroom apartments, private bath; 4/3-bedroom apartments, private bath. Kitchen, refrigerator, limited utensils, A/C, color TV, maid service, cots ($2.00). Modern structure. Rates: Sponsor $8.00, $5.00 each additional person. Active duty on orders, PCS/TAD/TDY have priority and make reservations. Other Space-A.

DV/VIP: PAO. EX-3364. 07+. Retirees Space-A.

Other: El Yuunque (L-EE-UN-KEE) rain forest with water falls, hiking trails, restaurant.

PUERTO RICO
Roosevelt Roads Naval Station, continued

TML Availability: Good, Oct-Mar. Difficult, Apr-Sep.

NOTE: 72 new Navy Lodge units to be available November 1990.

Cafeteria-865-3299	CPO Club-865-4853	Enlisted Club-865-4142
Locator-865-2000	Medical-865-4133	O'Club-865-3259/3273
Police-865-4123/4195	Snack Bar-865-4745	SDO/NCO-865-4311/4352

Congrats to Roosey Roads
New Navy Lodge Opens!

Happiness is....a real value in a warm resort area! Top it off with being across the street from a commissary and exchange and a kitchenette in your lodge unit, and you have real happiness bonus points or savings in the old pocketbook. And, staying on a military installation means camaraderie and increased safety as well.

On 3 March, the three-deck Navy Lodge located in Roosevelt Roads, Puerto Rico, opened to a crowd of well-wishers and military officials. Each of the 72 units has two double beds, private bath, kitchenette, air conditioning, cable TV, refrigerator, telephone, carpet, cookware, dishes, silverware, coffee pot/toaster and microwave ovens. And....the fee for this is only $35 per day.

There are also **two rooms equipped for the handicapped.** For those with large families, 12 of the 72 rooms are interconnecting units at $70 per day.

We talked with the new Navy Lodge Manager, Dorothy Glawson, and she tells us that you can see the ocean from the three-story Navy Lodge, but it is too long a walk to get there that way. There is a free bus, however, which can get you to the on-base beaches as well as other locations.

Reservations are handled toll-free through the convenient **1-800-NAVY INN** phone number. Retirees may make reservations one week in advance. The phone number for the Navy Lodge in Puerto Rico is **(809) 865-8282.**

Temporary Military Lodging Around the World — 203

FOREIGN COUNTRIES

ANTIGUA

Antigua Naval Facility (AN01R1)
St. Johns, West Indies
FPO Miami 34054-5000

TELEPHONE NUMBER INFORMAITON: Main installation numbers: Comm: 809-462-3171, ATVN: 854-1110 (ask for Antigua EX-398).

Location: On the northeast side of the island of Antigua, 1 mile from Coolidge Airport. NMC: St. Johns, 9 miles west.

Billeting Office: Quarterdeck, EX-398. 24 hours daily. Check in facility, check out 1200 hours daily. Government civilian employee billeting.

TML: TLF. Building 3. All ranks. PCS and TDY only. BOQ: 2/1-bedroom, private bath. Refrigerator, community kitchen, color TV, maid service, free washer/dryer, ice vending, bar in building. Building 1: 1/1-bedroom, private bath (female enlisted); 2/1-bedroom, latrine bath (enlisted). Refrigerator, maid service, free washer/dryer. Rates: Moderate. Duty can make reservations. Others Space-A.

DV/VIP: Adm Office, EX-386. O6+.

Other: Duty on leave restricted to $20.00 per day in purchases except snack bar and clubs. Retirees may use only club and medical facility due to SOFA. Support Facilities: Special Service, Snack Bar, Medical, Gas Station, BX, All Hands Club, Theater. Great beaches.

AUSTRALIA

Harold E. Holt Naval Communications Station (AU01R8)
FPO San Francisco 96680-1800

TELEPHONE NUMBER INFORMATION: Main installation numbers: Comm: 61-099-49-3587/3239, ATVN: 315-371-1945/3587/3239.

Location: In Exmouth, a remote community on the Northwest Cape of Western Australia. The nearest city is Perth, AU about 800 miles south; the nearest town of any size is Carnarvon, 250 miles to the south. One road connects all of these, following the coast.

Billeting Office: BEQ 4, 0700-1600 hours daily, EX-3588/27. Other hours, Security Office, EX-3332. Check in facility, check out 1200 hours daily. No government civilian employee billeting.

AUSTRALIA
Harold E. Holt Naval Communications Station, continued

TML: BEQ. Enlisted all grades. Duty only. 2/1-bedroom, latrine bath. Refrigerator, color TV in lounge, A/C, free washer/dryer, ice vending. Rates: no charge. Maximum 1 per room.

Other: No BX or commissary privileges for personnel not assigned to station due to SOFA. Commonwealth Pass obtained from Civil Commissioner of Exmouth needed to enter the base. Local "no frills" type lodging available at Caravan Park on Lefroy St, tel 099-49-1331, Norcape Lodge at Town Beach Rd, 099-49-1334, and the Potshot Inn, 099-49-1200. You must have your own camper to use park-type facilities. No pets due to quarantine requirements. Very warm in summer, Oct-Apr. Very casual dress.

TML Availability: Limited for duty only.

Cafeteria-3334	Enlisted Club-3510	Medical-3339
NCO Club-3510	O'Club-3571/3471	Police-3332
Snack Bar-3310		

BELGIUM

NATO/SHAPE Support Group (US) (BE01R7)
Hotel Raymond
APO New York 09088-5000

TELEPHONE NUMBER INFORMATION: Main installation numbers: Comm: 32-65-44-5500, (From Belgium dial 065-311131/32), ETS: 423-1110.

Location: From Bruxelles Airport take E-10 direct to Paris, exit at Mons, Belgium and follow signs to "GARE" (train station). Hotel is across from GARE. HE: p-35, E/3. NMC: Bruxelles, 50 miles north.

Billeting Office: No central billeting office. Priority I & II: AD, DOD civilian, PCS. Priority III: TDY, relative of hospital patient. Priority IV: TDY. Priority V: guest of AD/civilian at installation. Priority VI: leave, retirees. Note: Medal of Honor individual treated as Priority I. Check in 1300 hours, check out 1100 hours daily. EX-311131. Government civilian employee billeting.

TML: Hotel Raymond. All ranks. Leave or official duty. Accessible to handicapped. 68/1-bedroom, private bath. Refrigerator, color TV room & lounge, custodial service (except Sunday/holidays), essentials, free cribs/cots, free washer/dryer, cafeteria, food/ice vending. Modern structure. Renovated '88. Rates: Sponsor $27.00, adult (25 months & older) $4.50. Family of 3 $62.00 if in same room. Maximum 4 persons. All categories can make reservations. Accompanied dependents of active duty, disabled American veterans, military widows Space-A.

TML Availability: Fairly good. Best Oct-Mid May.

Cafeteria-44-7749	Enlisted Club-44-4954	Locator-44-5164
Medical-423-5820	NCO Club-44-5313	O'Club-44-5451
Police-065-223171		SDO/NCO-5410

Temporary Military Lodging Around the World — 205

BERMUDA

Bermuda Naval Air Station (BM01R1)
FPO New York 09560-5000

TELEPHONE NUMBER INFORMATION: Main installation numbers: Comm: 809-293-5316, ATVN: 938-5316.

Location: Bermuda is 600 miles east of Cape Hatteras, NC, in the Atlantic Ocean. NAS is on the north end of St David's Island near St George City. NMC: Hamilton, 6 miles southwest.

Billeting Office: Building 550. EX-5439. 24 hours daily. Check in at facility, check out 1200 hours daily. Government civilian employee billeting.

TML: BOQ/BEQ. Buildings 343, 344, 550, 632, 633. All ranks. Leave or official duty. Single rooms, hall bath. Refrigerator, A/C, TV lounge, maid service, washer/dryer, ice vending. Older structure, renovated. Rates: Officers $6.00, Enlisted $4.00, VIPs $9.00. Maximum 2 per room. Duty can make reservations. Others Space-A.

TML Availability: Good, Nov-Dec. Limited, other times.

Cafeteria-293-6116　　Medical-293-6514　　Police-293-6431
SDO/NCO-293-5316

CANADA

Argentia Naval Facility (CN02R1)
FPO New York 09597-5000

TELEPHONE NUMBER INFORMATION: Main installation numbers: Comm: 709-227-8555/8556, ATVN: 568-8555/8556.

Location: At the terminus of North Sydney (Nova Scotia) to Argentia (Newfoundland) Ferry Service. At Argentia there is access to the Trans-Canadian Highway, TCH-1, via CN-101, 25 miles northeast. The U.S. Naval Facility is in Argentia and is clearly marked. NMC: St. John's, Newfoundland, 80 miles northeast.

Billeting Office: ATTN: CBQ Manager, Box 10, U.S. Naval Facility, FPO New York 09597-5000. Billeting coordinated at Strain Memorial Hall, Building 848M. 24 hours daily. EX-8673. Check in facility, check out 1200 hours daily. Government civilian employee billeting.

TML: BEQ. Building 848M, Strain Memorial Hall. To reach it, turn right at intersection by railroad overpass, .5 miles to 10 story concrete building. Park in lower lot across the street from BQ. All ranks. Accessible to handicapped. Leave or official duty. 32/1-bedroom, shared bath; 5 separate bedrooms, private bath. Refrigerator, community kitchen, color TV room & lounge, free cribs/cots ($4.00), free washer/dryer, ice vending, maid service, color TV. Quarters on 4th deck. Meals available in galley on 2nd deck. Various clubs and vending machine on 1st deck. Older structure, renovated '88-90. Rates: $5.00 per person. Some DV/VIP lodging available in BEQ at rate of $8.00-$10.00 per person. Duty can make reservations. Others Space-A.

DV/VIP: Executive Officer, Building 848M, EX-5862. 06+.

206 — *Temporary Military Lodging Around the World*

CANADA
Argentia Naval Facility, continued

* Note: Retired personnel not authorized use of exchange or commissary.

Other: Great hunting and fishing area.

TML Availability: Best, Oct through June. More difficult, July through Sept.

Enlisted Club-227-8523   Galley-227-8625   NCO Club-227-8523
O'Club-227-8394   Police-227-8777   Snack B/Bowl-227-8482
SDO/NCO-227-8555

Goose Bay Air Base (CN03R1)
Labrador, CN APO-ISO

TELEPHONE NUMBER INFORMATION: Main installation numbers: Comm: 709-896-2461, ATVN: 622-2461.

Location: Must fly in or take the ferry from Newfoundland. RM: p-117, B/25. NMC: Happy Valley, 8 miles east.

Billeting Office: Building 565, EX-5555. 24 hours daily. Operated under contract to the Air Force.

TML: TAQ. All ranks. Leave or official duty. 4 rooms with 3 single beds per room, semi-private and latrine baths. Community kitchen, free cribs, ice vending, maid service, refrigerator, color TV room & lounge, washer/dryer. Older structure. Rates: Sponsor $4.00, adult $4.00, children over 12 $4.00. Duty can make reservations. Primarily for MAC crews returning from or going to Europe. Others can write to: Commander DET 1, 438 MAW/Goose Bay, McGuire AFB, NJ 08641.

TML Availability: Extremely limited year round.

CUBA

Guantanamo Bay Naval Station (CU01R1)
FPO New York 09593-5000

TELEPHONE NUMBER INFORMATION: Main installation numbers: Comm: 011-53-99-XXXX, ATVN: 723-3690/564-4063.

Location: In the southwest corner of the Republic of Cuba. Guantanamo Bay Naval Station is accessible only by air. NMC: Miami, FL 525 air miles northwest. Note: All personnel not assigned must have the permission of the Commander to visit Guantanamo Bay Naval Station.

Billeting Office: ATTN: BOQ Mgr. Building 1670, Deer Point Rd. Comm: 99-2402/3826/2238. ATVN: 564-4063. 24 hours daily. Check in facility, check out 1200 hours daily. Government civilian employee billeting.

TML: Navy Lodge. Naval Station, Box 38, FPO New York 09593-5000. All ranks. Leave or official duty. 0700-1800 daily. Check out 1200 hours daily. 26/1-bedroom, 2 double beds, studio couch, private bath. Kitchen, A/C, color TV, coin washer/dryer. Rates: $23.00 per unit. All categories can make reservations.

TML: BOQ/BEQ. Buildings 1660, 1661. All ranks. Leave or official duty. 20/1-bedroom, private (Officer); 18/1-bedroom, hall bath (Enlisted). Refrigerator,

Guantanamo Bay Naval Station, continued

CUBA

community kitchen (Officer, CPO), A/C, color TV room & lounge, maid service, free washer/dryer, ice vending. Modern structure. Rates: $2.00 per person. Duty can make reservations. Others Space-A.

DV/VIP: BOQ. Building 1670, EX-2402/4063. O6+.

TML Availability: Good most of the year except holidays.

All numbers below are Comm or ATVN extensions.

Cafeteria-4815/2311	CPO Club-2501/2379	Enlisted Club-2304/4733
Locator-4453/4366	Medical-4424/6395	O'Club-2132/2531
Police-4105/3813/4145	Snack Bar-2327/2652	SDO/NCO-4366

GERMANY

Amberg Sub-Community (GE59R7)
APO New York 09452-5000

TELEPHONE NUMBER INFORMATION: Main installation numbers: Comm: 49-09621-700-780/838, ETS: 476-5780/838.

Location: Take E-6 Autobahn east from Nürnberg, exit to E-12 northeast for 6 miles to Amberg, follow U.S. Forces signs to Pond Barracks. HE: p-40, G/2. NMC: Nürnberg, 38 miles southwest.

Billeting Office: None. Transient billets are in O'Club, Building 15. EX-785.

TML: Officers' Club, Building 15, Pond Barracks. All ranks. Leave or official duty. 4/1-bedroom and separate bedroom, shared bath; 1 suite, shared bath. Rates: $10.00-$30.00 per unit. Duty can make reservations.

DV/VIP: Determined by Community Cmdr. EX-805/806.

TML Availability: Limited.

Cons Dining-476-5748	Enlisted Club-476-5747	Locator-475-10
Medical-116	NCO Club-476-5747	O'Club-AMGC-746585
Police-114	Snack Bar-AMGC-72823	

Ansbach/Katterbach Community (GE60R7)
APO New York 09326-5000

TELEPHONE NUMBER INFORMATION: Main installation numbers: Comm: 49-0981-83-XXX (Ansbach), 49-09802-832-XXX (Katterbach); ETS: 468-7/8XXX (Ansbach), 467-2XXX (Katterbach); ATVN: 460-1110 Ask for ANS.

Location: Exit from E-12 Autobahn east or west to GE-14 or 13 north 4 miles. Follow US Forces signs to Katterbach Kaserne. HE: p-40, E/2. NMC: Nürnberg, 26 miles northeast.

Billeting Office: Katterbach BOQ Office. Comm: 09802-832-812. ETS:

GERMANY
Ansbach/Katterbach Community, continued

467-2812. Check in facility 0730-1630 M-Th, 0730-1500 F. Other times, Office of Deputy Cmdr, ETS: 468-8437. Check out 1000 hours daily. Government civilian employee billeting.

TML: Transient Facility. Building 5908. All ranks. Leave or official duty. 28/1-bedroom, private bath; 5 separate bedroom, private bath. Cribs/cots available, shared kitchenette with MW, maid service, color TV, VCR, utensils available, free washer/dryer. Older structure. Leave status rates: $15.00 1st person, $10.00 2nd person, $5.00 each additional person; duty status rates: 1st person $21.00, $15.00 2nd person, $9.00 each additional person. PCS in/out can make reservations 60 days in advance, 2 weeks in advance for TDY. Others Space-A.

DV/VIP: HHC, 1st AD. ETS: 468-8377. 06+. Retirees Space-A.

TML Availability: Good. Best in February, June, July and August.

Cafeteria-0981-87846	Locator-468-8425	Medical-09802-116
NCO Club-0981-87900	Police-114	O'Club-467-2704
Snack Bar-09802-356	SDO/NCO-811	

Augsburg Community (GE39R7)
APO New York 09178-5000

TELEPHONE NUMBER INFORMATION: Main installation numbers: Comm: 49-0821-448-XXXX, ETS: 434-XXXX, ATVN: 434-1110.

Location: From Munich-Stuttgart, Autobahn E-8, exit at "Augsburg West" and follow "US Military Facilties Augsburg" signs to various Kasernes. HE: p-40, F/4-5. NMC: Augsburg, in the city.

Billeting Office: ATTN: AETS-AUG-DEH-TB. Building 29, Reese Kaserne (Langemarckstrasse) housing office. EX-7270 or Comm: 0821-409001, 0730-1600 M-F. Check in facility, check out 1000 hours daily. Government civilian employee billeting.

TML: Guest House. Building 53, Reese Kaserne, Reinöl Strasse 74, Augsburg. All ranks. Leave or official duty. 34/1-bedroom, 1 bed, hall bath; 26 separate bedroom, private bath; 16/1-bedroom, 2 beds, shared bath; 3 suites with private bath. Refrigerator, color TV room & lounge, maid service, cribs/cots ($6.00), free washer/dryer, AAFES vending in building. Older structure, remodeled. Rates: Sponsor $20.00-$33.00, additional adult $26.00-$45.00, $6.00-$8.00 per child. Maximum 4 per room. Duty can make reservations. Others Space-A.

TML: Guest House. Buildings 180, 181, 182, Sheridan Kaserne. All ranks. Leave or official duty. 18/1-bedroom, hall bath; 3 separate bedroom suites, private bath. Refrigerator, color TV, maid service, free washer/dryer. Older structure. Rates: Sponsor $29.00 suites for 1 or 2 persons, $11.00 each additional person in suite, and room. Maximum 3 per suite, 2 per room. Duty can make reservations. Others Space-A.

DV/VIP: PAO. Determined by Commander. Retirees Space-A. Suites are open to all grades on a first come, first served basis.

Temporary Military Lodging Around the World — 209

GERMANY

Augsburg Community, continued

Other: There are also some Officers' quarters, SEQ which can be assigned to TDY or Space-A persons when no guest house spaces are available. Fugger Village, oldest social village in the world, is located in downtown Augsburg. Augsburg is over 2000 years old.

TML Availability: Good, Jan-Apr. Difficult, Oct-Nov.

Cafeteria-ABGC-403368 Enlisted Club-448-6514 Medical-449-4132
NCO Club-434-6443 O'Club-448-6115 Snack B-ABGC-403368
SDO/NCO-434-7414

Bad Kissingen Community (GE49R7)
APO New York 09330-5000

TELEPHONE NUMBER INFORMATION: Main installation numbers: Comm: 49-0971-86-XXX, ETS: 354-2XXX, ATVN: 350-1110 Ask for BKI.

Location: From the Kassel-Würzburg, E-70 Autobahn, exit Bad Kissingen/Hammelburg to GE-287 northwest for 9 miles. U S Forces signs mark directions to installations. HE: p-36, G/6. NMC: Schweinfurt, 12 miles southeast.

Billeting Office: Housing Office, Daley Barracks. EX-721. 0730-1600 hours daily. No government civilian employee billeting.

TML: Transient Billets. 11 Kurhausstrasse. EX-890. All ranks. Leave or official duty. Rooms have color TV, refrigerator, private bath. Rates: $18.00 1st person single rooms, $6.00 each additional person, $25.00 1st person rooms with living room, $7.00 each additional person.

TML Availability: Limited.

Cafeteria-BKIC-3743 Enlisted Club-354-2645 Medical-354-2724
NCO Club-354-2717 O'Club-354-2683 Police-354-2657

Bad Kreuznach Community (GE01R7)
APO New York 09252-5000

TELEPHONE NUMBER INFORMATION: Main installation numbers: Comm: 49-0671-609-XXXX, ETS: 490-XXXX, ATVN: 490-1110.

Location: Approximately 50 miles south from Frankfurt am Main, via Mainz to Bad Kreuznach Autobahn A-66 & A-60. Take B-41, at the east outskirt of the city, go south on Bosenheimer St, left on Alzyer St, to Nahe Club on the right, billeting next to club. HE: p-40, A/1. NMC: Bad Kreuznach, in city limits.

Billeting Office: ATTN: Family Housing Office, Building 5649, Mannheimerstrasse, EX-7246. Or Comm: 0671-77122. 0730-2300 hours daily. Check in facility, check out 1100 hours daily. Government civilian employee billeting. Confirmed reservations keys at MP station after duty hours.

TML: Guest House/BOQ/BEQ/DV/VIP. Building 5649 (GH), 5648 (DV/VIP). All ranks. Leave or official duty. 31/1-bedroom, shared bath; 3 suites, private bath

210 — *Temporary Military Lodging Around the World*

GERMANY
Bad Kreuznach Community, continued

(DV/VIP). Refrigerator, community kitchen, color TV, maid service, cribs ($2.00), cots ($4.00), free washer/dryer. Older structure. New TVs '87. Rates: Sponsor $16.00, adult $5.00, infant $2.00. Duty can make reservations. Others Space-A. Pets OK for $5.00 per night.

DV/VIP: Protocol Office, Rose Barracks, EX-6466. 06+. Retirees and lower grades Space-A.

Other: Beautiful landscape, spa area, not far from the Rhine Valley.

TML Availability: Good.

Cafeteria-BKHC-68370   Enlisted Club-490-5351   Locator-490-6274
NCO Club-490-5351   O'Club-490-6252   Police-114
Snack Bar-BKHC-68370 SDO/NCO-490-7105

Bad Tölz Community (GE02R7)
APO New York 09050-5000

TELEPHONE NUMBER INFORMATION: Main installation numbers: Comm: 49-08041-30-890, ETS: 441-4890, ATVN: 440-1110 Ask for BTZ.

Location: Between the Salzburg and Garmisch/Partenkirchen Autobahns on Nat-13. Exit Autobahn E-11 South at Holzkirchen and travel 22 km southwest on Nat-13. Signs mark Flint Kaserne. HE: p-92, H/2. NMC: Munich, 37 miles northwest.

Billeting Office: Building 1-W. EX-890. 0730-1600 hours duty days. Other hours SDO, EX-800. Check in facility, check out 1000 hours daily. Government civilian employee billeting in VOQ.

TML: VEQ. Buildings 102, 104. All ranks. Leave or official duty. 2/3-bedroom, shared bath; 2/4-bedroom, shared bath. Community kitchen, free cribs, kitchenette, maid service, color TV, utensils, free washer/dryer. Older structure. Rates: $15.00 per person. Maximum 6 per unit. Duty can make reservations. Others Space-A.

TML: VOQ/DV/VIP. Building 65. Officer 04+, Enlisted E7+. Leave or official duty. 1/1-bedroom, private bath; 2 separate bedrooms, private bath; Refrigerator, kitchenette (VIP only), limited utensils (VIP only), color TV, maid service, cribs. Older structure, remodeled. Rates: $30.00-$40.00 per night. Duty can make reservations. Others Space-A.

DV/VIP: Community Commander's office, ETS: 441-4760. 06+. E7-E9 and WO4 may use on a Space-A basis.

Other: Beautiful Bavarian Alps. AFRC Garmisch less than 1 hour drive south.

TML Availability: Fair. Difficult, December and June-August.

Cons Club-441-4619   Medical-441-4654   Snack Bar-BTZC-2583

Temporary Military Lodging Around the World — 211

GERMANY

Bamberg Community (GE34R7)
APO New York 09139-5000

TELEPHONE NUMBER INFORMATION: Main installation numbers: Comm: 49-0951-400-XXXX, ETS: 469-XXXX, ATVN: 460-1110 Ask for BBG.

Location: On GE 26/505. Warner Barracks, the main installation, is on the east side of the city between Zollner and Pödeldorter Strasses. Follow signs. HE: p-40, E/1. NMC: Nürnberg, 30 miles southeast.

Billeting Office: Guest House Office, Building 7678, Room 24, 2nd floor. EX-7596. 0900-2000 M-F, 0900-1800 Sa-Su. Other hours, Military Police, Building 7108. Check in facility, check out 1100 hours daily. Government civilian employee billeting.

TML: Guest Houses I & II. Buildings 7070, 7678. Zollner Strasse. All ranks. Leave or official duty. 13 rooms in Guesthouse I with 4 family rooms, shared bath; 4 single rooms, shared bath; 4 double rooms, shared bath; and 1 DV suite, private bath. 17 rooms in Guesthouse II with 9 family rooms, private bath; and 8 single rooms, private bath. Community kitchen, refrigerator (some rooms), color TV (some rooms), color TV lounge, maid service, free cribs (limited supply). Older structure, renovated '86. Rates: $23.00 per room and up in GH I; $17.00 an up in GH II. All categories can make reservations.

DV/VIP: Deputy Community Cmdr. 05+. Retirees and lower grades Space-A.

TML Availability: Limited.

Cafeteria-BBGC-39883   Enlisted Club-469-7556   Medical-469-8741/97
O'Club-469-8708   Police-469-7770   Snack Bar-BBGC-32271
SDO/NCO-469-7119

Baumholder Community (GE03R7)
APO New York 09034-5000

TELEPHONE NUMBER INFORMATION: Main installation numbers: Comm: 49-06783-6-XXXX, ETS: 485-1110 Ask for BHR+EX, ATVN: 485-1110 Ask for BHR+EX.

Location: From Kaiserslautern, take Autobahn 62 toward Trier, exit north at Freisen and follow signs to Baumholder and Smith Barracks. HE: p-39, F/G1. NMC: Kaiserslautern, 56 km southeast.

Billeting Office: Smith Barracks, Building 8076. EX-6188 or Comm: 06783-5182. 0800-1700 M-F. Other hours SDO, EX-7533. Check in 1300-1700, check out 1100 hours daily. Government civilian employee billeting.

TML: Lagerhof Transient Billeting. Building 8076. All ranks. Leave or official duty. 1/4-bedroom, private bath; 14/2-bedroom, private bath; 15/1-bedroom, private bath. Community kitchen, limited utensils, refrigerator, color TV lounge, maid service, free cribs/cots, free washer/dryer, color TVs. Older structure. Rates: PCS 1st person $20.00, 2nd person $15.00, additional persons $10.00; Space-A 1st person $16.00, 2nd person $12.00, additional persons $8.00. DVQ 1st person $32.00, 2nd person $15.00, additional persons $10.00. Children under 2 free. Duty can make reservations. Others Space-A.

GERMANY
Baumholder Community, continued

DV/VIP: Deputy Community Commander, EX-6300. 06/GS-12+.

Other: Nearby Idar Oberstein precious gems and stones. Trier with Roman ruins, Mosel Valley, vineyards, and a ski area (check with Special Services EX-6575/7182).

TML Availability: Very good.

Cafeteria-BHRC-5025   Enlisted Club-485-6281   Medical-485-6647
NCO Club-BHRC-5418   O'Club-BHRC-5014   Police-485-7547
Snack Bar-BHRC-5031   SDO/NCO-485-7533

Berchtesgaden AFRC (GE07R7)
APO New York 09029-5000
RESERVED FOR DESERT SHIELD/STORM RETURNEES ONLY.

TELEPHONE NUMBER INFORMATION: Main installation numbers: Comm: 49-08652-58-XXX, ETS: 441-5XXX.

Location: Exit the Munich-Salzburg Autobahn E-11 at Bad Reichenhall, south on GE-20, 18 kilometers to Berchtesgaden. HE: p-94, D/4. NMC: Munich, 100 miles northwest.

Description of Area: Nestled in the heart of the Bavarian Alps, just eight miles from the Austrian border, Berchtesgaden is a 1,200-year old storybook village with church spires framed by scenic mountains rising to nearly 9,000 feet.

Breathtaking scenery and a wide variety of sport and tour opportunities await the visitor to this popular all-season recreation spot. Skiers will love AFRC Berchtesgaden! The superbly designed ski facility is a great place to learn or enhance your skills. There are ski packages for beginners, intermediate skiers, and experts in downhill and cross country skiing. The Ski Austria program offers daily skiing on such well-known slopes as Flachau, Maria Alm, Hochkoenig, Zauchensee, Steinplatte, Jenner and Obertauern. There is group and individual mountaineering, golf at the Skytop Golf Course, four tennis courts, and kayaking and white-water rafting, and much, much more in sports of every variety.

There are tours to the "Sound of Music" city of Salzburg, Austria; or a visit to the world-class bobsled run, where the brave at heart can try their luck at controlling a racing luge; or dress in traditional miner's clothes and explorevast open rooms carved out of a salt mountain on the Salt Mine Tour; or visit the World War II bunkers, in the Obersalzberg Mountain, that were designed for Hitler and other leading Nazis; or take the Berchtesgaden Town Tour where you'll see the Royal Castle and visit a cuckoo clock factory and much more!

AFRC Berchtesgaden has lodgings for more than 700 guests in the historic General Walker Hotel, the Alpine Inn, the Berchtesgadener Hof, the Evergreen Lodge, the General McNair Hotel, and the Skytop Inn located next to the AFRC Golf Course.

TML Availability: Good except Jun-Aug and Christmas/New Year periods.

Reservations: Required up to 6 months in advance with deposit. Write to

GERMANY

Berchtesgaden AFRC, continued

Central Reservations, AFRC Berchtesgaden, APO NY 09029-5000. Or call Comm: 08652-58-623/823; ETS: 441-5623/823. For group reservations call Comm: 08652-58-666; ETS: 441-5666. Open 0730-2000 seven days a week. For child care information or reservations call ETS: 441-5652.

Eligibility: AD/Retired/DoD civilian assigned overseas. See Garmisch AFRC for more details on eligibility.

Rates: See Garmisch AFRC listing for all AFRC accommodation rates.

Facilities: APO, Commissary, Dispensary, Walker Movie Theater, The Studio '79 Disco, one bowling centers, Stars & Stripes Bookstore, art shop, gift shops, ESSO stations, child care center, sports shops, AMEXCO bank, class VI (Package Store), Strub Disco, PX/Foodland, chapel, beauty/barber shop, crystal Shop, restaurants & bars in hotels.

Activities: Swimming, golf, tennis, walking/hiking, great night life entertainment, ice skating, sledding, snow skiing, mountain climbing, kayaking & white water rafting. Full line of recreational equipment available.

Medical-441-5667   Police-441-5616

Berlin Community (GE26R7)
APO New York 09742-5000

TELEPHONE NUMBER INFORMATION: Main installation numbers: Comm: 49-030-819-XXXX, ETS: 332-XXXX, ATVN: 332-1110.

Location: Can be reached from the E-2, Helmstedt-Berlin Autobahn, by air to Tempelhof AB or via train from Frankfurt or Bremerhaven. HE: p-63, F/6. NMC: Berlin, in the city.

Billeting Office: Family Housing Branch. EX-6654. 0815-1600 hours M-F. Other hours Dahlem Guest House, EX-6425. Check in facility, check out 1100 hours daily. Government civilian employee billeting.

TML: Guest House. Dahlem Guest House, 19 Ihnestrasse. All ranks. Leave or official duty. 4/2-bedrooms, private bath; 3/4-bedrooms, private bath; 6/5-bed rooms, private bath; 8/6-bed rooms, private bath; 1 handicapped suite, private bath. Kitchen, maid service, washer/dryer, color TV. Older structure. Rates: $35.00-$42.00 first person, $5.00 each additional person. PCS can make reservations. Others Space-A.

TML: Guest House. Wannsee Hotel, Am Sandwerder. All ranks. Leave or official duty. Note: this is a new facility that opened for business in September '89. 12/2-bedroom, private bath; 4/4-bed suites, private bath. Color TV, maid service. Modern structure. Rates: $50.00-$55.00 first person, $15.00-$20.00 each additional person (price includes continental breakfast). TDY can make reservations. Others Space-A.

TML: Harnack House, 14-16 Ihnestrasse. All ranks. Leave or official duty. 1/7-bedroom, private bath; 1/5-bedroom, private bath; 3/4-bedrooms, private bath; 1/2-bedroom, private bath; 6/1-bedrooms, private bath. Color TV, maid service. Older structure. Rates: $35.00-$55.00 first person, $5.00-$7.00 each additional person. PCS can make reservations. Others Space-A.

GERMANY
Berlin Community, continued

DV/VIP: Protocol. Building 1, Room 2024-2032. EX-6933. 06+. Retirees Space-A.

Other: A great city that has everything. For a tour call Special Services, EX-6523.

TML Availability: Good, Feb-May and Aug-Nov. Difficult, other times.

Enlisted Club-332-6007 Locator-332-92/7475 Medical-116
NCO Club-332-6231 O'Club-332-6252 Police-332-3427
SDO/NCO-332-7222

Bindlach/Bayreuth Sub-Community (GE50R7)
APO New York 09411-5000

TELEPHONE NUMBER INFORMATION: Main installation numbers: Comm: 49-09208-83-XXX, ETS: 462-3XXX, ATVN: 460-1110 Ask for BDL.

Location: On GE-2, 60 miles north of Nürnberg, GE and north of Bayreuth, GE. Take the Bayreuth nord exit from GE-2 for 2 miles. US Forces signs direct to Christensen Barracks. HE: p-40, F/1. NMC: Bayreuth, 2 miles southwest.

Billeting Office: Guest House, Building 9350. Comm: 09208-1549, ETS: 462-3693 duty hours. Other hours SDO, ETS: 462-3801. Check in facility, check out 1200 hours daily. No government civilian employee billeting.

TML: TLF. All ranks. Leave or official duty. 10/1-bedroom, private bath. Maid service, kitchen available, cots/cribs, free washer/dryer. New structure. Rates: Sponsor $19.00, each additional person $10.00. Duty can make reservations. Others Space-A.

DV/VIP: Sub-Community Commander. EX-836. 06+. Retirees Space-A.

Other: Bayreuth is home of the Robert Wagner Opera House. Near many crystal and porcelain factories. Great ski area, call ITT ETS: 462-3648/3651.

TML Availability: Limited.

Enlisted Club-462-3634 Medical-116 NCO Club-462-3635
O'Club-462-3635 Police-114

Bitburg Air Base (GE04R7)
APO New York 09132-5000

TELEPHONE NUMBER INFORMATION: Main installation numbers: Comm: 49-06561-61-1110, ETS: 453-1110, ATVN: 453-1110.

Temporary Military Lodging Around the World — 215

GERMANY

Bitburg Air Base, continued

Location: From Trier, take Hwy B-51 North to Bitburg or Prüm, turn right at the "Bitburg Flugplatz" sign. HE: p-39, F/1. NMC: Trier, 17 miles south.

Billeting Office: Baron Inn, Building 101, Comm: 06561-62-1001. 24 hours daily. Check in facility, check out 1100 hours daily. Government civilian employee billeting.

TML: TLF. Baron Inn, Buildings 102, 124. All ranks. Leave or official duty. 20/1-bedroom, private bath; 42/2-bedroom, private bath. Kitchen, complete utensils, color TV room & lounge, maid service, free cribs/cots, free washer/dryer. Modern structure, remodeled. Rates: $24.00 per unit. Maximum 5 per room. Duty can make reservations. Others Space-A.

TML: VOQ. Buildings 101, 123. Officer 01-05. Leave or official duty. 6/1-bedroom, shared bath; 20/1-bedroom, private bath. Kitchen, limited utensils, color TV, maid service, free cribs/cots, free washer/dryer, ice vending. Modern structure. Rates: $9.00-$14.00 per person. Maximum 2 per room. Duty can make reservations. Others Space-A.

TML: VAQ. Building 101. Enlisted E1-E6. Leave or official duty. 12/1-bedroom, shared bath (SNCO); 54/1-bedroom, 2 beds, shared bath. Refrigerator, color TV, maid service, free cribs/cots, free washer/dryer, ice vending, coffee, iron, ironing boards. Modern structure. Rates: $6.50 per person. Duty can make reservations. Others Space-A.

TML: DVQ (DV/VIP). Building 101. Officer 06+, E9. Leave or official duty. EX-7200. 7/1-bedroom suites, private bath. Refrigerator, limited utensils, A/C, color TV, maid service, free cribs/cots, free washer/dryer, ice vending. Modern structure. Rates: $14.00 per person. Maximum 2 per room. Duty can make reservations. Others Space-A.

DV/VIP: Protocol Office, Building 116, EX-7200. 06/GS-15+. Retirees and lower grades Space-A.

Other: Beautiful walking trails and parks in Eifel area. Nearby Trier was 2000 years old in 1984 - oldest city in Germany.

TML Availability: Fairly good, Oct-Mar. Difficult, other times.

Cafeteria-BITC-2783	Enlisted Club-453-7544	Locator-453-7449
Medical-116	NCO Club-453-7544	O'Club-453-7543
Police-453-7400	Snack Bar-BITC-2783	SDO/NCO-453-7133

Bremerhaven Community (GE32R7)
APO New York 09069-5000

TELEPHONE NUMBER INFORMATION: Main installation numbers: Comm: 49-0471-893-XXXX, ETS: 342-XXXX, ATVN: 342-1110.

Location: Exit from the A-27 Autobahn and follow signs to Harbor House Hotel. HE: p-33, D/4. NMC: Bremerhaven, in the city.

Billeting Office: Harbor House Hotel. Buildings 602-604. 24 hours daily. EX-7604/7878/7657. Check in facility, check out 1100 hours daily. Government civilian employee billeting.

GERMANY
Bremerhaven Community, continued

TML: Guest House. Harbor House Hotel, Buildings 602-604. All ranks. Leave or official duty. 68/1-bedroom, shared bath; 11/1-bedroom, private bath; 5 separate bedrooms, private bath. Refrigerator, community kitchen, color TV room & lounge, maid service, cribs/cots ($5.00), free washer/dryer. Older structure, renovated 1 building. Rates: $10.00 per person, $5.00 infant in crib/cot. Maximum 3 adults or 2 adults/2 children per room. Duty can make reservations. Others Space-A. **Pets allowed on arrival or departure of PCS in/out.**

DV/VIP: Deputy Community Cmdr, EX-8094. O6+. Retirees and lower grades Space-A.

TML Availability: Good.

Medical-116
Police-342-8252
NCO Club-342-8272
Snack Bar-342-8069
O'Club-342-7600
SDO/NCO-342-8815

Butzbach Sub-Community (GE51R7)
APO New York 09077-5000

TELEPHONE NUMBER INFORMATION: Main installation numbers: Comm: 49-06033-82-XXXX, ETS: 343-2XXX, ATVN: 320-1110 Ask for BUT.

Location: On GE-3, 12 miles south of Giessen, GE. May be reached from the Frankfurt-Giessen E-3 Autobahn. HE: p-36, E/5. NMC: Giessen, 12 miles north.

Billeting Office: Transient Billeting Manager. EX-727. BOQ, #1 Ayers Kaserne, Kirchgöns. Check in facility, check out 1200 hours daily.

TML: BOQ. All ranks. Leave or official duty. Limited space for transients.

TML Availability: Very limited.

Enlisted Club-343-2705
NCO Club-343-2705
SDO/NCO-343-8111/8116
Locator-343-1110
Police-343-2829
Medical-343-2824
Snack Bar-64966

Chiemsee AFRC (GE08R7)
APO New York 09029-5000

TELEPHONE NUMBER INFORMATION: Main installation numbers: Comm: 49-08051-803172, ETS: 441-2355/396, TELEX: 56239 AFRC.

Location: Located directly off Munich-Salzburg Autobahn E-11 southeast of Munich. Buses use Feldeu exit; automobiles continue for 800 meters and exit when you see the sign for AFRC Chiemsee. HE: p-94, B/3. NMC: Munich, 50 miles northwest.

Description of Area: The AFRC Chiemsee Recreation Area is situated along the shores of Germany's largest lake—Chiemsee. Enjoy a variety of water sports such as canoeing, paddleboats, scuba diving, sailing, windsurfing or swimming. Or take advantage of the nearby Chiemgauer Alps, which offer opportunities for hiking, hang gliding and scenic panoramas of Chiemsee and

Chiemsee AFRC, continued

the Alps. For a ski vacation, AFRC Chiemsee is near Austrian resorts such as Kitzbühel and St. Johann. There are ski programs for beginners to experts. Night life at AFRC Chiemsee can include an evening with a gourmet meal in the Lake Hotel Bavarian Restaurant, dancing in the lake-front lounge, free movies, ice skating and swimming. Evening tours are offered to Munich and Salzburg, where you can go disco-hopping, visit charming restaurants, beer cellars, wine parlors, or just enjoy either of these beautiful cities after dark.

AFRC Chiemsee has the Chiemsee Park Hotel and Chiemsee Lake Hotel with accommodations for more than 300 guests. A modern travel camp offering shower and camp store facilities is also available. There are 110 camp sites with 220 volt electrical hook-ups and nearby laundromats, bathhouses with hot showers, and campstores. TML Availability: Good.

Season of Operation: Year round.

Reservations: Required up to six months in advance with deposit. Write to AFRC Chiemsee Reservations, APO NY 09029-5000. Or call Comm: 08051-803172/803173; ETS: 441-2355/396. Open 0700-2000 hours M-F, 0730-1800 Sa-Su. For Travel Camp reservations call Comm: 08051-8733 or 08061-802719/306 or ETS: 4412-719/306.

Eligibility: AD/Retired/DOD civilian assigned overseas. See Garmisch AFRC listing for more details.

Rates: See Garmisch AFRC listing for all AFRC accommodation rates.

Facilities: Includes but not limited to: Snackbar, laundromat, Lake Hotel, restaurants & bars, check cashing, child care center, sports equipment rental, boat rental/launch, ESSO Station nearby, ice, and recreation room.

Activities: Unlimited summer, winter and mountain sports.

Darmstadt Community (GE37R7)
APO New York 09175-5000

TELEPHONE NUMBER INFORMATION: Main installation numbers: Comm: 49-06151-69-XXXX, ETS: 348-XXXX, ATVN: 394-1110 Ask for DST.

Location: Accessible from the E-5 and E-67 autobahns. One miles south of downtown Darmstadt. Follow signs to Jefferson Village. HE: p-40, B/1. NMC: Darmstadt, 1 miles north.

Billeting Office: Building 4091, Jefferson Village. 0730-1615 M-F. EX-7111 or Comm: 06151-68111. Other hours, Staff Duty Officer EX-6557/7423. Check in facility, check out 1000 hours daily. Government civilian employee billeting.

TML: Guest House. Building 4091, Jefferson Village. All ranks. Leave or official duty. 24 single rooms, shared bath; 13 suites, private bath. Refrigerator, community kitchen, limited utensils, color TV, maid service,

GERMANY
Darmstadt Community, continued

cribs/cots ($1.50), free washer/dryer, VCRs in rooms and over 300 tapes available. Older structure, remodeled. Rates: Single $15.00-$24.00, suites $25.00-$39.00. Sofa bed $10.00. Maximum 4 per room. Duty and disabled American veterans can make reservations. Others Space-A.

Other: Stars & Stripes European edition is published here. Hunting museum of Kranichstein, north of Darmstadt. Great wild food dishes in the park or Hotel.

TML Availability: Good, Sep. More difficult, Oct-Jun.

Cafeteria-348-6546   Enlisted Club-348-7395   Medical-97
NCO Club-348-7395   O'Club-348-7191   Police-348-7351
Snack Bar-348-6546

Frankfurt Community (GE05R7)
APO New York 09710-5000

TELEPHONE NUMBER INFORMATION: Main installation numbers: Comm: 49-069-151-XXXX, ETS: 320-XXXX, ATVN: 320-1110.

Location: The Ambassador Arms Hotel is on the corner of Miguel Allee and Hansa Allee within the General Creighton Abrams Complex in Frankfurt. HE: p-39, B/1. NMC: Frankfurt, 2 km southeast.

Billeting Office: Ambassador Arms Hotel, Building 2351, Sioli Str 2351. EX-7441. 0800-1700 M-F. Check in facility, check out 1100 hours daily. Government civilian employee billeting.

TML: Guest House DV/VIP. Buildings 2351/52/63/66/71. All ranks. Leave or official duty. Accessible to handicapped. EX-5738 or Comm: 069-550641. 187 rooms, 339 bed spaces (with 5 VIP suites, 9 kitchen suites, 1/2/3-bedroom apartments). Color TV, refrigerator, maid service, free cribs/cots, coin washer/dryer, facilities for handicapped. Rates: TDY/PCS Sponsor $25.00 (shared room and bath); $40.00 (private room and shared bath); $45.00 (private room and bath); Sponsor $50.00 (DVQ suites); each additional person $15.00. Duty can make reservations. Others Space-A.

NOTE: The Ambassador Arms offers all its guests a complimentary breakfast during the following hours: 0630-0830 M-F, 0800-1000 Sa/Su. Sunday brunch is offered at the Terrace Club between 1030-1330 hours at regular price.

NOTE: In March 1989, AFRC Europe's first branch reservations office opened in Frankfurt. Telephone numbers for the office are Comm: 069-568075/568077/568078.

DV/VIP: COFS, V Corps, Creighton Abrams Building. EX-7141. 07+. Retirees and lower grades Space-A through Protocol only.

TML Availability: Good, winter. Difficult, summer.

Cafeteria-FKTC-558138   Enlisted Club-325-5749   Locator-320-1110
Medical-325-6111   NCO Club-325-5466   O'Club-320-5002
Police-325-7637   SDO/NCO-325-5810   SDO/NCO-320-5810

GERMANY

Fulda Community (GE35R7)
APO New York 09146-5000

TELEPHONE NUMBER INFORMATION: Main installation numbers: Comm: 49-0661-86-XXXX, ETS: 321-3XXX, ATVN: 320-1110 Ask for FDA.

Location: Take the Fulda Nord exit from E-7 Autobahn to GE-27 South. In Downs Barracks. HE: p-36, F/5. NMC: Frankfurt, 65 miles southwest.

Billeting Office: Building 7307, 2nd floor (across st from O'Club). 0800-1700 M-F. Comm: 0661-78689. ETS: 321-3632. Other hours SDO, Building 8112, ETS: 321-3803. Check in facility, check out 1200 hours daily. Government civilian employee billeting.

TML: BOQ. Buildings 7307, 7309. All ranks. Leave or official duty. 20 separate bedrooms, shared bath; 11/1-bedroom, 2 beds, shared bath; 8/1-bedroom, shared bath; 1/1-bedroom suite, living room, private bath, (DV/VIP). Four community kitchens, limited utensils, refrigerator, range, maid service. Older structure. Rates: Separate bedroom, suite $15.00, double room $11.00, single room $7.00. Duty can make reservations. Others Space-A.

DV/VIP: Office Deputy Cmdr, EX-604. 06+.

TML Availability: Good, Sep-May.

Cafeteria-FDAC-75566 Enlisted Club-321-3637 Locator-321-1110
Medical-116 NCO Club-321-3615 O'Club-321-3637
Police-114 Snack Bar-FDAC-75566 SDO/NCO-321-3583/803

Garmisch AFRC (GE10R7)
APO New York 09053-5000

TELEPHONE NUMBER INFORMATION: Main installation numbers: Comm: 49-08821-750-575, ETS: 440-2575.

Location: Take Autobahn E-6 south from Munich to Garmisch. From Austria take national roads numbered 2 or 187. HE: p-92, F/3. MNC: Munich, 60 miles north.

Description of Area: Garmisch has been Germany's leading winter recreation and sports area since hosting the 1936 Winter Olympic Games. Located 60 miles south of Munich, Garmisch sits at the foot of Germany's highest mountain, the Zugspitze. For 35 years AFRC Garmisch has been providing a wide range of sports activities including skiing, indoor tennis, arts and crafts, children's programs and a wide variety of tours. AFRC Garmisch provides the means for quality economy vacations.

There is a full range of ski programs from beginner to expert. There are great golf opportunities, tennis indoor and outdoor, kayaking, white-water rafting, windsurfing, mountaineering, arts and crafts and much more.

AFRC Garmisch offers four hotels (Abrams, Sheridan Plaza, Patton, Von Steuben) and the Haus Flora and a modern travel camp with total accommodations for more than 1,300 guests. The travel camp has over 100 trailer and 70 tent sites.

GERMANY
Garmisch AFRC, continued

TML Availability: Good except June-Aug and Christmas/New Year periods. The Army Executive Agency in charge of Armed Forces Rec Centers is building a large new hotel in Garmisch over the next few years to replace existing structures that it currently leases for AFRC use. As updated information becomes available, it will be published in Military Living's R&R Report.

Season of Operation: Year round.

Reservations: Required up to six months in advance with deposit. Write to AFRC Central Reservations, APO NY 09053-5000. Or call Comm: 08821-750-575; ETS: 440-2575. Open 0730-2000 hours M-F, 0730-1830 hours Sa-Su. For Travel Camp reservations call Comm: 08821-750-848; ETS: 440-2848.

Eligibility: In general, all U.S. Forces military and civilian personnel stationed in the USEUCOM area of responsibility and their family members, and visiting immediate family (when accompanied by the sponsor) may stay in AFRC hotels and camping areas. Also included are civilian U.S. citizens employed by the U.S. government agencies and supporting institutions located in the Federal Republic of Germany, such as USO, Red Cross, and others. Also fully authorized are Canadian Armed Forces peronnel and their family members (when accompanied by a sponsor stationed in the FRG). U.S. military personnel stationed outside USEUCOM, retired U.S. military and British Army of the Rhine (stationed in the FRG) personnel and family members (when accompanied by the sponsor) are authorized space-available accommodations. As of 1 July 1989, all restrictions governing use of AFRC facilities by retired U.S. military personnel were lifted.

Rates: See AFRC accommodation rates quoted below.

Facilities: APO, AMEXCO Bank, beauty/barber shop, commissary, dispensary, chapel, Snack-O-Mat, AAFES Garage, library, sports shop, rec room, Alpine Theater, art shop, Bavarian Shop, class VI (Package Store), dental clinic, Foodland, PX, Stars & Stripes Bookstore, arts & crafts shop, child care center, hotel restaurants & bars, TV room and much more.

Activities: Swimming, tennis, wind surfing, hang gliding, arts & crafts, ice skating, snow skiing, golf, kayaking/rafting, mountain climbing/hiking/walking tours, great entertainment & shows.

Armed Forces Recreation Center (AFRC) Accommodation Rates:

	E1-E5		Others	
GARMISCH	Single	Double	Single	Double
Room (no bath)	$17.00	$24.00	$21.00	$28.00
Room (w/bath)	$31.00	$39.00	$36.00	$44.00
Family Suites	ask for availability and price			
BERCHTESGADEN				
Room (no bath)	$17.00	$24.00	$21.00	$28.00
Room (w/bath)	$31.00	$39.00	$36.00	$44.00
Family Suites	ask for availability and price			
CHIEMSEE				
Lake View	$39.00	$42.00	$46.00	$49.00
Mountain View	$33.00	$36.00	$39.00	$42.00

Temporary Military Lodging Around the World — 221

GERMANY

Garmisch AFRC, continued

Family Suites   ask for availability and price

Prices are subject to change without notice.

Other: Holiday Inn and Hotel Alpengruss are contract hotels and arrangements must be made with the billeting office in advance.

Medical-440-2816   **Police-440-2801**

Gelnhausen Sub-Community (GE89R7)
APO NY 09091-5000

TELEPHONE NUMBER INFORMATION: Main installation numbers: Comm: 49-06051-81-XXX, ETS: 321-2XXX, ATVN: 320-1110 Ask for GLN.

Location: Take E-66 Autobahn northeast from Frankfurt for 25 miles, exit to GE-40 North and Gelnhausen. HE: p-38, F/6. NMC: Frankfurt, 25 miles southwest.

Billeting Office: O'Club, Building 1617. EX-708. Check in facility, check out 1100 hours daily.

TML: TLQ. O'Club, Building 1617. Officer all grades. Leave or official duty. 6/1-bedroom, private bath. Rates: $10.00 per person. Duty can make reservations. Others Space-A. Also try BOQ, Building 1804, ETS: 321-2864.

TML Availability: Limited.

Enlisted Club-321-2604   Medical-116   O'Club-321-4281
Police-114   Snack Bar-321-4282   SDO/NCO-321-7275

Giessen Community (GE23R7)
APO New York 09169-5000

TELEPHONE NUMBER INFORMATION: Main installation numbers: Comm: 49-0641-402-XXXX, ETS: 343-XXXX, ATVN: 343-1110.

Location: Autobahn E-5 to Giessener Ring and take Grunberg exit. Follow signs to Giessen General Depot. HE: p-36, E/5. NMC: Giessen, in the city.

Billeting Office: ATTN: Guest House. Building 32. Comm: 0641-46215. ETS: 343-6422. 0730-1600 hours daily. Other hours SDO, Building 1. ETS: 343-8434. Check in facility, check out 1200 hours daily. No government civilian employee billeting.

TML: Guest House. Building 63, Giessen General Depot. All ranks. Leave or official duty. 26/1-bedroom, latrine bath; 3/1-bedroom suites, private bath (DV/VIP). Community kitchen, color TV, maid service, free cribs/cots, free washer/dryer. Older structure. Rates: $9.50 per person. Maximum 3 per unit. Duty can make reservations. Others Space-A.

TML: Guest House. Building 4118, Butzbach. All ranks. Leave or official duty. 5/1-bedroom, latrine bath. Community kitchen, color TV, maid service.

GERMANY
Giessen Community, continued

Older structure. Rates: $9.50 per person. Maximum 3 persons. Duty can make reservations. Others Space-A. **Pets allowed.**

DV/VIP: Cmdr. ETS: 343-8434. Determined by Cmdr.

TML Availability: Good.

Cafeteria-343-6413 Enlisted Club-343-6183 Locator-343-1110
Medical-116 NCO Club-343-6113 O'Club-343-6431
Police-343-6362 SDO/NCO-343-6303

Göppingen Community (GE06R7)
APO New York 09454-5000

TELEPHONE NUMBER INFORMATION: Main installation numbers: Comm: 49-07161-618-XXX, ETS: 425-3XXX, ATVN: 425-1110.

Location: 3 km northeast of Göppingen, off B-10, follow signs for Cooke Barracks. HE: p-40, C/3. NMC: Stuttgart, 50 km northwest.

Billeting Office: ATTN: AETSGPN-DEH-H, Cooke Barracks Housing Area, Building 304. EX-536. 0700-1900 hours M-F, 0700-1600 Sa-Su. Check in facility, check out 1100 hours daily. Government civilian employee billeting.

TML: Guest House/TLF. Building 304. All ranks. Leave or official duty. 32/2-bedroom suites, private bath; or 64/1-bedroom, shared bath. Community kitchen, color TV lounge, maid service, free washer/dryer. Older structure, renovated. Rates: Sponsor $19.00, each additional person $10.00. Maximum 4 per suite, 2 per room + 1 crib ($2.00 extra). PCS in/out have priority, followed by TDY. Others Space-A.

TML Availability: Fairly good. Best, Jan-Apr, Aug-Oct.

Cafeteria-425-3608 Comm Club-425-3552 O'Club-425-3540
Police-425-3827

Grafenwöhr Training Area (GE11R7)
APO New York 09114-5000

TELEPHONE NUMBER INFORMATION: Main installation numbers: Comm: 49-09641-83-XXXX, ETS: 475-XXXX, ATVN: 475-1110.

Location: From Autobahn E-6 exit at Pegnitz/Grafenwöhr, follow signs to training area. HE: p-40, F/1. NMC: Nürnberg, 90 km southwest.

Billeting Office: Building 214, Opposite O'Club. EX-6182/7188. 0730-1900 hours daily. Other hours, Hq, Building 621, EX-8306. Check in billeting, check out 1000 hours daily. No government civilian employee billeting.

TML: Guest House. Building 211. All ranks. Leave or official duty. 12/1-bedroom, hall bath; 4 separate bedroom, private bath; 5/2-bedroom, hall bath; 2/3-bedroom, private bath. Kitchen, community kitchen, color TV, maid service, free cribs, cots ($7.00), free washer/dryer, ice vending. Older structure,

GERMANY

Grafenwöhr Training Area, continued

renovated. Rates: Sponsor $13.00-$18.00, each additional person $7.00. Maximum $52.00 per family. Duty can make reservations. Others Space-A.

TML: VOQ. Building 209. Officer all grades. Leave or official duty. 3/1-bedroom, private bath; 13 separate bedroom, private bath; 10 separate bedrooms, shared bath. Refrigerator, color TV, maid service, free cribs, cots ($10.00), free washer/dryer. Older structure, renovated '87. Rates: Sponsor $18.00, each additional person $10.00. Maximum 2-3 persons per room. Duty can make reservations. Others Space-A.

DV/VIP: Protocol Office, 7th Army Training Command. 06+. ETS: 475-8316. Retirees and lower grades Space-A.

TML Availability: Difficult. Best, Nov-Mar.

Cafeteria-GFNC-515   Enlisted Club-475-6168   Medical-116
NCO C-475-6144   O'Club-475-6200   Police-475-8319
SDO/NCO-475-6332/8324

Hahn Air Base (GE12R7)
APO New York 09109-5000

TELEPHONE NUMBER INFORMATION: Main installation numbers: Comm: 49-6543-51-7679, ETS: 450-1110, ATVN: 450-1110.

Location: On Hwy 327 between Morbach and Kastellaun, 2 kilometers from Sohren on B-50. HE: p-39, G/1. NMC: Frankfurt, 65 miles east.

Billeting Office: Building 407, Main St. EX-7679. 24 hours daily. Check in billeting, check out 1200 hours daily. Government civilian employee billeting in contract hotels.

TML: TLF. Buildings 1380. All ranks. Leave or official duty. 19 separate bedroom suites, private bath. Kitchen, limited utensils, color TV room & lounge, maid service, essentials, free cribs/cots, free washer/dryer, ice vending. Older structure. Renovated and remodeled '89. Rates: $24.00 per room. Maximum 5 persons in Building 1380. Duty can make reservations. Others Space-A.

TML: VOQ. Building 407. All ranks. Leave or official duty. 8 separate bedroom suites, private bath (VOQ VIP); 2 separate bedroom suites, private bath (VAQ VIP); 72/1-bedroom, shared bath. Kitchen, color TV room & lounge, maid service, free cribs/cots, free washer/dryer, ice vending. Older structure. Rates: $7.50 (VAQ), $8.00 (VOQ), $14.00 (DV), under 2 years free. Maximum 2 per room. Duty can make reservations. Others Space-A.

DV/VIP: Protocol Office, 50th TFW/CCE, Building 401. EX-7221. 06+. Retirees Space-A.

Other: Cities of Trier, Berncastle and Cochen are within easy driving distance.

TML Availability: Limited, all year.

GERMANY
Hahn Air Base, continued

Cafeteria-450-6167 Locator-450-7747 Medical-450-7430
NCO Club-450-7543 O'Club-450-7566 Police-450-7795
SDO/NCO-450-7679

Hanau Community (GE13R7)
APO New York 09165-5000

TELEPHONE NUMBER INFORMATION: Main installation numbers: Comm: 49-06181-88-1110, ETS: 322-1110, ATVN: 322-1110.

Location: From Autobahn 66 to Highway 8 or 40 to Hanau, New Argonner and Pioneer Housing Area south of Highway 8. Clearly marked. HE: p-36, E/6. NMC: Frankfurt, 15 miles west.

Billeting Office: ATTN: Billeting Office, Building 318, Pioneer Housing. ETS: 322-8947. 0730-1200/1230-1530 M,Tu,Th, 0730-1200/1230-1530 W, 0730-1200/1230-1515 F. Other hours, SDO, Building 4, Pioneer Kaserne. Check in billeting, check out 0900 hours daily. Government civilian employee billeting.

TML: Guest House. Building 318, Pioneer Housing. All ranks. Leave or official duty. 6/2-bedroom, private bath; 8/3-bedroom, private bath; 7/4-bedroom, private bath. Cribs/cots, maid service, refrigerator, color TV, free washer/dryer. Older structure. Rates: Sponsor $30.00, each additional person $10.00. Maximum 2 per room. Duty can make reservations. Others Space-A. **Pets OK with $25.00 non-refundable fee + $2.00 per pet per night.**

TML: Guest House. Building 203, New Argonner. All ranks. Leave or official duty. 32/1-bedroom, 2 beds, private bath. Cribs/cots, refrigerator, color TV, maid service, free washer/dryer. Older structure, renovated '88/89. Rates: same as Guest House above. Maximum 2 per room. Duty can make reservations. Others Space-A. **Pets OK with $25.00 non-refundable cleaning fee + $2.00 per pet per night.**

TML: VOQ. Building 204. Officer all grades. Leave or official duty. 2/1-bedroom suites, 2 beds, living room, private bath. Refrigerator, community kitchen, cribs/cots, color TV, maid service, free washer/dryer. Older structure, renovation scheduled for '90. Rates: same as Guest Houses. Maximum 2 per room. Duty can make reservations. Others Space-A.

DV/VIP: PAO, Building 1202. Comm: 06181-13654. 06+. Retirees and lower grades Space-A.

TML Availability: Difficult.

Cafeteria-HNUC-55169 Enlisted Club-322-8565 Locator-322-8351
Medical-116 NCO Club-322-8696 O'Club-322-8209
Police-114 Snack Bar-HNUC-55169 SDO/NCO-322-8708

Heidelberg Community (GE33R7)
APO New York 09102-5000

TELEPHONE NUMBER INFORMATION: Main installation numbers: Comm: 49-06221-57-XXXX, ETS: 370-XXXX, ATVN: 370-XXXX.

Temporary Military Lodging Around the World — 225

GERMANY

Heidelberg Community, continued

Location: Access from the E-5 and E-67 Autobahns. A spur off the E-67 Autobahn terminates in Heidelberg. Follow signs to Mark Twain Village and Patrick Henry Village. HE: p-40, B/2. NMC: Heidelberg, in the city.

Billeting Office: Building 4527, North Lexington Avenue, Patrick Henry Village. 24 hours. EX-6941/8128. Check in facility, check out 1100 hours daily. Government civilian employee billeting.

TML: Guest House. Building 4527, North Lexington Village, Patrick Henry Village. All ranks. Leave or official duty. 164/1-bedroom, shared bath; 14 separate bedroom, private bath; 6/2-bedroom, private bath; 86/1-bedroom, private bath. Refrigerator, community kitchen, color TV, maid service, cribs/cots, washer/dryer. Older structure, renovated. Rates: varies widely according to status and type of room. Call. PCS can make reservations. Others Space-A. **Pets allowed with one day room charge and $2.00 per day service charge.**

DV/VIP: SGS, HQ USAREUR. ETS: 370-8707. 06/GS-15+. Retirees and lower grades Space-A.

Other: University of Heidelberg, Students' Inns, Roten Ochsen (Red Ox), Zum Sepp'l side by side on the Hauptstrasse. The Castle above the city on the mountain.

TML Availability: Difficult, all year.

Cafeteria-HPGC-24424	Enl Club-370-8241	Locator-370-6832
Medical-370-6978	NCO Club-370-8241	O'Club-370-7040
Police-114	Snack Bar-HPGC-24423	SDO/NCO-370-8500

Heilbronn Community (GE38R7)
APO New York 09176-5000

TELEPHONE NUMBER INFORMATION: Main installation numbers: Comm: 49-07131-58-XXXX, ETS: 426-2XXX, ATVN: 370-1110 Ask for HBN.

Location: Off Autobahn E-81 South near the intersections of E-81 and E-6. In the south end of city, follow signs to Wharton Kaserne. HE: p-40, C/3. NMC: Heidelberg, 30 miles northwest.

Billeting Office: Building 201/204 Herbert Hoover Strasse. EX-523/496/497 duty hours. Other hours EX-806. Check in facility, check out 1200 hours daily. Government civilian employee billeting.

TML: BOQ. Building 201/204, Herbert Hoover Strasse. Officer all grades. Leave or official duty. Limited number of rooms for transients, shared bath. Maid service, free washer/dryer. Older structure. Rates: Moderate. Duty can make reservations. Others Space-A.

DV/VIP: Deputy Community Cmdr, EX-462. 06+. Retirees Space-A.

TML Availability: Varies.

Cafeteria-HBNC-53121	Enlisted Club-426-2528	Locator-426-92
Medical-426-2888	NCO Club-HBNC-53186	O'Club-HBNC-53132

GERMANY
Heilbronn Community, continued

Police-114   Snack Bar-HBNC-53121 SDO/NCO-426-2462/400

Hessisch-Oldendorf Air Station (GE45R7)
APO New York 09669-5000

TELEPHONE NUMBER INFORMATION: Main installation numbers: Comm: 49-05152-74-XXX, ATVN: 331-6XXX.

Location: A NATO forces base. Thirty miles from Hannover, GE. HE: p-36, E/1. NMC: Hannover, 30 miles northeast.

Billeting Office: Building 4, Dawson Dr. 0700-2200 M-F, 1200-2000 Sa-Su. EX-201. Other hours, Security Police, EX-204. Check in billeting, check out 1100 hours daily. Government civilian employee billeting.

TML: VAQ. Buildings 4, 6. Enlisted E1-E6. Leave or official duty. 6/1-bedroom, shared bath; 7/2-bedroom, hall bath. Refrigerator, community kitchen, color TV, maid service, free cots, free washer/dryer, ice vending. Modern structure. Rates: $6.00 per person. No children. All categories can make reservations.

TML Availability: Limited. Best, Dec-May.

Cafeteria-629   Enlisted Club-299   Locator-204
Medical-260/204   O'Club-351   Police-204/211
Snack Bar-356/237   SDO/NCO-EX-212

Idar-Oberstein Sub-Community (GE53R7)
APO New York 09322-5000

TELEPHONE NUMBER INFORMATION: Main installation numbers: Comm: 49-06781-61-XXXX, ETS: 492-XXXX, ATVN: 485-1110 Ask for IDN.

Location: On GE-41 northeast of Birkenfeld; may be reached from the E-6, Mannheim-Saarbrucken Autobahn. HE: p-40, A/2. NMC: Kaiserslautern, 30 miles south.

Billeting Office: Building 9032, Strassburg Kaserne in the Algenrodt section of the city. EX-6713. 24 hours. Check in facility, check out 1000 hours daily. Government civilian employee billeting.

TML: TLQ. Same as billeting office. All ranks. Leave or official duty. 12/1-bedroom, shared bath. Refrigerator, community kitchen, limited utensils, maid service, cribs $1.50, free washer/dryer. Older structure, renovated. Rates: Sponsor $8.00, each additional person $4.00. Duty can make reservations. Others Space-A.

Other: Semiprecious gem cutting center of Europe.

TML Availability: Good, winter months.

Locator-492-92   Medical-492-6886   NCO Club-492-6749
O'Club-492-6776

Temporary Military Lodging Around the World — 227

GERMANY

Kaiserslautern Community (GE30R7)
APO New York 09012-5000

TELEPHONE NUMBER INFORMATION: Main installation numbers: Comm: 49-0631-411-XXXX, ETS: 483-XXXX, ATVN: 489-1110.

Location: Off the E-6 Mannheim-Saarbrucken Autobahn. Take Mitte exit for Vogelweh Housing Area. Follow signs to housing area or Kapun Barracks (AS). HE: p-40, A/2. NMC: Kaiserslautern, 3 miles northeast.

Billeting Office: Building 1002, Rheinland Pfalz Haus. 24 hours daily. Comm: 0631-411-7190/7649; ETS: 489-7190/7649 (Vogelweh Office). Under AF control at Ramstein AB. Comm: 06371-47-7193/6082; ETS: 480-7193/6082 (Ramstein Office). Check in facility, check out 1300 hours daily. Government civilian employee billeting.

TML: Guest House. Building 1002. All ranks. Leave or official duty. 225 units, shared bath; suites, private bath. Community kitchen each floor, coin washer/dryer, color TV, radio. 16/1-bedroom, private bath, living room, suites (DV/VIP). Older structure, renovated. Rates: $10.00 per person. Duty can make reservations. Others Space-A.

DV/VIP: PAO. Ramstein AB. Comm: 06371-47-7193. 06+. Retirees Space-A.

Other: The city hall (Rathaus) is the highest in Germany, elegant restaurant in the penthouse. Pfaltztheater, opera, operetta, plays and ballet. Visit Harry's gift shop, 5-11 Mannheimer Strasse, Comm: 0631-67081 for gifts, known around the world by military families.

TML Availability: Good.

Cafeteria-KLNC-57653	Enlisted Club-483-7330	Locator-483-92
Medical-116	NCO Club-489-7261	O'Club-489-6000
Police-114	Snack Bar-KLNC-57653	SDO/NCO-483-8674

Karlsruhe Community (GE14R7)
APO New York 09164-5000

TELEPHONE NUMBER INFORMATION: Main installation numbers: Comm: 49-0721-759-XXXX, ETS: 376-XXXX, ATVN: 370-1110 Ask for KRE.

Location: Take the Karlsruhe exit off Autobahn E-4. Follow signs to Smiley Barracks. HE: p-40, B/3. NMC: Karlsruhe, in the city.

Billeting Office: Building 9942, Tennessee Ave. EX-6010. 24 hours daily. Check in facility, check out 1000 hours daily. Government civilian employee bileting.

TML: Guest House. Karlsruhe Lodge. Buildings 9941, 9942. All ranks. Leave or official duty. 88 rooms, shared bath; 4 suites, private bath. Kitchen (suites), refrigerator, community kitchen, limited utensils, color TV room & lounge, maid service, free cribs/cots, free washer/dryer, ice vending, microwave. Older structure. Rates: Sponsor $20.00, each additional person $8.00. Maximum 2 adults, 1 child. Duty can make reservations. Others Space-A. **Pets OK ($2.00 per pet per day plus one day room rent).** DA Lodging Operation of the Year Award (small category) for 1988.

GERMANY
Karlsruhe Community, continued

TML Availability: Good, Sep-Mar. More difficult, other times.

Cafeteria-376-7239	Enlisted Club-376-6285	Medical-376-6541
NCO Club-376-6285	O'Club-376-6441	Police-376-6123
Snack Bar-376-7239	SDO/NCO-376-6433/6362	

Landstuhl Army Medical Center (GE40R7)
APO New York 09180-5000

TELEPHONE NUMBER INFORMATION: Main installation numbers: Comm: 49-06371-86-XXXX, ETS: 486-XXXX, ATVN: 483-1110.

Location: Take the Landstuhl exit from the E-6 Mannheim-Saarbrücken Autobahn. Follow signs for "2nd General Hospital". HE: p-40, A/2. NMC: Kaiserslautern, 10 miles northeast.

Billeting Office: ATTN: LBAQ. Building 305. EX-7267. Ramstein AB, 24 hours daily. Check in facility, check out 1100 hours daily. Government civilian employee billeting.

TML: BOQ/BAQ. Building 3752. All ranks. Leave or official duty. 99/1-bedroom, 2 beds, shared bath. Community kitchen, refrigerator, color TV, maid service, free cribs/cots, free washer/dryer. Older structure, remodeled. Rates: $10.00 per person, Maximum $20.00 per room. Duty can make reservations. Others Space-A.

DV/VIP: Community Cmdr. EX-7183. 06+.

TML Availability: Good, Nov-Feb. Difficult, summer months.

Enlisted Club-486-7198	Locator-486-7183	Medical-486-8107
NCO Club-486-7198	O'Club-486-7244	Police-486-7660

Mainz Community (GE41R7)
APO New York 09185-0029

TELEPHONE NUMBER INFORMATION: Main installation numbers: Comm: 49-06131-48-XXXX, ETS: 334-XXXX, ATVN: 320-1110 Ask for MNZ.

Location: Take the Mainz exit from the E-61 Autobahn to GE B-9. Follow the signs to Martin Luther King Village. HE: p-40, A/1. NMC: Mainz, in the city.

Billeting Office: Building 6706, Martin Luther King Village. Comm: 06131-38650. ETS: 334-7396. 0600-2000 M-F. 0800-1600 Sa-Su. Check in facility, check out 1200 hours daily. Government civilian employee billeting.

TML: TLQ. Building 6706. All ranks. Leave or official duty. 16 separate bedroom suites, private bath. Kitchen, color TV, maid service, cribs ($1.00), free washer/dryer, ice vending. Older structure, renovated '87. Rates: Sponsor $25.00, if sharing $17.50 each. Maximum $45.00 per room. Maximum 5 per room. Duty can make reservations. Others Space-A. TDY/PCS have priority.

Temporary Military Lodging Around the World — 229

GERMANY

Mainz Community, continued

DV/VIP: Protocol Office. 05+. Retirees Space-A.

Other: City of Mainz, Rhine River cruises.

TML Availability: Good, all year.

Cafeteria-MNZC-37644 Enlisted Club-334-3709 Medical-116
NCO Club-334-7380 O'Club-334-7380 Police-334-7111

Mannheim Community (GE43R7)
APO New York 09086-5000

TELEPHONE NUMBER INFORMATION: Main installation numbers: Comm: 49-0621-730-XXXX, ETS: 382-XXXX Coleman, 380-XXXX Funari, ATVN: 380-1110.

Location: Accessible from the E-5 or E-67 Autobahns. Take the Viernheim exit, follow signs to Benjamin Franklin Housing Area on Fürther Strasse. HE: p-40, B/2. NMC: Mannheim, 8 miles southwest.

Billeting Office: Building 312, Benjamin Franklin Housing Area (BFHA), Fürther Strasse. 0630-1800 daily. Comm: 0621-730-8118/6547. ETS: 380-8118/6547.

TML: Transient Hotel. Building 380, Benjamin Franklin Housing Area, Fuerther Strasse. All ranks. Leave or official duty. Maid service, washer/dryer. VIP suites have honor bars. Older structure, renovated. Rates: Sponsor $25.00, dependents $11.00; $35.00 for suites. Duty can make reservations. Others Space-A.

TML: Guesthouse. Building 312. All ranks. Leave or official duty. Accessible to handicapped. 3/1-bedroom, private bath; 39/2-bedroom, private bath. Community kitchen, rollaways/cribs, ice vending, kitchenette, maid service, refrigerator, special facilities for disabled American veterans, cable color TV, free washer/dryer. Older structure, renovated. Rates: $25.00 per adult, $11.00 per child. Maximum $46.00 per family. Duty can make reservations. Others Space-A. **Contract hotel available for pets.**

Other: Modern National Theater. Old Observatory, constructed in 1722, and ancient Mannheim castle, completed in 1720.

TML Availability: Good, July-Sept, Dec-June. Difficult, Sept.-Nov.

Cafeteria-735906 Enlisted Club-380-6157 Locator-380-92
Medical-116 NCO Club-380-6370 O'Club-MHNC-731333
Police-380-7118/6322 Snack B-MHNC-783325 SDO/NCO-380-8168

Munich Community (GE15R7)
APO New York 09407-5000

TELEPHONE NUMBER INFORMATION: Main installation numbers: Comm: 49-089-6229-6011, ETS: 440-6011, ATVN: 440-1110.

GERMANY
Munich Community, continued

Location: Munich can be reached from both Autobahns E-8 or E-9. Follow the Salzburg Autobahn signs on Mittlerer Ring, watch for signs indicating directions to McGraw Kaserne. HE: p-40, G/5. NMC: Munich, in the city.

Billeting Office: Building 13, McGraw Kaserne, 239 Tegernsee Land Strasse, 8000 Muenchen 90. EX-6011. 24 hours daily. Check in facility, check out 1100 hours daily.

TML: Guest House. Desk, Building 13, McGraw Kaserne. All ranks. Leave or official duty. Accessible to handicapped. 135 separate bedrooms, shared bath; 6/1-bedroom suites, private bath (VIP); 33/2-bedroom, shared bath; 24/3-bedroom, shared bath; 24/4-bedroom, shared bath; 24/4-bedroom, shared bath. Kitchen (some), community kitchen (some), refrigerator (some), complete utensils (some), essentials, food vending, special facilities for handicapped veterans (6 units), color TV, maid service, free cribs, cots ($5.00), free washer/dryer (some). Older structure. Renovated '89 new carpets/TVs. Rates: Single $25.00; VIP $40.00, double $32.00; VIP $45.00. All categories can make reservations.

DV/VIP: DCC, USMCA, Building 54, Room 218, EX-8300/6244. 06+. Retirees and lower grades Space-A.

TML Availability: Good. Best, Nov-May.

Locator-440-1110
SDO/NCO-440-8300
Burger King-699-0166
Medical-440-7295
Snack Bar-440-6171
Police-440-6179
Baskin Robins-699-0106

Neubreucke Sub-Community (GE54R7)
APO New York 09305-5000

TELEPHONE NUMBER INFORMATION: Main installation numbers: Comm: 49-06782-13-XXX, ETS: 493-7XXX, ATVN: 485-1110 Ask for NEU.

Location: On GE-41, near Baumholder. Follow signs to Neubruecke Hospital. HE: p-39, G/1. NMC: Baumholder, 9 miles east.

Billeting Office: Building 9965. 0730-1700 M-F. Comm: 06782-13-287/416. ETS: 493-7287/7416. After duty hours contact Security Police, Building 9920. Comm: 06782-13-415/309. Check in facility 1300-1700 hours, check out 1100 hours daily. Government civilian employee billeting.

TML: Guest House. Buildings 9961, 9966. All ranks. Leave or official duty. Accessible to handicapped. 55/2-bedroom, shared bath; 4 separate bedroom, private bath. Refrigerator, community kitchen, limited utensils, color TV, maid service, cribs, washer/dryer. Older structure, remodeled. Rates for personnel on leave/vacation: Sponsor $14.00 ($22.00 for suites), adult $10.00, child $6.00. Rates for active duty personnel: Sponsor $18.00, adult $13.00, child $8.00. Others Space-A.

Other: Recreation center and women's USO center.

TML Availability: Best, Sep-Apr. Difficult, May-Aug.

GERMANY

Neubreucke Sub-Community, continued

Cafeteria-6638 NCO Club-493-7219 Medical-116
O'Club-493-7219 Police-114

Neu-Ulm Community (GE28R7)
APO New York 09035-5000

TELEPHONE NUMBER INFORMATION: Main installation numbers: Comm: 49-0731-809-XXXX, ETS: 427-XXXX, ATVN: 427-XXXX.

Location: South of the E-8 Munich-Stuttgart Autobahn. Take the Ulm Ost exit south for 4 miles. HE: p-40, D/4-5. NMC: Stuttgart, 50 miles northwest.

Billeting Office: No central billeting office. Donau Casino Combined Club. 24 hours daily. Comm: 0731-7401. ETS: 427-6290. Other hours, CQ, Building 202, Wiley Barracks. Check in facility, check out 1100 hours daily. Government civilian employee billeting.

TML: Donau Casino Club. E6+, GS-13+, O6+. Leave or official duty. 9/1-bedroom, private bath; 7/1-bedroom, semi-private bath. 1 separate bedroom suite, private bath (DV/VIP). Refrigerator, color TV, maid service, cribs ($5.00), rollaways ($10.00), free washer/dryer. Older structure, renovated. Rates: Adult, single $35.00; adult, double $45.00; child under 5 $5.00. Maximum $78.00 per family. Reservations accepted for GS-13+ and O6+.

DV/VIP: Deputy Community Commander, Building 131. Comm: 0731-74881. ATVN: 427-6601. O6+. Retirees and lower grades Space-A.

Other: On the Danube River. Munster cathedral in New Ulm has the tallest church steeple in the world.

TML Availability: Good year round.

Enlisted Club-427-6492 Locator-427-6213 Medical-ULMC-85245
NCO Club-427-6492 O'Club-427-6290 Police-427-6648
SDO/NCO-427-6647

Nürnberg Community (GE44R7)
APO New York 09696-5000

TELEPHONE NUMBER INFORMATION: Main installation numbers: Comm: 49-0911-700-XXXX, ETS: 460-XXXX, ATVN: 460-1110.

Location: Access from Autobahns E-3 (east-west), E-6 (east-west), E-9 (north-south). Also from GE-2 & 4 (north-south) and GE-8 & 14 (east-west). The Bavarian American Hotel is located in the center of the city across from the main train station. HE: p-40, F/2. NMC: Nürnberg, in the city.

Billeting Office: Bavarian American Hotel, Bahnfof Strasse 3. Comm: 0911-23440. ETS: 460-6632. 24 hours. Also, W. O. Darby Kaserne, 460-6888. Check in facility, check out 1200 hours daily. Government civilian employee billeting.

GERMANY
Nürnberg Community, continued

TML: Hotel. All ranks. Leave or official duty. 130 single/double room, shared bath/private bath; 10 separate bedroom suites, private bath. Color TV, lounge, maid service, cribs/cots, coin washer/dryer. No room service. Restaurant/bar in hotel, mini-shop, newsstand, new TV, game rooms. Older structure. Rates: $22.00 per person, $40.00 for suites (PCS/TDY). All categories Space-A. Check the telephone numbers above for BOQ/BEQ space in the area.

DV/VIP: Deputy Community Commander, EX-6696. 06+. Retirees Space-A.

Other: Toy Manuf area of GE, Christmas market for decorations.

TML Availability: Good, Oct-Apr. Difficult, other times.

Cafeteria-460-6578   Enlisted Club-460-4634   Locator-92
Medical-460-5744   NCO Club-460-6668   O'Club-460-6589
Police-460-6600   Snack B-NBGC-706841   SDO/NCO-460-8306

Pirmasens Community (GE42R7)
APO New York 09189-5000

TELEPHONE NUMBER INFORMATION: Main installation numbers: Comm: 49-06331-86-XXXX, ETS: 495-XXXX, ATVN: 495-1110 Ask for PMS.

Location: On the triangle of GE-10 from Zweibrücken and GE-270 from Kaiserslautern. HE: p-39, G/2. NMC: Pirmasens, 1 miles southeast.

Billeting Office: ATTN: AERP-EH-U. Building 4535, Bundestrasse 10. EX-6535/7393. 0730-1800 M-F. Other hours SDO, Building 4624. EX-6444. Check in after 1300, check out 1000 hours daily. Government civilian employee billeting.

TML: Guest House. Building 4535. All ranks. Leave or official duty. Accessible to handicapped. 29/1-bedroom, private bath; 16/1-bedroom, shared bath; 2 separate bedroom, private bath. Refrigerator, community kitchen, color TV, maid service, free cribs/cots, free washer/dryer. Older structure, renovated '89. Rates: Sponsor $19.00, adult $4.00, child $4.00, infant $2.00. Maximum 3 per room. Duty can make reservations. Others Space-A.

TML: DV/VIP. Building 4537. Office 06+. 2 separate bedroom suites, private bath. Kitchen, complete utensils, color TV, maid service, cribs/cots. Older structure, new TVs/carpets '87. Rates: call for rates. Maximum 3 per suite. Duty can make reservations. Others Space-A.

DV/VIP: 59th Ordnance Brigade, SGS Office. Building 4616. EX-7383. 06+. Retirees and lower grades Space-A.

TML Availability: Good, Dec, Jan. Difficult, May-Aug.

Cafeteria-PMSC-65757   Medical-116   Enlisted Club-495-6530
O'Club-495-6520   Police-114   Snack Bar-PMSC-65757
SDO/NCO-495-6444

Temporary Military Lodging Around the World — 233

GERMANY

Ramstein Air Base (GE24R7)
APO New York 09094-5000

TELEPHONE NUMBER INFORMATION: Main installation numbers: Comm: 49-06371-47-XXXX, ETS: 480-XXXX, ATVN: 480-1110.

Location: Two exits from Mannheim-Saarbrücken E-6 Autobahn, marked Flugplatz Ramstein. Also, west on B-40 to Landstuhl Strasse, turn right follow signs to Flugplatz Ramstein. HE: p-39, G/2. NMC: Kaiserslautern, 12 miles east.

Billeting Office: ATTN: Reservations. Building 305, Washington Ave. EX-7864/7345. 0730-1800 M-Th, 0730-1630 F. Check in facility, check out 1200 hours daily. Government civilian employee billeting.

TML: Crew Quarters. Buildings 538 (Officer), 2408 (Enlisted). Leave or official duty. 62/1-bedroom, shared bath. Refrigerator, color TV room & lounge, maid service, free cots, free washer/dryer, ice vending. Modern structure Rates: $10.00 per person. Note: quarters are for crew members only.

TML: TLQ. Buildings 303, 1004. All ranks. Leave or official duty. 2/1-bedroom, private bath; 77/2-bedroom, private bath. Kitchen, limited utensils, color TV room & lounge, maid service, free cribs/cots, free washer/dryer, ice vending. Modern structure. Rates: $24.00 per unit. Maximum 4 per unit. Duty can make reservations. Others Space-A.

TML: TAQ. Buildings 1003, 2408, 2409, 3752, 3756. Enlisted all grades. Leave or official duty. 674/1-bedroom, 2 beds, shared bath; 2 separate bedroom suites, private bath. Refrigerator, community kitchen (some), limited utensils, color TV room & lounge, maid service, free cribs/cots, washer/dryer, ice vending. Modern structure. Rates: $10.00 per person. Maximum $20.00 per family. Duty can make reservations. Others Space-A.

TML: VOQ. Buildings 304-306, 530, 540, 541, 1002, 3751, 3754. Officer all grades. 533/1-bedroom, shared bath & private bath; 27 separate bedrooms, private bath. Kitchen (some), refrigerator, limited utensils, color TV room & lounge, maid service, free cribs/cots, free washer/dryer, ice vending. Modern structure. Rates: $10.00 per person. Maximum $20.00 per family. Duty can make reservations. Others Space-A.

TML: DV/VIP. Building 1018. Officer 06+. Leave or official duty. See numbers under Protocol below. 11 separate bedroom suites, private bath. Refrigerator, limited utensils, color TV, washer/dryer, ice vending. Modern structure, renovated. Rates: $18.00 per person. Maximum $54.00 per family. Maximum 3 person. Duty can make reservations. Others Space-A.

DV/VIP: Protocol, Building 201. Comm: 06371-4851. ATVN: 480-7558. 06+. Retirees Space-A.

TML Availability: Very good all year. Best, winter months.

Cafeteria-480-6162
NCO Club-480-5637
Snack Bar-480-6061
Locator-480-6120/6989
O'Club-480-6066
Medical-486-8260
Police-480-5323

GERMANY

Rhein Main Air Base (GE16R7)
APO New York 09057-5000

TELEPHONE NUMBER INFORMATION: Main installation numbers: Comm: 49-069-699-1110, ETS: 330-1110, ATVN: 330-1110.

Location: Adjacent to Frankfurt International Airport of E-5 Autobahn to Darmstadt. HE: p-40, B/1. NMC: Frankfurt, 10 miles north.

Billeting Office: Building 7265-7267, Aerial Port Quarters. EX-7682/83. 0730-1630 hours daily (an information recording is operational after hours). Other hours, Deputy Manager, EX-7266. Check in billeting, check out 1000 hours daily. Government civilian employee billeting if civilian Air Force on official duty.

TML: Aerial Port Quarters (Hotel), Building 110. Officer all grades. Leave or official duty. 250/2-bedroom, shared bath; 12/4-bedroom, private bath; 4/1-bedroom, private bath. Refrigerator, color TV, maid service, free cribs, washer/dryer, ice vending. Older structure. Rates: $10.00 per person. Maximum $20.00 per room. Maximum 2 per room. Duty can make reservations. Others Space-A.

TML: VAQ. Building 345. Enlisted all ranks. Leave or official duty. 5/1-bedroom, private bath; 173 separate bedrooms, hall bath. Refrigerator, color TV room & lounge, maid service, free washer/dryer. Older structure. Rates: $8.00 per person. Maximum $16.00 per room. Maximum 2 per room. Duty can make reservations. Others Space-A.

DV/VIP: Protocol, 435 TAW/CCP, Building 110, Room 150. EX-6059. 06+/civilian equivalent. Retirees and lower grades Space-A.

Other: Visit Frankfurt's famous Fairgrounds (Messa), exhibits of all types.

TML Availability: Good, Dec-Jan. Difficult, other times.

Cafeteria-69-1181	Enlisted Club-7997	Locator-7691/7348
Medical-7307	NCO Club-7121	O'Club-7120
Police-114/7177	Snack Bar-69-3076	SDO/NCO-330-7801

Schwäbisch Hall Sub-Community (GE17R7)
APO New York 09025-5000

TELEPHONE NUMBER INFORMATION: Main installation numbers: Comm: 49-0791-45-XXX, ETS: 426-4XXX, ATVN: 460-1110 Ask for SHL.

Location: Take B-14 or B-19 exit from Heilbronn/Nürnberg Autobahn. Go through Schwäbisch Hall, follow signs to Ellwagen/Dolan Barracks. HE: p-40, C/4. NMC: Stuttgart, 50 km northeast.

Billeting Office: Building 371. EX-530. 0730-1600 hours daily. Other hours CQ, Building 314, EX-527. Check in facility, check out 1100 hours daily.

Temporary Military Lodging Around the World — 235

GERMANY

Schwäbisch Hall Community, continued

TML: Guest House. Building 371. All ranks. Leave or official duty. 3/1-bedroom, private bath; 19 separate bedrooms, hall bath; 1/2-room VIP suite, private bath. Refrigerator, community kitchen, color TV, maid service. Older structure. Rates: Single occupant $20.00, double occupancy $25.00; TDY rates: single occupant $30.00, double occupancy $36.00. Maximum 3 per room. All categories can make reservations.

DV/VIP: Commander. EX-525. 06+.

TML Availability: Good, Oct-Apr. Difficult, other times.

Cafeteria-SHLC-2269	Enlisted Club-426-4536	Medical-426-4566
NCO Club-426-4536	O'Club-426-4608	Police-426-4807
Snack Bar-SHLC-2269	SDO/NCO-426-4525/827	

Schweinfurt Community (GE48R7)
APO New York 09033-5000

TELEPHONE NUMBER INFORMATION: Main installation numbers: Comm: 49-09721-96-XXXX, ETS: 354-XXXX, ATVN: 350-1110 Ask for SFT.

Location: 9 miles east of Kassel-Würzburg, E-70 Autobahn. On GE-303, 2 miles past GE-B19. Follow US Forces signs. HE: p-40, D/1. NMC: Schweinfurt, in the city.

Billeting Office: Billeting Manager. Building 89. 0730-2000 hours M-F. Comm: 09721-82931. ETS: 354-6245. After hours contact SDO, Building 1, Comm: 09721-96288, ATVN: 354-6288. Check in facility, check out 1000 hours daily. Government civilian employee billeting.

TML: Guest House. Bradley Inn. Building 89. All ranks. Leave or official duty. 8/1-bedroom, 2 beds, private bath; 8/1-bedroom, 1 bed, private bath; 34 separate bedrooms, private bath; 2/2-bedroom, private bath. Community kitchen, refrigerator (some), utensils, color TV, maid service, free cribs/cots, free washer/dryer, vending machine. Older structure, renovated. Rates: Sponsor $29.00, each additional person $10.00. Maximum $69.00 per family. Duty can make reservations. Others Space-A.

DV/VIP: Chief, Housing Office. Building 251. Comm: 09721-96448. 03/GS-12+. Retirees and lower grades Space-A.

TML Availability: Good, all year.

Cafeteria-SFTC-82334	Enl Club-354-6330	Locator-354-6748
Medical-STFC-82397	NCO Club-354-6330	O'Club-354-6398
Police-STFC-802160	Snack Bar-354-63320	SDO/NCO-354-6288

Sembach Air Base (GE18R7)
APO New York 09136-5000
RUNWAY CLOSED. LIMITED BASE SUPPORT.

TELEPHONE NUMBER INFORMATION: Main installation numbers: Comm: 49-06302-67-XXXX, ETS: 496-XXXX, ATVN:496-1110.

Location: From the E-12 Autobahn exit A-6 marked Enkenbach-Alsenborn and follow B-48 in the direction of Bad Kruznach. Immediately past town of Munchweiller right to Sembach AB. Also, accessible from B-40 North. HE: p-40, A/2. NMC: Kaiserslautern 14 km west.

236 — *Temporary Military Lodging Around the World*

GERMANY
Sembach Air Base, continued

Billeting Office: ATTN: SVH. Building 216, Radar Ave (known as Dorm Row). EX-7588/7149. 24 hours daily. Check in billeting, check out 1200 hours daily. Government civilian employee billeting.

TML: VOQ/DV/VIP. Building 110, 1st, 2nd and 3rd floors. EX-6194. Officer all grades. Leave or official duty. Accessible to handicapped. 42/1-bedroom, shared bath; 9 separate bedroom suites, private bath (DV/VIP). Refrigerator, community kitchen, limited utensils, color TV, maid service, free cribs/cots, free washer/dryer, ice vending. Older structure. Rates: $6.00 per person rooms, $10.00 per person suites. Maximum 3 per unit. Duty can make reservations. Others Space-A.

TML: VAQ. Building 216 Enlisted all grades. Leave or official duty. 73/1-bedroom, 2 beds, hall bath. Maid serivce. Older structure. Rates: $6.00 per person. No families. Duty can make reservations. Others Space-A.

DV/VIP: 66ECW/CCE, Building 112, EX-7960. 06+. Retirees Space-A.

TML Availability: Difficult. Best, Dec-Jan.

Cafeteria-496-7741	Enlisted Club-496-6626	Locator-496-7535
Medical-116	NCO Club-496-6625	O'Club-496-7611
Police-496-7171	Snack Bar-496-7571	SDO/NCO-496-6625

Spangdahlem Air Base (GE19R7)
APO New York 09126-5000

TELEPHONE NUMBER INFORMATION: Main installation numbers: Comm: 49-06565-61-1110, ETS: 452-1110, ATVN: 452-1110.

Location: From the Koblenz-Trier Autobahn E-1 exit at Wittlich, to B-50 West toward Bitburg. The AB is near Binsfeld 24 km west of Wittlich. Signs mark the AB entrance. HE: p-39, F/1. NMC: Trier, 21 miles southeast.

Billeting Office: ATTN: 52 SVS/SVH/Billeting, Building 38, Goodfellow Dr. EX-6504. 24 hours daily. Check in facility, check out 1100 hours daily. No government civilian employee billeting.

TML: VOQ/VAQ. Building 38. All ranks. Leave or official duty. 47 rooms in VOQ with private bath; 96 bed spaces in VAQ with shared bath. Refrigerator, color TV, maid service, washer/dryer, ice vending. Older structure. Rates: $6.00. Maximum 2 persons. Duty can make reservations. Others Space-A.

TML: TLF. All ranks. Leave or official duty. 56 separate rooms, private bath. Cribs, ice vending, kitchenette, maid service, color TV, complete utensils, washer/dryer. Modern structure. Rates $24.00 per unit. Duty can make reservations. TLF is for families and singles PCS in/out.

DV/VIP: Cmdr, 52 TFW/CC, EX-6434. Determined by Cmdr. 06+. Retirees Space-A.

TML Availability: Limited all year. Best, Nov-Dec.

Cafeteria-452-6615	Enlisted Club-452-6588	Locator-452-6038
Medical-452-6588	NCO Club-452-6588	O'Club-452-6530
Police-452-6666	SDO/NCO-452-6141	

Temporary Military Lodging Around the World — 237

GERMANY

Stuttgart Community (GE20R7)
APO New York 09154-5000

TELEPHONE NUMBER INFORMATION: Main installation numbers: Comm: 49-0711-819-XXXX, ETS: 420-XXXX, ATVN: 420-1110.

Location: Can be reached from both E-11 and E-70 Autobahns. Look for signs to Robinson Barracks. HE: P-40, C/4. NMC: Stuttgart, within city limits.

Billeting Office: Building 169. Comm: 0711-859-523. ETS: 420-6209. 0730-1630 hours daily. Check in facility, check out 1100 hours daily. Government civilian employee billeting.

TML: Guest House. Building 169. Hilltop Hotel at Robinson Barracks. All ranks. Leave or official duty. Check in 1400 hours daily. 60/1-bedroom, shared bath; 4 separate bedroom suites, private bath (DV/VIP). Refrigerator, color TV room & lounge, maid service, cribs/cots, free washer/dryer. Older structure, renovated '86-'87. Rates: For PCS/TDY, $40.00-$130.00 for 1-6 persons, $15.00 each additional person; for leave and other Space-A, $30.00-$55.00 for 1-6 persons, $5.00 each additional person. Maximum 2 adults/2 children under 5 per room. Duty can make reservations. Others Space-A.

DV/VIP: Cmdr. ETS: 420-2038. 06/GS-15+. Retirees Space-A.

TML Availability: Very limited, all year.

Enlisted Club-420-6377   Medical-116   NCO Club-420-6377
O'Club-420-6129   Police-420-8317   Snack Bar-859518
SDO/NCO-420-6095

Templehof Central Airport (GE25R7)
APO New York 09611-5000

TELEPHONE NUMBER INFORMATION: Main installation numbers: Comm: 49-30-819-XXXX, ATVN: 332-1110.

Location: At Platz der Luftbrücke, intersection of Columbia Damm and Tempelhofer Damm Streets. HE: city map 6, Berlin (West). NMC: Berlin, in the city.

Billeting Office: ATTN: 7350th ABG/SVH, Building D2. EX-5574. Columbia House, O'Club, EX-5591. 24 hours daily. Check in facility, check out 1300 hours daily. Government civilian employee billeting.

TML: Guest House/VOQ. Buildings C2, D2. All ranks. Leave or official duty. 24/1-bedroom, hall bath; 13 separate bedrooms, shared bath. VAQ and suites also available. Refrigerator, community kitchen, maid service, cribs/cots, washer/dryer, ice vending. Older structure, renovated. Rates: $5.00-$8.00 per person. Maximum 3-6 per unit. All categories can make reservations. Others Space-A.

DV/VIP: Protocol Office. EX-5151. 06+. Retirees Space-A.

TML Availability: Good.

Dining Fac-332-5696   Enlisted Club-332-5318   Locator-332-5511
NCO Club-332-5318   O'Club-332-5005   Police-332-5314
Snack Bar-332-5224   SDO/NCO-332-5224

238 — *Temporary Military Lodging Around the World*

GERMANY

Wertheim Sub-Community (GE52R7)
APO New York 09047-5000

TELEPHONE NUMBER INFORMATION: Main installation numbers: Comm: 49-09342-75-XXX, ETS: 355-5XXX, ATVN: 350-1110 Ask for WRT.

Location: Take the Marktheidenfeld-Wertheim exit from the Frankfurt-Nürnberg E-3 Autobahn. HE: p-40, D/1. NMC: Würzburg, 25 miles west.

Billeting Office: Building 6, O'Club. 0800-1700 hours daily. EX-689. Check in facility, check out 1100 hours daily. No government civilian employee billeting.

TML: TLQ. O'Club, Building 6. All ranks. Leave or official duty. 21/1-bedroom, 2 beds, hall bath; 2/2-bedroom, 2 beds each, hall bath; 1/2-bedroom suite, living room, private bath. Refrigerator, color TV lounge, maid service, cribs $1.50, free washer/dryer, ice vending. Older structure. Renovated. Rates: $6.00 first bed, $4.00 each additional bed, suites $25.00. Duty can make reservations. Others Space-A.

DV/VIP: Deputy Community Commander. ETS: 355-5724/5800. O6+. Retirees Space-A.

TML Availability: Good, Feb-Apr.

Cafeteria-WRTC-7130	Enlisted Club-355-5688	Locator-355-92
Medical-355-5695	NCO Club-355-5688	O'Club-355-5689
Police-355-5818	Snack Bar-WRTC-7130	SDO/NCO-355-5648/783

Wiesbaden Community (GE27R7)
APO New York 09457-5000

TELEPHONE NUMBER INFORMATION: Main installation numbers: Comm: 49-06121-82-XXXX, 78-XXXX, ETS: 337/339-XXXX, ATVN: 320-1110 Ask for WBN.

Location: Accessible from Autobahns E-3, E-5, E-61. Take exits marked Wiesbaden Air Base to Berlinerstrasse then Frankfurterstrasse to billeting office. HE: p-40, A/1. NMC: Wiesbaden, in the city.

Billeting Office: American Arms Hotel, 17 Frankfurterstrasse. 24 hours daily, Comm: 06121-343035. ETS: 339-3314. Amelia Earhart Hotel, Konrad Adenauer Ring 39, Comm: 06121-816368, ETS: 337-6200. Check in facility, check out 1200 hours daily. Government civilian employee billeting.

TML: Amelia Earhart Hotel, adjacent to USAF hospital. Enlisted all ranks. Leave or official duty. 376/1-bedroom, private bath. Refrigerator, color TV room and lounge, maid service, free cribs/cots, free washer/dryer. Some units DV/VIP suites with hair dryer, make-up mirror, microwave ovens, bar, quad-plex stereo. Reservations for E7-E9, used by all grades after 1600 hours daily. Modern structure. TLA Rates: $35.00 1st person, $25.00 2nd person, $15.00 each additional person; TDY Rates: $40.00-$50.00 single occupant, $30.00-$40.00 per person shared occupancy, $20.00-$30.00 second occupant, $20.00 each additional person in suites. Duty can make reservations. Others Space-A.

TML: American Arms Hotel, 17 Frankfurterstrasse. All ranks. Leave or official duty. 108/1-bedroom, shared bedroom; 22 separate bedroom, private bath; 1/2-bedroom suite, private bath. Community kitchen, refrigerator, color TV room and lounge, maid service, free cribs/cots, coin washer/dryer, ice vending. Modern structure. Restaurant, bar, barber and concessions in hotel. Rates: Same as Amelia Earhart Hotel. Duty can make reservations. Others Space-A. Also, on Wiesbaden Air Base there are 92 Transient Officer.

Temporary Military Lodging Around the World — 239

GERMANY

Wiesbaden Community, continued

billets, and 172 Transient Enlisted billets, call ETS: 339-6525 for info and accommodations.

DV/VIP: Contact hotel manager at either hotel listed above. 06+. Retirees and lower grades Space-A.

Other: Hainerberg Shopping Center is 3 blocks away in the center of Wiesbaden, the cultural capital of the state of Hessen.

TML Availability: Good, Nov-Mar. Difficult, other times.

Exchange-WBNC-719081	Cafeteria-WBNC-701596	Enlisted Club-339-3351
Locator-WBNC-785055	Medical-885-441	NCO Club-339-3421
O'Club-337-5111/4413	Police-114	SDO/NCO-EX-5088

Wildflecken Community (GE86R7)
APO New York 09026-5000

TELEPHONE NUMBER INFORMATION: Main installation numbers: Comm: 49-09745-1239, ATVN: 326-3553/3964.

Billeting Office: Building 32, 16th St, 0730-1545 M-F, other hours Building 7, Room 109, ATVN: 326-3824. Check in billeting, check out 1100 hours. Government civilian employee billeting.

TML: Guesthouse. Building 2. All ranks. 9/1-bedroom, private and hall bath; 1 separate bedroom, private bath; 3/2-bedroom, hall bath. Refrigerator, community kitchen, limited utensils, color TV, cribs ($5.00), washer/dryer. Rates: Sponsor $10.00, each additional person $5.00. All categories can make reservations. Duty personnel have priority. **Pets OK for $1.00 per night.**

TML: VOQ/VEQ. Building 25. All ranks. 29/1-bedroom, hall bath. Refrigerator, wardrobe, desk, TV, maid service, cribs ($10.00), washer/dryer. Rates: $10.00 per person. All categories can make reservations. Duty personnel have priority.

TML: VOQ/VEQ. Building 26. All ranks. 27/1-bedroom, hall bath; 1 separate bedroom, hall bath. Refrigerator, maid service, washer/dryer. Rates: $8.00 per person.

TML: DVQ. Building 50. Officer 06+, Enlisted E-9. 4 separate bedroom, private bath. Kitchenette, complete utensils, color TV, maid service, cribs ($15.00). Rates: $15.00 per person. All categories can make reservations. Duty personnel have priority.

TML Availability: Best, Dec, Jan, Feb. Difficult, Aug, Sept, Oct.

Enlisted Club-326-3603	Locator-326-3471	Medical-326-3662
NCO Club-326-3603	O'Club-326-3443	Snack Bar-09745-684

Worms/Northpoint/Weierhof Community (GE31R7)
APO New York 09058-3879

TELEPHONE NUMBER INFORMATION: Main installation numbers: Comm: 49-06241-48-XXXX, ETS: 383-XXXX, ATVN: 383-1110.

Location: Take the Worms exit from the Mannheim-Saarbrücken E-6 Autobahn. Follow the signs to Thomas Jefferson Village. HE: p-40, B/2. NMC: Worms, in the city.

GERMANY
Worms/Northpoint/Weierhof Community, continued

Billeting Office: Building 5032, Liebenauer Strasse. EX-7374/7763. 0730-1830 M-F. Other hours, OOD, Building 5814, EX-7234. Check in facility, check out 1200 hours daily. Government civilian employee billeting.

TML: TLF. All ranks. Leave or official duty. 15/1-bedroom, shared bath; 5 VIP suites, 4 family suites, separate bedroom, living room, private bath, bar. Refrigerator, color TV, VCR on request, cribs/cots ($2.00). Older structure. Rates: Sponsor $21.00, each additional person $4.50 (rooms); Sponsor $32.00, each additional person $4.50 (VIP suites). TDY can make reservations. Others Space-A.

TML Availability: Good, Nov-Apr. Difficult, other times.

Cafeteria-WMSC-43305	Enlisted Club-491-2744	Locator-383-92
Medical-116	NCO Club-383-7689	O'Club-383-7420
Police-114	Snack Bar-WMSC-43305	SDO/NCO-383-7234/7103

Würzburg Community (GE21R7)
APO New York 09801-5000

TELEPHONE NUMBER INFORMATION: Main installation numbers: Comm: 49-0931-889-XXXX, ETS: 350-XXXX, ATVN: 350-1110.

Location: From west on Autobahn E-3 take Heidingsfield exit to Rottendorfer Strasse north to Leighton Barracks. Take first right after Hq Building 6, proceed to Building 2. HE: p-40, D/1. NMC: Würzburg, 1 miles south.

Billeting Office: ATTN: Guest House, CZN-161. Building 2, Leighton Barracks. EX-6383. 0730-1600 hours. Other hours SDO, Building 6, EX-6283. Check in facility, check out 0900 hours daily. Government civilian employee billeting.

TML: Guest House, Building 2. All ranks. Leave or official duty. 22/2-bedroom, latrine bath. Refrigerator, BW TV, maid service, cribs $2.00, free washer/dryer. Older structure. Rates: Sponsor $14.00, each additional person $4.00. Maximum family $30.00. Duty can make reservations. Others Space-A.

TML: DV/VIP. Building 2, Officer 06+. Leave or official duty. EX-8308/8306. 2 separate bedroom suites, private bath. Kitchen, complete utensils, color TV, maid service, cribs $2.00, free washer/dryer. Older facility. Rates: Sponsor $16.00, each additional person $4.00. Maximum 3 persons. Duty can make reservations. Others Space-A.

DV/VIP: SGS, Protocol, Building 6. EX-8308/8306. 06/GS-15+. Retirees Space-A.

Other: Marienberg Castle. Annual Mozart Festival in summer. Famous Franken wine in the light of a thousand candles at the Würzburg Castle. See the old walled city of Rothenburg on the Talber, easy drive south of Würzburg.

TML Availability: Good, Oct-Mar. Difficult, other times.

Cafeteria-WBGC-706689	Enlisted Club-350-6238	Locator-350-98
Medical-116	NCO Club-350-6112	O'Club-350-6413
Police-114	Snack Bar-WBGC-706689	

Zweibrücken Air Base (GE22R7)
APO New York 09860-5000
CLOSED

GERMANY

Canadians Put Out The Welcome Mat!
Lodging for two....Under $11 U.S.

Sometimes, I get a little discouraged at R&R. How can I possible keep coming up with new bargains showing military how to *"travel on less per day...the military way?"* Then, out of the blue I learn of something new—from one of our subscribers, from the U.S. military directory, from a research trip or from another source.

Today is one of those happy days! We received the nicest letter from the Director General of Personnel Services at National Defence Headquarters in Ottawa, Canada.

"Since its inception in 1971, the **Temporary Military Lodging Around The World** book has been utilized by the Canadian Military. As stated in the introduction—once purchased the book pays for itself many times over. It is surprising that is has not made it on the best selling list, especially during these financially trying times. *(Ed's Note—Our books, which are characterized as Directories, are not eligible for consideration for that list.)*

"The purpose of this letter is to forward an addition for inclusion in the next edition under Canada in the Foreign Countries section. Canadian Forces Base Trenton is the largest air base in the Canadian Forces and is centrally located in Ontario, but not too far from Fort Drum and Griffis Air Force Base in New York.

"We look forward to welcoming our American military neighbours, active and retired, to Canadian Forces Base Trenton and the Yukon Lodge."

The new information will be included in the next edition of **Temporary Military Lodging Around The World**. Meanwhile, here is some basic info for our subscribers' use. The main installation phone numbers for the Canadian Forces Base Trenton, in Trenton, Ontario, are (613) 392-2811; ATVN or DSN 827-7011. Trenton is 100 miles east of Toronto on Hwy 401. There is no central billeting office. The Canadian address is: Base Commander, Attn: Yukon Lodge, Canadian Forces Base Trenton, Astra, Ontario KOK 1 BO.

Lodging is available at the Yukon Lodge, Bldg 76 and 77. It is available to all ranks, officer and enlisted. It may be used on leave or official duty, phone (613) 965-3793; desk is open 24 hours. Check out time is noon daily. There are 55 rooms with various 1-5 bedroom semi-private and private bath. Rooms have color TV, clock-radio, telephone, maid service, free cribs, coin washer/dryers. Yukon Lodge is an older structure. Rates are $6 Canadian plus tax per person (at press-time, this was $5.24 U.S. plus tax—figured at 1 U.S. dollar being worth 1.1445 Canadian dollars).

There are a limited number of DV/VIP accommodations for 0-6 and above (Colonel/Navy/USCG/PHS Captain). For these arrangements, call Base Protocol (613) 965-3379 (ATVN/DSN 827-3379).

We at R&R will look forward to hearing from our first subscribers who accept the hospitality of our Canadian Armed Forces friends.

Zweibrücken Community (GE29R7)
APO New York 09052-5000

TELEPHONE NUMBER INFORMATION: Main installation numbers: Comm: 49-06332-86-XXXX, ETS: 494-XXXX, ATVN: 494-1110.

Location: Take the Neurkirchen exit fm the Mannheim-Saarbrücken E-6 Autobahn. Follow signs to Kreuzberg Kaserne on Landstuhler Strasse. HE: p-39, G/2. NMC: Zweibrücken, in the city.

Billeting Office: Building 4206. EX-7166/6566. Duty days 0800-1630 hours. Other hours, SDO, Building 4000, ETS: 494-7145. Check in facility, check out 1200 hours. Government civilian employee billeting.

TML: BOQ. Building 4206. All ranks. Leave or official duty. 8/1-bedroom, shared bath; 4 separate bedrooms, private bath, suites. Refrigerator, color TV, maid service, free cribs/cots. Older structure. Rates: Sponsor $6.00, adult $4.00, maximum 4 persons per unit. Duty can make reservations. Others Space-A. **Pets allowed with approval of Deputy Community Cmdr.**

DV/VIP: Deputy Community Cmdr. EX-6647. 06+. Retirees Space-A.

242 — Temporary Military Lodging Around the World

GERMANY
Zweibrücken Community, continued

Other: Famous Zweibrücken Rose Garden, more than 70,000 roses on view.

TML Availability: Good year round.

Cafeteria-ZBNC-2982
Medical-116
Police-114

Enlisted Club-494-6642
NCO Club-494-6129
Snack Bar-494-6412

Locator-494-92
O'Club-494-6642
SDO/NCO-494-7145

GREECE

Hellenikon Air Base (GR01R9)
APO New York 09223-5000
CLOSED

Iraklion Air Station (GR02R9)
APO New York 09291-5000

TELEPHONE NUMBER INFORMATION: Main installation numbers: Comm: 30-81-761-281/2/3, ATVN: 668-1110.

Location: On the Greek Island of Crete. From Iraklion Airport, right at main entrance past the Greek Military base, next left. Straight for 20 minute drive to Gournes, AS on the left. HE: p-85, B/3. NMC: Iraklion, 8 miles west.

Billeting Office: ATTN: 7276th ABG/SVH. Building 208, North St. EX-3942/3842. 0730-2330 hours duty days. Other hours, Security Police EX-3246. Check in billeting, check out 1300 hours daily.

TML: TLF. Evina Villas. All ranks. Leave or official duty. 4/1-bedroom, private bath; 11/2-bedroom, private bath. Kitchen, complete utensils, color TV room & lounge, maid service, free cribs/cots, ice vending. Modern structure. Rates: $20.00 per family. Duty can make reservations. Others Space-A.

Temporary Military Lodging Around the World — 243

Iraklion Air Station, continued

GREECE

TML: VAQ. Royal Hotel. Enlisted all grades. Leave or official duty. 21/1-bedroom, hall bath. Refrigerator, color TV room & lounge, maid service. Modern structure.

Rates: $6.00 per person. Maximum 2 per room. Duty can make reservations. Others Space-A.

TML: VOQ. Building 208. Officer all grades, Enlisted E7-E9. Leave or official duty. 16/1-bedroom, shared bath; 4 separate bedroom, private bath (DV/VIP). A/C, color TV room & lounge, maid service, free cots, free washer/dryer, ice vending. Modern structure. Rates: $6.00 per person for rooms, maximum $18.00 per family; $10.00 per person DV/VIP. Duty can make reservations. Others Space-A.

DV/VIP: Building 208, Section 1. EX-3556. 06+. Retirees and lower grades Space-A.

Other: Knossos Palace, Archeological Site.

TML Availability: Good, winter and early spring. Difficult, summer months.

Cafeteria-3215	Enlisted Club-3316	Locator-3859/3426
Medical-3525	O'Club-3316	Police-3426
Snack Bar-3215		

HONG KONG

China Fleet Club (HK01R8)
Fleet House, 6 Arsenal Street
Wanchai, Hong Kong

TELEPHONE NUMBER INFORMATION: Main installation number: Comm: 852-5-296001.

Location: Located at 6 Arsenal Street, Wanchai, Hong Kong. Call for driving directions. NMC: Hong Kong, in the city.

Billeting Office: None. Check in at front desk. Comm: 5-296001.

TML: Service club. All ranks. Leave or official duty. The China Fleet Club is a non-government temporary military lodging facility which has provided lodging for active duty and retired American, British, and other NATO service personnel for many years. The club has 38 twin-bedded rooms, all of which have a private bath and color TV. Facilities included a restaurant, meeting room, lounges, auditorium, bowling alley, squash courts and a sauna. One of the club's featured attractions is a two-floor shopping mall which is administered by the U.S. Navy Contracting Department. Prices are closely monitored, vendors are carefully screened, so many high quality bargains are always on hand. Rates: HK$400 per night for officers, HK$300 per night for enlisted. Reservations can be secured with a check for one night's stay per week booked. All categories can make reservations.

TML Availability: Unknown.

244 — *Temporary Military Lodging Around the World*

ICELAND

Keflavik Naval Station (IC01R7)
FPO New York 09571-0334

TELEPHONE NUMBER INFORMATION: Main installation numbers: Comm: 354-25-0111 (From IC 22490), ATVN: 450-0111 (From USA), ATVN: 228-0111 (From Europe).

Location: IAP shares landing facilities with Naval Station. From Reykjavik seaport take Hwy S follow signs to Keflavik. Well marked. Naval Station is 4 km before town of Keflavik. HE: p-1, A/2. NMC: Reykjavik, 35 miles north.

Billeting Office: ATTN: BOQ. Building 761. EX-4333. 24 hours daily. Check in at billeting, check out 1200 hours daily. No government civilian employee billeting.

TML: Navy Lodge. Naval Station, Box 10. Building 786. All ranks. Leave or official duty. Comm: 354-25-2000-EX-7594. 31/1- & 2-bedroom, private bath. Kitchen (11 units), community kitchen, color TV room & lounge, maid service, free cribs/cots, coin washer/dryer, ice vending. Older structure. Rates: $20.00-28.00 per unit. Maximum 6 persons. All categories can make reservations.

TML: BOQ/BEQ. Buildings 636, 761, 762. All ranks. Leave or official duty. 61/1-bedroom, private bath; 4 separate bedrooms, private bath. Color TV room & lounge, maid service, free washer/dryer. Older structure. Rates: $5.50 per person. Duty can make reservations. Others Space-A.

DV/VIP: Commander Iceland Defense Force, Box 1, FPO NY 09571-5000. EX-4414. 05+. Retirees Space-A.

Other: A great undiscovered outdoor vacation land.

TML Availability: Lodge, good in winter months; billeting, fair. Lodge, difficult, Apr-Aug; billeting, poor.

All numbers are Commercial or ATVN extensions.

Cafeteria-2149/5287	Enlisted Club-4115	Locator-22490
Medical-3301	NCO Club-6126	O'Club-7004
Police-2000	Snack Bar-2149/5287	SDO/NCO-2100

ITALY

Admiral Carney Park (IT03R7)
Naples, IT
FPO New York 09521-1000

TELEPHONE NUMBER INFORMATION: Main installation numbers: Comm: 39-081-526-1579, ATVN: 625-4834.

Location: On the west coast of IT in Admiral Carney Park, 7 miles from Naples and 5 miles from US Naval Support Activity, Naples. HE: p-51, E/6. NMC: Naples, 7 miles south.

ITALY

Admiral Carney Park, continued

Billeting Office: NAVSUPPACT Rec Servicec, Box 13, US Naval Support Activity, FPO New York 09521-1000. Comm: 081-526-1579. ATVN: 625-4834. Reservations required. Check in facility, check out 1030 hours daily. Operates year round.

TML: Rec Facility. All ranks. Leave only. Accessible to handicapped. 26/1-bedroom cottages, latrine bath. Kitchenette, refrigerator, complete utensils, washer/dryer, all essential furniture. Rates: $25.00 per cabin. Maximum 4 per cabin. All categories can make reservations up to 3 months in advance.

Other: Pompeii, Herculanum, Isles of Capri, Ischia are nearby. Full rec park. For more details see Military RV, Camping & Rec Areas Around The World.

TML Availability: Good, winter months. Difficult, summer months.

Aviano Air Base (IT04R7)
APO New York 09293-5000

TELEPHONE NUMBER INFORMATION: Main installation numbers: Comm: 39-434-66-7520, ATVN: 632-7520.

Location: Adjacent to town of Aviano in Pordenone province. Thirty miles east of Udine, IT and 50 miles northeast of Venice. From A-28 North exit Pordenone to IT-159 for 8 miles to Aviano AB. HE: p-93, C/4. NMC: Pordenone, 8 miles north.

Billeting Office: Building 256, Ritchie St. 24 hours daily. Comm: 0434-65-2306. ATVN: 632-7262. Check in facility, check out 1200 hours daily. Government civilian employee billeting.

TML: VOQ/VAQ/TAQ. Buildings 230, 232, 273, 274. All ranks. Leave or official duty. 20 double rooms, private bath; 2/1-bedroom, private bath, suites (DV/VIP). Dependents OK. Rates: Moderate.

DV/VIP: PAO, Building T-8, Room 204, Comm: 04493-7-331. 06+.

TML Availability: Good, Dec-Jan. More difficult, other times.

Enlisted Club-2493	NCO Club-2493	Police-2200
SDO/NCO-2673		

Camp Darby (IT10R7)
APO New York 09019-5000

TELEPHONE NUMBER INFORMATION: Main installation numbers: Comm: 39-050-54-7111, ETS: 633-7225.

Location: Located midway between Livorno & Pisa. From Autostrade A-1 take Pisa Sud exit. Turn left and continue to end of road, left onto Via Aurelia (SS 1), right to S. Piero A'Grado & follow Camp Darby signs. HE: p-50, A/3. NMC: Pisa, 6 miles north.

Billeting Office: Building 303, EX-7225. Check in facility, check out 1000 hours daily. Reservations for Sea Pines Lodge 0700-2200 hours daily, EX-7225. Rec area open year round.

TML: Sea Pines Lodge. Building 836. All ranks. Leave or official duty. 24/1-bedroom, private bath. Sleeps up to 4 persons, 1 double or 2 twin beds, 2

ITALY
Camp Darby, continued

bunk beds. Refrigerator, community kitchen, limited utensils, color TV room & lounge, maid service, cribs ($3.00), cots ($5.00), washer/dryer. Modern structure. Rates: $25.00 1 person, $35.00 2 persons, $40.00 3 persons, $45.00 4 persons. Pets allowed, $3.50 per night + $50.00 damage deposit.

DV/VIP: Commander, 8th Support Group, Building 302. Comm: 050-54-7505. 06/GS-13+. Retirees Space-A.

Other: Famous Leaning Tower of Pisa 6 miles away, walled city of Lucca 20 miles, and Florence, the art city, 75 miles away.

TML Availability: Good, winter months. Difficult, summer months.

Cons Club-7462   Police-7575   SDO/NCO-7575/7083

Comiso Air Station (IT11R7)
APO New York 09694-5000

TELEPHONE NUMBER INFORMATION: Main installation numbers: Comm: 39-932-73-1111, ATVN: 628-1110.

Location: The air station is located 14 miles northwest of Ragusa in the southeast corner of the island of Sicily. RM: p-53, E/5. NMC: Ragusa, 14 miles southeast.

Billeting Office: ATTN: 487 CSG/SVH, Building 241, Vittoria Rd, 0800-2400 daily. EX-2560. Check in billeting, check out 1200 hours. No government civilian employee billeting.

TML: TLF. Building 201. All ranks. Leave or official duty. Accessible to handicapped. 32 separate bedrooms, private bath. A/C, free cribs/cots, ice vending, kitchenette, housekeeping service, refrigerator, color TV, complete utensils, washer/dryer. Modern structure. Rates: $24.00 per room. Pets allowed with $100.00 deposit for demages.

TML: VAQ. Building 241. Enlisted all grades. Leave or official duty. Accessible to handicapped. 15/1-bedroom, private bath. A/C, community kitchen, free cots, ice vending, maid service, refrigerator, color TV in room and lounge, washer/dryer, vending machines. Modern structure. Rates: $6.00 per person. Maximum 2 per unit. Duty can make reservations. Others Space-A.

TML: VOQ. Building 241. Officer all grades. Leave or official duty. Accessible to handicapped. 10/1-bedroom, private bath/shared bath; 3 separate bedrooms, private bath. A/C, free cots, ice vending, maid service, refrigerator, color TV, free washer/dryer. New TVs/drapes in 1989. Modern structure. Rates: $6.00 per person. Duty can make reservations. Others Space-A.

DV/VIP: Protocol Office, Building 107, Comm: 932-73-2608, ATVN: 628-2787. 06/GS-14+.

TML Availability: Best, Dec. though March. Difficult during summer months.

Enlisted Club-EX-2385   Locator-EX-2354   Medical-116
NCO Club-EX-2385   O'Club-EX-2385   Police-EX-2313
Snack Bar-EX-2607   SDO/NCO-EX-2439

Temporary Military Lodging Around the World — 247

ITALY

La Maddalena Navy Support Office (IT13R7)
FPO New York 09533-0051

TELEPHONE NUMBER INFORMATION: Main installation numbers: Comm: 39-789-722318, ATVN: 726-2141.

Location: Located on the northern tip of the island of Sardinia. Take the main road (IT-125) north from Olbia to Palau, then take a 15 minute ferry ride to La Maddalena and follow signs to the installation. HE: p-54, C/1. NMC: Olbia, 28 miles southeast.

Billeting Office: Calabro Hall, 0800-1700 daily. Comm: 790223, ATVN: 726-1223. For Reservations call Comm: 722-318, ATVN: 726-2971. After hours contact NSO at Comm: 790-338. Check in facility, check out anytime.

TML: BEQ/BOQ. Building 300. All ranks. Leave or official duty. Accessible to handicapped. 17/1-bedroom, 1 bed, shared bath; 36/1-bedroom, 2 beds, shared bath; 12 separate bedrooms, private bath. A/C, ice vending, maid service, refrigerator, color TV, washer/dryer. New TVs in 1989. Modern structure. Rates: no charge. Maximum 2 per room.

DV/VIP: Protocol Office, Building 300, Apt 9. Comm: 722318, ATVN: 726-2141. 06+ Lower grades may use if BOQ is full.

TML Availability: Best after Sept. Difficult during summer months.

Enlisted Club-84283   Medical-EX-275   Police-EX-244
Snack Bar-EX-253   SDO/NCO-EX-338

Naples Naval Support Activity (IT05R7)
FPO New York 09521-1000

TELEPHONE NUMBER INFORMATION: Main installation numbers: Comm: 39-81-724-1110, ATVN: 625-1110.

Location: In Naples, a large port city south of Rome on the N-S Autostrada (toll road) and IT-1. HE: p-51, E/6. NMC: Naples, in the city.

Billeting Office: BEQ. Building 71. EX-4842. Check in facility, check out 1200 hours daily. Government civilian employee billeting.

TML: BEQ. Building 71. Enlisted all grades. Leave or official duty. Single rooms, hall and latrine bath. Refrigerator, color TV lounge, essentials, maid service, free washer/dryer, food/ice vending, microwaves in lounges. Older structure. New carpets/TVs '89. New quarters complex anticipated '92. Rates: $4.00 per person. Dependents not authorized. Duty can make reservations. Others Space-A.

DV/VIP: Building 70, EX-4567, NSA Protocol Office.

Other: The following support facility are available: AMEXCO, APO, auto craft/hobby, bank, car rental, package store, convenience store, medical, ITT, coin washer/dryer, outdoor rec equipment, BX, snack bar, theater, nursery, O'Club, CPO Club, Enlisted Club, Rod & Gun Club, and chaplain.

TML Availability: Extremely limited. Best, winter.

Cafeteria-4591   Enlisted Club-4794   Locator-4556
Medical-300/301   NCO Club-4794   Police-4686
SDO/NCO-4546

248 — *Temporary Military Lodging Around the World*

ITALY

San Vito dei Normanni Air Station (IT07R7)
APO New York 09240-5000

TELEPHONE NUMBER INFORMATION: Main installation numbers: Comm: 39-0831-42-1110, ATVN: 622-1110 .

Location: Island on the the heel of Italy's boot midway between the port cities of Brindisi and the town of San Vito dei Normanni. The AS is on SS-379 serving the area. Four miles from the Adriatic shore. Follow the signs to "U S Base". HE: p-52, G/2. NMC: Brindisi, 5 miles south.

Billeting Office: Building 455, Jefferson Ave. 0700-0100 daily. EX-3906. Check in facility, check out 1100 hours daily. Government civilian employee billeting.

TML: TLQ/VOQ/VAQ/DVQ. Buildings 601-603, 435. All ranks. Leave or official duty. 15/1-bedroom, hall bath; 10/1-bedroom, private bath; 33 separate bedrooms, private bath. Kitchen, complete utensils, A/C, color TV room & lounge, maid service, free cribs/cots, free washer/dryer, ice vending. Modern structure, renovated. Rates: $6.00-$10.00 per person (VOQ/VAQ/DVQ), $24.00 per unit (TLQ). Duty can make reservations. Others Space-A.

DV/VIP: Protocol Office. ATVN: 622-3482. O6/GS-15+. Retirees & lower grades Space-A.

TML Availability: Best, Nov.-Apr. More difficult, other times.

Cafeteria-3640	Consolidated Club-3691	Locator-3408
Medical-3511	Police-114	Snack Bar-3640
SDO/NCO-1110		

Sigonella Naval Air Station (IT01R7)
FPO New York 09523-5000

TELEPHONE NUMBER INFORMATION: Main installation numbers: Comm: 39-095-56-1110 (NAS I), 86-1110 (NAS II), ATVN: 624-1110.

Location: On the east coast of the Island of Sicily. Accessible from A-19 or IT-417. HE: p-53, E/4. NMC: Catania, IT, 10 miles northeast.

Billeting Office: ATTN: PAO, Air Term, EX-5575. 24 hours daily. Check in facility, check out 1200 hours daily. Government civilian employee billeting.

TML: BOQ/BEQ. All ranks. Leave or official duty. EX-2300/1. 42/1-bedroom, private bath; 11 separate bedroom suites, private bath (DV/VIP). A/C, color TV, maid service, free washer/dryer, ice vending. Older structure. Rates: $8.00 per person. Maximum $25.00 per family. Maximum 3 per unit. Duty can make reservations. Others Space-A.

DV/VIP: PAO, Building 545. EX-5251/5252. O6+. Retirees Space-A. No dependents under age of 15 permitted.

Other: Mount Etna, active, snow-capped volcano. Taormina, resort area.

TML Availability: Good, Dec.-Jan. Difficult, other times.

Cafeteria-4272	Enlisted Club-4263/4	Locator-0
Medical-4333 (NAS I)	O'Club-4204	Police-4201/2
Snack Bar-5469	SDO/NCO-5253/5255	

Temporary Military Lodging Around the World — 249

ITALY

Vicenza Palladio (IT06R7)
Caserma Carlo Ederle
APO New York 09168-5000

TELEPHONE NUMBER INFORMATION: Main installation numbers: Comm: 39-0444-51-5190, ATVN: 634-7301.

Location: Take the Vicenza east exit from the Number 4 Autostrada which runs from Trieste to Milano. Follow signs to Caserma Carlo Ederle or SETAF Hq's. HE: p-91, H/6. NMC: Vicenza, in the city.

Billeting Office: Building 136, 8th St. 0600-2000 hours daily. Comm: 0444-51-5190. ATVN: 634-7301. Other hours, SDO in Building 109, EX-7711. Check in facility, check out 0900 hours daily. Government civilian employee billeting.

TML: Guest House/DVQ. Building 136. All ranks. Leave or official duty. Accessible to handicapped. 25/3-bedroom suites, private bath; 24 DVQ suites, private bath. Kitchen, complete utensils, A/C (DVQ only), color TV, maid service, cots, cribs ($10.00), VCRs. Modern structure, remodeled '87. Rates: Sponsor $24.00, each additional person $10.00 (Guest House); Sponsor $35.00, each additional person $10.00 (DVQ). Maximum 6 per room. Reservations are required. **Pets $5.00 per day.**

DV/VIP: Vicenza Billeting Activity, Hq 22nd ASG/USMCAV, DEH, Building 136, Room 601, ATVN: 634-7712. 05/GS-15+. Retirees Space-A.

Other: Cities of Venice and Verona in easy driving distance.

TML Availability: Good, Oct-Nov. Difficult, May-Sep.

Cafeteria-500447	NCO Club-7869	O'Club-7886
Police-7626	Snack Bar-7013	SDO/NCO-7711

JAPAN

Atsugi Naval Air Facility (JA14R8)
FPO Seattle 98767-5000

TELEPHONE NUMBER INFORMATION: Main installation numbers: Comm: 81-462-51-1520-EX, ATVN: Dial Comm number then ask for EX-6880/1/2/3.

Location: In central Japan off Tokyo Bay. Yokohama is 15 miles east and Tokyo is 28 miles northeast. Camp Zama is 5 miles north. NMC: Tokyo, 28 miles northeast.

Billeting Office/Navy Lodge: Building 987. Navy Lodge. Box 10. FPO Seattle 98767. All ranks. Leave or official duty. Accessible to handicapped. ATVN: 228-6880. 0700-2300 hours daily. Check out 1100 hours. 30/1-bedroom, 2 double beds, private bath. Kitchen, free cribs, essentials, ice vending, maid service, refrigerator, special facilities for disabled American veterans, color TV lounge, washer/dryer. Modern structure. Rates: $30.00 per unit. Maximum 4 persons per unit. All categories can make reservations.

TML Availability: Extremely limited. Best Jan-May.

250 — *Temporary Military Lodging Around the World*

JAPAN

Camp S. D. Butler Marine Corps Base (JA07R8)
FPO Seattle 98773-5000

TELEPHONE NUMBER INFORMATION: Main installation numbers: Comm: 81-098892-5111, ATVN: 635-2191/3749.

Location: Four miles south of Okinawa City on Hwy 330 at Camp Foster 2 miles north of Futenma. NMC: Naha, 7 miles south.

Billeting Office: ATTN: FACS, Billeting/Housing Coordinator. Building 11. ATVN: 635-2191/3749. 0730-2400 daily. Other hours, Building 1, OOD. ATVN: 635-7218/2644. Check in facility, check out 1200 hours daily. Government civilian employee billeting.

TML: TLF. Courtney Lodge. Building 2540, Camp Courtney. All ranks. Leave or official duty. ATVN: 622-9578. 16 suites, private bath. Refrigerator, A/C, cable color TV room & lounge, maid service, cribs/cots, coin washer/dryer. Modern structure. Rates: $25.00 per unit. Maximum 3 per unit.

TML: TLF. Hansen Lodge. Building 2540, Camp Hansen. All ranks. Leave or official duty. ATVN: 623-4511. Same as Courtney except 18/1-bedroom, shared bath. Older structure. Rates: $8.00 per room. Maximum 2 per room. Reservations accepted.

TML: Kuwae Lodge. Building 400, Camp Lester. All ranks. Leave or official duty. ATVN: 634-0214. 165 rooms with kitchen. Washer/dryer, playroom, rec rooms. Rates: $22.00-$26.00 single, $44.00-$46.00 double adjoining rooms, $66.00-$70.00 3 room suite. Reservations accepted 30 days in advance.

TML: TQ. Building 11, Camp Foster. All ranks. Leave or official duty. ATVN: 635-2191/3749. 20 separate bedroom, living room, private bath. Kitchen, A/C, color TV, maid service, free washer/dryer, video cassette reception in room. Older structure, renovated. Rates: vary according to rank and status. Duty can make reservations. Others Space-A.

TML: VOQ. Buildings 217, 219, MCAS(H), Futenma. Officer all grades. Leave or official duty. Same as above except: 12/1-bedroom, private bath; 4 separate bedroom, private bath; 2 suites, maximum 2 per suite. Maximum 1 per room. Rates: same as Camp Foster. Duty can make reservations. Others Space-A.

TML: DV/VIP. Buildings 340, 341, 344, Coral Hill. Call for eligible grades. Leave or official duty. ATVN: 635-2191/3749 (Protocol). 5/3-bedroom cottages, private bath; 1/4-bedroom cottage, private bath. Kitchen, utensils, color TV, maid service, free washer/dryer. Older structure. Rates: vary according to rank, status, and number of dependents. Maximum 6 per unit. Duty can make reservations. Others Space-A.

TML: DV/VIP. Buildings 4205, 4222, 4515. Same as above. Rates: vary according to rank, status, and number of dependents.

DV/VIP: Protocol Office, Building 1, SD Bulter MCB, ATVN: 635-7274. Protocol Office, Building 4225, III MEF, Camp Courtney, ATVN: 622-7749. Protocol Office, Building 1, 1st MAW, SC Butler MCB, ATVN: 635-2901.

TML Availability: Good. Best, Aug-Mar. More difficult, other times.

Cafeteria-635-4100	Enlisted Club-635-4842	Locator-635-7456
Medical-634-1756	NCO Club-635-5242	Police-635-7441

Temporary Military Lodging Around the World — 251

JAPAN

Camp Zama (JA06R8)
APO San Francisco 96343-5000

TELEPHONE NUMBER INFORMATION: Main installation numbers: Comm: 81-4062-51-1520 (ask for 233-3293 or 233-4474), ATVN: 233-3293, 233-4474.

Location: 25 miles south of Tokyo or north of Yokohama. Excellent rail service. NMC: Tokyo, 25 miles north.

Billeting Office: ATTN: AJGH-EH-HB, Building 563, Sand St. ATVN: 233-3293/4474. 24 hours daily. Check in facility, check out 1200 hours daily. Government civilian employee billeting.

TML: Guest House. Building 780. All ranks. Leave or official duty. 1st floor accessible to handicapped. 5/1-bedroom, hall bath and latrine bath; 14/2-bedroom, hall bath and latrine bath; 2/3-bedroom, private bath. Utensils, refrigerator, community kitchen, microwave, A/C, color TV, maid service, cribs/cots ($3.00), free washer/dryer. Older structure. Rates: Sponsor $10.00-$18.00 depending on rank, $5.00 each additional person. Duty can make reservations. Others Space-A.

TML: Guest House, Coe Hall. All ranks. Leave or official duty. 1st floor accessible to handicapped. 6 separate bedroom, 4 with private bath, 2 with hall bath/latrine bath; 3/2-bedroom, 1 with private bath, 2 with hall bath/latrine bath. 1/3-bedroom, hall bath/latrine bath. A/C, cots ($3.00), kitchenette, maid service, color TV, complete utensils, free washer/dryer. Older structure. Rates: Sponsor $13.00-$18.00, $4.00 each additional person. Duty can make reservations. Others Space-A.

TML: VOQ/VEQ. Building 742. All ranks. Leave or official duty. 1st floor accessible to handicapped. 38/1-bedroom, private bath. Refrigerator, bar stocked, cribs/cots ($5.00), community kitchen, A/C, color TV and VCR, maid service, free washer/dryer, vending machine. Modern structure. Renovated 1988/89. Rates: Sponsor $12.00, $3.00 each additional person. Duty can make reservations. Others Space-A. **Pets boarded at clinic for $4.00 per night.**

TML: DVQ. Building 550. Officer O6+. Leave or official duty. 1st floor accessible to handicapped. 12 separate bedroom, private bath. A/C, community kitchen, cots/cribs ($5.00), maid service, refrigerator, TV and VCR, washer/dryer in building. Modern structure. New carpeting/TVs in 1989. Rates: Sponsor: $15.00, $5.00 each additional person. Duty can make reservations. Others Space-A. **Pets boarded at clinic for $4.00 per day.**

DV/VIP: USARJ Protocol Office, Building 101. EX-3-4019. O7+. Retirees Space-A.

TML Availability: Guest House good, Oct-Apr. Difficult, other times. VOQ/VEQ difficult most of the time.

Cafeteria-233-4255   Cons Club-233-4253   Medical-233-8455
Police-233-3473   Snack Bar-233-4534   SDO/NCO-233-3514

Iwakuni Marine Corps Air Station (JA12R8)
FPO Seattle 98764-5001

TELEPHONE NUMBER INFORMATION: Main installation numbers: Comm: 81-0827-21-4171, ATVN: 236-5409.

Location: Facing the Inland Sea on the south portion of the island of Honshu, 450 miles southwest of Tokyo, .5 miles off JA-188 on JA-189. NMC: Hiroshima, 25 miles north.

Billeting Office: Building 603. Comm: 0827-21-4171-EX-3181. ATVN: 236-5409.

JAPAN
Iwakuni Marine Corps Air Station, continued

24 hours daily. Check in Building 603, check out 1200 hours daily. Government civilian employee billeting.

TML: Transient Billeting. Buildings 330, 420, 511, 603, 611. All ranks. Leave or official duty. Some facilities accessible to handicapped. EX-3221. 19/1-bedroom, latrine bath (Enlisted); 51 separate bedroom, private bath (SNCOs and Officers); 1/2-bedroom, private bath (DV-Shogun House); 17/1-bedroom, two beds, latrine bath (enlisted). Kitchenette (Building 603), refrigerator, limited utensils (Building 603), A/C, color TV, maid service, cribs/cots, ice vending. Modern structure. Rates: Sponsor and adults $5.00 for Officers, $4.00 for SNCOs and $3.00 for E-5 and below, 12 and under $2.00. Duty can make reservations. Others Space-A.

DV/VIP: Protocol Office, Building 360, ATVN: 236-4211.

TML Availability: Good. Difficult, Feb. and Mar.

Enlisted C-3506/3122	Locator-3114/4211	Medical-5571
NCO Club-3363	O'Club-3480	Police-3222
Snack Bar-4773		

Kadena Air Base (JA08R8)
APO San Francisco 96239-5000

TELEPHONE NUMBER INFORMATION: Main installation numbers: Comm: 81-61172-41100, ATVN: 630-1110.

Location: Take Hwy 58 North from Naha to Kadena's Gate 1 on the right immediately north of USMC Air Station Futenma. NMC: Naha, 12 miles south.

Billeting Office: ATTN: 18 SVS/SVH. Building 332, Beeson Ave. ATVN: 634-1100. Comm: 81-61172-43817. 24 hours daily. Check in at billeting, check out 1200 hours daily. Government civilian employee billeting.

TML: TLF. Family Quarters. Building 437. All ranks. Leave or official duty. Accessible to handicapped. 58 apartments. A/C, refrigerator, kitchen, complete utensils, color TV, maid service, free cribs, free rollaway, free washer/dryer. Modern structure. Rates: $35.00 per unit. Maximum 6 persons per unit. Duty can make reservations. Others Space-A.

TML: VAQ. Buildings 317, 322, 504, 506, 509, 510. Enlisted all grades. 58/1-bedroom, private bath. 120 separate bedrooms, semi-private bath. 30/2-bedroom, private bath. A/C, maid service, refrigerator, color TV, free washer/dryer. Rates: $5.50 per person per night. Maximum 2 persons. Duty can make reservations. Others Space-A.

TML: VOQ. Buildings 304, 306, 311, 314, 315, 316, 318, 502, 508, 512. Officer all grades. 157/1-bedroom, private bath. 40 separate bedroom, semi-private bath. A/C, maid service, refrigerator, color TV, free washer/dryer. Rates: $8.50 per person. Maximum 2 persons. Duty can make reservations. Others Space-A.

TML: DV/VIP. Buildings 315, 78, 2024. Officer O6+. Leave or official duty. 20/1-bedroom, private bath. 2/3-bedroom, private bath. A/C, essentials, kitchen, complete utensils, maid service, color TV lounge, free washer/dryer. Rates: $8.50 per person. Duty can make reservations. Others Space-A.

DV/VIP: Protocol Office, Building 10. ATVN: 634-3548. O6+.

Other: Aerial Port for Okinawa, JA. Great Space-A departure point, JA, RK, RP all 3 hours flying time.

Kadena Air Base, continued

JAPAN

TML Availability: Good, Dec-Jan. Difficult, spring & summer.

Cafeteria-633-3183
NCO Club-634-0740
Locator-634-1110
O'Club-634-4878
Medical-634-3333
Police-634-2475

Misawa Air Base (JA03R8)
APO San Francisco 96519-5000

TELEPHONE NUMBER INFORMATION: Main installation numbers: Comm: 81-176-53-5181, ATVN: 226-1110.

Location: On the northeast portion of the Island of Honshu, 400 miles north of Tokyo. NMC: Hachinohe City, 17 miles southeast.

Billeting Office: Building 669. EX-3526. 24 hours daily. Check in billeting, check out 1200 hours daily.

TML: TLF. Buildings 696-699. All ranks. Leave or official duty. 16/2-bedroom apartments, shared bath. Kitchen, refrigerator, utensils, color TV, maid service, free cribs/cots, free washer/dryer, ice vending. Older structure. Rates: $28.00-$48.00 per unit. Duty can make reservations. Others Space-A.

TML: VOQ. Buildings 662, 664, 674. Officer 01-06. Leave or official duty. 16/1-bedroom, private bath, cottages; 8/2-bedroom, shared bath. Community kitchen, refrigerator, color TV, maid service, free washer/dryer, ice vending. Older structure, renovated. Rates: $8.00 per person. Duty can make reservations. Others Space-A.

TML: VAQ. Building 669. Enlisted all grades. Leave or official duty. 20/1-bedroom, latrine bath; 2 separate bedroom, private bath, suites (E9). Refrigerator, color TV, maid service, free washer/dryer, ice vending. Rates: $8.00 per person. Duty can make reservations. Others Space-A.

TML: DV/VIP. Building 17. Officer 06+ (M&F). Leave or official duty. 5/1-bedroom, private bath, suites. Refrigerator, A/C, color TV, maid service. Modern structure, renovated. Rates: $8.00 per person. Duty can make reservations. Others Space-A.

DV/VIP: 432 TFW/CCE. EX-4804. 06+. Retirees Space-A.

Other: BX, cafeteria, commissary, gas station, medical, NCO Club, O'Club, package store, theater. Call 17653-5181-0000 for information.

TML Availability: Good, Nov-Dec. Difficult, other times.

The New Sanno US Forces Center (JA01R8)
APO San Francisco 96503-5000

TELEPHONE NUMBER INFORMATION: Main installation numbers: Comm: 81-03-440-7871-EX-7121, ATVN: 229-7121 (reservations).

Location: At 4-12-20 Minami Azabu, Minato-ku, Tokyo 106, a five minute walk from nearest subway station, Hiroo. NMI: Tokyo Administrative Facility, 10 miles.

Description of Area: The New Sanno US Forces Center, which opened in October 1983, is located in a quiet residential area not far from downtown Tokyo. In fact it's only a five-minute walk from The New Sanno to the nearest subway station, Hiroo, so that all the tourist attractions that make Tokyo an exciting city

JAPAN
New Sanno US Forces Center, continued

to visit are easily accessible to New Sanno guests. The New Sanno is a completely modern hotel which offers its military guests the finest accommodations and food service at affordable rates. Each of the 149 guest rooms features modern furnishings and a private bath, as well as the comfort of central air conditioning. Two of the suites are traditional Japanese-style for guests who want to enjoy the full flavor of the Orient. Guests of the New Sanno will find three restaurants located within the facility: Emporium, a family restaurant; Wellingtons, which features fine dining, and Kikuya, a Japanese-style steak house. Also available are a cocktail lounge and a convenient 24-hour snack bar. Entertainment and special events are scheduled on a regular basis in The New Sanno's main ballroom which can seat up to 500 guests.

If you are interested in touring local attractions, or desire tickets for theater, concerts or sports events, the travel service at The New Sanno can make all the necessary arrangements. The travel service can also book your airline or steamship reservations for other portions of your itinerary. If you are traveling on commercial airlines and arriving at Tokyo's Narita International Airport, an economical airport express bus is available to transport you into the city and directly to the front door of the New Sanno. Bus transportation is also available for Space-A travelers arriving at Yokota Air Base. Up-to-date information on the bus schedule is available at the Yokota MAC terminal. The New Sanno is a joint-services facility operated by the Navy but supported by all branches of the U S military (active duty, retired and active duty reserve) and their dependents as well as DoD Civilian employees assigned to Japan.

Reservations: It is recommended that you make reservations preferably 1 month in advance with 1 night's deposit for each room reserved. Reservations must be accompanied by name, rank or grade, service, duty status, SSN, full address and telephone number of requesting individual. Also indicate clearly the dates of your arrival and departure, the number of adults and children in the party, and number of rooms needed, if more than one. Deposits can be charged to VISA, MasterCard, American Express, or Diner's Club by giving your card number, signature, and its expiration date. Deposits can be refunded only if notice of cancellation is received three (3) days or more before arrival date. For reservations write: The New Sanno, APO San Francisco 96503-5000. Comm: 81-3-440-7871-EX-7121, ATVN: 229-7121 (reservations), TELEX: 242-7125 SANTEL J, FAX: 229-7102. Check-out time is 1200 hours. Special requests for a late check-out will be accommodated when conditions permit for a charge. Check-in cannot be assured before 1500 hours.

Eligibility: Active duty, retirees, their guests and dependents and surviving spouses; reservists with orders or pay vouchers to prove active duty status; federal civilian employees and non-DoD personnel with DoD orders assigning them to, or authorizing travel through, Japan, or documentation that they are traveling under the auspices of the US Embassy, Tokyo, or the UN Command.

Room Rates for the New Sanno U S Forces Center

Room Type	No.	I*	II*	III*	IV*
Single (Queen bed)	43	$25	$32	$38	$52
Double (Queen + single bed)	78	$35	$41	$48	$65
King Suite (King + sofa)	17	$50	$54	$58	$76
Twin Suite (Twins + sofa)	3	$50	$54	$58	$76
Family Suite (Qn + bunk rm)	2	$50	$61	$72	$90
Family Room (Delux Twin)	1	$50	$61	$72	$90
Japanese Suite	2	$63	$68	$74	$94

*I: E1-E5 and comparable DoD civilian grades; *II: E6-03, WO1-WO4, comparable DoD civilian grades, (disabled American veterans, unremarried widows, orphans with DD1173); *III: 04-010 and comparable DoD civilian grades; *IV: retired and non-DoD personnel.

TML Availability: Good, most of the year.

Temporary Military Lodging Around the World — 255

JAPAN

Okuma Resort—Okinawa (JA09R8)
Kadena AB, APO San Francisco 96239-5000

TELEPHONE NUMBER INFORMATION: Main installation numbers: Comm: 81-098-041-5164, ATVN: 634-4322.

Location: On Hwy 58, 50 miles north of Kadena AB. Left off Hwy 58 before Hentona. NMC: Naha, JA 62 miles south.

Billeting Office: ATTN: Leisure Resources Center, Schilling Rec Center, 18th CSW/SSRS, APO San Francisco 96239-5000. Building 116. Reservation required up to 60 days in advance. 0700-2200 hours daily (summer), W-M (winter). Check in 1500 hours at facility, check out 1100 hours daily. Operates year round.

TML: Rec Cabana's. All ranks. Leave or official duty. 7 cabana's with 64 rooms, private bath/share bath. Refrigerator, A/C, color TV (some), maid service, free cribs/cots ($3.00), free washer/dryer, ice vending (small fee), fully furnished. Concrete block construction. Rates: $15.00 1 room, 2 double beds, single bath; $20.00 1 room, 1 single/1 double or 2 double beds, private bath; $25.0 2-room or VIP suites. 2 single/2 double or 4 double beds, private bath. All categories can make reservations.

DV/VIP: Protocol, Building 10, 313 Air Division, Kadena AB, Okinawa. EX-0106. 06+. Retirees and lower grades Space-A.

Other: Great beach rec area. For full details see Military Living's Military RV, Camping & Rec Areas Around The World.

TML Availability: Good, Nov-Dec. Difficult, other times.

Tama Hills Recreation Center (JA10R8)
Yokota Air Base
APO San Francisco 96328-5000

TELEPHONE NUMBER INFORMATION: Main installation numbers: Comm: 81-0423-77-7009, ATVN: 224-3421/3422.

Location: Fifteen miles southeast of Yokota AB. NMC: Tokyo, 45 mile train ride.

Billeting Office: 475 ABW/SSRL, Yokota AB, APO San Francisco 96328-5000. 24 hours daily. ATVN: 224-3409. For reservations call Comm: 0423-77-7009 or ATVN: 224-3420/3421. Check in at facility, check out 1100 hours daily. Operates year round. Reservations required with first days rent.

TML: Rec Lodge and cabins. All ranks. Leave or official duty. Reservations required. 18/1-bedroom, private bath, and 10 separate bedroom, private bath; 6 cottages, private bath. Refrigerator, A/C, color TV, maid service, cots, washer/dryer (.50), ice vending. Rates: $20.00 per person leave status; $15.00 per person active duty. All categories can make reservations. **Pets allowed.**

Other: Great Rec Area near Tokyo. For complete details see Military RV, Camping & Rec Areas Around The World.

TML Availability: Good, Oct-Mar. Difficult, other times.

Cafeteria-224-3421-EX-22/51   Police-224-3421-EX-40

256 — *Temporary Military Lodging Around the World*

JAPAN

Tokyo Administration Facility (JA02R8)
APO San Francisco 96503-0004

TELEPHONE NUMBER INFORMATION: Main installation numbers: Comm: 81-03-440-7881, ATVN: 229-3270/3345.

Location: At #7-23-17 Roppongi, Minato-ku, Tokyo. Near Imperial Palace and 10 miles by taxi from New Sanno Hotel. NMC: Tokyo, in the city.

Billeting Office: Building 1, Room 419, Hardy Barracks. EX-3270/3345. 24 hours daily. Check in at facility, check out 1200 hours daily. Government civilian employee billeting.

TML: VOQ/BEQ. All ranks. Leave or official duty. EX-3270/3345. 19/1-bedroom, shared bath; 2 separate bedroom suites, private bath. Refrigerator, community kitchen, A/C, color TV, maid service, cribs, free washer/dryer. Older structure. Remodeled July '87. Rates: Sponsor $10.00-$15.00, each additional person $2.00-5.00. Maximum per family $30.00. Reservation info not provided. **Pets allowed.**

DV/VIP: Call Camp Zama, Building 101, Room W-223. ATVN: 233-4019, for assistance.

TML Availability: Good. Best months Jan-May.

Cafeteria-229-3480

Yokosuka Fleet Activities (JA05R8)
Box 40, Code 450
FPO Seattle 98762-5000

TELEPHONE NUMBER INFORMATION: Main installation numbers: Comm: 81-0468-26-1911, (Dial 011 from JA), ATVN: 234-1110.

Location: About 20 miles south of Tokyo and 25 miles north of Yokohama. NMC: Tokyo, 20 miles north. Excellent train service.

Billeting Office: Building G-22, Clements St. Comm: 0468-26-1911-EX-7777, ATVN: 234-7777 (BEQ); Comm: 0468-26-1911-EX-7317, ATVN: 234-7317 (BOQ). 24 hours daily. Navy Lodge: Fleet Activities, Code 700, FPO Seattle 98762-5000. Check in facility, check out before 1200 hours daily. Government civilian employee billeting.

TML: Navy Lodge. Building J-197-J-200 (main building). All ranks. Leave or official duty. EX-7270. 81/1-bedroom, private bath; 27/2-bedroom, private bath; 19/1-bedroom, hall bath. Kitchen (12 room), refrigerator (all), utensils, A/C, color TV room & lounge, maid service, free cribs/cots, coin washer/dryer, ice vending. Modern structure '80. Rates: $19.00 latrine bath, $27.00 private bath. Maximum 6 persons each unit. No dependent children without sponsor. Reservations accepted.

TML: BEQ. Buildings 1492, 1721. Enlisted all grades. Leave or official duty. 232/1-bedroom, 3 beds, private bath. Refrigerator, A/C, color TV room & lounge, maid service, free washer/dryer. Modern structure. Rates: $3.00 per person. Maximum 3 per room. Duty can make reservations. Others Space-A.

TML: BOQ. Buildings 1556, 1723. Officer all grades. Leave or official duty. 95/1-bedroom, private bath. Kitchen, A/C, color TV room and lounge, maid service, free washer/dryer, barber shop. Modern structure. Rates: $5.00 per person. Duty can make reservations. Others Space-A. Note: most rooms have only 1 single bed.

Temporary Military Lodging Around the World — 257

JAPAN

Yokosuka Fleet Activities, continued

TML: CPOQ. Building 1475. Enlisted E7-E9. Leave or official duty. 62/1-bedroom, private bath. Refrigerator, community kitchen, A/C, color TV room & lounge, maid service, free washer/dryer, ice vending. Modern structure. Rates: $2.00 per person. Duty can make reservations. Others Space-A. Note: all beds are singles with limited room for cots.

TML: Other. NASU Lodge. 100 miles north of Tokyo. Rec Service Office. EX-5613/7306. Two-story wood-frame building accommodates up to 26 persons. Japanese style floor and bath. Kitchen and lodging requirements. Near many rec areas for skiing, fishing, hiking, horseback riding. Reservations taken 1 month in advance. Call for rates. Group rates available. All ranks.

DV/VIP: Protocol Office, Comm: 0468-26-1911-EX-5685, ATVN: 234-7317. 07+. Retirees Space-A.

TML Availability: Good. Somewhat difficult, June-Sep.

Cafeteria-7386/5782	CPO Club-7751	Enlisted Club-7718
Locator-213	O'Club-7318	Police-5347
Snack Bar-6183	SDO/NCO-5000	

Yokota Air Base (JA04R8)
APO San Francisco 96328-5000

TELEPHONE NUMBER INFORMATION: Main installation numbers: Comm: 81-425-52-2511, ATVN: 248-1101.

Location: Take JA-16 South from Tokyo. AB is 1 mile west of Fussa JA. Clearly marked. NMC: Tokyo, 35 miles northeast.

Billeting Office: ATTN: SVH Billeting. Building 10, Bobzien Ave & 1st St. Comm: 425-52-2511-EX-5-7712. ATVN: 225-9270. 24 hours daily. Check in billeting, check out 1200 hours daily. Government civilian employee billeting.

TML: TLF. Building 10. All ranks. Leave or official duty. EX-9270. 31/4-bedroom, shared bath. Kitchen, utensils, A/C, color TV room & lounge, maid service, free cribs, free washer/dryer, special facilities for handicapped. Modern structure. Rates: $32.00 per room. Duty can make reservations. Others Space-A. **Limited pet care available on base.**

TML: VOQ. Buildings 14, 120, 131-134. Officer all grades. Leave or official duty. EX-9270. 136/1-bedroom, private bath; 15 separate bedroom, private bath, suites. Refrigerator, A/C, color TV, maid service, free washer/dryer. Older structure. Rates: $8.00 per person. Duty can make reservations. Others Space-A.

TML: BOQ. Buildings 116, 117, 220, 413. Officer all grades. Leave or official duty. EX-9355. 232 separate bedroom, private bath. Kitchen, A/C (Building 220, 413), free washer/dryer. Modern structure. Rates: not provided. **Caged birds & fish only.**

TML: VAQ. Building 16. Enlisted all grades. Leave or official duty. EX-9270. 80/1-bedroom, latrine bath; 22/2-bedroom. Refrigerator, A/C, color TV, maid service, free washer/dryer. Older structure. Rates: $6.00 per person. Maximum 4 per unit. Duty can make reservations. Others Space-A.

TML: DV/VIP. SNCO Suites. Building 32. Enlisted E7-E9. Leave or official duty. EX-9270. 3/1-bedroom, private bath, suite. Refrigerator, A/C, black and white TV, maid service, free washer/dryer. Modern structure. Rates: $10.00 per person. Duty can make reservations. Others Space-A.

JAPAN
Yokota Air Base, continued

TML: DV/VIP. Buildings 13, 17, 32. Officer O6+ (M&F). Leave or official duty. EX-9270. 9 separate bedroom, private bath, suites; 4/2-bedroom, private bath, suites. Kitchen, utensils, A/C, color TV, maid service, free cribs, free washer/dryer. Older structure. Rates: $10.00 per person. Duty can make reservations. Others Space-A.

DV/VIP: 5th AF/CSP, EX-5-4141. O6+. Retirees and lower grades Space-A.

Other: Tokyo - hundreds of varied attractions.

TML Availability: Good, Oct-Mar. Difficult, other times.

Cafeteria-225-8550	Enlisted Club-225-2337	Locator-225-8390
Medical-225-9111	NCO Club-225-2330	O'Club-225-8619
Police-116	Snack Bar-225-8549	

KOREA

Chinhae Naval Facility (RK06R8)
FPO Seattle 98769-5000

TELEPHONE NUMBER INFORMATION: Main installation numbers: Comm: 82-51 Ask for Chinhae, ATVN: 720-8767.

Location: On the east coast of Korea, south of Pusan. Take the Seoul-Pusan expressway to Pusan, exit and continue along the coast for 25 miles south.

Billeting Office: Cmdr's Office, duty hours. EX-8767. Check in facility, check out 1200 hours daily.

TML: Officers' Club. Officer all grades. Leave or official duty. 6/1-bedroom, 2 double beds, private bath. A/C, telephone, maid service. Older structure, renovated. Rates: Moderate. Duty can make reservations. Others Space-A.

TML Availability: Good.

CPO Club-549	Enlisted Club-555	Medical-595
O'Club-550	Snack Bar-558	

Dragon Hill Lodge (RK09R8)
HQ EUSA
APO San Francisco 96301-5000

TELEPHONE NUMBER INFORMATION: Main installation number: 82-2-7918-2305.

Location: Located on South Post, Yongsan, in Seoul. From Kimpo International Airport, enter the Olympics Stadium Expressway 88 for approximately 15 miles, then take the Panpo Bridge exit and cross the bridge. Look for the Capital Hotel on the right side as you come off the bridge. Stay on the right side of the road and do not go under ground where the road splits. Go to the major intersection and turn left (one mile from bridge), enter the 2nd gate on the left side (gate 10) and proceed to the Lodge. NMC: Seoul, in the city.

KOREA

Dragon Hill Lodge, continued

Billeting Office: None. Check in at front desk. Comm: 82-2-7918-2222. ATVN: 738-2222.

TML: Brand new 1990 Lodge. All ranks. Leave or official duty. Accessible to handicapped. 267/1-bedroom, private bath; 10/2-bedroom, private bath. A/C, cots ($10.00), cribs, ice vending, kitchenette, maid service, special facilities for handicapped, color TV, complete utensils, washer/dryer, VCRs. Modern structure. Rates: $35.00-$55.00 per room for personnel on leave/vacation status; $75.00 per room for active duty personnel on TDY or PCS. Maximum 4 persons. All categories can make reservations. **Pets can be boarded at vet clinic near Gate 17, South Post.**

TML Availability: Good. Best, Oct-May.

Locator-724-6830	Medical-737-3545	NCO Club-737-8681
O'Club-721-7324	Police-724-6363/4300	

Kunsan Air Base (RK05R8)
APO San Francisco 96264-5000

TELEPHONE NUMBER INFORMATION: Main installation numbers: Comm: 82-42-282-4110, (From RK 1-011-82-282-4110), ATVN: 272-4110.

Location: On the west central coast of RK. Exit from Seoul-Pusan expressway, directions to AB clearly marked. NMC: Kunsan City, 7 miles north.

Billeting Office: ATTN: 8CSG/SVH. Building 309, West 9th St. Comm: 1-011-82-282-4604. ATVN: 272-4604. 24 hours daily. Check in billeting. Check out 1100 hours daily. Government civilian employee billeting.

TML: VOQ. Building 392. Officer all grades. Leave or official duty. EX-4604. 21/1-bedroom, latrine bath. Refrigerator, A/C, color TV, maid service, free washer/dryer. Older structure. Rates: Moderate. Duty can make reservations. Others Space-A.

TML Availability: Limited.

Locator-272-4351	Medical-272-4333	NCO Club-272-4312
O'Club-272-4494	Police-272-4944	Snack Bar-272-4912

Kwang Ju Air Base (RK08R8)
APO San Francisco 96324-5000

TELEPHONE NUMBER INFORMATION: Main installation numbers: Comm: 82-62 Ask for EX-920637 then for 4768, ATVN: 784-6477.

Location: Five miles from city of Kwang Ju on the main road. Take PIA exit from Highway 3 then take the first left. Drive over overpass, then take the first right to the Base. NMC: Kwang Ju, 5 miles southwest.

Billeting Office: ATTN: 6171 ABS/SVH. Building 214, across from community club. EX-652. 0600-2100 hours daily. Other hours Security Police, EX-401. Check in facility, check out 1200 hours daily. No government civilian employee billeting. Dependents not authorized.

TML: VAQ. Enlisted all grades. Leave or official duty. Accessible to handicapped. 48/1-bedroom, shared bath; 6 separate bedroom, private bath. Refrigerator, utensils, microwave, A/C, color TV room & lounge, maid service, free washer/dryer, ice

KOREA
Kwang Ju Air Base, continued

vending. Modern structure. Rates: $6.00 per person. Duty can make reservations. Others Space-A.

TML: VOQ. Building 244. Officer all grades. Leave or official duty. Accessible to handicapped. 12/1-bedroom, private bath; 8/2-bedroom, private bath. Refrigerator, limited utensils, A/C, color TV room & lounge, maid service, free washer/dryer, ice vending. Modern structure. Rates: $6.00 per person. Duty can make reservations. Others Space-A.

TML Availability: Good, Sep-Oct. Difficult, Feb-Mar.

Enlisted Club-EX-774　　Locator-EX-654　　Police-EX-401
SDO/NCO-EX-560

Naija Hotel AFRC (RK01R8)
CFSSC-Korea, CFSSA-III
APO San Francisco 96301-0074
CLOSED

Scoop
New Navy Contract Lodge in Naples, Italy

The Hotel Residence Costa Bleu at Pinetamare is a Navy contract hotel located about 30 minutes from Navy headquarters in Naples, Italy. The hotel was badly need for incoming and outgoing Navy personnel in the Naples area. It is very popular with an occupancy rate of over 85%.

The hotel has 101 units ranging from efficiencies up to four bedroom units. As U.S. military on orders receive a Temporary Lodging Allowance (TLA), the rates are in accordance with those current allowances. Presently, they run from $63.88 for a single, $98.28 for a double and up to $221.13 for seven persons. We are told that comparable facilities are much more expensive "on the economy." If space is available, personnel on leave and retirees may use the hotel, but at the same rates as those on TLA. Payment is made in U.S. dollars.

The Hotel Residence Costa Bleu is located in Pinetamare, right on the seaside in a resort area. Each unit has a full service kitchen and a terrace. Larger units have two baths and there is a clothes washer in each room. The hotel has a restaurant and lounge, and many more are in the area nearby. In addition, the hotel contract provides a theater, swimming pool and beach club.

For information call from the U.S. 011-34-81-509-7120. Susan Carbone is the contact. The address is: Hotel Residence Costa Bleu, Parco Marina, Riviera Fontana Bleu, Pinetamare, Caserta 81030.

According to Navy Lodge officials, this is their only contract lodge in operation. Remember, you read it in R&R first! These kind of tips are your dividends for being a R&R subscriber.

Naija Hotel AFRC, continued

KOREA

Osan Air Base (RK04R8)
APO San Francisco 96570-5000

TELEPHONE NUMBER INFORMATION: Main installation numbers: Comm: 82-332-284-4110, (From RK 1-011-82-284-4110), ATVN: 284-4110.

Location: Off the Seoul-Pusan expressway 38 miles south of Seoul. Directions to AB clearly marked. Adjacent to Song Tan City. NMC: Seoul, 38 miles north.

Billeting Office: ATTN: 51 CSG/SVH (PACAF), Building 771, EX-4672/6768. 24 hours daily. Check in billeting, check out 1200 hours daily. Government civilian employee billeting.

TML: TLF. Building 1007. All ranks. Leave or official duty. 17 separate bedroom, sleeps 5, private bath. Kitchen, complete kitchen, A/C, color TV, maid service, free cribs, free washer/dryer. Modern structure. Rates: $24.00 per unit. Maximum 5 per unit. Duty can make reservations. Others Space-A.

TML: VOQ. Buildings 1001, 1003. Officer all grades. Leave or official duty. 65/1-bedroom, private bath. Kitchen, limited utensils, A/C, color TV, maid service, free cribs, free washer/dryer. Modern structure. Rates: $8.00 per person. Maximum $24.00 per unit. Maximum 3 persons. Duty can make reservations. Others Space-A.

TML: VOQ/VAQ. Officer Building 771. All ranks. Leave or official duty. 258/1-bedroom/2 beds, latrine bath. Refrigerator, community kitchen, limited utensils, A/C, color TV, maid service, free washer/dryer. Modern structure. Rates: $6.00 per person. Maximum $8.00 per family. Duty can make reservations. Others Space-A.

TML: DV/VIP. On Hill 180. Officer O6+. Leave or official duty. 11/1-bedroom, private and semi-private baths; 1 separate bedroom suite, private bath. Refrigerator, A/C, color TV, maid service, free cribs/cots, free washer/dryer. Modern structure. Rates: $10.00 per person. Maximum 2 persons. Duty can make reservations. Others Space-A.

DV/VIP: Protocol Officer, 314th AD. EX-4-6700. O6+. Retirees and lower grades Space-A.

TML Availability: Best, Nov-Feb. Difficult, other times.

Cafeteria-3136	**Enlisted Club**-6931	**Locator**-6700/4597
Medical-118	**NCO Club**-6665	**O'Club**-6749
Police-116	**Snack Bar**-3136	

KOREA

Suwon Air Base (RK03R8)
APO San Francisco 96461-5000

TELEPHONE NUMBER INFORMATION: Main installation numbers: Comm: 82-331-288-4110, (From RK 1-011-288-4110), ATVN: 288-4110.

Location: Off the Seoul-Pusan expressway, clearly marked. NMC: Seoul, 20 miles north.

Billeting Office: Attn: Chief of Services. Building 2126. EX-5105. 24 hours daily. Check in billeting, check out 1300 hours daily. Government civilian employee billeting.

TML: TAQ/BOQ/DV/VIP. Building 2126. All ranks. Leave or official duty. EX-5105. 5/1-bedroom, private bath (DV/VIP); 27/1-bedroom/2 beds, shared bath (VOQ); 28/1-bedroom/2 beds, shared bath (TAQ). Refrigerator, A/C, color TV, maid serivce, free washer/dryer, ice vending. Modern structure. Rates: Moderate. Maximum 2 per unit. Duty can make reservations. Others Space-A.

DV/VIP: Building 2126, Front Desk, EX-5105. 06+. Retirees and lower grades Space-A.

TML Availability: Very Good.

Cafeteria-288-5558	Locator-288/5105/5288	NCO Club-288-5400
O'Club-288-5400	Police-288-4819	Snack Bar-288-5558

Yongsan Army Garrison (RK07R8)
APO San Francisco 96301-5000

TELEPHONE NUMBER INFORMATION: Main installation numbers: Comm: 82-2-7914-8205/8184, ATVN: 724-8205/8184.

Location: In the Yongson district of Seoul. NMC: Seoul, in the city.

Billeting Office: Billeting Office. Building 1112. EX-8205/8184. 24 hours daily. Check in facility, check out 1200 hours daily. No government civilian employee billeting.

TML: VOQ. Buildings 8102, 8103, 8104. Officer all grades, Enlisted E7-E9. Official duty only. 3 separate bedroom suites, private bath; 1/2-bedroom, shared bath. Refrigerator, A/C, cribs, color TV, maid service, washer/dryer. Modern structure. Rates: $15.00 per person. Maximum $20.00 per family. Duty can make reservations. Others Space-A.

TML: VEQ. Buildings 4110. Enlisted E1-E6. Leave or official duty. 29 separate bedroom, latrine bath. Refrigerator, community kitchen, A/C, color TV, maid service, washer/dryer. Modern structure. Rates: $4.00 per room. Duty can make reservations. Others Space-A.

TML: DVQ. Buildings 3723, 4464, 4468, 4436. Officer 07+ or civilian equivalent. Leave or official duty. Comm: 7913-3315. 9 separate bedroom, private bath. Community kitchen, kitchenette, complete utensils, cribs, color TV, A/C, maid service. Modern structure. Rates: Sponsor $25.00, adults $12.50, children $5.00. Duty can make reservations. Others Space-A.

DV/VIP: Sec Joint Stall, Protocol Branch, SJS-P, HHC, EUSA, Building 2472. Comm: 7913-3315, ATVN: 723-3315. 07+ or civilian equivalent. Lower grades Space-A.

Temporary Military Lodging Around the World — 263

KOREA

Yongsan Army Garrison, continued

TML Availability: Good, but reserve early.

Enlisted Club-293-5148 Medical-293-4581 NCO Club-293-5094
O'Club-293-4389 SDO/NCO-738-7621/5569

NETHERLANDS

Schinnen Community (NT02R7)
APO New York 09011-0029

TELEPHONE NUMBER INFORMATION: Main installation numbers: Comm: 31-045-26-2230, ATVN: None.

Location: Take Autobahn A-2, A-76 or E-9. Also NE-39, exit at Schinnen, cross railroad tracks, turn left to base, Hendrik Kamp. HE: p-35, G/2. NMC: Maastricht, NT, 15 miles southwest.

Billeting Office: Officers' Club, or US Protocol Office, Building H58. Comm: 045-26-2230 (reservations). 0800-2230 hours duty days. Call Comm: 045-26-3188 after hours. Check in facility, check out 1200 hours daily. Government civilian employee billeting in local hotels.

TML: Officers' Club. Officer all grades. Leave or official duty. 20 double rooms, private bath; 2/1-bedroom, private bath suites (DV/VIP). Dependents OK. Rates: Moderate.

DV/VIP: PAO, Building T-8, Room 204, Comm: 04493-7-331. O6+.

Other: Margraten American War Cemetery. Maastricht building from Middle Ages.

TML Availability: Limited.

Enl Club-045-26-3228 Locator-04493-7-199 Medical-045-26-3177
NCO Club-045-26-3197 O'Club-045-26-3188 Police-04493-7-323
Snack Bar-04493-7-336

Sösterberg Air Base (NT01R7)
APO New York 09292-5000

TELEPHONE NUMBER INFORMATION: Main installation numbers: Comm: 31-03463-5-8499, ATVN: 363-8499.

Location: On Utrechtsweg between Utrecht and Amersfoort in Huis ter Heide. Take the turn to Den Dolder. HE: p-34, D-E/4. NMC: Utrecht, NT, 8 miles southwest.

Billeting Office: ATTN: 32 TFS/SVH. Building 31. W. S. Camp. 24 hours daily. EX-8499. Check in billeting, check out 1200 hours daily.

TML: TAQ. Building 31. Enlisted all grades. Leave or official duty. 4/1-bedroom, private bath; 13/2-bedrooms, shared bath. Color TV, maid service, cribs, refrigerator. Modern structure. Rates: Not specified, call. Duty can make reservations. Others Space-A.

TML: VOQ. Building A-27. Officer all grades. Leave or official duty. 5/1-bedroom,

NETHERLANDS
Sösterberg Air Base, continued

shared bath. Refrigerator, color TV, maid service, free cribs/cots. Older structure. Rates: $6.50 per person. Maximum $13.00 per family. Duty can make reservations. Others Space-A.

DV/VIP: Protocol, Building 101. EX-8132. O6+. Retirees and lower grades Space-A.

TML Availability: Good, Oct-Feb. Difficult, other times.

Cafeteria-363-8590   Enlisted Club-363-8540   Locator-363-8599
Medical-363-8540   NCO Club-363-8590   O'Club-363-8592
Police-363-3012   SDO/NCO-363-8561

PANAMA

Fort Clayton (PN02R3)
APO Miami 34004-5000

TELEPHONE NUMBER INFORMATION: Main installation numbers: Comm: 507-87-3105, ATVN: 287-3105.

Location: Near the Pacific Ocean entrance to the Panama Canal. Take Gaillard Hwy toward the Miraflores Locks. NMC: Panama City, 8 miles southwest.

Billeting Office: Building 518, Hospital Rd, Fort Clayton. EX-4451/3251. 0700-1530 M-F. Check in billeting, check out 1100 hours daily.

TML: Guest House. Building 518. All ranks. Leave or official duty. 34/1-bedroom, private bath; 5 separate bedroom, private bath. Refrigerator, A/C, color TV room and lounge, maid service, free cribs/folding beds, free washer/dryer, ice vending. Dining hall. Older structure. Rates: maximum $33.00 per family on leave, $39.00 per family on active duty. Duty can make reservations. Others Space-A.

TML: Gulick Guesthouse. Building 402, Ft. Espinar. All ranks. Leave or official duty. Comm: 289-4828/4081. 12/1-bedroom; 2 separate bedroom. A/C, community kitchen, cribs/cots, ice vending, maid service, refrigerator, color TV room and lounge, washer/dryer. Rates: maximum $24.00-$40.00 per family. Duty can make reservations. Others Space-A.

TML: VOQ. Building 119, Quarry Heights. Enlisted E7+/Officer all grades. Leave or official duty. Comm: 282-4899. 13 separate bedroom, shared bath. Refrigerator, A/C, color TV, maid service, vending machine. Older structure. Rates: maximum $33.00-$38.00 per family. Duty can make reservations. Others Space-A.

TML: DV/VIP. Building 77, Casa Caribe, Ft Amador Housing Area. Enlisted E9/Officer O6+. Leave or official duty. EX-5057/8. 4/1-bedroom suites, private bath; 2 separate bedroom, private bath. Refrigerator, A/C, color TV, maid service, free washer/dryer. Central kitchen, breakfast served. Rates: maximum $37.00-$40.00 per family. Duty can make reservations. Others Space-A.

DV/VIP: Protocol Office, Building 95, Room 171. EX-287-5057/8. E9/O6+. Retirees and lower grades Space-A.

TML Availability: Good, Oct-May. Difficult, other times.

Enlisted Club-287-3849   Locator-287-3105   Medical-282-5222
NCO Club-287-4716   Police-287-4401   Snack Bar-287-4718
SDO/NCO-287-3107

PANAMA

Howard Air Force Base (PN01R3)
APO Miami 34001-5000

TELEPHONE NUMBER INFORMATION: Main installation numbers: Comm: 507-84-3010, ATVN: 284-3010.

Location: Adjacent to Thatcher Hwy (K-2) on Pacific side of Panama. RM: p-119, I/25. NMC: Panama City, 10 miles west.

Billeting Office: Building 708. EX-4919/5306. 24 hours daily. Check in billeting, check out 1200 hours daily. No government civilian employee billeting.

TML: TLQ. Building 1511. All ranks. Leave or official duty. EX-4914/4556. 6/2-bedroom apts. Kitchen, complete utensils, A/C, color TV, maid service, free cribs/cots, free washer/dryer. Older structure, new carpets '87. Rates: $24.00 per room per night. Maximum 6 per room. Duty can make reservations. Others Space-A.

TML: TAQ. Buildings 186, 710. Enlisted E1-E6. Leave or official duty. 52 rooms, shared/latrine bath. Refrigerator, A/C, color TV, maid service, free washer/dryer, ice vending. Older structure. Rates: $5.50 per person, maximum 2 persons. Duty reservations. Others Space-A.

TML: BEQ. Building 519. Enlisted E7-E9. Offical duty only. 22 separate bedroom, private bath. Kitchen, A/C, washer/dryer. Older structure. Rates: No charge. Permanent party only. No dependents.

TML: BOQ. Buildings 19, 21. Officer all ranks. Official duty only. 48 separate bedroom, private bath. Kitchen, A/C, washer/dryer. Rates: No charge. Permanent party only. No dependents.

TML: VOQ. Buildings 13, 14, 117, 119, 174. Officer all grades. Leave or official duty. 2/1-bedroom, private bath; 32 separate bedroom, private bath. Refrigerator, A/C, color TV, maid service, washer/dryer, ice vending. Older structure, remodeled. Rates: $8.50 per person, maximum $17.00 per family. Maximum 2 per room. Duty can make reservations. Others Space-A.

TML: DV/VIP. Buildings 16, 119, 519. Officer 06+. Leave or official duty. 1 separate bedroom suite, private bedroom; 1/2-bedroom suite, private bath; 1/3-bedroom suite, private bedroom. Kitchen, utensils, A/C, color TV, maid service, washer/dryer, ice vending. Rates: $8.50 per person. Maximum 2 per room. Duty can make reservations. Others Space-A.

DV/VIP: USAFSO/CCP, Howard, EX-84-4601. 06+. Retirees and lower grades Space-A.

TML Availability: Difficult at all times.

Cafeteria-84-3927	Locator-84-3010	Medical-84-4100
NCO Club-84-4189	O'Club-84-4860	SDO/NCO-84-5663

Quarry Heights Post (PN03R3)
APO Miami 34003-5000

TELEPHONE NUMBER INFORMATION: Main installation numbers: Comm: 507-82-3602, ATVN: 285-6110.

Location: Adjacent to Panama City. Clearly marked. NMC: Panama City, in the city.

PANAMA
Quarry Heights Post, continued

Billeting Office: Building 119. 0800-1700 hours daily. EX-3602/3439. Check in facility, check out 1200 hours daily. Government civilian employee billeting.

TML: Guest House (O'Club). Building 119. All ranks. Leave or official duty. 14/1-bedroom, shared bath. Refrigerator, A/C, BW TV, maid service, free cribs/cots, free washer/dryer. Older structure, remodeled. Rates: Moderate. Duty can make reservations. Others Space-A.

Other: Only facilities available at this location are O'Club and Package Store. See other Panama listings for support activities.

TML Availability: Good.

PHILIPPINES

Camp John Hay USAF Recreation Center (RP02R8)
San Francisco 96298-5000

CLOSED

Camp John Hay, continued   **PHILIPPINES**

Clark Air Base (RP03R8)
APO San Francisco 96274-5000
CLOSED

PHILIPPINES

Grande Island Recreation Center (RP01R8)
U S Naval Station, Subic Bay
FPO San Francisco 96651-1009

TELEPHONE NUMBER INFORMATION: Main installation numbers: Comm: 63-384-9222/32/40, (Fm RP 344-9222), ATVN: 382-3011-EX-4-7222.

Location: Off base. Grande Island is at the mouth of Subic Bay. It is 2 hours by car from Manila or Clark AB and a 30 minute shuttleboat ride from Subic Bay Naval Station.

Description of Area: Man's imagination and a beautiful tropical island have combined to create the most unique recreational facility in the world--Grande Island. Once a fortress guarding the entrance to Subic Bay, Grande Island is now a self-contained recreation center. Facilities are provided for a variety of recreation-oriented activities including swimming (pool/beach), scuba and snorkeling, softball, tennis, volleyball, basketball, pitch-n-putt golfing, and a glass-bottom boat for viewing the sea life around the island. A small Navy Exchange retail store and the Reef Restaurant are also on the Island.

NMI: On base.

Season of Operation: year round.

Reservations: Required. Cottage, hotel, and party reservations can be made up to 60 days in advance. Grande Lodge reservations can be made up to 30 days in advance for individual rooms and up to 1 year for group bookings for the entire facility. Write to: Recreation Services Department, Box 12, US Naval Station, FPO San Francisco 96651-1009. Comm: 63-884-922/9232, ATVN: 882-3011-EX-4-1101.

Eligibility: Active duty military personnel, retired military personnel, DOD civilian employees stationed overseas.

Accommodations and Rates:

Cottages	Hillside	Beach
1 Bedroom		$14.00
2 Bedroom	$14.00	$16.00
3 Bedroom		$18.00
4 Bedroom	$20.00	$22.00
8 Bed Fleet Quonset		$16.00

Hotel			
Single	$10.00	Economy with A/C	$10.00
Double	$12.00	Economy	$6.00
Efficiency	$14.00	Cubicles (4-6 beds)	$2.00
Suite Efficiency	$17.00	Extra beds	$2.00

Grande Lodge	
Double	$10.00
Double A/C	$12.00
Entire Facility	$102.00

There are 14 Cottages and 10 double rooms in the Grande Lodge plus the Hotel.

Temporary Military Lodging Around the World — 269

PHILIPPINES

Grande Island Recreation Center, continued

Shuttle Boat Schedule - Depart Fleet Landing

Mon-Fri	Sat., Sun., & Hol.	
0530	0530	1600
0800	0650	1700
1000	0800	1800
1200	0900	1900
1400	1000	2100
1600	1100	2200
1800	1200	
2000	1300	
2130	1400	
2245	1500	

Subic Bay Naval Station (RP04R8)
FPO San Francisco 96651-0003

TELEPHONE NUMBER INFORMATION: Main installation numbers: Comm: 63-384-1101, ATVN: 344-1101.

Location: About 100 miles northwest of Manila, across the Bataan peninsula on the west coast of Luzon. NMC: Manila, 100 miles southeast.

Billeting Office: Navy Lodge, Box 39, Naval Station, FPO San Francisco 96651-0003. Comm: 384-8840/8991. 24 hours daily. Check in facility, check out 1200 hours daily. Government civilian employee billeting.

TML: Navy Lodge. Building 893. All ranks. Leave or official duty. 72/1-bedroom, 2 beds, private bath. Kitchenette, AC, color TV, maid service, free cribs/rollaways (limited number), coin washer/dryer, ice vending. Modern structure. Rates: $32.00 per unit. Maximum 2 adults and 3 children. All categories can make reservations.

TML: BOQ. Buildings 294, 663. Officer 04-. Leave or official duty. EX-9216/9585. 1 bedroom, 2-3 beds each, shared bath. A/C, color TV, maid service. Older structure. Rates: Moderate. Duty can make reservations. Others Space-A.

TML: BEQ. Building 489, Barracks No. 3. Enlisted E7+. Leave or official duty. EX-9198. 32/1-bedroom, shared bath. A/C, color TV, maid service, community refrigerator. Older structure. Rates: Moderate. Also, Barracks 1, 2, 4, & 7 for accompanied E6. Same details as above. Duty can make reservations. Others Space-A.

TML: DV/VIP. Buildings 195, 107. Officer 05+. Leave or official duty. EX-9813/9821. 1/1-bedroom, private bath; kitchen, color TV, maid service (Quonset hut, 07+). 2/2-bedroom suites, private bath; color TV, maid service (06+). 10/1-bedroom, private bath; color TV, maid service (05+). Older structure. Renovated. Rates: Moderate. Duty can make reservations. Others Space-A.

DV/VIP: Flag Sec, COMNAVPHIL, EX-9813/9821. 05+. Retirees Space-A.

TML Availability: Good.

Cafeteria-29268
Med-Available
Police-99

Enl Club-Available
CPO Club-Available
Snack Bar-29259

Locator-1101
O'Club-Available

PORTUGAL

Lajes Field, Azores (PO01R7)
APO New York 09406-5000

TELEPHONE NUMBER INFORMATION: Main installation numbers: Comm: 351-95-52101, ATVN: 723-1410 (CONUS direct), 858-1110 (Via Andrews AFB, MD), 236-1110 (Via RAF Croughton, UK).

Location: On Terceira Island (Azores PO) 20 miles long & 12 miles wide. Lajes Field is 2 miles west of Praia da Vitoria, PO, on Mason Hwy. NMC: Lisbon, 850 miles east.

Billeting Office: Building T-166, EX-5178/7283. 24 hours daily. Check in facility, check out 1200 hours. Government civilian employee billeting.

TML: TLQ. Building T-306. All ranks. Leave or official duty. Accessible to handicapped. 30/1-bedroom apartments, living room, private bath. Kitchenette, color TV, free cribs/cots, free washer/dryer. Modern structure. Rate: $15.00-$30.00 per room. Maximum 5 per room. Active duty PCS out with family can make reservations. Others Space-A. **Pets allowed in TLF kennel.**

DV/VIP: Contact billeting office. 06+. Retirees and lower grades Space-A.

Other: A warm and economical spot to spend a few days.

TML Availability: Best, Nov-Apr. Difficult, May-Oct.

Cafeteria-22211	Enlisted Club-23265	Locator-6130/23222
Medical-23237	NCO Club-23265	O'Club-23195
Police-23222	Snack Bar-6290	SDO/NCO-23202

SPAIN

Moron Air Base (SP01R7)
APO New York 09282-5000

TELEPHONE NUMBER INFORMATION: Main installation numbers: Comm: 34-54-84-1039/1122 (from CONUS), 954-84-1039/1122 (from Spain), ATVN: 722-1110.

Location: Sevilla, Spain to Alcala, Spain on N-334, pass Alcala to SE-333. At intersection of SE-342 and B-333 proceed on SE-342 to Moron AB. Base well marked. NMC: Sevilla, 40 miles northwest.

Billeting Office: ATTN: 7120 ABF/SVH. Building P-303, 1st St. EX-2798. 24 hours daily. Check in facility, check out 1200 hours daily. Government civilian employee billeting. ATTENTION: AD not assigned in Spain, retired personnel, widow(ers), government civilian employees not assigned in Spain, dependents of all groups, are not permitted to purchase any articles free of Spanish taxes on any military installation, i.e. Foodland. Military ID card holder visitors to Spain are permitted to make purchases in open messes, Stars & Stripes, and billeting. Also, personnel arriving by military air at Torrejon AB and Rota NAS are advised to contact security or passenger service for immigration clearance. This notice applies to other Spanish listings.

Temporary Military Lodging Around the World — 271

SPAIN

Moron Air Base, continued

TML: VOQ/VAQ/DV/VIP. Building P-303. All ranks. Leave or official duty. 55 separate bedroom, shared bath. Some DV suites, private bath. Refrigerator, community kitchen, A/C, color TV lounge, maid service, free washer/dryer. Modern structure. Rates: $9.00 per person VOQ, $8.00 per person VAQ, $14.00 DV/VIP. Maximum 2 plus one crib per unit. Duty can make reservations. Others Space-A.

DV/VIP: Billeting, EX-2798. Determined by Commander. Retirees Space-A.

TML Availability: Good Nov-March, fairly good April-Oct.

All numbers are Comm or ATVN extensions.

Comm Club-2416	Dining Fac-2249	Locator-1110
Medical-2069	Police-2132	SDO/NCO-2401

Rota Naval Air Station (SP02R7)
Box 2, FPO New York 09540-5000

TELEPHONE NUMBER INFORMATION: Main installation numbers: Comm: 34-56-862780, (From Spain but outside the province of Cadiz dial 956-862780), ATVN: 727-0111.

Location: On Spain's South Atlantic Coast. Accessible from E-25 South and SP-342 West. HE: map p-61, C-5. NMC: Cadiz, 22 miles south.

Billeting Office: Building 1610, Flor St. EX-2567/2568. 0830-1700 hours daily. Check in 24 hours daily at facility, check out 1200. Government civilian employee billeting.

TML: Navy Lodge. Naval Station, Box 17, Building 1674. All ranks. Leave or official duty. EX-2643. 22/1-bedroom, private bath. Kitchen, utensils, A/C, color TV room & lounge, maid service, free cribs/cots, coin washer/dryer, beauty shop. Modern structure. Rates: $25.00 per unit. Maximum 5 persons. All categories can make reservations.

TML: BOQ. Building 39. Officer all grades. Leave or official duty. EX-2510/2511. 116/1-bedroom, shared bath; 38 separate bedroom, private bath (10 DV/VIP suites). Refrigerator, community kitchen, A/C, color TV lounge, maid service, free cribs, free washer/dryer, 2 rec rooms, conference room. Modern structure. Rates: $4.00 per person, infant $1.00. 2 per unit except suites 4 per unit. Duty can make reservations. Others Space-A.

TML: BEQ. Buildings 37-39. Enlisted all grades. Leave or official duty. EX-2460. 300/1-bedroom, latrine bath; 22/1-bedroom, hall bath (E7+). Refrigerator (22/1-bedroom only), color TV lounge, maid service, free washer/dryer. Modern structure, remodeled. Rates: $2.00 per person, maximum 1-4 persons per unit. Duty can make reservations. Others Space-A.

DV/VIP: Protocol Office. Building 1, 2nd floor. EX-2744. 06+. Retirees Space-A.

TML Availability: Good, winter months. Difficult, Jun-Sep.

Enlisted Club-2317	Medical-2225	NCO Club-EX-2433
O'Club-EX-2509	Pizza-7213	Police-2000
SDO/NCO-2222		

SPAIN

Torrejon Air Base (SP03R7)
APO New York 09283-5000

TELEPHONE NUMBER INFORMATION: Main installation numbers: Comm: 34-1-665-7777, ATVN: 723-1110.

Location: From Madrid, take N-11 northeast toward Barcelona, immediately past the airport at Barajas. HE: p-59, D/2. NMC: Madrid, 17 miles southwest.

Billeting Office: ATTN: 401 SVS/SVH. Don Quixote Inn. Building 121. EX-3150/1844. From Madrid, Comm: 665-3150. 0800-1700 hours daily. Check in facility, check out 1100 hours daily. Government civilian employee billeting.

TML: TLF. Building 123. All ranks. Leave or official duty. 150/1-bedroom, shared bath. Refrigerator, color TV, maid service, free cribs/cots, free washer/dryer. Older structure, renovated. Rates: $24.00. Duty can make reservations. Others Space-A. No pets but kennels available on base and in the Madrid area.

TML: VOQ/VAQ. All grades. Leave or official duty. 279/1-bedroom, shared bath. Refrigerator, color TV, in-house movie channel, maid service, free cribs/cots, free washer/dryer. Older structure. Rates: $14.00 per person. Duty can make reservations. Others Space-A. No pets but kennels available on base and in the Madrid area.

DV/VIP: Hq 16AF/CCO, Building 105, EX-5496. 06+. Retirees Space-A. 14/2-bedroom suites, private bath. Rates: $14.00 per person.

TML Availability: Good, Nov-Mar. Difficult, other times.

All numbers are Comm or ATVN extensions.

Locator-1841	Medical-3402	NCO Club-5760
O'Club-5791	Police-5400	SDO/NCO-5105

Zaragoza Air Base (SP04R7)
APO New York 09286-5000

TELEPHONE NUMBER INFORMATION: Main installation numbers: Comm: 34-76-326711 (from US), 976-326711 (from Spain) ATVN: 724-1110.

Location: From French border crossing Gerona, take Autopista 2, 4 hours to base. From Madrid, take National Hwy N-11 to base. HE: p-56, H/5. NMC: Zaragoza 12 miles northeast.

Billeting Office: Building 900. EX-2141/2715. 24 hours daily. Check in facility, check out 1200 hours daily. Government civilian employee billeting.

TML: VOQ. Building 900. Officer all grades. Leave or official duty. Accessible to handicapped. 60/1-bedroom, private bath; 48/1-bedroom, shared bath. Kitchen (60 units), refrigerator, limited utensils, A/C, color TV, maid service, cribs, free washer/dryer, ice vending. Older structure. Rates: $11.00 per person. Maximum 2 per room. Duty can make reservations. Others Space-A.

TML: VAQ. Building 827, 829, 831, 833. Enlisted all grades. Leave or official duty. 357/1-bedroom, latrine bath. Refrigerator, color TV room & lounge, maid service, free washer/dryer, ice vending. Modern structure, renovated. Rates: $8.50 per person. Maximum 2-4 per room. Duty can make reservations. Others Space-A.

TML: DV/VIP. Buildings 829, 900. Officer 06+, Enlisted E7-E9. Leave or official duty. EX-2558. 2/1-bedroom, private bath; 7 separate bedroom, private bath (6

SPAIN

Zaragoza Air Base, continued

have kitchen). Refrigerator, complete utensils, A/C, color TV room & lounge, maid service, cribs, free washer/dryer, ice vending. Older structure. Rates: $10.00 per person. Maximum 4 per unit. Duty can make reservations. Others Space-A.

DV/VIP: PAO. EX-2558. O6/CMSgt/GS-15+. Retirees Space-A.

Other: Within easy driving distances of international ski and beach resorts.

TML Availability: Good, Dec and June. Difficult, other times.

All numbers are Comm or ATVN extensions.

Cafeteria-2795	Enlisted Club-2347	Locator-2210/2141
Medical-2116	NCO Club-2347	O'Club-2763
Police-2178		SDO/NCO-113/2000

TURKEY

Ankara Air Station (TU01R9)
APO New York 09254-5000

TELEPHONE NUMBER INFORMATION: Main installation numbers: Comm: 90-4-125-9943, ATVN: 672-5000.

Location: From Esenboga Airport take bus or taxi to Balgat. NMC: Ankara, in the city.

Billeting Office: ATTN: 7217th ABG/SVH. Building 135, Karyagdi Sokak 13, Cankaya, Ankara. Comm: 90-4-138-9453. ATVN: 672-3128/3183. 24 hours daily. Check in billeting, check out 1300 hours daily.

TML: VOQ (Building 123), VAQ (Building 135). All ranks. Leave or official duty. VOQ: 7 bed spaces in 4 apts, shared bath, in O'Club, downtown Ankara. Kitchen, utensils, color TV, maid service, free washer/dryer. VAQ: 45 bed spaces in 11/3-bedroom apts, shared bath, in downtown Ankara. Kitchen (7 units), refrigerator and MW in other units, utensils, color TV, maid service, free washer/dryer. Note: TV for video only. No English speaking stations in Ankara. Modern structure. Rates: $8.00-$14.00 per person. Duty can make reservations. Others Space-A. Pets OK if on leash. There is a 20-unit TLF facility and Airmen's BEQ on Ankara AS. $24.00 per unit for TLF.

DV/VIP: Hq TUSLOG, Building 2001, EX-3198. E9/O6+. Retirees and lower grades Space-A.

TML Availability: Good, Oct-May. Difficult, other times.

Cafeteria-234	Locator-4116	Medical-PTT-125-2329
NCO Club-3296	O'Club-3104	Police-2241

Incirlik Air Base (TU03R9)
APO New York 09289-5000

TELEPHONE NUMBER INFORMATION: Main installation numbers: Comm: 90-71-119062/111285, ATVN: 676-1110.

TURKEY
Incirlik Air Base, continued

Location: From Adana, east on E-5 for 3 miles, left at sign for Incirlik. Base is clearly marked. NMC: Adana, 3 miles west.

Billeting Office: ATTN: 39 CSS/SVH. Building 952, 6th St. 24 hours daily. Check in facility, check out 1100-1200 hours daily. EX-6709/86. Government civilian employee billeting.

TML: TLF. Building 1066, Hodja. All ranks. Leave or official duty. 49 separate bedroom, living room, dining room, private bath. Kitchen, complete utensils, A/C, color TV room & lounge, maid service, free cribs/cots, free washer/dryer, ice vending, facilities for disabled American veterans, irons, clock-radios, microwave. Modern structure. Rates: $20.00 per unit. TDY/PCS can make reservations. Others Space-A.

TML: VOQ. Buildings 934/36/38/40/52, 1010/12. Officer all grades. Leave or official duty. 24/1-bedroom, shared bath; 64/1-bedroom, private bath; 12/1-bedroom, 2 beds, private bath (may be reservations for air crews). Refrigerator, A/C, color TV room & lounge, maid service, free washer/dryer. Older structure, renovated. Rates: $6.00 per person. Maximum $12.00 per room. Duty can make reservations. Others Space-A.

TML: VAQ. Buildings 1004/42/44/46/48/50/52, 902/04/06/08/18/20. Enlisted all grades. Leave or official duty. 36/1-bedroom, 2 beds, private bath, (may be reserved for air crews); 156/1-bedroom, 2/3 beds, latrine bath (E1-E6) (no females or children due to latrine bath); 2 separate bedroom suites, private bath (E7-E9) (7 day limit). Refrigerator, A/C, color TV, maid service, free washer/dryer. Older structure, renovated. Rates: $6.00 per person. Maximum $12.00 per room. Duty can make reservations. Others Space-A.

TML: DV/VIP. Building 1072. Officer 06+. Leave or official duty. 6 separate bedroom suites, private bath. Kitchen, limited utensils, A/C, color TV, maid service, free washer/dryer, ice vending, alcoholic beverages and soft drinks stocked in room on "Honor System." Older structure. Rates: $6.00 per person. Maximum $12.00 per unit. Duty can make reservations. Others Space-A. Also, 95/1-bedroom, private bath, contract quarters for TDY, funded travel orders only.

DV/VIP: Protocol Office, 39 TACG/CCE. EX-6347. E9, 06/GS-15+. Retirees and lower grades Space-A.

Other: Castle ruins, museums.

TML Availability: Good all year.

Cafeteria-6981	Enlisted Club-6010	Locator-6289
Medical-6666	NCO Club-6010	O'Club-6967
Police-3200		SDO/NCO-6376

Izmir Air Station (TU04R9)
APO New York 09224-5000

TELEPHONE NUMBER INFORMATION: Main installation numbers: Comm: 90-51-145360, ATVN: 675-1110.

Location: In the center of Izmir on the central west coast of Turkey. HE: p-82, G/6. NMC: Izmir, in the city.

Billeting Office: Kordon Hotel. ATVN: 675-1110-EX-3490. 0730-1700 daily. Check in facility, check out 1200 hours daily. Government civilian employee billeting.

Temporary Military Lodging Around the World — 275

TURKEY

Izmir Air Station, continued

TML: TLQ. Kordon Hotel. All ranks. Leave or official duty. Accessible to handicapped. 72/1-bedroom, private bath; 6/2-bedroom, private bath; 6 DV suites, private bath. Refrigerator, A/C, color TV room & lounge, maid service, free cribs/cots, washer/dryer, ice vending. Part modern and part older, renovated structure. Rates: $20.00-$32.00 per room. Maximum 3 per unit. Duty can make reservations. TDY/PCS have priority. Others Space-A.

DV/VIP: Protocol Office, 7241 ABG/CCE. Facility #48, Room 603. ATVN: 675-1110-EX-3341. O6+/E9. Retirees and lower grades Space-A.

TML Availability: Good, except May-Oct.

Enlisted Club-3482   Medical-3357   NCO Club-3482
O'Club-3482   Police-3222   SDO/NCO-3222

Sinop Army Field Station (TU02R9)
APO New York 09133-5000

TELEPHONE NUMBER INFORMATION: Main installation numbers: Comm: 90-3761-5431/5432, ATVN: 672-1110 Ask for Sinop.

Location: Take the coastal highway west from Samsun until you reach Sinop. There are no major highways that connect Sinop to the rest of Turkey. There is daily bus service to Samsun (3 hour trip), and Istanbul (12 hour trip). There is a community airport in Samsun. NMC: Samsun 100 miles east.

Billeting Office: Building S-512, Barbaros Cadisi. 0730-1630 hours M-F. EX-213. Other hours, DEH EX-345, or SDO/MP EX-222/256. Check in facility, check out 1200 hours daily. Government civilian employee billeting.

TML: Hotel Melia Kasim, Hotel 117-Sinop, Karakum Hotel. All ranks. Leave or official duty. 120/1-bedroom, private bath. Color TV, maid service, free washer/dryer. Modern structure. Rates: $35.00 per room. Maximum 2 per room. All categories can make reservations. Others Space-A. Note: limited DVQ facilities. Call for information.

DV/VIP: PAO, ATTN: IAEN-DPCA. EX-209/334. O6/GS-16+. Retirees and lower grades Space-A.

Other: Sinop is a small fishing village of 18,000 people. Founded in 1200 BC, it has artifacts from Greek, Roman, Byzantine, and Ottoman periods in museums.

TML Availability: Fairly good. Best, Sep-May. Access to the installation requires prior approval of commander.

Cafeteria-267   Locator-0   Medical-331
NCO Club-363   O'Club-223   Police-222
Snack Bar-276   SDO/NCO-0

UNITED KINGDOM

RAF Alconbury (UK01R7)
APO New York 09238-5000

TELEPHONE NUMBER INFORMATION: Main installation numbers: Comm: 44-0480-82-3000, ATVN: 223-3000.

UNITED KINGDOM
RAF Alconbury, continued

Location: From London, take A-1 North to A-604, exit marked RAF Alconbury, follow signs. Approximately 65 miles north of London. HE: p-13, D/3. NMC: Huntingdon, 4 miles east.

Billeting Office: ATTN: 10th SVS/SVH. Building 639, Texas St. EX-3670. 24 hours daily. Check in facility, check out 1300 hours daily. Government civilian employee billeting.

TML: VOQ. Buildings 639, 640. Officer all grades. Leave or official duty. 58/1-bedroom, 2 beds, shared bath; 6 suites, private bath (DV/VIP). Refrigerator, color TV room & lounge, maid service, free cribs/cots, free washer/dryer, facilities for disabled American veterans. Modern structure. Rates: Moderate for rooms, $14.00 per person for suites. Maximum 2 per suite. Duty can make reservations. Others Space-A.

TML: TAQ. Building 652. Enlisted all ranks. 22/2-bedroom, shared bath; 4/1-bedroom suites, shared bath; 3 separate bedroom suites, private bath. Refrigerator, color TV, maid service, free washer/dryer. Modern structure. Rates: $6.00 per person rooms; $10.00-$14.00 per person suites. Duty can make reservations. Others Space-A.

TML: All ranks TLF also available. 20 suites, private bath. $24.00 per unit.

DV/VIP: Hq 10th TRW. EX-2111/2112. O6+. Retirees and lower grades Space-A.

TML Availability: Good, Aug-Mar. Difficult, other times.

Cafeteria-3610	Enlisted Club-2513	Locator-2565
Medical-116	NCO Club-3567	O'Club-3382
Police-114	Snack Bar-3426	

RAF Bentwaters/Woodbridge (UK12R7)
APO New York 09755-5000

TELEPHONE NUMBER INFORMATION: Main installation numbers: Comm: 44-0394-43-3000, ATVN: 225-1110.

Location: Take A-12 North from Ipswich to exit signs east on B-1069 to Melton, for twin bases of RAF Bentwaters/Woodbridge. HE: p-13, F/1. NMC: Ipswich, 15 miles southeast.

Billeting Office: ATTN: 81 SVS/SVH. Building 629, behind the NCO Club. 24 hours daily. EX-1844/2281. Check in facility, check out 1200 hours daily. Government civilian employee billeting.

TML: TLF. Buildings 166-168, 174-175. All ranks. Leave or official duty. 40 separate bedrooms, private bath. Kitchen, complete utensils, color TV, maid service, free cribs, free washer/dryer, ice vending. Modern structure. Rates: $25.00 per unit. Maximum 5 per unit. Duty can make reservations. Others Space-A.

TML: VAQ. Building 759. Enlisted all grades. Leave or official duty. 45 rooms with semi-private bath. Modern structure. Rates: $7.50 per person, maximum $15.00 per room. Duty can make reservations. Others Space-A.

TML: BOQ. Building 629. Officer all grades. Leave or official duty. 23/1-bedroom, semi-private bath (4 with private bath). Refrigerator, cable color TV room and lounge, maid service, cribs, free washer/dryer. Older structure, renovated '88. Rates: $8.50 per person. Maximum $17.00 per room. Duty can make reservations. Others Space-A.

Temporary Military Lodging Around the World — 277

UNITED KINGDOM

RAF Bentwaters/Woodbridge, continued

DV/VIP: PAO. 81st TFW/CCP, EX-2101/02/05. O6+. Retirees and lower grades Space-A.

Other: These are twin bases located seven miles apart.

TML Availability: Seasonal. Fairly good over-all. Best, Dec-Mar.

Cafeteria-0394-420263	Enlisted Club-2659	Locator-2673
Medical-2574	NCO Club-2659	O'Club-2256
Police-2204	Snack Bar-0394-420263	

Brawdy Wales Naval Facility (UK02R7)
FPO New York 09519-5000

TELEPHONE NUMBER INFORMATION: Main installation numbers: Comm: 44-437-760654, (From UK Haverfordwest 437-5452), ATVN: 391-4356.

Location: From London, take M-4 to Swansea, A-40 to Haverfordwest, A-487 to Brawdy. HE: p-12, C/2. NMC: Haverfordwest, Wales, UK 10 miles south.

Billeting Office: Naval Facility, EX-5452/4356/4236. 0800-1600 hours daily. Check in facility, check out as arranged. No government civilian employee billeting.

TML: RAF Berthing Facilities. All ranks. Leave or official duty. Arrange by telephone EX-5452 with Naval Facility Brawdy. Rooms in the Officers' or Enlisted Mess. Color TV lounge, free washer/dryer. Older structure. Rates: Moderate. All categories can make reservations.

Following support facilities are available: Exchange, Package Store, Commissary, Gas Station, Clubs/Messes.

TML Availability: Depends on berthing requirements at the time.

Snack Bar-2951

Burtonwood Army Depot (UK03R7)
APO New York 09075-3738

TELEPHONE NUMBER INFORMATION: Main installation numbers: Comm: 44-0925-36611, ATVN: 243-1110.

Location: Near Warrington, Cheshire, UK. From Motorway 62, Liverpool is 17 miles west, Manchester is 22 miles east. HE: p-11, B/4.

Billeting Office: Header House, Gate 12. 0800-1600 hours duty days. Comm: 0925-36611-EX-320. ATVN: 243-1320. Other hours, SDO. Comm: 0925-36611. ATVN: 243-1208. Check in facility, check out 1100 hours daily. Government civilian employee billeting.

TML: VOQ/DV/VIP. VOQ, all ranks. DV/VIP, 06/GS-15+. Leave or official duty. 6/3-bedroom, shared bath. Kitchen, utensils, A/C, color TV lounge, maid service, free cribs, free washer/dryer. Older structure, renovated. Rates: Sponsor $16.00, each additional person $8.00. Duty can make reservations. Others Space-A. Note: Limited TML at Caerwent Storage Activity located in South Wales 5 miles east of Chepstow. Access via A-48 main highway.

DV/VIP: PAO. Comm: 0925-36611-EX-310. O6/GS-15+. Retirees and lower grades Space-A.

278 — *Temporary Military Lodging Around the World*

UNITED KINGDOM
Burtonwood Army Depot, continued

The following facilities are available: PX, Commissary, APO, Gas Station, Nursery, Package Store, Army Community Services, Snack Bar, Chaplain, Theater.

TML Availability: Limited.

RAF Chicksands (UK04R7)
APO New York 09193-5000

TELEPHONE NUMBER INFORMATION: Main installation numbers: Comm: 44-462-812571-EX-400, (From UK Hitchin 0462-812571), ATVN: 234-1110.

Location: From London, take M-1 North to Luton, A-6 North to A-507 or A-600 to Shefford. Both A-507 and A-600 pass one of the Chicksands RAF gates. HE: p-13, D/1. NMC: Bedford, 10 miles northwest.

Billeting Office: Building 403, Wellington Dr. Comm: 816868. ATVN: 234-2400. 24 hours daily. Check in facility, check out 1100 hours daily. No government civilian employee billeting.

TML: VAQ. Building 403/4. Enlisted E1-E6. Leave or official duty. 67/1-bedroom, latrine bath; 6 separate bedroom, private bath. Refrigerator, color TV room & lounge, maid service, free cribs/cots, free washer/dryer, ice vending. Older structure. Rates: $8.00 per person. Maximum $16.00 per family. Duty can make reservations. Others Space-A.

TML Availability: Good, winter. Difficult, summer.

Cafeteria-EX-2588	Enlisted Club-EX-2448	Locator-EX-2382
Medical-EX-2387	NCO Club-EX-2448	O'Club-EX-2399
Police-EX-2213	Snack Bar-EX-2588	

Edzell Naval Security Group Activity (UK06R7)
FPO New York 09518-5000

TELEPHONE NUMBER INFORMATION: Main installation numbers: Comm: 44-356-4431, (From UK Edzell 0356-4431), ATVN: 229-1110.

Location: From Aberdeen take A-92 to A-94 South, follow Perth/Dundee signs. Last town before Edzell is Lawrencekirk look for RAF Edzell signs to base. HE: p-6, G/6. NMC: Aberdeen, 40 miles north.

Billeting Office: Campbell Hall. Comm: EX-218. 24 hours daily. Check in facility, check out 1200 hours daily. No government civilian employee billeting.

TML: Navy Lodge. All ranks. Comm: EX-251. 1000-1700 M-F, 1000-1330 Sa. 8/2-bedroom mobile homes, private bath. Kitchen, complete utensils, color TV, maid service, free cribs, coin washer/dryer, snack machine. Older structure. Rates: $30.00 per unit, sleeps 4-6 persons. Duty can make reservations. PCS priority. Others Space-A.

TML: BOQ. Officers' Open Mess. Officer all grades. Leave or official duty. Comm: EX-218. ATVN: 229-4218. 8 separate bedroom, private bath. Kitchen, limited utensils, maid service, free washer/dryer. Modern structure. Rates: Moderate. Maximum 4-5 persons per unit. Duty can make reservations. Others Space-A.

Temporary Military Lodging Around the World — 279

UNITED KINGDOM

Edzell Naval Security Group Activity, continued

TML: BEQ. Building 333. Enlisted all grades. Leave or official duty. Extensions same as BOQ. 106/1-bedroom, 2-beds, private bath. Refrigerator, color TV lounge, maid service, free washer/dryer. Modern structure. Rates: Moderate. Duty can make reservations. Others Space-A.

DV/VIP: PAO, Building 22, Comm: 010-03564-431-EX-337. ATVN: 229-4337. 07+.

Other: Edzell Castle.

TML Availability: Good, Nov-Feb. Difficult, other times.

All numbers are Comm or ATVN extensions.

Cafeteria-253	Enlisted Club-298/252	Locator-336/351
Medical-266	O'Club-237	Police-208
Snack Bar-270		SDO/NCO-232

RAF Fairford (UK11R7)
APO New York 09125-5000

CLOSED

RAF Greenham Common/Welford (UK05R7)
APO New York 09150-5000

TELEPHONE NUMBER INFORMATION: Main installation numbers: Comm: 44-0635-51-2000, ATVN: 266-1110.

Location: Take M-4 from Heathrow Airport, exit 13, Newbury, A-34 South for 1 mile to Newbury and GC/W RAF. HE: p-13, BC/3. NMC: Newbury, Berks, 4 miles north.

Billeting Office: Building 24, Barracks Rd, EX-2363. 24 hours daily. Check in

UNITED KINGDOM
RAF Greenham Common/Welford, continued

facility, check out 1200 hours daily. Government civilian employee billeting in VOQ.

TML: TLF. Building 221. All ranks. Leave or official duty. 1/2-bedroom cottage, private bath. Kitchen, complete utensils, color TV, maid service, free washer/dryer. Older structure, renovated. Rates: $24.00 per night. Duty and retired can make reservations. Others Space-A.

TML: VAQ. Buildings 31, 32. Enlisted all grades. Leave or official duty. 12/1-bedroom, latrine bath; 7 separate bedroom, private bath. Refrigerator, TV, free washer/dryer. Rates: $7.50 per person. Maximum $15.00 double, $7.50 single. Maximum 3 persons double, 1 single. Duty can make reservations. Others Space-A.

TML: VAQ (RAF Welford). Enlisted all grades. Leave or official duty. 7/2-bedroom, private bath. Kitchen, utensils, TV, maid service, free washer/dryer. Modern structure. Rates: $7.50 per person. Maximum $30.00 per family. Duty can make reservations. Others Space-A.

TML: Greenham Lodge. Building 228. Officer all grades. Leave or official duty. 15/2-bedroom, private bath; 5 separate bedroom suites, private bath. Kitchen (3 units), refrigerator, community kitchen, TV, maid service, free washer/dryer, ice vending. Older structure. Rates: $12.00 per person. Maximum $48.00 per family. Maximum 6 per unit. Duty can make reservations. Others Space-A.

DV/VIP: Protocol Office, EX-2424. 06+. Retirees Space-A.

Other: Littlecote House, 15 miles west, Portsmouth Naval Harbor.

TML Availability: Limited. Best, December.

All numbers are Comm or ATVN extensions.

Cafeteria-2208	Enlisted Club-2213	Locator-2222
Medical-2116	NCO Club-2213	O'Club-2858
Police-2200	Snack Bar-2208	

RAF Lakenheath (UK07R7)
APO New York 09179-5000

TELEPHONE NUMBER INFORMATION: Main installation numbers: Comm: 44-0638-52-1110, ATVN: 226-1110.

Location: From London, go north on the M-1 to the A-11 to the A-1065. HE: p-13, EF/1. NMC: Cambridge, 30 miles south.

Billeting Office: Building 956. EX-1844/2177. 24 hours daily. Check in facility, check out 1000 hours daily. No government civilian employee billeting.

TML: TLF. Various buildings. All ranks. Leave or official duty. 31 units, private bath. Kitchen, complete utensils, color TV, maid service, cribs/cots, free washer/dryer. Modern structure. Rates: $24.00 per unit. Duty can make reservations. Others Space-A.

TML: VAQ. Building 980. All ranks. 32 shared bedroom (E1-E6), shared bath. 2 SNCO bedrooms (E7-E8) with private kitchen. Otherwise shared kitchen, color TV, maid service, free washer/dryer. Older structure. Rates: $8.00 per person shared rooms, $10.00 per person SNCO rooms. Maximum 2 persons. Duty can make reservations. Others Space-A.

RAF Lakenheath, continued UNITED KINGDOM

TML: VOQ. Building 978. All ranks. Leave or official duty. 28 separate bedroom, private bath. cribs, kitchenette, maid service, color TV, washer/dryer. Rates: $8.00 per person. Maximum $16.00 per unit. Maximum 2 per unit. Duty can make reservations. Others Space-A.

TML: DV/VIP. Various buildings. Officer O6+, Enlisted E9. Leave or official duty. Comm: 0638-52-3502. ATVN: 226-3502. 8 separate bedroom, private bath. Kitchenette, cribs, color TV, maid service, washer/dryer. Older structure. Rates: $10.00 per person. Maximum $20.00 per suite. Maximum 3 per suite. Children not authorized. Duty can make reservations. Others Space-A.

DV/VIP: 48 TFW/CCP, Building 1156. EX-3500. O6+ & E9. Retirees and lower grades Space-A.

Other: Shuttle Bus to RAF Mildenhall departs 50 minutes after the hour 0650-1450.

TML Availability: Limited.

All numbers are Comm or ATVN extensions.

Cafeteria-3170	Locator-1841	Medical-2226
NCO Club-2207	O'Club-3636	Police-3631
Snack Bar-2578		

London Service Clubs (UK13R7)

Union Jack Club
Sandell Street, Waterloo
London, SE1 8UJ, United Kingdom

TELEPHONE NUMBER INFORMATION: Comm: 44-01-928-4814, ATVN: None.

Location: Opposite Waterloo Station (train), central London. HE: p-13, D/3. NMC: London, in the city.

Billeting Office: Address as above. The club embodies the original Women's Services and Families Club. Allied Forces are welcomed and granted Temporary Honorary Membership. 24 hours. Check in 1300 hours, check out 1000 hours daily.

TML: Club/Hotel. All ranks. Leave only. Reservations accepted. All charges include VAT. Check accepted when supported by cheque card. Meals paid for when taken, 10% discount for 7 days booking or more, deposit of one night when booking, refundable if cancelled 48 hours in advance of arrival.

Other: 208 single rooms and 63 twin-bed rooms all with wash basins, H/C water, with baths, showers, and waterclosets centrally located on each floor. Also, as of summer '91, 52 single rooms with private bath; 20 doubles with private bath; and 8 family suites, each with a twin-bed in 1 room, a double-bunk bed in another, and a private bath. Bring own soap and towels. Bar, color TV, launderette, reading and writing rooms, conference and banquetting areas. Rates: Excellent public transportation service, limited car parking facilities. Club will provide rates and other info upon request. An Officers' Annex has recently been opened consisting of a bar/anteroom, a dining room, and bedroom accommodations for individuals and families. All serving and retired officers are eligible. Price $17.25 single to $55.10 family suite.

Note: this is a private club and is not government/military billeting.

TML Availability: Good, but book early.

UNITED KINGDOM
London Service Clubs, continued

Victory Services Club
63/79 Seymour Street, London W2 2HF

TELEPHONE NUMBER INFORMATION: Comm: 44-01-723-4474, ATVN: None.

Location: Two blocks from the Marble Arch station, easy walking distance to the American Embassy, Navy Annex, Mayfair and Oxford Streets. HE: p-13, D/3. NMC: London, in the city.

Billeting Office: Address as above. This is a members only club. The following are eligible to join. A.) Serving and ex-service personnel of all ranks of the Armed Forces of the Crown, including those of the Commonwealth and members of NATO Forces stationed in the UK. B.) Spouses of members of the club. C.) Widows and widowers of ex-service personnel. The membership year is from 1 April and 31 March. Membership Fees: 10.00 pounds annually, 150.00 pounds lifetime. Write to club for an application and further details.

TML: Club/hotel. All ranks. Bedroom accommodations for 400 members (with 59 double bedrooms for married members. Rates: without private shower/bath: 14.00-16.75 pounds single room, 25.95-30.25 pounds twin-bedded room, 6.00-7.00 pounds per child 3-12 years; with private shower/bathroom: 17.80-21.20 pounds single room, 34.30-39.70 pounds twin bedded rooms, 45.00-51.60 pounds family suite, 8.00-10.00 pounds per child 3-12 years. Checks accepted when supported by a cheque card. Club facilities include a modern restaurant/grill room, bars, lounges, ballroom, game room, television rooms and library. Rates: double rooms for married couples 33.00 pounds, single rooms 13.20 pounds. All categories can make reservations.

TML Availability: Good but book early.

Note: other non-government **TML** in London is available at the **Portsmouth Royal Sailors Home Club,** Queen Street, Portsmouth, PO1, 3HS, telephone 0705-824231; and the **Royal Fleet Club,** 9-12 Morice Square, Davenport, Plymouth PL1 4PQ, telephone 0752-52723.

RAF Mildenhall (UK08R7)
APO New York 09127-5000

TELEPHONE NUMBER INFORMATION: Main installation numbers: Comm: 44-0638-51-2407/2203/2989/1844, ATVN: 238-2407/2203/2989/1844.

Location: From London or Cambridge follow A-11(M) to Newmarket and Barton Mills. Take A-1101 for 2.5 miles through Mildenhall Town to Beck Row Village and the AB. HE: p-13, E/1. NMC: Cambridge, 30 miles southwest.

Billeting Office: 513 SVS/SVH, Billeting Manager, Building 459. Comm: 0638-51-2726. ATVN: 238-2726. 24 hours daily. Check in facility, check out 1100 hours daily. Government civilian employee billeting.

TML: TLF. Building 104. All ranks. EX-2989. 40/2-bedroom apartments, private bath. Kitchen, microwave, complete utensils, color TV, maid service, free cribs, free washer/dryer. Modern structure. Rates: $24.00 per unit. Maximum 4 per room. Duty can make reservations. Others Space-A.

TML: VAQ. 100 and 400 area. Enlisted all grades. Leave or official duty. Shared rooms with open bay restrooms. Rates: $8.00 per person. Duty can make reservations. Other Space-A.

TML: VOQ. 200 and 400 area. Officer all grades. Leave or official duty. 1-bedroom,

UNITED KINGDOM

RAF Mildenhall, continued

TML: DV/VIP. Office 06+. Leave or official duty. 1-bedroom suites, private bath. Rates: Moderate. Duty can make reservations. Others Space-A.

DV/VIP: Protocol Office, 3rd AF, Building 239. EX-2132. 07+. Retirees and lower grades (06) Space-A.

Other: The largest and most active Space-A airport in the UK. Shuttle Bus to Lakenheath RAF departs MAC Term 35 minutes after hours 0635-1435, 1720, 1820.

TML Availability: Extremely limited. Best, Nov-Dec.

All numbers Comm or ATVN extensions.

Cafeteria-2689	Enlisted Club-2683	Locator-2669
Medical-2657	NCO Club-2323	O'Club-2615
Police-2667	Snack Bar-2488	SDO/NCO-2121

RAF Upper Heyford/Croughton (UK09R7)
APO New York 09194-5000

TELEPHONE NUMBER INFORMATION: Main installation numbers: Comm: 44-0869-23-4449, ATVN: 263-1110.

Location: From London, to Oxford, use M-40, then either A-423 (Oxford-Banbury) or A-43 (Oxford-Northampton), signs to base. HE: p-13, C/2. NMC: Oxford, 12 miles south.

Billeting Office: ATTN: 20th SVS/SVH. Building 73, Castle St, back of O'Club. 24 hours daily. Comm: 0869-23-4905/4557. ATVN: 263-4905/4557. Check in facility, check out 1100 hours daily. Government civilian employee billeting.

TML: TLF. All ranks. Leave or official duty. 120/1-bedroom; 24 separate bedroom. A/C. cots/cribs, ice vending, kitchenette, maid service, color TV room and lounge, utensils, free washer/dryer. Older structure, remodeled '89. Rates: $7.00-$24.00 per night. Maximum 2 per room. Duty can make reservations. Others Space-A.

TML: TLF. Building 41. All ranks. Leave or official duty. Accessible to handicapped. 24/1-bedroom. Cribs/cots, kitchenette maid service, refrigerator, color TV room and lounge, complete utensils, washer/dryer. Older structure, remodeled. Rates: $7.00-$24.00 per night. Duty can make reservations. Others Space-A.

DV/VIP: Building 74, EX-4557. 06+. Retirees and lower grades Space-A.

Other: City of Oxford. Blenheim Palace, George Washington's ancestral home.

TML Availability: Good, Nov-Feb. Difficult, Mar-Oct.

Cafeteria-4600	Enlisted Club-4423	Locator-4975
Medical-116	NCO Club-4284	O'Club-4424
Police-4337	Snack Bar-4582	SDO/NCO-4816

284 — *Temporary Military Lodging Around the World*

UNITED KINGDOM

RAF Wethersfield (UK10R7)
APO New York 09120-5000
CLOSED

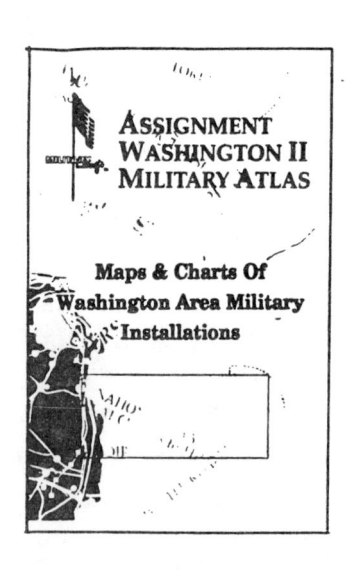

ASSIGNMENT WASHINGTON II MILITARY ATLAS

Maps & Charts Of Washington Area Military Installations

You can get this book at wholesale prices by ordering 25 or more copies. Call (703) 237-0203 for more information.

APPENDIX A

COUNTRY AND STATE ABBREVIATIONS
(used in this book)

COUNTRY ABBREVIATIONS

AN-Antigua
AU-Australia
BE-Belgium
BM-Bermuda
CN-Canada
CU-Cuba
GE-West Germany (and Berlin)
GR-Greece
GU-Guam*
HK-Hong Kong
IC-Iceland
IT-Italy
JA-Japan
MW-Midway*
NT-Netherlands

PN-Portugal
PO-Portugal (Azores)
PR-Puerto Rico*
RP-Republic of Korea
RP-Republic of the Philippines
SP-Spain
TU-Turkey
UK-United Kingdom
US-United States

*US Possession or Territory

STATE ABBREVIATIONS

AK-Alaska
AL-Alabama
AR-Arkansas
AZ-Arizona
CA-California
CO-Colorado
CT-Connecticut
DC-District of Columbia
DE-Delaware
FL-Florida
GA-Georgia
HI-Hawaii
IA-Iowa
ID-Idaho
IL-Illinois
IN-Indiana
KS-Kansas
KY-Kentucky
LA-Louisiana
MA-Massachusetts
MD-Maryland
ME-Maine
MI-Michigan
MN-Minnesota
MO-Missouri
MS-Mississippi

MT-Montana
NE-Nebraska
NC-North Carolina
ND-North Dakota
NH-New Hampshire
NJ-New Jersey
NM-New Mexico
NV-Nevada
NY-New York
OH-Ohio
OK-Oklahoma
OR-Oregon
PA-Pennsylvania
RI-Rhode Island
SC-South Carolina
SD-South Dakota
TN-Tennessee
TX-Texas
UT-Utah
VA-Virginia
VT-Vermont
WA-Washington
WI-Wisconsin
WV-West Virginia
WY-Wyoming

APPENDIX B

General Abbreviations

This appendix contains general abbreviations used in this book. Commonly understood abbreviations and standard abbreviations found in addresses have not been included in order to save space.

A
AAF-Army Airfield
AAFES-Army/Air Force Exchange System
AB-Air Base
A/C-Air Conditioning
AD-Active Duty
AF-Air Force
AFB-Air Force Base
AFRC-Air Force Reserve Center
AFRC-Armed Forces Recreation Center
AFRES-Air Force Reserve
ANG-Air National Guard
APO-Army Post Office
AS-Air Station
ATVN-Automatic Voice Network

B
BAQ-Bachelor Airmens' Quarters
BEQ-Bachelor Enlisted Quarters
BOQ-Bachelor Officers' Quarters

C
CG-Coast Guard
Cmdr-Commander
CO-Commanding Officer
Comm-Commercial Telephone System
Cons-Consolidated
CPO-Chief Petty Officer
CSM-Command Sergeant Major

D
DO-Duty Officer
DoD-Department of Defense
DV-Distinguished Visitor

E
EX-Telephone Extension

F
FPO-Fleet Post Office
FTS-Federal Telephone System

H
HE-Hallwag Europe (atlas)
Hq-Headquarters

K
Km-Kilometer

M
Marine Corps
MCB-Marine Corps Base
MCAS-Marine Corps Air Station

N
NAB-Naval Amphibious Base
NAS-Naval Air Station
NB-Naval Base
NCO-Noncommissioned Officer
NG-National Guard
NMC-Nearest Major City
NS-Naval Station
NSWC-Naval Surface Weapon Center
NTC-Naval Training Center
NWC-Naval Weapons Center

O
O'Club-Officers' Club
OD-Officer of the Day
OIC-Officer in Charge

P
PCS-Permanent Change of Station

R
RAF-Royal Air Force
Rec-Recreation
RM: p-Rand McNally Atlas (page)

S
SDO-Staff Duty Officer
Space-A-Space-Available

T
TAD-Temporary Attached Duty
TAQ-Temporary Airmens' Quarters
TDY-Temporary Duty
TEQ-Temporary Enlisted Quarters
TLF-Temporary Lodging Facility
TLF-Transient Lodging Facility
TLQ-Temporary Living Quarters
TML-Temporary Military Lodging
TOQ-Transient Officers' Quarters
TV-Television

Appendix B, continued

U
US-United States
USA-United States Army
USAF-United States Air Force
USCG-United States Coast Guard
USMC-United States Marine Corps
USN-United States Navy

V
VAQ-Visiting Airmens' Quarters
VEQ-Visiting Enlisted Quarters
VIP-Very Important Person
VOQ-Visiting Officer Quarters

MILITARY TRIVIA LOVERS - HERE'S THE BOOK FOR YOU!

Do you know where the famous flag raised over Iwo Jima during World War II is on display? How about General Patton's ivory handled revolvers? Or the world's first atomic submarine? Or "Anzio Annie," the only surviving German railroad gun from World War II? When and where did George Washington surrender for the first and only time during his military career? If you don't know the answers to these questions but wish you did, then you need Military Living's newest book, *U.S. Military Museums, Historic Sites & Exhibits.*

Written by Bryce D. Thompson, the compact, easy-to-use book is your guide to the following: Army, Navy, Marine Corps, Air Force, Coast Guard and N.O.A.A. Museums; other military museums; sites associated with the histories of all military powers in the U.S. and its territories; aviation and maritime museums having significant military collections; historic warships; submarines and boats; and NASA visitor centers and space museums.

The new book is published in both a soft cover edition and a hardcover gift edition, also suitable for libraries. Look for *U.S. Military Museums, Historic Sites & Exhibits* at your nearest military exchange and save! If not available, call Military Living in Falls Church, VA at (703) **237-0203.** Books may be ordered with your Visa, MasterCard or American Express card. Or, send your order to Military Living at PO Box 2347, Falls Church, VA 22042-0347. The soft cover mailed to your address is $16.45 and the hardcover gift edition is $26.45. Virginia addressees must add 4.5% sales tax.

P.S. Thinking of buying it as a gift? Let Military Living ship direct with our gift card from you. Easy ... and a thoughtful gift as well!

288 — *Temporary Military Lodging Around the World*

APPENDIX C

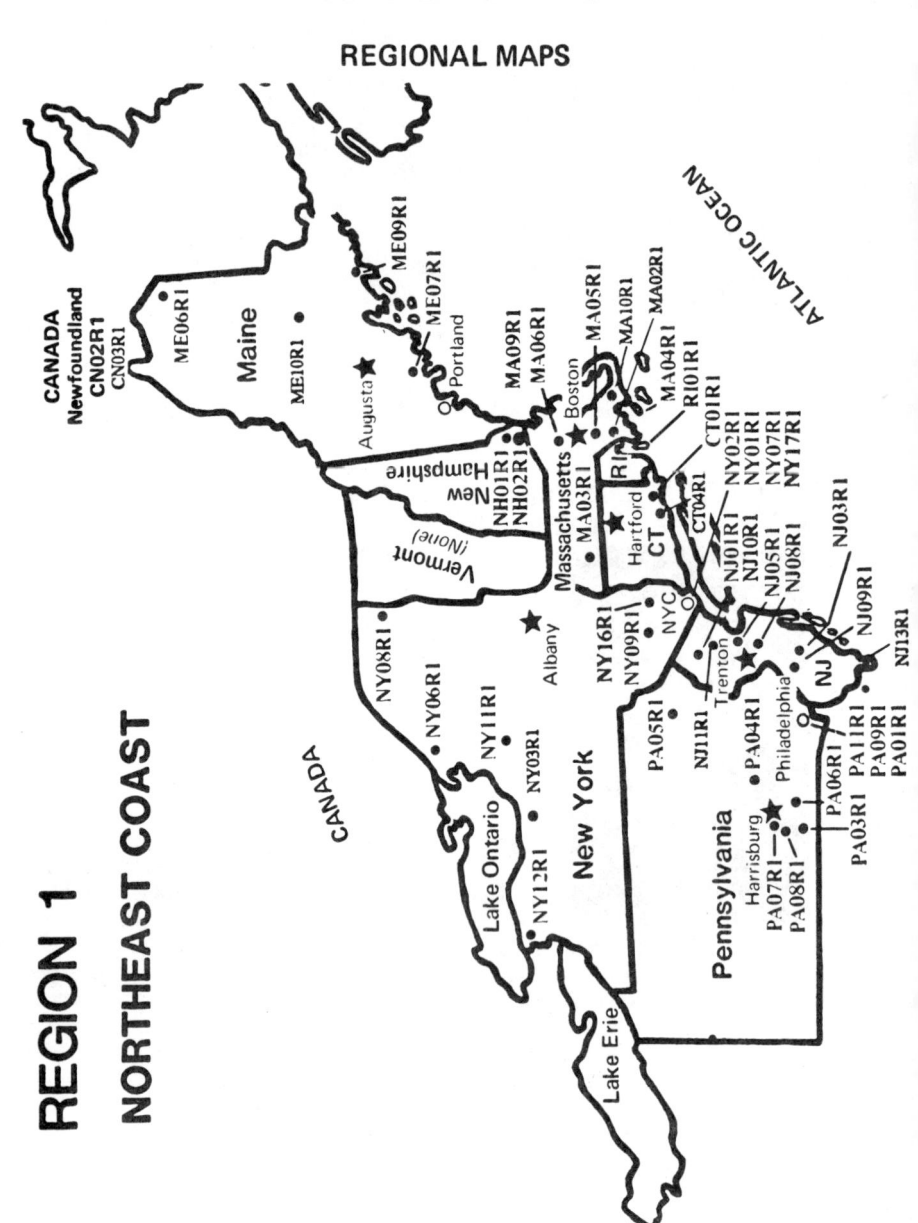

REGIONAL MAPS

**REGION 1
NORTHEAST COAST**

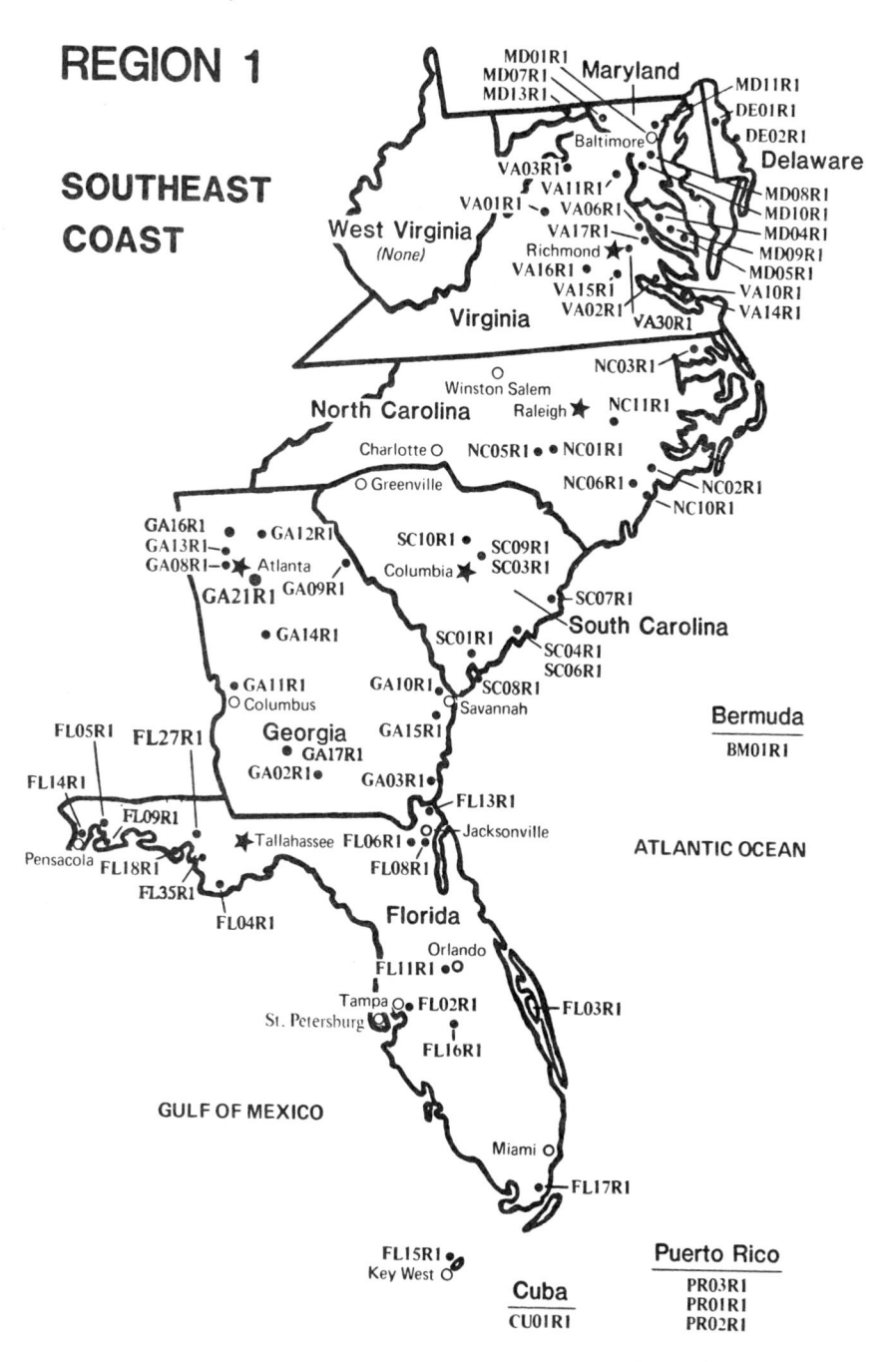

Temporary Military Lodging Around the World — 289

APPENDIX C, cont'd

REGION 1

SOUTHEAST COAST

Maryland: MD01R1, MD07R1, MD13R1, MD11R1, MD08R1, MD10R1, MD04R1, MD09R1, MD05R1

Delaware: DE01R1, DE02R1

West Virginia (None)

Virginia: VA03R1, VA11R1, VA01R1, VA06R1, VA17R1, VA16R1, VA15R1, VA02R1, VA30R1, VA10R1, VA14R1

North Carolina: NC03R1, NC11R1, NC05R1, NC01R1, NC06R1, NC02R1, NC10R1

South Carolina: SC10R1, SC09R1, SC03R1, SC07R1, SC01R1, SC04R1, SC06R1, SC08R1

Georgia: GA16R1, GA13R1, GA08R1, GA12R1, GA21R1, GA09R1, GA14R1, GA11R1, GA10R1, GA15R1, GA17R1, GA02R1, GA03R1

Florida: FL05R1, FL27R1, FL14R1, FL09R1, FL18R1, FL35R1, FL04R1, FL13R1, FL06R1, FL08R1, FL11R1, FL02R1, FL03R1, FL16R1, FL17R1, FL15R1

Bermuda: BM01R1

ATLANTIC OCEAN

GULF OF MEXICO

Cuba: CU01R1

Puerto Rico: PR03R1, PR01R1, PR02R1

APPENDIX C, cont'd

REGION 1
WASHINGTON D.C. METRO AREA

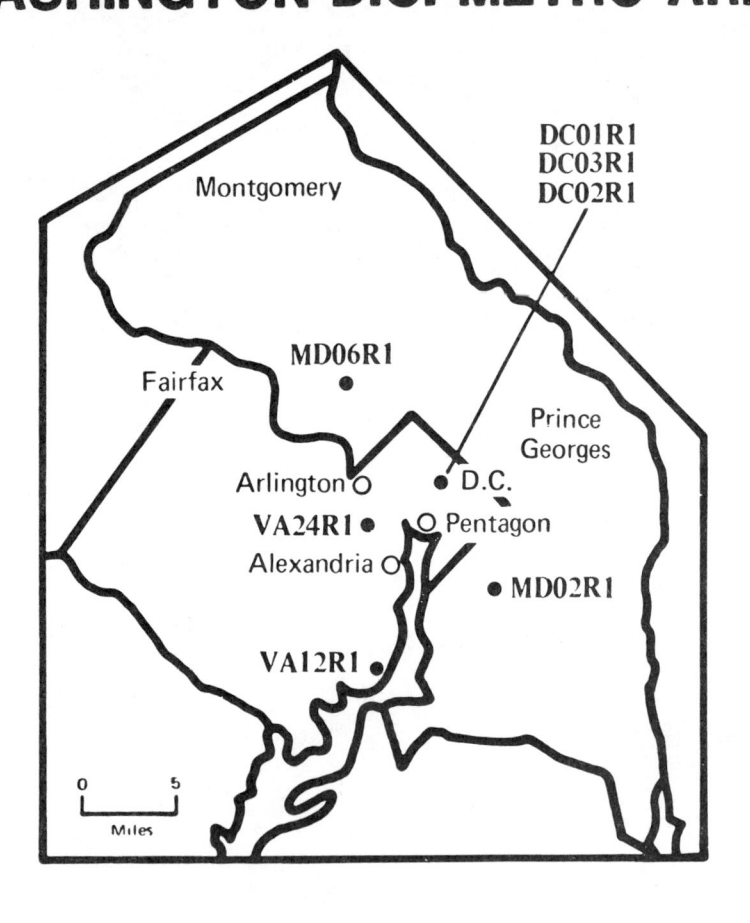

- DC01R1
- DC03R1
- DC02R1
- Montgomery
- MD06R1
- Fairfax
- Prince Georges
- Arlington
- D.C.
- VA24R1
- Pentagon
- Alexandria
- MD02R1
- VA12R1

0 — 5 Miles

APPENDIX C, cont'd

REGION 1
NORFOLK AREA

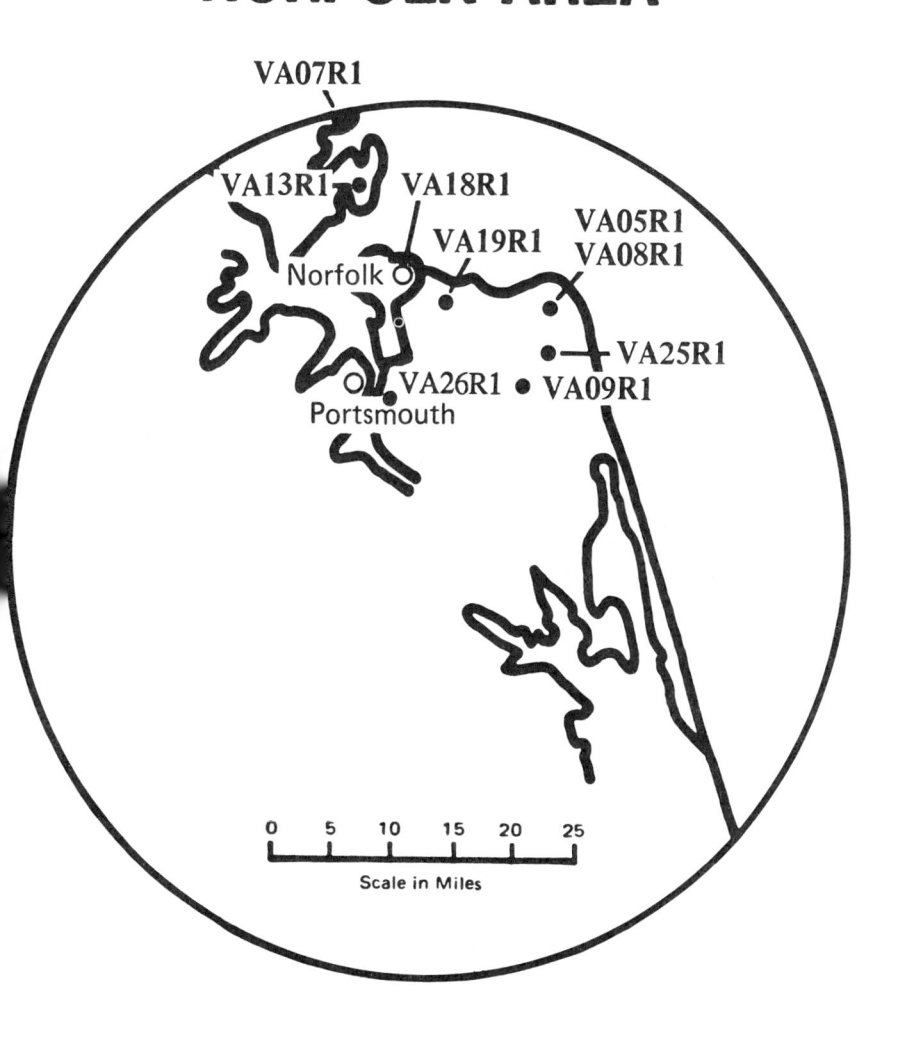

APPENDIX C, cont'd

REGION 2
NORTHEAST CENTRAL

Temporary Military Lodging Around the World — 293

APPENDIX C, cont'd

REGION 2
SOUTHEAST CENTRAL

Missouri
- MO02R2
- Kansas City ○
- St. Louis ○
- MO04R2 ★ Jefferson City
- MO01R2 ●
- MO03R2 ●

Kentucky
- Cincinnati ○
- ★ Frankfort
- ○ Louisville
- ○ Lexington
- KY01R2
- KY02R2

Tennessee
- ★ Nashville
- Knoxville ○
- TN01R2
- ○ Memphis
- TN02R2

Arkansas
- ○ Fort Smith
- AR01R2
- AR02R2
- ★ Little Rock
- AR03R2

Mississippi
- MS01R2
- MS04R2 ★ Jackson
- Meridian ○
- MS02R2
- MS03R2

Alabama
- Huntsville ○
- AL06R2
- Birmingham ○
- AL01R2
- Tuscaloosa ○
- AL03R2 ● ● AL04R2
- ★ Montgomery
- AL02R2
- Mobile ○
- AL08R2

Louisiana
- Shreveport ○
- LA01R2
- LA07R2 LA05R2
- Baton Rouge ★
- New Orleans ○
- LA11R2
- LA06R2

GULF OF MEXICO

APPENDIX C, cont'd

REGION 3
NORTHWEST CENTRAL

APPENDIX C, cont'd

REGION 3
SOUTHWEST CENTRAL

New Mexico
- Santa Fe
- Albuquerque
- NM03R3
- NM02R3
- NM04R3
- NM05R3
- Las Cruces
- El Paso
- TX06R3

Oklahoma
- OK05R3
- Tulsa
- Oklahoma City
- OK04R3
- OK02R3
- OK01R3
- Lawton

Texas
- Amarillo
- TX20R3
- Lubbock
- TX37R3
- TX21R3
- Ft. Worth
- Dallas
- TX12R3
- TX09R3
- TX14R3
- Waco
- TX02R3
- TX24R3
- TX07R3
- Austin
- TX27R3
- Houston
- Del Rio
- TX05R3
- San Antonio
- TX28R3
- TX26R3
- TX18R3
- TX03R3
- TX25R3
- TX19R3
- TX23R3
- TX43R3
- Corpus Christi
- TX10R3
- TX42R3
- TX22R3

MEXICO

Republic of Panama
- PN01R3
- PN02R3
- PN03R3

GULF OF MEXICO

296 — *Temporary Military Lodging Around the World*

APPENDIX C, cont'd

REGION 4
WEST COAST

Temporary Military Lodging Around the World — 297

APPENDIX C, cont'd

REGION 4
SAN FRANCISCO AREA

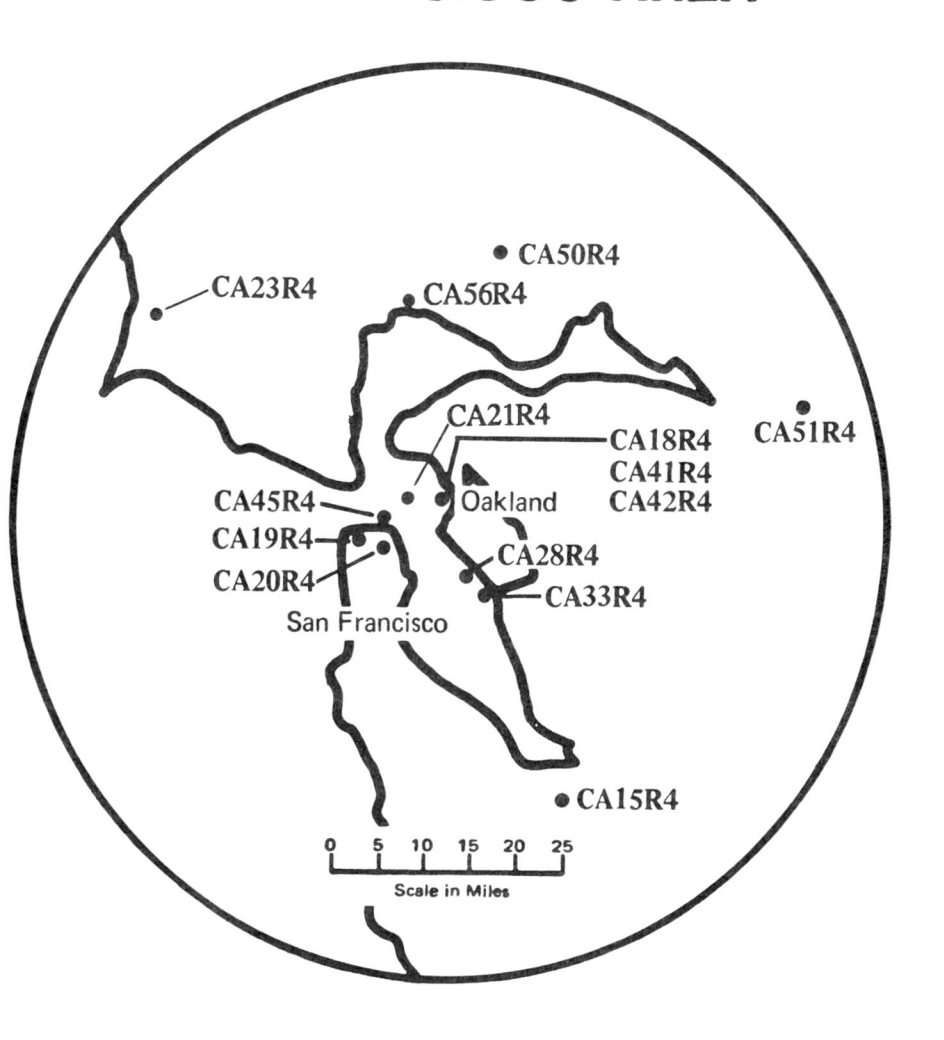

APPENDIX C, cont'd

REGION 4
LOS ANGELES AREA

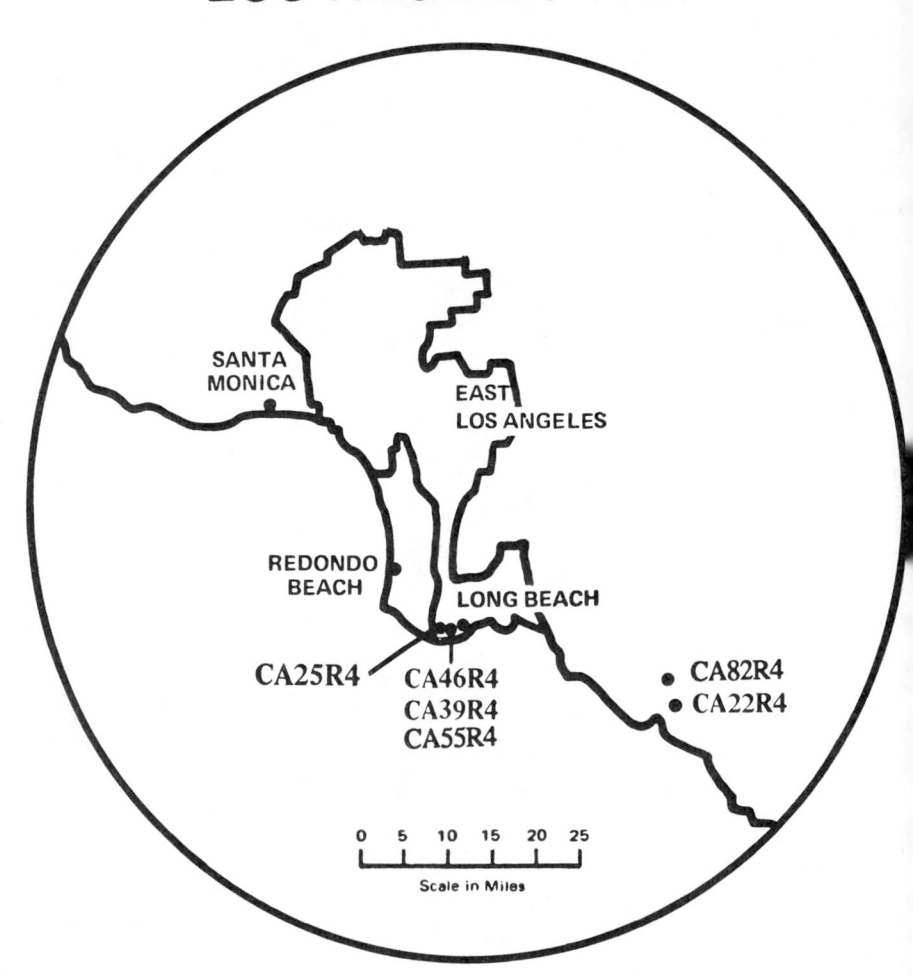

APPENDIX C, cont'd

REGION 4
SAN DIEGO AREA

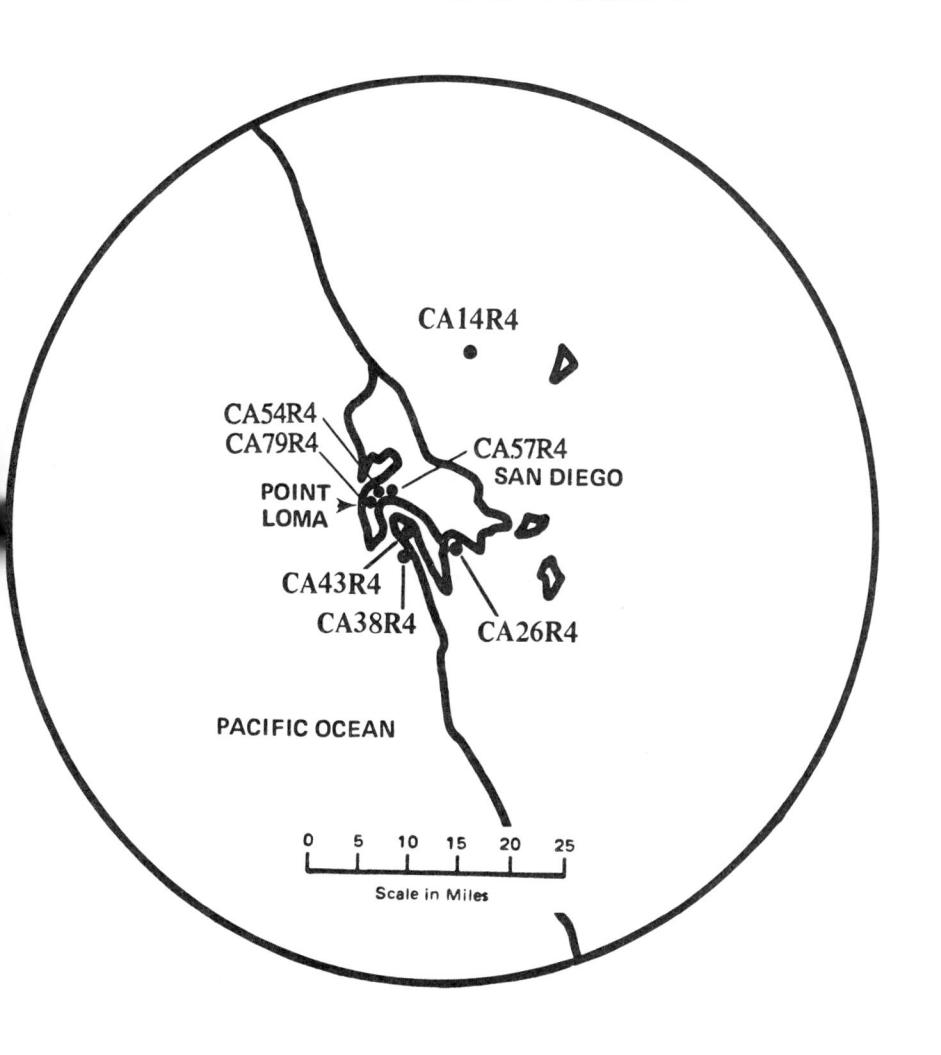

CA14R4

CA54R4
CA79R4
POINT LOMA
CA57R4
SAN DIEGO

CA43R4
CA38R4
CA26R4

PACIFIC OCEAN

0 5 10 15 20 25
Scale in Miles

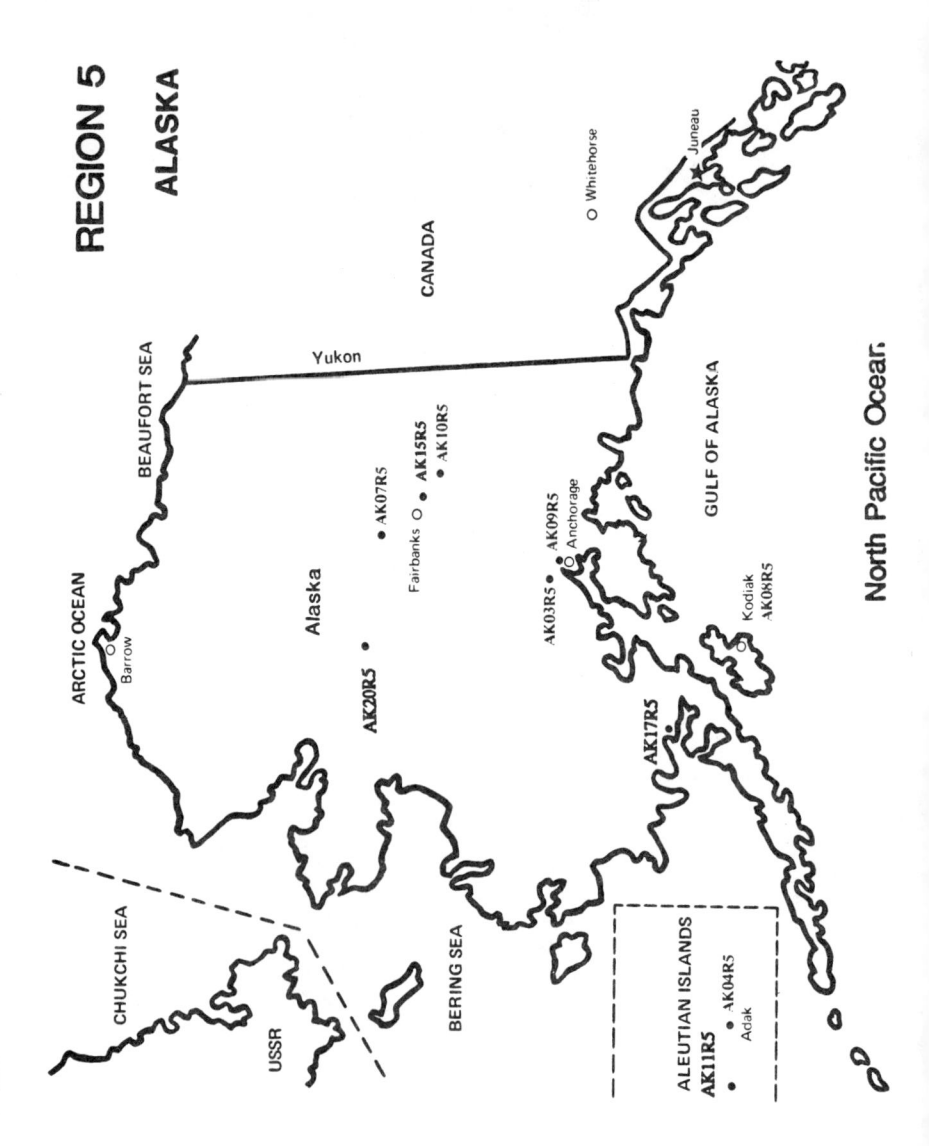

300 — *Temporary Military Lodging Around the World*

APPENDIX C, cont'd

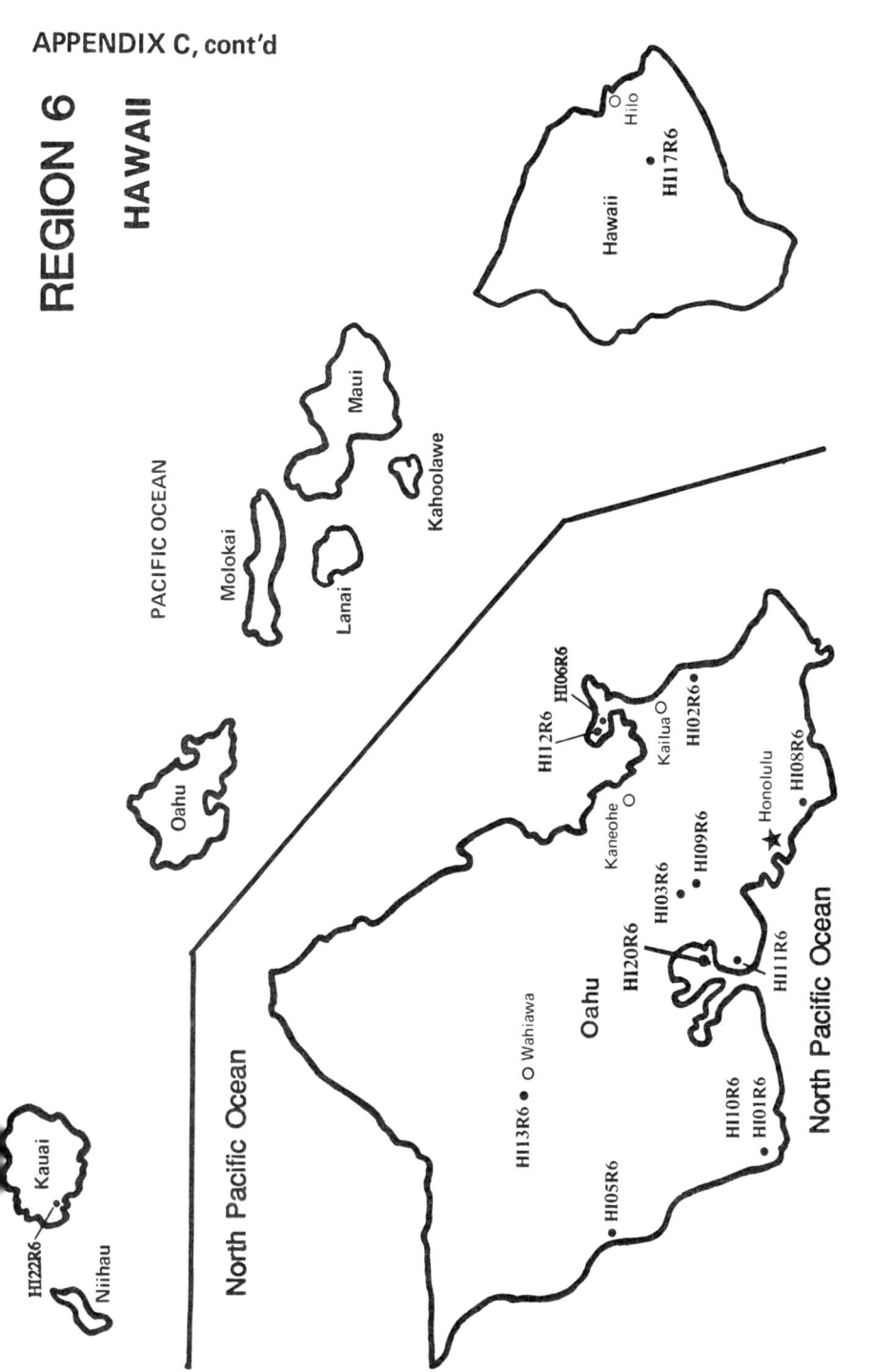

APPENDIX C, cont'd

REGION 6 — HAWAII

APPENDIX C, cont'd

REGION 7
UNITED KINGDOM

Iceland
IC01R7

Scotland
- Inverness
- UK06R7
- Glasgow
- Edinburgh
- JK29R7

NORTH SEA

IRISH SEA

England
- Newcastle
- York
- Leeds
- Liverpool
- UK03R7
- Sheffield
- Nottingham
- Peterborough
- Norwich
- Birmingham
- UK01R7
- UK07R7
- UK08R7
- Cambridge
- UK04R7
- Ipswich
- UK12R7
- UK09R7
- UK10R7 CLOSED
- Oxford
- UK11R7
- UK13R7
- London
- Bristol
- UK05R7
- UK18R7
- Dover

Wales
- UK02R7
- Brawdy
- Cardiff

Celtic Sea

Southampton

Plymouth

Strait of Dover

ENGLISH CHANNEL

Temporary Military Lodging Around the World — 303

APPENDIX C, cont'd

REGION 7
SPAIN/PORTUGAL

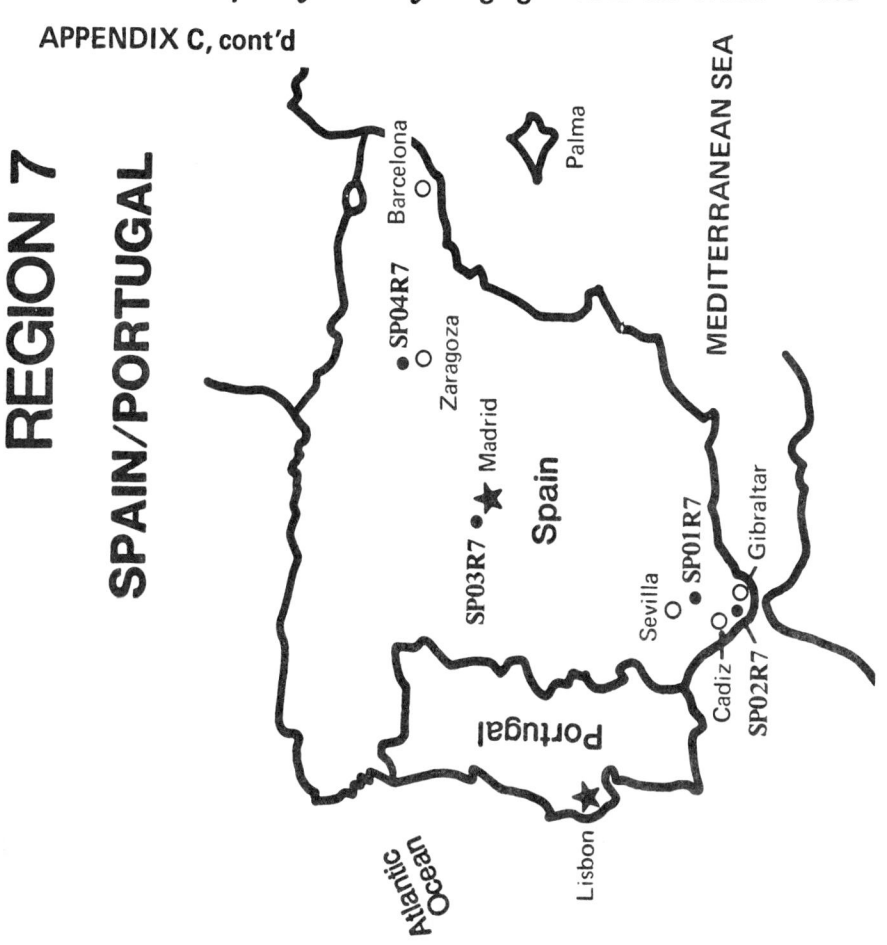

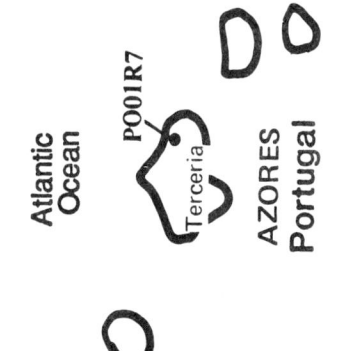

Spain / Portugal map with locations:
- Barcelona
- Palma
- SP04R7 / Zaragoza
- SP03R7 / Madrid
- Sevilla
- SP01R7
- Cadiz / SP02R7
- Gibraltar
- Lisbon
- MEDITERRANEAN SEA
- Atlantic Ocean

AZORES, Portugal:
- PO01R7 / Terceria
- Atlantic Ocean

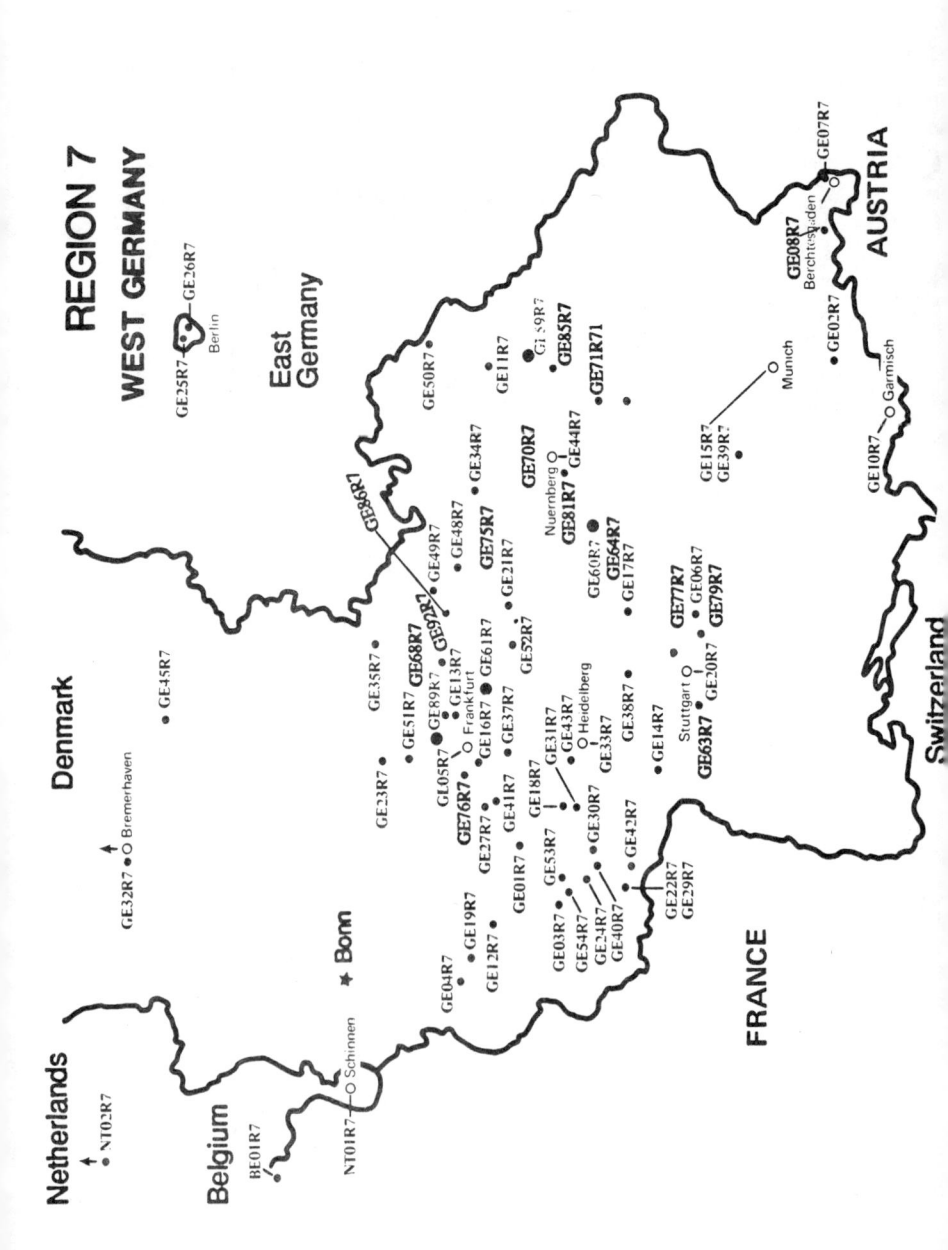

APPENDIX C, cont'd

REGION 7
WEST GERMANY

Temporary Military Lodging Around the World — 305

APPENDIX C, cont'd

REGION 7
ITALY

- IT04R7 (near Udine)
- IT06R7 (Verona/Vicenza)
- IT10R7 (Pisa)
- IT13R7 (Sardinia)
- IT03R7 (Naples)
- IT05R7 (Naples)
- IT07R7
- IT12R7 (Sardinia)
- IT01R7 (Sicily)
- IT11R7 (Sicily)

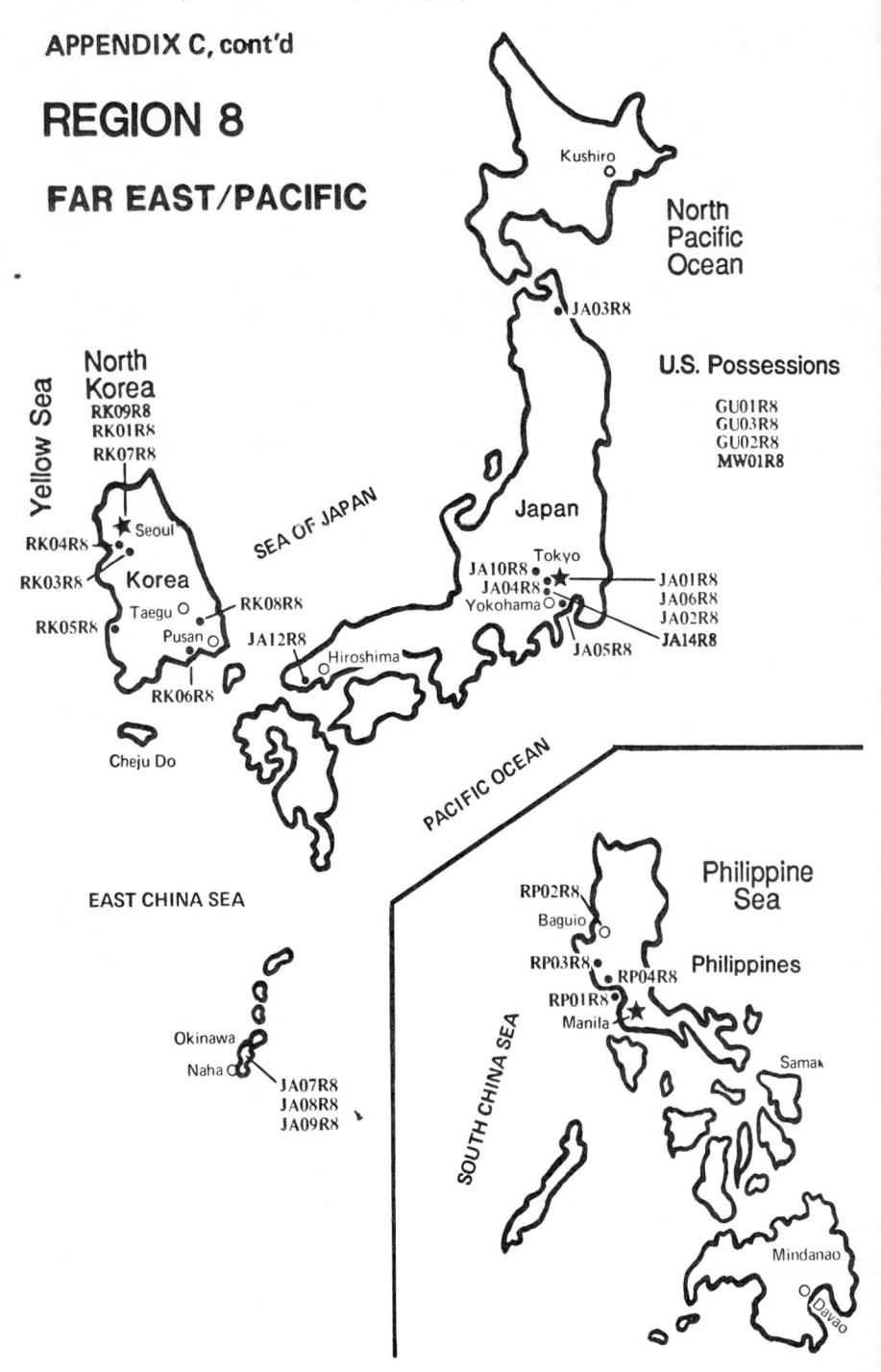

APPENDIX C, cont'd

REGION 8

FAR EAST/PACIFIC

North Korea
RK09R8
RK01R8
RK07R8

RK04R8
RK03R8
RK05R8
RK08R8
RK06R8

Korea — Seoul, Taegu, Pusan
Cheju Do

Japan — Kushiro, Tokyo, Yokohama, Hiroshima
JA03R8
JA10R8
JA04R8
JA01R8
JA06R8
JA02R8
JA14R8
JA05R8
JA12R8

U.S. Possessions
GU01R8
GU03R8
GU02R8
MW01R8

Okinawa — Naha
JA07R8
JA08R8
JA09R8

Philippines — Baguio, Manila, Samar, Mindanao, Davao
RP02R8
RP03R8
RP04R8
RP01R8

Temporary Military Lodging Around the World — 307

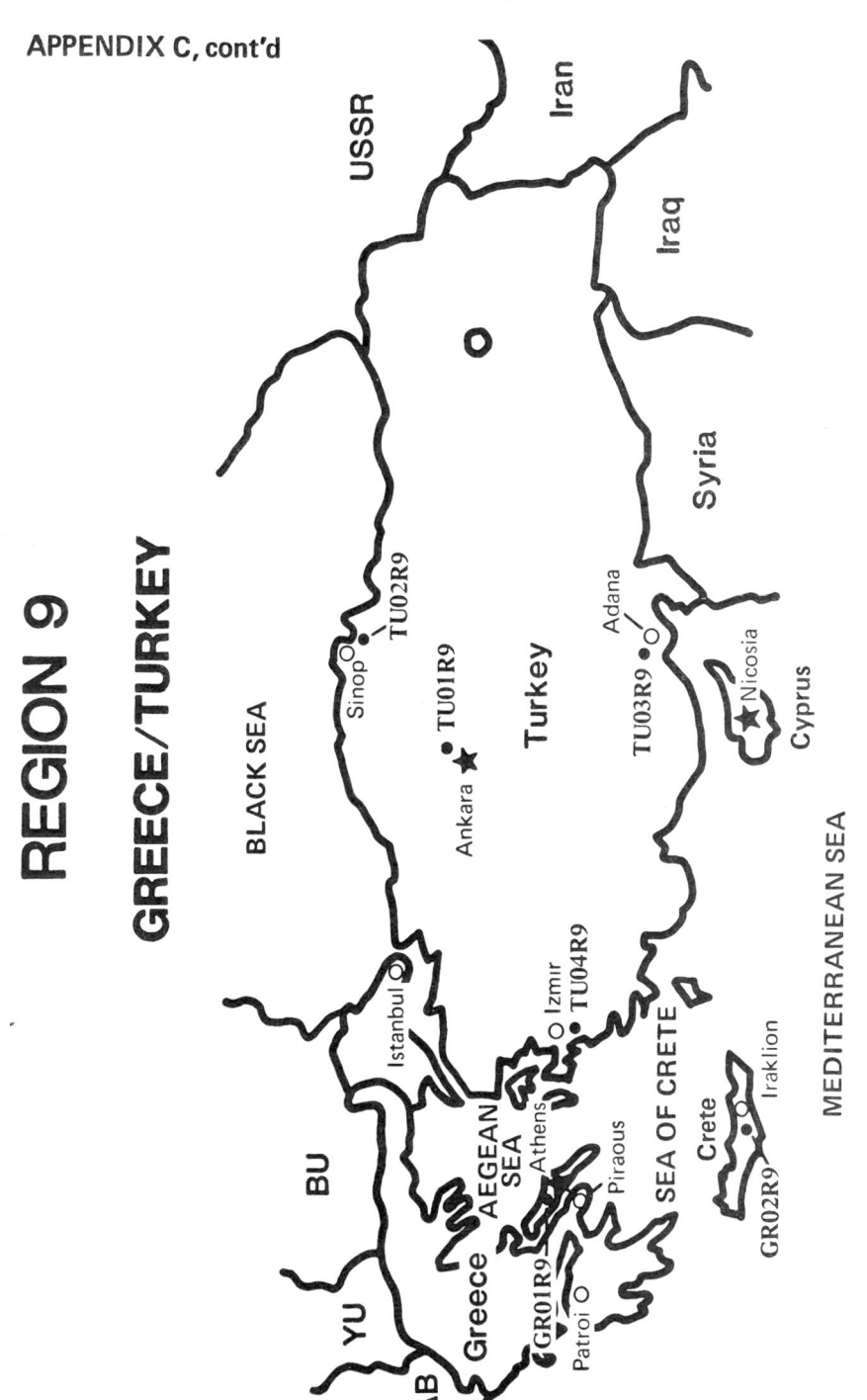

APPENDIX C, cont'd

REGION 9
GREECE/TURKEY

APPENDIX D

Temporary Military Lodging Questions and Answers

Answers below are based on information available to us at press time. Due to the fact that policies differ from installation to installation, these general answers must be accepted only as guides...not rules. Specific questions should be directed to each individual installation at the time of your visit. Policies often change.

1.) What types of lodging are available on military installations? There are numerous types of lodging. They range from very modern, modular-constructed, complete housekeeping units which will sleep a family of five with all the amenities found in a good motel (plus a furnished kitchenette) such as found in Navy Lodges, to the old faithful guest houses...relics of World War II, which are often barracks-type buildings. Some may have been improved while others are definitely sub-standard. Some are the modern hotel type such as the Hale Koa (Hawaii), the New Sanno (Japan) and Dragon Hill (Yongson, Korea). There are also the modern motel type such as the Super 8's at Governor's Island, Fort Bliss, and Fort Drum. Somewhere in between, you will find the VOQ type accommodations that usually consist of private rooms with a shared bath between rooms. If you are the "picky" type, we suggest you take a look before signing in, if possible.

2.) Were the units mentioned above constructed with tax dollars? According to information given TML, the answer on most of the lodging is an emphatic "NO." The newer construction was built from non-appropriated funds or grants from welfare funds, generated from profits from Exchanges, etc. The exception to this is in cases where old unused family housing initially built with appropriated funds has been converted into temporary lodging facilties.

3.) What does space-available (Space-A) mean? The purpose of having lodging on military installations is to accommodate duty personnel and those arriving or departing an installation on permanent change of station (PCS) orders. Those on orders generally have first priority on all lodging. After these needs have been met, if there is any space left over, leave personnel may utilize the facilities on a space-available basis. During the summer months, space-available lodging may be more difficult to obtain than during the spring, fall, and winter.

4.) How about advance reservations? While many installations will accept reservations from those on duty, leave travelers will generally find that they cannot make reservations in advance but are accepted on a space-a basis on arrival at the billeting office. As we are listing the lodging of five different services in this book, the rules may vary greatly from place to place. Please call in advance to check on specific policies on making reservations at the time of your trip. You may be surprised and find that the place you want to visit will accept your reservation.

5.) Can retirees use military lodging? Definitely...usually on the same space-available basis as active duty on leave. Retirees will also find that they are welcome to use the lodging on many installations overseas, even though they may be restricted from using the commissary or exchange in most overseas areas due to the Status of Forces Agreement.

6.) Are Reservists eligible for TML? Reservists drawing retired pay - the grey or the blue ID card - are entitled on the same basis as other retirees to use TML for themselves and their dependents. Reservists at a base on inactive duty for training may use TML during that period, and their

Appendix D, continued

dependents are eligible. Reservists on active duty for training may use TML on a space-available basis along with accompanying dependents. Usually, they have a lower priority than active duty. During that period of time, family members are also eligible for the use of commissaries and exchanges. Air Force facilities will accept family members of the Air National Guard or Air Force Reserve when on active duty and/or in training.

Red ID card holders and their dependents have occasionally been allowed to use TML. Since rules can differ from place to place, we recommend that you inquire at each location if interested.

7.) Your book often refers to Autovon (ATVN) phone numbers. What are they? Autovon (Automatic Voice Network) numbers are military phone numbers which are to be used only by those on **official business**. Such numbers can normally be dialed only from a military installation and are monitored to assure their use is not violated. As many of our readers use military lodging and facilities while traveling on duty, and many government offices use our book as a reference guide, we publish the Autovon numbers, when available, as a service to them.

8.) What is DV/VIP lodging? It is lodging for distinguished official visitors. Some installations will have a few rooms or a small guest house available for them. If these facilities are not being used by official visitors, many installations will often extend the courtesy of their use to qualified active duty personnel on leave status or retirees on a day-to-day space-available basis. Most military installations we surveyed referred to DV/VIP as grades 06 and above. Just a few included lower officer grades and senior NCOs in this category. The Marine Corps calls their distinguished visitors lodging Distinguished Guest Quarters (DGQ's). Since 1977, we have noted that many more Air Force bases are providing DV/VIP lodging for their senior NCOs. Those in the DV/VIP category should check our listings in this book for more complete information and inquire at each installation upon arrival. Distinguished visitors will usually find that it is best to make advance reservations through the Protocol Office or Visitor's Bureau of the installation concerned. In some cases, the billeting office has authority to place personnel in the quarters and coordinates the visit for the traveler.

9.) My husband is enlisted. What chance do we have at staying in military lodging? Better than ever. In the past few years, concentrated efforts have been made to provide more temporary lodging for enlisted members. Please notice in our listing the numerous references to quarters for all ranks. In the newer Air Force Transient Living Quarters, Navy Lodges, and Army Guest Houses, rank has absolutely no privileges. All ranks are accommodated on an equal basis. Policies may vary on other types of lodging. At some places, enlisted have priority.

10.) May 100% DAVs use TML? Most military lodging units accept 100% DAVs on a space-available basis if it is possible. In fact, the Hale Koa R&R hotel specifically mentions 100% DAVs in their brochure as being eligible. One problem that 100% DAVs have encountered has been caused by the color of their ID card. It is the same color (buff or butterscotch) as carried by family members. Many times 100% DAVs are turned away from facilities which require family members to be accompanied by their sponsor. The "ID card-checking authority" assumes this military member is not a military member but a "dependent" or family member. Watch for more info on this subject in Military Living's R&R report.

Appendix D, continued

11.) How about Navy - Bachelor Quarters (BQ)? We are told that a few Bachelor Enlisted Quarter (BEQ) locations have unsuitable facilities for family members (central latrines, etc.). However, most BEQs have suitable facilities. Also, Bachelor Officer Quarters (BOQs) are almost always suitable. They will generally accept family members accompanying their sponsor. Rules can vary from installation to installation. If a Navy Lodge is not available, always ask about the possible use of the BOQ.

12.) What about widows, widowers, and unaccompanied dependents? We have better news to report in this new edition of TML. Dependents of active duty personnel who are involved in a PCS move may now use TML and may make reservations at the installation they are leaving and at the new one to which they are assigned. They may also use TML en route on a space-available basis. This includes TML in TLFs and in VOQs or VAQs.

Unaccompanied dependents of military members on leave and also widows/ers of deceased members may use TML on a space-available basis in VAQs or VOQs if this policy has been approved by the base commander. (Therefore, this may NOT be in effect at all Air Force installations.) This does not include the use of TLFs.

Other services generally have always allowed unaccompanied military family members to use TML on a space-available basis. This, of course, has and will continue to differ from installation to installation. The new Navy Lodge brochure, however, states "Dependent children are welcomed at Navy Lodges only when accompanied by a parent or guardian authorized to utilize Navy Lodges."

MILITARY Living's
R&R
SPACE-A REPORT
FOR ALL RANKS &
ALL SERVICES
ACTIVE OR RETIRED
FAMILY MEMBERS & WIDOWS/ERS
**6 TIMES YEARLY
TRAVEL NEWSLETTER**

SEE THE CENTRAL ORDER COUPONS

IN THE BACK OF THIS BOOK

APPENDIX E

Billeting Regulations and Navy Lodge Information

Army Billeting Operations Regulations

The following has been extracted from Army Regulation 210-11, effective 15 July 1983.

Army regulation 210-11 prescribes policies, procedures, and instructions relating to the billeting function, which encompasses the management and operation of unaccompanied personnel housing (UPH) to include permanent party and temporary duty (TDY)) and guest house (GH) accommodations under the jurisdiction of the Department of the Army (DA).

Objectives. The objectives of the UPH and GH program are to provide: a.) Adequate housing for eligible military and DOD civilian personnel, permanently assigned or in a TDY status. b.) Short-term accommodations for military personnel and families (arriving or departing incident to permanent change of station (PCS)) and authorized visitors.

Transient Quarters Operations. Quarters will be identified by use as follows. a.) Visiting Officer Quarters (VOQ) and Visiting Enlisted quarters (VEQ). VOQ and VEQ support TDY military and civilian personnel to include distinguished visitors who normally use DVQ. b.) Guest Houses (GH). GHs provide short-term accommodations for accompanied and unaccompanied military personnel and eligible DOD civilians arriving or departing installations incident to PCS. Also included are active military personnel on leave, active or retired military personnel in military hospitals, and guests of service members. Retired military personnel and families may occupy GHs if space is available.

Each category of transient quarters (e.g. VOQ, VEQ, DVQ, or GH) will be a separate operation. Twenty-four hour check-in and check-out service should be provided. When twenty-four hour service is not appropriate, another installation activity may assist visitors arriving during non-duty hours.

Services and Supplies. As a minimum, the following services will be provided. a.) In-room maid service. b.) Bathroom facilities with two towels and one washcloth per occupant daily, cloth bathmat, soap, and toilet paper. c.) One clean drinking glass or cup per occupant. d.) Minimum of one trash receptacle or one wastebasket per room. e.) Information on service charges, telephone service, post transportation, taxis, other local transportation, religious services, dining facilities, post exchange, post recreational activities, commercial laundry, washers and dryers, commissary, and emergency and medical facilities. f.) Vending machines to provide soft drinks, candy, cigarettes, and if washing machines are available, small packaged laundry soap. g.) When kitchen facilities are not available in GH, provisions for warming baby formula and bottles. h.) Alarm clock or radio or wakeup service.

Guest House Operations. GHs may be established as hotel- or motel-like furnished rooms, furnished apartments or houses, or other facilities. The use of GHs is a privilege afforded military personnel, with or without families, and eligible DOD civilians primarily to assist in moves incident to PCS. GHs will be voluntarily occupied except as otherwise prescribed, and occupants will pay a service charge established by the installation commander. The

Appendix E, continued

occupants will be advised of the rates and method of payment prior to occupancy.

Personnel having priority I status for occupancy of GHs are: active duty military of all grades (and eligible DOD civilians in foreign areas), accompanied or unaccompanied, departing or arriving incident to PCS; visiting relatives and guests of patients in military hospitals or military patients in local hospitals; active and retired military personnel and other personnel undergoing outpatient medical treatment who must stay overnight near a military medical facility. Note: installation commanders may establish priorities within priority I to meet special needs.

Personnel having priority II status for occupancy of GHs are: friends and relatives visiting service personnel stationed at the installation.

Unless prohibited by international agreement, the following personnel may occupy GHs on a space-available basis: military personnel in a leave, pass, or transient status; retired military personnel in a transient status; other personnel in a transient status who are entitled to dependency benefits.

Reservations. Only personnel in priority I may reserve GHs. Reservations will be on a first-come basis without regard to rank. Reservations should not be accepted more than 60 days in advance. Requests must include expected arrival time and date. Members on PCS will provide a copy of PCS orders or the special order number, date, and issuing headquarters with the reservation request.

Personnel visiting hospital patients must give the patient's name with the reservation request. Reservations are conditional pending confirmation of patient status.

Navy Lodges

Navy Lodge Mission. The Navy Lodge mission is to provide U.S. military personnel accompanied by dependents under Permanent Change of Station (PCS) orders with clean, comfortable, temporary lodging accommodations while they are seeking a permanent residence.

At Naval hospitals, the Navy Lodge mission is to provide authorized personnel with clean, comfortable, temporary accommodations with the following priorities. Priority I: members of the immediate family of in-patients who are seriously or critically ill and sponsors of children who are undergoing or convalescing from serious surgery. Priority II: members of the immediate family of all other in-patients.

Reservations. Reservations will be held only until 1800 hours unless advance deposit has been received. Check-in time is normally 1500 hours; earlier arrivals will be accommodated when possible. Reserved accommodations have priority over guests holding accommodations who wish to extend their length of stay. Since January 1986, MasterCards and VISA cards have been accepted as payment for room rental.

MasterCards and VISA cards are also now accepted for guaranteed reservations. Accompanied PCS personnel may make reservations at any time. Retirees can make reservations 10 days in advance. Other categories can make reservations 21 days in advance. Four new Navy Lodges are scheduled to be opened in 1990: Patuxent River NAS (50 units), Staten Island Naval

Appendix E, continued

Base (50 units), Roosevelt Roads Naval Station (72 units), Key West Naval Air Station (26 units). In addition, Memphis Naval Air Station is scheduled for a 22 unit increase in 1990. **The toll-free reservations number for all Navy Lodges in CONUS is 1-800-NAVY-INN. New Jersey residents may dial 1-201-323-1103 or ATVN 624-1103. The ATVN number for reservations if dialing from overseas is 565-2027.** Reservations at OCONUS and foreign-area Navy Lodges should be made by contacting the Lodge directly by phone or through the mail.

With regard to Navy permament party housing operations, **Unaccompanied Officer Personnel Housing (UOPH) and Unaccompanied Enlisted Personnel Housing (UEPH) facilities have been re-designated as Bachelor Officer Quarters (BOQ) and Bachelor Enlisted Quarters (BEQ). BOQ and BEQ facilities both admit retirees and other transients on a space-available basis.** Lodging facilities exist at approximately 175 Naval installations around the world. All Exchange personnel (active & retired) and "Grey Area" retired reservists (not yet age 60) are eligible to use Navy Lodges.

Marine Corps Billeting Operations Regulations

The following has been extracted from the Real Property Facilities Manual, Volume XI, Marine Corps Bachelor Housing Management dated 28 October 1985 and updated thru 10 November 1988.

Transient Quarters Operation. Transient quarters are operated primarily to provide a service to duty transient personnel and TAD students. Adequate quarters shall be set aside to accommodate TAD transient personnel. When designated transient quarters are fully occupied, transients may voluntarily occupy permanent party quarters.

The following personnel are entitled to designated TAD transient quarters on a confirmed reservation basis: a.) Military personnel and DOD civilians on TAD orders. b.) U.S. and foreign civilians traveling as guests of the Armed Forces. c.) Reserve personnel in TAD status, unit training status, and annual trainees on individual orders. d.) TAD foreign nationals or foreign military trainees engaged in or sponsored by military assistance or similar training programs unless prohibited by the Status of Forces Agreement (SOFA). e.) Family members on medical TAD orders. f.) Military personnel with or without family members, arriving or departing for overseas installations on PCS when TLF or permanent housing is not immediately available. g). Families of members overseas.

The following personnel may occupy designated transient quarters on a space-available basis: a.) Retirees, military personnel on leave, family members, or guests of military personnel assigned to the activity if TLF space is not available. b.) DOD civilian employees and their families arriving or departing incident to PCS when TLFs are not available. c.) Guests of the activity commander. Non-duty transients shall be advised at the time of registration that occupancy is strictly on a day-to-day, space-available basis and that they must vacate not later than the following day if the quarters are required for duty transients.

Distinguished Guest Quarters (DGQ's) are also available to accommodate the frequent travel of high ranking officials, both civilian and military. DGQ's are under the control of the installation commander.

Appendix E, continued

Services and Supplies. As a minimum, transient quarters should provide the same facilities, services, and supplies which would ordinarily be provided a permanent BOQ/BEQ resident of the same grade. Transient units should be considered adequate only when meal facilities (commercial or government) are available during reasonable hours for three meals a day, within a reasonable walking distance or with transportation provided.

The following services and supplies are required in all units used for transient personnel: a.) Twenty-four hour check-in or check-out service, 24-hour wake-up service, or issue of an alarm clock. b.) Custodial service in all common-use areas. c.) Daily maid service. d.) Change of bed linens when guests depart, or once a week minimum for long-term guests. e.) At least one towel, bar of soap, and drinking glass per guest. f.) Lock and key for doors to all separate units, and inside and outside locks or latches on all bathroom facilities between rooms.

Coast Guard Temporary Guest Housing Facility Policies

The following has been extracted from Coast Guard Commandant Publication P1710.14 dated 18 January 1989.

Most large Coast Guard installations have developed guest housing in response to the need for temporary lodging for Coast Guard members and their families. These facilities are operated and managed by the Coast Guard Nonappropriated Fund Activity (NAFA). Since each installation manages its own GH, each has its own rules and regulations regarding usage.

Guest housing was developed mainly for use by active duty Coast Guard members and their families traveling under PCS orders; however, Coast Guard personnel in other than PCS status and members of the other uniformed services are allowed to use some Coast Guard guest housing facilities. It is always advisable to call the facility you intend to visit to determine your eligibility.

Air Force Billeting Operations Regulations

The following has been extracted from Air Force Regulation 90-9 dated 31 October 1984 and updated thru 27 March 1989.

Transient Quarters Operation. Transient Quarters are operated to provide a service to duty transient personnel and TDY students. The operation of transient quarters is based on the need of the services and the availability of quarters at an installation.

Personnel Eligible for Transient Quarters: The following personnel are eligible to occupy Visiting Officer Quarters (VOQ) and Visiting Enlisted Quarters (VEQ) commensurate with their grade on a space-confirmed basis. The order in which the following are listed does not indicate a priority: a.) TDY personnel, including crew members. b.) TDY U.S. civilian employees, and civilians traveling under competent authority. c.) Members of the Air National Guard and Air Force Reserve on annual tours, school tours, special tours of active duty, or active duty for training. d.) Members of the Air National Guard and Air Force Reserve on inactive duty training. e.) TDY or TDY student, foreign military, or civilian personnel sponsored through security assistance, allied exchange, or foreign liaison programs. f.) USAFA and AFROTC cadets traveling on official orders. g.) Aircraft passengers on official orders or emergency leave at aerial ports of embarkation, if aerial port

Appendix E, continued

quarters are not available. h.) Dependents on medical TDY orders. i.) Military and civilian personnel using military aircraft in TDY or PCS status who, for reasons beyond their control, remain overnight (RON) at locations other than their TDY or PCS location. j.) Contract engineering and technical services personnel (CETSP). k.) Guests of the armed forces as determined by the installation commander. l.) Applicants for an Air force commission. m.) Active duty personnel on emergency leave. n.) Unaccompanied personnel, including civilians, entitled to permanent quarters who are temporarily without permament housing due to PCS travel orders. o.) Military and civilian personnel and their families arriving or departing an overseas location incident to PCS, if no other government temporary lodging is available. p.) Military and civilian personnel in a TDY status to nearby locations who desire government quarters in lieu of commerical quarters. q.) Personnel on permissive TDY orders.

The following personnel are eligible to occupy VOQ/VEQ on a space-available basis. Maximum stay is 30 days during any one visit. Extensions must be approved by the installation commander. The order in which the following are listed does not indicate a priority: a.) Dependents accompanying official TDY personnel. b.) Married military and civilian personnel with their families in CONUS who are temporarily without permanent housing due to PCS orders, only when TLFs (see below) are not available. c.) Unaccompanied personnel entitled to permanent quarters who arrive or depart incident to PCS and are temporarily without permanent housing. d.) Dependents of members who are patients in Air Force hospitals, only if TLF not available. e.) Retirees and retirement eligible Reservists in a nonduty status (who have DD Form 2 AF Res with a copy of ARPC certificate of retirement eligibility) and their dependents. f.) Active duty members and their dependents on ordinary leave, environmental and morale leave (EML), or travel status. g.) U.S. civilians and their dependents on EML orders from overseas duty assignments, only if TLF is not available. h.) Active status and/or in training Air National Guard and Air Force Reserve members and their dependents. i.) Space-available passengers aboard military aircraft interrupted short of destination, or passengers arriving at ports for space-available travel on departing military flights. j.) AFROTC cadets, organizations, and youth groups when approved by the installation commander. k.) Civilian Air Patrol (CAP) members on official visits. Note: transient dependents of deceased military members and dependents unaccompanied by their active or retired military sponsor, or U.S. civilian sponsor in overseas areas, may occupy transient quarters when approved by the installation commander.

Temporary Lodging Facility Operations. Temporary Lodging Facilities (TLFs) are operated to provide temporary housing to authorized personnel at the lowest possible cost consistent with giving good service.

Eligibility For and Assignment to TLFs. Personnel listed below are eligible to occupy TLFs. Assignments are made without regard to rank and on a first-come-first-served basis. Following personnel have priority 1 status: a.) Active duty military members accompanied by their dependents or their dependents alone, incident to PCS, separation, or retirement. b.) Civilian and military friends and relatives of patients in Air Force hospitals. c.) Hospital outpatients. d.) Personnel who are accompanied by dependents and in permissive TDY, ordinary leave, or terminal leave status, and traveling for the purpose of house hunting in conjunction with PCS, retirement, or separation.

Following personnel have priority 2 status: a.) Military members and dependents on leave or delay en route. b.) Military and civilian personnel,

Appendix E, continued

whether or not accompanied by dependents, on TDY when VOQ or VAQ facilities are fully occupied. c.) Retired military members and dependents. d.) Unaccompanied married personnel and unmarried members being joined by or acquiring dependents. e.) Unaccompanied married personnel and unmarried members incident to PCS, if neither transient nor permanent party government quarters are available. f.) Civilians accompanied by their dependents incident to PCS, active status Air National Guard and Air Force Reserve not in a duty status and their dependents.

Following personnel have priority 3 status: a.) Friends and relatives of assigned military personnel. Note: Personnel in priorities 2 and 3 are accommodated on a space-available basis and are required to vacate quarters no later than the next day after quarters are required by personnel in priority 1.

Reservations. Only personnel in priority 1 may request advance reservations. Reservation request should include expected arrival time and date. Reservations will not be held beyond 1700 hours unless the billeting office is notified in advance of personal needs for a later arrival time. Normal check out time is 1200 hours.

Services and Supplies. Maid service is normally supplied on a daily basis, to include light dusting and vacuuming as required, clean towels and glasses, cleaning of bathroom, emptying of trash containers, and bedmaking with weekly changing of linen unless there is a change in occupant(s).

MILITARY Livings..
R&R SPACE-A REPORT
OUR OTHER PUBLICATION

Did you know that Military Living publishes a separate travel newsletter? It is completely different from our local magazine. Published six times yearly, the *R&R Space-A Report* keeps subscribers informed of important news regarding military recreation. The main topics covered are military space-available air travel, temporary military lodging and military RV, camping and rec areas around the world. Our readers learn FIRST about changes which may affect their travels.

News about military discounts in civilian hotels, motels and attractions are also included. Our readers use the *R&R Space-A Report* as a central clearing house of information. Sometimes, just one tip from one of their letters can save you a lot of hassles and/or money. For subscription info, call Military Living at (703) 237-0203 or see the handy coupon in the back of this book. Thanks!

Temporary Military Lodging Around the World — 317

APPENDIX F

Installations That Did Not Respond
To Our Request for Information

Various sources have suggested that the following installations may have temporary military lodging facilities. These installations, however, did not respond to our request for information, so we cannot positively confirm or deny the existence of TML facilities at the following locations.

UNITED STATES

Alaska
Galena Airport (AK20R5)
King Salmon Airport (AK17R5)
Shemya Air Force Base (AK11R5)

California
Mare Island Naval Station (CA56R4)
San Diego Marine Corps Recruit Depot (CA57R4)
San Diego Naval Training Center (CA54R4)
Tustin Marine Corps Air Station (CA82R4)

Connecticut
Long Island Sound Coast Guard Group (CT04R1)

Florida
Panama City Naval Coastal Systems Center (FL35R1)

Georgia
Atlanta Naval Air Station (GA16R1)

Hawaii
Barking Sands Pacific Missile Range Facility (HI22R6)

New Jersey
Cape May Coast Guard Training Center ((NJ13R1)
Earle Naval Weapons Station (NJ11R1)

New York
Seneca Army Depot (NY03R1)

Ohio
Defense Construction Supply Center (OH05R2)

Virginia
Defense General Supply Center (VA30R1)
Norfolk Naval Shipyard (VA26R1)

FOREIGN COUNTRIES

Germany
Bad-Aibling Sub-Community (GE91R7)
Bad Hersfeld Sub-Community (GE92R7)
Böblingen/Sindelfingen Sub-Community (GE63R7)
Crailsheim Sub-Community (GE64R7)
Friedberg/Bad Nauheim Sub-Community (GE68R7)
Herzo Base Sub-Community (GE70R7)
Hohenfels Sub-Community (GE71R7)
Kitzingen Sub-Community (GE75R7)
Lindsey Air Station (GE76R7)
Lugwigsburg/Kornwestheim Sub-Community (GE77R7)
Nellingen Sub-Community (GE79R7)
Schwabach Sub-Community (GE81R7)
Vilseck Sub-Community (GE85R7)

Panama
Fort Sherman (PN06R3)
Panama Canal Naval Station (PN09R3)

Saudi Arabia
Dhahran Community (SA01R9)
Riyadh Community (SA03R9)

Appendix F, continued

United Kingdom
High Wycombe Air Station (UK18R7)
RAF Machrihanish (Scotland) (UK29R7)

MEET THE CRAWFORD FAMILY

Roy Crawford, Jr., Marketing Manager

Ann & Roy Crawford, Publishers

Temporary Military Lodging Around the World — 319

HOTEL/MOTEL DIRECTORY

Military families enjoy using military lodging because they feel at home there. Unfortunately, many times, particularly during peak season, military lodging can be fully occupied.

In view of this, we surveyed a number of hotels/motels throughout the U.S., asking if they wanted to offer special military rates to military I.D. card holders. By offering military rates, they are expressing a desire to attract you to their lodging facilities. While the exact price may change, you should be able to obtain their current military rate.

Should you have difficulty obtaining a military rate at the hotels/motels listed, ask to speak with a management representative and show them their listing, which they previously authorized. If this is not satisfactory, you may choose to try elsewhere. In any case, always show your military I.D. and establish the price to be paid before signing in. Also, please mention their listing in Military Living's *Temporary Military Lodging Around the World*.

ENLARGED SAMPLE LISTING

HOTEL NAME
HOTEL ADDRESS

CRAWFORD INN FALLS CHURCH
137 Washington Street
Falls Church, Virginia 22046   *HOTEL TELEPHONE*
(703) 237-0203 / 800-555-1212
M $49 C $52 R $55 1, 2, 3, 4, 5, 6, 7

Lodging INDEX

M = Single Military Rate
C = Single Corporate Rate
R = Single Regular Rate
1 = Rates may vary due to exchange rates
2 = Restaurant nearby or on premises
3 = Swimming Pool
4 = Free Parking
5 = Courtesy car available
6 = Accommodations for handicapped
7 = Complimentary breakfast

ALABAMA

Charter House Inn
U.S. Rt.84 Bypass-E
Andalusia, Alabama 36420
(205) 222-7511 / (800) 443-9110
M $35.50 C $38 R $39.50 2, 3, 4, 6

Sheraton Inn
2195 Ross Clark Circle, S.E.
Dothan, Alabama 36301
(205) 794-8711
M $37 C $40 R $40 2, 3, 4, 6

Best Western Bradbury Inn
180 South Beltline
Mobile, Alabama 36608
(205) 343-9345/(800) 528-1234
M $40 C $47 R $49 1, 2, 3, 4, 6

Days Inn South
1705 Dauphin Island Parkway
Mobile, Alabama 36605
(205) 471-6114 / (800) 325-2525
M $21.95 C $28 R $33 2, 3, 4, 6

Econo Lodge (Economy Inn)
1119 Government Street
Mobile, Alabama 36604
(205) 433-8800 / (800) 446-6900
M $23.25 C $24.25 R $26.95 2, 3, 4, 6

Radisson Admiral Semmes
251 Government Street
Mobile, Alabama 36608
(205) 432-8000 / (800) 333-3333
M $40 C $68 R $78 1, 2, 3

Governors House Hotel
2705 East South Boulevard
Montgomery, Alabama 36116
(205) 288-2800 / (800) 334-8459
M $33.39 C $53 R $60 1, 2, 3, 4, 5, 6

Inn South
I-65 & Southern Blvd.
Montgomery, Alabama 36105
(205) 288-7999/(800) 642-0890 AL only
M $27 C $31 R $31 2, 4, 6

State House Inn
924 Madison Ave. (downtown)
Montgomery, Alabama 36104
(205) 265-0741 / AL only (800) 552-7099
M $33 C $38 R $42 2, 3, 4, 6

ALABAMA

Ozark Holiday Inn
151 Hwy. 231 North
Ozark, Alabama 36360
(205) 774-7300
M $34 C $36 R $38 1, 2, 3, 4, 6

ALASKA

Clarion Hotel Anchorage
4800 Spenard Road
Anchorage, Alaska 99517-3236
(907) 243-2300 / (800) 544-0553
M $80 C $105 R $115 1, 2, 4, 5, 6

Kobuk Motel
1104 E. 5th
Anchorage, Alaska 99501
(907) 274-1650
M $45 R $52 1, 2

Mush Inn Motel
333 Concrete Street
Anchorage, Alaska 99501
(907) 277-4554
M $54-95 C $54-95 R $60 1, 2, 4, 6

Captain Bartlett Inn
1411 Airport Way
Fairbanks, Alaska 99701
(907) 454-1888 / (800) 544-7528
M $59.50 C $79.50 R $99.50 1, 2, 3, 4, 5, 6

ARIZONA

Holiday Inn
245 London Bridge Road
Lake Havasu, Arizona 86403
(602) 855-4071 / 1-800-HOLIDAY
M $35 C $39 R $47 2, 3, 4, 5, 6

Holiday Inn Mesa
1600 S. Country Club Drive
Mesa, Arizona 85210
(602) 964-7000 / (800) 999-MESA
M $39-45 C $49-79 R $69-89 1, 2, 3, 4, 6

ARIZONA

Doubletree Suite Hotel Phoenix Gateway Center, 320 N. 44th Street
Phoenix, Arizona 85008
(602) 225-0500
M$52 C$115-125 R$125-135 1, 2, 3, 4, 5, 6, 7

Hampton Inn I-17
8101 N. Black Canyon Hwy.
Phoenix, Arizona 85021
(602) 864-6233 / (800)- HAMPTON
M $35-48 C $37-51 R $43-61 1, 2, 3, 4, 6

Holiday Inn Corporate Center
2532 W. Peoria Avenue
Phoenix, Arizona 85029
(602) 943-2341 / (800) 843-3663
M $52 Sgl C $53-77 R $55-79 3, 4, 6

Inn Suites at Phoenix Squaw Peak
1615 E. Northern
Phoenix, Arizona 85020
(602) 997-6285 / (800) 842-4242
M $39 C $59 R $69 1, 2, 3, 4, 6

Ramada Inn - Union Hills
2641 W. Union Hills Drive
Phoenix, Arizona 85027
(602) 978-2222 / (800) 228-2828
M $52 C $65 R $79 2, 3, 4, 6

Holiday Inn - Scottsdale
5101 N. Scottsdale Road
Scottsdale, Arizona 85250
(602) 945-4392
M $29-60 C $51-113 R $56-118 1, 2, 3, 4, 6

Inn Suites at Scottsdale's
7707 E. McDowell Road
Scottsdale, Arizona 85257
(602) 941-1202 / (800) 842-4242
M $34 C $48 R $58 1, 2, 3, 4, 6

Comfort Inn
5300 S. 56th Street
Tempe, Arizona 85283
(602) 820-7500 / (800) 221-2200
M $29-35 C $30-36 R $34-39 2, 3, 4, 6

Inn Suites - Tempe
1651 W. Baseline Road
Tempe, Arizona 85253
(602) 897-7900 / (800) 842-4242
M $39 C $56 R $65 1, 2, 3, 4, 6

ARIZONA

Lexington Hotel Suites - Tempe
1660 W. Elliot Road
Tempe, Arizona 85283
(602) 345-8585 / (800) 53-SUITE
M $45-48 C $57-67 R $69-84 2, 3, 4, 6

Ramada Hotel Airport East
1600 S. 52nd Street
Tempe, Arizona 85281
(602) 967-6600 / (800) 678-9955
M $52 C $67 R $79 2, 3, 4, 5, 6

Best Western Executive Inn
333 W. Drachman
Tucson, Arizona 85705
(602) 791-7551
M $35 C $38 R $40-50 1, 2, 3, 4

Inn Suites of Tucson
6201 N. Oracle Road
Tucson, Arizona 85704
(602) 297-8111 / (800) 842-4242
M $45 C $59 R $69 1, 2, 3, 4, 6

The Lodge on the Desert
306 N. Alvernon Way
Tucson, Arizona 85711
(602) 325-3366 / 1-800-456-5634
M $40 C $40 R $66 1, 2, 3, 4, 6

Palm Court Inn
4425 E. 22nd Street
Tucson, Arizona 85711
(602) 745-1777 / (800) 288-1650
M $25 C $32 R $38 1, 2, 3, 4

Ramada Downtown
404 N. Freeway I-10 & Mary St.
Tucson, Arizona 85745
(602) 624-8341 / (800) 228-2828
M $48 incl tax & breakfast 2, 3, 4, 5, 6

Tanque Verde Inn
7007 E. Tanque Verde
Tucson, Arizona 85715
(602) 298-2300 / (800) 822-8484
M $48 C $49.50 R $55 1, 2, 3, 4, 6

Best Western CHILTON INN & Conference Center, 300 E. 32nd Street
Yuma, Arizona 85364
(602) 344-1050 / (800) 528-1234
M $43 tax incl C $45 R $53-60 1, 2, 3, 4, 5, 6

ARIZONA

Inn Suites at Yuma
1450 Castle Dome Road
Yuma, Arizona 85364
(602) 783-8341 / (800) 842-4242
M $45 C $54 R $59

Yuma Inn Motel
260 S. 4th Avenue
Yuma, Arizona 85364
(602) 782-4592
M $18-25 C $21-28 R $25-35 1, 2, 3, 4

ARKANSAS

Fayetteville Hilton Hotel
70 North East Street
Fayetteville, Arkansas 72701
(501) 442-5555 / (800) HILTONS
M $40 C $55 R $55 1, 2, 3, 4, 5, 6

Mountain Inn
21 S. College Avenue
Fayetteville, Arkansas 72701
(501) 521-1000 / (800) 336-7133
M $27+tax C $29+tax R $29.95+tax 1, 2, 3, 4, 5

Days Inn
10524 West Markham Street
Little Rock, Arkansas 72205
(501) 225-7366 / (800) 325-2525
M $35 C $35 R $42 2, 3, 4, 6

Riverfront Hilton Inn
#2 Riverfront Place
North Little Rock, Arkansas 72114
(501) 371-9000 / (800) HILTONS
M $40 C $61 R $53-63 3, 4, 5, 6

CALIFORNIA

Grand Hotel
One Hotel Way
Anaheim, California 92802
(714) 776-9510 / H.S.I. (800) 421-6662
M $52 C $80 R $85-100 1, 2, 3, 4, 6

Quality Hotel & Conference Center
616 Convention Way
Anaheim, California 92802
(714) 750-3131 / (800) 228-5151
M $42 C $55 R $79 1, 3, 4, 6

CALIFORNIA

Sandman Inn
921 S. Harbor Blvd.
Anaheim, CA 92805 / (714) 956-5730
CA 800-372-6644 / US 800-235-3399
M $30-50 C $34-52 R $44-64 1, 2, 3, 4, 5, 6

Sheraton Anaheim Hotel
1015 W. Ball Road
Anaheim, California 92802
(714) 778-1700 / (800) 325-3535
M $50 C $87 R $100 1, 2, 3, 4, 6

Super 8 Lodge
1511 E. Main St.
Barstow, California 92311
(619) 256-0860 / (800) 843-1991
M $46 R $53 1, 2, 3, 6

Days Inn Hotel-San Francisco Int'l Airport
777 Airport Boulevard
Burlingame, California 94010
(415) 342-7772 / (800) 451-6641
M $58 C $65 R $69 1, 2, 3, 4, 5, 6, 7

Executive Inn (Suites)
1300 Camden Avenue
Campbell, California 95008
(408) 559-3600 / (800) 888-3611
M $55 C $70 R $75 1, 2, 4, 6

Red Carpet Inn
1311 South Santo Antonio Drive
Colton, California 92324
(714) 824-9020
M $29.95 C $32 R $36 1, 2, 3, 4, 5, 6

Concord Hilton
1970 Diamond Boulevard
Concord, CA 94520 / (415) 827-2000
US (800) 826-6688 / CA (800) 826-2644
M $59 C $104 R $114 2, 3, 4, 5, 6

Quality Suites Hotel Irvine/El Toro
23192 Lake Center Drive
El Toro, California 92630
(714) 380-9888 / (800) 228-5151
M $69 C $69 R $79 1, 2, 3, 4, 6

Affordable Deluxe Inn
1250 W. Valley Parkway
Escondido, CA 92025 (10 min from Miramar)
(619) 741-7117 / (800) 654-6942
M $30 C $37 R $44 1, 2, 3, 4, 6

CALIFORNIA

Best Western Franciscan Inn-Fallbrook
1635 S. Mission Road
Fallbrook, California 92028
(619) 728-6174 / (800) 528-1234
M $42-55 C $42-55 R $45-60 1, 2, 3, 4, 5, 6

Heritage Inn (Fullerton)
333 E. Imperial Highway
Fullerton, California 92635
(714) 447-9200
M $30+10%tx C $49.95 R $62 1, 2, 3, 4, 6

Consort Legacy Hotel
1160 N. Vermont Avenue
Hollywood, California 90029
(213) 660-1788 / (800) 445-6120
M $50 max 4 C $56 max 4 R $70 2, 3, 4, 5, 6

Holiday Inn, Irvine
17941 Von Karman
Irvine, California 92714
(714) 863-1999 / (800) HOLIDAY
M $49 C $78-85 R $83-90 1, 2, 3, 4, 5, 6

La Jolla Village Inn
3299 Holiday Court
La Jolla, California 92037
(619) 453-5500 / (800) 345-9995
M $67 C $65 R $75 1, 2, 3, 4, 5, 6

Holiday Inn Laguna Hills
25205 La Paz Road
Laguna Hills, California 92653
(714) 586-5000 / (800) HOLIDAY
M $62 C $65 R $69 1, 2, 3, 4, 5, 6, 7

Best Western Lakewood Inn
11727 E. Carson Street
Lakewood (Long Beach), California 90715
(213) 402-4200 / (800) 528-1234
M $42 C $43 R $45 3, 4, 6

Residence Inn by Marriott
4111 E. Willow
Long Beach, California 90815
(213) 595-0909 / (800) 331-3131
M $80 (4+days) C $104 R $109 2, 3, 4

Budget Inn - Los Angeles Downtown
1710 West 7th Street
Los Angeles, California 90017
(213) 483-3470
M $35 C $35 R $39 1, 2, 3, 4, 6

CALIFORNIA

Executive Motor Inn
457 S. Mariposa Avenue
Los Angeles, California 90020
(213) 380-6910
M $34 C $34 R $38 2, 3, 4

Hyatt Regency Los Angeles
711 South Hope Street
Los Angeles, California 90017
(213) 683-1234 / (800) 233-1234
M $75-84 C $160 R $175 1, 2, 6

The Quality Hotel
5249 West Century Boulevard
Los Angeles, California 90045
(213) 645-2200 / (800) 228-5151
M $51 C $52 R $52 1, 2, 3, 5, 6

Comfort Inn Milpitas
66 S. Main Street
Milpitas, California 95035
(408) 262-7666 / (800) 228-5150
M $40 C $40 R $45 2, 3, 4, 6

A Great Place to Stay in Monterey

LONE OAK MOTEL

$36 For 2
Through May
Sunday thru Thursday
Please present this ad at check in.

- Rooms with Hot Tubs, Fireplace & Steambaths available.
- Indoor Spa
- HBO and ESPN
- Free Local Calls and Coffee
- Spacious Family Units

**2221 N. Fremont St.
Monterey, CA
(408) 372-4924**

CALIFORNIA

Super 8 Motel - Milpitas
485 South Main Street
Milpitas, California 95035
(408) 946-1615 / (800) 843-1991
M $36-72 C $36-72 R $40-80 2, 4, 6

Cypress Gardens Inn
1150 Munras Avenue
Monterey, California 93940
(408) 373-2761 / (800) 433-4732
M $39-89 C $39-89 R $49-89 1, 2, 3, 4, 7

El Adobe Inn
936 Munras Avenue
Monterey, California 93940
(408) 372-5409 / (800) 433-4732
M $39-79 C $39-79 R $49-79 1, 2, 4, 7

Lone Oak Motel
2221 N. Fremont Street
Monterey, California 93940
(408) 372-4924
M $36-68 C $36-72 R $36-76 1, 4, 6

Ramada Inn
24630 Sunnymead Blvd.
Moreno Valley, California 92388-3798
(714) 243-0088
M $28 C $40 R $39 2, 3, 4, 5, 6

Fireside Inn
730 Morro Avenue
Morro Bay, California 93442
(805) 772-2244 / CA (800) 444-0562
M $42 C $42 R $50 1, 2, 4, 6

Sunset Travelodge
1080 Market Avenue
Morro Bay, California 93442
(805) 772-1259 / (800) 255-3050
M $40 C $40 R $50 1, 2, 3, 4

Villager Motel
1098 Main Street
Morro Bay, California 93442
(805) 772-1235 / CA (800) 444-0782
M $38 C $38 R $48 1, 2, Indoor jacuzzi spa

Rodeway Inn, Mountain View
55 Fairchild Drive
Mountain View, California 94043
(415) 967-6856 / (800) 228-2000
M $45 C $45 R $50 2, 3, 4, 6

CALIFORNIA

Newark-Fremont Hilton
39900 Balentine Drive
Newark, California 94560
(415) 490-8390 / (800) HILTONS
M $58 C $84-104 R $94-114 2, 3, 4, 5, 6

Hyatt Regency Oakland
1001 Broadway
Oakland, California 94607
(415) 893-1234 / (800) 233-1234
M $69 C $109 R $120 1, 2, 3, 6

Red Lion Hotel/Ontario
222 N. Vineyard
Ontario, California 91764
(714) 983-0909 / (800) 547-8010
M $55 C $94 R $99 1, 2, 3, 4, 5, 6

Radisson Palm Springs Resort
1600 N. Indian Avenue
Palm Springs, California 92262-4602
(619) 327-8311 / (800) 333-3333
M $55-65 R $89-119 1, 2, 3, 4, 5, 6

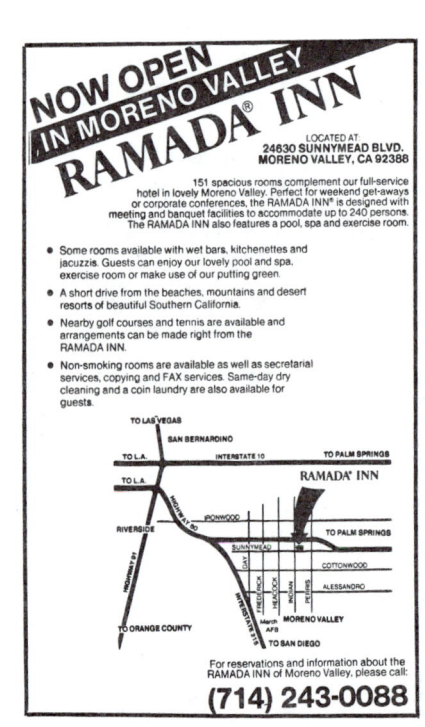

NOW OPEN IN MORENO VALLEY

RAMADA INN

LOCATED AT:
24630 SUNNYMEAD BLVD.
MORENO VALLEY, CA 92388

151 spacious rooms complement our full-service hotel in lovely Moreno Valley. Perfect for weekend get-aways or corporate conferences, the RAMADA INN® is designed with meeting and banquet facilities to accommodate up to 240 persons. The RAMADA INN also features a pool, spa and exercise room.

- Some rooms available with wet bars, kitchenettes and jacuzzis. Guests can enjoy our lovely pool and spa, exercise room or make use of our putting green.
- A short drive from the beaches, mountains and desert resorts of beautiful Southern California.
- Nearby golf courses and tennis are available and arrangements can be made right from the RAMADA INN.
- Non-smoking rooms are available as well as secretarial services, copying and FAX services. Same-day dry cleaning and a coin laundry are also available for guests.

For reservations and information about the RAMADA INN of Moreno Valley, please call:

(714) 243-0088

CALIFORNIA

Best Western Pasadena Inn
3570 E. Colorado Boulevard
Pasadena, California 91107
(818) 796-9100 / (800) 528-1234
M $44 C $44 R $50 1, 2, 3, 4, 6

Best Western Pasadena Royale
3600 E. Colorado Boulevard
Pasadena, California 91107
(818) 793-0950 / (800) 528-1234
M $46 C $46 R $52 1, 2, 3, 4, 6

B/W Sunrise Hotel King Harbor Marina
400 North Harbor Drive
Redondo Beach, California 90277
(213) 376-0746 / (800) 528-1234
M $70-72 C $70-72 R $80-100 1, 2, 3, 4, 5, 6

Super 8 Lodge
4317 Madison Avenue
Sacramento, California 95842
(916) 334-7430 / (800) 843-1991
M $41 R $45 1, 2, 3, 4, 6

Super 8 Lodge
294 E. Hospitality Lane
San Bernardino, California 92408
(714) 381-1681 / (800) 843-1991
M $42 R $46 1, 2, 3, 4, 6

Circle 8 Motor Inn
543 Hotel Circle South
San Diego, California 92108
(619) 297-8800 / (800) 345-9995
M $42.50 C $42.50 R $45.50 1, 2, 3, 4, 5, 6

Comfort Inn
719 Ash Street
San Diego, California 92101
(619) 232-2525 / (800) 228-5150
M $40-50 C $40-50 R $47-57 1, 2, 4, 5

Hanalei Hotel
2270 Hotel Circle
San Diego, California 92108
(619) 297-1101
M $55 C $69 R $80-98 1, 2, 3, 4, 5, 6

Holiday Inn Mission Valley
595 Hotel Circle South
San Diego, California 92108
(619) 291-5720 / (800) HOLIDAY
M $59 C $62 R $65 2, 3, 4, 6

CALIFORNIA

Horton Park Plaza Hotel
901 Fifth Avenue
San Diego, California 92101
(619) 232-9500 / (800) 443-8012
M $67 C $99 R $99-149 1, 2, 5, 6

Howard Johnson
1430 7th Avenue
San Diego, California 92101
(619) 696-0911 / (800) 654-2000
M $45-55 C $47-57 R $52-60 1, 2, 3, 4, 5,

Humphrey's Half Moon Inn
2303 Shelter Island Drive
San Diego, California 92106
(619) 224-3411 / (800) 345-9995
M $67 C $75 R $79 1, 2, 3, 4, 5, 6

Kona Kai
1551 Shelter Island Drive
San Diego, California 92106
(619) 222-1191 / (800) 231-9589
2, 3, 4, 6

COME TO SAN DIEGO'S BEACH & TENNIS RESORT

only **$67** per room per night

FREE BREAKFAST

- Nursery Service
- Beach Front
- Racquetball
- Ocean Views
- Health Spa
- Tennis
- Children's Activities
- Stars & Stripes Cruises Available

KONA KAI
BEACH & TENNIS RESORT
1551 Shelter Island Dr.
San Diego, CA 92106
(619) 222-1191   (800) 231-9589

CALIFORNIA

Loma Lodge
3202 Rosecrans Street
San Diego, California 92110
(619) 222-0511 / (800) 266-0511
M$30.95 s or dbl C$30.95 R$30.95 1, 2, 3, 4

Ramada Inn - Hotel Circle
2151 Hotel Circle South
San Diego, California 92108
(619) 291-6500 (800) 345-9995
M $49.50 C $49 R $59 1, 2, 3, 4, 5, 6

Ramada Inn - Old Town
2435 Jefferson Street
San Diego, California 92110
(619) 260-8500 / 1-800-228-2828
M $57 C $57 R $59 1, 2, 3, 4, 5, 6

Seapoint Hotel
4875 N. Harbor Drive
San Diego, California 92106
(619) 224-3621 / (800) 345-9995
M $49.50 C $49 R $59 1, 2, 3, 4, 5, 6

Amsterdam Hotel
749 Taylor Street
San Francisco, California 94108
(415) 673-3277 / (800) 637-3444
M $38-52 C $40-56 R $42-59 1, 2

Handlery Union Square Hotel
351 Geary Street
San Francisco, California 94105
(415) 781-7800 / (800) 522-5455
M $65, C $75-100 R $90 1, 3, 6

Holiday Inn Civic Center
50 Eighth Street
San Francisco, California 94103
(415) 626-6103 / (800) HOLIDAY
M $66 C $86 R $84-111 2, 3, 4, 6

Marines' Memorial Club
609 Sutter Street
San Francisco, California 94102
(415) 673-6672
M $55 Single Mem Reg $55 2, 3, 6

Mosser Victorian Hotel
54 Fourth Street
San Francisco, CA 94103 / (415) 986-4400
CA (800) 831-4224 / US 800-227-3804
M $37-39 C $37-39 R $39-46 1, 6

CALIFORNIA

marines' memorial club
IN SAN FRANCISCO

- 1st Class Hotel Rooms ($40-$55)
- Luxurious Suites (from $70)
- Skyroom Dining Room/Lounge
- Banquet and Meeting Rooms
- Theatre   • Health Club/Pool

If you're not a member—*you should be!*

Prestigious Location
Membership in this unique organization is offered to former and retired members of all branches of the U.S. Armed Forces.
Membership Dept., Marines' Memorial Club
609 Sutter St., San Francisco, CA 94102
(415) 673-6672
800-5-MARINE   800-3-MARINE in CA.

Pacific Heights Inn
1555 Union Street
San Francisco, California 94123
(415) 776-3310 / (800) 523-1801
M $49-55 C $58-64 R $65-69 1, 2, 4, 6

Powell Hotel
28 Cyril Magnin Street
San Francisco, California 94102
(415) 398-3200 / (800) 368-0700
M $55 C $70 R $75 1, 2

Powell West Hotel
111 Mason Street
San Francisco, California 94102
(415) 771-1200 / (800) 368-0700
M $60 C $80 R $88 1, 2

Quality Hotel San Francisco
2775 Van Ness Avenue
San Francisco, California 94109
(415) 928-5000 / (800) 228-5151
M $59-76 C $65-81 R $68-108 1, 2, 4

CALIFORNIA

Senator Hotel
519 Ellis Street, San Francisco, CA 94109
(415) 775-0506 / CA (800) 782-0990
US (800) 624-4525
M $33 C $34.20 R $38-45 1, 2, 4, 5

Comfort Suites
121 E. Grand Avenue
South San Francisco, CA 94080
(415) 589-7766 / (800) 228-5150
M $55 C $69 R $72 2, Jacuzzi, 4, 5, 6

Comfort Inn
1215 S. 1st Street
San Jose, California 95110
(408) 280-5300 / (800) 228-5150
M $45 C $50 R $50 1, 2, 4, 6

Executive Inn (Suites)
3930 Monterey Road
San Jose, California 95111
(408) 281-8700 / (800) 292-7667
M $50 C $55 R $60 1, 2, 4, 6

Best Western Royal Oak Motor Hotel
214 Madonna Road
San Luis Obispo, California 93401
(805) 544-4410
M $50 C $52-63 R $57-65 1, 2, 3, 4, 5, 6

Sands Motel
9355 Hearst Drive
San Simeon, California 93452
(805) 927-3253 / CA (800) 444-0779
M $40 C $40 R $50 1, 2, 3, 4

Howard Johnson Lodge
2700 Hotel Terrace
Santa Ana, California 92705
(714) 432-8888 / (800) 654-2000
M $38 R $51 1, 2, 3, 4, 6

Ramada Hotel
2726 S. Grand Avenue
Santa Ana, California 92705
(714) 966-1955 / (800) 888-5540
M $55 C $69 R $75 2, 3, 4, 5, 6

Saddleback Inn
1660 E. First Street
Santa Ana, California 92701
(714) 835-3311 / (800) 854-3911
M $32-45 C $55-65 R $65-75 1, 2, 3, 4, 5, 6

CALIFORNIA

Woolley's Petite Suites
2721 Hotel Terrace Road
Santa Ana, California 92705
(714) 540-1111 / Call collect
M $59 C $57 R $62 2, 3, 4, 5, 6

Santa Clara Airport Hotel
2151 Laurelwood Road
Santa Clara, California 95054
(408) 988-8411
M $45-50 C $85-130 R $95-140 1, 2, 3, 4, 5, 6

Santa Maria Inn
801 South Broadway
Santa Maria, California 93454
(805) 928-7777 / (800) 462-4276
M $69 C $85 R $92 1, 2, 3, 4, 6

Los Robles Lodge
925 Edwards Avenue
Santa Rosa, CA 95401 /(707) 545-6330
CA (800) 552-1001 / US (800) 255-6330
M $54 C $54 R $60 2, 3, 4, 5, 6

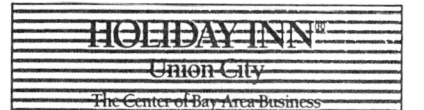

HOLIDAY INN
Union City
The Center of Bay Area Business

Location: Centralized Bay Area location. Easy access to three main airports – San Francisco, Oakland, and San Jose. Located at Interstate 840 Alvarado-Niles exit. Complimentary airport shuttle from three airports with prior reservation.
Accommodations: 266 First Class guest rooms. 7 luxury suites.
Meeting Facilities: Over 10,000 sq. ft. of meeting and banquet facilities. Accommodating groups of 10 to 600.
Rates: Special group rates, corporate rates and deluxe weekend packages available.
Dining and Entertainment: Three outstanding restaurants.
- Marco Polo – Specializing in continental cuisine.
- La Terrasse – Resplendent garden ambiance
- Furusato – World renowned Japanese restaurant
- Le Carrousel – European accent. Disco entertainment and weekday happy hours.

Recreation: Facilities include tennis, racquetball, exercise room, sauna, spa and outdoor swimming pool.
For reservations call toll free 800-Holiday or contact hotel directly at (415) 489-2200.
Commissions: 10%.

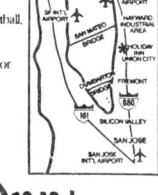

Holiday Inn

UNION CITY/HAYWARD
32083 Alvarado/Niles Road
Union City, CA 94587

CALIFORNIA

Cornerstone B&B Inn
1308 Main Street
St. Helena, California 94574
(707) 963-1891
M $45-95 R $65-135 1, 2, 4

Holiday Inn Torrance-Gateway
19800 S. Vermont
Torrance, California 90502
(213) 781-9100 / (800) HOLIDAY
M $69 C $82-88 R $85-100 1, 2, 3, 4, 5, 6

Holiday Inn
32083 Alvarado Niles Road
Union City, California 94587
(415) 489-2200
M $55 C $69 R $71 2, 3, 4, 5, 6

Comfort Inn Vallejo
1185 Admiral Callaghan Lane
Vallejo, California 94591
(707) 648-1400 / (800) 828-1185
M $42 C $44 R $51 1, 2, 3, 4, 6

CALIFORNIA

Ventura Beach Travelodge
929 E. Thompson Boulevard
Ventura, California 93001
(805) 648-2557 / (800) 255-3050
M $38 C $38 R $48 1, 2, 3, 4

Hyatt Westlake Plaza Hotel
880 South Westlake Boulevard
Westlake Village, California 91361
(805) 497-9991 / (800) 223-1234
M $80 C $110 R $125 2, 3, 4, 6

Warner Center Marriott
21850 Oxnard Street
Woodland Hills, California 91367
(818) 887-4800
M $80

COLORADO

Holtze Executive Village
15403 E. 1st Avenue
Aurora, Colorado 80011
(303) 361-6200 / (800) 422-2092
M $30 C $40 R $45 2, 3, 4, 5

Best Western Raintree Inn Airport
1645 Newport Drive
Colorado Springs, Colorado 80916
(719) 597-7000 / (800) 824-3662
M $42 C $55 R $60 2, 3, 4, 5, 7

Comfort Inn
8280 Highway 83
Colorado Springs, Colorado 80920
(303) 598-6700 / (800) 221-2222
M $35-39 C $35-39 R $45-49 2, 3, 4, 6

Ramada Inn East
520 N. Murray Blvd.
Colorado Springs, Colorado 80907
(303) 596-7660 / (800) 2-RAMADA
M $36 C $36-48 R $40-58 1, 2, 3, 4, 5, 6

Ramada Inn North
I-25 at Garden of the Gods Road
Colorado Springs, Colorado 80907
(303) 594-0700 / (800) 2-RAMADA
M $36 C $36-48 R $40-58 1, 2, 3, 4, 5, 6

The Best Defense...

For a comfortable stay while visiting your Industry Partners in the San Fernando Valley.

We're offering a *Military Rate* of *$80 per night*, on space availability. Active Military I.D. Card required at check-in.. For 10 or more rooms a night, call our Sales Office **(818) 887-4800** for reservations.

WARNER CENTER **Marriott**
WOODLAND HILLS

·21850 Oxnard Street,
Woodland Hills, California 91367

COLORADO

Executive Tower Inn
1405 Curtis Street
Denver, Colorado 80202
(303) 571-0300 / (800) 525-6651
M $45 C $78 R $80 2, 3, 5, 6

Holiday Inn Denver Downtown
1450 Glenarm Place
Denver, CO 80202 / (303) 573-1450
(800) 423-5128 / (800) 423-2201
M $45 C $60 R $76 2, 3, 4, 6

Stapleton Plaza Hotel & Fitness Center
3333 Quebec Street
Denver, Colorado 80207
(303) 321-3500 / (800) 950-6070
M $57 ($63 Pkg) C $74 R $79 2, 3, 4, 5, 6

Warwick Hotel
1776 Grant Street
Denver, Colorado 80203
(303) 861-2000 / (800) 525-2888
M $59 C $89 R $114 2, 3, 5, 6

Best Western Raintree Inn Denver Southwest, 3605 South Wadsworth
Lakewood, Colorado 80235
(303) 989-6900 / (800) 824-3662
M $42 C $48 R $55 2, 3, 4, 5, 6, 7

CONNECTICUT

Quality Inn Groton
404 Bridge Street
Groton, Connecticut 06340
(203) 445-8141 / 1-800-221-2222
M $46.25 C $54.50 R $75 1, 2, 3, 4

Hampton Inn
129 Plains Road (Exit 36 off I-95)
Milford, Connecticut 06460
(203) 874-4400 / (800) HAMPTON
M $44 C $48-60 R $48-60 2, 4, 6

Regal Inn
1605 Whalley Avenue
New Haven, Connecticut 06515
(203) 389-9504
M $35 C $32 R $35-38 1, 2, 4

HOLTZE

EXECUTIVE VILLAGE

A Hotel You Can Come Home To

TYPICAL UNIT PLAN

- Hotel Rooms or beautifully equipped one or two bedroom units
- Continental breakfast and hospitality hour
- Jacuzzi, pool, saunas, weightroom and even bicycles for check-out
- Cable TV with free movie channels
- Daily Maid Service

15403 E. 1st Avenue
Aurora, CO 80011
(303) 361-6200 • 1-800-422-2092

HOLTZE

Call For Our Best Rates/Daily, Weekly, Monthly

CONNECTICUT

Travelodge-New London South
Exit 74, Interstate 95
Niantic, Connecticut 06357
(203)739-5483 / (800) 255-3050
M $35-48 C $40-52 R $52 1, 2, 3, 4

Stratford Ramada
225 Lordship Boulevard
Stratford, Connecticut 06497
(203) 375-8866 / (800) 2-RAMADA
M $59 C $59 R $59 1, 2, 3, 4, 5, 6

Howard Johnson Plaza Hotel
88 Union Street
Waterbury, Connecticut 06702
(203) 575-1500 / (800) 654-2000
M $55 C $56 R $60 2, 3, 4, 5

DELAWARE

Days Inn
900 Churchman Road
Newark, Delaware 19713
(302) 368-2400 / (800) 325-2525
M $51 C $51 R $61 2, 3, 4, 6

District of Columbia

Cherry Blossom Travelodge DC/Arlington
3030 Columbia Pike
Arlington, Virginia 22204
(703) 521-5570 / (800) 255-3050
M $45 C $53 2, 3, 4

Embassy Square Suites
2000 N Street, N.W.
Washington, D.C. 20036
(202) 659-9000 / 1-800-424-2999
M $69 C $129 R $139 1, 2, 3, 6, 7

THE WHITE HOUSE, THE SMITHSONIAN AND ALL OF WASHINGTON, D.C.

FOR ONLY $69*

The Embassy Square Suites...in the heart of Washington, D.C....ideally located only 1 block from Metro Subway. *Featuring:* • 250 spacious suites with fully equipped kitchens • Complimentary continental breakfast • Outdoor courtyard with swimming pool • Ample underground parking • Chic dining and entertainment nightly • Special family rates—kids under 16 stay free with parents

EMBASSY SQUARE SUITES

2000 N STREET, NW, WASHINGTON, DC 20036
(202) 659-9000 Call Toll Free 1-800/424-2999

*Rates are available to active & retired Military personnel with I.D. Rates are offered on a limited availability basis, and subject to change without notice.

MILITARY BREAK.

We at Travelodge know military families enjoy using military lodging. Unfortunately, many times, particularly during peak moving seasons, military lodging can be fully occupied. At Travelodge we try to help by offering a clean, comfortable room at a great low rate. So call now and get your military rate from Travelodge today.

DISTRICT OF COLUMBIA
Washington, D.C./Arlington
3030 Columbia Pike
Arlington, VA
(703) 521-5570

MASSACHUSETTS
Bedford (Boston Area)
285 Great Road
(617) 275-6120

Natick (Boston Area)
1350 Worcester Road
(508) 655-2222

Pittsfield
16 Cheshire Road (Route 8)
(413) 443-5661

NEW JERSEY
Cherry Hill/Mt. Laurel (Philadelphia Area)
State Highway 73 at NJ Turnpike, Exit 4
(609) 234-7000

PENNSYLVANIA
Chambersburg
565 Lincoln Way East
(717) 264-4187

Gettysburg
10 East Lincoln Avenue
(717) 334-6235

Lancaster
2101 Columbia Avenue
(717) 397-4201

VERMONT
Shelburne
1907 Shelburne Road
(802) 985-8037

VIRGINIA
Williamsburg
1408 Richmond Road
(804) 220-2367

Winchester
1825 Dominion Avenue
(703) 665-0685

For Reservations Call: 1-800-255-3050

Travelodge®
Inns • Hotels • Suites

© 1990 Trusthouse Forte Hotels, Inc.

District of Columbia

Hotel Lombardy
2019 I Street, N.W.
Washington, D.C. 20006
(202) 828-2600 / (800) 424-5486
M $78 C $95 R $95 2

Master Hosts Inn
1917 Bladensburg Road
Washington, D.C. 20002
(202) 832-8600 / (800) 251-1962
M $42 C $42 R $55 2, 3, 4

Quality Hotel Downtown
1315 16th Street, N.W.
Washington, D.C. 20036
(202) 232-8000 / (800) 368-5689
M $77 C $82 R $90-110 1, 2

Washington Plaza Hotel
Massachusetts and Vermont Ave. N.W.
Washington, D.C. 20005
(202) 842-1300 / (800) 424-1140
M $78 C $98 R $115-135 2, 3, 6, 7

FLORIDA

Comfort Inn - Mayport
2401 Mayport Road
Atlantic Beach, Florida 32233
(904) 249-0313
M $36.50 C $39.50 R $44 1, 2, 3, 4, 6

Holiday Inn Gulfview
521 S. Gulfview Blvd., Clearwater Beach,
FL 34630 / (813) 447-6461 / (800) HOLIDAY
M 47.50-71.50 C 50.50-120.50 R 55.50-125.50
2, 3, 4, 6

Holiday Inn University of Miami
1350 S. Dixie Highway, U.S. #1 South
Coral Gables, Florida 33146
(305) 667-5611 / (800) HOLIDAY
M $49 C $59 R $71 2, 3, 4

Crestview Holiday Inn
I-10 & St. Hwy. 85
Crestview, Florida 32536
(904) 682-6111
M $33 C $35.10 R $39 2, 3, 4, 6

FLORIDA

Fort Lauderdale Airport Hilton Hotel
1870 Griffin Road
Dania, FL 33004 / (305) 920-3300
FL 1-800-654-8266 / US 1-800-426-8578
M $52 C $89-105 R $75-180 1, 3, 4, 5, 6

The Westin Cypress Creek
400 Corporate Drive
Fort Lauderdale, Florida 33334
(305) 772-1331 / (800) 228-3000
M $60 C $145 R $155 1, 2, 3, 4, 6

Travelodge Fort Lauderdale/Sunrise
1251 E. Sunrise Boulevard
Fort Lauderdale, Florida 33304
(305) 763-6601 / (800) 255-3050
M $35 C $37 R $45 1, 2, 3, 4

Days Inn
6651 Darter Court
Fort Pierce, Florida 34945
(407) 466-4066 / (800) 325-2525
M $38-42 C $39-45 R $45-60 1, 2, 3, 4, 6

Howard Johnson Hollywood Beach Resort
Inn, 2501 North Ocean Drive
Hollywood Beach, Florida 33019
(305) 925-1411 / (800) 423-9867
M $47-87 C $55-115 R $55-135 1, 2, 3, 4, 6

Best Western Bradbury Suites
8277 Western Way
Jacksonville, Florida 32256
(904) 737-4477 / (800) 528-1234
M $46 C $57 R $59 1, 2, 3, 4, 6

Comfort Suites
8333 Dix Ellis Trail
Jacksonville, Florida 32256
(904) 739-1155 / (800) 221-2222
M $44 C $52 R $58 2, 3, 4, 6, 7

Sheraton Orlando North
600 N. Lake Destiny Drive
Maitland, Florida 32751
(407) 660-9000 / (800) 325-3535
M $54 C $102 R $115 1, 2, 3, 4, 5, 6

Holiday Inn of Merritt Island
260 E. Merritt Island Causeway
Merritt Island, Florida 32952
(407) 452-7711
M $39 C $42 R $49 3, 4, 6

FLORIDA

Everglades Hotel
244 Biscayne Boulevard
Miami, Florida 33132
(305) 358-0983 / (800) 327-5700
M $50 C $69 R $75 2, 3

Golden Nugget Beach Resort
18555 Collins Avenue
Miami Beach, Florida 33160
(305) 932-1445 / 1-800-327-0694
Rates vary with location & season 2, 3, 4

Holiday Inn-International Airport South
1101 N.W. 57th Avenue
Miami, Florida 33126
(305) 266-0000 / (800) HOLIDAY
M $45-65 C $46-70 R $46-72 1, 2, 3, 4, 5, 6

Holiday Inn Orlando West
2815 East Highway 50
Ocoee, Florida 34761
(407) 656-5050 / (800) 327-5429
3, 4

Orlando A Howard Johnson-Westpark Hotel
304 W. Colonial Drive
Orlando, Florida 32802
(407) 843-8700 / (800) 523-3405
M $45-65 C $55-65 R $55-110 1, 2, 3, 4, 6

Orlando Marriott International Drive
8001 International Drive
Orlando, Florida 32819
(407) 351-2420 / (800) 228-9290
M $59 C $105 R $105-135 1, 3, 4, 6

Park Inn International Orlando-North
736 Lee Road
Orlando, FL 32810 / (407) 647-1112
FL (800) 432-5549 / US (800) 262-7003
M $35 C $40 R $46 2, 3, 4, 6 (limited)

Palm Beach Gardens Marriott
4000 RCA Boulevard
Palm Beach Gardens, Florida 33410
(407) 622-8888 / (800) 228-9290
M $57 C $125 R $135 2, 3, 4, 6

LaBrisa Motor Inn
5711 E. Highway 98
Panama City, Florida 32404
(904) 871-2345 / (800) 523-4369
M $25 C $25 R $28 1, 2, 3, 4

FLORIDA

Residence Inn by Marriott - Pensacola
7230 Plantation Road
Pensacola, Florida 32504
(904) 479-1000 / (800) 331-3131
M $51 C $69 R $73 1, 2, 3, 4, 6

Ebb Tide Apartments & Motel
300 Briny Avenue
Pompano Beach, Florida 33062
(305) 941-7200
Rates vary w/season 2, 3, 4

Traders Ocean Resort
1600 S. Ocean Blvd.
Pompano Beach, FL 33062 / (305) 941-8400
FL (800) 533-5565 / US (800) 325-5220
Fax 305-941-1024/M$43-65 C $45-69 1, 2, 3, 4

Ponce de Leon Resort & Convention Center
P.O. Box 98, 4000 U.S. #1 North
St. Augustine, FL 32085 / (904) 824-2821
FL (800) 228-2821 / US (800) 824-2821
M $50 C $60 R $65 1, 2, 3, 4, 6

LA BRISA Motor Inn

Panama City, Florida

MINUTES FROM TYNDALL A.F.B.
SPECIAL MILITARY RATES

5711 East Highway 98
Panama City, FL 32404
Phone: 904/871-2345

Toll Free 1-800-523-4369

FLORIDA

Colony Plaza Hotel
2600 W. Highway 50
West Orlando (Ocoee), Florida 34761
(407) 656-3333 / (800) 821-0136
M $38 C $38 R $45-60 1, 2, 3, 4

John Henry's Inn
1701 E. Busch Boulevard
Tampa, Florida 33612
(813) 933-7681
M $20 C $28 R $32 1, 2, 3, 4, 6

Ramada Airport Hotel & Conference Center
5303 W. Kennedy Boulevard
Tampa, Florida 33609
(813) 877-0534 / (800) 2-RAMADA
M $45 C $55 R $59 2, 3, 4, 5, 6

GEORGIA

Best Way Inn
144 14th Street
Atlanta, Georgia 30318
(404) 873-4171
M $29-40 C $29-40 R $31-42 2, 3, 4

Best Western Bradbury Suites
4500 Circle 75 Parkway
Atlanta, Georgia 30339
(404) 956-9919 / (800) 528-1234
M $60 C $62 R $64 1, 2, 3, 4, 6

Days Hotel at Lenox
3377 Peachtree Road, N.E.
Atlanta, Georgia 30326
(404) 264-1111 / (800) 325-2525
M $59 C $69 R $79 1, 2, 3, 4, 5, 6

Executive Villas Hotel
5735 Roswell Road
Atlanta, Georgia 30342
(404) 252-2868 / (800) 241-1013
M 1BR $46 2BR $59 3BR $80 2, 3, 4, 6

Lanier Plaza
418 Armour Drive
Atlanta, Georgia 30324
(404) 873-4661 / (800) 554-8444
M $53 C $60 R $65-75 3, 4, 6, 7

Rodeway Inn Midtown
1470 Spring Street
Atlanta, Georgia 30309
(404) 872-5821 / (800) 654-6200
M $52 C $65 R $72 2, 3, 4, 5, 6

Super 8 Motel Atlanta N.W.
4502 Circle 75 Parkway
Atlanta, Georgia 30339
(404) 955-3388 / (800) 843-1991
M $29.95 C $29.95 R $29.95 1, 2, 4, 6

Best Western Bradbury Suites
1062 Claussen Road
Augusta, Georgia 30907
(404) 733-4656 / (800) 528-1234
M $44 C $56 R $58 1, 2, 3, 4, 6

Comfort Inn Augusta
629 Frontage Road, I-20 & Bobby Jones Expwy
Augusta, Georgia 30957
(404) 855-6060 / (800) 228-5150
M $38 C $38 R $45 2, 3, 4, 5, 6

Colony Plaza Hotel

West Orlando (OCOEE), FL 34761
Colony Plaza Hotel   (407) 656-3333
Canada & US Toll Free 1-800-821-0136
Directions: FL Tpk. Exit 267 go East on Hwy 50, 1/2 mile on right. Off I-4 exit on Colonial & 50, go West 10 1/2 miles—hotel on left.

MILITARY SPECIAL

Off to Disney World!

1990
$38.00
per room/per night

**For 1 to 4 Persons!
Each Room Has
Two Double Beds**
10% Tax Not Included

Non-Commissionable

- This coupon may not be used in conjunction with any other coupon offer.
- Based on space availability.
- Offer not valid unless this coupon presented to desk clerk upon check-in.

Valid thru Dec. 1990

GEORGIA

The Partridge Inn
2110 Walton Way
Augusta, Georgia 30904
(404) 737-8888 / (800) 476-6888
M $55 C $60 R $70 1, 2, 3, 4, 6

Charter House Inn
U.S. Hwy 27 South & 84 Bypass
Bainbridge, Georgia 31717
(912) 246-8550 / (800) 768-8550
M $35 C $36 R $37 2, 3, 4, 6

Howard Johnson-Atlanta Airport South
I-285 & Riverdale Road
College Park (ATLANTA), Georgia 30349
(404) 996-4321 / (800) 241-3092
M $42 C $44 R $50 2, 3, 4, 5, 6

The Jekyll Island Club Hotel - A Radisson Resort, 371 Riverview Drive
Jekyll Island, Georgia 31520
(912) 635-2600 / (800) 333-3333
M $69 C $86 R $79-109 2, 3, 4, 6

Kingsland Super 8 Motel
I-95 & Hwy. 40, Exit 2
Kingsland, Georgia 31548
(912) 729-6888 / (800) 843-1991
M $27.88 C $27.88 R $30.88 1, 2, 4, 6

Best Western Bradbury Inn
5985 Oakbrook Parkway
Norcross, Georgia 30093
(404) 662-8175 / (800) 528-1234
M $46 C $56 R $58 1, 2, 3, 4, 6

Rodeway Inn
I-95 & U.S. 17
P.O. Box 429, Richmond Hill, GA 31324
(912) 756-3376 / (800) 228-2000
M $25 C $25 R $27 1, 2, 3, 4

Charter House Inn
2710 Osborne Street
St. Marys, Georgia 31558
(912) 882-6250 / (800) 768-6250
M $36 C $36 R $38 2, 3, 4, 6

Best Western Bradbury Suites
2060 Crescent Centre Boulevard
Tucker, Georgia 30084
(404) 496-1070 / (800) 528-1234
M $65 C $67 R $69 1, 2, 3, 4, 6

Make my diem!

For business or pleasure, save in Atlanta with Per Diem Plus.™

When you or your family are in Atlanta for business or pleasure, you can count on Rodeway Inn to make your diem. Stop at the Rodeway Inn-Midtown and get a clean, comfortable room at a single rate of $52 plus tax – guaranteed to meet the published government per diem. No problems. No hassles. Call for information and reservations on our Special Services Hotline, set up exclusively for government, military, and CRC personnel. Next trip stay at Rodeway. And let us make your diem.

For information and reservations, call our Special Services Hotline:

800-654-6200

RODEWAY INN

HAWAII

Continental Surf Hotel
2426 Kuhio Avenue
Honolulu, Hawaii 96815
(808) 531-5235/(800) 367-5004 Cont. U.S.
M $41-47 C $37-42 R $47-62 1, 2

Kaulana Kai Hotel
2425 Kuhio Avenue
Honolulu, Hawaii 96815
(808) 922-7777 / (800) 367-5666
Single Regular Rate $70

Queen Kapiolani Hotel
150 Kapahulu Avenue
Honolulu, Hawaii 96815
(808) 531-5235/(800) 367-5004 Cont. U.S.
M $57-81 C $65-83 R $79-112 1, 2, 3

Waikiki Hana Hotel
2424 Koa Avenue
Honolulu, Hawaii 96815
(808) 531-5235/(800) 367-5004 Cont. U.S.
M $47-73 C $56-75 R $55-84 1, 2

Waikiki Marina Hotel
1956 Ala Moana Boulevard
Honolulu, Hawaii 96815
(808) 955-0714 / (800) 367-6070
M $52-66 R $58-73 1, 2, 3

ILLINOIS

Best Western Bradbury Suites
2111 South Arlington Heights Road
Arlington Heights, Illinois 60005
(312) 956-1400 / (800) 528-1234
M $75(inc tax) C $69 R $74 1, 2, 4, 6

The Inn at University Village
625 S. Ashland
Chicago, Illinois 60607
(312) 243-7200 / (800) 662-5233
M $50 C $95-110 R $140 1, 2, 4, 5, 6

Days Inn Decatur
333 North Wyckles Road
Decatur, Illinois 62522
(217) 422-5900 / (800) 325-2525
M $33.95 C $33.95 R $32.95-36.95 2, 4, 6

ILLINOIS

Holiday Inn O'Hare/Mannheim
1450 E. Touhy
Des Plaines, Illinois 60018
(708) 296-8866 / (800) HOLIDAY
M $55 C $64 R $71-79 3, 4, 5, 6

Granite City Lodge
1200 19th Street
Granite City, Illinois 62040
(618) 876-2600
M $25 C $25 R $27 1, 3, 4, 6

Hotel Moraine - Across from Ft. Sheridan
700 N. Sheridan Road
Highwood, Illinois 60040
(708) 433-4100 / (800) 433-4101
M $55 C $64 R $85 1, 2, 3, 4, 6

Holiday Inn Joliet
411 Larkin Avenue
Joliet, Illinois 60436
(815) 729-2000 / (800) HOLIDAY
M $49 C $59 R $60-65 2, 3, 4, 6

The Inn at University Village

$50* PLUS TAX

MILITARY RATE

Minutes From Downtown
Free Parking
Free Shuttle Service

625 SOUTH ASHLAND AVENUE AT HARRISON
CHICAGO, IL 60607 • 312/243-7200

1•800•662•5233 NATIONWIDE

*Rates good on space availability only.
Single or double occupancy.

EXPECT THE FINEST

Temporary Military Lodging Around the World — 337

ILLINOIS

Days Inn Melrose Park
1900 N. Mannheim Road
Melrose Park, Illinois 60160
(708) 681-3100 / (800) 325-2525
M $40 C $40 R $41-51 1, 2, 4

Holiday Inn Mt. Prospect
200 East Rand
Mount Prospect, Illinois 60056
(312) 255-8800
M $49 C $58 R $60 2, 3, 4, 5

Travelodge Chicago/Naperville
1617 Naperville Road
Naperville, Illinois 60563
(708) 505-0200 / (800) 255-3050
M $37.36 C $38-45 R $43-48 1, 2, 4, 6

Quincy Travelodge
200 South 3rd Street
Quincy, Illinois 62301
(217) 222-5620 / (800) 255-3050
M $33 C $33 R $37 1, 2, 3, 4, 5, 6

Days Inn/Richmond-Lake Geneva
11200 North Route 12
Richmond, Illinois 60071
(815) 678-4807 / (800) 325-2525
M $35 C $35 R $33-43 1, 2, 3, 4, 6

Best Western at O'Hare
10300 W. Higgins Road
Rosemont, Illinois 60018
(708) 296-4958 / (800) 528-1234
M $51 C $61 R $63-66 1, 2, 3, 4, 5, 6

Days Inn O'Hare South
3801 N. Mannheim Road
Schiller Park, Illinois 60176
(708) 678-0670 / (800) 325-2525
M $43 C $43 R $45-59 1, 2, 3, 4, 5

Days Inn Shorewood
19747 Frontage Road
Shorewood, Illinois 60435
(815) 741-8664 / (800) 325-2525
M $45 C $48 R $50 1, 2, 3, 4

Urbana Travelodge
409 West University Avenue
Urbana, Illinois 61801
(217) 328-3521 / (800) 255-3050
M $36 C $36 R $38 1, 2, 3, 4, 6

ILLINOIS

Waukegan Travelodge
222 Grand Avenue
Waukegan, Illinois 60085
(312) 244-8950 / (800) 255-3050
M $42 C $42 R $48 1, 2, 3, 4, 6

Palwaukee Motor Inn
1090 S. Milwaukee Avenue
Wheeling, Illinois 60090
(708) 537-9100
M $39 C $45 R $48-50 1, 2, 3, 4

INDIANA

Hammond Hotel
7813 Indianapolis Boulevard
Hammond, Indiana 46324
(219) 844-7780
M $39 C $42 R $46 1, 2, 3, 4, 6

Quality Inn Castleton Suites
8275 Craig Street
Indianapolis, Indiana 46250
(317) 841-9700
M $48 C $51 R $55 1, 2, 4, 6

Rodeway Inn East-Indianapolis
7050 East 21st Street
Indianapolis, Indiana 46219
(317) 352-0481 / (800) 228-2000
M $31.90 C $31.90 R $34 1, 2, 3, 4, 6

West Lafayette Travelodge
200 Brown Street
West Lafayette, Indiana 47906
(317) 743-9661 / (800) 255-3050
M $35 C $35 R $38 1, 2, 3, 4, 6

KANSAS

Super 8 Lodge
1708 West Wyatt Earpp
Dodge City, Kansas 67801
(316) 225-3924 / (800) 843-1991
M $24.88 C $26.88 R $28.88 1, 2, 3, 4

Comfort Inn
1621 Super Plaza
Hutchinson, Kansas 67501
(316) 663-7822 / (800) 228-5150
C $27.95 C $29.95 R $32.95 1, 2, 3, 4

KANSAS

Quality Inn City Center
15 West 4th
Hutchinson, Kansas 67501
(316) 663-1211 / (800) 228-5151
M $25.95 C $29.95 R $33.95 1, 2, 3, 4

Liberty Inn
1133 S. Washington
Junction City, Kansas 66441
(913) 238-1141 / (800) 2-RAMADA
M $21 C $21 R $23 1, 2, 3, 4, 6

Holiday Inn Downtown
424 Minnesota Avenue
Kansas City, Kansas 66101
(913) 342-6919
M $41 C $49 R $53 1, 2, 3, 4, 7

Lawrence Travelodge
801 Iowa Street
Lawrence, Kansas 66044
(913) 842-5100 / (800) 255-3050
M $30 C $32 R $36 1, 2, 3, 4, 6

Ramada Inn
3rd and Delaware
Leavenworth, Kansas 66048
(913) 651-5500 / (800) 2-RAMADA
M $33 C $35 R $37-45 1, 2, 3, 4, 6

Guesthouse Apartment Hotel
9775 Lenexa Drive
Lenexa, Kansas 66215
(913) 541-4000 / (800) 828-4994
M $54 C $54 R $59 1, 2, 3, 4, 6

Howard Johnson's
3839 S. W. Topeka
Topeka, Kansas 66609
(913) 266-4700 / (800) 2-RAMADA
M $30 C $30 1, 2, 3, 4, 5, 6

Ramada Inn Downtown
420 E. 6th Street
Topeka, Kansas 66607
(913) 234-5400 / (800) 2-RAMADA
M $43 C $49 R $66 1, 2, 3, 4, 5, 6

Ramada Inn South
3847 S. W. Topeka
Topeka, Kansas 66609
(913) 267-1800 / (800) 2-RAMADA
M $30 C $34 R $46 1, 2, 3, 4, 5, 6

KANSAS

Holiday Inn®
Downtown

OVERLOOKING RIVER CITY U.S.A.

JUST MINUTES FROM GREYHOUND AND HORSE RACING

$41.00 Single $49.00 Double

FREE BREAKFAST WITH THIS COUPON

I-70 at the Minnesota Exit
424 Minnesota Ave.
Kansas City, Kansas
913-342-6919
(Some restrictions may apply.)

Ramada Hotel at Broadview Place
400 W. Douglas
Wichita, Kansas 67202
(316) 262-5000 / (800) 2-RAMADA
M $50 C $60 R $64 1, 2, 3, 4, 5, 6

Scotsman Inn - East
465 S. Webb Road
Wichita, Kansas 67207
(316) 684-6363 / (800) 477-7268
R $25.95 1, 2, 4, 6

Wichita Hilton East
549 S. Rock Road
Wichita, Kansas 67207
(316) 686-7131 / (800) HILTONS
M $49 C $75 R $75-91 2, 3, 4, 5

The Wichita Royale
125 N. Market
Wichita, Kansas 67202
(316) 263-2101 / (800) 876-0240
M $45 C $65 R $75 1, 2, 3, 4, 5

KENTUCKY

Capital Plaza Hotel
405 Wilkinson Boulevard
Frankfort, Kentucky 40601
(502) 227-5100 / (800) 372-2727
M $45 C $58 1, 2, 3, 4, 6

Hyatt Regency Lexington
400 W. Vine Street
Lexington, Kentucky 40507
(606) 253-1234 / (800) 233-1234
M $50 C $105 R $120 1, 2, 3, 4, 5, 6

Lexington Hilton Inn
1938 Stanton Way, I-75 at Newtown Pike
Lexington, Kentucky 40511
(606) 259-1311
M $47 C $64 R $72 2, 3, 4, 5, 6

Radisson Plaza Hotel
Broadway & Vine
Lexington, Kentucky 40507
(606) 231-9000 / (800) 333-3333
M $50-60 C $89 R $99 2, 3, 4, 5, 6

Days Inn Hotel
101 E. Jefferson Street
Louisville, Kentucky 40202
(502) 585-2200 / (800) 325-2525
M $37 C $41 R $49 2, 3, 4, 5, 6

Louisville/Hurstbourne Travelodge
9340 Blairwood Road
Louisville, Kentucky 40222
(502) 425-8010 / (800) 255-3050
M $30 C $33-47 R $35-49 1, 2, 4, 6

Super 8 Motel
395 Redmar Boulevard
Radcliff, Kentucky 40160
(502) 352-1888 / (800) 843-1991
M $29.88 C $29.88 R $31.88 2, 4, 6

LOUISIANA

Sheraton Baton Rouge Hotel
4728 Constitution
Baton Rouge, Louisiana 70808
(504) 925-2244 / (800) 325-3535
M $45 C $56 R $69 1, 2, 3, 4, 5, 6

LOUISIANA

Holiday Inn
I-12 & Hwy. 190, P.O. Box 1759
Covington, Louisiana 70434
(504) 893-3580 / (800) HOLIDAY
M $43 C $48 R $55 1, 2, 3, 4, 6

Holiday Inn / Westbank
100 Westbank Expressway
Gretna, Louisiana 70053
(504) 366-2361
M $28 R $28 2, 3, 4, 6

Dauphine Orleans Hotel
415 Dauphine Street
New Orleans, Louisiana 70003
(504) 586-1800 / (800) 521-7111
M $55 C $75 R $90 1, 3, 4, 5

La Salle Hotel
1113 Canal Street
New Orleans, Louisiana 70112
(504) 523-5831 / (800) 521-9450
M $35.10 R $39 2

MARYLAND

Holiday Inn - Chesapeake House
1007 Beards Hill Road
Aberdeen, Maryland 21001
(301) 272-8100
M $56 C $64 R $69 1, 2, 3, 4, 6

Comfort Inn Northwest
10 Wooded Way
Baltimore, Maryland 21222
(301) 484-7700 / (800) 228-5150
M $45 C $45 2, 3, 4, 6

Days Inn West
6700 Security Boulevard
Baltimore, Maryland 21207
(301) 281-1800 / (800) 325-2525
M $48 C $53 2, 3, 4, 5, 6

Ramada Hotel
1701 Belmont Avenue
Baltimore, Maryland 21207
(301) 265-1100 / (800) 2-RAMADA
M $50 C $60 R $72 2, 3, 4, 5, 6

MARYLAND

Sheraton International Hotel
On Baltimore/Washington International Airport
Baltimore, Maryland 21240
(301) 859-3300 / (800) 638-5858
M $63 R $99 2, 3, 4, 5, 6

Shoney's Inn
1401 Bloomfield Avenue
Baltimore, Maryland 21227
(301) 646-1700 / (800) 222-2222
M $49 C $49 R $59 2, 3, 4, 6

Holiday Inn Calverton
4095 Powder Mill Road
Beltsville, Maryland 20705
(301) 937-4422 / (800) HOLIDAY
M $62 C $73 R $79 2, 3, 4, 6

American Inn of Bethesda
8130 Wisconsin Avenue
Bethesda, Maryland 20814
(301) 656-9300 / 1-800-323-7081
M $50 C $58 R $65 2, 3, 4

Days Inn Camp Springs Hotel
5001 Mercedes Boulevard
Camp Springs, Maryland 20746
(301) 423-2323 / (800) 325-2525
M $44 C $45 R $50 2, 3, 4, 5, 6

Colony South Hotel
7401 Surratts Road
Clinton, Maryland 20735
(301) 856-4500 / (800) 537-1147
M $58 C $75 R $80 1, 2, 3, 4, 5, 6

Days Inn of Frederick
Exit 54 I-70, Exit 31A I-270
5646 Buckeystown Pike, Frederick, MD 21701
(301) 694-6600 / (800) 325-2525
M $40.60 C $40.60 R $45 1, 2, 3, 4, 6

Econo Lodge Frederick
420 Prospect Boulevard
Frederick, Maryland 21701
(301) 695-6200 / (800) 446-6900
M $29-36 C $36.90 R $41 2, 3, 4, 6

Econo Lodge Gaithersburg
18715 North Frederick Avenue
Gaithersburg, Maryland 20879
(301) 963-3840 / (800) 446-6900
M $40-42 C $42.30 R $47 2, 4, 6

MARYLAND

La Plata Super 8 Motel
729 N. Highway 301
La Plata, Maryland 20646
(301) 934-3465
M 10% C 10% 1, 2, 4, 5, 6

Budget Host Valencia Motel
10131 Washington Blvd., U.S. 1
Laurel, Maryland 20707
(301) 725-4200 / (800) 336-4366
R $38-45 1, 2, 4, 6

Howard Johnson Hotel
#1 Second Street
Laurel, Maryland 20707
(301) 725-8800 / (800) 654-2000
M $39 C $39 R $42-50 1, 2, 3, 4, 5

Belvedere Motor Inn
60 Main Street
Lexington Park, Maryland 20653
(301) 863-6666
M $35 R $37 1, 2, 3, 4, 6

Congressional Park Days Inn
1775 Rockville Pike
Rockville, Maryland 20850
(301) 881-2300 / (800) 255-1775
M $68 C $85 R $94 1, 2, 4, 5, 6

Days Inn Rockville
16001 Shady Grove Road
Rockville, Maryland 20850
(301) 948-4300
M $51 C $51 R $55 1, 2, 3, 4, 6

Holiday Inn Waldorf
One St. Patrick Drive
Waldorf, Maryland 20603
(301) 645-8200 or 7-843-3350
M $49 C $49 R $55 2, 3, 4, 6

MASSACHUSETTS

Days Inn Burlington
30 Wheeler Road
Burlington, Massachusetts 01803
(617) 272-8800
M $73 C $99 R $109 1, 2, 3, 4, 5, 6

MASSACHUSETTS

Red Carpet Inn
6 Bourn Bridge Cul-de-sac, Rt. 28
Buzzards Bay, Massachusetts 02532
(508) 759-2711
M $35-42 R $38 1, 4

Comfort Inn at the Parwick Centre
450 Memorial Drive
Chicopee, Massachusetts 01020
(413) 739-7311 / (800) 228-5150
M $43 C $48 R $48-63 1, 2, 4, 6

The Earl of Sandwich Motor Manor
378 Route 6A
East Sandwich, MA 02537 (Cape Cod)
(508) 888-1415
M $30-60 C $30-65 R $35-85 1, 2, 4, 6

Days Inn - Framingham
30 Worcester Road
Framingham, Massachusetts 01701
(508) 875-6151 / (800) 325-2525
M $56 C $62 R $73 1, 2, 3, 4, 5, 6

Hampton Inn-North Andover/Lawrence
224 Winthrop Avenue
Lawrence, Massachusetts 01843
(508) 975-4050 / (800) HAMPTON
M $48 R $55-63 1, 2, 4, 6

Sheraton Needham Hotel
100 Cabot Street
Needham, Massachusetts 02194
(617) 444-1110 x615 / (800) 325-3535
M $70 C $110 R $135 2, 4, 6

Days Inn - Newton
399 Grove Street
Newton, Massachusetts 02162
(617) 969-5300 / (800) 325-2525
M $73 C $89-97 R $99-107 1, 2, 3, 4, 6

Days Inn Saugus
999 Broadway, Rt. 1
Saugus, Massachusetts 01906
(617) 233-1800 / (800) 325-2525
M $45 C $75 R $89 1, 2, 4, 5, 6

Days Inn Woburn
19 Commerce Way
Woburn, Massachusetts 01801
(617) 935-7110 / (800) 325-2525
M $65 C $90 R $102 1, 2, 3, 4, 5, 6

MICHIGAN

Detroit/Dearborn Travelodge
23730 Michigan Avenue
Dearborn, Michigan 48124
(313) 565-7250 / (800) 255-3050
M $38 C $40-65 R $43-68 1, 2, 4, 6

Days Inn Downtown Detroit
231 Michigan Avenue
Detroit, Michigan 48226
(313) 965-4646 / (800) 325-2525
M $54 C $69 R $79 2, 3, 6

Detroit Airport Marriott
Detroit Metro Airport
Detroit, Michigan 48242
(313) 941-9400 / (800) 228-9290
M $60 C $115 R $120 2, 3, 4, 5

Residence Inn by Marriott
5777 Southfield Service Drive
Detroit, Michigan 48228
(313) 441-1700 / (800) 331-3131
M $66 C $93 R $103 2, 3, 4, 6

Radisson Suite Hotel
37529 Grand River Avenue
Farmington Hills, Michigan 48331
(313) 477-7800 / (800) 333-3333
M $49 C $79 R $85 2, 3, 4, 6

Detroit/Novi Travelodge
21100 Haggerty Road
Northville, Michigan 48167
(313) 349-7400 / (800) 255-3050
M $36 C $39-54 R $43-56 1, 2, 4, 6

Detroit/Southfield Travelodge
27650 Northwestern Highway
Southfield, Michigan 48034
(313) 353-6777 / (800) 255-3050
M $36 C $39-54 R $43-56 1, 2, 4, 6

MINNESOTA

Best Western Bradbury Suites
7770 Johnson Avenue
Minneapolis, Minnesota 55435
(612) 893-9999 / (800) 528-1234
M $54 C $65 R $67 1, 2, 4, 6

MINNESOTA

Days Inn Minneapolis North
1501 Freeway Blvd., exit Shingle Creek Pkwy.
Minneapolis, Minnesota 55430
(612) 566-4140 / (800) 325-2525
M $40 C $48 R $56 1, 2, 3, 4, 6

Minneapolis Marriott Minnetonka
5801 Opus Parkway
Minnetonka, Minnesota 55343
(612) 935-5500 / (800) 627-6714
M $55 C $105 R $119 1, 2, 3, 4, 6

Red Carpet Inn
235 Withers Harbor Drive
Red Wing, Minnesota 55066
(612) 388-1502 / (800) 251-1962
M $33.21 C $36.90 R $36.90 1, 3, 4, 6

MISSISSIPPI

Rienzi Inn
6007 Highway 90 East
Pascagoula, Mississippi 39567
(601) 769-6200
M $18 C $19.95 R $19.95 1, 2, 3, 4

MISSOURI

The Elms Resort Hotel
Regent and Elms Boulevard
Excelsior Springs, Missouri 64024
(816) 637-2141 / (800) 843-3567
M $39 Sun-Th C $39 Sun-Th R $79 1, 2, 3, 4

Holiday Inn Sports Complex
4011 Blue Ridge Cutoff
Kansas City, Missouri 64133
(816) 353-5300, ext 155
M $45 C $56 R $64 2, 3, 4, 6

Econo Lodge St. Louis/St. Charles
I-70 & Zumbehl Road, 3040 W. Clay Street
St. Charles, Missouri 63301
(314) 946-9992 / (800) 446-6900
M $25 C $25 R $29.95 2, 4, 6

St. Louisian Hotel
1133 Washington Avenue
St. Louis, Missouri 63101
(314) 421-4727
M $32 C $35 R $45 1, 2, 3, 4, 5

THE ELMS RESORT HOTEL

It's never been easier to have a good time.

- 113 deluxe guest rooms and suites
- State-of-the-art exercise room
- Complete spa facilities
- 10 private environmental rooms
- Hair salon • Restaurant
- 18 hole championship golf course
- Meeting rooms
- Tennis courts
- Free Showtime cable T.V.
- Special group rates

Special Military Rates Available.

For Reservations call 1-800-THE ELMS or 816/637-2141

Regent & Elms Blvd. • Excelsior Springs, Mo.

NEW

GUESTHOUSE APARTMENT HOTEL

"There's someplace like home."

About half the cost of other all-suites

- Serving Metropolitan Kansas City
- Low daily/weekly/monthly rates
- Separate bedroom with phone and desk
- Fully equipped kitchen
- Color Cable TV, ESPN, HBO, CNN
- Non-smoker's suites
- Health club privileges included
- Minutes to military locations!

GUESTHOUSE APARTMENT HOTEL

9775 Lenexa Drive   1-800-828-4994
(Facing I-35, 2 Blks South of 95th St.)

MONTANA

Super 8 Lodge & Lionshead Resort
1545 Targhee Pass Highway
West Yellowstone, Montana 59758
(406) 646-9584 / (800) 843-1991
M $33.88 C $33.88 R $38.88 1, 2, 4, 6

NEBRASKA

Ramada Inn
2301 N.W. 12th Street
Lincoln, Nebraska 68501
(402) 475-5911 / (800) 2-RAMADA
M $36 C $36 R $38-48 1, 2, 3, 4, 5, 6

NEVADA

Circus Circus Hotel/Casino
2880 Las Vegas Boulevard South
Las Vegas, Nevada 89114-4967
(702) 734-0410 / (800) 634-3450
R $19-44 1, 2, 3, 4, 6

Holiday Inn Reno-Downtown
1000 East Sixth Street
Reno, Nevada 89512
(702) 786-5151 / (800) 648-4877
M $39 C $49 R $55 1, 2, 3, 4, 6

NEW HAMPSHIRE

Eastern Inns
P.O. Box 775, Rte. 16
N. Conway, New Hampshire 03860
(603) 356-5447 / (800) 628-3750
M $48 C $55 R $55-65 1, 2, 3, 4

Airport Economy Inn
7 Airport Road
West Lebanon, New Hampshire 03784
(603) 298-8888
M $39.50-45 C $39.50-45 R $43.50-50 1, 2, 4, 6

NEW JERSEY

The Royal Inn
120 Evergreen Place
East Orange, New Jersey 07018
(201) 677-3100 / (800) 257-3303
M $54 C $54 R $60-75 1, 2, 3, 4, 6

Sheraton Meadowland Hotel
Sheraton Plaza Drive
East Rutherford, New Jersey 07073
(201) 896-0500 / (800) 325-3535
M $75 C $135 R $119-160 1, 2, 3, 4, 5, 6

Days Inn - Atlantic City/Pleasantville
1150 Tilton Road
Pleasantville, New Jersey 08232
(609) 641-4500 / (800) 325-2525
M $44 C $45 R $80 1, 2, 3, 4, 6

Palace Hotel
2600 Tonnele Avenue
North Bergen, New Jersey 07047
(201) 866-0400 / (800) 548-4206
M $60 C $65 R $70 2, 3, 4

Holiday Inn
109 9th Avenue
Runnemede, New Jersey 08078
(609) 939-4200 / 1-800-HOLIDAY
M $50 C $65 R $74 2, 3, 4, 6

Days Hotel Secaucus
455 Harmon Meadow Boulevard
Secaucus, New Jersey 07094
(201) 617-8888
M $71.20 C $82 R $90 2, 4, 5, 6

NEW MEXICO

Royal Hotel of Albuquerque
4119 Central Avenue, N.E.
Albuquerque, New Mexico 87108-1160
(505) 265-3585 / (800) 843-8572
M $29.90 C $31.90 R $38.90 2, 3, 4, 5, 6

NEW YORK

Days Hotel LaGuardia
100-15 Ditmars Boulevard
East Elmhurst, New York 11369
(718) 898-1225/ (800) 325-2525
M $115 C $120 R $125 1, 2, 3, 4, 5, 6

The Inn at Fort Drum
4205 Po Valley Road, P.O. Box 201
Fort Drum, New York 13602
(315) 773-7777
M $42 R $42 2, 4, 6

Freeport Motor Inn & Boatel
445 S. Main Street
Freeport, New York 11520
(516) 623-9100
M $57 C $60 R $64 2, 4

Travelodge International Hotel
JFK Airport
Jamaica, New York 11430
(718) 995-9000 / (800) 255-3050
M $93 C $105 R $120 2, 4, 5, 6

America's Waking Up To Us

When you wake up in our Days Hotel you know you're going to have a great day.

We're centrally located just minutes from Manhattan, and all its exciting attractions... and we're right around the corner from Queens, Shea Stadium and Flushing Meadow Park.

Our location isn't all we have to offer, we have 224 spacious guest rooms, conference and exhibit space, dine in our gracious restaurant and than relax in our lounge.

For more information and reservations call
(718) 898-1225
or
Toll Free
800-325-2525

DAYS HOTEL
100-15 Ditmars Boulevard
East Elmhurst, N.Y. 11369

NEW YORK

Days Inn North
400 7th North Street
Liverpool, New York 13088
(315) 451-1511 / (800) 325-2525
M $49 C $56 R $56
1, 2, 3, 4, 5

Beekman Tower
3 Mitchell Place
New York, New York 10017
(212) 355-7300 / (800) ME-SUITE
M $107 R $165 1, 2

Dumont Plaza
150 E. 34th Street
New York, New York 10016
(212) 481-7600 / (800) ME-SUITE
M $107 R $180 2

Eastgate Tower
222 East 39th Street
New York, New York 10016
(212) 687-8000 / (800) ME-SUITE
M $107 R $175 1, 2

Lyden House
320 E. 53rd Street
New York, New York 10022
(212) 888-6070 / 1-800-ME-SUITE
M $107 R $175 1, 2

Milford Plaza (Best Western)
270 W. 45th Street
New York, New York 10036
(212) 869-3600 / (800) 221-2690
M $85 C $88 R $95-135 7

Plaza Fifty
155 E. 50th Street
New York, New York 10022
(212) 751-5710 / (800) ME-SUITE
M $107 R $180 1, 2

Shelburne Murray Hill
303 Lexington Avenue
New York, New York 10016
(212) 689-5200 / (800) ME-SUITE
M $107 R $175 1, 2

NEW YORK

Southgate Tower
371 Seventh Avenue
New York, New York 10001
(212) 563-1800 / (800) ME-SUITE
M $105-107 R $160 2

Days Inn of Plattsburgh
I-87 & Route 3
Plattsburgh, New York 12901
(518) 561-0403 / (800) 325-2525
M $36-46 C $38-48 R $41-51 1, 2, 3, 4, 6

Holiday Inn
P.O. Box 3159, Greenville Turnpike & Rt. 23
Port Jervis, New York 12771
(914) 856-6611 / (800) 465-4329
M $44 C $60 R $64 1, 2, 3, 4, 6

Quality Inn, North
1308 Buckley Road
N. Syracuse, New York 13212
(315) 451-1212 / (800) 221-2222
M $49 C $65 R $65 2, 3, 4, 5

Red Carpet Inn
Northern Lights on Route 11
N. Syracuse, New York 13212
(315) 454-3266 / (800) 251-1962
M $35-40 C $35-40 R $35-45 1, 2, 3, 4, 6

Sheraton Utica Hotel & Conference Center
200 Genesee Street
Utica, New York 13502
(315) 797-8010
M $60-78 C $73 R $78-84 1, 2, 3, 4, 5, 6

NORTH CAROLINA

Innkeeper Motor Lodge of Fayetteville
1720 Skibo Road
Fayetteville, North Carolina 28303
(919) 867-7659
M $34-44 C $35-45 R $37-47 1, 2, 3, 4, 6

Days Inn Raleigh-Crabtree
6329 Glenwood Avenue, U.S. 70
Raleigh, North Carolina 27612
(919) 781-7904 / (800) 325-2525
M $33.75 C $38 R $42 1, 2, 3, 4, 6

NORTH CAROLINA

Mission Valley Inn
2110 Avent Ferry Road
Raleigh, North Carolina 27606
(919) 828-3173 / (800) 223-2252
M $35-47 C $53 R $59 2, 3, 4, 5, 6

Days Inn Raleigh Airport/RTP
I-40 & Exit 284, Airport Blvd.
Box 13525 RTP, North Carolina 27709-3525
(919) 469-8688 / (800) 325-2525
M $43.95 C $49 R $55 1, 2, 3, 4, 5, 6

St. Regis Resort Hotel
Box 4000 North Topsail Shores
Sneads Ferry, North Carolina 28460
(919) 328-0778 / (800) 682-4882
M 25% dis C 25% dis R $69 less dis. 1, 3, 4

Mid Pines - A Clarion Resort
1010 Midland Road
Southern Pines, North Carolina 28387
(919) 692-2114 / (800) 323-2114
M $52-80 C $53-85 R $72-95 1, 2, 3, 4, 5, 6

OHIO

Holiday Inn - Beachwood
3750 Orange Place
Beachwood, Ohio 44122
(216) 831-3300 / (800) HOLIDAY
M $52 C $70-80 R $80-90 1, 2, 3, 4, 5, 6

Drawbridge Inn
I-75 & Buttermilk Pike
Fort Mitchell, KY 41017 (Greater Cincinnati)
(606) 341-2800 / (800) 354-9793
1, 2, 3, 4, 5, 6

Holiday Inn - North
2235 Sharon Road
Cincinnati, Ohio 45241
(513) 771-0700 / (800) HOLIDAY
M $45 C $65 R $69 2, 3, 4, 6

Budget Inn of America
14043 Brookpark Road
Cleveland, Ohio 44142
(216) 267-2350
M $30.95 C $32.95 R $35.95 2, 4, 5

OHIO

Days Hotel I-480
4600 Northfield Road
Cleveland, Ohio 44128
(216) 663-4100 / (800) 325-2535
M $46 C $59 R $70 2, 3, 4, 6

Ramada University Hotel
3110 Olentangy River Road
Columbus, Ohio 43202
(614) 267-7461 / (800) 228-2828
M $49 C $55 R $59 2, 3, 4, 5, 6

Travelodge/Columbus-Worthington
7480 N. High Street
Columbus, Ohio 43235
(614) 431-2525 / (800) 255-3050
M $34 C $34 R $37 2, 4, 6

Radisson Hotel Toledo
101 North Summit
Toledo, Ohio 43604
(419) 241-3000 / (800) 333-3333
M $45 C $65 R $69 1, 2, 5, 6

Cleveland/Willoughby Travelodge
34600 Maplegrove Road
Willoughby, Ohio 44094
(216) 585-1900 / (800) 255-3050
M $30 C $34-51 R $36-53 1, 2, 4, 6

OKLAHOMA

Best Western Trade Winds Courtyard Inn
2128 Gary Freeway
Clinton, Oklahoma 73601
(405) 323-2610 / (800) 528-1234
M $27.50 C $30 R $33 2, 3, 4

Ramada Inn
601 N. 2nd
Lawton, Oklahoma 73507 (Also Fort Sill)
(405) 355-7155/ (800) 2-RAMADA
M $31-33 C $33 R $36-38 1, 2, 3, 4, 5, 6

Days Inn Northwest
2801 N.W. 39th
Oklahoma City, Oklahoma 73112
(405) 946-0741 / (800) 325-2525
M $25 C $25 R $27 1, 3, 4, 6

OKLAHOMA

Days Inn South
2616 S. Interstate 35
Oklahoma City, OK 73129 (exit S. 29th St.)
(405) 677-0521 / (800) 325-2525
M $24.95 C $27.90 R $31 1, 2, 3, 4, 6

Lexington Hotel Suites
1200 S. Meridian
Oklahoma City, Oklahoma 73108
(405) 943-7800 / (800) 53-SUITE
M $38 C $43 R $45 1, 2, 3, 4, 6

Stratford House Inn
1110 Charles Page Boulevard
Sand Springs, Oklahoma 74063
(918) 245-0283
M $33.30 C $35 R $37 1, 2, 4, 6

Stratford House Inn-Riverside
114 East Skelly Drive
Tulsa, Oklahoma 74035
(918) 743-2009
M $28.95 C $29.95 R $32.95 1, 2, 4, 6

Stratford Towers
3355 East Skelly Drive
Tulsa, Oklahoma 74135
(918) 744-4263
M $26.95 C $29.95 R $29.95 1, 2, 4

PENNSYLVANIA

Days Inn Suites
1329 Bristol Pike
Bensalem, Pennsylvania 19020
(215) 245-5222 / (800) 325-2525
M $56 C $66 R $79 3, 4, 6

Holiday Inn - Chambersburg
1095 Wayne Avenue
Chambersburg, Pennsylvania 17201
(717) 263-3400 / (800)-HOLIDAY
M $46 C $48 R $48 2, 3, 4, 6

Sheraton Inn Greensburg
108 Sheraton Drive, Route 30 East
Greensburg, Pennsylvania 15601
(412) 836-6060
1, 2, 3, 4, 6

PENNSYLVANIA

Howard Johnson Lodge
Rte. 202 North & South Gulph Road
King of Prussia, Pennsylvania 19406
(215) 265-4500 / (800) 654-2000
M $65-72 C $70-76 R $74-83 1, 2, 3, 4

Quality Inn/Lebanon-Hershey
625 Quentin Road
Lebanon, Pennsylvania 17042
(717) 273-6771 / (800) 228-5151
M $44 C $51 R $57 1, 2, 3, 4, 6

Holiday Inn Mechanicsburg
5401 Carlisle Pike
Mechanicsburg, Pennsylvania 17055
(717) 697-0321 / (800) HOLIDAY
M $45 C $64 R $75 2, 3, 4, 6

Howard Johnson Hotel
11580 Roosevelt Boulevard
Philadelphia, Pennsylvania 19116
(215) 464-9500
M $45 C $55 R $65 1, 2, 3, 4, 6

Philadelphia Airport Marriott
4509 Island Avenue
Philadelphia, Pennsylvania 19153
(215) 365-4150
M $69 C $115 R $125 2, 3, 4, 5, 6

Quality Inn Historic Downtown Suites
1010 Race Street
Philadelphia, Pennsylvania 19107
(215) 922-1730 / (800) 628-8932
M $68 C $80 R $85 1, 2, 6

Wyndham Franklin Plaza Hotel
17th and Vine Streets
Philadelphia, Pennsylvania 19103
(215) 448-2000 / (800) 822-4200
M $69-72 C $105 R $145 1, 2, 3, 6

Pittsburgh Green Tree Marriott
101 Marriott Drive
Pittsburgh, Pennsylvania 15205
(412) 922-8400 / (800) 228-9290
M $54 C $112 R $120 2, 3, 4, 5, 6

Enjoy Complete Satisfaction at your Military Reunion at SHERATON INN GREENSBURG!

We've served the following Reunions:

3471st Ordinance M.A.M. Company
157th Engineer Combat Battalion
51st Medical Battalion
194th General Hospital - World War II
478th AAAAW Battalion Association
National 4th Infantry Division
Tri-State Fighting 69th's
163rd AAA Gun Battery
501 Battery "C" AAA Gun Battalion

ENJOY!!! RELAX!!! ENOY!!!

- Conveniently Located on Route 30
- Close To Two PA Turnpike Exits #7 & #8
- Comfortable Sleeping Rooms
- Fine Dining Room
- Live Entertainment in the Lounge
- Special Theme Nights
- Racquetball and Golf Course on Premises
- Delicious Food
- Weekend Packages
- USAIR's Allegheny Commuter Plan Service to Nearby Latrobe Airport

Sheraton Inn Greensburg
The hospitality people of ITT

ROUTE 30 EAST, 100 SHERATON DRIVE
GREENSBURG, PENNSYLVANIA 15601

RHODE ISLAND

Howard Johnson Lodge
20 Jefferson Boulevard
Warwick, Rhode Island 02888
(401) 467-9800 / (800) 654-2000
M $54 C $59 R $69 1, 2, 3, 4, 5, 6

SOUTH CAROLINA

Charleston Marriott Hotel
4770 Marriott Drive
Charleston, South Carolina 29418
(803) 747-1900 / (800) 228-9290
M$51-54 C$95-110 R$105-120 1, 2, 3, 4, 5, 6

Ramada Inn Airport
I-26 at West Montague Avenue
Charleston, South Carolina 29418
(803) 744-8281 / (800) 272-6232
M $47 C $48 R $48-68 1, 2, 3, 4, 5

Best Western Bradbury Suites
7525 Two Notch Road
Columbia, South Carolina 29223
(803) 736-6666 / (800) 528-1234
M $48 C $54 R $56 1, 2, 3, 4, 6

Ramada Hotel Northeast
8105 Two Notch Road
Columbia, South Carolina 29212
(803) 736-5600 / (800) 228-2828
M $45 C $52 R $56 1, 2, 3, 4, 5, 6

Holiday Inn
1014 Montague
Greenwood, South Carolina 29646
(803) 223-4231
M $35 2, 3, 4, 6

The Spa on Port Royal Sound
239 Beach City Road
Hilton Head Island, South Carolina 29928
(803) 681-7500 / (800) 428-2228
M 10% discount 1, 2, 3, 4

Days Inn Surfside Pier Hotel
15 S. Ocean Boulevard
Surfside Beach (Myrtle Beach), SC 29575
(803) 238-4444 / (800) 533-7599
1, 2, 3, 4, 6

SOUTH CAROLINA

Holiday Inn West
101 Outlet Boulevard
Myrtle Beach, South Carolina 29577
(803) 236-1000 / (800) 847-2707
M $39 C $49 R $65 1, 2, 3, 4, 5, 6

Sheraton Atlantic Shores Resort
2701 S. Ocean Boulevard
Myrtle Beach, South Carolina 29577
(803) 448-2518 / (800) 992-1055
M $39-73 C $39-89 R $49-119 1, 2, 3, 4, 5, 6

Park Inn International Hotel
226 N. Washington Street
Sumter, South Carolina 29150
(803) 775-2323 / (800) 982-4469
M $30 C $36.95 R $38.95 1, 2, 3, 4, 6

SOUTH DAKOTA

Luxury Lodge Motel
130 E. Illinois, P.O. Box 437
Spearfish, South Dakota 57783
(605) 642-2728
M $33 C $35 R $38 1, 2, 4

TENNESSEE

Hermitage Hotel
231 6th Avenue N.
Nashville, Tennessee 37219
(615) 244-3121 / (800) 251-1908
M $52 C $83 R $88 1, 2, 6

TEXAS

AmeriSuites by Howard Johnson
6800 I-40 West
Amarillo, Texas 79106
(806) 358-7943 / (800) 654-2000
M $38 C $40 R $42 1, 2, 3, 4, 5, 6

Harvey Hotel-Amarillo
3100 West I-40
Amarillo, Texas 79102
(806) 358-6161 / (800) 922-9222
M $46 C $55 R $65 2, 3, 4, 5, 6, 7

AmeriSuites
By HOWARD JOHNSON

Attention all military personnel!!

AmeriSuites offers you MORE for less!!
Why settle for just a room?

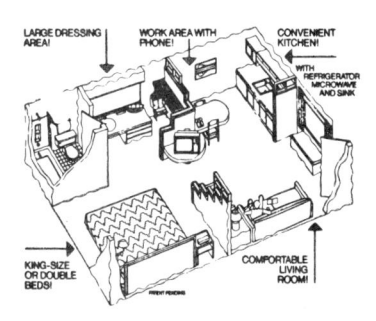

FREE!
- CONTINENTAL BREAKFAST BUFFET
- MORNING PAPER
- AIRPORT TRANSPORTATION AT MOST LOCATIONS
- COURTYARD SWIMMING POOL AND SPA

■ AMARILLO

■ EL PASO

■ IRVING

■ SAN ANTONIO

Ask about our military and extended stay rates.

1-800-654-2000

Rates subject to room availability.

AMERICA'S • AFFORDABLE • ALL-SUITE • HOTEL℠

TEXAS

Holiday Inn - Amarillo
1911 I-40 East & Ross
Amarillo, Texas 79102
(806) 372-8741 / (800) 465-4329
M $41 C $58 R $60 2, 3, 4, 5, 6

Comfort Inn
1601 E. Division Street
Arlington, Texas 76011
(817) 261-2300 / (800) 228-5150
M $33 C $38 R $42 1, 2, 3, 4, 6

Days Inn Austin
8210 I-35 N.
Austin, Texas 78753
(512) 835-2200 / (800) 325-2525
M $26 C $32 R $33 1, 2, 3, 4, 5, 6

Holiday Inn Northwest Plaza
8901 Business Park Drive, 183 at MOPAC
Austin, Texas 78759
(512) 343-0888 / (800) HOLIDAY
M $45 C $60 R $60 2, 3, 4, 5, 6

Comfort Inn
104 South Texas Avenue
College Station, Texas 77840
(409) 846-7333 / (800) 221-2222
M $35-52 C $36-53 R $39-54 1, 2, 3, 4, 5, 6

Manor House Inn
2504 Texas Avenue South
College Station, Texas 77840
(409) 764-9540 / (800) 231-4100
M $35 C $40 R $45 1, 2, 3, 4, 5, 6

Corpus Christi Marriott Hotel
707 N. Shoreline
Corpus Christi, Texas 78401
(512) 882-1700 / (800) 228-9290
M $49-53 C $76-99 R $86-109 1, 3, 4, 6

Holiday Inn Corpus Christi Airport
5549 Leopard Street
Corpus Christi, Texas 78408
(512) 289-5100 / 1-800-HOLIDAY
M $42 C $49 2, 3, 4, 6

TEXAS

Holiday Inn - Emerald Beach
1102 S. Shoreline
Corpus Christi, Texas 78401
(512) 883-5731
M $45 C $55 R $65 2, 3, 4, 6, 7

Ramada Inn Bay Front
601 Shoreline Boulevard
Corpus Christi, Texas 78401
(512) 883-7271
M $38 C $38 R $41 1, 2, 3, 4, 6

Best Value Inn
9737 Harry Hines Boulevard
Dallas, Texas 75220
(214) 257-2411
M $19.95 C $19.95 R $22.95 1, 2, 3, 4, 6

Bristol Suites Hotel
7800 Alpha Road
Dallas, Texas 75240
(214) 233-7600 / (800) 922-9222
M $74 C $99 R $130 2, 3, 4, 5, 6, 7

Colony Parke Hotel
6060 N. Central Expressway
Dallas, TX 75206 / (214) 750-6060
TX (800) 441-9258 / US (800) 527-1808
M $49 C $70 R $75 2, 3, 4, 6

Harvey Hotel-Addison
14315 Midway Road
Dallas, Texas 75244
(214) 980-8877 / (800) 922-9222
M$74 C$79 R$120 2, 3, 4, 5, 6, 7 dinner

Harvey Hotel-Dallas
7815 LBJ Freeway
Dallas, Texas 75240
(214) 960-7000 / (800) 922-9222
M$69 C$74 R$89 2, 3, 4, 5, 6, 7 dinner

Hyatt Regency DFW
P.O. Box 619014, Inside DFW Airport
DFW Airport, Texas 75261
(214) 453-1234 / (800) 233-1234
M $69 C $105 R $120 1, 2, 3, 4, 6

Quality Hotel Market Center
2015 Market Center Boulevard
Dallas, Texas 75207
(214) 741-7481 / (800) 421-2555
M $45 C $50 R $65-75 3, 4, 5, 6

TEXAS

The Residence Inn by Marriott
13636 Goldmark Drive
Dallas, Texas 75240
(214) 669-0478 / (800) 331-3131
M $69 C $80 R $89 2, 3, 4, 6

Rodeway Inn (Love Field Airport)
3140 West Mockingbird Lane
Dallas, Texas 75235
(214) 357-1701 / (800) 228-2000
M $34 C $34 R $37-39 2, 3, 4, 5

Duncanville Inn
202 Jellison Boulevard
Duncanville, Texas 75116
(214) 296-0345
M $29.95 C $32 R $35 1, 2, 3, 4, 6

AmeriSuites by Howard Johnson
8250 Gateway East
El Paso, Texas 79907
(915) 591-9600 / (800) 654-2000
M $47 C $47 R $49 1, 2, 3, 4, 5, 6

Holiday Inn Mid City
4800 Gateway East
I-10 & Raynolds exit
El Paso, Texas 79905
(915) 533-7521 / (800) HOLIDAY
M $35 C $40 R $43 2, 3, 4, 5, 6

The Inn at Fort Bliss
1744 Victory Avenue
Fort Bliss, Texas 79906
(915) 565-7777
M $31.75 R $31.75 4, 6

Days Inn, Downtown
600 Commerce
Fort Worth, Texas 76102
(817) 332-6900 / (800) 325-2525
M $40 C $43 R $45 2

Holiday Inn North & Conference Center
2540 Meacham Boulevard
Fort Worth, Texas 76106
(817) 625-9911 / (800) HOLIDAY
M $45 C $56 R $59 2, 3, 4, 6

La Quinta - Northeast Fort Worth
7920 Bedford-Euless Road
Fort Worth, Texas 76118
(817) 498-2750 / (800) 531-5900
M $34 C $35 R $38 1, 2, 3, 4, 5

TEXAS

Park Central Hotel
1010 Houston Street
Fort Worth, Texas 76102
(817) 336-2011 / (800) 245-PARK (7275)
M $36 C $40 R $44 2, 3, 4

Ramada Inn Grand Prairie
402 E. Safari Parkway
Grand Prairie, Texas 75050
(214) 263-4421 / (800) 2-RAMADA
M $32-37 C $38 R $43 1, 2, 3, 4

Harvey Suites-Houston Medical Center
6800 South Main Street
Houston, Texas 77030
(713) 528-7744 / (800) 922-9222
M$62 C$64 R$84 2, 3, 4, 5, 6, 7 dinner

Houston Marriott Astrodome
2100 S. Braeswood
Houston, Texas 77030
(713) 797-9000 / (800) 228-9290
M $55 C $85 R $95 1, 2, 3, 4, 6

Ramada Hotel Northwest
12801 Northwest Freeway
Houston, Texas 77040
(713) 462-9977 / (800) 2-RAMADA
M $47 C $59 R $62.80 2, 3, 4, 6

Residence Inn Houston-Astrodome
7710 S. Main Street
Houston, Texas 77030
(713) 660-7993 / (800) 331-3131
M $58 C $70 R $79 2, 3, 4, 6

AmeriSuites by Howard Johnson
3950 W. Airport Freeway
Irving, Texas 75062
(214) 790-1950 / (800) 654-2000
M $42.50 C $49 R $54 1, 2, 3, 4, 5, 6

Harvey Hotel - DFW Airport
4545 W. John Carpenter Freeway
Irving, Texas 75063
(214) 929-4500 / (800) 922-9222
M $74 C $92 R $109 2, 3, 4, 5, 6

Harvey Suites Hotel
4550 W. John Carpenter Freeway
Irving, Texas 75063
(214) 929-4499 / (800) 922-9222
M $74 C $94 R $94 2, 3, 4, 5, 6, 7

TEXAS

Fort Hood/Killeen Hilton Hotel
803 East Central Texas Expressway
Killeen, Texas 76541
(800) 825-6009 / (800) HILTONS
M $37 C $47 R $57 1, 2, 3, 4, 5, 6

Killeen Hilton Hotel
803 East Central Texas Expressway
Killeen, Texas 76541
(800) 825-6009 / (800) HILTONS
M $37 C $47 R $57 1, 2, 3, 4, 5, 6

Park Inn International
3120 Estes Parkway
Longview, Texas 75601 (Estes at I-20)
(214) 753-4884 / (800) 527-PARK
M $35-41 C $37-43 R $39-45 1, 2, 3, 4

Hotel Faust
240 South Seguin
New Braunfels, Texas 78130
(512) 625-7791
M $29 C $35 R $42 1, 2, 4, 6

Harvey Hotel-Plano
1600 N. Central Expressway
Plano, Texas 75074
(214) 578-8555 / (800) 922-9222
M$74 C$74 R$94 2, 3, 4, 5, 6, 7 dinner

AmeriSuites by Howard Johnson
10950 Laureate Drive
San Antonio, Texas 78249
(512) 691-1103 / (800) 654-2000
M $40 C $40 R $42 1, 2, 3, 4, 5, 6

AmeriSuites by Howard Johnson
11221 San Pedro Avenue
San Antonio, Texas 78216
(512) 342-4800 / (800) 654-2000
M $45 C $49 R $51 1, 2, 3, 4, 5, 6

Days Inn North Loop
2635 N.E. Loop 410
San Antonio, Texas 78217
(512) 653-9110
M $29 C $34 R $42 2, 3, 4, 5

EconoLodge Airport San Antonio
333 N.W. Loop 410
San Antonio, Texas 78216
(512) 344-4581
M $32.95 C $32.95 R $36.95 1, 2, 3, 4, 5, 6

TEXAS

Holiday Inn Downtown/Market Square
318 W. Durango
San Antonio, Texas 78204
(512) 225-3211 / (800) HOLIDAY
M $47 C $61 R $61 2, 3, 4, 6

Plaza San Antonio Hotel
555 S. Alamo
San Antonio, Texas 78205
(512) 229-1000 / (800) 421-1172
M $65 C $115 R $120-140-160 1, 2, 3

Scotsman Inn - East
211 No. W. W. White
San Antonio, Texas 78219
(512) 359-7268 / (800) 677-7268
R $25.95 1, 2, 3, 4, 6

Scotsman Inn - Northeast
5710 Industry Park Drive
San Antonio, Texas 78218
(512) 662-7400 / (800) 688-7268
R $24.95 1, 2, 3, 4, 6

Super 8 Motel of San Antonio
11027 IH 35 N.
San Antonio, Texas 78233
(512) 637-1033 / (800) 843-1991
M $25.88 C $30.88 R $32.88 1, 3, 4, 6

Texas Guestel Suites
13101 E. Loop 1604 N.
San Antonio, Texas 78233
(512) 655-9491 / 1-800-537-4238
M $35 C $44 R $49 1, 2, 3, 4, 5

Ten West Motor Inn
19793 I-10 West
San Antonio, Texas 78257
(512) 698-3991
M $25 C $27.50 R $30 1, 2, 3, 4, 6

Sheraton Inn - Sherman
3605 Highway 75 South
Sherman, Texas 75090
(214) 868-0555
M $40 C $53 R $58 2, 3, 4, 6

Best Western Raintree Inn
5701 Padre Boulevard
South Padre Island, Texas 78597
(512) 761-4913 / (800) 824-3662
M 25%off rr C 15%off rr R $48-108 1, 3, 4, 6

TEXAS

Sheraton South Padre Island Beach Resort
310 Padre Boulevard
South Padre Island, Texas 78597
(512) 761-6551 / (800) 325-3535
M $55-130 C $70-120 R $80-130 1, 2, 3, 4, 6

The Ramada Inn
I-30 and Summerhill Road
Texarkana, Texas 75501
(214) 794-3131 / (800) 2-RAMADA
M $30 C $36 R $39-45 1, 2, 3, 4, 5, 6

Econolodge Motel
795 South I-35 East
Waxahachie, Texas 75165
(214) 937-4982
M $30.60 R $34.50 2, 3, 4, 6

UTAH

Millstream Motel
1450 Washington Boulevard
Ogden, Utah 84404
(801) 394-9425 / 1-800-ALL-UTAH
M $24 C $24 R $26 1, 2, 4, 5

Quality Inn South
4465 Century Drive
Salt Lake City, Utah 84123
(801) 268-2533 / (800) 228-5151
M $37 C $41 R $49 1, 2, 3, 4, 5, 6

VIRGINIA

Comfort Inn - Mt. Vernon
7212 Richmond Highway
Alexandria, Virginia 22306
(703) 765-9000 / (800) 433-2546
M $53 C $53 R $63 2, 3, 4, 6

Guest Quarters Suite Hotel
100 S. Reynolds Street
Alexandria, Virginia 22304
(703) 370-9600 / (800) 424-2900
M $81-89 C $115 R $125-135 1, 2, 3, 4, 5

Best Western Arlington
2480 S. Glebe Road
Arlington, Virginia 22206
(703) 979-4400 / (800) 426-6886
M $64.95 C $86 R $91 1, 2, 3, 4, 5, 6, 7

VIRGINIA

Days Hotel Crystal City/National Airport
2000 Jefferson Davis Highway
Arlington, Virginia 22202
(703) 920-8600
M $61 C $61 R $73 2, 3, 4, 5

Quality Hotel Arlington
1200 N. Courthouse Road
Arlington, Virginia 22201
(703) 524-4000 / (800) 228-5151
M $64 C $81 1, 2, 3, 4, 5, 6

Rosslyn Westpark Hotel
1900 N. Fort Myer Drive
Arlington, Virginia 22209
(703) 527-4814 / (800) 368-3408
M $77 C $89 R $97 1, 2, 3, 4, 6

Sheraton Crystal City Hotel
1800 Jefferson Davis Highway
Arlington, Virginia 22202
(703) 486-1111 / (800) 325-3535
M $79-82 C $125 R $135 1, 2, 3, 4, 5, 6

Sheraton National Hotel
900 S. Orme Street
Arlington, Virginia 22204
(703) 521-1900 / (800) 325-3535
M $79-82 C $105 R $115 1, 2, 3, 4, 5, 6

Quality Inn, Fairfax
11180 Main Street
Fairfax, Virginia 22030
(703) 591-5900 / (800) 223-1223
M $54.50 C $54.50 R $60.50 1, 2, 3, 4, 6

Hampton Inn
1813 West Mercury Boulevard
Hampton, Virginia 23666
(804) 838-8484 / (800) 426-7866
M $36 C $40 R $44 1, 2, 4, 6

Holiday Inn Hampton-Coliseum Hotel &
Conference Center, 1815 W. Mercury Blvd.
Hampton, Virginia 23666
(804) 838-0200 / (800) 842-9370
M $50 C $54 R $58 1, 2, 3, 4, 5, 6

Sheraton Harrisonburg
1400 E. Market St., I-81 & US 33, exit 64E
Harrisonburg, Virginia 22801
(703) 433-2521 / (800) 325-3535
M $47 C $60 R $73 1, 2, 3, 4, 6

VIRGINIA

Comfort Inn
200 Elden Street
Herndon, Virginia 22070
(703) 437-7555
M $56 C $56 R $66 2, 4, 5, 6

Days Inn - Leesburg
721 E. Market
Leesburg, Virginia 22075
(703) 777-6622 / (800) 325-2525
M $43 C $45 R $50 1, 2, 3, 4, 6

Leesburg Westpark Hotel
59 Clubhouse Drive, S.W.
Leesburg, Virginia 22075
(703) 777-1910
M $40 C $40 R $45 1, 2, 3, 4, 6

Tysons Westpark Hotel
8401 Westpark Drive
McLean, Virginia 22102
(703) 734-2800 / (800) 533-3301
M $77/59 C $84 R $89 1, 2, 3, 4, 5, 6

Holiday Inn Newport News
6128 Jefferson Avenue
Newport News, Virginia 23605
(804) 826-4500 / (800) 465-4329
M $42.40 C $48 R $52 2, 3, 4, 6

TDY Inn
15910 Warwick Boulevard
Newport News, Virginia 23602
(804) 888-6667
M $45 R $55 1, 2, 4, 5, 6

Econo Lodge/Azalea Gardens
1850 E. Little Creek Road
Norfolk, Virginia 23518
(804) 588-8888 / (800) 446-6900
M $27.85 C $27.85 R $30.95 1, 2, 3, 4, 7

Norfolk Airport Hilton
1500 N. Military Highway
Norfolk, Virginia 23502
(804) 466-8000 / (800) 422-7474
M $51 C $79-99 R $85-117 2, 3, 4, 5, 6

Sheraton Reston Hotel
11810 Sunrise Valley Drive
Reston, Virginia 22091
(703) 620-9000 / (800) 325-3535
M $81-84 C $99 R $104 1, 2, 3, 4, 5, 6

VIRGINIA

Comfort Suites Hotel
8710 Midlothian Turnpike
Richmond, Virginia 23235
(804) 320-8900 / (800) 228-5150
M $48 C $50 R $58-68 1, 2, 3, 4, 6

Ramada Inn South
2126 Willis Road
Richmond, Virginia 23237
(804) 271-1281 / (800) 228-2828
M $42 C $47 R $51-58 1, 2, 3, 4, 6

The Virginia Inn
5701 Chamberlayne Road
Richmond, Virginia 23227
(804) 266-7616 / (800) 776-4667
M $40 C $40 R $42 1, 2, 3, 4

The Best Western Springfield Inn
6550 Loisdale Court
Springfield, Virginia 22150
(703) 922-9000 / (800) 528-1234
M $54-64 C $57-68 R $62-68 1, 2, 3, 4, 6

Days Inn
1587 Springhill Road
Vienna, Virginia 22182
(703) 448-8020 / (800) 325-2525
M $61 C $61 R $73 2, 3, 4, 6

Residence Inn by Marriott-Tysons Corner
8616 Westwood Center Drive
Vienna, Virginia 22182
(703) 893-0120 / (800) 331-3131
M $92-127 C $118 1, 2, 3, 4, 6

Sheraton Premiere at Tysons Corner
8661 Leesburg Pike, Tysons Corner
Vienna, Virginia 22182
(703) 448-1234 / (800) 325-3535
M $81-84 C $130 R $144 1, 2, 3, 4, 5, 6

The Cavalier Hotel
42nd & Oceanfront
Virginia Beach, VA 23451 / (804) 425-8555
VA (800) 582-8324 / US (800) 446-8199
M $50-60 C $50-60 R $75-130 1, 2, 3, 4, 5, 6

Best Western Virginia Inn
900 Capitol Landing Road
Williamsburg, Virginia 23185
(804) 229-1655
M $35-49 R $39-59 1, 2, 3, 4, 6

VIRGINIA

Holiday Inn Patriot
3032 Richmond Road
Williamsburg, Virginia 23185
(804) 565-2600 / (800) 446-6001
3, 4, 6

Williamsburg Westpark Hotel
1600 Richmond
Williamsburg, Virginia 23185
(804) 229-1134 / (800) 446-1062
M $27-48 C $29-55 R $35-55 1, 2, 3, 4

Holiday Inn
I-81 & U.S. 50 East
Winchester, Virginia 22601
(703) 667-3300 / (800) HOLIDAY
M $44.13 C $47-59 R $49-61 1, 2, 3, 4, 5, 6

WASHINGTON

Mt. Vernon Travelodge
1910 Freeway Drive
Mt. Vernon, Washington 98273
(206) 428-7020 / (800) 255-3050
M $39 C $37 R $44 1, 2, 3, 4, 6

Coachman Inn
5563 Highway 20
Oak Harbor, Washington 98277
(206) 675-0727 / (800) 635-0043
M $38 C $38 R $39.50 1, 2, 3, 4, 5, 6

Rodeside Lodge
12501 Aurora Avenue North
Seattle, WA 98133 / (206) 364-7771
US 1-800-227-7771 / WA 1-800-637-0636
M $36-38 C $36-38 R $40-55 1, 2, 3, 4, 5, 6

WISCONSIN

Midway Motor Lodge
3033 W. College Avenue
Appleton, Wisconsin 54914
(414) 731-4141 / (800) 528-1234
M $44 C $51 R $54 1, 3, 4, 5

Island Inn Resort & Convention Centre
529 Park Plaza Drive
La Crosse, Wisconsin 54601
(608) 784-9500 / (800) 447-9676
M $41 C $46 1, 3, 4, 5, 6

WISCONSIN

Quality Inn West Towne Suites
650 Grand Canyon Drive
Madison, Wisconsin 53719
(608) 833-4200 / (800) 228-5150
M $45 C $51 R $55 2, 4, 6

Rafters Motor Inn
I-90/94 & Highway 80
New Lisbon, Wisconsin 53950
(608) 562-5141 / (800) 341-8000
M $31.05 C $28.50 R $34.50-37.50 2, 4, 6

Country Hospitality Inn
737 Avon Road
Sparta, Wisconsin 54660
(608) 269-3110 / (800) 456-4000
M $33.25 C $33.25 R $36.95 1, 2, 3, 4, 6

Econo Lodge
2005 N. Superior Avenue
Tomah, Wisconsin 54660
(608) 372-9100 / (800) 446-6900
M $29.65 C $29.65 R $32.95 1, 2, 3, 4, 6

Days Inn
P.O. Box 381, Highway 12
Wisconsin Dells, Wisconsin 53965
(608) 254-6444 / (800) 325-2525
M $30-45 C $30-45 R $31-50 1, 2, 3, 4, 6

WYOMING

Holiday Inn
204 W. Fox Farm Road
Cheyenne, Wyoming 82007
(307) 638-4466 / (800) HOLIDAY
M $37 C $47 R $52 2, 3, 4, 5, 6

Super 8 Motel Douglas
314 Russell Avenue
Douglas, Wyoming 82633
(307) 358-6800 / (800) 843-1991
M $24.20 C $24.20 R $26.20 2, 4, 6

Management/Financial

Armed Forces Financial Network
For AFFN ATM locations nearest you
Call 1-800-662-AFFN

Travel Agencies

Personalized Travel
Your Space-A Backup System
8330 Boone Blvd., Suite 745
703-761-4080 / 800-237-6971
FAX 703-893-6394

Ann, Roy Crawford, Sr., and Roy Crawford, Jr., the publishers of Temporary Military Lodging Around the World, *request that you kindly show this book and its civilian hotel directory to the General Managers of hotels you visit which want to encourage military ID card holders to patronize their establishments. Please give them our address so they may contact us about the next new edition of this book or one of our other helpful travel books.*

Thank you.

Military Living Publications
P.O. Box 2347
Falls Church, VA 22042-0347
(703) 237-0203, FAX 237-2233

356 — *Temporary Military Lodging Around the World*

MILITARY Living's
Family of Publications

Phone orders are accepted with Visa, American Express and Mastercard.

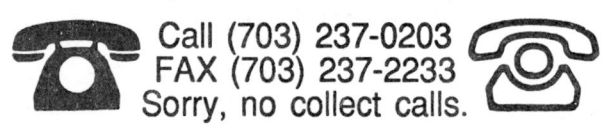

Call (703) 237-0203
FAX (703) 237-2233
Sorry, no collect calls.

CENTRAL ORDER COUPON

MILITARY Living

MILITARY LIVING PUBLICATIONS
P.O. Box 2347, Falls Church, VA 22042-0347
Telephone (703) 237-0203 • FAX 237-2233

Item	Publications	Qty	Item	Publications	Qty
#14 #17	**U.S. Military Installation Map.** Lists over 550 military installations & rec areas. (folded) **$5.95** (2 wall maps unfolded in a hard tube) **$15.00**		#9	**U.S. Forces Travel and Transfer Guide Europe and Near East Areas.** The complete military guide to Europe. **$16.95**	
#13	**Military RV, Camping & Rec Areas Around the World.** You can have fun with this book. **$10.95**		#11	**U.S. Military Museums, Historic Sites & Exhibits.** A great, practical book. One of a kind. Has photo insert, Smyth binding and presentation page. (Hard Cover) **$26.95**	
#1	**Military Space-A Air Opportunities Around the World.** The one everyone is talking about! **$15.95**		#15 #16	**COLLECTOR'S ITEM! Desert Shield Commemorative Maps.** (folded) **$7.00** (2 unfolded wall maps in a hard tube) **$16.00**	
#12	**Temporary Military Lodging Around the World** Our all time best seller. **$12.95**		#6	**Assignment Washington II Military Atlas.** Maps & Charts of Washington Area Military Installations **$8.95**	
#8	**U.S. Forces Travel and Transfer Guide, USA and Caribbean Areas.** This book should be in every car. **$10.95**		#21	**R&R Space-A Report.** The world-wide travel newsletter. 5 yrs.-$47.00 2 yrs.-$22.00 3 yrs.-$30.00 (6 issues) 1 yr.-$14.00	
	Subtotal: $			Subtotal: $	

*If you are an R&R Space-A subscriber, you may deduct $1.00 per book on books only. (No discount on the R&R Report itself or on the U.S. Road Map.)
For 1st Class Mail, add $1.00 per book.
Mail Order Prices are for U.S. APO & FPO addresses. Please consult Publisher for International Mail Price. Sorry, no billing.
GREAT FUND RAISERS! Please write for wholesale rates.

Publisher's Note: *Assignment Washington* **is out of stock. All new version, with maps, will be available in early '91.**

Total $_____

VA addressees add 4 1/2% sales tax $_____ (Books & Map only)

Total Amount $_____ Enclosed

We're as close as your telephone...by using our Telephone Ordering Service. We honor VISA, American Express, MasterCard, Carte Blanche and Diners. Call us at (703) 237-0203 and order today! Sorry, no collect calls. Or...fill out the info in the mail order coupon below.

Name:_____ ☐ Active Duty

Street:_____ ☐ Retired

City:_____ ☐ Widower

State/Zip Code_____ ☐ 100% Disabled Veteran

Phone:_____ ☐ Guard Reservist
(with area code)
Signature:_____ ☐ Other_____

Rank:_____ or Rank of Sponsor_____

Branch of Service:_____

Please mail check or money order to: **Military Living, P.O. Box 2347, Falls Church, VA 22042-0347**

358 — *Temporary Military Lodging Around the World*

Space-A Travel Newsletter
(Space-A Air ... Space-A RV & Camping ... Space-A Temporary Military Lodging)

FREE COPIES FOR PURCHASERS of THIS BOOK

"TRAVEL ON LESS PER DAY.... THE MILITARY WAY"

We'd like to acquaint you with our travel newsletter, Military Living's R&R Space-A Report. It gives late breaking info on Space-A air travel, new info on military camping and rec areas, and temporary military lodging plus informative and helpful reader trip reports.

We'll send you two back issues (a $4.00 value) if you will send $2.00 to cover cost of processing, postage and handling.

To get your copies, send your name and address and $2.00 to:

Military Living R&R (Dept. SA)
Box 2347
Falls Church, Virginia 22042-0347

Note: We regret that this must be a one-time offer and may not be used to extend a current R&R Space-A Report subscription or combined with any other discount.

Temporary Military Lodging Around the World — 359

MILITARY Living's
Family of Publications

- MILITARY LODGING
- MILITARY SPACE A AIR — Opportunities Around The World
- Forces Travel Guide Europe and Near East Areas
- U.S. Forces Travel Guide U.S.A and Caribbean Areas
- U.S. Military Museums, Historic Sites & Exhibits
- Military RV, Camping & Rec Areas
- UNITED STATES MILITARY INSTALLATION ROAD MAP — ISBN 0-914862-28-6
- MILITARY Living
- ASSIGNMENT WASHINGTON II MILITARY ATLAS — Maps & Charts Of Washington Area Military Installations
- R&R SPACE-A REPORT
- DESERT SHIELD — Saudi Arabia

Phone orders are accepted with Visa, American Express and Mastercard.

Call (703) 237-0203
FAX (703) 237-2233
Sorry, no collect calls.

TRANSFERRING TO WASHINGTON, D.C. AREA?

MOVING TO WASHINGTON COUPON

"One Shot" Help

MOVING TO WASHINGTON?
Make one call or send this coupon & help will be on its way. As a military wife, one of my chief goals is to boost military family morale . . . so mail this coupon today & help will be on its way.
Hope to hear from you soon.

Ann Crawford, Publisher
Military Living Magazine

TO: Mrs Ann Crawford, Publisher, Military Living
P.O. Box 2347, Falls Church, VA 22042-0347
Phone: (703) 237-0203, FAX (703) 237-2233

Our Family Is:
- [ ] Army
- [ ] Navy
- [ ] Air Force
- [ ] Marine
- [ ] Coast Guard
- [ ] P.H.S.
- [ ] NOAA
- [ ] Other
- [ ] Active
- [ ] Retired
- [ ] 100% DAV

Military member's name/rank: _____ Spouses Name _____

Address: _____
City/State/Zip: _____
Tel: _____ Total number in family: _____ Number of children: _____

Area assigned to: _____
We expect to arrive: _____
We would like info, if possible, on the following:
- [ ] House [ ] Apt. [ ] Condo
- [ ] Renting [ ] Buying
- [ ] Car
- [ ] Furniture
- [ ] Major Appliances
- [ ] Short Term Housing
- [ ] Military Lodging
- [ ] Hotel/Motel [ ] B & B
- [ ] Short Term Apt.
- [ ] Banking/Checking Accounts
- [ ] Employment Opportunities for spouse
- [ ] Real Estate Career Opportunities
- [ ] Legal Services/Settlement Atty.
- [ ] College Opportunities
- [ ] Investment Opportunities
- [ ] Travel in nearby areas
- [ ] Back Issues of **Military Living**
- [ ] Window Treatments
- [ ] Dentist [ ] Doctor

Type of job: _____

Temporary Military Lodging Around the World — 361

Space-A Travel Newsletter
(Space-A Air ... Space-A RV & Camping ... Space-A Temporary Military Lodging)

FREE COPIES FOR PURCHASERS of THIS BOOK

"TRAVEL ON LESS PER DAY.... THE MILITARY WAY"

We'd like to acquaint you with our travel newsletter, Military Living's R&R Space-A Report. It gives late breaking info on Space-A air travel, new info on military camping and rec areas, and temporary military lodging plus informative and helpful reader trip reports.

We'll send you two back issues (a $4.00 value) if you will send $2.00 to cover cost of processing, postage and handling.

To get your copies, send your name and address and $2.00 to:

Military Living R&R (Dept. SA)
Box 2347
Falls Church, Virginia 22042-0347

Note: We regret that this must be a one-time offer and may not be used to extend a current R&R Space-A Report subscription or combined with any other discount.

CENTRAL ORDER COUPON

MILITARY Living

MILITARY LIVING PUBLICATIONS
P.O. Box 2347, Falls Church, VA 22042-0347
Telephone (703) 237-0203 • FAX 237-2233

Item	Publications	Qty	Item	Publications	Qty
#14	U.S. Military Installation Map. Lists over 550 military installations & rec areas. (folded) **$5.95**		#9	U.S. Forces Travel and Transfer Guide Europe and Near East Areas. The complete military guide to Europe. **$16.95**	
#17	(2 wall maps unfolded in a hard tube) **$15.00**				
#13	Military RV, Camping & Rec Areas Around the World. You can have fun with this book. **$10.95**		#11	U.S. Military Museums, Historic Sites & Exhibits. A great, practical book. One of a kind. Has photo insert, Smyth binding and presentation page. (Hard Cover) **$26.95**	
#1	Military Space-A Air Opportunities Around the World. The one everyone is talking about! **$15.95**		#15	COLLECTOR'S ITEM! Desert Shield Commemorative Maps. (folded) **$7.00**	
			#16	(2 unfolded wall maps in a hard tube) **$16.00**	
#12	Temporary Military Lodging Around the World Our all time best seller. **$12.95**		#6	Assignment Washington II Military Atlas. Maps & Charts of Washington Area Military Installations **$8.95**	
#8	U.S. Forces Travel and Transfer Guide, USA and Caribbean Areas. This book should be in every car. **$10.95**		#21	R&R Space-A Report. The world-wide travel newsletter. 5 yrs.-$47.00 2 yrs.-$22.00 3 yrs.-$30.00 (6 issues) 1 yr.-$14.00	

Subtotal: $ _____ | Subtotal: $ _____

*If you are an R&R Space-A subscriber, you may deduct $1.00 per book on books only. (No discount on the R&R Report itself or on the U.S. Road Map.)
For 1st Class Mail, add $1.00 per book.
Mail Order Prices are for U.S. APO & FPO addresses. Please consult Publisher for International Mail Price. Sorry, no billing.
GREAT FUND RAISERS! Please write for wholesale rates.

Publisher's Note: *Assignment Washington* is out of stock. All new version, with maps, will be available in early '91.

Total $ _____

VA addressees
add 4 1/2% sales tax $ _____
(Books & Map only)

Total Amount $ _____
Enclosed

We're as close as your telephone...by using our Telephone Ordering Service. We honor VISA, American Express, MasterCard, Carte Blanche and Diners. Call us at (703) 237-0203 and order today! Sorry, no collect calls. Or...fill out the info in the mail order coupon below.

Name: _____

Street: _____

City: _____

State/Zip Code: _____

Phone: _____
(with area code)
Signature: _____

Rank: _____ or Rank of Sponsor _____

Branch of Service: _____

☐ Active Duty
☐ Retired
☐ Widower
☐ 100% Disabled Veteran
☐ Guard Reservist
☐ Other _____

Please mail check or money order to: **Military Living, P.O. Box 2347, Falls Church, VA 22042-0347**

Temporary Military Lodging Around the World — 363

NEW TML!

Information about TML facilities at the installations listed below reached us after the first printing of this edition of *Temporary Military Lodging Around the World* went to press. For this second printing, we have included all the information that limited space allows us to. For more details, contact the billeting office directly at the numbers listed below.

UNITED STATES

CALIFORNIA

TUSTIN MARINE CORPS AIR STATION (CA86R4), Tustin MCAS, CA 92710-5000. Main installation numbers: Comm: 714-726-3011. ATVN: 997-3011.

Location: Off I-5 in Orange County. Exit I-5 at Red Hill Ave. Proceed west for 5.5 miles to the AS main gate. RM: p-15, L/16. NMC: Irvine, 1 mile south.

Billeting Office: Building 20-A, Moffett/Cross Streets. EX-7983. 0700-1530 M-F. Check in facility, check out 1100 hours. No government civilian employee billeting.

TML: DV/VIP. Quarters C. Officer 04+. Leave or official duty. 1/2-bedroom, private bath suite. Kitchenette, maid service, color TV, utensils. Older structure. Rates: Moderate. Maximum 4 persons. All categories Space-A. Active duty 07+ bumps other categories.

DV/VIP: Command Secretary, Building 4. Comm: 726-7301. 06+. Retirees and lower grades Space-A.

FLORIDA

PANAMA CITY NAVAL COASTAL SYSTEMS CENTER (FL35R1), Panama City, FL 32407-5000. Main installation numbers: 904-234-4011. ATVN: 436-4011.

Location: Located on US-98 at the foot of the Hathaway Bridge in Panama City Beach. RM: p-21, X/7. NMC: Panama City, adjacent.

Billeting Office: Housing Referral, Building 126, Crag Road. Comm: 234-4425/4248. ATVN: 436-4425/4248. 0800-1600 M-F. Check in billeting, check out 1100 hours. Government civilian employee billeting.

TML: BOQ (Building 349)/BEQ (Building 304). All ranks. Leave or official duty. BOQ: 47 rooms, private bath. BEQ: 29 rooms, shared bath, 58 rooms, private bath. A/C, cots ($6.00), ice vending, kitchenette (BOQ), refrigerator only (BEQ), maid service, color TV (limited in BEQ), utensils (BOQ only). BOQ is modern structure. Rates: $6.00 per person BOQ, $4.00-$6.00 per person BEQ. Duty can make reservations. Others Space-A.

DV/VIP: Public Affairs Office, Building 110, Code 055. Comm: 235-5467. 06/GS-15+. Retirees Space-A in Public Affairs is contacted

HAWAII

BARKING SANDS PACIFIC MISSILE RANGE FACILITY (HI04R6), Kekaha, Kauai, HI 96752-0128. Main installation numbers: Comm: 808-335-4111. ATVN: 471-4111.

Location: From airport at Lihue take HI-50 west for approximately 30 miles. RM: p-7, B/2. NMC: Waimea, 8 miles south.

Billeting Office: None. Check in after 1400 at MWR office. Reservations are required by application only at least 60 days in advance. Address: Beach Cottages

New TML, continued

Reservation, MWRPMRF, Barking Sands, Kekaha, Kauai, HI 96752-0128. Comm: 808-335-4446. ATVN: 471-6446. Check in MWR office, Check out 1200 hours.

TML: Cottages. All ranks. Leave or official duty. 6/2-bedroom cottages, private bath. Kitchen, utensils, microwave, washer/dryer. Rates: $35.00 per cottage. Maximum 6 per cottage.

OHIO

DEFENSE CONSTRUCTION SUPPLY CENTER (OH05R2), Columbus, OH 43216-5000. Main installation numbers: Comm: 614-238-3131. ATVN: 850-3131.

Location: From I-270 (Beltway), take exit 39 to Broad Street West. The main gate is at 3990 Broad Street. RM: p-77, SJ/25. NMC: Columbus, in city limits.

Billeting Office: Building 201, Officers' Club, Foyle and Washington Streets, 0830-1630 M-F. EX-2694. After hours, EX-2111. Check in billeting, check out 1100 hours.

TML: TLQ. Building 201. All ranks. Leave or official duty. 3/1-bedroom private bath; 5/1-bedroom, hall bath; 2/2-bedroom, private bath. A/C, cribs, kitchenette (some), maid service, color TV, washer/dryer. Modern structure. Rates: $24.00 per unit. Half price if PCS. Duty can make reservations. Others Space-A.

DV/VIP: Building 11-13. ATVN: 850-2168. Retirees Space-A.

OVERSEAS

GERMANY

KITZINGEN SUB-COMMUNITY (GE75R7), APO New York 09031-5000. Main installation numbers: Comm: 44-09321-305-113. ETS: 355-113.

Location: From Würzburg, take highway B-8 southeast approximately 12 miles to Kitzingen. HE: p-40, D/1. NMC: Würzburg, 10 miles south.

Billeting Office: Building 166, Richtholenstrasse. Comm: 09321-31836. 0800-2300 M-F. After hours Comm: 09321-32732. Check in facility, check out 1100 hours. Government civilian employee billeting.

TML: Officers' Club Guesthouse. Building 166. Officer all ranks. Leave or official duty. 10 rooms and 2 suites. Cots ($10.00), cribs ($5.00), maid service, refrigerator, TV room and lounge, free washer/dryer. Modern structure. Rates: $25.00-$35.00 per couple. Maximum 4 per persons room.